DISCOVER MCGRAW-HILL NETWORKS™

AN AWARD-WINNING SOCIAL STUDIES PROGRAM DESIGNED TO FULLY SUPPORT YOUR SUCCESS.

» Aligns to the Massachusetts State Standards

» Engages you with interactive resources and compelling stories

» Provides resources and tools for every learning style

» Empowers targeted learning to help you be successful

UNDERSTANDING IS THE FOUNDATION OF ACHIEVEMENT

Clear writing, real-life examples, photos, interactive maps, videos, and more will capture your attention and keep you engaged so that you can succeed.

You will find tools and resources to help you read more effectively.

networks

FOCUS YOUR TIME AND YOUR EFFORT

LEARNSMART®

No two students are alike! We built LearnSmart® so that all students can work through the key material they need to learn at their own pace.

YOUR TIME MATTERS

LearnSmart with SmartBook™ adapts to you as you work, guiding you through your reading so you can make every minute count.

DISCOVER A PERSONALIZED READING EXPERIENCE

Every student experiences LearnSmart® differently. The interactive challenge format highlights content and helps you identify content you know and don't know.

RETAIN MORE INFORMATION

LearnSmart® detects content you are most likely to forget and will highlight what you need to review.

networks™

BE THE STUDENT YOU WANT TO BE

STUDENTS WHO UNDERSTAND THE WORLD WILL BE THE ADULTS WHO CAN CHANGE IT.

DISCOVER IT ALL ONLINE!

1. Go to connected.mcgraw-hill.com

2. Enter your username and password from your teacher.

3. Click on your book.

4. Select your chapter and lesson, or explore the Resource Library.

networks

GO ONLINE AND START EXPLORING!

(t)McGraw-Hill Education; (b)Julia Goss/Flickr Open/Getty Images

WORLD
GEOGRAPHY
and Ancient Civilizations I

Richard G. Boehm, Ph.D.

Jackson J. Spielvogel, Ph.D

DISCOVER MCGRAW-HILL NETWORKS™, AN AWARD-WINNING SOCIAL STUDIES PROGRAM DESIGNED TO FULLY SUPPORT YOUR SUCCESS. Networks™.

- Aligns to the National Geography Standards
- Aligns to the National Council for the Social Studies Standards
- Engages you with interactive resources and compelling stories
- Provides resources and tools for every learning style
- Empowers target learning to help you be successful

UNDERSTANDING IS THE FOUNDATION OF ACHIEVEMENT

Clear writing, real-life examples, photos, interactive maps, videos, and more will capture your attention and keep you engaged so that you can succeed.

You will find tools and resources to help you read more effectively.

mheducation.com/prek-12

Send all inquiries to:
McGraw-Hill Education
8787 Orion Place
Columbus, OH 43240

ISBN: 978-0-07-700840-6
MHID: 0-07-700840-5

Printed in the United States of America.

5 6 7 LWI 25 24 23 22

AUTHORS

SENIOR AUTHOR

Richard G. Boehm, Ph.D., was one of the original authors of *Geography for Life: National Geography Standards,* which outlined what students should know and be able to do in geography. He was also one of the authors of the *Guidelines for Geographic Education*, in which the Five Themes of Geography were first articulated. Dr. Boehm has received many honors, including "Distinguished Geography Educator" by the National Geographic Society (1990), the "George J. Miller Award" from the National Council for Geographic Education (NCGE) for distinguished service to geographic education (1991), "Gilbert Grosvenor Honors" in geographic education from the Association of American Geographers (2002), and the NCGE's "Distinguished Mentor Award" (2010). He served as president of the NCGE, has twice won the Journal of Geography award for best article, and also received the NCGE's "Distinguished Teaching Achievement." Presently, Dr. Boehm holds the Jesse H. Jones Distinguished Chair in Geographic Education at Texas State University in San Marcos, Texas, where he serves as director of The Gilbert M. Grosvenor Center for Geographic Education. His most current project includes the production of the video-based professional development series, *Geography: Teaching With the Stars*. Available programs may be viewed at www.geoteach.org.

SENIOR AUTHOR

Jackson J. Spielvogel is Associate Professor of History Emeritus at The Pennsylvania State University. He received his Ph.D. from The Ohio State University, where he specialized in Reformation history under Harold J. Grimm. His work has been supported by fellowships from the Fulbright Foundation and the Foundation for Reformation Research. At Penn State, Spielvogel helped inaugurate the Western civilization courses, as well as a popular course on Nazi Germany. His book, *Hitler and Nazi Germany,* was published in 1987 (seventh edition, 2014). He is also the author of *Western Civilization,* published in 1991 (ninth edition, 2015). Spielvogel is the coauthor (with William Duiker) of *World History,* first published in 1998 (eighth edition, 2016). Spielvogel has won five major university-wide teaching awards. In 1988–1989, he held the Penn State Teaching Fellowship, the university's most prestigious teaching award. He won the Dean Arthur Ray Warnock Award for Outstanding Faculty Member in 1996 and the Schreyer Honors College Excellence in Teaching Award in 2000.

CONTRIBUTING AUTHORS

Jay McTighe has published articles in a number of leading educational journals and has coauthored 10 books, including the best-selling *Understanding by Design* series with Grant Wiggins. McTighe also has an extensive background in professional development and is a featured speaker at national, state, and district conferences and workshops. He received his undergraduate degree from the College of William and Mary, earned a master's degree from the University of Maryland, and completed post-graduate studies at the Johns Hopkins University.

Dinah Zike, M.Ed., is an award-winning author, educator, and inventor recognized for designing three-dimensional, hands-on manipulatives and graphic organizers known as Foldables®. Foldables are used nationally and internationally by parents, teachers, and other professionals in the education field. Zike has developed more than 180 supplemental educational books and materials. Two of her books (*Envelope Graphic Organizers*™ and *Foldables® and VKVs® for Phonics, Spelling, and Vocabulary PreK-3rd*) were each awarded *Learning* Magazine's Teachers' Choice Award for Professional Development in 2014. Two other books (*Notebook Foldables®* and *Foldables®, Notebook Foldables®, & VKVs® for Spelling and Vocabulary 4th–12th*) were each awarded *Learning* Magazine's Teachers' Choice Award for 2011. In 2004 Zike was honored with the CESI Science Advocacy Award. She received her M.Ed. from Texas A&M, College Station, Texas.

CONTRIBUTING AUTHORS

Doug Fisher Ph.D. and Nancy Frey Ph.D. are professors in the School of Teacher Education at San Diego State University. Fisher's focus is on literacy and language, with an emphasis on students who are English Learners. Frey's focus is on literacy and learning, with a concentration in how students acquire content knowledge. Both teach elementary and secondary teacher preparation courses, in addition to their work with graduate and doctoral programs. Their shared interests include supporting students with diverse learning needs, instructional design, and curriculum development. Fisher and Frey are coauthors of numerous articles and books, including *Better Learning Through Structured Teaching, Checking for Understanding, Background Knowledge*, and *Improving Adolescent Literacy*. They are coeditors (with Diane Lapp) of the NCTE journal *Voices From the Middle*.

CONSULTANTS AND REVIEWERS

ACADEMIC CONSULTANTS

William H. Berentsen, Ph.D.
Professor of Geography and
  European Studies
University of Connecticut
Storrs, Connecticut

David Berger, Ph.D.
Ruth and I. Lewis Gordon
  Professor of Jewish History
Dean, Bernard Revel Graduate
  School
Yeshiva University
New York, New York

R. Denise Blanchard, Ph.D.
Professor of Geography
Texas State University–San
  Marcos
San Marcos, Texas

Brian W. Blouet, Ph.D.
Huby Professor of Geography
  and International Education
The College of William
  and Mary
Williamsburg, Virginia

Olwyn M. Blouet, Ph.D.
Professor of History
Virginia State University
Petersburg, Virginia

Maria A. Caffrey, Ph.D.
Lecturer, Department of
  Geography
University of Tennessee
Knoxville, Tennessee

So-Min Cheong, Ph.D.
Associate Professor of Geography
University of Kansas
Lawrence, Kansas

Alasdair Drysdale, Ph.D.
Professor of Geography
University of New Hampshire
Durham, New Hampshire

Rosana Ferreira, Ph.D.
Assistant Professor of
  Geography and Atmospheric
  Science
East Carolina University
Greenville, North Carolina

Eric J. Fournier, Ph.D.
Associate Professor of Geography
Samford University,
Birmingham, Alabama

Matthew Fry, Ph.D.
Assistant Professor of Geography
University of North Texas
Denton, Texas

Douglas W. Gamble, Ph.D.
Professor of Geography
University of North Carolina
Wilmington, North Carolina

Gregory Gaston, Ph.D.
Professor of Geography
University of North Alabama
Florence, Alabama

Jeffrey J. Gordon, Ph.D.
Associate Professor of Geography
Bowling Green State University
Bowling Green, Ohio

Alyson L. Greiner, Ph.D.
Associate Professor of Geography
Oklahoma State University
Stillwater, Oklahoma

William J. Gribb, Ph.D.
Associate Professor of
  Geography
University of Wyoming
Laramie, Wyoming

Joseph J. Hobbs, Ph.D.
Professor of Geography
University of Missouri
Columbia, Missouri

Ezekiel Kalipeni, Ph.D.
Professor of Geography and
  Geography Information
  Science
University of Illinois
Urbana, Illinois

Pradyumna P. Karan, Ph.D.
Research Professor of
  Geography
University of Kentucky
Lexington, Kentucky

Christopher Laingen, Ph.D.
Assistant Professor of
  Geography
Eastern Illinois University
Charleston, Illinois

Jeffrey Lash, Ph.D.
Associate Professor of
  Geography
University of Houston–Clear
  Lake
Houston, Texas

Jerry T. Mitchell, Ph.D.
Research Professor of
  Geography
University of South Carolina
Columbia, South Carolina

Thomas R. Paradise, Ph.D.
Professor, Department of
  Geosciences and the King
  Fahd Center for Middle East
  Studies
University of Arkansas
Fayetteville, Arkansas

David Rutherford, Ph.D.
Assistant Professor of Public
  Policy and Geography
Executive Director, Mississippi
  Geographic Alliance
University of Mississippi
University, Mississippi

Dmitrii Sidorov, Ph.D.
Professor of Geography
California State University
Long Beach, California

Amanda G. Smith, Ph.D.
Professor of Education
University of North Alabama
Florence, Alabama

Jeffrey S. Ueland, Ph.D.
Associate Professor of
  Geography
Bemidji State University
Bemidji, Minnesota

Fahui Wang, Ph.D.
Professor of Geography
Louisiana State University
Baton Rouge, Louisiana

TEACHER REVIEWERS

Precious Steele Boyle, Ph.D.
Cypress Middle School
Memphis, TN

Jason E. Albrecht
Moscow Middle School
Moscow, ID

Jim Hauf
Berkeley Middle School
Berkeley, MO

Elaine M. Schuttinger
Trinity Catholic School
Columbus, OH

Mark Stahl
Longfellow Middle School
Norman, OK

Mollie Shanahan MacAdams
Southern Middle School
Lothian, MD

Sara Burkemper
Parkway West Middle Schools
Chesterfield, MO

Alicia Lewis
Mountain Brook Junior High
  School
Birmingham, AL

Steven E. Douglas
Northwest Jackson Middle
  School
Ridgeland, MS

LaShonda Grier
Richmond County Public
  Schools
Martinez, GA

Samuel Doughty
Spirit of Knowledge Charter
  School
Worcester, MA

CONTENTS

Norbert Millauer/AFP/Getty Images

CHAPTER 1

David Hay Jones/Science Source

CHAPTER 2

CONTENTS

CONTENTS

Lebrecht Music and Arts Photo Library/Alamy

CHAPTER 9

Scala/Art Resource, NY

CHAPTER 10

Italian School/The Bridgeman Art Library/Getty Images

CHAPTER 11

CONTENTS

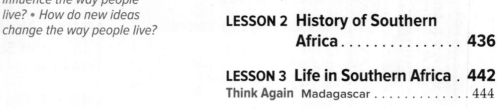

CONTENTS

Werner Forman/Art Resource, NY

CHAPTER **21**

The Americas **605**

FEATURES

Think Again?

Thinking Like a Geographer

EXPLORE the CONTINENT

GLOBAL CONNECTIONS

What Do You **Think?**

FEATURES

FEATURES

MAPS

UNIT 4: CENTRAL AMERICA, THE CARIBBEAN ISLANDS, AND SOUTH AMERICA

CHARTS, GRAPHS, DIAGRAMS, AND INFOGRAPHICS

Videos

Lessons have videos to help you learn more about your world!

networks ONLINE RESOURCES

Interactive Graphic Organizers

Interactive Images

⌄ Games

HOW TO USE THE ONLINE STUDENT EDITION

TO THE STUDENT

Welcome to McGraw-Hill Education's **Networks** Online Student Learning Center. Here you will access your Online Student Edition, as well as many other learning resources.

① LOGGING ON TO THE STUDENT LEARNING CENTER

Using your Internet browser, go to connected.mcgraw-hill.com.

Enter your username and password or create a new account using the redemption code your teacher gave you.

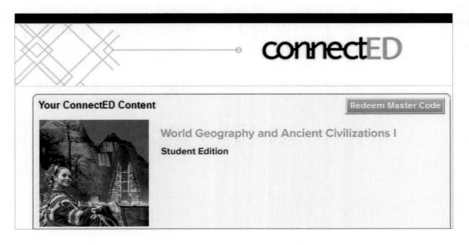

② SELECT YOUR PROGRAM

Click your program to launch the home page of your Online Student Learning Center.

HOW TO USE THE ONLINE STUDENT EDITION

Using Your Home Page

(1) **HOME PAGE**

To return to your home page at any time, click the program's title in the top left corner of the page.

(2) **QUICK LINKS MENU**

Use this menu to access:
- Messages
- Notes (your personal notepad)
- The online Glossary
- The online Atlas

(3) **HELP**

For videos and assistance with the various features of the Networks system, click Help.

(4) **MAIN MENU**

Use the menu bar to access:
- The Online Student Edition
- Skills Builder (for activities to improve your skills)
- Test Prep
- Resource Library
- Assignments
- Assessments
- LearnSmart

(5) **ONLINE STUDENT EDITION**

Go to your Online Student Edition by selecting the chapter and lesson and then click Go.

(6) **ASSIGNMENTS**

Recent assignments from your teacher will appear here. Click the assignment or click See All to see the details.

(7) **RESOURCE LIBRARY**

Use the carousel to browse the Resource Library.

HOW TO USE THE ONLINE STUDENT EDITION

Using Your Online Student Edition

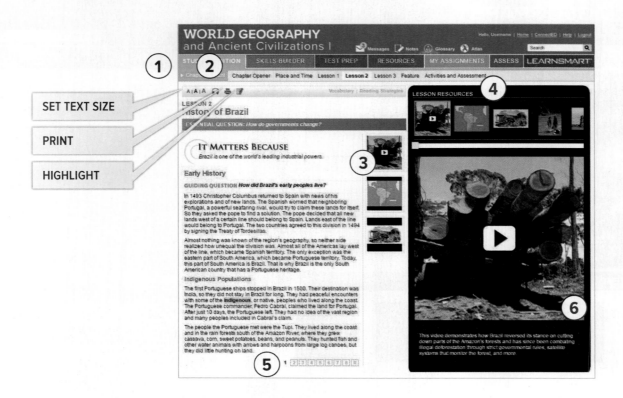

SET TEXT SIZE

PRINT

HIGHLIGHT

(1) LESSON MENU

- Use the tabs to open the different lessons and special features in a chapter.
- Clicking on the unit or chapter title will open the table of contents.

(2) AUDIO EDITION

Click on the headphones symbol to have the page read to you. MP3 files for downloading each lesson are available in the Resource Library.

(3) RESOURCES FOR THIS PAGE

Resources appear in the middle column to show that they go with the text on this page. Click the images to open them in the viewer.

(4) LESSON RESOURCES

Use the carousel to browse the interactive resources available in this lesson. Click on a resource to open it in the viewer below.

(5) CHANGE PAGES

Click here to move to the next page in the lesson.

(6) RESOURCE VIEWER

Click on the image that appears in the viewer to launch an interactive resource, including:

- Lesson Videos
- Photos and Slide Shows
- Maps
- Charts and Graphs
- Games
- Lesson Self-Check Quizzes

Reading Support in the Online Student Edition

Your Online Student Edition contains several features to help improve your reading skills and understanding of the content.

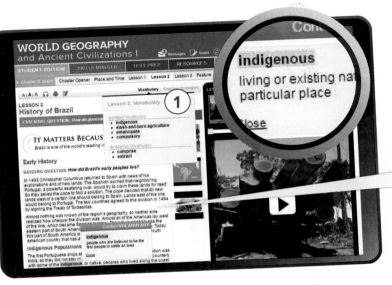

1 LESSON VOCABULARY

Click Vocabulary to bring up a list of terms introduced in this lesson.

VOCABULARY POP-UP

Click on any term highlighted in yellow to open a window with the term's definition.

2 NOTES

Click Notes to open the note-taking tool. You can write and save any notes you want in the Lesson Notes tab.

Click on the Guided Notes tab to view the Guided Reading Questions. Answering these questions will help you build a set of notes about the lesson.

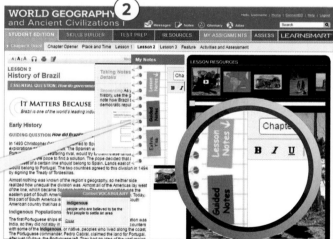

3 GRAPHIC ORGANIZER

Click Reading Strategies to open a note-taking activity using a graphic organizer.

Click the image of the graphic organizer to make it interactive. You can type directly into the graphic organizer and save or print your notes.

HOW TO USE THE ONLINE STUDENT EDITION

Using Interactive Resources in the Online Student Edition

Each lesson of your Online Student Edition contains many resources to help you learn the content and skills you need to know for this subject.

Networks provides many kinds of resources. This symbol shows that the resource is a slide show.

① LAUNCHING RESOURCES

Clicking a resource in the viewer launches an interactive resource.

② QUESTIONS AND ACTIVITIES

When a resource appears in the viewer, one or two questions or activities typically appear beneath it. You can type and save your answers in the answer boxes and submit them to your teacher.

③ INTERACTIVE MAPS

When a map appears in the viewer, click on it to launch the interactive map. You can use the drawing tool to mark up the map. You can also zoom in and turn layers on and off to display different information. Many maps have animations and audio as well.

④ CHAPTER FEATURE

Each chapter begins with a feature called *Place and Time*. This feature includes a map and time line to help you understand when and where the events in this chapter took place.

The map and time line are both interactive. You can click on the map and the time line to access an interactive version.

HOW TO USE THE ONLINE STUDENT EDITION

Activities and Assessment

1 **CHAPTER ACTIVITIES AND ASSESSMENT**

At the end of each chapter is the Activities and Assessment tab. Here you can test your understanding of what you have learned. You can type and save answers in the answer boxes and submit them to your teacher.

When a question or an activity uses an image, graph, or map, it will appear in the viewer.

Finding Other Resources

There are hundreds of additional resources available in the Resource Library.

2 **RESOURCE LIBRARY**

Click the Resources tab to find collections of Primary Sources, Biographies, Skills Activities, and the Reading Essentials and Study Guide.

You can search the Resource Library by lesson or keyword.

Click the star to mark a resource as a favorite.

REFERENCE ATLAS

ATLAS KEY

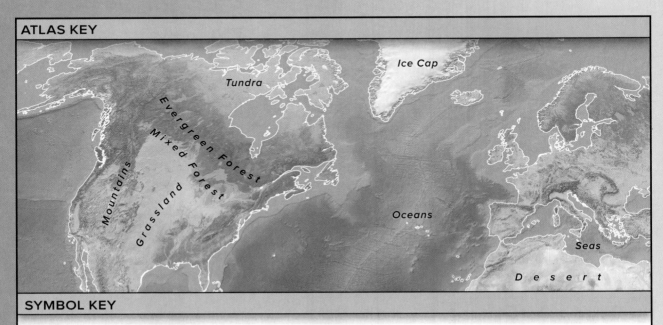

SYMBOL KEY

.... Claimed boundary

——— International boundary
(political map)

——— International boundary
(physical map)

⊗ National capital

○ State/Provincial capital

• Towns

▼ Depression

▲ Elevation

 Dry salt lake

Lake

Rivers

Canal

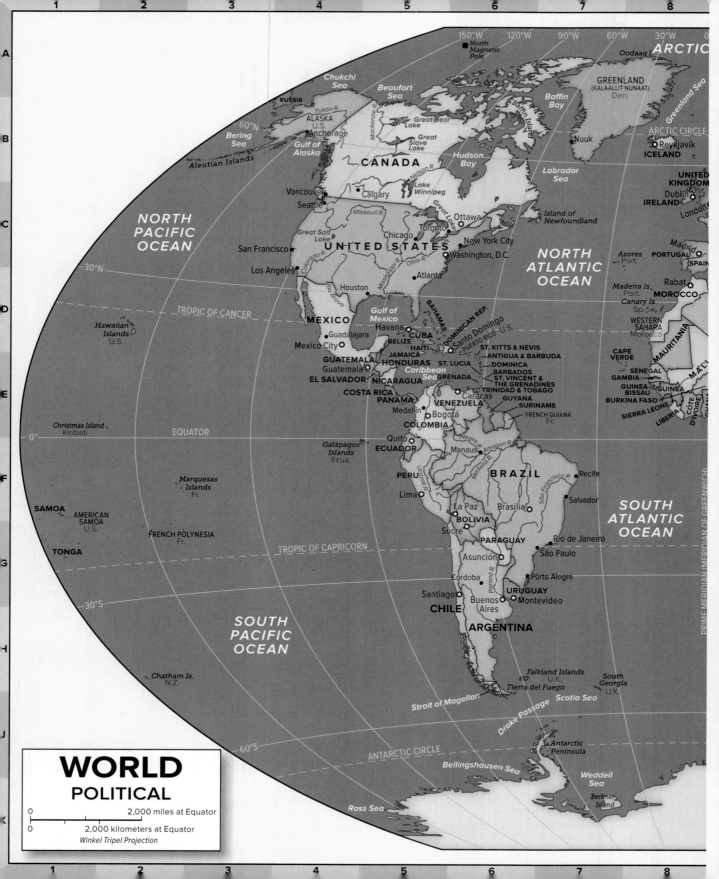

WORLD
POLITICAL

0 ————————— 2,000 miles at Equator

0 ————————— 2,000 kilometers at Equator

Winkel Tripel Projection

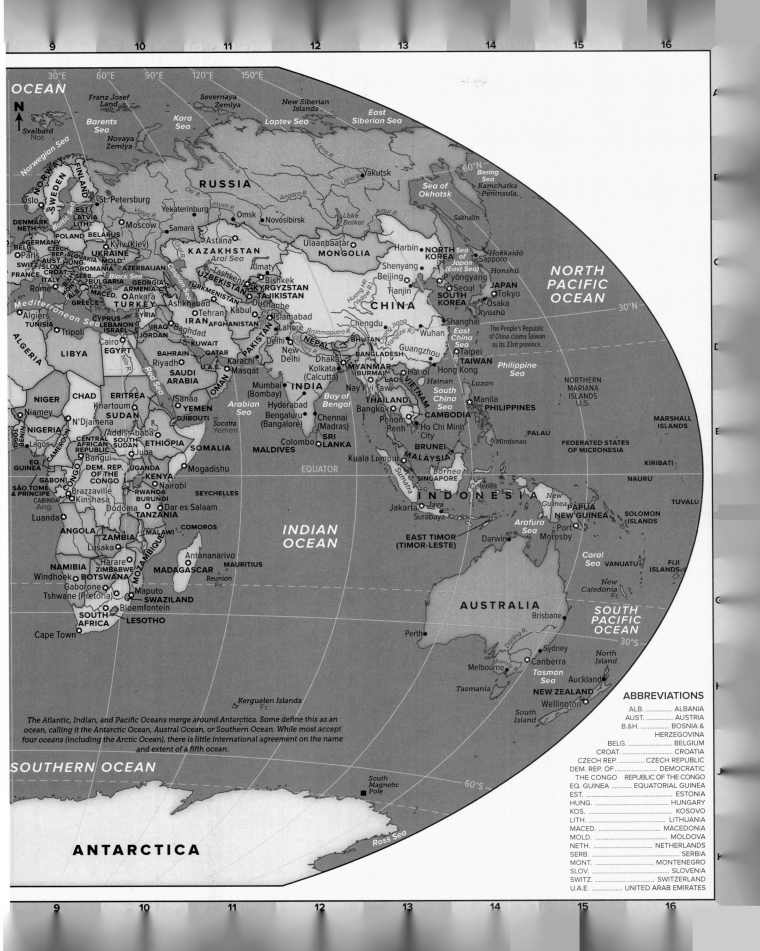

OCEAN

N

Svalbard
Nor.
Franz Josef
Land
Severnaya
Zemlya
New Siberian
Islands
Barents
Sea
Novaya
Zemlya
Kara
Sea
Laptev Sea
East
Siberian Sea
Norwegian Sea
NORWAY
SWEDEN
FINLAND
Oslo
St. Petersburg
Yekaterinburg
Omsk
Novosibirsk
RUSSIA
Lena R.
Yakutsk
60°N
Bering
Sea
Kamchatka
Peninsula
Sea of
Okhotsk
DENMARK
NETH.
EST.
LATVIA
LITH.
Moscow
Samara
Astana
Ulaanbaatar
Harbin
Sakhalin
BELG.
GERMANY
POLAND
BELARUS
CZECH
REP. Slovakia
UKRAINE
KAZAKHSTAN
Aral Sea
Almaty
Bishkek
MONGOLIA
NORTH
KOREA
Shenyang
Sea of
Japan
(East Sea)
Hokkaidō
Sapporo
Paris
SWITZ.
FRANCE
AUST. HUNG.
CROAT. SERB.
SLOV.
ROMANIA
MOLD.
BULGARIA
AZERBAIJAN
UZBEKISTAN
KYRGYZSTAN
Beijing
Tianjin
P'yŏngyang
Seoul
SOUTH
KOREA
JAPAN
Tokyo
Osaka
Honshū
Kyūshū
NORTH
PACIFIC
OCEAN
Rome
ITALY
B.&H.
MONT.
KOS.
MACED.
GREECE
ARMENIA
GEORGIA
TURKEY
Ankara
Ashkhabad
TURKMENISTAN
TAJIKISTAN
Dushanbe
CHINA
Chengdu
Huang He
(Yellow R.)
Chang Jiang
(Yangtze R.)
Wuhan
Shanghai
East
China
Sea
30°N
The People's Republic
of China claims Taiwan
as its 23rd province.
Black Sea
Caspian Sea
Mediterranean Sea
CYPRUS
SYRIA
LEBANON
ISRAEL
IRAN
Tehran
Kabul
AFGHANISTAN
Islamabad
Lahore
Brahmaputra R.
NEPAL
BHUTAN
BANGLADESH
Guangzhou
Hong Kong
Taipei
TAIWAN
Philippine
Sea
Algiers
TUNISIA
Tripoli
ALGERIA
LIBYA
EGYPT
Cairo
Nile R.
JORDAN
IRAQ
Baghdad
KUWAIT
QATAR
BAHRAIN
U.A.E.
Riyadh
SAUDI
ARABIA
OMAN
PAKISTAN
Karachi
Masqat
Delhi
New
Delhi
Ganges R.
Dhaka
MYANMAR
(BURMA)
Nay Pyi Taw
Kolkata
(Calcutta)
Hanoi
LAOS
VIETNAM
South
China
Sea
Hainan
Luzon
Manila
PHILIPPINES
NORTHERN
MARIANA
ISLANDS
U.S.
MARSHALL
ISLANDS
NIGER
CHAD
ERITREA
Khartoum
SUDAN
Sanaa
YEMEN
Red Sea
Arabian
Sea
Mumbai
(Bombay)
Hyderabad
INDIA
Bengaluru
(Bangalore)
Bay of
Bengal
Chennai
(Madras)
THAILAND
Bangkok
CAMBODIA
Phnom
Penh
Ho Chi Minh
City
NIGER
Niamey
BENIN
NIGERIA
Lagos
CENTRAL
AFRICAN
REPUBLIC
N'Djamena
Addis Ababa
DJIBOUTI
Socotra
Yemen
SOMALIA
Colombo
SRI
LANKA
MALDIVES
BRUNEI
MALAYSIA
Kuala Lumpur
SINGAPORE
PALAU
FEDERATED STATES
OF MICRONESIA
KIRIBATI
EQUATOR
CAMEROON
EQ.
GUINEA
GABON
CONGO
SÃO TOMÉ
& PRÍNCIPE
CABINDA
Ang.
Banqui
DEM. REP.
OF THE
CONGO
Brazzaville
Kinshasa
SOUTH
SUDAN
Juba
UGANDA
KENYA
Nairobi
RWANDA
BURUNDI
Mogadishu
SEYCHELLES
Mindanao
INDONESIA
Sumatra
Borneo
Celebes
New
Guinea
PAPUA
NEW GUINEA
Port
Moresby
SOLOMON
ISLANDS
NAURU
TUVALU
Luanda
ANGOLA
TANZANIA
Dodoma
Dar es Salaam
ZAMBIA
Lusaka
MALAWI
MOZAMBIQUE
COMOROS
INDIAN
OCEAN
Jakarta
Surabaya
Java
Arafura
Sea
Darwin
EAST TIMOR
(TIMOR-LESTE)
Coral
Sea
VANUATU
New
Caledonia
Fr.
FIJI
ISLANDS
NAMIBIA
Windhoek
BOTSWANA
Gaborone
Tshwane (Pretoria)
ZIMBABWE
Harare
Antananarivo
MADAGASCAR
MAURITIUS
Reunion
Fr.
Maputo
SWAZILAND
AUSTRALIA
Brisbane
SOUTH
PACIFIC
OCEAN
30°S
SOUTH
AFRICA
Bloemfontein
LESOTHO
Cape Town
Perth
Murray R.
Darling R.
Melbourne
Sydney
Canberra
North
Island
Tasmania
Auckland
Tasman
Sea
NEW ZEALAND
Wellington
South
Island
Kerguelen Islands
Fr.

The Atlantic, Indian, and Pacific Oceans merge around Antarctica. Some define this as an
ocean, calling it the Antarctic Ocean, Austral Ocean, or Southern Ocean. While most accept
four oceans (including the Arctic Ocean), there is little international agreement on the name
and extent of a fifth ocean.

SOUTHERN OCEAN

South
Magnetic
Pole
60°S

ANTARCTICA

Ross Sea

ABBREVIATIONS

ALB.	ALBANIA
AUST.	AUSTRIA
B.&H.	BOSNIA & HERZEGOVINA
BELG.	BELGIUM
CROAT.	CROATIA
CZECH REP.	CZECH REPUBLIC
DEM. REP. OF THE CONGO	DEMOCRATIC REPUBLIC OF THE CONGO
EQ. GUINEA	EQUATORIAL GUINEA
EST.	ESTONIA
HUNG.	HUNGARY
KOS.	KOSOVO
LITH.	LITHUANIA
MACED.	MACEDONIA
MOLD.	MOLDOVA
NETH.	NETHERLANDS
SERB.	SERBIA
MONT.	MONTENEGRO
SLOV.	SLOVENIA
SWITZ.	SWITZERLAND
U.A.E.	UNITED ARAB EMIRATES

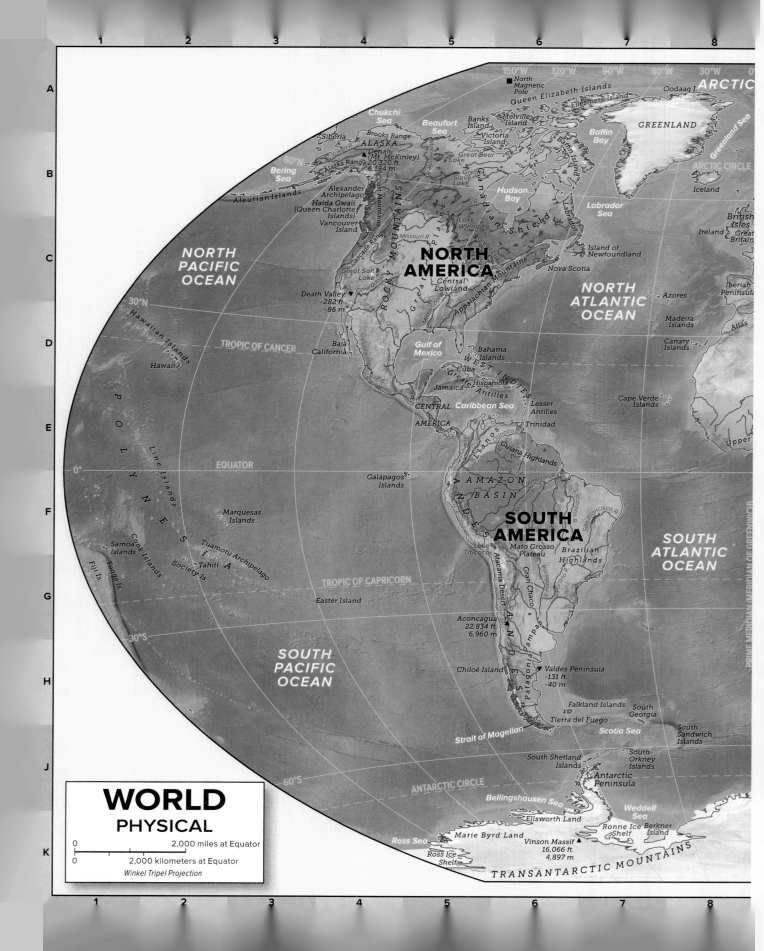

WORLD
PHYSICAL

0   2,000 miles at Equator

0   2,000 kilometers at Equator

Winkel Tripel Projection

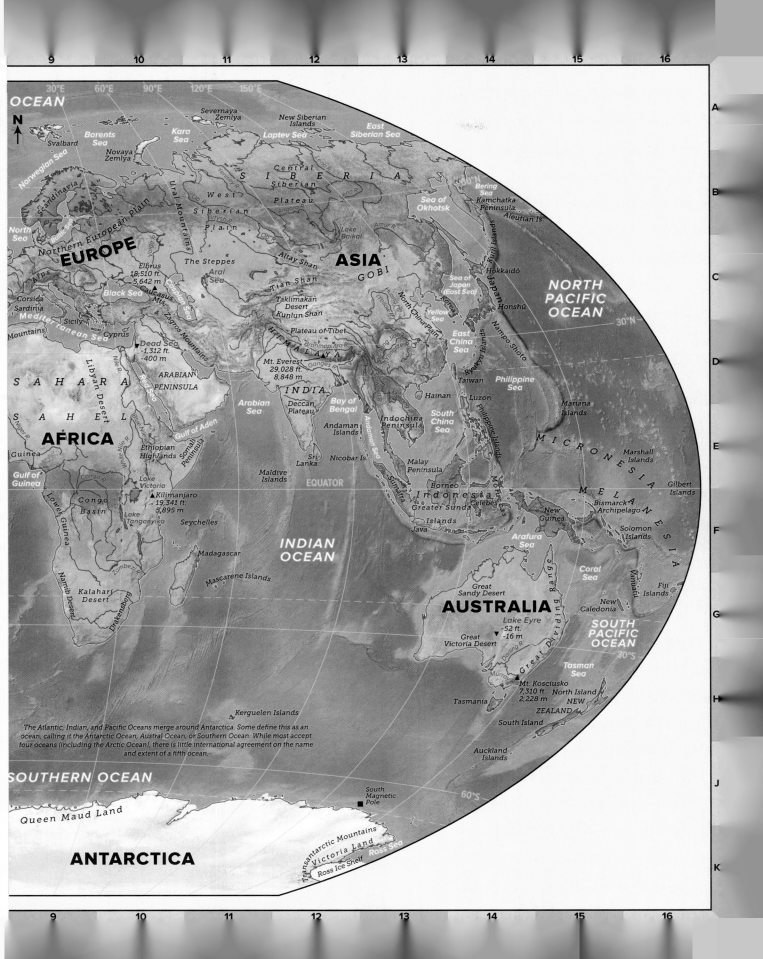

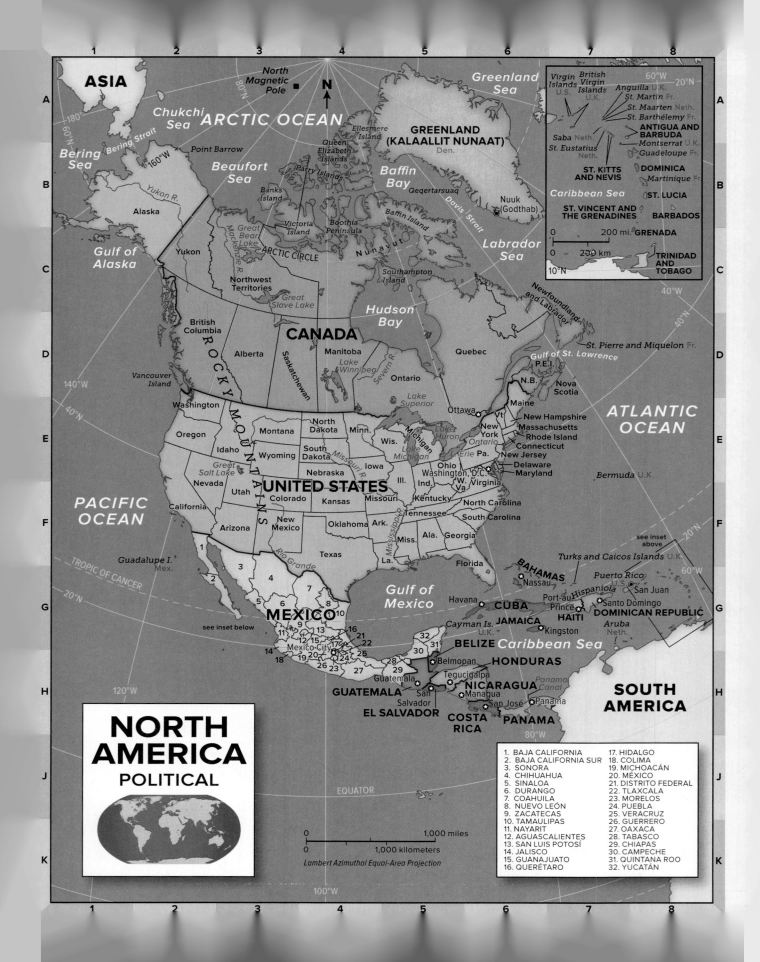

NORTH AMERICA
POLITICAL

1. BAJA CALIFORNIA
2. BAJA CALIFORNIA SUR
3. SONORA
4. CHIHUAHUA
5. SINALOA
6. DURANGO
7. COAHUILA
8. NUEVO LEÓN
9. ZACATECAS
10. TAMAULIPAS
11. NAYARIT
12. AGUASCALIENTES
13. SAN LUIS POTOSÍ
14. JALISCO
15. GUANAJUATO
16. QUERÉTARO
17. HIDALGO
18. COLIMA
19. MICHOACÁN
20. MÉXICO
21. DISTRITO FEDERAL
22. TLAXCALA
23. MORELOS
24. PUEBLA
25. VERACRUZ
26. GUERRERO
27. OAXACA
28. TABASCO
29. CHIAPAS
30. CAMPECHE
31. QUINTANA ROO
32. YUCATÁN

0   1,000 miles
0   1,000 kilometers
Lambert Azimuthal Equal-Area Projection

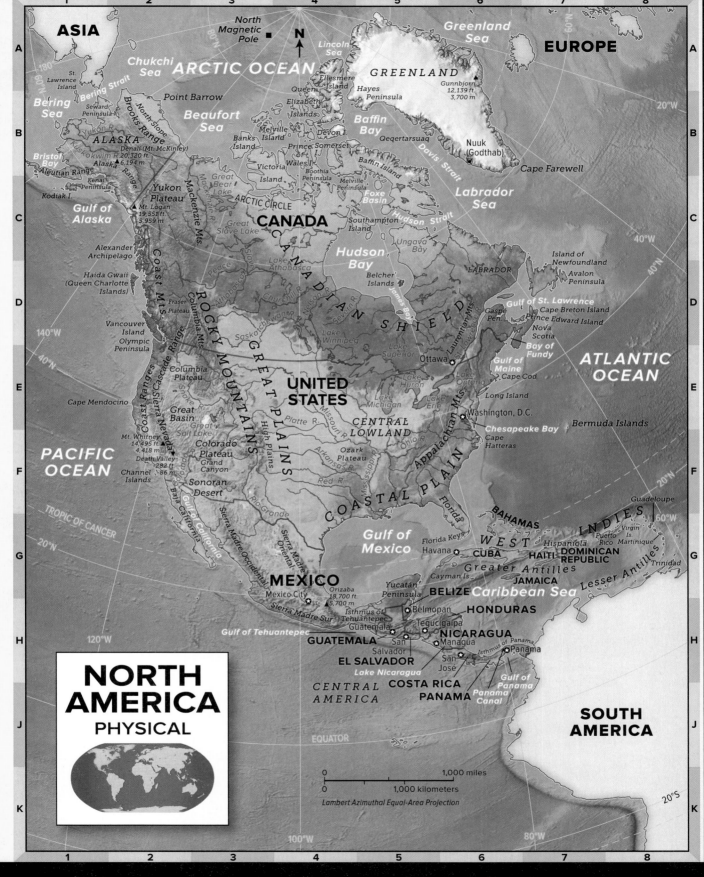

NORTH AMERICA
PHYSICAL

ASIA

EUROPE

Greenland Sea

Chukchi Sea ARCTIC OCEAN

North Magnetic Pole

N

Lincoln Sea

GREENLAND

Point Barrow

Ellesmere Island

Hayes Peninsula

Gunnbjorn 12,139 ft. 3,700 m

Queen Elizabeth Islands

Beaufort Sea

North Slope

Bering Strait

St. Lawrence Island

Bering Sea

Seward Peninsula

ALASKA

Brooks Range

Yukon R.

Denali (Mt. McKinley) 20,320 ft. 6,194 m

Melville Island

Banks Island

Devon I.

Somerset I.

Prince of Wales I.

Boothia Peninsula

Baffin Bay

Qeqertarsuaq

Nuuk (Godthab)

Cape Farewell

Davis Strait

Bristol Bay

Aleutian Range

Kuskokwim R.

Alaska Range

Kenai Peninsula

Kodiak I.

Gulf of Alaska

Mt. Logan 19,551 ft. 5,959 m

Yukon Plateau

Great Bear Lake

ARCTIC CIRCLE

Mackenzie Mts.

Victoria Island

Melville Peninsula

Baffin Island

Foxe Basin

Hudson Strait

Labrador Sea

Island of Newfoundland

Avalon Peninsula

Alexander Archipelago

Haida Gwaii (Queen Charlotte Islands)

Vancouver Island

Olympic Peninsula

Coast Mts.

Fraser Plateau

Columbia Mts.

Great Slave Lake

CANADA

Slave R.

Peace R.

Athabasca R.

Lake Athabasca

CANADIAN SHIELD

Hudson Bay

Belcher Islands

Southampton Island

Ungava Bay

LABRADOR

Gulf of St. Lawrence

Gaspé Pen.

Cape Breton Island

Prince Edward Island

Nova Scotia

Bay of Fundy

ATLANTIC OCEAN

140°W

Columbia Plateau

ROCKY MOUNTAINS

Columbia R.

Churchill R.

Saskatchewan R.

Nelson R.

Severn R.

Lake Winnipeg

Lake Superior

Laurentian Mts.

Ottawa

Lake Ontario

Gulf of Maine

Cape Cod

Cape Mendocino

Cascade Range

Sierra Nevada

Coast Ranges

Snake R.

Great Basin

Great Salt Lake

GREAT PLAINS

High Plains

Platte R.

Missouri R.

Lake Michigan

Lake Huron

Lake Erie

CENTRAL LOWLAND

Appalachian Mts.

Washington, D.C.

Long Island

Chesapeake Bay

Cape Hatteras

Bermuda Islands

PACIFIC OCEAN

Mt. Whitney 14,495 ft. 4,418 m

Death Valley -282 ft. -86 m

Colorado Plateau

Grand Canyon

Ozark Plateau

Arkansas R.

Ohio R.

Mississippi R.

Channel Islands

Sonoran Desert

Baja California

Sierra Madre Occidental

Rio Grande

Red R.

COASTAL PLAIN

Florida

TROPIC OF CANCER

120°W

Gulf of California

MEXICO

Mexico City

Sierra Madre Oriental

Sierra Madre Sur

Orizaba 18,700 ft. 5,700 m

Isthmus of Tehuantepec

Gulf of Tehuantepec

Gulf of Mexico

Florida Keys

Havana

CUBA

BAHAMAS

WEST

Greater Antilles

Cayman Is.

JAMAICA

INDIES

Hispaniola

HAITI

DOMINICAN REPUBLIC

Puerto Rico

Virgin Is.

Martinique

Guadeloupe

Lesser Antilles

Trinidad

20°N

Yucatán Peninsula

BELIZE

Belmopan

Caribbean Sea

GUATEMALA

Guatemala

Tegucigalpa

HONDURAS

NICARAGUA

Managua

Isthmus of Panama

Panama

CENTRAL AMERICA

San Salvador

EL SALVADOR

Lake Nicaragua

San José

COSTA RICA

PANAMA

Gulf of Panama

Panama Canal

SOUTH AMERICA

EQUATOR

0   1,000 miles

0   1,000 kilometers

Lambert Azimuthal Equal-Area Projection

20°S

80°W

100°W

60°W

40°W

20°W

20°N

40°N

60°N

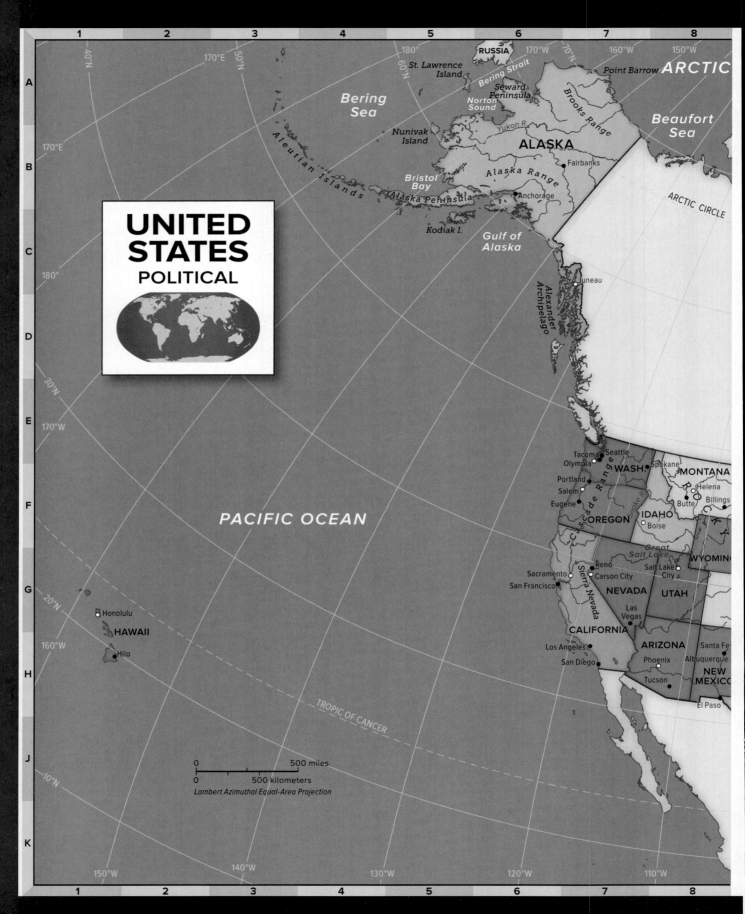

UNITED STATES
POLITICAL

PACIFIC OCEAN

Bering Sea

St. Lawrence Island
Bering Strait
Seward Peninsula
Norton Sound
Nunivak Island
Yukon R.
ALASKA
Brooks Range
Point Barrow
ARCTIC
Beaufort Sea
ARCTIC CIRCLE
Fairbanks
Alaska Range
Anchorage
Bristol Bay
Alaska Peninsula
Kodiak I.
Gulf of Alaska
Juneau
Alexander Archipelago
Aleutian Islands

RUSSIA

Honolulu
HAWAII
Hilo

TROPIC OF CANCER

Tacoma Seattle
Olympia Spokane
WASH.
Portland
Salem
Eugene
OREGON
MONTANA
Helena
Butte Billings
IDAHO
Boise
Snake R.
Great Salt Lake
WYOMING
Salt Lake City
Reno
Carson City
Sacramento
San Francisco
NEVADA
UTAH
Las Vegas
CALIFORNIA
Los Angeles
San Diego
ARIZONA
Phoenix
Tucson
Santa Fe
Albuquerque
NEW MEXICO
El Paso

Sierra Nevada
Cascade Range

| 0 | 500 miles |
| 0 | 500 kilometers |

Lambert Azimuthal Equal-Area Projection

40°N
170°E
50°N
180°
170°E
60°N
170°W
180°
30°N
170°W
20°N
160°W
10°N
150°W
140°W
130°W
120°W
110°W
170°W
160°W
150°W
70°N

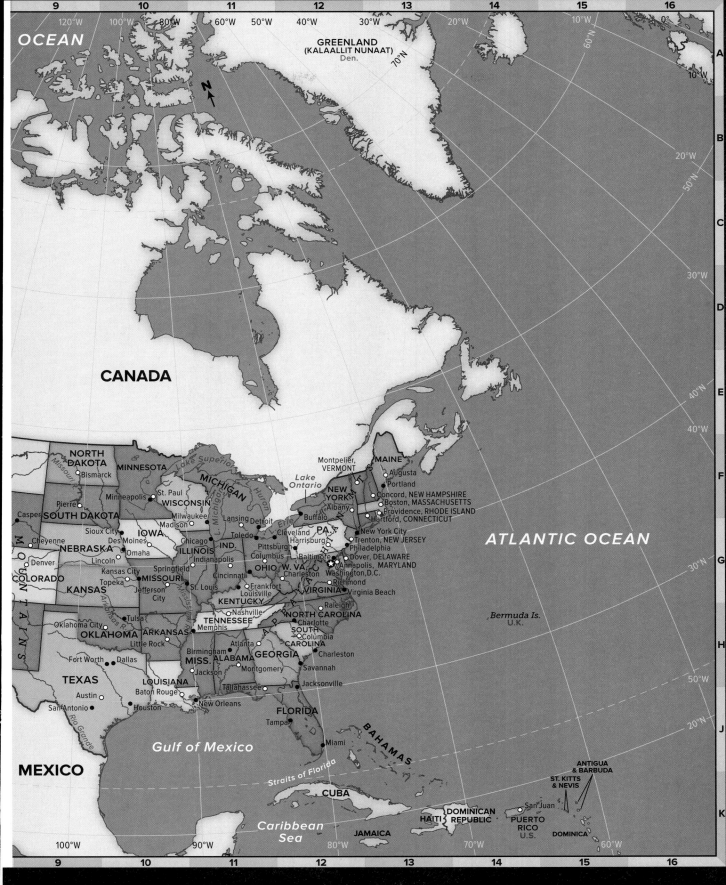

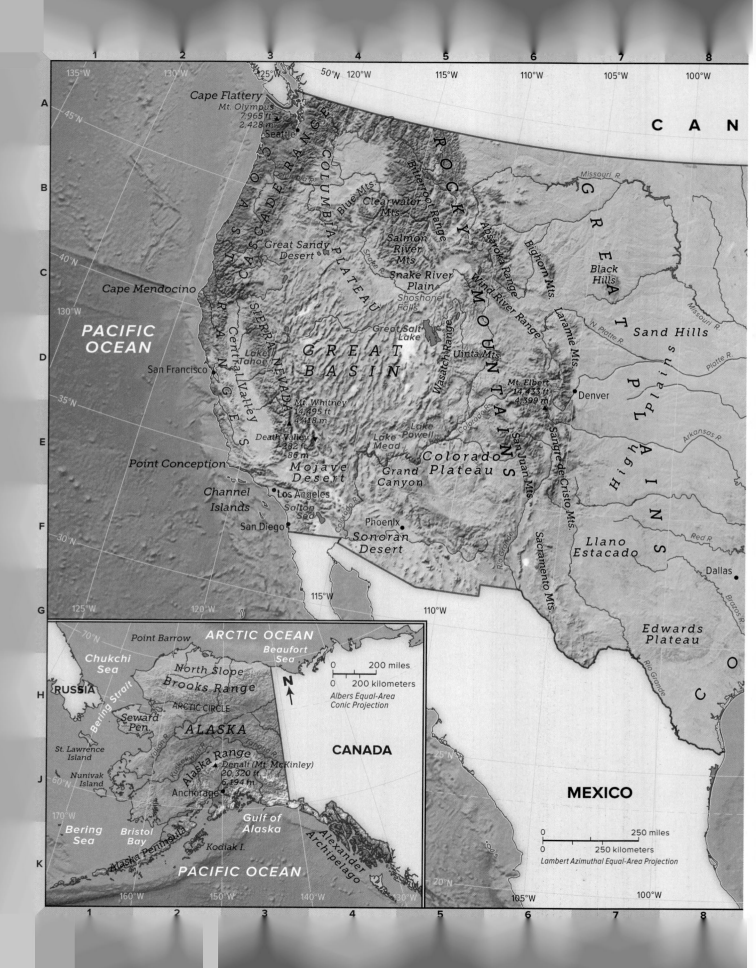

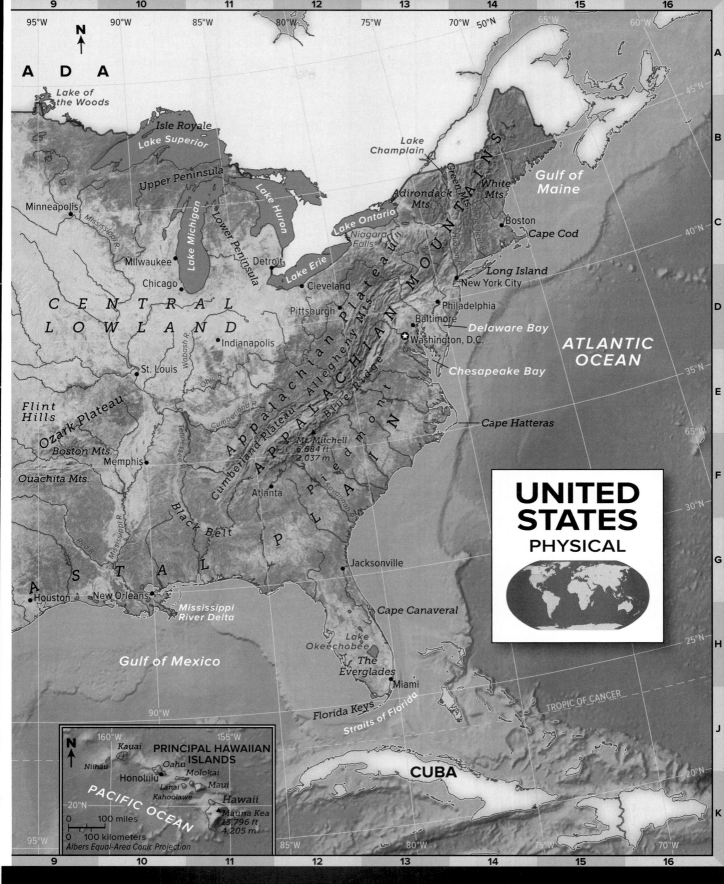

UNITED STATES PHYSICAL

PRINCIPAL HAWAIIAN ISLANDS

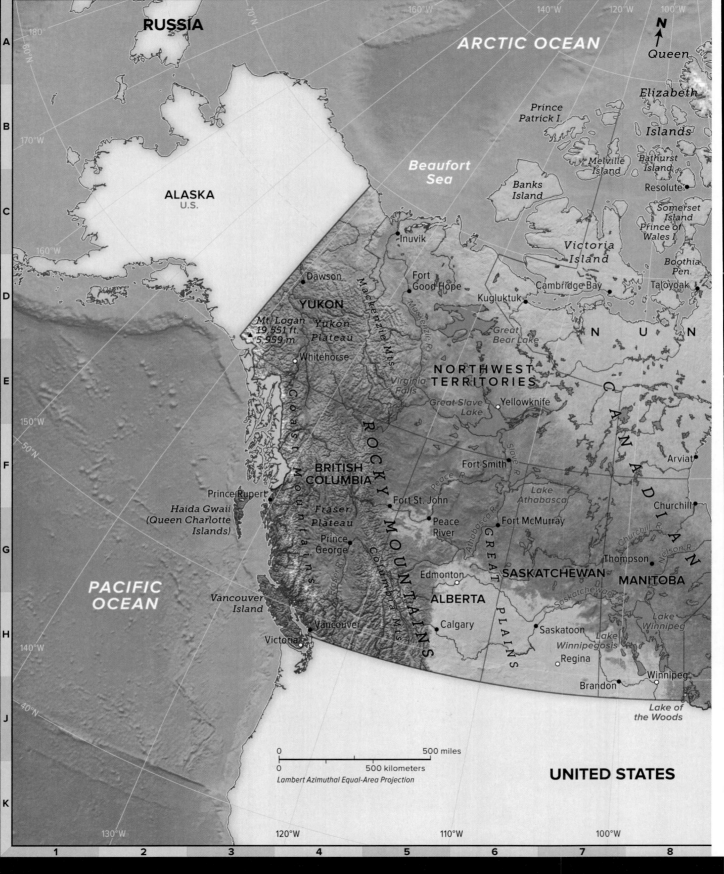

RUSSIA

ARCTIC OCEAN

N
Queen

Elizabeth

Prince
Patrick I.

Islands

Melville
Island

Bathurst
Island

Resolute

ALASKA
U.S.

Beaufort
Sea

Banks
Island

Somerset
Island
Prince of
Wales I.

Boothia
Pen.

Inuvik

Dawson

Fort
Good Hope

Kugluktuk

Victoria
Island

Cambridge Bay

Talóyoak

YUKON

▲ Mt. Logan
19,551 ft.
5,959 m

Yukon
Plateau

Whitehorse

N U N

Great
Bear Lake

NORTHWEST
TERRITORIES

Virginia
Falls

Great Slave
Lake

Yellowknife

C A N A D I A N

Fort Smith

Arviat

BRITISH
COLUMBIA

Fraser
Plateau

Prince Rupert

Haida Gwaii
(Queen Charlotte
Islands)

Prince
George

Fort St. John

Peace
River

Lake
Athabasca

Fort McMurray

Churchill

Thompson

GREAT

SASKATCHEWAN

MANITOBA

PACIFIC
OCEAN

Vancouver
Island

Vancouver

Victoria

Edmonton

ALBERTA

Calgary

Saskatoon

Lake
Winnipegosis

Regina

Brandon

PLAINS

Lake
Winnipeg

Winnipeg

Lake of
the Woods

0   500 miles

0   500 kilometers
Lambert Azimuthal Equal-Area Projection

UNITED STATES

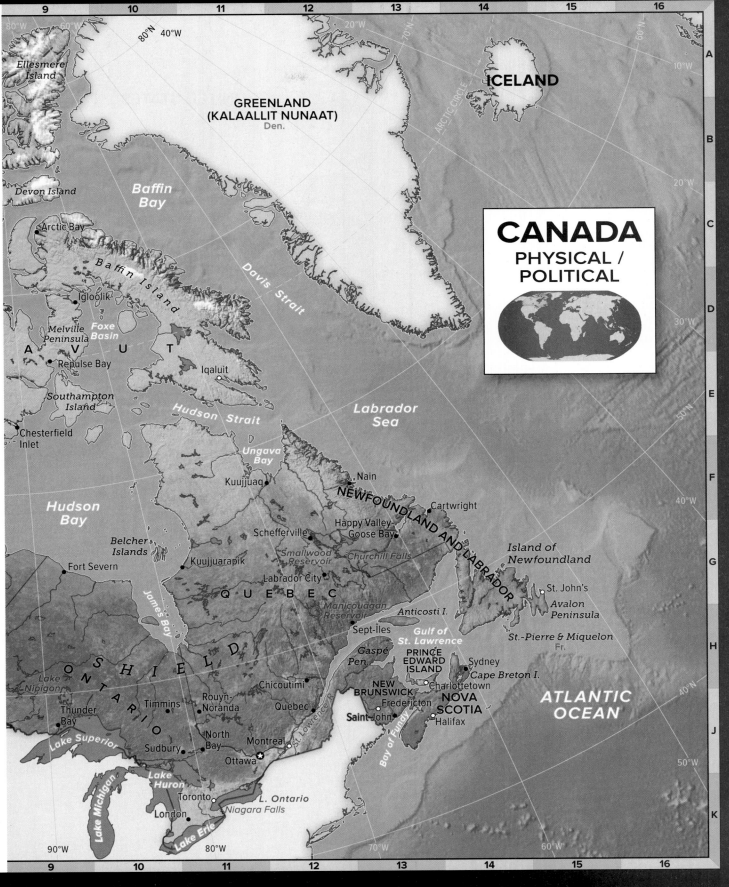

CANADA
PHYSICAL / POLITICAL

ICELAND

GREENLAND
(KALAALLIT NUNAAT)
Den.

Ellesmere
Island

Baffin
Bay

Devon Island

Arctic Bay

B a f f i n I s l a n d

Davis Strait

Igloolik

Melville
Peninsula

Foxe
Basin

N U N A V U T

Repulse Bay

Southampton
Island

Iqaluit

Hudson Strait

Chesterfield
Inlet

Labrador
Sea

Ungava
Bay

Hudson
Bay

Nain

Kuujjuaq

NEWFOUNDLAND

Belcher
Islands

Schefferville

Happy Valley-
Goose Bay

Cartwright

AND LABRADOR

Fort Severn

Kuujjuarapik

Smallwood
Reservoir

Churchill Falls

Island of
Newfoundland

QUEBEC

Labrador City

St. John's

Manicouagan
Reservoir

Avalon
Peninsula

Anticosti I.

St.-Pierre & Miquelon
Fr.

Sept-Îles

Gulf of
St. Lawrence

S H I E L D

Gaspé
Pen.

PRINCE
EDWARD
ISLAND

Sydney
Cape Breton I.

Lake
Nipigon

O N T A R I O

Chicoutimi

Charlottetown

ATLANTIC
OCEAN

Timmins

Rouyn-
Noranda

Quebec

NEW
BRUNSWICK

NOVA
SCOTIA

Thunder
Bay

Fredericton

Lake Superior

North
Bay

St. Lawrence R.

Saint John

Halifax

Sudbury

Montreal

Bay of Fundy

Lake
Michigan

Lake
Huron

Ottawa

Toronto

L. Ontario

London

Niagara Falls

Lake Erie

James Bay

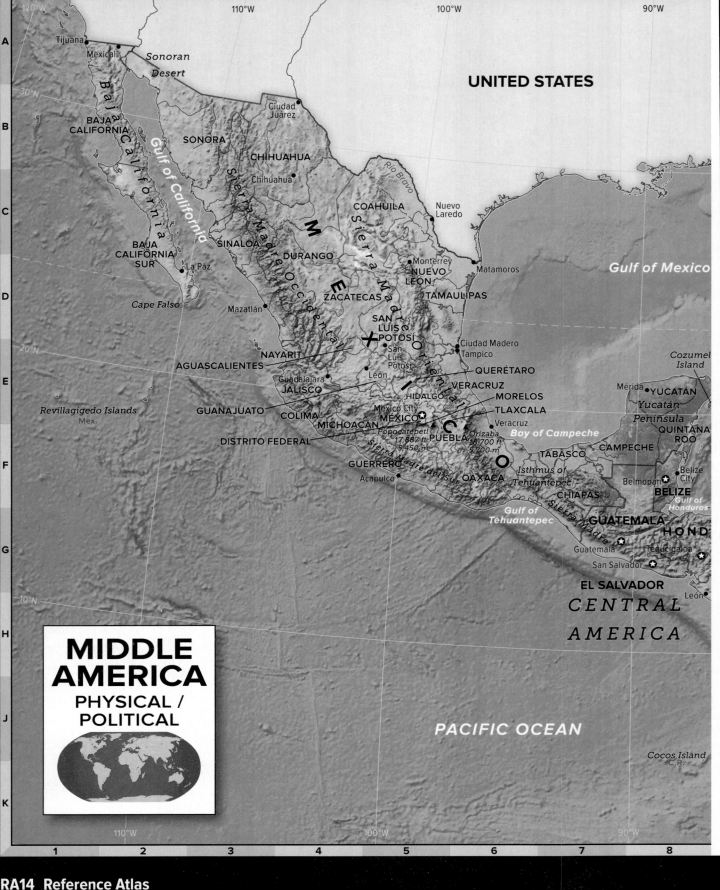

MIDDLE
AMERICA
PHYSICAL /
POLITICAL

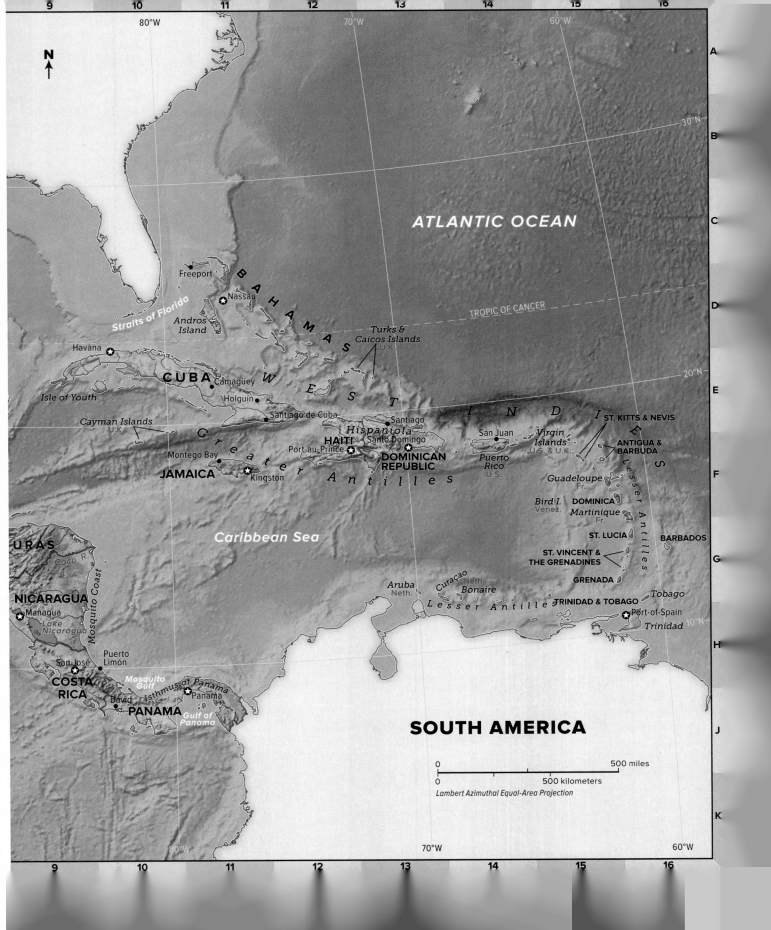

South America Political

Caribbean Sea

1 2 3 4 5 6 7 8

80°W   40°W

N

0   1,000 miles
0   1,000 kilometers
Lambert Azimuthal Equal-Area Projection

VENEZUELA
Caracas ✪
Lake Maracaibo   Orinoco R.   **GUYANA**
Bogotá ✪   **SURINAME**
                         Angel Falls   Georgetown ✪   Paramaribo ✪
                         Total drop   Cayenne •
                         3,212 ft. 979 m   *GUIANA HIGHLANDS*   **FRENCH GUIANA**
COLOMBIA
                         Río Negro   Boundary claimed   *Marajó Island*
Quito ✪   by Suriname
ECUADOR   *A M A Z O N*   *Amazon R.*   EQUATOR   0°
0°   0°

Marañón R.   *Amazon R.*
                         B A S I N   *Tapajós R.*
PERU   *S e l* *v a s*
                         Purus R. *Madeira R.*
                                                BRAZIL   *Araguaia R.* *São Francisco R.*
Lima ✪   *Ucayali R.*   *Xingu R.* *Tocantins R.*
                         ■   *B R A Z I L I A N*
Machu Picchu   *MATO GROSSO PLATEAU*
                         La Paz ✪   Brasília ✪
Lake Titicaca   **BOLIVIA**   *H I G H L A N D S*
                         ✪ Sucre
20°S   *Altiplano* *Salar de Uyuni* *CHACO* *Paraguay R.*   20°S

TROPIC OF CAPRICORN   **PARAGUAY**   *Iguazú Falls*
San Ambrosio I.   *GRAN*   ✪ Asunción
San Félix I.   *A*   *Paraná R.*
                         N   *Uruguay R.*
                         D
CHILE   *E*   *P A M P A S*
                         S   *Colorado R.*
         Acóncagua   Buenos Aires ✪ **URUGUAY**
Juan Fernández Is.   22,834 ft.   Montevideo ✪
                         6,960 m   **ARGENTINA**   *Río de la Plata*
         Santiago ✪   *ATLANTIC OCEAN*

Colorado R.
Negro R.

40°S   Chiloé Island   *P*   Valdés Peninsula   40°S
                         A   -131 ft.
                         T   -40 m
         Taitao   *A*   *Gulf of San Jorge*
PACIFIC   Peninsula *G*
OCEAN   *O*
         Wellington I.   *N*   Laguna del Carbón   *Falkland Islands*
                         I   -344 ft.   *(Islas Malvinas)*
                         A   -105 m
                                                       • Stanley
                         Tierra del Fuego
Strait of Magellan   *Cape Horn*   *South Georgia Island*

100°W   80°W   60°W   40°W   20°W

SOUTH AMERICA
PHYSICAL

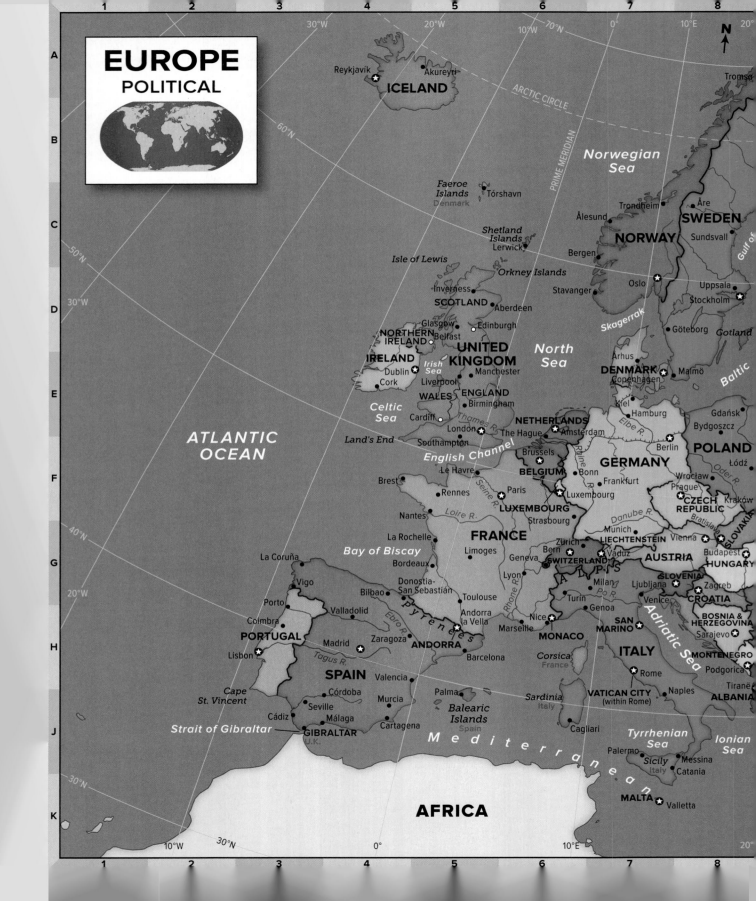

EUROPE
POLITICAL

N

Reykjavík · Akureyri
ICELAND

ARCTIC CIRCLE

Tromsö

Norwegian Sea

Faeroe Islands · Tórshavn
Denmark

Trondheim · · Åre

Ålesund · **SWEDEN**

Shetland Islands · **NORWAY** · Sundsvall
Lerwick

Isle of Lewis Bergen

Orkney Islands · Stavanger · Oslo ☆ · Uppsala

Inverness · Stockholm

SCOTLAND · Aberdeen *Skagerrak* · Göteborg · *Gotland*

Glasgow · Edinburgh Århus

NORTHERN Belfast · · Malmö
IRELAND **UNITED** · · **DENMARK** ☆
KINGDOM *North Sea* Copenhagen *Baltic*

IRELAND · Manchester Kiel

Dublin ☆ *Irish Sea* Hamburg · *Gdańsk*

Cork · Liverpool · Bydgoszcz

ENGLAND · Birmingham **NETHERLANDS** · Berlin ☆ **POLAND**

WALES The Hague · Amsterdam ☆
Cardiff · *Thames R.* *Elbe R.* · Łódź

Celtic Sea London ☆ · **GERMANY** Wrocław ·

Land's End Southampton Brussels ☆ *Rhine* · Prague ☆ *Oder R.*

English Channel **BELGIUM** Bonn · · Frankfurt **CZECH** Kraków

Le Havre · **GERMANY** · **REPUBLIC**

Brest · Paris · Luxembourg · Bratislava

Rennes · **LUXEMBOURG** · Munich · Vienna ☆ **SLOVAKIA**

Seine R. Strasbourg · *Danube R.* · **LIECHTENSTEIN** · Budapest ☆

Nantes · *Loire R.* Zürich · Vaduz ☆ **AUSTRIA** **HUNGARY**

FRANCE Bern ☆ · **SLOVENIA**

La Rochelle · · Geneva **SWITZERLAND** Ljubljana ☆ · Zagreb ☆

Bay of Biscay Limoges · Lyon · Milan · Venice **CROATIA**

La Coruña · Bordeaux · · Turin · *Po R.* · Genoa **BOSNIA &**

Vigo · Donostia- · · **SAN** **HERZEGOVINA**

Porto · San Sebastián · Nice **MARINO** Sarajevo ☆

Bilbao Toulouse · Marseille · **MONACO** · **MONTENEGRO**

Coímbra · **ANDORRA** **ITALY** Podgorica ☆

Valladolid Andorra · *Corsica* Rome ☆ Tiranë ☆

PORTUGAL la Vella France **VATICAN CITY** Naples · **ALBANIA**

Madrid ☆ Zaragoza · **ANDORRA** (within Rome)

Lisbon ☆ Barcelona *Tyrrhenian Sea* *Ionian Sea*

Cape St. Vincent **SPAIN** Valencia *Sardinia* · Cagliari

Córdoba · Palma Italy

Cádiz · Seville · Murcia *Balearic Islands* Palermo · *Sicily*

Málaga Cartagena Spain · Italy · Messina

Strait of Gibraltar **GIBRALTAR** **MALTA** ☆ · Catania

U.K. *Mediterranean* · Valletta

ATLANTIC OCEAN

Pyrenees
Ebro R.
Tagus R.

AFRICA

A commonly accepted division between Asia and Europe—here marked by a gray line—is formed by the Ural Mountains, Ural River, Caspian Sea, Caucasus Mountains, and the Black Sea with its outlets, the Bosporus and the Dardanelles.

Europe/Asia boundary

ASIA

ASIA

Barents Sea

Tobseda

Pechora

URAL MOUNTAINS

LAPLAND

Murmansk

Kirovsk

Kola Peninsula

White Sea

Umba

Ivalo

Kiruna

Kemi

Luleå

Umeå

Oulu

FINLAND

Kem'

Arkhangel'sk

Severodvinsk

Syktyvkar

Northern Dvina R.

Perm

Vaasa

Kuopio

Lake Onega

Pori

Tampere

Lake Ladoga

Kirov

Ufa

Turku

Helsinki

St. Petersburg

RUSSIA

Gulf of Bothnia

Sea

Tallinn

ESTONIA

Novgorod

Yaroslavl'

Kazan'

Orenburg

LATVIA

Riga

Tver'

Moscow

Nizhniy Novgorod

Samara

Ural R.

Daugavpils

Oral

LITHUANIA

Vilnius

Vitsyebsk

Smolensk

Ryazan'

Penza

Saratov

Kaunas

Kaliningrad

BELARUS

Minsk

Bryansk

Volga R.

Warsaw

Homyel'

Kursk

KAZAKHSTAN

Vistula R.

Chernihiv

Don R.

Volgograd

Sumy

L'viv

Kyiv (Kiev)

Kharkiv

Astrakhan

Carpathian Mts.

Vinnytsya

Dnieper R.

Poltava

Dniester R.

UKRAINE

Donets'k

Caspian Sea

Dnipropetrovs'k

Rostov

MOLDOVA

Stavropol'

Chişinău

Sea of Azov

Kerch

Grozny

Odessa

Crimea

Simferopol'

Caucasus Mountains

AZERBAIJAN

ROMANIA

Sevastopol'

Yalta

GEORGIA

Baku

Belgrade

Bucharest

Constanţa

SERBIA

Balkan Mts.

Varna

Black Sea

KOSOVO

Priština

BULGARIA

Bosporus

Sofia

Skopje

Istanbul

MACEDONIA

TURKEY

Thessaloníki

Dardanelles

Sea of Marmara

GREECE

Aegean Sea

ASIA

Athens

Peloponnese

Rhodes

Nicosia

Iráklion

Crete

Greece

CYPRUS

Sea

0   400 miles

0   400 kilometers

Lambert Azimuthal Equal-Area Projection

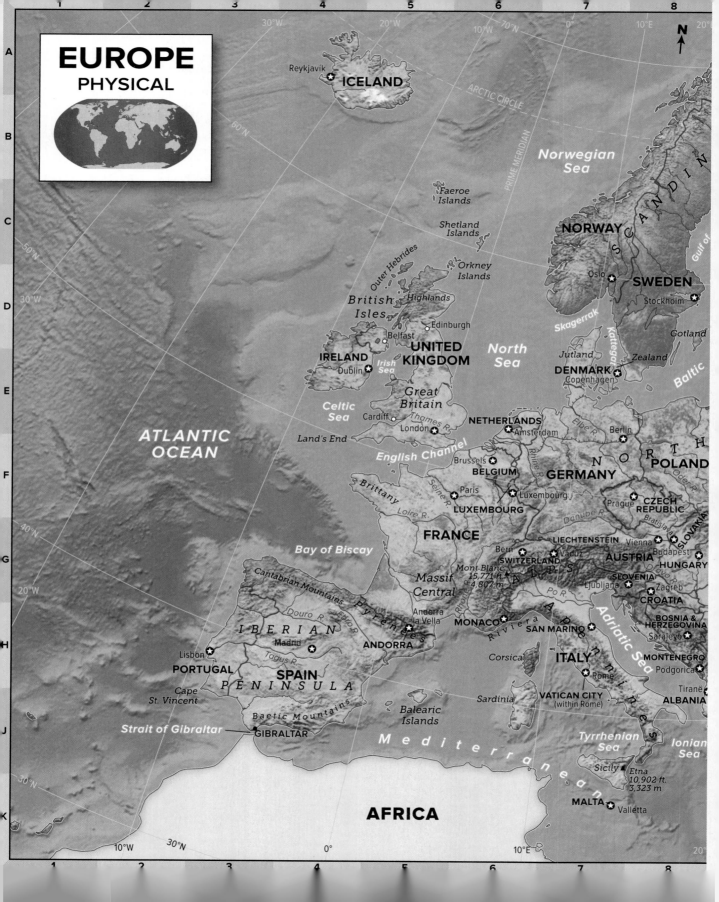

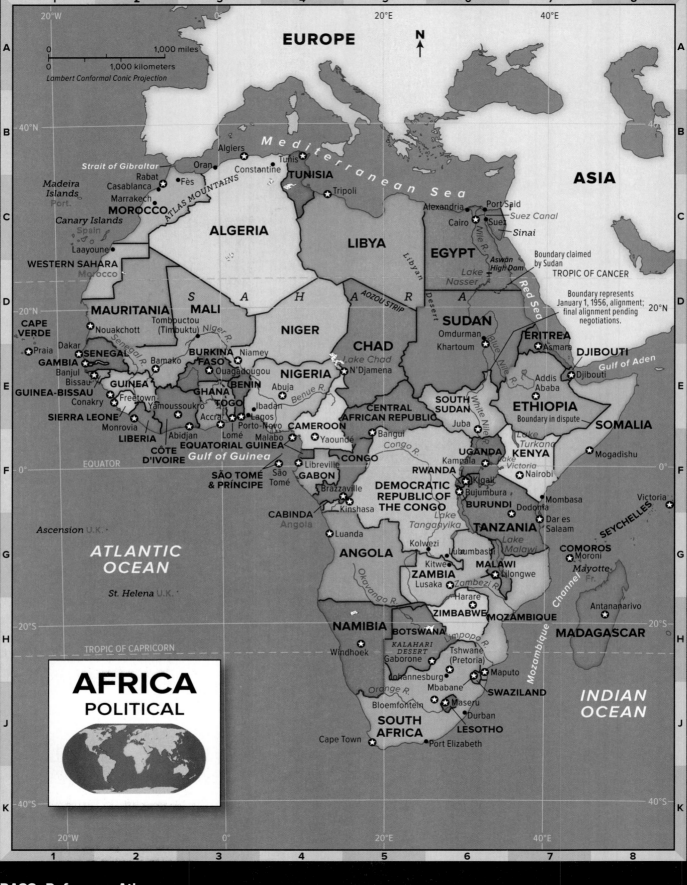

AFRICA
POLITICAL

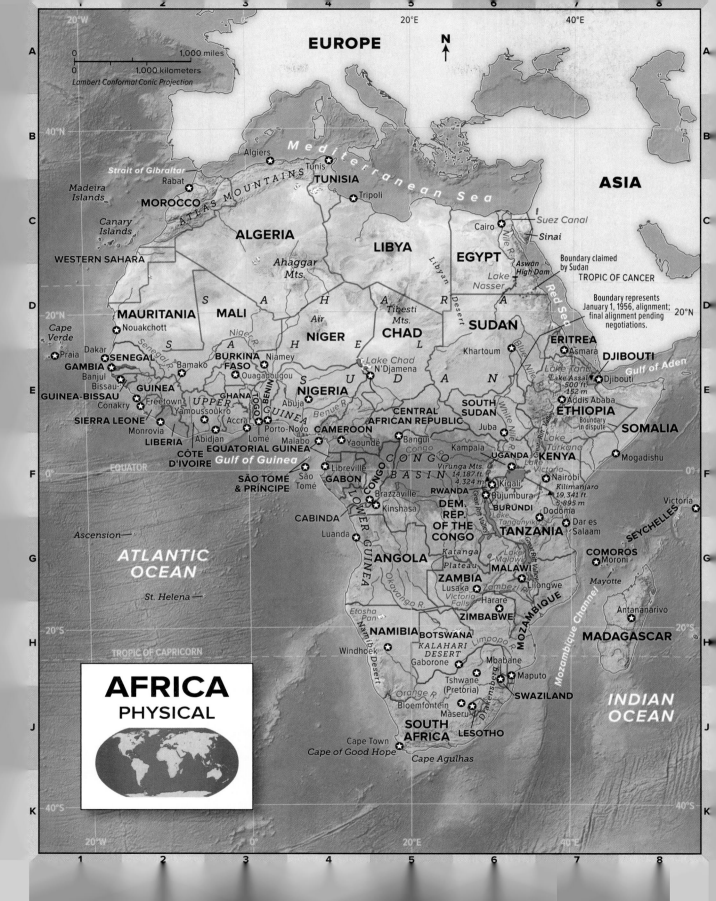

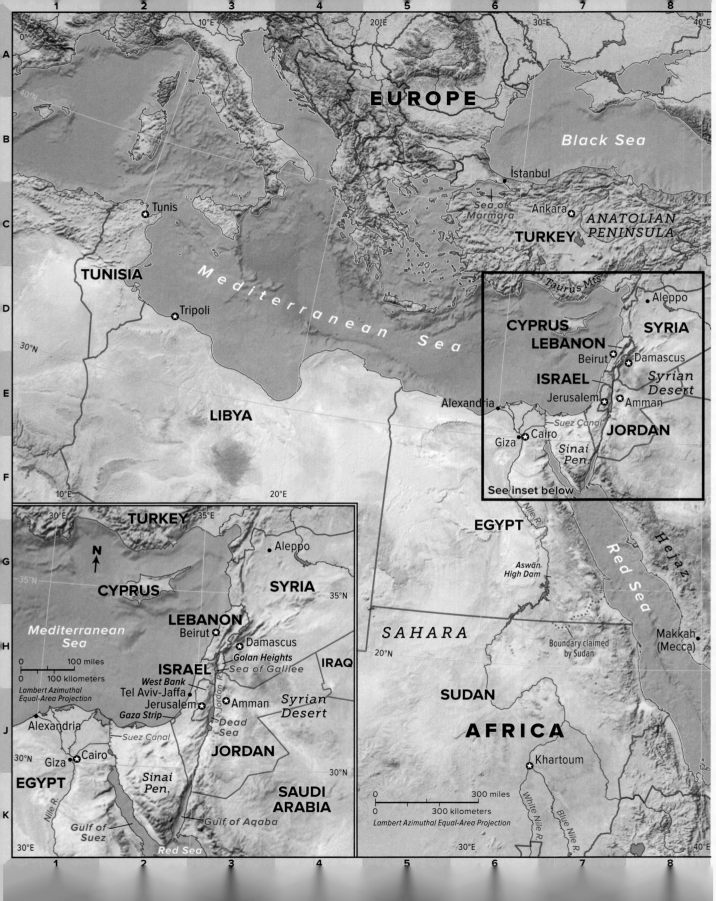

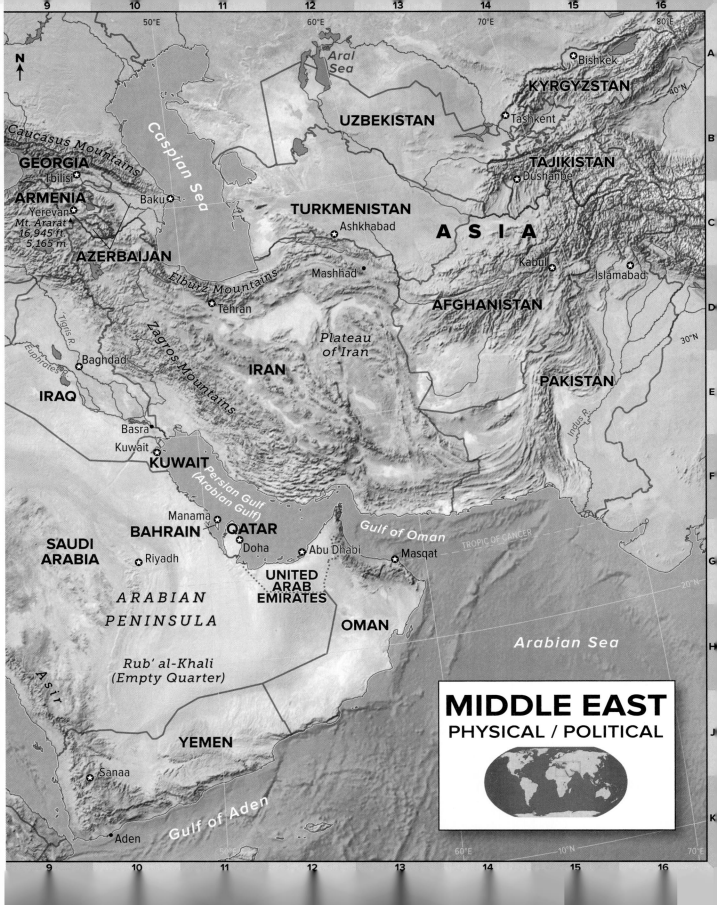

MIDDLE EAST
PHYSICAL / POLITICAL

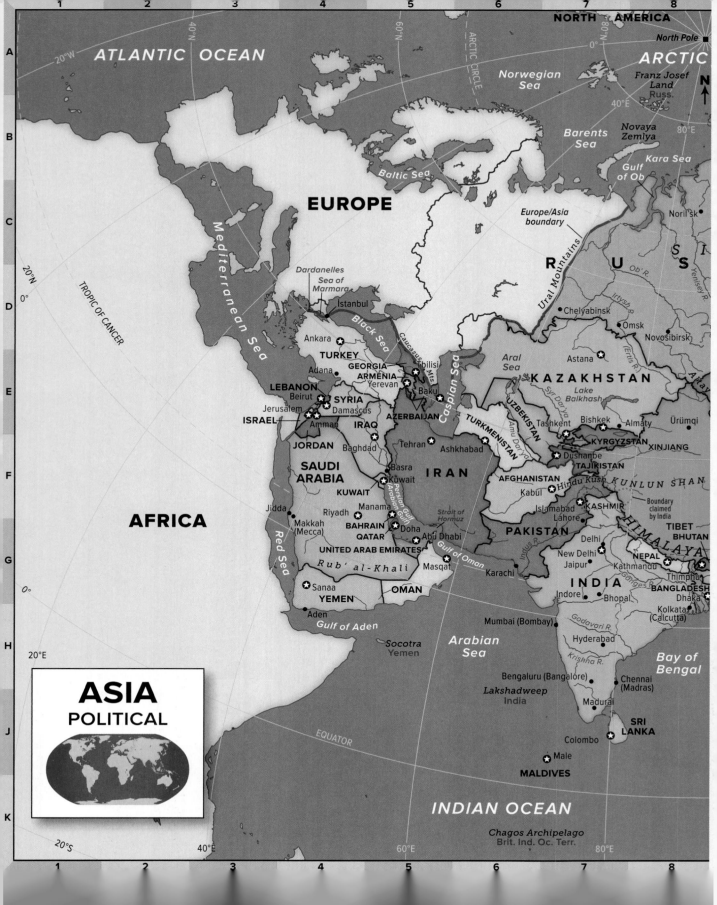

ASIA
POLITICAL

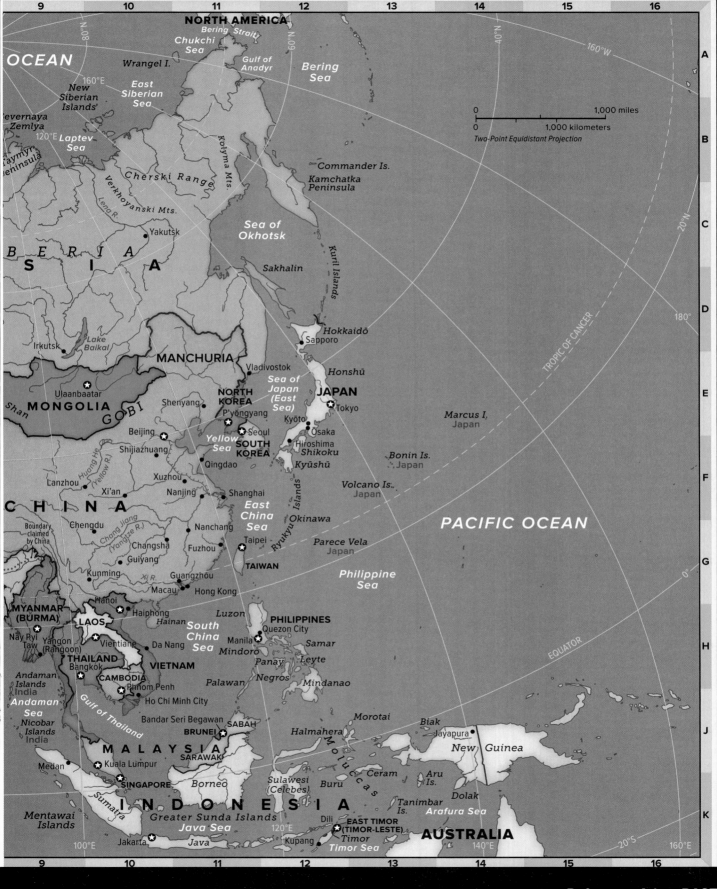

9   **10**   **11**   **12**   **13**   **14**   **15**   **16**

OCEAN

NORTH AMERICA

Chukchi Sea

Wrangel I.

Bering Strait

Gulf of Anadyr

Bering Sea

160°E

New Siberian Islands

East Siberian Sea

Severnaya Zemlya

120°E

Laptev Sea

Taymyr Peninsula

Cherski Range

Kolyma Mts.

~ *Commander Is.*

Kamchatka Peninsula

Verkhoyanski Mts.

Lena R.

S I B E R I A

Yakutsk

Sea of Okhotsk

Sakhalin

Kuril Islands

Irkutsk

Lake Baikal

MANCHURIA

Vladivostok

Hokkaidō

Sapporo

Honshū

Ulaanbaatar

MONGOLIA

Shan

GOBI

Shenyang

NORTH KOREA

P'yŏngyang

Sea of Japan (East Sea)

JAPAN

Tokyo

Beijing

Seoul

SOUTH KOREA

Kyōto

Ōsaka

Shijiazhuang

Yellow Sea

Hiroshima

Shikoku

Marcus I, Japan

Lanzhou

Huang He (Yellow R.)

Xuzhou

Qingdao

Kyūshū

Xi'an

Nanjing

Shanghai

Bonin Is. Japan

C H I N A

Chengdu

Chong Jiang (Yangtze R.)

Nanchang

East China Sea

Boundary claimed by China

Changsha

Fuzhou

Okinawa

Volcano Is. Japan

Guiyang

Ryukyu Islands

Taipei

Kunming

Xi R.

Guangzhou

TAIWAN

Parece Vela Japan

Macau

Hong Kong

PACIFIC OCEAN

Hanoi

MYANMAR (BURMA)

Haiphong

Philippine Sea

LAOS

Hainan

Luzon

Nay Pyi Taw

Yangon (Rangoon)

Vientiane

Da Nang

PHILIPPINES

Quezon City

THAILAND

Bangkok

South China Sea

Manila

Samar

Andaman Islands India

VIETNAM

Mindoro

Leyte

CAMBODIA

Phnom Penh

Panay

Andaman Sea

Ho Chi Minh City

Palawan

Negros

Mindanao

Nicobar Islands India

Gulf of Thailand

Bandar Seri Begawan

SABAH

Morotai

Biak

BRUNEI

Halmahera

Jayapura

Medan

Kuala Lumpur

M A L A Y S I A

SARAWAK

Ceram

New Guinea

SINGAPORE

Borneo

Sulawesi (Celebes)

Buru

Moluccas

Aru Is.

Dolak

Sumatra

I N D O N E S I A

Tanimbar Is.

Arafura Sea

Mentawai Islands

Greater Sunda Islands

Java Sea

120°E

Dili

EAST TIMOR (TIMOR-LESTE)

AUSTRALIA

100°E

Jakarta

Java

Kupang

Timor

Timor Sea

140°E

160°E

20°S

0   1,000 miles

0   1,000 kilometers

Two-Point Equidistant Projection

60°N

40°N

160°W

20°N

180°

TROPIC OF CANCER

0°

EQUATOR

A

B

C

D

E

F

G

H

J

K

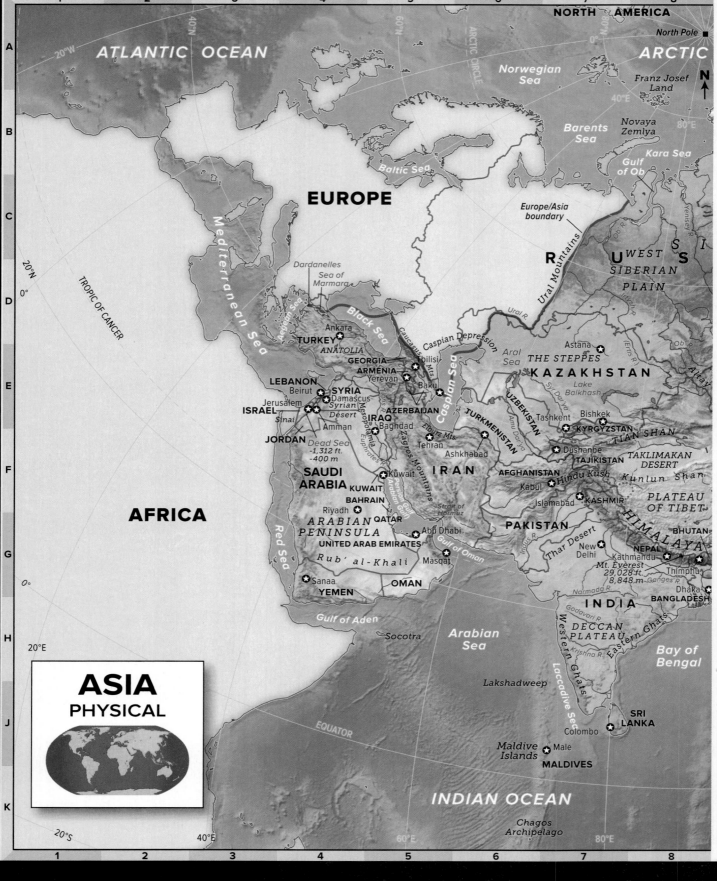

ASIA
PHYSICAL

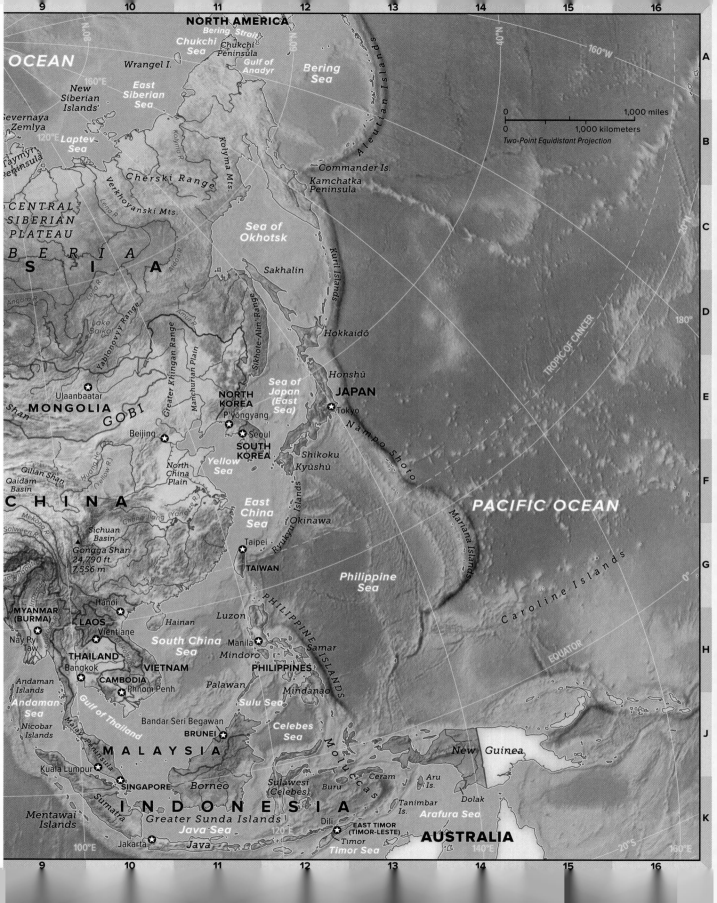

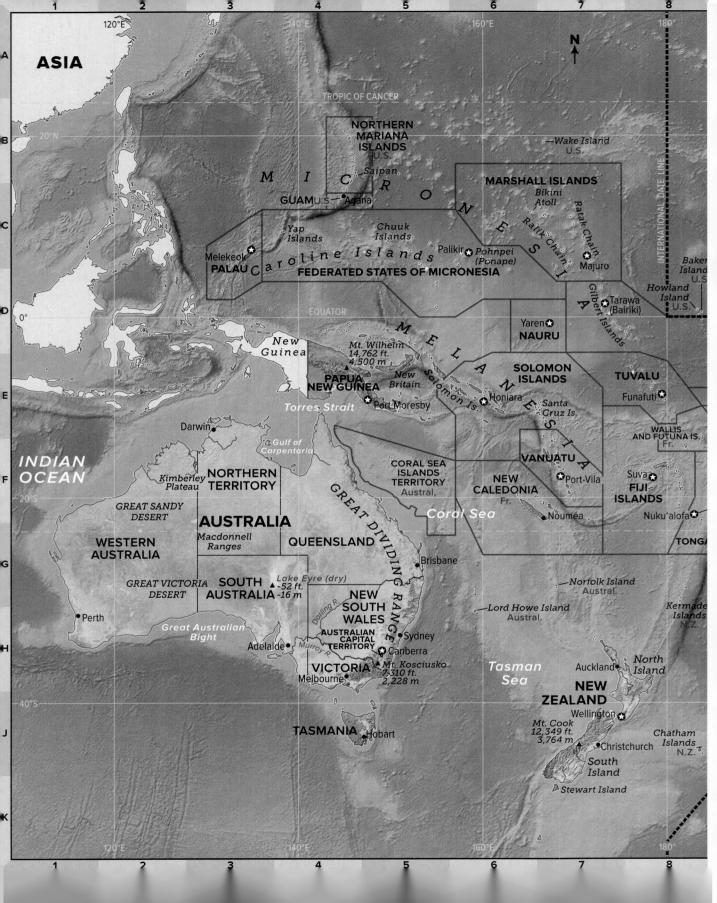

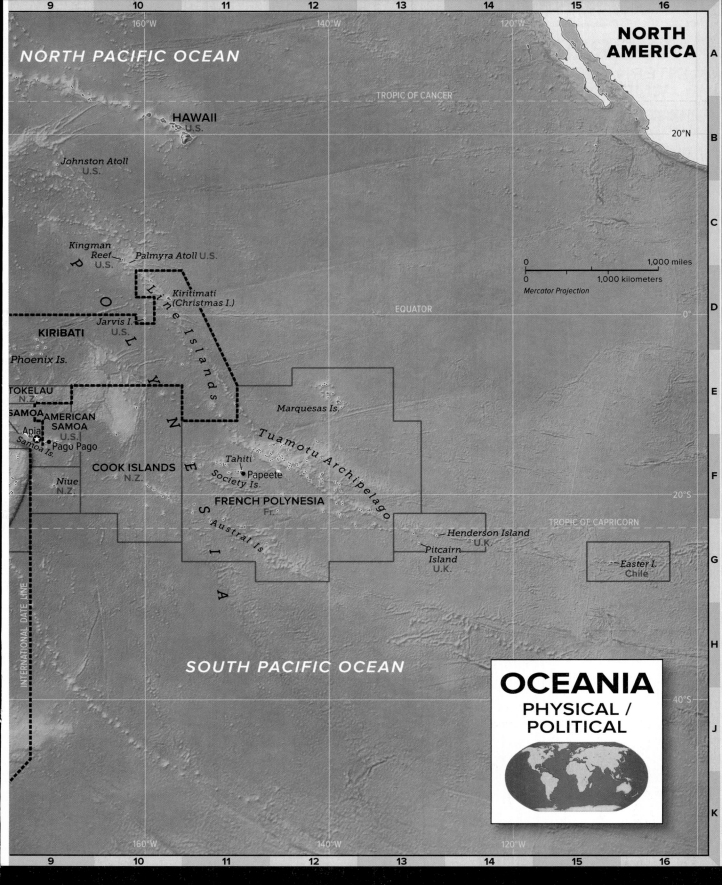

NORTH PACIFIC OCEAN

NORTH
AMERICA

TROPIC OF CANCER

20°N

HAWAII
U.S.

Johnston Atoll
U.S.

Kingman
Reef
U.S.

Palmyra Atoll U.S.

Kiritimati
(Christmas I.)

Jarvis I.
U.S.

EQUATOR   0°

KIRIBATI

Line Islands

Phoenix Is.

TOKELAU
N.Z.

SAMOA

AMERICAN
SAMOA
U.S.

Apia

Pago Pago

Samoa Is.

Marquesas Is.

Tuamotu Archipelago

COOK ISLANDS
N.Z.

Niue
N.Z.

Tahiti

Papeete

Society Is.

FRENCH POLYNESIA
Fr.

Austral Is.

P O L Y N E S I A

20°S

TROPIC OF CAPRICORN

Henderson Island
U.K.

Pitcairn
Island
U.K.

Easter I.
Chile

INTERNATIONAL DATE LINE

SOUTH PACIFIC OCEAN

40°S

0   1,000 miles
0   1,000 kilometers
Mercator Projection

OCEANIA
PHYSICAL /
POLITICAL

9   10   11   12   13   14   15   16

160°W   140°W   120°W

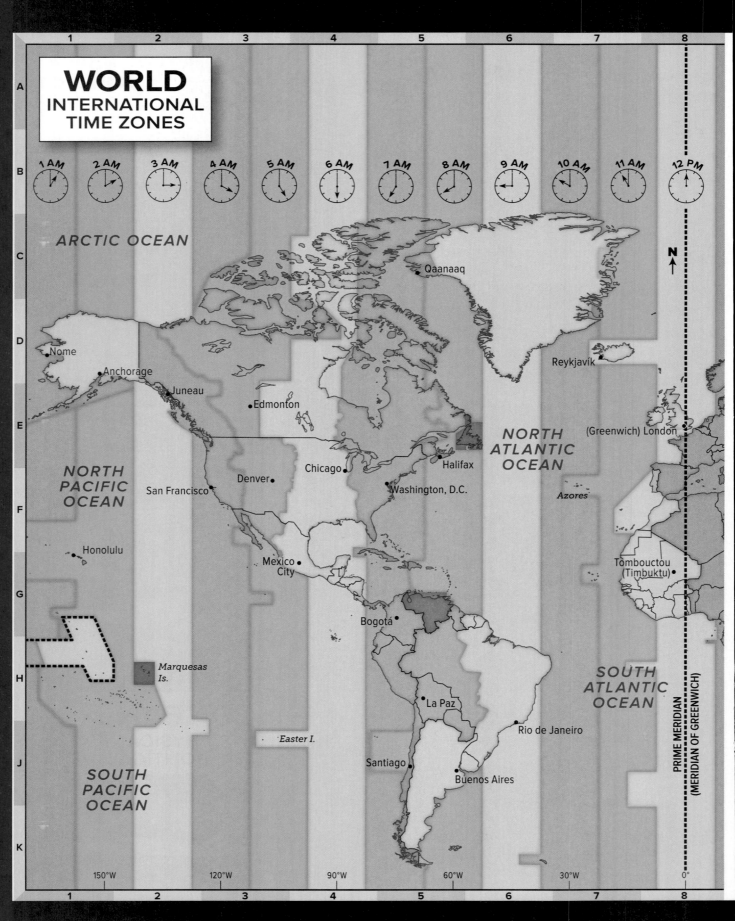

WORLD
INTERNATIONAL TIME ZONES

1 AM   2 AM   3 AM   4 AM   5 AM   6 AM   7 AM   8 AM   9 AM   10 AM   11 AM   12 PM

ARCTIC OCEAN

N

Qaanaaq

Nome

Reykjavik

Anchorage

Juneau

Edmonton

(Greenwich) London

NORTH ATLANTIC OCEAN

NORTH PACIFIC OCEAN

Chicago

Halifax

San Francisco

Denver

Washington, D.C.

Azores

Honolulu

Tombouctou (Timbuktu)

Mexico City

Bogotá

SOUTH ATLANTIC OCEAN

Marquesas Is.

La Paz

Rio de Janeiro

Easter I.

SOUTH PACIFIC OCEAN

Santiago

Buenos Aires

PRIME MERIDIAN (MERIDIAN OF GREENWICH)

150°W   120°W   90°W   60°W   30°W   0°

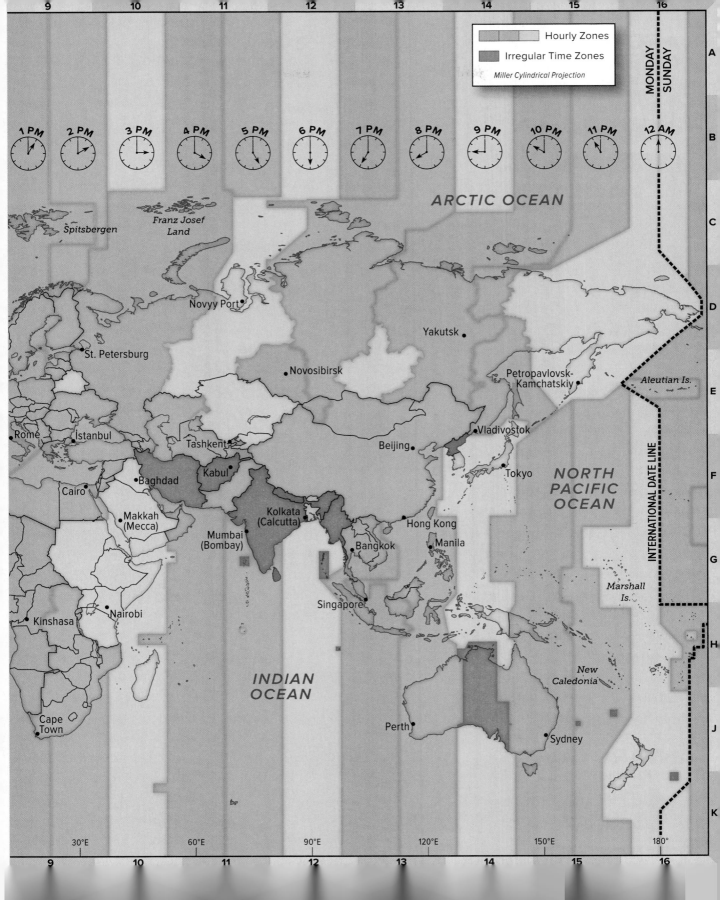

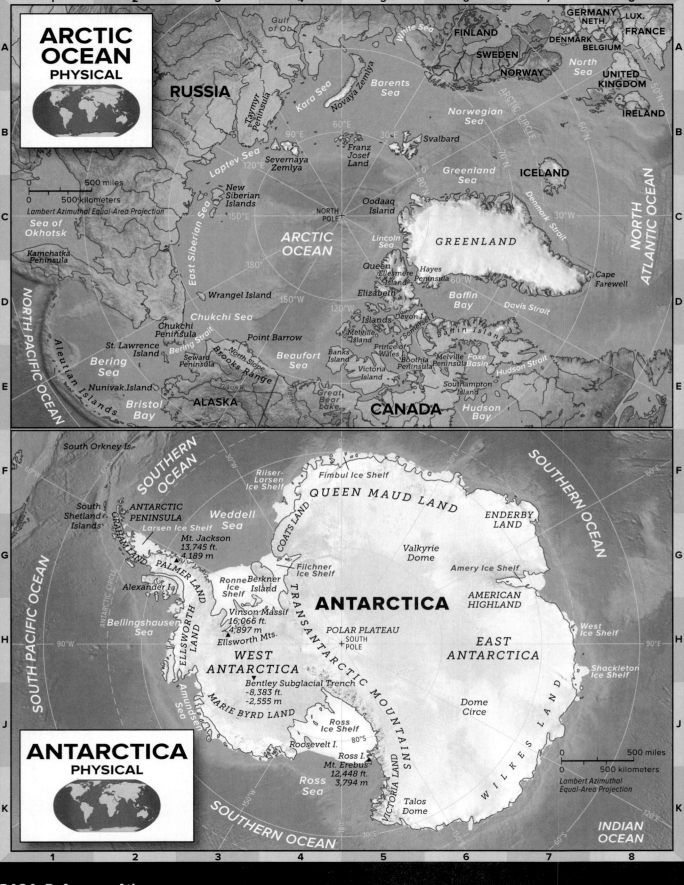

ARCTIC OCEAN
PHYSICAL

RUSSIA

Gulf of Ob

Taymyr Peninsula

Yenisey R.

White Sea

Kara Sea

Novaya Zemlya

Barents Sea

FINLAND

SWEDEN

NORWAY

DENMARK

GERMANY
NETH.
LUX.
FRANCE
BELGIUM

North Sea

UNITED KINGDOM

IRELAND

Lena R.

Laptev Sea

Severnaya Zemlya

ARCTIC CIRCLE

50°N

60°N

70°N

90°E

60°E

30°E

Franz Josef Land

Svalbard

Norwegian Sea

Greenland Sea

ICELAND

NORTH ATLANTIC OCEAN

New Siberian Islands

East Siberian Sea

120°E

150°E

180°

NORTH POLE

0°

80°N

Oodaaq Island

Lincoln Sea

Denmark Strait

GREENLAND

30°W

Cape Farewell

500 miles

500 kilometers

Lambert Azimuthal Equal-Area Projection

Sea of Okhotsk

Kamchatka Peninsula

Wrangel Island

150°W

ARCTIC OCEAN

120°W

Queen Elizabeth Islands

Ellesmere Island

Hayes Peninsula

60°W

Baffin Bay

Davis Strait

Chukchi Peninsula

Chukchi Sea

Point Barrow

Devon I.

Melville Island

Somerset I.

Baffin Island

NORTH PACIFIC OCEAN

Aleutian Islands

St. Lawrence Island

Bering Strait

Seward Peninsula

Brooks Range

North Slope

Beaufort Sea

Banks Island

Prince of Wales I.

Boothia Peninsula

Melville Peninsula

Foxe Basin

Bering Sea

Nunivak Island

Yukon R.

Victoria Island

Southampton Island

Hudson Strait

Bristol Bay

ALASKA

Great Bear Lake

Mackenzie R.

CANADA

Hudson Bay

ANTARCTICA
PHYSICAL

South Orkney Is.

SOUTHERN OCEAN

60°W

30°W

Riiser-Larsen Ice Shelf

Fimbul Ice Shelf

QUEEN MAUD LAND

SOUTHERN OCEAN

South Shetland Islands

ANTARCTIC PENINSULA

GRAHAM LAND

Weddell Sea

Larsen Ice Shelf

COATS LAND

ENDERBY LAND

PALMER LAND

Mt. Jackson 13,745 ft. 4,189 m

Filchner Ice Shelf

Valkyrie Dome

Amery Ice Shelf

ANTARCTIC CIRCLE

Alexander I.

Ronne Ice Shelf

Berkner Island

ANTARCTICA

AMERICAN HIGHLAND

SOUTH PACIFIC OCEAN

90°W

Bellingshausen Sea

ELLSWORTH LAND

Vinson Massif 16,066 ft. 4,897 m

Ellsworth Mts.

TRANSANTARCTIC MOUNTAINS

POLAR PLATEAU

SOUTH POLE

EAST ANTARCTICA

90°E

West Ice Shelf

Shackleton Ice Shelf

WEST ANTARCTICA

Bentley Subglacial Trench -8,383 ft. -2,555 m

Dome Circe

WILKES LAND

Amundsen Sea

MARIE BYRD LAND

80°S

Ross Ice Shelf

Roosevelt I.

Ross Sea

Ross I.
Mt. Erebus 12,448 ft. 3,794 m

VICTORIA LAND

Talos Dome

500 miles

500 kilometers

Lambert Azimuthal Equal-Area Projection

150°W

180°

150°E

120°E

60°E

60°S

70°S

SOUTHERN OCEAN

INDIAN OCEAN

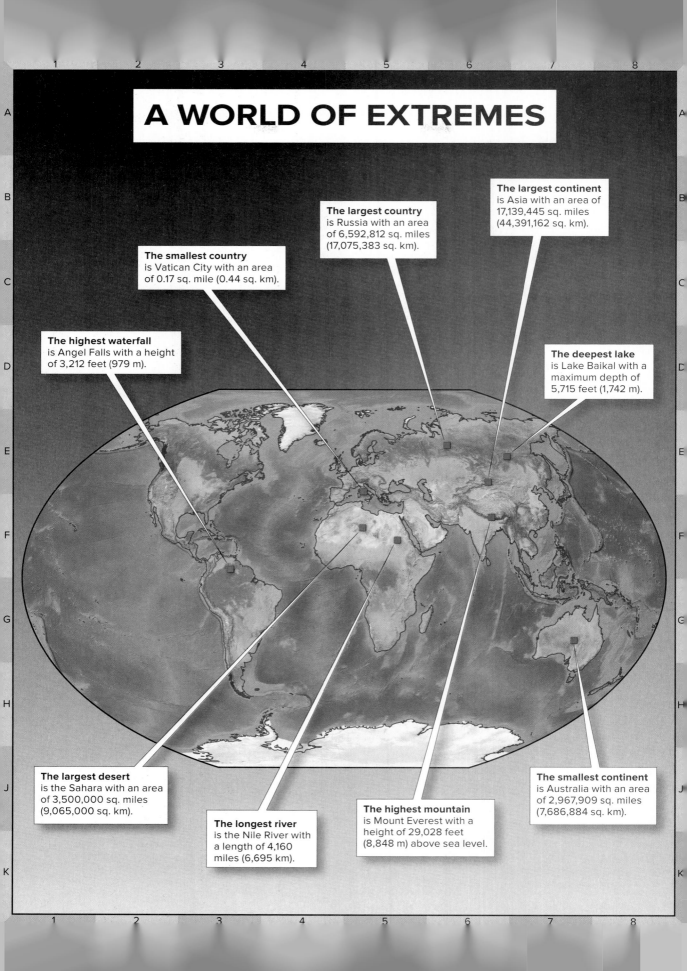

A WORLD OF EXTREMES

The largest continent
is Asia with an area of
17,139,445 sq. miles
(44,391,162 sq. km).

The largest country
is Russia with an area
of 6,592,812 sq. miles
(17,075,383 sq. km).

The smallest country
is Vatican City with an area
of 0.17 sq. mile (0.44 sq. km).

The deepest lake
is Lake Baikal with a
maximum depth of
5,715 feet (1,742 m).

The highest waterfall
is Angel Falls with a height
of 3,212 feet (979 m).

The largest desert
is the Sahara with an area
of 3,500,000 sq. miles
(9,065,000 sq. km).

The smallest continent
is Australia with an area
of 2,967,909 sq. miles
(7,686,884 sq. km).

The longest river
is the Nile River with
a length of 4,160
miles (6,695 km).

The highest mountain
is Mount Everest with a
height of 29,028 feet
(8,848 m) above sea level.

GEOGRAPHIC DICTIONARY

Archipelago

Ocean

Gulf

Volcano

Reservoir

Isthmus

Plateau

Highlands

Canyon

Cliff

Cape

Bay

Harbor

Reef

Island

Channel

Peninsula

archipelago a group of islands

basin area of land drained by a given river and its branches; area of land surrounded by lands of higher elevations

bay part of a large body of water that extends into a shoreline, generally smaller than a gulf

canyon deep and narrow valley with steep walls

cape point of land that extends into a river, lake, or ocean

channel wide strait or waterway between two landmasses that lie close to each other; deep part of a river or other waterway

cliff steep, high wall of rock, earth, or ice

continent one of the seven large landmasses on the Earth

delta flat, low-lying land built up from soil carried downstream by a river and deposited at its mouth

divide stretch of high land that separates river systems

downstream direction in which a river or stream flows from its source to its mouth

escarpment steep cliff or slope between a higher and lower land surface

glacier large, thick body of slowly moving ice

gulf part of a large body of water that extends into a shoreline, generally larger and more deeply indented than a bay

harbor a sheltered place along a shoreline where ships can anchor safely

highland elevated land area such as a hill, mountain, or plateau

hill elevated land with sloping sides and rounded summit; generally smaller than a mountain

island land area, smaller than a continent, completely surrounded by water

isthmus narrow stretch of land connecting two larger land areas

lake a sizable inland body of water

lowland land, usually level, at a low elevation

mesa broad, flat-topped landform with steep sides; smaller than a plateau

mountain land with steep sides that rises sharply (1,000 feet or more) from surrounding land; generally larger and more rugged than a hill

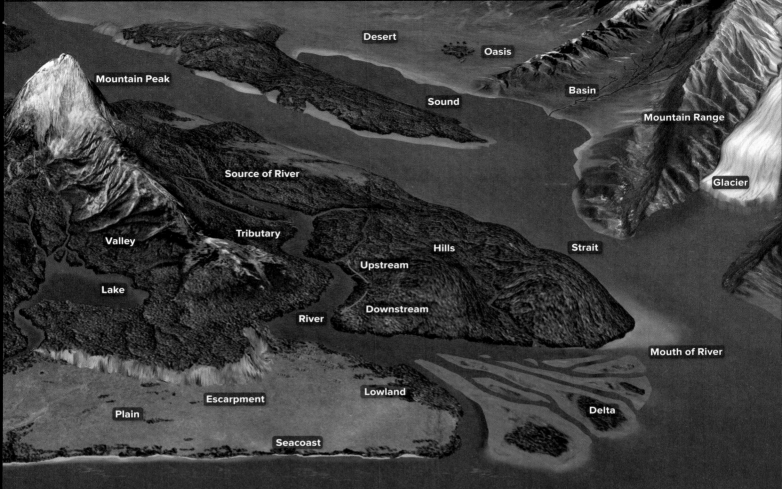

mountain peak pointed top of a mountain

mountain range a series of connected mountains

mouth (of a river) place where a stream or river flows into a larger body of water

oasis small area in a desert where water and vegetation are found

ocean one of the four major bodies of salt water that surround the continents

ocean current stream of either cold or warm water that moves in a definite direction through an ocean

peninsula body of land jutting into a lake or ocean, surrounded on three sides by water

physical feature characteristic of a place occurring naturally, such as a landform, body of water, climate pattern, or resource

plain area of level land, usually at low elevation and often covered with grasses

plateau area of flat or rolling land at a high elevation, about 300 to 3,000 feet (90 to 900 m) high

reef a chain of rocks, coral or sand at or near the surface of the water

river large natural stream of water that runs through the land

sea large body of water completely or partly surrounded by land

seacoast land lying next to a sea or an ocean

sound broad inland body of water, often between a coastline and one or more islands off the coast

source (of a river) place where a river or stream begins, often in highlands

strait narrow stretch of water joining two larger bodies of water

tributary small river or stream that flows into a large river or stream; a branch of the river

upstream direction opposite the flow of a river; toward the source of a river or stream

valley area of low land usually between hills or mountains

volcano mountain or hill created as liquid rock and ash erupt from inside the Earth

SCAVENGER HUNT

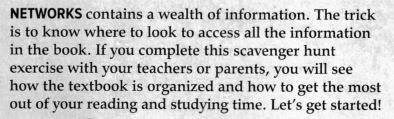

NETWORKS contains a wealth of information. The trick is to know where to look to access all the information in the book. If you complete this scavenger hunt exercise with your teachers or parents, you will see how the textbook is organized and how to get the most out of your reading and studying time. Let's get started!

1 How many lessons are in Chapter 2?

2 What does Unit 1 cover?

3 Where can you find the Essential Questions for each lesson?

4 In what three places can you find information on a Foldable?

5 How can you identify content vocabulary and academic vocabulary in the narrative?

6 Where do you find graphic organizers in your textbook?

7 You want to quickly find a map in the book about the world. Where do you look?

8 Where would you find the latitude and longitude for Dublin, Ireland?

9 If you needed to know the Spanish term for *earthquake*, where would you look?

10 Where can you find a list of all the charts in a unit?

THE WORLD

UNIT 1

Chapter 1	Chapter 2	Chapter 3	Chapter 4
What Does a Historian Do?	The Geographer's World	Physical Geography	Early Humans and the Agricultural Revolution

EXPLORE the WORLD

Geography is the study of Earth and all of its variety. When you study geography, you learn about the planet's land, water, plants, and animals. Some people call Earth "the water planet." Do you know why? Water—in the form of streams, rivers, lakes, seas, and oceans—covers nearly 70 percent of Earth's surface.

(1) BODIES OF WATER Underseas explorers can still experience the thrill of investigating uncharted territory— one of Earth's last frontiers. Almost all of the Earth's water consists of a continuous body of water that circles the planet. This body of water makes up five oceans: the Pacific, the Atlantic, the Indian, the Southern, and the Arctic.

(2) LANDFORMS Landforms are features of the land, such as mountains, valleys, and canyons. Landforms influence where people live and how they relate to their environment.

3 NATURAL RESOURCES Natural resources are products of Earth that people use to meet their needs. Solar energy is power produced by the heat of the sun. Sun and wind are renewable resources. These resources cannot be used up.

FAST **FACT**

Earth's longest mountain range is under water.

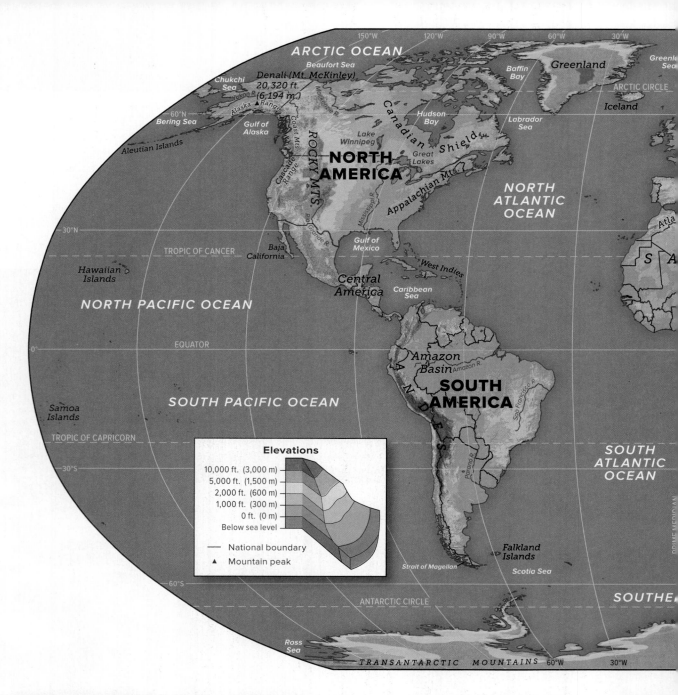

Elevations

10,000 ft. (3,000 m)	
5,000 ft. (1,500 m)	
2,000 ft. (600 m)	
1,000 ft. (300 m)	
0 ft. (0 m)	
Below sea level	

— National boundary

▲ Mountain peak

THE WORLD

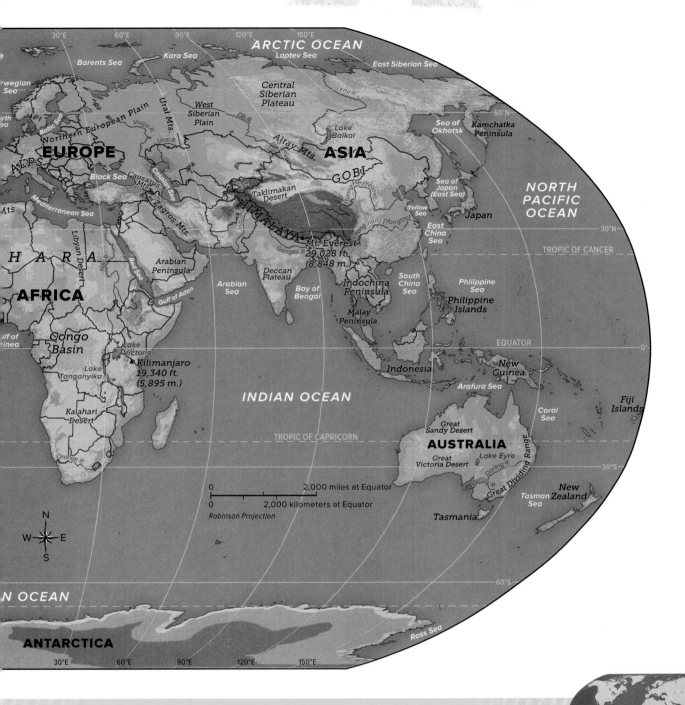

ARCTIC OCEAN
Laptev Sea
East Siberian Sea
Barents Sea
Kara Sea
Norwegian Sea
Baltic Sea
Central Siberian Plateau
Lena R.
West Siberian Plain
Ural Mts.
Ob R.
Volga R.
Ural R.
Northern European Plain
EUROPE
ALPS
Black Sea
Caucasus Mts.
Caspian Sea
Mediterranean Sea
Mts.
Zagros Mts.
Libyan Desert
Nile R.
Red Sea
Arabian Peninsula
Gulf of Aden
HARA
AFRICA
Gulf of Guinea
Congo Basin
Lake Victoria
Lake Tanganyika
Kilimanjaro 19,340 ft. (5,895 m.)
Kalahari Desert
Orange R.
Altay Mts.
ASIA
Lake Baikal
GOBI
Taklimakan Desert
HIMALAYA
Mt. Everest 29,028 ft (8,848 m.)
Indus R.
Brahmaputra R.
Ganges R.
Huang He (Yellow)
Chang Jiang (Yangtze)
Deccan Plateau
Arabian Sea
Bay of Bengal
Indochina Peninsula
Malay Peninsula
Sea of Okhotsk
Kamchatka Peninsula
Sea of Japan (East Sea)
Japan
Yellow Sea
East China Sea
South China Sea
Philippine Sea
Philippine Islands
NORTH PACIFIC OCEAN
60°N
30°N
TROPIC OF CANCER
EQUATOR
Indonesia
New Guinea
Arafura Sea
INDIAN OCEAN
TROPIC OF CAPRICORN
Great Sandy Desert
AUSTRALIA
Great Victoria Desert
Lake Eyre
Darling R.
Murray R.
Great Dividing Range
Coral Sea
Fiji Islands
Tasman Sea
New Zealand
Tasmania
0   2,000 miles at Equator
0   2,000 kilometers at Equator
Robinson Projection
N W E S
ANTARCTICA
Ross Sea
30°E   60°E   90°E   120°E   150°E
30°S
60°S
0°
N OCEAN
30°E   60°E   90°E   120°E   150°E

PHYSICAL

MAP SKILLS

1 **THE GEOGRAPHER'S WORLD** What part of South America has the highest elevation?

2 **THE GEOGRAPHER'S WORLD** What body of water is located west of Greenland?

3 **PLACES AND REGIONS** How would you describe southern Africa?

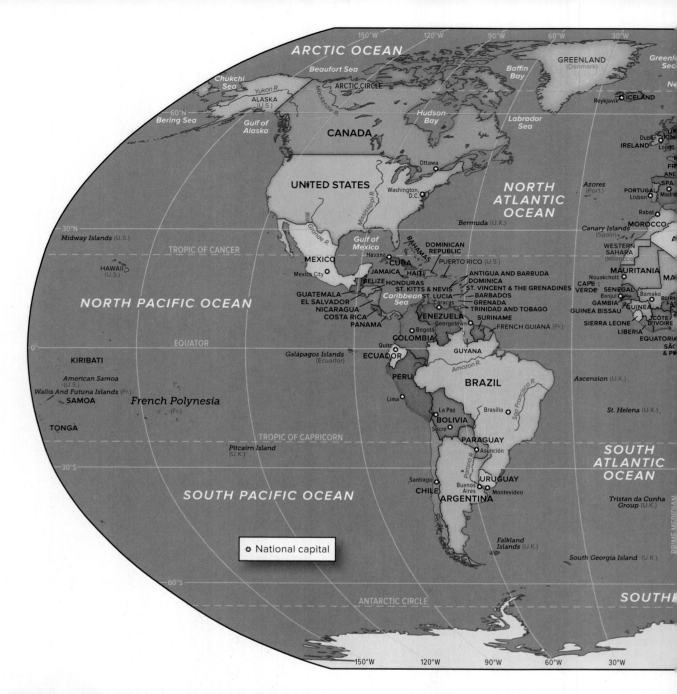

THE WORLD

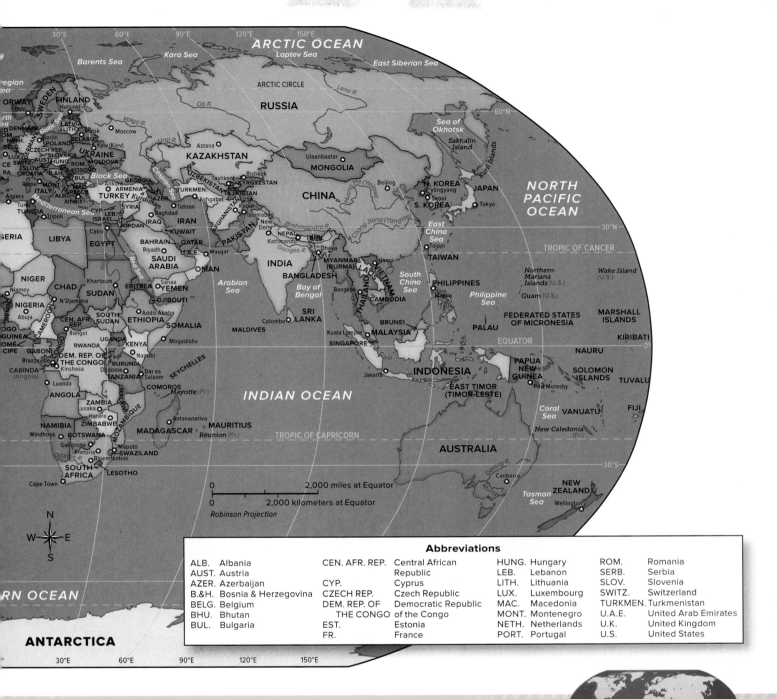

ARCTIC OCEAN

Barents Sea | Kara Sea | Laptev Sea | East Siberian Sea

ARCTIC CIRCLE

ORWAY SWEDEN FINLAND
Oslo Helsinki

RUSSIA

Ob R. | Lena R. | 60°N

Volga R. | Astana | Sea of Okhotsk

Moscow | Sakhalin Island

Ural R. | KAZAKHSTAN | Ulaanbaatar | Kuril Islands

MONGOLIA | Bishkek | Beijing | N. KOREA | JAPAN
P'yŏngyang | NORTH PACIFIC OCEAN

Tashkent | KYRGYZSTAN | S. KOREA | Seoul | Tokyo

UZBEKISTAN | TAJIKISTAN | Huang He (Yellow)

TURKMEN. | Ashgabat | CHINA | East China Sea

TURKEY Kurdistan | Tehran | AFGHANISTAN | Kabul | Chang Jiang (Yangtze) | 30°N

SYRIA | IRAQ | IRAN | Islamabad | New Delhi | NEPAL | BHU. | Kathmandu | Dhaka | Taipei | TROPIC OF CANCER

LEB. | Baghdad | JORDAN | KUWAIT | PAKISTAN | Brahmaputra R. | TAIWAN

ISRAEL | BAHRAIN | QATAR | Riyadh | U.A.E. | Masqat | Ganges R. | MYANMAR (BURMA) | LAOS | VIETNAM | Hanoi

LIBYA | EGYPT | SAUDI ARABIA | OMAN | INDIA | BANGLADESH | South China Sea | PHILIPPINES | Northern Mariana Islands (U.S.) | Wake Island (U.S.)

NIGER | CHAD | SUDAN | ERITREA | Sanaa | YEMEN | Arabian Sea | Bay of Bengal | Bangkok | THAILAND | CAMBODIA | Manila | Philippine Sea | Guam (U.S.)

NIGERIA | Niamey | N'Djamena | SRI LANKA | BRUNEI | PALAU | FEDERATED STATES OF MICRONESIA | MARSHALL ISLANDS

Abuja | CEN. AFR. REP. | ETHIOPIA | SOMALIA | Colombo | MALDIVES | Kuala Lumpur | MALAYSIA | KIRIBATI

Bangui | UGANDA | KENYA | Mogadishu | SINGAPORE | EQUATOR | NAURU

DEM. REP. OF THE CONGO | RWANDA | Nairobi | JAKARTA | INDONESIA | PAPUA NEW GUINEA | SOLOMON ISLANDS | TUVALU

CABINDA (Angola) | Kinshasa | BURUNDI | SEYCHELLES | Port Moresby

Luanda | TANZANIA | Dar es Salaam | EAST TIMOR (TIMOR-LESTE)

ANGOLA | ZAMBIA | COMOROS | Mayotte (Fr.) | INDIAN OCEAN | Coral Sea | VANUATU | FIJI

NAMIBIA | ZIMBABWE | Antananarivo | MAURITIUS | New Caledonia (Fr.)

Windhoek | BOTSWANA | MADAGASCAR | Réunion (Fr.) | TROPIC OF CAPRICORN

Gaborone | Maputo | SWAZILAND | AUSTRALIA | 30°S

SOUTH AFRICA | LESOTHO | Canberra | NEW ZEALAND

Cape Town | Tasman Sea | Wellington

2,000 miles at Equator
2,000 kilometers at Equator
Robinson Projection

RN OCEAN

ANTARCTICA

30°E | 60°E | 90°E | 120°E | 150°E

Abbreviations

ALB.	Albania	CEN. AFR. REP.	Central African Republic	HUNG.	Hungary	ROM.	Romania
AUST.	Austria			LEB.	Lebanon	SERB.	Serbia
AZER.	Azerbaijan	CYP.	Cyprus	LITH.	Lithuania	SLOV.	Slovenia
B.&H.	Bosnia & Herzegovina	CZECH REP.	Czech Republic	LUX.	Luxembourg	SWITZ.	Switzerland
BELG.	Belgium	DEM. REP. OF THE CONGO	Democratic Republic of the Congo	MAC.	Macedonia	TURKMEN.	Turkmenistan
BHU.	Bhutan			MONT.	Montenegro	U.A.E.	United Arab Emirates
BUL.	Bulgaria	EST.	Estonia	NETH.	Netherlands	U.K.	United Kingdom
		FR.	France	PORT.	Portugal	U.S.	United States

POLITICAL

MAP SKILLS

1 **PLACES AND REGIONS** How would you describe the region north of Australia?

2 **THE GEOGRAPHER'S WORLD** Which country is located west of Egypt?

3 **THE GEOGRAPHER'S WORLD** What is the capital of Mongolia?

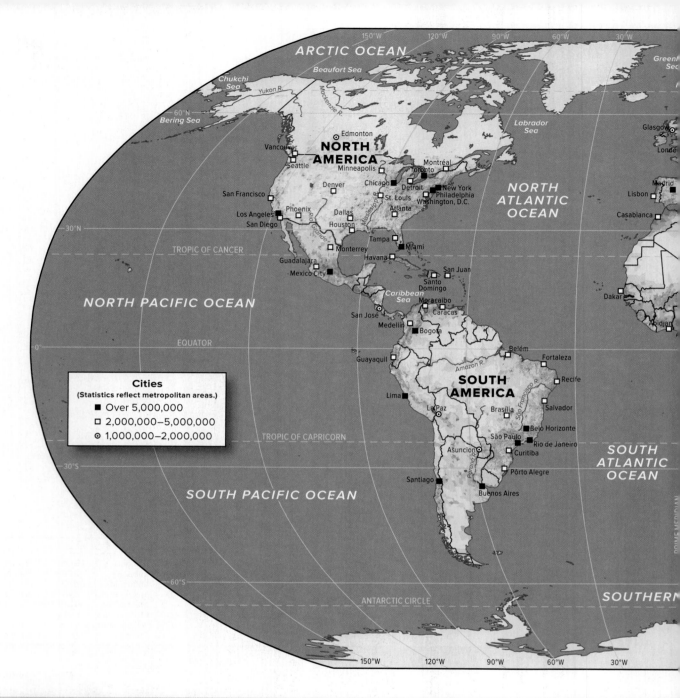

ARCTIC OCEAN

Beaufort Sea

Chukchi
Sea

Yukon R.

Bering Sea

60°N

Labrador
Sea

Greenl

Glasgow

London

NORTH
AMERICA

Edmonton

Vancouver
Seattle

Mackenzie R.

Montréal

Toronto

NORTH
ATLANTIC
OCEAN

Madrid

Lisbon

Minneapolis

Denver

Chicago

Detroit

New York

St. Louis

Philadelphia

San Francisco

Washington, D.C.

Atlanta

Casablanca

Los Angeles

Phoenix

Dallas

Houston

San Diego

Rio Grande

30°N

Tampa

Mississippi R.

TROPIC OF CANCER

Monterrey

Miami

Havana

Guadalajara

Mexico City

San Juan

Santo
Domingo

NORTH PACIFIC OCEAN

Caribbean
Sea

Maracaibo

Caracas

Dakar

San José

Medellín

Bogotá

Abidjan

EQUATOR

Guayaquil

Belém

Fortaleza

Amazon R.

SOUTH
AMERICA

Recife

São Francisco R.

Cities
(Statistics reflect metropolitan areas.)
■ Over 5,000,000
□ 2,000,000–5,000,000
⊙ 1,000,000–2,000,000

Lima

Brasília

Salvador

La Paz

Belo Horizonte

São Paulo

Rio de Janeiro

TROPIC OF CAPRICORN

Asunción

Curitiba

SOUTH
ATLANTIC
OCEAN

30°S

Pôrto Alegre

Santiago

SOUTH PACIFIC OCEAN

Buenos Aires

Paraná R.

60°S

ANTARCTIC CIRCLE

SOUTHERN

150°W   120°W   90°W   60°W   30°W

THE WORLD

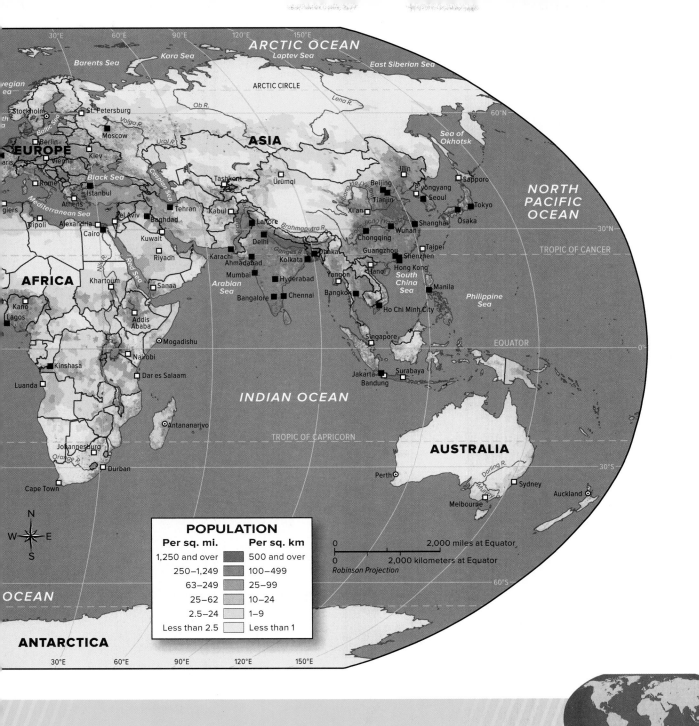

POPULATION

Per sq. mi.		Per sq. km
1,250 and over		500 and over
250–1,249		100–499
63–249		25–99
25–62		10–24
2.5–24		1–9
Less than 2.5		Less than 1

0   2,000 miles at Equator

0   2,000 kilometers at Equator

Robinson Projection

POPULATION DENSITY

MAP SKILLS

1 **PLACES AND REGIONS** What parts of South America are the most densely populated?

2 **PLACES AND REGIONS** Which part of Africa has the lowest population density?

3 **ENVIRONMENT AND SOCIETY** In general, what population pattern do you see in Europe?

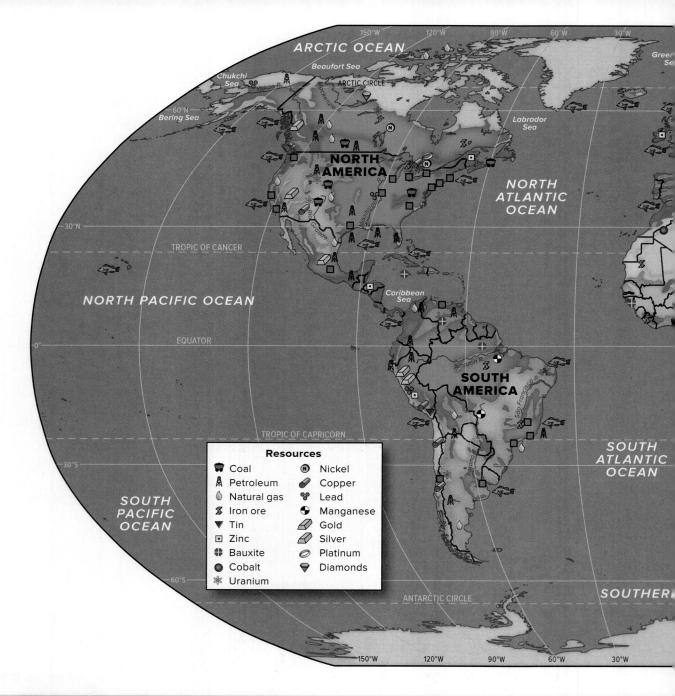

Resources

- 🐾 Coal
- 🛢 Petroleum
- 💧 Natural gas
- ⚡ Iron ore
- ▼ Tin
- ▣ Zinc
- ▦ Bauxite
- ⬤ Cobalt
- ✳ Uranium
- Ⓝ Nickel
- ▬ Copper
- ✦ Lead
- ◕ Manganese
- ▱ Gold
- ▱ Silver
- ⬭ Platinum
- ▽ Diamonds

THE WORLD

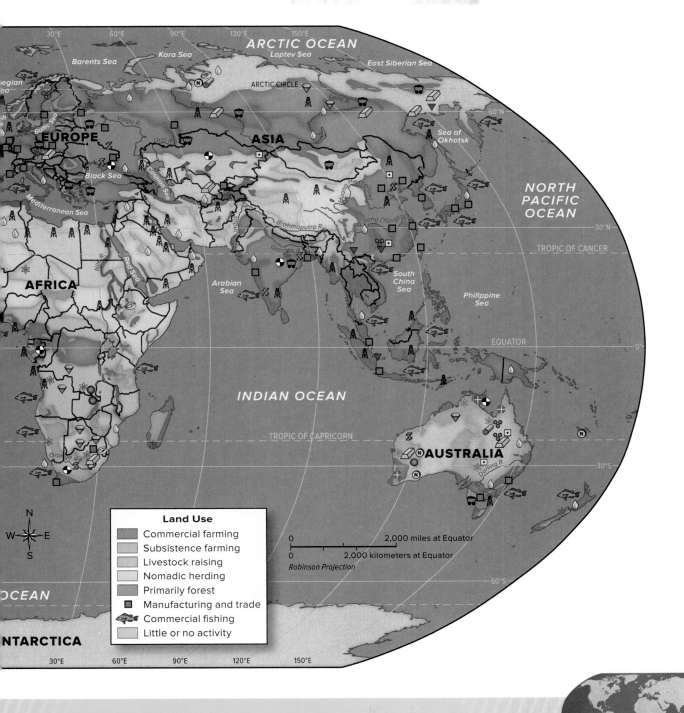

Land Use

- Commercial farming
- Subsistence farming
- Livestock raising
- Nomadic herding
- Primarily forest
- Manufacturing and trade
- Commercial fishing
- Little or no activity

0   2,000 miles at Equator

0   2,000 kilometers at Equator

Robinson Projection

ECONOMIC RESOURCES

MAP SKILLS

1 **ENVIRONMENT AND SOCIETY** What economic activity is found along most coastal regions?

2 **HUMAN GEOGRAPHY** Describe the general use of land in North Africa.

3 **PLACES AND REGIONS** Which area produces oil—North America or Australia?

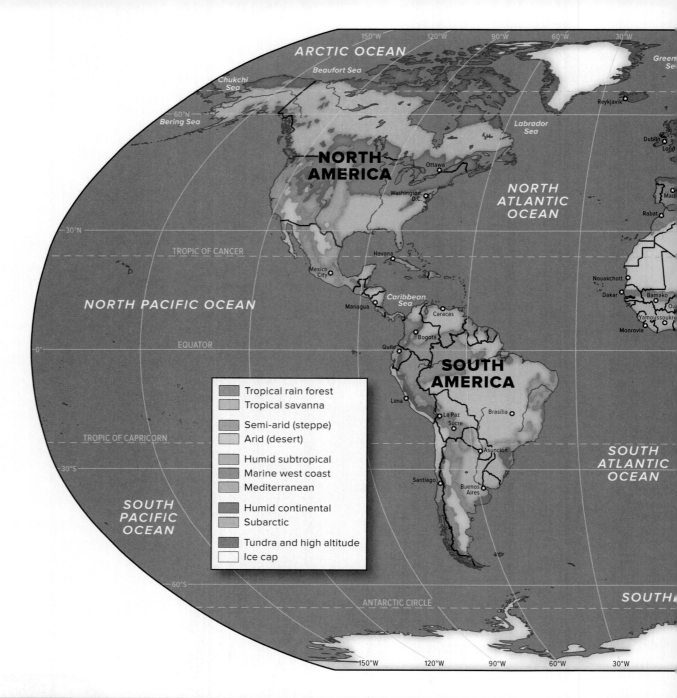

THE WORLD

Tropical rain forest
Tropical savanna

Semi-arid (steppe)
Arid (desert)

Humid subtropical
Marine west coast
Mediterranean

Humid continental
Subarctic

Tundra and high altitude
Ice cap

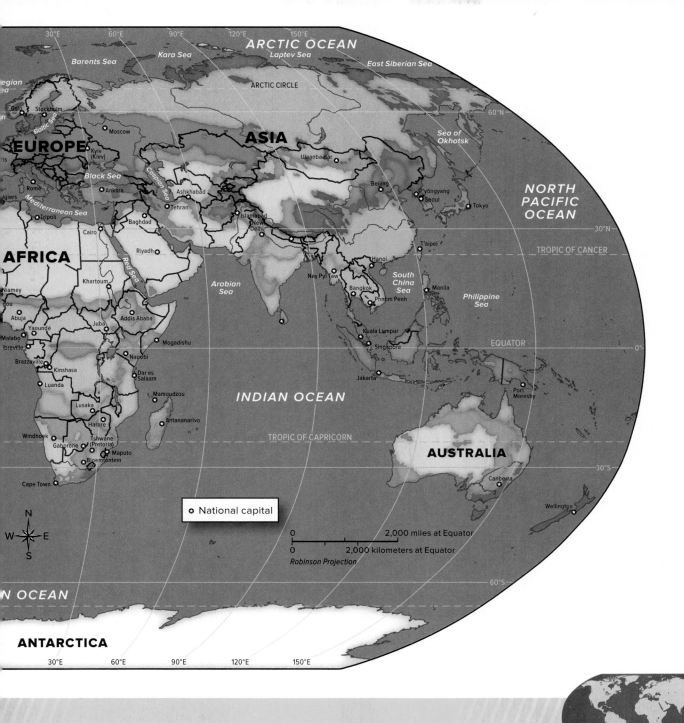

ARCTIC OCEAN

Barents Sea

Kara Sea

Laptev Sea

East Siberian Sea

ARCTIC CIRCLE

60°N

Oslo
Stockholm

Moscow

EUROPE

ASIA

Kyiv (Kiev)

Black Sea

Ulaanbaatar

Sea of Okhotsk

NORTH PACIFIC OCEAN

Rome
Algiers
Ankara
Ashkhabad

Beijing

P'yŏngyang
Seoul

Tokyo

Mediterranean Sea
Tripoli
Tehran
Baghdad

Islamabad
New Delhi

30°N

T'aipei

TROPIC OF CANCER

Cairo

AFRICA

Riyadh

Hanoi

Khartoum

Red Sea

Arabian Sea

Nay Pyi Taw

Bangkok

South China Sea

Manila

Philippine Sea

Niamey
Abuja
Yaoundé
Malabo
Libreville

Juba

Addis Ababa

Mogadishu

Phnom Penh

Kuala Lumpur
Singapore

EQUATOR

0°

Brazzaville
Kinshasa

Nairobi

Jakarta

Luanda

Dar es Salaam

INDIAN OCEAN

Port Moresby

Lusaka

Mamoudzou

Antananarivo

Harare

TROPIC OF CAPRICORN

AUSTRALIA

Windhoek
Gaborone
Tshwane (Pretoria)
Bloemfontein

Maputo

Canberra

30°S

Cape Town

Wellington

○ National capital

0   2,000 miles at Equator
0   2,000 kilometers at Equator
Robinson Projection

60°S

N OCEAN

ANTARCTICA

30°E   60°E   90°E   120°E   150°E

N
W   E
S

CLIMATE

MAP SKILLS

1 **PHYSICAL GEOGRAPHY** Which climate zones appear in northern North America?

2 **THE GEOGRAPHER'S WORLD** Which continent receives more rain—Australia or South America? Why?

3 **PHYSICAL GEOGRAPHY** In general, how does the climate of southern Africa compare with the climate of northern Africa?

netw⊙rks
There's More Online!

◀ *A museum employee places the head on a statue in the Terra-cotta Warriors exhibit at the Dresden Energy Museum.*

What Does a Historian Do?

Norbert Millauer/AFP/Getty Images

THE STORY MATTERS ...

Hundreds of terra-cotta warriors stood, silent and without expression, in the empty exhibit hall. They were replicas of the original statues found in China in 1974. Since their discovery, the warriors, dating from 210 B.C., have fascinated historians.

The mystery of the warriors captured the imaginations of people all over the world. Museums asked for a chance to show the statues in their cities. Researchers carefully created exact replicas of the statues that would be strong enough to travel around the world. Museum workers assembled heads, arms, and bodies in exactly the correct order. Thousands of visitors came to marvel at the beautiful and mysterious warriors.

ESSENTIAL QUESTIONS

- Why is history important?
- How do we learn about the past?
- How do you research history?

Place & Time: Historians in the 21st Century

Many people are historians. Some study written records of a war that happened decades ago. Some study dinosaur bones and other ancient artifacts from millions of years in the past. Family historians may be the ones you are most familiar with. They are the relatives who remember when everyone's birthday is and can tell you what your great-grandparents did for a living.

Museums display artifacts and other historical information for everyone to see. Archaeologists add to displays as new discoveries are made.

Step Into the Place

IMAGE FOCUS There are many ways to study the past. Look at the photos.

1 ANALYZING VISUALS Where do people find information about the past?

2 IDENTIFYING What tools do people use to study the past?

3 CRITICAL THINKING
Making Connections Where could you go to learn about the history of your community?

Historians and students use many types of research tools. Computers are valuable resources for locating data.

Credit: PunchStock

Step Into the Time

TIME LINE The time line shows different periods in history. What name is given to the first time period in history?

WORLD HISTORY

Prehistory up to 3500 B.C.		Ancient History 3500 B.C. to A.D. 500	
B.C. 4000	B.C. 3000	B.C. 2000	

Middle Ages
A.D. 500 to A.D. 1400

Modern History
after A.D. 1400 to present

| B.C. 1000 | A.D. 1 | A.D. 500 | A.D. 1000 | A.D. 1500 |

LESSON 1

What Is History?

ESSENTIAL QUESTION

• Why is history important?

IT MATTERS BECAUSE
Events of the past created the world we live in, and knowing history can help us make decisions about the future.

Why Study History?

GUIDING QUESTION *What types of things can history reveal about the past?*

History is the study of the people and events of the past. History explores both the way things change and the way things stay the same. History tells the story of the ways that cultures change over time.

People who study history are called historians. A historian's job is to examine the causes, or reasons, that something happened in the past. They also look for the effects, or results, of the event. They ask, "What happened?" and "Why did it happen?" They ask, "How did things change?" and "How has it influenced today?" Sometimes they ask, "What would have happened if . . . ?"

History explains why things are the way they are. The invention of the wheel in prehistoric times paved the way for the use of horse-drawn carts in later time periods. The carts were a step toward the invention of the automobile in modern times. Today, cars are an **integral** part of our culture.

Learning about the past helps us understand the present. It helps us make decisions about the future. Historical instances of conflict and cooperation are examples we can learn from. We can use that knowledge when we face similar choices.

Reading HELPDESK

Taking Notes: *Categorizing*

Use a graphic organizer like the one shown here to list the important details about studying history.

Studying History		
Reasons to Study History	Measuring Historical Time	People Who Study Time

Content Vocabulary

• **era**
• **archaeology**
• **artifact**
• **paleontology**

• **fossil**
• **anthropology**
• **species**

Studying history helps us understand how we fit into the human story. Some of the clues are the languages we speak, the technologies we use, and the pastimes we enjoy. All these are results of events that happened in the past. History teaches us who we are.

☑ PROGRESS CHECK

Explaining Why is it important to understand cause and effect when studying the past?

Measuring Time

GUIDING QUESTION *What are historical periods?*

To study the past, historians must have a way to identify and describe when things happened. They do that by measuring and labeling time in different ways.

Periods of History

One way to measure time is to label groups of years. For example, a group of 10 years is called a **decade**. A group of 100 years is known as a *century*. Centuries are grouped into even longer time periods. Ten centuries grouped together is called a *millennium*, which is a period of 1,000 years.

Historians also divide the past into larger blocks of time known as **eras.** *Prehistory* is the first of these long periods. Prehistory is the time before people developed writing.

The ancient Roman Forum has been called the most important meeting place in all of history. Today, it stands next to the buildings of modern Rome. Different historical eras are represented by both ancient and modern buildings.

©Jean-Pierre Lescourret/Corbis

era a large division of time

Academic Vocabulary

integral essential; necessary

decade a group or set of 10 years

Writing was invented about 5,500 years ago. The period known as *Ancient History* comes next. It ends c. A.D. 500 (c., or circa, means "about"). Historians call the time period between about A.D. 500 and about A.D. 1400 the *Middle Ages*, or the medieval period. *Modern History* begins about A.D. 1400. It continues to the present day.

Calendars

A *calendar* is a system for arranging days in order. Different cultures in the world have developed about 40 different calendars.

Some cultures developed calendars based on nature, such as the cycle of the moon. The Chinese and Jewish calendars base their months on the appearance of the new moon. The ancient Egyptians also based one of their calendars on the moon.

Julian Calendar

The calendar we use today is based in part on a calendar developed by Julius Caesar, a Roman leader. This calendar is called the Julian calendar, and it started counting years at the **founding** of Rome. A year on the Julian calendar was 365¼ days long. The calendar added an extra day every four years. The year with the extra day was called a leap year. However, the Julian calendar was still not **precisely,** or exactly, right. It lost several minutes each year, which added up to about one lost day every 128 years.

The Gregorian calendar is named for its creator, Pope Gregory XIII. Why is it important that most of the world uses a form of the calendar he developed?

Gregorian Calendar

By A.D. 1582, the Julian calendar was losing time—about 10 days. Pope Gregory XIII decided to create a new calendar. First, he started counting from the birth of Jesus. Next, he ordered that the days between October 4th and October 15th of that year be dropped from the calendar. Like the Julian calendar, the Gregorian calendar includes leap years. However, in the Gregorian calendar, no century year will be a leap year unless it is divisible by 400, such as the years 1600 or 2000. That way, it will take thousands of years before there is another lost day.

Reading HELPDESK

Academic Vocabulary

found to create or set up something, such as a city
precise exact

Reading Strategy: *Context Clues*

Context clues are words or phrases that give hints about the meaning of another word. Which phrase provides a clue about the meaning of the word *precisely*?

Not all countries accepted the Gregorian calendar right away. It took more than three centuries for the calendar to be recognized around the world. Today, most of the world uses this calendar. Like the Gregorian calendar, other calendars are also based on events of religious importance. The Jewish calendar begins about 3,760 years before the Gregorian calendar. According to Jewish tradition, that is when the world was created. Muslims date their calendar from the time that Muhammad, their first leader, left the city of Makkah (Mecca) to go to Madinah (Medina). This was the year A.D. 622 in the Gregorian calendar.

This stone calendar was made by the Minoans, people who lived on ancient Crete.

Dating Events

In the Gregorian calendar, the years before the birth of Jesus are known as "B.C.," or "before Christ." The years after are called "A.D.," or *anno domini*. This phrase comes from the Latin language and means "in the year of the Lord."

To date events before the birth of Jesus, or "B.C.," historians count backwards from A.D. 1. There is no year "0." The year before A.D. 1 is 1 B.C. (Notice that "A.D." is written before the date and "B.C." is written after the date.) For example, on the time line below, the founder of Buddhism was born about 563 B.C., or 563 years before the birth of Jesus. To date events after the birth of Jesus, or "A.D.," historians count forward, starting at A.D. 1. A date in the first 100 years after the birth of Jesus is between A.D. 1 and A.D. 100. Therefore, on the time line below, Buddhism spread to China in A.D. 100, or 100 years after the birth of Jesus.

To avoid a religious reference in dating, many historians prefer to use the initials B.C.E. ("before the common era") and C.E. ("common era"). These initials do not change the numbering of the years.

Using Time Lines

A time line is another way to track the passage of time. Time lines show the order of events within a period of time. They also show the amount of time between events. Most time lines are divided into even sections of time. Events are placed on a time line at the date when the event occurred.

INFOGRAPHIC

Time lines can trace the growth and decline of civilizations. This time line tracks the events of ancient India.

1 **IDENTIFYING** Around what year did the Mauryan Empire's Golden Age begin?

2 **CRITICAL THINKING** *Analyzing* Which dates and events on this time line give information about the Aryans?

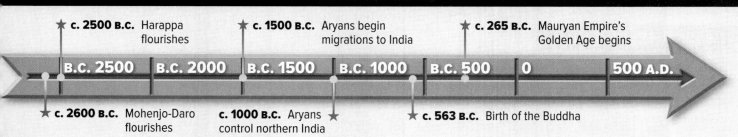

ANCIENT INDIA

c. 2500 B.C. Harappa flourishes

c. 1500 B.C. Aryans begin migrations to India

c. 265 B.C. Mauryan Empire's Golden Age begins

B.C. 2500 | B.C. 2000 | B.C. 1500 | B.C. 1000 | B.C. 500 | 0 | 500 A.D.

c. 2600 B.C. Mohenjo-Daro flourishes

c. 1000 B.C. Aryans control northern India

c. 563 B.C. Birth of the Buddha

Nimatallah/Art Resource, NY

**Heinrich Schliemann
(A.D. 1822–1890)**

As a boy, Heinrich Schliemann (SHLEE • MAHN) loved stories about ancient Greece. He dreamed of finding Troy, an ancient city destroyed during the Trojan War.

In 1871, Schliemann began to dig through a human-made mound in Hissarlik (HIH • suhr • LIHK), Turkey. Two years later, he uncovered the remains of a mysterious ancient city in the area where Troy had stood. Some archaeologists believe that Schliemann actually found Troy. Others are unsure. Nevertheless, his work led to the discovery of many ancient Greek treasures. Because of his work, Schliemann is considered the founder of prehistoric Greek archaeology.

▶ **CRITICAL THINKING**
Making Inferences Archaeologists study and catalog evidence they find. What might be the historical value of uncovering evidence of an entire city?

Usually, the dates on a time line are evenly spaced. Sometimes, however, a time line covers events over too many years to show on one page. In this case, a slanted or jagged line might be placed on the time line. This shows that a certain period of time is omitted from the time line.

Time lines help historians make sense of the flow of events. A time line can be a single line, or it can be two or more lines stacked on top of each other. Stacked time lines are called multilevel time lines.

☑ **PROGRESS CHECK**

Applying When would a historian use a calendar? When would a historian use a time line?

Digging Up the Past

GUIDING QUESTION *What do students of prehistory look for?*

Since the invention of writing, people have recorded important events. These written records give historians a window to the past. Students of prehistory look into an even deeper past, one without writing. They must find a different kind of window.

History and Science

These historians use science to study history. As scientists, they study physical evidence to learn about our ancestors.

Archaeology (ahr·kee·AHL·luh·jee) is the study of the past by looking at what people left behind. Archaeologists dig

Build Vocabulary: *Word Parts*

The suffix *-ology* means "the study of." The suffix *-ist* means "a person who." For example, *biology* is the study of life. A *biologist* is a person who studies life. What do archaeologists, paleontologists, and anthropologists do?

Reading**HELP**DESK

archaeology the study of objects to learn about past human life
artifact an object made by people
paleontology the study of fossils

fossil plant or animal remains that have been preserved from an earlier time
anthropology the study of human culture and how it develops over time
species a class of individuals with similar physical characteristics

in the earth for places where people once lived. They never know what they will find. They often discover **artifacts** (AHR·tih·FAKTS)—objects made by people. Common artifacts include tools, pottery, weapons, and jewelry. Archaeologists study artifacts to learn what life was like in the past.

Paleontology (PAY·lee·AHN·TAH·luh·jee) also looks at prehistoric times. Paleontologists study fossils to learn what the world was like long ago. **Fossils** are the remains of plant and animal life that have been preserved from an earlier time.

Anthropology (AN·thruh·PAH·luh·jee) is the study of human culture and how it develops over time. Anthropologists study artifacts and fossils, too. They look for clues about what people valued and believed.

Human Discoveries

In 1974, a team led by paleontologist Donald Johanson made an exciting find in Ethiopia in Africa. They discovered a partial skeleton of a human ancestor who lived more than 3.2 million years ago. Lucy, as she was called, was about three and a half feet tall (1.07 m) and weighed about 60 pounds (27.2 kg). She had long arms and short legs, and she walked upright.

Lucy belonged to the species *Australopithicus afarensis*. A **species** is a class of individuals with similar physical characteristics. Lucy lived long before the species called *Homo sapiens* evolved. All modern human beings belong to this species. The term *Homo sapiens* is Latin for "wise man." Scientists believe that Homo sapiens probably developed about 150,000 to 195,000 years ago.

✓ PROGRESS CHECK

Comparing How are archaeologists, paleontologists, and anthropologists like detectives?

Kevin Fujii/Associated Press

Connections to
TODAY
How Lucy Got Her Name

The night that Lucy was discovered, the team that found her was listening to the song "Lucy in the Sky with Diamonds" by the singing group the Beatles. They nicknamed the skeleton "Lucy," which was more attractive than her official name, AL 288-1.

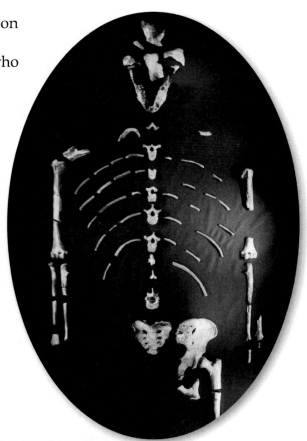

Scientists have found and pieced together about 40 percent of Lucy's skeleton.

LESSON 1 REVIEW

Review Vocabulary

1. Explain what a historical *era* is.

2. Compare and contrast *artifacts* and *fossils*.

Answer the Guiding Questions

3. *Making Connections* Name one example of how the past influences daily life today.

4. *Listing* Identify different ways that historians measure time.

5. *Describing* How do historians learn about people who lived in the earliest historical eras?

6. **INFORMATIVE/EXPLANATORY** How would a historian describe your life? Write a short essay that identifies the era in which you live and the artifacts that tell about your culture.

How Does a Historian Work?

There's More Online!

- How do we learn about the past?

IT MATTERS BECAUSE
Knowing how historians work helps us understand historical information.

What Is the Evidence?

GUIDING QUESTION *What types of evidence do historians use to understand the past?*

Historians ask questions about the information they find from the past. Why did some nations go to war? How were the people affected by that war? How did events of the past change people's lives? These questions help us focus on historical problems.

To learn the answers to the historical questions, historians look for **evidence** (EH·vuh·duhnts). Evidence is something that shows proof or an indication that something is true. Evidence could be in the form of material objects, such as a soldier's uniform or scraps of pottery from an archaeological dig.

Other evidence may appear in documents or written materials that were created during a historical event. Historians use the evidence they read in historical **sources** to interpret what happened in the past.

Primary and Secondary Sources

Historians look for clues about the past in primary and secondary sources. **Primary sources** are firsthand pieces of evidence. They were written or created by the people who saw or experienced an event. Primary sources include letters, diaries, or government records. Literature or artwork from a particular time

Reading**HELP**DESK

Taking Notes: *Sequencing*

As you read, think about the steps in finding and evaluating evidence. Use the sequence chart to note the steps in the process.

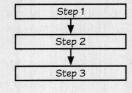

Step 1

Step 2

Step 3

Content Vocabulary
- evidence
- primary source
- secondary source
- point of view
- bias
- conclusion
- scholarly

and place is a primary source. Spoken interviews and objects, such as tools or clothing, are also primary sources. Primary sources help historians learn what people were thinking while the events took place. They use the sources to find evidence that explains historical events.

Historians also use **secondary sources**. Secondary sources are created after an event. They are created by people who were not part of the historical event. The information in secondary sources is often based on primary sources. Examples of secondary sources are biographies, encyclopedias, history books, and textbooks.

A secondary source contains background information. Secondary sources also offer a broad view of an event. However, a historian must use primary sources to find new evidence about a subject.

Reliable Sources

Suppose you were studying the history of England and you wanted to know how ancient people lived. You might look in a book called the *Domesday Book*. This book was created in A.D. 1086 by administrators under William I. The book is a primary source from the period. It contains information about the people of England at the time it was written.

These sculptures of warriors are evidence of life in China during the Qin Dynasty. They give archaeologists and historians information about China's culture and its first emperor.

evidence something that shows proof that something is true

primary source firsthand evidence of an event in history

secondary source a document or written work created after an event

Academic Vocabulary

source document or reference work

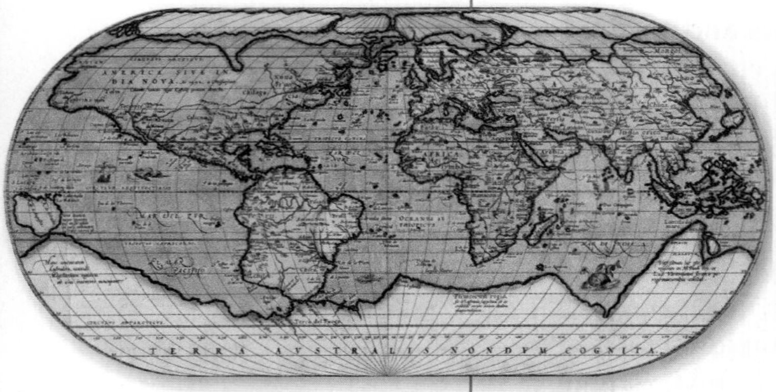

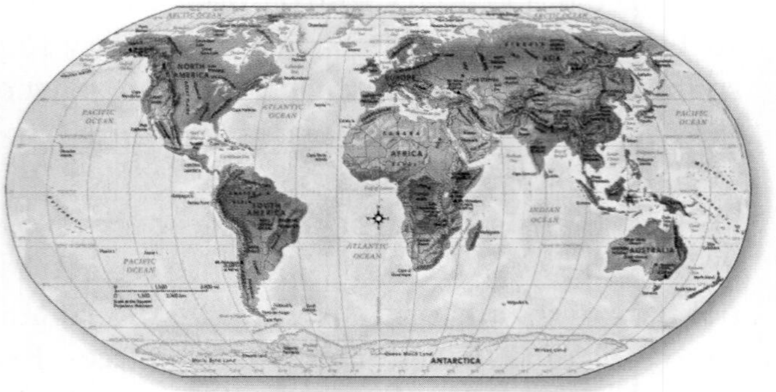

Maps can be primary sources. The map on the left was created around A.D. 1500. How does it compare with the modern world map on the right? What can historians learn by comparing these maps?

Connections to TODAY

The Census

In A.D. 1086, King William I of England decided to collect information about the land and people in his country. Today, our government collects similar data every 10 years in the U.S. Census. Questions in the census do not include details about mills and animals as in the *Domesday Book*. They instead focus on age, race, and living arrangements. The census information is a primary source about the people who live in the United States.

The *Domesday Book* is a long list of manors and the names of their owners. It includes details about how many workers worked the land. It lists the number of fishponds, mills, and animals owned by each person. It also estimates the value of each property. The historian's job is to analyze and interpret the information from primary sources. They consider where and when a source was created. They also look for the reasons that the source was created. Was it a secret letter? Was it a document created for the king, such as the *Domesday Book*? Was it written so that all the people in a town or country would read it?

What Is Point of View?

Historians interpret the document and the reasons it was created. Then they form an opinion about whether the source is trustworthy and reliable in its facts. This step is important since each source was written with a particular **point of view** or general attitude about people or life. The authors of primary sources use their points of view to decide what information is important and what to include in the document. Historians evaluate a primary source to find its point of view. They decide if it has a trustworthy viewpoint.

Sometimes a point of view is expressed as a **bias** or an unreasoned, emotional judgment about people and events. Sources with a bias cannot always be trusted.

✓ PROGRESS CHECK

Explaining What is a historian's job when looking at primary sources?

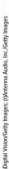

(l)Digital Vision/Getty Images; (r)Antenna Audio, Inc./Getty Images

Reading HELPDESK

point of view a personal attitude about people or life

bias an unreasoned, emotional judgment about people and events

Writing About History

GUIDING QUESTION *How do we write about history?*

When historians write about an event, they interpret the information from primary sources to draw conclusions and make inferences.

Making an inference means choosing the most likely explanation for the facts at hand. Sometimes the inference is simple. For example, if you see a person who is wearing a raincoat walk into a room with a dripping umbrella, you can infer that it is raining outside. The dripping umbrella and the raincoat are the evidence that combine with your prior knowledge about weather to infer that it is raining.

Making inferences about historical events is more complex. Historians check the evidence in primary sources and compare it to sources already known to be trustworthy. Then, they look at secondary sources that express different points of view about an event. In this way, historians try to get a clear, well-rounded view of what happened. The inference they make is how they explain what happened in the past. This explanation is based on the evidence in primary and secondary sources.

For example, you might read the *Domesday Book* to analyze the types of animals raised in 1086. You could add this knowledge to additional evidence from another source about grain that was planted. Then, you could think about what you know to be true about food. You might use all of this information to make an inference about the types of food people ate in eleventh-century England.

This cave painting was made during the Paleolithic era. It is a primary source.

▶ **CRITICAL THINKING**
Analyzing Primary Sources
What information does the painting give historians?

Yoko Aziz/Age fotostock

Looking at History

Professional historians become experts on their historical subject. Historians gather artifacts and data about a subject and then write what they have learned from the study. Such writing may become an article in a **scholarly** (SKAH·luhr·lee) journal, or magazine. It may become a book on the specific subject.

In most cases, historical books and articles are reviewed by other scholars for accuracy. Experts in the field will review the sources and write their own articles. They evaluate how the historian has interpreted the facts. This study of historical interpretations is called historiography. Historians must keep accurate notes and be careful that their inferences are reasonable.

Focusing Research

Some historians keep their areas of study very narrow. For example, someone could spend an entire career investigating the events that occurred on a single day, such as the day in the year A.D. 79 that Mount Vesuvius, a volcano in the region that is now Italy, erupted and destroyed the city of Pompeii. This subject is a **finite** place and time. Other historians focus on broader subjects. For example, some historians study the economic history of a period. Others study the political history of a country during a certain period of time. Still others might study military history, the history of medicine, or the history of technology in a certain place.

Drawing Conclusions

A **conclusion** (kuhn·KLOO·zhun) is a final decision that is reached by reasoning. You draw conclusions all the time. For example, you may notice that a friend often wears T-shirts from music concerts that he has attended. You might also remember he can never get together on Thursday nights because he has guitar lessons on Thursdays. Based on these two clues, you could draw the conclusion that your friend is really interested in music. Historians draw conclusions in the same way. They look for facts and evidence in their primary and secondary sources. Then, they use reasoning to make a judgment or draw a conclusion.

If you were researching World War I, this photo of American soldiers could help you. Using photos as evidence is a good way to expand information. What do you think these soldiers are waiting for?

Hulton Archive/Getty Images

Reading HELP DESK

scholarly concerned with academic learning or research

conclusion a decision reached after examining evidence

Academic Vocabulary

finite limited; having boundaries

interpretation an explanation of the meaning of something

Historical Interpretations

Sometimes historians disagree about their **interpretations** of the facts. For example, historians disagree about how to evaluate the historical figure of Genghis Khan. There are historians who argue that Genghis Khan was a fierce and bloodthirsty warrior. Some have expressed horror at the tremendous destruction that Genghis Khan's fierce soldiers brought as they conquered new lands. Yet some historians see Genghis Khan differently. They look at the way Genghis Khan ruled his great Mongol empire. Sources show that this was a time of peace, prosperity, and stability in a huge portion of central and eastern Asia. The people living in the Mongol empire enjoyed a remarkable degree of religious tolerance, higher learning, and consistent laws.

Genghis Khan and his Mongol warriors expanded the Mongol Empire. The violence of their invasions contrasted with the peace inside the empire.

Which conclusion is correct? Was Genghis Khan a ruthless warrior or a strong, intelligent leader of a great land? A historian may rely on evidence to support either position. However, it is the job of the historian to evaluate the primary sources and explain why both interpretations can be argued.

 **PROGRESS CHECK**

Analyzing Why do historians draw different conclusions about events of the past?

LESSON 2 REVIEW

Review Vocabulary

1. Name one way a *primary source* is different from a *secondary source.*

2. Why does a historian have to understand what *point of view* is?

Answer the Guiding Questions

3. *Drawing Conclusions* Why does drawing a conclusion come at the end of a research process?

4. *Making Generalizations* How does a primary source help a historian understand the past?

5. *Assessing* Explain why some historians differ in their interpretations of historical events.

6. **INFORMATIVE/EXPLANATORY** Think of the reading you do every day. In a short paragraph, give an example of one primary source and one secondary source that you have read recently. Explain why each example fits into the category you have chosen.

What Do You Think?

Should Artifacts Be Returned to Their Countries of Origin?

Imagine you were an archaeologist who found an important ancient artifact in another country. You would want to take that artifact home with you and display it in a museum. The country where you found the artifact might raise a protest. They may want the object to stay in their own country. Many such artifacts are displayed in museums far away from their country of origin. Who has the biggest claim to them? Should artifacts be returned to the countries in which they were found?

TEXT: "Who's Right? Repatriation of Cultural Property," by Malcolm Bell III and James Cuno, Bureau of International Information Programs, U.S. Department of State, November 2, 2010.
PHOTO: Tim Graham/Getty Images

Yes

PRIMARY SOURCE

❝The Oxford English Dictionary defines "repatriate" as "to restore (an artifact or other object) to its country of origin." Many artifacts. . . have special cultural value for a particular community or nation. When these works are removed from their original cultural setting, they lose their context and the culture loses a part of its history. A request for repatriation of an artifact. . . usually has a strong legal basis. The antiquity was exported illegally, probably also excavated [dug up] illegally, and most importantly, it is now defined by U.S. courts as stolen property. Even in the United States, where private property rights are greatly respected, the government claims ownership of antiquities from federal lands—and would request their repatriation if they were to be privately excavated and exported.❞

—**Malcolm Bell III, professor emeritus, University of Virginia**

The Cairo Museum holds countless artifacts from Egypt's long history. An example is this famous golden burial mask of Pharaoh Tutankhamen.

The Metropolitan Museum of Art in New York is visited by millions of people every year. The museum's collection includes treasures from all over the world, including this sphinx of the Egyptian pharaoh Amenhotep II.

No

PRIMARY SOURCE

// History is long and untidy. Territory held today by a given nation-state in the past likely belonged to a different political entity [unit], one with other descendents. Does ancient Hellenistic [Greek] art made and found in Afghanistan, once on the edge of the Greek empire, belong to Greece or to Afghanistan? To which modern nation do they belong? The lines designating [assigning] claims to art and culture are not clear-cut.

I would argue that within the limits of the law, museums, wherever they are, should be encouraged to acquire works of art representative of the world's many and diverse cultures. This can be through purchase or long-term loan and working in collaboration [cooperation] with museums and nations around the world. These collections encourage a cosmopolitan [international] view of the world and promote a historically accurate understanding of the fluidity [constantly changing] of culture. //

—**James Cuno, president and Eloise W. Martin Director of the Art Institute of Chicago**

What Do You Think?

1 *Identifying* Why is repatriation a legal issue according to Bell?

2 *Contrasting* How do the arguments of Bell and Cuno differ?

CRITICAL THINKING

3 *Problem Solving* Describe a compromise that might solve a conflict over ownership of artifacts.

LESSON 3

Researching History

ESSENTIAL QUESTION

• How do you research history?

IT MATTERS BECAUSE
Knowing where to find information about your subject will make it easier to complete research projects and other schoolwork.

Planning Your Project

GUIDING QUESTION *How do you begin a research project?*

The first step in a history research project is to identify your topic. A topic should not be too broad (The Middle Ages) or too narrow (Middlebury, England, 1535). To test your topic, try looking it up in an encyclopedia. If there is no entry for your topic, it may be too small. If there are many entries, or a very long entry, the topic may be too large. Selecting a topic that is workable is the most important part of the project.

After you choose a topic, you need to decide what you want to learn about it. Create six questions to help you find out *who, what, when, where, why,* and *how.* Then write each question at the top of a note card. These cards will become your research tools. You may need to add additional cards as you research.

Choosing Research Materials

After selecting a topic and creating your question cards, the next step is to gather your research materials. Begin with general reference books, such as encyclopedias and textbooks, or your notes from class. Next, try looking for books about your subject at the library. Your research material must be nonfiction, rather than fiction or persuasive writing.

Reading **HELP**DESK

Taking Notes: *Finding the Main Idea*

As you read, look for the main idea of each section. Use a graphic organizer like this one to write the details that support the main idea.

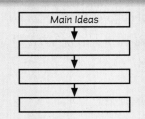

Main Ideas

Content Vocabulary
• credentials   • .edu
• URL   • .org
• .gov   • plagiarize

32   *What Does a Historian Do?*

Distinguishing Fact From Opinion

Scan each possible source to determine if the source is trustworthy. Look for opinion statements in the text. This will give you a clue that a resource could be biased or untrustworthy. Remember, a statement of fact expresses only what can be proven by evidence. A statement of opinion expresses an attitude. It is a conclusion or judgment about something that cannot be proven true or false. Historical research should rely on facts and primary sources rather than opinions.

Making Notes

As you find information, make a note about it on your cards. Your notes should be in your own words and in complete sentences. On the back of each card, make notes about the books in which you found the information.

☑ PROGRESS CHECK

Explaining Why is it important to distinguish fact from opinion in historical writing?

Researching on the Internet

GUIDING QUESTION *How do you safely research on the Internet?*

Looking for information on the Internet is quick and rewarding. However, it can be a challenge to find out if the information you located is true. Good historians follow a few important guidelines as they gather information.

Authorship

Many articles on the Internet are unsigned. A reader has no way of knowing who wrote the content and whether the author is an expert on the subject. However, reliable articles will be signed by well-known experts on the subject. The authors will include details about their **credentials** (kreh·DEN·shulz), or evidence that they are experts.

Web sites such as these may be reliable for certain subjects. There are many clues on a Web site to let you know if it will have reliable information.

(tl)Library of Congress; (c)NASA; (b)National Archive

credentials something that gives confidence that a person is qualified for a task

Check it Out!

If you answer NO to any of the questions below, the Web page or Web site is probably not a reliable resource.

- Is the authorship of the article clear?
- Can you easily find out who is responsible for the Web site?
- Has the Web page been updated recently?
- Does the writing seem balanced or does it contain a bias toward one point of view?

There are other ways to decide if an article is worth using for research. You can look at the homepage for the article. If the article is on the site of a university, government office, or museum, it is probably reliable. For example, suppose you find a signed article about the foods eaten by American colonists. You find that the article is published by an academic journal at a university. You can assume that this page is a better source than an unsigned article about the same subject by a blogger on a cooking Web site.

Web URLs

A uniform resource locator, or **URL,** is the address of an online resource. The ending on a URL tells a great deal about the content. A URL that ends in **.gov** is most likely a government entity. This site probably contains accurate **data.** This data is usually as up to date as possible.

A URL that ends in **.edu** is usually a site for an educational institution, such as a college or university. Most .edu sites pride themselves on accuracy. However, it is possible that documents on these sites may contain opinions in addition to facts.

Nonprofit organizations usually use **.org** at the end of their URLs. These sites may be very accurate. However, these groups often gather information to support their cause. Their sites may contain biased information, and they often contain opinions.

You have gathered information and answered the questions on your note cards. Then organize your cards into categories. Once your cards are sorted, you can use them as an outline for writing your research paper.

☑ **PROGRESS CHECK**

Speculating What are the consequences of using an Internet resource with biased information?

Writing Without Bias

GUIDING QUESTION *How do you interpret historical events accurately?*

You have chosen a good topic. You have created your question cards and used them while reading encyclopedia articles and library books. You have also used your cards while reviewing reliable Internet resources about your topic. You have turned the answers on your question cards into an outline. Now you are ready to write your research report. As you work, be aware of some important guidelines for writing about history.

URL abbreviation for *uniform resource locator*; the address of an online resource

.gov the ending of a URL for a government Web site

.edu the ending of a URL for a Web site for an educational institution

.org the ending of a URL for an organization

plagiarize to present someone's work as your own without giving that person credit

Academic Vocabulary

data information, usually facts and figures

violate to disobey or break a rule or law

Plagiarism

To **plagiarize** (PLAY·juh·RYZ) is to present the ideas or words of another person as your own without offering credit to the source. Plagiarism is similar to forgery, or copying something that is not yours. It also **violates** copyright laws. These laws prevent the unauthorized use of a writer's work. If you copy an idea or a written text exactly word-for-word, that is plagiarism. Some scholars have ruined their careers through plagiarism. They used content from books or the Internet without citing the source or giving credit.

To avoid plagiarism, follow these rules:

- Put information in your own words.
- When you restate an opinion from something you read, include a reference to the author: "According to Smith and Jones, . . ."
- Always include a footnote when you use a direct quotation from one of your sources.

"I didn't write the book report. I downloaded and printed it directly from the Internet, but I did collate and staple it myself."

Cartoons can make plagiarism seem humorous, but it is illegal and can lead to serious consequences.

Ancient History and Modern Values

Avoid using modern ideas to evaluate a historical event. For example, a scholar of women's history may want to apply modern ideas to women's rights in historical settings. Ideas have changed over time. Drawing conclusions about women's attitudes in the Middle Ages using modern ideas would be a mistake. Your evaluations of history should be based on the evidence, not on today's understanding of rights and society.

☑ **PROGRESS CHECK**

Listing What is one way to avoid plagiarism when writing about history?

LESSON 3 REVIEW

Review Vocabulary

1. Why is it against the law to *plagiarize*?

2. Which URL ending would identify a Web site for a charity?

   a. .org **b.** .gov **c.** .edu

Answer the Guiding Questions

3. ***Assessing*** How do you know if a resource in a library book can be trusted?

4. ***Listing*** Identify the clues you would look for to decide if an online resource is trustworthy.

5. ***Determining Cause and Effect*** What is one negative effect that can come from applying modern values to a historical event?

6. **ARGUMENT** Your teacher does not want students to use the Internet for research. Write two paragraphs in which you persuade the teacher that the Internet can be a reliable source of information.

Write your answers on a separate piece of paper.

1 Exploring the Essential Question

INFORMATIVE/EXPLANATORY Using information you have read in this chapter, give three reasons why we study history.

2 21st Century Skills

ANALYZE AND INTERPRET MEDIA Research a historical subject of your choice. Find three reliable sources and at least one source that would not be considered reliable. Write a paragraph that analyzes the online resources you discovered. Describe why each source is reliable or unreliable.

3 Thinking Like a Historian

SEQUENCING Create a personal time line using the terms *before my birth* and *after my birth*. Fill in the time line with three key events that happened before and three key events that happened after you were born.

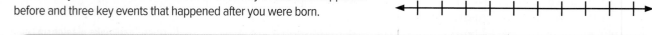

4 GEOGRAPHY ACTIVITY

Lewis and Clark expedition journal from the explorations of the Louisiana Territory

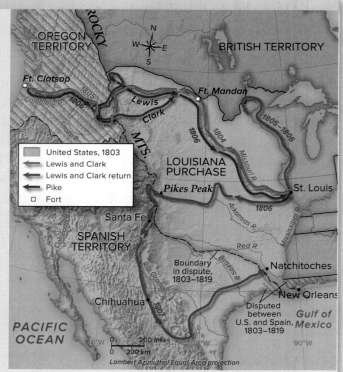

Modern map of Lewis and Clark journey, 1803

Comparing Sources

Which map is a primary source? Which is a secondary source? Include definitions of these terms in your answer. Then, explain why each source is useful to a historian.

Directions: Write your answers on a separate piece of paper.

CHECKING FOR UNDERSTANDING

1 Define each of these terms.

A. era	**F.** secondary source
B. artifact	**G.** point of view
C. fossil	**H.** bias
D. evidence	**I.** conclusion
E. primary source	

REVIEW THE GUIDING QUESTIONS

2 *Explaining* What does a historian do?

3 *Identifying* In the Gregorian calendar, what do "B.C." and "A.D." mean? How are they used in dating events?

4 *Defining* What is a primary source? What is a secondary source? Give an example of each.

5 *Listing* List three ways to avoid plagiarism.

6 *Identifying* What is the purpose of a time line? Use the time line about ancient India in this chapter to answer the following questions:

A. What is the earliest event on the time line?

B. In which year did the Aryans bring Hindu ideas to India?

C. Which event occurs between c. 1000 B.C. and c. 265 B.C.?

D. How long was it from when Harappa flourished to when the Aryans controlled northern India?

7 *Describing* How are history and archaeology similar? How are they different?

8 *Discussing* What might you do to help determine whether information you find on the Internet contains reliable information?

9 *Explaining* Why do scholars review historical books and articles?

CRITICAL THINKING

10 *Comparing and Contrasting* Compare and contrast paleontology and anthropology. Provide an example of each.

11 *Formulating Questions* What questions should you ask when you choose an event or time period to study?

12 *Differentiating* How do calendars and time lines differ, even though they might include the same events?

13 *Recognizing Relationships* How are primary sources and secondary sources about the same event related?

14 *Hypothesizing* Why do you think historians have different interpretations of historical facts?

15 *Explaining* How can the study of history help us make decisions about the future?

16 *Sequencing* In researching a protest about a war that occurred fifty years ago, what steps would you follow to find and evaluate evidence?

17 *Assessing* Would you be more likely to use a Web site with a URL that ends in .org or .gov as a source for a research project? Why?

18 *Determining Cause and Effect* Why should you avoid using modern ideas to evaluate a historical event? Give an example.

19 *Distinguishing Fact from Opinion* Decide which of the following statements is an opinion and which is a fact. Explain which statement would be best used for historical research and why.

A. Tutankhamen died after ruling Egypt for nine years.

B. Egyptians were better rulers than the Hyksos.

20 *Reasoning* Why does point of view matter to a historian when interpreting sources?

Need Extra Help?

If You've Missed Question	1	2	3	4	5	6	7	8	9	10	11	12	13	14	15	16	17	18	19	20
Review Lesson	1,2	1	1	2	3	1	1	3	2	1	1	1	2	2	1	2	3	3	3	2

DBQ SHORT RESPONSE

"Historians do not perform heart transplants, improve highway design, or arrest criminals. ... History is in fact very useful, actually indispensable [necessary], but the products of historical study are less tangible [physical], sometimes less immediate, than those that stem from some other disciplines."

—Excerpt from "Why Study History?" by Peter N. Stearns

21 Which part of this passage is fact? Which part is opinion?

22 According to Stearns, why is the usefulness of history difficult to identify?

EXTENDED RESPONSE

23 *Narrative* Write two paragraphs that identify primary sources and secondary sources about your life. Would these sources be biased? Explain.

STANDARDIZED TEST PRACTICE

DBQ ANALYZING DOCUMENTS

24 *Identifying* Historian William H. McNeill wrote an essay explaining why people should study history.

"[We] can only know ourselves by knowing how we resemble and how we differ from others. Acquaintance [familiarity] with the human past is the only way to such self knowledge. ...

In [studying history], eternal and unchanging truth does not emerge. Only inspired, informed guesses about what mattered and how things changed through time. ... Not very good, perhaps; simply the best we have in the unending effort to understand ourselves and others ..."

—Excerpt from "Why Study History?" by William H. McNeill

According to McNeill, what do people gain from the study of history?
A. They discover absolute truth.
B. They discover that the past was not very good.
C. They learn more about themselves.
D. They learn to give their best effort in what they do.

25 *Identifying Point of View* With which statement would McNeill agree?
A. Studying history is a waste of time.
B. We have much to learn from history.
C. History has no influence on the present time.
D. We should look to history for the answers to all of our questions.

Need Extra Help?

If You've Missed Question	**21**	**22**	**23**	**24**	**25**
Review Lesson	2	1	3	1	1

THE GEOGRAPHER'S WORLD

ESSENTIAL QUESTION • *How does geography influence the way people live?*

David Hay Jones/Science Source

A glaciologist drills for an ice sample.

Lesson 1
How Geographers View the World

Lesson 2
The Geographer's Tools

The Story Matters...

Since ancient times, people have drawn maps to show their known world. As people explored, they came into contact with different places and people, which expanded their understanding of the world. Today, what we know about the world continues to grow as geographers study the world's environments with the latest technology. More importantly, by understanding the connections between humans and the environment, geographers can find solutions to significant problems.

FOLDABLES
Study Organizer

Go to the Foldables® library in

Geographer's View
Geographer's Tools

the back of your book to make a Foldable® that will help you take notes while reading this chapter.

THE GEOGRAPHER'S WORLD

Geography is the study of Earth in all of its variety. When you study geography, you learn about the physical features and the living things—humans, plants, and animals—that inhabit Earth.

Step Into the Place

MAP FOCUS Use the map to answer the following questions.

1 **THE GEOGRAPHER'S WORLD** What are the names of the large landmasses on the map?

2 **THE GEOGRAPHER'S WORLD** What are the names of the large bodies of water on the map?

3 **THE GEOGRAPHER'S WORLD** What do you think the blue lines are that appear within the landmasses?

4 CRITICAL THINKING **Analyzing** How is this world map similar to other maps you have seen?

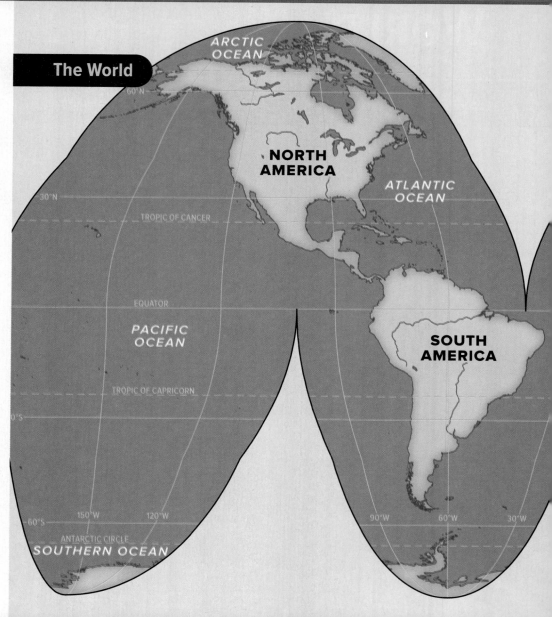

The World

ARCTIC OCEAN

60°N

NORTH AMERICA

ATLANTIC OCEAN

30°N

TROPIC OF CANCER

EQUATOR

PACIFIC OCEAN

SOUTH AMERICA

TROPIC OF CAPRICORN

30°S

150°W   120°W   90°W   60°W   30°W

60°S

ANTARCTIC CIRCLE

SOUTHERN OCEAN

Step Into the Time

DESCRIBING Choose an event from the time line and write a paragraph describing how it might have changed how people understood or viewed the world in which they lived.

150 Ptolemy creates atlas of known world

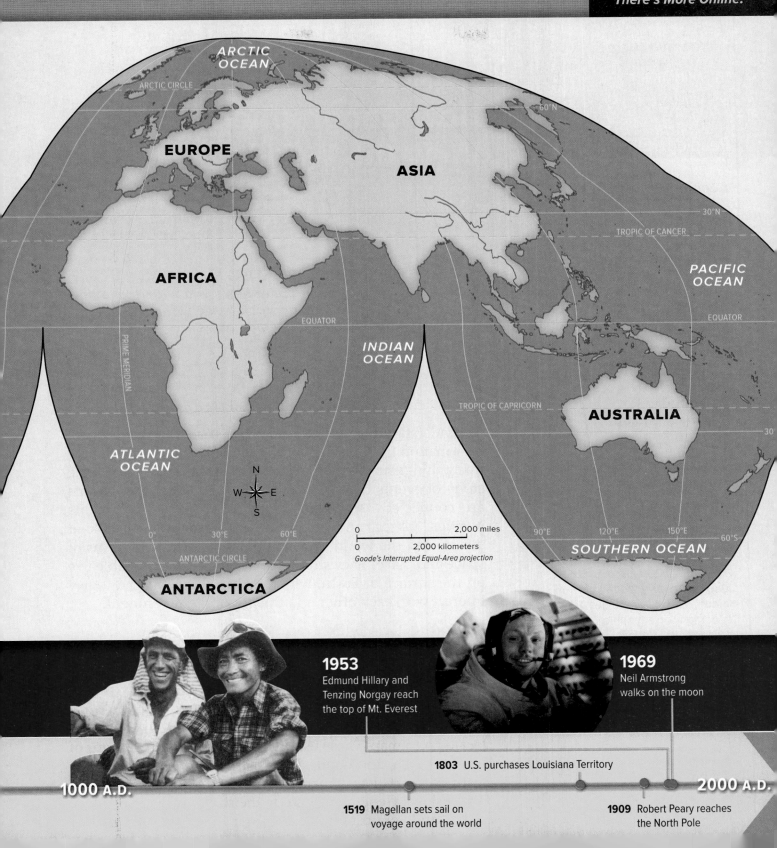

ARCTIC CIRCLE

60°N

EUROPE

ASIA

30°N

TROPIC OF CANCER

AFRICA

PACIFIC OCEAN

EQUATOR

INDIAN OCEAN

EQUATOR

TROPIC OF CAPRICORN

AUSTRALIA

30

ATLANTIC OCEAN

N
W E
S

0°   30°E   60°E

0   2,000 miles
0   2,000 kilometers
Goode's Interrupted Equal-Area projection

90°E   120°E   150°E   60°S

SOUTHERN OCEAN

ANTARCTIC CIRCLE

ANTARCTICA

1953
Edmund Hillary and
Tenzing Norgay reach
the top of Mt. Everest

1969
Neil Armstrong
walks on the moon

1803 U.S. purchases Louisiana Territory

1000 A.D.

2000 A.D.

1519 Magellan sets sail on
voyage around the world

1909 Robert Peary reaches
the North Pole

Reading**HELP**DESK

Academic Vocabulary

- dynamic
- component

Content Vocabulary

- geography
- spatial
- landscape
- relative location
- absolute location
- latitude
- Equator
- longitude
- Prime Meridian
- region
- environment
- landform
- climate
- resource

TAKING NOTES: *Key Ideas and Details*

Identifying As you read the lesson, list the five themes of geography on a graphic organizer like the one below.

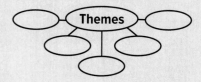

Themes

Lesson 1
How Geographers View the World

ESSENTIAL QUESTION • *How does geography influence the way people live?*

IT MATTERS BECAUSE
Thinking like a geographer helps you understand how the world works and appreciate the world's remarkable beauty and complexity.

Geographers Think Spatially

GUIDING QUESTION *What does it mean to think like a geographer?*

An understanding of the world is based on a combination of information from many sources. Biology is the study of how living things survive and relate to one another. History is the study of events that occur over time and how those events are connected. **Geography** is the study of Earth and its peoples, places, and environments. Geographers look at people and the world in which they live mainly in terms of space and place. They study such topics as where people live on the surface of Earth, why they live there, and how they interact with each other and the physical environment.

Thinking Spatially

Geography, then, emphasizes the spatial aspects of the world. **Spatial** refers to Earth's features in terms of their locations, their shapes, and their relationships to one another.

Physical features such as mountains and lakes can be located on a map. These features can be measured in terms of height, width, and depth. Distances and directions to other features can be determined. The human world also has spatial dimensions. Geographers study the size and shape of cities, states, and countries. They consider how close or far apart these human features are to one another. Geographers also think about the relationships between human features and physical features.

But thinking spatially is more than just the study of the location or size of things. It means looking at the characteristics of Earth's features. Geographers ask what mountains in different locations are made of. They examine what kinds of fish live in different lakes. They study the layout of cities and think about how easy or difficult it is for people to move around in them.

The Perspective of Place

Locations on Earth are made up of different combinations of physical and human characteristics. Physical features such as climate, landforms, and vegetation combine with human features such as population, economic activity, and land use. These combinations create what geographers call places.

Places are locations on Earth that have distinctive characteristics that make them meaningful to people. The places where we live, work, and go to school are important to us. Our home is an important place. Even small places such as our bedroom or a classroom often have a unique and special meaning. In the same way, larger locations, such as our hometown, our country, or even Earth, are places that have meaning for people.

One way that geographers learn about places is by studying landscapes. **Landscapes** are portions of Earth's surface that can be viewed at one time and from one location. They can be as small as the view from the front porch of your home, or they can be as large as the view from a tall building that includes the city and surrounding countryside.

The geography theme of *place* describes all of the characteristics that give an area its own special quality.

▶ CRITICAL THINKING
Describing What are the characteristics that make a place like Times Square in New York City special?

José Fuste Raga/age Fotostock

Whether we visit a landscape or we look at photographs of the landscape, it can tell us much about the people who live there. Geographers look at landscapes and try to explain their unique combinations of physical and human features. As you study geography, notice the great variety in the world's landscapes.

The Perspective of Experience

Geography is not something you learn about only in school or just from books. Geography is something you experience every day.

We all live in the world. We feel the change of the seasons. We hear the sounds of birds chirping and of car horns honking. We walk on sidewalks and in forests. We ride in cars along streets and highways. We shop in malls and grocery stores. We fly in airplanes to distant places. We surf the Internet or watch TV and learn about peoples and events in our neighborhood, our country, and the world.

This is all geography. By learning about geography in school, we can better appreciate and understand this world in which we live.

A Changing World

Earth is **dynamic**, or always changing. Rivers shift course. Volcanoes suddenly erupt, forming mountains or collapsing the peaks of mountains. The pounding surf removes sand from beaches.

The things that people make change, too. Farmers shift from growing one crop to another. Cities grow larger. Nations expand into new areas.

Geographers, then, study how places change over time. They try to understand what impact those changes have. What factors made a city grow? What effect did a growing city have on the people who live there? What effect did the city's growth have on nearby communities and on the land and water near it? Answering questions like these is part of the field of geography.

☑ READING PROGRESS CHECK

Describing How is geography related to history?

The Five Themes of Geography

GUIDING QUESTION *How can you make sense of a subject as large as Earth and its people?*

Geographers use five themes to organize information about the world. These themes help them view and understand Earth.

Location

Location is where something is found on Earth. There are two types of location. **Relative location** describes where a place is compared to another place. This approach often uses the cardinal directions—north, south, east, and west. A school might be on the east side of town. Relative location can also tell us about the characteristics of

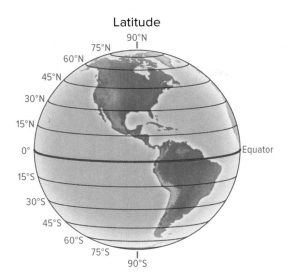

Latitude

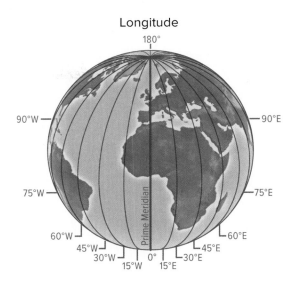

Longitude

a place. For example, knowing that New Orleans is near the mouth of the Mississippi River helps us understand why the city became an important trading port.

Absolute location is the exact location of something. An address like 123 Main Street is an absolute location. Geographers identify the absolute location of places using a system of imaginary lines called latitude and longitude. Those lines form a grid for locating a place precisely.

Lines of **latitude** run east to west, but they measure distance on Earth in a north-to-south direction. One of these lines, the **Equator**, circles the middle of Earth. This line is equally distant from the North Pole and the South Pole. Other lines of latitude between the Equator and the North and South Poles are assigned a number from 1° to 90°. The higher the number, the farther the line is from the Equator. The Equator is 0° latitude. The North Pole is at 90° north latitude (90° N), and the South Pole is at 90° south latitude (90° S).

Lines of **longitude** run from north to south, but they measure distance on Earth in an east-to-west direction. They go from the North Pole to the South Pole. These lines are also called *meridians*. The **Prime Meridian** is the starting point for measuring longitude. It runs through Greenwich, England, and has the value of 0° longitude. There are 180 lines of longitude to the east of the Prime Meridian and 180 lines to the west. They meet at the meridian 180°, which is the International Date Line.

Geographers use latitude and longitude to locate anything on Earth. In stating absolute location, geographers always list latitude first. For example, the absolute location of Washington, D.C., is 38° N, 77° W.

Lines of latitude circle Earth parallel to the Equator and measure the distance north or south of the Equator in degrees. Lines of longitude circle the Earth from the North Pole to the South Pole. These lines measure distances east or west of the Prime Meridian.

▶ CRITICAL THINKING
The Geographer's World At what degree latitude is the Equator located?

Disney World, located in Orlando, Florida, attracts millions of visitors every year.
▶ CRITICAL THINKING
Human Geography What effect do you think Disney World has on the surrounding communities?

Place

Another theme of geography is place. The features that help define a place can be physical or human.

Why is Denver called the "Mile High City"? Its location one mile above sea level gives it a special character. Why does New Orleans have the nickname "the Crescent City"? It is built on a crescent-shaped bend along the Mississippi River. That location has had a major impact on the city's growth and how its people live.

Region

Although places are unique, two or more places can share characteristics. Places that are close to one another and share some characteristics belong to the same **region**. For example, Los Angeles and San Diego are located in southern California. They have some features in common, such as nearness to the ocean. Both cities also have mostly warm temperatures throughout the year.

In the case of those two cities, the region is defined using physical characteristics. Regions can also be defined by human characteristics. For instance, the countries of North Africa are part of the same region. One reason is that most of the people living in these countries follow the same religion, Islam.

Geographers study region so they can identify the broad patterns of larger areas. They can compare and contrast the features in one region with those in another. They also examine the special features that make each place in a region distinct from the others.

(t)Aerial Archives/Alamy; (inset)Ilene MacDonald/Alamy

Human-Environment Interaction

People and the environment interact. That is, they affect each other. The physical characteristics of a place affect how people live. Flat, rich, well-watered soil is good for farming. Mountains full of coal can be mined. The environment can present all kinds of hazards, such as floods, droughts, earthquakes, and volcanic eruptions.

People affect the environment, too. They blast tunnels through mountains to build roadways and drain swamps to make farmland. Although these actions can improve life for some people, they can also harm the environment. Exhaust from cars on the roadways can pollute the air, and turning swamps into farms destroys natural ecosystems and reduces biological diversity.

The **environment** is the natural surroundings of a place. It includes several key features. One is **landforms**, or the shape and nature of the land. Hills, mountains, and valleys are types of landforms. The environment also includes the presence or absence of a body of water. Cities located on coastlines, like New York City, have different characteristics than inland cities, like Dallas.

Weather and climate also play a role in how people interact with their environment. The average weather in a place over a long period of time is called its **climate**. Alaska's climate is marked by long, cold, wet winters and short, mild summers. Hawaii's climate is warm year-round. Alaskans interact with their environment differently in December than Hawaiians do.

Another **component**, or part, of the environment is **resources**. These are materials that can be used to produce crops or other products. Forests are a resource because the trees can be used to build homes and furniture. Oil is a resource because it can be used as a source of energy.

Movement

Geographers also look at how people, products, ideas, and information move from one place to another. People have many reasons for moving. Some move because they find a better job.

Academic Vocabulary

component part

In 2005, Hurricane Katrina devastated the Gulf Coast and the city of New Orleans (left). Years later, many houses remain abandoned (right).
▶ CRITICAL THINKING
Physical Geography What hazards does the environment present?

THE SIX ESSENTIAL ELEMENTS

Element	Definition
The World in Spatial Terms	Geography is the study of the location and spatial relationships among people, places, and environments. Maps reveal the complex spatial interactions.
Places and Regions	The identities of individuals and peoples are rooted in places and regions. Distinctive combinations of human and physical characteristics define places and regions.
Physical Systems	Physical processes, like wind and ocean currents, plate tectonics, and the water cycle, shape Earth's surface and change ecosystems.
Human Systems	Human systems are things like language, religion, and ways of life. They also include how groups of people govern themselves and how they make and trade products and ideas.
Environment and Society	Geography studies how the environment of a place helps shape people's lives. Geography also looks at how people affect the environment in positive and negative ways.
The Uses of Geography	Understanding geography and knowing how to use its tools and technologies helps people make good decisions about the world and prepares people for rewarding careers.

Being aware of the six essential elements will help you sort out what you are learning about geography.

▶ CRITICAL THINKING

Identifying The study of volcanoes, ocean currents, and climate is part of which essential element?

Sometimes, people are forced to move because of war, famine, or religious or racial prejudice. Movement by large numbers of people can have important effects. People may face shortages of housing and other services. If new arrivals to an area cannot find jobs, poverty levels can rise.

In our interconnected world, a vast number of products move from place to place. Apples from Washington State move to supermarkets in Texas. Oil from Saudi Arabia powers cars and trucks across the United States. All this movement relies on transportation systems that use ships, railroads, airplanes, and trucks.

Ideas can move at an even faster pace than people and products. Communications systems, such as telephone, television, radio, and the Internet, carry ideas and information all around the Earth. Remote villagers on the island of Borneo watch American television shows to learn about life in the United States. Political protestors in Egypt use text messaging and social networking sites to coordinate their activities. The geography of movement affects us all.

The Six Essential Elements

The five themes are one way of thinking about geography. Geographers also divide the study of geography into six essential elements. Elements are the topics that make up a subject. Calling them *essential* means they are necessary to understanding geography.

✓ READING PROGRESS CHECK

Determining Central Ideas How is the theme of location related to the theme of place?

Skill Building

GUIDING QUESTION *How will studying geography help you develop skills for everyday life?*

Have you ever used a Web browser to find a route from your home to another place? If so, your search took you to a Web site that provides maps. If you followed that map to your destination, you were using a geography skill.

Interpreting Visuals

Maps are one tool geographers use to picture the world. They use other visual images, as well. These other visuals include graphs, charts, diagrams, and photographs.

Graphs are visual displays of numerical information. They can help you compare information. Charts display information in columns and rows. Diagrams are drawings that use pictures to represent something in the world or an abstract idea. A diagram might show the steps in a process or the parts that make up something.

Critical Thinking

Geographers ask analytical questions. For example, geographers might want to know why earthquakes are more likely in some places than in others. That question looks at causes. They might ask, How does climate affect the ways people live? Such questions examine effects.

Geographers might ask how the characteristics of a place have changed over time. That is a question of analysis. Or they could ask why people in different nations use their resources differently. That question calls on them to compare and contrast.

Learning how to ask—and answer—questions like these will help sharpen your mind. In addition to understanding geography better, you will also be able to use these skills in other subjects.

✓ **READING PROGRESS CHECK**

Analyzing How do geographers use visuals?

Include this lesson's information in your Foldable®.

LESSON 1 REVIEW

Reviewing Vocabulary
1. Why is it not possible to state the *absolute location* of a river?

Answering the Guiding Questions
2. *Determining Central Ideas* Why do geographers study more than a place's location and dimensions?

3. *Analyzing* Does the environment of a place involve physical or human characteristics?

4. *Identifying* What are two examples of a human system?

5. *Analyzing* Why do geographers need to use visuals other than maps?

6. *Informative/Explanatory Writing* Describe the physical and human characteristics of your community.

Reading**HELP**DESK

Academic Vocabulary

- sphere
- convert
- distort

Content Vocabulary

- hemisphere
- key
- scale bar
- compass rose
- map projection
- scale
- elevation
- relief
- thematic map
- technology
- remote sensing

TAKING NOTES: *Key Ideas and Details*

Describing As you read the lesson, identify three parts of a map on a graphic organizer. Then, explain what each part shows.

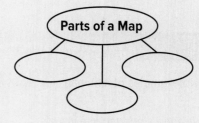

Parts of a Map

Lesson 2
The Geographer's Tools

ESSENTIAL QUESTION • *How does geography influence the way people live?*

> ### IT MATTERS BECAUSE
> *The tools of geography help you understand the world.*

Using Globes and Maps

GUIDING QUESTION *What is the difference between globes and maps?*

If you close your eyes, you can probably see your neighborhood in your mind. When you do, you are using a mental map. You are forming a picture of the buildings and other places and where each is located in relation to the others.

Making and using maps is a big part of geography. Of course, geographers make maps that have many parts. Their maps are more detailed than your mental map. Still, paper maps are essentially the same as your mental map. Both are a way to picture the world and show where things are located.

Globes

The most accurate way to show places on Earth is with a globe. Globes are the most accurate because globes, like Earth, are **spheres**; that is, they are shaped like a ball. As a result, globes represent the correct shapes of land and bodies of water. They show distances and directions between places more correctly than flat images of Earth.

The Equator and the Prime Meridian each divides Earth in half. Each half of Earth is called a **hemisphere**. The Equator divides Earth into sections called the Northern and Southern Hemispheres. The Prime Meridian, together with the International Date Line, splits Earth into the Eastern and Western Hemispheres.

Maps

Maps are not round like globes. Instead, maps are flat representations of the round Earth. They might be sketched on a piece of paper, printed in a book, or displayed on a computer screen. Wherever they appear, maps are always flat.

Maps **convert**, or change, a round space into a flat space. As a result, maps **distort** physical reality, or show it incorrectly. This is why maps are not as accurate as globes are, especially maps that show large areas or the whole world.

Despite this distortion problem, maps have several advantages over globes. Globes have to show the whole planet. Maps, though, can show only a part of it, such as one country, one city, or one mountain range. As a result, they can provide more detail than globes can. Think how large a globe would have to be to show the streets of a city. You could certainly never carry such a globe around with you. Maps make more sense if you want to study a small area. They can focus on just that area, and they are easy to store and carry.

Maps tend to show more kinds of information than globes. Globes generally show major physical and political features, such as landmasses, bodies of water, the countries of the world, and the largest cities. They cannot show much else without becoming too difficult to read or too large. However, some maps show these same features. But maps can also be specialized. One map might illustrate a large mountain range. Another might display the results of an election. Yet another could show the locations of all the schools in a city.

☑ **READING PROGRESS CHECK**

Analyzing What is the chief disadvantage of maps?

Academic Vocabulary

sphere a round shape like a ball

convert to change from one thing to another

distort to present in a manner that is misleading

A set of imaginary lines divides Earth into hemispheres.

▶ CRITICAL THINKING

The Geographer's World What line divides Earth into Eastern and Western Hemispheres?

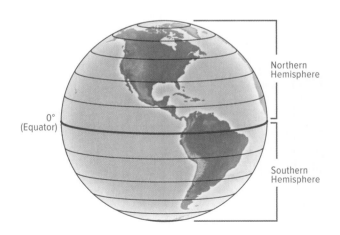

Northern Hemisphere

0°
(Equator)

Southern Hemisphere

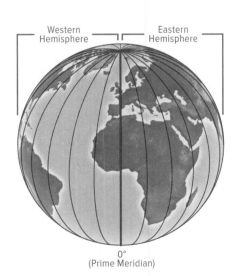

Western Hemisphere

Eastern Hemisphere

0°
(Prime Meridian)

All About Maps

GUIDING QUESTION *How do maps work?*

You will find maps in many different places. You can see them in a subway station. Subway maps indicate the routes each train takes. In a textbook, a map might show new areas that were added to the United States at different times. At a company's Web site, a map can locate all its stores in a city. The map of a state park would tell visitors what activities they can enjoy in each area of the park. Each of these maps is different from the others, but they have some traits in common.

Parts of a Map

Maps have several important elements, or features. These features are the tools that convey information.

The map title tells what area the map will cover. It also identifies what kind of information the map presents about that area. The **key** unlocks the meaning of the map by explaining the symbols, colors, and lines. The **scale bar** is an important part of the map. It tells how a measured space on the map corresponds to actual distances on Earth. For example, by using the scale bar, you can determine how many miles in the real world each inch on the map represents. The **compass rose** shows direction. This map feature points out north, south, east, and west. Some maps include insets that show more detail for smaller areas, such as cities on a state map. Many maps show latitude and longitude lines to help you locate places.

Map Projections

To convert the round Earth to a flat map, geographers use **map projections**. A map projection distorts some aspects of Earth in order to represent other aspects as accurately as possible on a flat

Many different kinds of maps are available because maps are useful for showing a wide range of information.

▶ CRITICAL THINKING

Describing What is the difference between a large-scale and a small-scale map?

(l)Chris Wallace/Alamy; (r)Peter Bischoff/Getty Images

map. Some projections show the correct size of areas in relation to one another. Other map projections emphasize making the shapes of areas as accurate as possible.

Some projections break apart the world's oceans. By doing so, these maps show land areas more accurately. They clearly do not show the oceans accurately, though.

Mapmakers, known as cartographers, choose which projection to use based on the purpose of the map. Each projection distorts some parts of the globe more or less than other parts. Finally, mapmakers think about what part of Earth they are drawing and how large an area they want to cover.

Map Scale

Scale is another important feature of maps. As you learned, the scale bar relates distances on the map to actual distances on Earth. The scale bar is based on the scale at which the map is drawn. **Scale** is the relationship between distances on the map and on Earth.

Maps are either *large scale* or *small scale*. A large-scale map focuses on a smaller area. An inch on the map might correspond to 10 miles (16 km) on the ground. A small-scale map shows a relatively larger area. An inch on a small-scale map might be the same as 1,000 miles (1,609 km).

Each type of scale has benefits and drawbacks. Which scale to use depends on the map's purpose. Do you want to map your school and the streets and buildings near it? Then you need a large-scale map to show this small area in great detail. Do you want to show the entire United States? In that case, you need a small-scale map that shows the larger area but with less detail.

Types of Maps

The two types of maps are general purpose and thematic. The type depends on what kind of information is drawn on the map. General-purpose maps show a wide range of information about an area. They generally show either the human-made features of an area or its natural features, but not both.

Political maps are one common type of general-purpose map that shows human-made features. They show the boundaries of countries or the divisions within them, like the states of the United States. They also show the locations and names of cities.

Physical maps display natural features such as mountains and valleys, rivers, and lakes. They picture the location, size, and shape of these features. Many physical maps show **elevation**, or how much above or below sea level a feature is. Maps often use colors to present this information. A key on the map explains what height above or below sea level each color represents.

Physical maps usually show **relief**, or the difference between the elevation of one feature and the elevation of another feature near it.

Thinking Like a Geographer

Relief

Relief is the height of a landform compared to other nearby landforms. If a mountain 10,000 feet (3,048 m) high rises above a flat area at sea level, the relief of the mountain equals its elevation: 10,000 feet. If the 10,000-foot high mountain is in a highland region that is 4,000 feet (1,219 m) above sea level, its relief is *less than* its elevation—only 6,000 feet (1,829 m). The difference in height between it and the land around it is much less than its absolute height. *What would be the relief of a mountain 7,500 feet (2,286 m) high compared to its highest foothill, at 3,000 feet (914 m) high?*

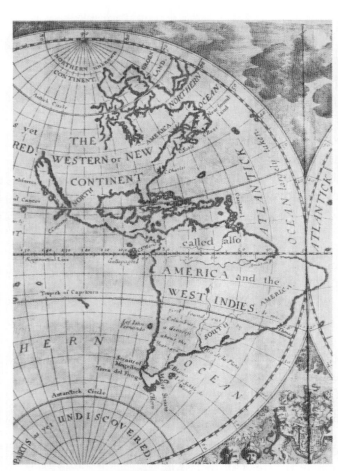

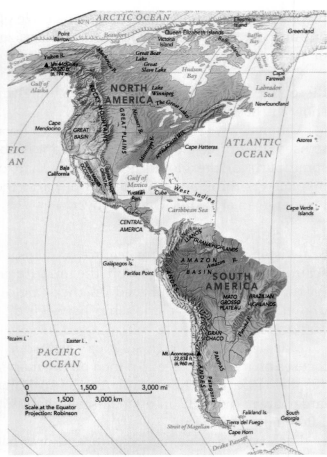

(l)Kathy Collins/Getty Images; (r)Antenna Audio - Inc./Getty Images

Cartography is the science of making maps. As knowledge of Earth grew, maps became increasingly accurate.

▶ **CRITICAL THINKING**

The Geographer's World Describe two ways in which the historical map differs from the present-day map.

Elevation is an absolute number, but relief is relative. It depends on other landforms that are nearby. The width of the colors on a physical map usually shows the relief. Colors that are narrow show steep places, and colors that are wide show gently sloping land.

Thematic maps show more specialized information. A thematic map might indicate the kinds of plants that grow in different areas. That kind of map is a vegetation map. Another could show where farming, ranching, or mining takes place. That kind of map is called a land-use map. Road maps show people how to travel from one place to another by car. Just about any physical or human feature can be displayed on a thematic map.

☑ **READING PROGRESS CHECK**

Describing How do the two main types of maps differ?

Geospatial Technologies

GUIDING QUESTION *How do geographers use geospatial technologies?*

Have you seen maps on cell phones and GPS devices in cars? These electronic maps are an example of geospatial technologies. **Technology** is any way that scientific discoveries are applied to practical use. Geospatial technologies can help us think spatially.

They provide practical information about the locations of physical and human features.

Global Positioning System

GPS devices work with a network called the Global Positioning System (GPS). This network was built by the U.S. government. Parts of it can be used only by the U.S. armed forces. Parts of it, though, can be used by ordinary people all over the world. The GPS has three elements.

The first element of this network is a set of more than 30 satellites that orbit Earth constantly. The U.S. government launched the satellites into space and maintains them. The satellites send out radio signals. Almost any spot on Earth can be reached by signals from at least four satellites at all times.

The second part of the network is the control system. Workers around the world track the satellites to make sure they are working properly and are on course. The workers reset the clocks on the satellites when needed.

The third part of the GPS system consists of GPS devices on Earth. These devices receive the signals sent by the satellites. By combining the signals from different satellites, a device calculates its location on Earth in terms of latitude and longitude. The more satellite signals the device receives at any time, the more accurately it can determine its location. Because satellites have accurate clocks, the GPS device also displays the correct time.

GPS is used in many ways. It is used to track the exact location and course of airplanes. That information helps ensure the safety of flights. Farmers use it to help them work their fields. Businesses use it to guide truck drivers. Cell phone companies use GPS to provide services. And of course, GPS in cars helps guide us to our destinations.

Geographic Information Systems

Another important geospatial technology is known as a geographic information system (GIS). These systems consist of computer hardware and software that gather, store, and analyze geographic information. The information is then shown on a computer screen. Sometimes it is displayed as maps. Sometimes the information is shown in other ways. Companies and governments around the world use this new tool.

A GIS is a powerful tool because it links data about all kinds of physical and human features with the locations of those features. Because computers can store and process so much data, the GIS can be accurate and detailed.

People select what features they want to study using the GIS. Then they can combine different features on the same map and analyze the patterns.

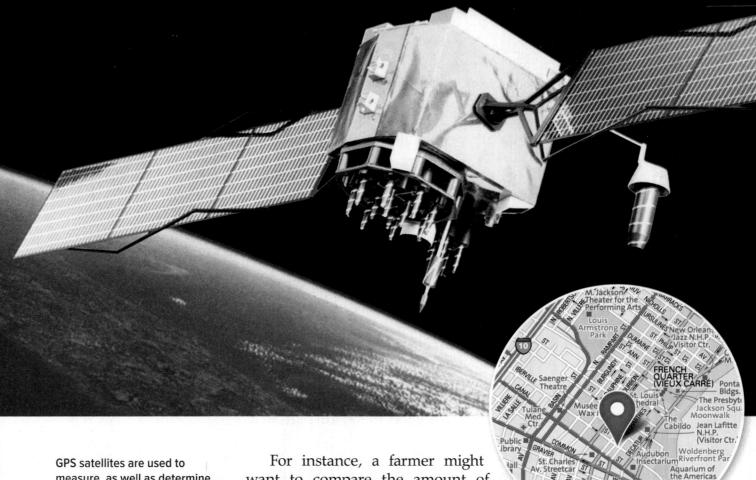

GPS satellites are used to measure, as well as determine, location on Earth. Some cell phones receive this satellite information, allowing people to locate places in a city (inset map).

▶ CRITICAL THINKING

Analyzing Why is it important for geographers to know exactly where places are located on Earth?

For instance, a farmer might want to compare the amount of moisture in the soil to the health of the plants. At the same time, he or she could add soil types around the farm to the comparison. The farmer could then use the results of the analysis to answer all kinds of questions. What plants should I plant in different locations? How much irrigation water should I use? How can I drive the tractor most efficiently?

Satellites and Sensors

Since the 1970s, satellites have gathered data about Earth's surface. They do so using remote sensing. **Remote sensing** simply means getting information from far away. Most early satellite sensors were used to gather information about the weather. Weather satellites helped save lives during disasters by providing warnings about approaching storms. Before satellites, tropical storms were often missed because they could not be tracked over open water.

Satellites gather information in different ways. They may use powerful cameras to take pictures of the land. They can also pick up other kinds of information, such as the amount of moisture in the soil, the amount of heat the soil holds, or the types of vegetation that

are present. In the early 2000s, scientists used satellites and GIS technology to help conserve the plants and animals that lived in the Amazon rain forest. Using the technology, scientists can compare data gathered from the ground to data taken from satellite pictures. Land use planners use this information to help local people make good decisions about how to use the land. These activities help prevent the rain forest from being destroyed.

Some satellites gather information regularly on every spot in the world. That way, scientists can compare the information from one year to another. They look for changes in the shape of the land or in its makeup, spot problems, and take steps to fix them.

Limits of Geospatial Technology

Geospatial technologies allow access to a wealth of information about the features and objects in the world and where those features and objects are located. This information can be helpful for identifying and navigating. By itself, however, the information does not answer questions about why features are located where they are. These questions lie at the heart of understanding our world. The answers are crucial for making decisions about this world in which we live.

It is important to go beyond the information provided by geospatial technologies. We must build understanding of peoples, places, and environments and the connections among them.

✓ READING PROGRESS CHECK

Analyzing How could remote sensing be used as part of a GIS?

Include this lesson's information in your Foldable®.

LESSON 2 REVIEW

Reviewing Vocabulary

1. Why do maps *distort* the way Earth's surface really looks?

Answering the Guiding Questions

2. *Identifying* Why are maps generally more useful than globes?

3. *Identifying* Suppose a map had the title "Russia: Land Use and Resources." What kinds of information will the map show and about what area?

4. *Identifying* Are road maps general-purpose maps or thematic maps? Explain your answer.

5. *Analyzing* How could GIS help businesses make better decisions?

6. *Informative/Explanatory Writing* Describe your neighborhood in a paragraph and then draw a map of it. Include the relevant features of a map and label them.

What Do You Think?

TEXT: Andrew Lavoie, "THE ONLINE ZOOM LENS: WHY INTERNET STREET-LEVEL MAPPING TECHNOLOGIES DEMAND RECONSIDERATION OF THE MODERN-DAY TORT NOTION OF 'PUBLIC PRIVACY,'" Georgia Law Review 00168300, Winter 2009, Vol. 43, Issue 2; PHOTO: (b)incamerastock/ Alamy

Are Street-Mapping Technologies an Invasion of People's Privacy?

Suppose you are curious about a place you have never visited. Instead of going in person, you might be able to get a 360-degree view from your computer. Services like Google Street View and Bing Streetside display panoramic images of public roadways and buildings. The photos are taken by cameras attached to roving vehicles. They capture whatever is happening at the time, which means they sometimes capture random bystanders, too. Some people argue that street-level mapping programs violate the right to privacy. They point out that individuals' pictures can appear on the mapping Web sites without their knowledge or consent. Do tools like Street View intrude too much on people's privacy?

Yes!

" Privacy encompasses the right to control information disseminated [spread] about oneself. . . . Personal behavior disclosures that occur as a result of Internet street-level mapping technologies almost certainly violate this personal right to choose which face to display to the world. . . . A person may not mind that their friends and family know of their participation in certain socially stigmatizing [disapproved of] activities; an entirely new issue arises, however, should the entire public suddenly discover that the person is [doing something questionable.] . . . Internet street-level mapping scenes depart from being simply a record of what a member of the public could have seen on the street [because] on the Internet, images can be—and often are—saved onto users' hard drives for later dissemination. Thus, compromising [reputation-damaging] images, even if removed by Google after the fact, can be released to the public in an ever-widening wake [path]. "

—Andrew Lavoie, Georgia attorney

Users can view high-resolution imagery from Google Earth or Street View on their screens.

A camera mounted on a car provides the technology for Google Street View.

No !

PRIMARY SOURCE

" At Google we take privacy very seriously. Street View only features imagery taken on public property and is not in real time. This imagery is no different from what any person can readily capture or see walking down the street. Imagery of this kind is available in a wide variety of formats for cities all around the world. While the Street View feature enables people to easily find, discover, and plan activities relevant to a location, we respect the fact that people may not want imagery they feel is objectionable featured on the service. We provide easily accessible tools for flagging inappropriate or sensitive imagery. . . . [U]sers can report objectionable images. Objectionable imagery includes nudity, certain types of locations (for example, domestic violence shelters) and clearly identifiable individuals. . . . We routinely review takedown requests and act quickly to remove objectionable imagery. "

—Stephen Chau, product manager for Google Maps

What Do You Think? DBQ

❶ *Identifying* What types of images does Google consider inappropriate?

❷ *Citing Text Evidence* What points does Andrew Lavoie make to argue that Street View invades people's privacy?

Critical Thinking

❸ *Identifying Point of View* Describe a situation when Street View could be useful and one when it could embarrass or endanger someone. Do you think the benefits outweigh the privacy concerns?

Directions: Write your answers on a separate piece of paper.

1 Use your **FOLDABLES** to Explore the Essential Question.
INFORMATIVE/EXPLANATORY WRITING Take a few moments to think about the physical geography and human geography where you live. Then write a short essay explaining how your area's geography impacts how your family lives, works, and plays.

2 21st Century Skills
INTEGRATING VISUAL INFORMATION What did your town or city look like 100 years ago? Work in groups of four or five and find historical photos or old maps of your community. Compare those to the way the community looks today. Write captions identifying the photos, and explain how the community has changed. Present your information as a slide show.

3 Thinking Like a Geographer
PLACES AND REGIONS Create a graphic organizer like the one shown here to describe the different types of maps geographers use.

4 **GEOGRAPHY ACTIVITY**

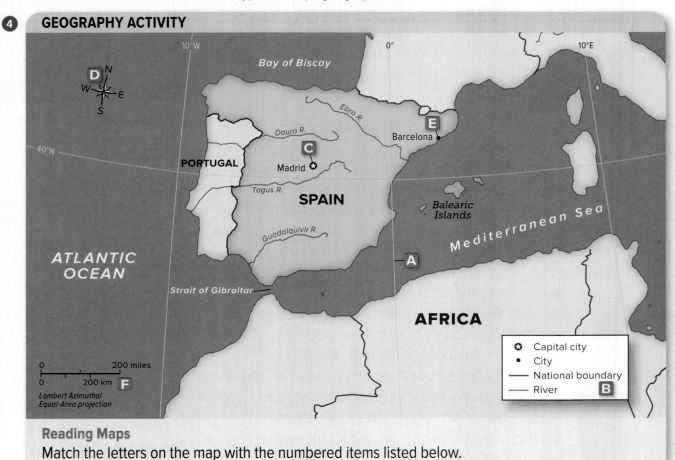

Reading Maps
Match the letters on the map with the numbered items listed below.

1. map key
2. compass rose
3. Prime Meridian
4. scale bar
5. city
6. capital

REVIEW THE GUIDING QUESTIONS

Directions: Choose the best answer for each question.

1 Lines of latitude measure distance on Earth
   A. in a north-to-south direction.
   B. in miles.
   C. in an east-to-west direction.
   D. in kilometers.

2 Which of these cities are located in the same region?
   F. Los Angeles and Dallas
   G. New York and Boston
   H. Chicago and Miami
   I. Atlanta and San Francisco

3 The average weather that occurs in a place over a long period of time is called its
   A. environment.
   B. relative location.
   C. climate.
   D. landscape.

4 What is the name of the line that divides Earth into sections called the Northern and Southern Hemispheres?
   F. the Prime Meridian
   G. the International Date Line
   H. the Tropic of Capricorn
   I. the Equator

5 Which part of a map shows the primary directions north, south, east, and west?
   A. key
   B. compass rose
   C. scale bar
   D. map projection

6 Which type of map would you use to locate your state's boundaries?
   F. political map
   G. land-use map
   H. road map
   I. physical map

DBQ ANALYZING DOCUMENTS

❼ IDENTIFYING In the excerpt below, two geographers summarize the content of their geography book.

"In this book we . . . investigate the world's great geographic realms [areas]. We will find that each of these realms possesses a special combination of cultural . . . and environmental properties [characteristics]."

—from H.J. de Blij and Peter O. Muller, *Geography*

Which theme of geography is represented by these geographic realms?

A. human-environment interaction   C. movement

B. location   D. region

❽ IDENTIFYING Which of these would be an example of the environmental characteristics of a realm?

F. plants and animals that live there

G. language and religion of the people who live there

H. nationalities of the people living there

I. type of government found in the realm

SHORT RESPONSE

"Hurricanes, wildfires, floods, earthquakes, and other natural events affect the Nation's economy, . . . property, and lives. . . . The USGS gathers and disseminates [gives out] real-time hazard data to relief workers, conducts long-term monitoring and forecasting to help minimize the impacts of future events, and evaluates conditions in the aftermath of disasters."

—from United States Geological Service, *The National Map—Hazards and Disasters*

❾ ANALYZING Why would the natural disasters named in this excerpt affect the nation's economy?

❿ IDENTIFYING POINT OF VIEW How could relief workers benefit by having maps that show areas that were hit by a natural disaster?

EXTENDED RESPONSE

Write your answer on a separate piece of paper.

⓫ INFORMATIVE/EXPLANATORY WRITING Imagine that you were with Lewis and Clark when they explored and mapped the western United States. Choose any location along their route and write a journal entry describing the landforms, animals, plants, and people you would have seen.

Need Extra Help?

If You've Missed Question	❶	❷	❸	❹	❺	❻	❼	❽	❾	❿	⓫
Review Lesson	1	1	1	1	2	2	1	1	1	2	2

GEOGRAPHY: REALMS, REGIONS, AND CONCEPTS, Twelfth Edition, by H. J. de Blij and Peter O. Muller. Copyright © 2006 by H. J. de Blij and Peter O. Muller. Published by John Wiley & Sons, Inc.; From "THE NATIONAL MAP—HAZARDS AND DISASTERS." National Geospatial Program Office, Fact Sheet 2009-3010. U.S. Geological Survey, Department of the Interior/USGS. The USGS home page is http://www.usgs.gov.

PHYSICAL GEOGRAPHY

ESSENTIAL QUESTION • *How does geography influence the way people live?*

Carsten Peter/National Geographic/Getty Images

A geologist prepares to enter the crater of Ambryn Island volcano.

network**s**

There's More Online about Earth's Physical Geography.

CHAPTER **3**

Lesson 1
Planet Earth

Lesson 2
A Changing Earth

Lesson 3
Land and Water

The Story Matters...

Earth is part of a larger physical system called the solar system. Earth's position in the solar system makes life on our planet possible. The planet Earth has air, land, and water that make it suitable for plant, animal, and human life. Major natural forces inside and outside of our planet shape its surface. Some of these forces can move suddenly and violently, causing disasters that dramatically affect life on Earth.

FOLDABLES
Study Organizer

Go to the Foldables® library in the back of your book to make a Foldable® that will help you take notes while reading this chapter.

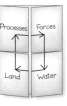

Continents sit on large bases called plates. As these plates move on top of Earth's fluid mantle, the continents move. Sometimes, the plates collide with each other or slide under each other, creating earthquakes or volcanoes.

Step Into the Place

MAP FOCUS Use the map to answer the following questions.

1 PHYSICAL GEOGRAPHY Where are most of the world's volcanoes located?

2 PHYSICAL GEOGRAPHY How many plates are underneath Australia?

3 CRITICAL THINKING Integrating Visual Information Why do you think the edge of the Pacific Ocean is often called the Ring of Fire?

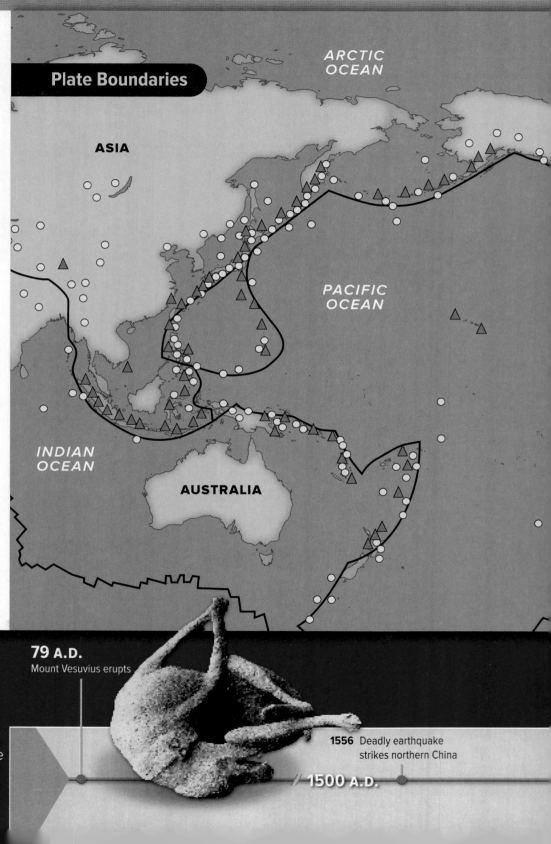

Plate Boundaries

ARCTIC OCEAN

ASIA

PACIFIC OCEAN

INDIAN OCEAN

AUSTRALIA

Step Into the Time

DRAWING EVIDENCE Choose one event from the time line and explain how the natural forces that shape the physical geography of a particular place can have a worldwide impact.

79 A.D. Mount Vesuvius erupts

1556 Deadly earthquake strikes northern China

1500 A.D.

ARCTIC OCEAN

EUROPE

NORTH AMERICA

ATLANTIC OCEAN

AFRICA

INDIAN OCEAN

PACIFIC OCEAN

SOUTH AMERICA

N
W · E
S

○ Earthquake
▲ Volcano
— Plate boundary

0   2,000 miles
0   2,000 kilometers
Miller projection

2005
Hurricane Katrina strikes southeastern United States

2011
Earthquake, tsunami near Japan triggers nuclear accident

1931 Floods in China leave 80 million homeless

1700 A.D.   **1800 A.D.**   **1900 A.D.**   **2000**

1906 Earthquake, fire devastate San Francisco

2010 Haiti earthquake kills more than 220,000 people

networks

There's More Online!

☑ **CHART/GRAPH** Climate Zones

☑ **ANIMATION** Earth's Rotation

☑ **IMAGE** Rain Shadow

☑ **SLIDE SHOW** Effects of Climate Change

☑ **VIDEO**

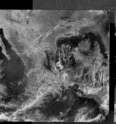

Lesson 1
Planet Earth

ESSENTIAL QUESTION • *How does geography influence the way people live?*

IT MATTERS BECAUSE
We learn about the processes that change Earth.

Looking at Earth

GUIDING QUESTION *What is the structure of Earth?*

Earth is one planet among a group of planets that revolve around the sun. The sun is just one of hundreds of millions of stars in our galaxy. Because the sun is so large, its gravity causes the planets to constantly **orbit**, or move around, it. The sun is the center of the solar system in which we live. Earth is a member of the solar system—planets and the other bodies that revolve around our sun.

Earth and the Sun

Life on Earth could not exist without heat and light from the sun. Earth's orbit holds it close enough to the sun—about 93 million miles (150 million km)—to receive a constant supply of light and heat energy. The sun, in fact, is the source of all energy on Earth. Every plant and animal on the planet needs the sun's energy to survive. Without the sun, Earth would be a cold, dark, lifeless rock floating in space.

As Earth orbits the sun, it rotates, or spins, on its axis. The **axis** is an imaginary line that runs through Earth's center from the North Pole to the South Pole. Earth completes one rotation every 24 hours. As Earth rotates, different areas are in sunlight and in darkness. The part facing toward the sun experiences daylight, while the part facing away has night. Earth makes one **revolution**, or complete trip around the sun, in 365¼ days. This is what we define as one year. Every four

(l to r)NASA/NOAA/GSFC/Suomi NPP/VIIRS/Norman Kuring; Martin Puddy/The Image Bank/Getty Images; Ariadne Van Zandbergen/
Lonely Planet Images/Getty Images; Scott Warren/Aurora/Getty Images

ReadingHELPDESK

Academic Vocabulary

• **accurate**

Content Vocabulary

• **orbit**
• **axis**
• **revolution**
• **atmosphere**
• **solstice**
• **equinox**
• **climate**
• **precipitation**
• **rain shadow**

TAKING NOTES: *Key Ideas and Details*

Summarize As you read, complete a graphic organizer about Earth's physical system.

Element	Description
Hydrosphere	
Lithosphere	
Atmosphere	
Biosphere	

years, the extra fourths of a day are combined and added to the calendar as February 29th. A year that contains one of these extra days is called a leap year.

Inside Earth

Thousands of miles beneath your feet, Earth's heat has turned metal into liquid. You do not feel these forces, but what lies inside affects what lies on top. Mountains, deserts, and other landscapes were formed over time by forces acting below Earth's surface—and those forces are still changing the landscape.

If you cut an onion in half, you will see that it is made up of many layers. Earth is also made up of layers. An onion's layers are all made of onion, but Earth's layers are made up of many different materials.

Layers of Earth

The inside of Earth is made up of three layers: the core, the mantle, and the crust. The center of Earth—the core—is divided into a solid inner core and an outer core of melted, liquid metal. Surrounding the outer core is a thick layer of hot, dense rock called the mantle. Scientists calculate that the mantle is about 1,800 miles (2,897 km) thick. The mantel also has two parts. When volcanoes erupt, the glowing-hot lava that flows from the mouth of the volcano is magma from Earth's outer mantle. The inner mantle is solid, like the inner core. Magma is melted rock. The outer layer is the crust, a rocky shell forming the surface of Earth. The crust is thin, ranging from about 2 miles (3.2 km) thick under oceans to about 75 miles (121 km) thick under mountains.

DIAGRAM SKILLS >

Crust
about 31 to 62 miles thick (50 to 100 km)

Mantle
about 1,770 miles thick (2,850 km)

Outer core
about 1,400 miles thick (2,253 km)

Inner core
about 1,500 miles in diameter (2,414 km)

EARTH'S LAYERS
Earth is comprised of several layers.

Identifying What is the innermost layer of Earth called?

NASA/NOAA/GSFC/Suomi NPP/VIIRS/Norman Kuring

The deepest hole ever drilled into Earth is about 8 miles (13 km) deep. That is still within Earth's crust. The farthest any human has traveled down into Earth's crust is about 2.5 miles (4 km) deep. Still, scientists have developed an **accurate** picture of the layers in Earth's structure. One important way that scientists do this is to study vibrations from deep within Earth. The vibrations are caused by earthquakes and explosions underground. From their observations, scientists have learned what materials are inside Earth and estimated the thickness and temperature of Earth's layers.

Earth's Physical Systems

Powerful processes operate below Earth's surface. Processes are also at work in the physical systems on the surface of Earth. Earth's physical systems consist of four major subsystems: the hydrosphere, the lithosphere, the atmosphere, and the biosphere.

About 71 percent of Earth's surface is water. The hydrosphere is the subsystem that consists of Earth's water. Water is found in oceans, seas, lakes, ponds, rivers, groundwater, and ice. Only 3 percent of the water on Earth is freshwater.

Only about 29 percent of Earth's surface is land. Land makes up the part of Earth called the lithosphere. Landforms are the shapes that occur on Earth's surface. Landforms include plains, hills, plateaus, mountains, and ocean basins, the land beneath the ocean.

The air we breathe is part of the **atmosphere**, the thin layer of gases that envelop Earth. The atmosphere is made up of about 78 percent nitrogen, 21 percent oxygen, and small amounts of other gases. The atmosphere is thickest at Earth's surface and gets thinner higher up. Ninety-eight percent of the atmosphere is found within 16 miles (26 km) of Earth's surface. Outer space begins at 100 miles (161 km) above Earth, where the atmosphere ends.

The biosphere is made up of all that is living on the surface of Earth, close to the surface, or in the atmosphere. All people, animals, and plants live in the biosphere.

Academic Vocabulary

accurate correct

Earth is sometimes called the "water planet" because about 71 percent of it is covered with water. Almost 97 percent of this water, however, is salt water.

☑ READING PROGRESS CHECK

Identifying Which of Earth's layers is between the crust and the outer core?

Seasons

GUIDING QUESTION *How does Earth's orbit around the sun cause the seasons?*

Fruits such as strawberries, grapes, and bananas cannot grow in cold, icy weather. Yet grocery stores across America sell these ripe, colorful fruits all year, even in the middle of winter. Where in the world is it warm enough to grow fruit in January? To find the answer, we start with the tilt of Earth.

Earth is tilted 23.5 degrees on its axis. If you look at a globe that is attached to a stand, you will see what the tilt looks like. Because of the tilt, not all places on Earth receive the same amount of direct sunlight at the same time.

As Earth orbits the sun, it stays in its tilted position. This means that one-half of the planet is always tilted toward the sun, while the other half is tilted away. As a result, Earth's Northern and Southern Hemispheres experience seasons at different times.

On about June 21, the North Pole is tilted toward the sun. The Northern Hemisphere is receiving the direct rays of the sun. The sun appears directly overhead at the line of latitude called the Tropic of Cancer. This day is the summer **solstice**, or beginning of summer, in the Northern Hemisphere. It is the day of the year that has the most hours of sunlight during Earth's 24-hour rotation.

Six months later—about December 22—the North Pole is tilted away from the sun. The sun's direct rays strike the line of latitude known as the Tropic of Capricorn. This is the winter solstice—when winter occurs in the Northern Hemisphere and summer begins in the Southern Hemisphere. The days are short in the Northern Hemisphere but long in the Southern Hemisphere.

DIAGRAM SKILLS >

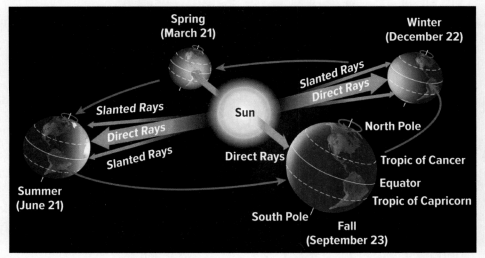

SEASONS
The tilt of Earth as it revolves around the sun causes the seasons to change.

▶ **CRITICAL THINKING**
Analyzing Why are the seasons reversed in the Northern and Southern Hemispheres?

Midway between the two solstices, about September 23 and March 21, the sun's rays are directly overhead at the Equator. These are **equinoxes**, when day and night in both hemispheres are of equal length—12 hours of daylight and 12 hours of nighttime everywhere on Earth.

☑ READING PROGRESS CHECK

Identifying When it is winter in the Southern Hemisphere, what season is it in the Northern Hemisphere?

Factors That Influence Climate

GUIDING QUESTION *How do elevation, wind and ocean currents, weather, and landforms influence climate?*

The sun's direct rays fall year-round at low latitudes near the Equator. This area, known as the Tropics, lies mainly between the Tropic of Cancer and the Tropic of Capricorn. The Tropics circle the globe like a belt. If you lived in the Tropics, you would experience hot, sunny weather most of the year because of the direct sunlight. Outside the Tropics, the sun is never directly overhead. Even when these high-latitude areas are tilted toward the sun, the sun's rays still hit Earth indirectly at a slant. This means that no sunlight at all shines on the high-latitude regions around the North and South Poles for as much as six months each year. Thus, climate in these regions is always cool or cold.

Water swirls down the street of a small town in India after heavy rains.

▶ CRITICAL THINKING

Analyzing How does elevation influence climate?

Martin Puddy/The Image Bank/Getty Images

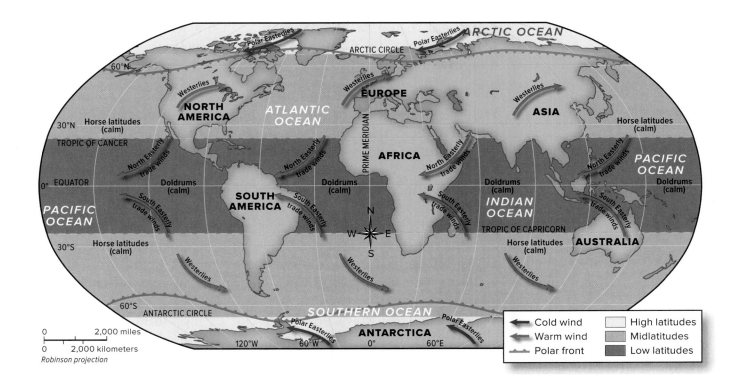

Elevation and Climate

At all latitudes, elevation influences climate. This is because Earth's atmosphere thins as altitude increases. Thinner air retains less heat. As elevation increases, temperatures decrease by about 3.5°F (1.9°C) for every 1,000 feet (305 m). For example, if the temperature averages 70°F (21.1°C) at sea level, the average temperature at 5,000 feet (1,524 m) is only 53°F (11.7°C). A high elevation will be colder than lower elevations at the same latitude.

Wind and Ocean Currents

In addition to latitude and elevation, the movement of air and water helps create Earth's climates. Moving air and water help circulate the sun's heat around the globe.

Movements of air are called winds. Winds are the result of changes in air pressure caused by uneven heating of Earth's surface. Winds follow prevailing, or typical, patterns. Warmer, low-pressure air rises higher into the atmosphere. Winds are created as air is drawn across the surface of Earth toward the low-pressure areas. The Equator is constantly warmed by the sun, so warm air masses tend to form near the Equator. This warm, low-pressure air rises, and then cooler, high-pressure air rushes in under the warm air, causing wind. This helps balance Earth's temperature.

MAP SKILLS

1 **PHYSICAL GEOGRAPHY** In what general direction does the wind blow over Africa?

2 **PHYSICAL GEOGRAPHY** What air currents flow over the midlatitudes?

Just as winds move in patterns, cold and warm streams of water, known as currents, circulate through the oceans. Warm water moves away from the Equator, transferring heat energy from the equatorial region to higher latitudes. Cold water from the polar regions moves toward the Equator, also helping to balance the temperature of the planet.

Weather and Climate

Weather is the state of the atmosphere at a given time, such as during a week, a day, or an afternoon. Weather refers to conditions such as hot or cold, wet or dry, calm or stormy, or cloudy or clear. Weather is what you can observe any time by going outside or looking out a window. **Climate** is the average weather conditions in a region or an area over a longer period. One useful measure for comparing climates is the average daily temperature. This is the average of the highest and lowest temperatures that occur in a 24-hour period. In addition to the average temperature, climate includes typical wind conditions and rainfall or snowfall that occur in an area year after year.

Rainfall and snowfall are types of precipitation. **Precipitation** is water deposited on the earth in the form of rain, snow, hail, sleet, or mist. Measuring the amount of precipitation in an area for one day provides data about the area's weather. Measuring the amount of precipitation for one full year provides data about the area's climate.

Landforms

It might seem strange to think that landforms such as mountains can affect weather and climate, but landforms and landmasses change the strength, speed, and direction of wind and ocean

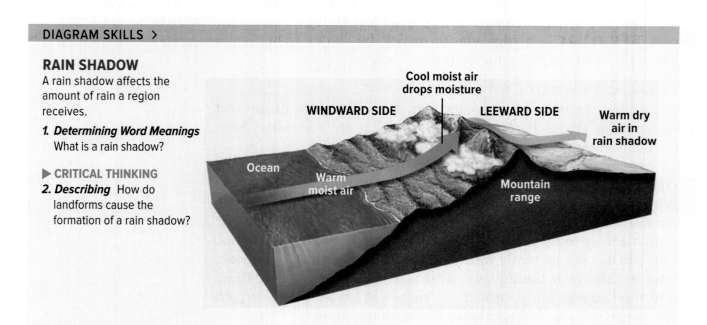

DIAGRAM SKILLS >

RAIN SHADOW
A rain shadow affects the amount of rain a region receives.

1. Determining Word Meanings What is a rain shadow?

▶ CRITICAL THINKING
2. Describing How do landforms cause the formation of a rain shadow?

Cool moist air drops moisture

WINDWARD SIDE   LEEWARD SIDE   Warm dry air in rain shadow

Ocean   Warm moist air   Mountain range

currents. Wind and ocean currents carry heat and precipitation, which shape weather and climate. The sun warms the land and the surface of the world's oceans at different rates, causing differences in air pressure. As winds blow inland from the oceans, they carry moist air with them. As the land rises in elevation, the atmosphere cools. When masses of moist air approach mountains, the air rises and cools, causing rain to fall on the side of the mountain facing the ocean. The other side of the mountain receives little rain because of the rain shadow effect. A **rain shadow** is a region of reduced rainfall on one side of a high mountain; the rain shadow occurs on the side of the mountain facing away from the ocean.

☑ **READING PROGRESS CHECK**

Determining Word Meanings Do the terms *weather* and *climate* mean the same thing? Explain.

Different Types of Climate Zones

GUIDING QUESTION *What are the characteristics of Earth's climate zones?*

Why do Florida and California have so many amusement parks? These places have cold or stormy weather at times, but their climates are generally warm, sunny, and mild, so parks can stay open all year.

The Zones

In the year 1900, German scientist Wladimir Köppen invented a system that divides Earth into five basic climate zones. Climate zones are regions of Earth classified by temperature, precipitation, and distance from the Equator. Köppen used names and capital letters to label the climate zones as follows: Tropical (A); Desert (B); Humid Temperate (C); Cold Temperate (D); and Polar (E). Years later, a sixth climate zone was added: High Mountain (F).

The climate in a zone affects how people live and work.
▶ CRITICAL THINKING
Identifying What are two useful measures for comparing climates in different areas?

Each climate zone also can be divided into smaller subzones, but the areas within each zone have many similarities. Tropical areas are hot and rainy, oftentimes with dense forests. Desert areas are always dry, but they can be cold or hot, depending on their latitude. Humid temperate areas experience all types of weather with changing seasons. Cold temperate climates have a short summer season but are generally cold and windy. Polar climates are very cold, with ice and snow covering the ground most of the year. High mountain climates are found only at the tops of high mountain ranges such as the Rockies, the Alps, and the Himalaya. High mountain climates have variable conditions because the atmosphere cools with increasing elevation. Some of the highest mountaintops are cold and windy and stay white with snow all year.

Different types of plants grow best in different climates, so each climate zone has its own unique types of vegetation and animal life. These unique combinations form ecosystems of plants and animals that are adapted to environments within the climate zone. A biome is a type of large ecosystem with similar life-forms and climates. Earth's biomes include rain forest, desert, grassland, and tundra. All life is adapted to survive in its native climate zone and biome.

A caribou grazes on a tundra field in Alaska. Animals that live in that environment have unique adaptations that help them survive.

U.S. Fish & Wildlife Service/Erwin & Peggy Bauer

Changes to Climate

Many scientists say climates are changing around the world. If this is true, the world could experience new weather patterns. These changes might mean more extreme weather in some places and milder weather in others. Human activities can affect weather and climate. For example, people have cut down millions of square miles of rain forests in Central and South America. As a result, fewer trees are available to release moisture into the air. The result is a drier climate in the region.

Metal, asphalt, and concrete surfaces in cities absorb a huge amount of heat from the sun. An enormous mass of warmer air builds up in and around the city, affecting local weather.

In recent years, scientists have become aware of a problem called global warming. Global warming is an increase in the average temperature of Earth's atmosphere. Industries created by humans dump polluting chemicals into the atmosphere. Many scientists say that a buildup of this pollution is contributing to the increasing temperature of Earth's atmosphere.

If the temperature of the atmosphere continues to rise, all of Earth's climates could be affected. Changes in climate may result in altering many natural ecosystems. Another consequence is that the survival of some plant and animal species will be threatened. It is also likely to be expensive and difficult for humans to adapt to these changes.

✔ **READING PROGRESS CHECK**

Identifying In which one of the six major climate zones do you live?,

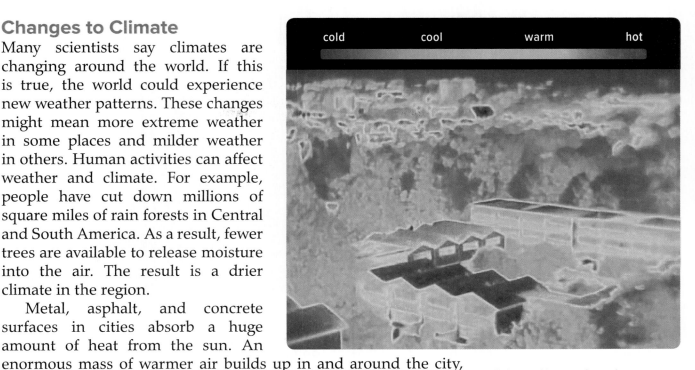
cold   cool   warm   hot

A thermal image shows heat escaping from the roofs of buildings.

▶ **CRITICAL THINKING**

Analyzing Why do sites in large cities tend to get very warm?

Include this lesson's information in your Foldable®.

LESSON 1 REVIEW

Reviewing Vocabulary
1. Write a sentence comparing the two terms below.
   a. revolution   **b.** solstice

Answering the Guiding Questions
2. ***Identifying*** What are the parts of our solar system?

3. ***Describing*** How does Earth's orbit around the sun cause the seasons?

4. ***Determining Central Ideas*** What factors determine the climate of an area?

5. ***Describing*** Identify Earth's six major climate zones. Describe the characteristics of the zones.

6. ***Narrative Writing*** Imagine that you live on a planet that is not tilted on its axis. What might this planet's seasons be like? How might life on this planet differ from life on Earth? Write a fictional narrative that addresses these questions.

Reading**HELP**DESK

Academic Vocabulary

- **intense**

Content Vocabulary

- **continent**
- **tectonic plates**
- **fault**
- **earthquake**
- **Ring of Fire**
- **tsunami**
- **weathering**
- **erosion**
- **glacier**

TAKING NOTES: *Key Ideas and Details*

Identify As you read, use a graphic organizer like this one to describe the external forces that have shaped Earth.

External Forces

Lesson 2
A Changing Earth

ESSENTIAL QUESTION • *How does geography influence the way people live?*

IT MATTERS BECAUSE
Internal and external forces change Earth, the setting for human life.

Forces of Change

GUIDING QUESTION *How was the surface of Earth formed?*

Since Earth was formed, the surface of the planet has been in constant motion. Landmasses have shifted and moved over time. Landforms have been created and destroyed. The way Earth looks from space has changed many times because of the movement of continents.

Earth's Surface

A **continent** is a large, continuous mass of land. Continents are part of Earth's crust. Earth has seven continents: Asia, Africa, North America, South America, Europe, Antarctica, and Australia. The region around the North Pole is not a continent because it is made of a huge mass of dense ice, not land. Greenland might seem as big as a continent, but it is classified as the world's largest island. Each of the seven continents has features that make it unique. Some of the most interesting features on the continents are landforms.

Even though you usually cannot feel it, the land beneath you is moving. This is because Earth's crust is not a solid sheet of rock. Earth's surface is like many massive puzzle pieces pushed close together and floating on a sea of boiling rock. The movement of these pieces is one of the major forces that create Earth's land features. Old mountains are worn down, while new mountains grow taller. Even the continents move.

Plate Movements

Earth's rigid crust is made up of 16 enormous pieces called **tectonic plates**. These plates vary in size and shape. They also vary in the amount they move over the more flexible layer of the mantle below them. Heat from deep within the planet causes plates to move. This movement happens so slowly that humans do not feel it. But some of Earth's plates move as much as a few inches each year. This might not seem like much, but over millions of years, it causes the plates to move thousands of miles.

Movement of surface plates changes Earth's surface features very slowly. It takes millions of years for plates to move enough to create landforms. Some land features form when plates are crushed together. At times, forces within Earth push the edge of one plate up over the edge of a plate beside it. This dramatic movement can create mountains, volcanoes, and deep trenches in the ocean floor.

At other times, plates are crushed together in a way that causes the edges of both plates to crumble and break. This event can form jagged mountain ranges. If plates on the ocean floor move apart, the space between them widens into a giant crack in Earth's crust. Magma rises through the crack and forms new crust as it hardens and cools. If enough cooled magma builds up that it reaches the surface of the ocean, an island will begin to form.

Powerful forces within Earth cause the Old Faithful geyser in Yellowstone National Park (left) to erupt. Those forces also cause lava to flow from Mount Etna volcano in Italy (right).

▶ CRITICAL THINKING
Describing What causes plates to move?

(l)©Jeff Vanuga/Corbis; (r)MARCELLO PATERNOSTRO/AFP/Getty Images

People attempt to cross a collapsed bridge after a powerful earthquake in the Philippines.

▶ CRITICAL THINKING

Describing What causes earthquakes?

Academic Vocabulary

intense great or strong

Sudden Changes

Change to Earth's surface also can happen quickly. Events such as earthquakes and volcanoes can destroy entire areas within minutes. Earthquakes and volcanoes are caused by plate movement. When two plates grind against each other, faults form. A **fault** results when the rocks on one side or both sides of a crack in Earth's crust have been moved by forces within Earth. **Earthquakes** are caused by plate movement along fault lines. Earthquakes also can be caused by the force of erupting volcanoes.

Various plates lie at the bottom of the Pacific Ocean. These include the huge Pacific Plate along with several smaller plates. Over time, the edges of these plates were forced under the edges of the plates surrounding the Pacific Ocean. This plate movement created a long, narrow band of volcanoes called the **Ring of Fire**. The Ring of Fire stretches for more than 24,000 miles (38,624 km) around the Pacific Ocean.

The **intense** vibrations caused by earthquakes and erupting volcanoes can transfer energy to Earth's surface. When this energy travels through ocean waters, it can cause enormous waves to form on the water's surface. A **tsunami** is a giant ocean wave caused by volcanic eruptions or movement of the earth under the ocean floor. Tsunamis have caused terrible flooding and damage to coastal areas. The forces of these mighty waves can level entire coastlines.

☑ READING PROGRESS CHECK

Determining Central Ideas Earth's surface plates are moving. Why don't we feel the ground moving under us?

Other Forces at Work

GUIDING QUESTION *How can wind, water, and human actions change Earth's surface?*

What happens when the tide comes in and washes over a sand castle on the beach? The water breaks down the sand castle. Similar changes take place on a larger scale across Earth's lithosphere. These changes happen much slower—over hundreds, thousands, or even millions of years.

TED ALJIBE/AFP/Getty Images

Weathering

Some landforms are created when materials such as rocks and soil build up on Earth's surface. Other landforms take shape as rocks and soil break down and wear away over time. **Weathering** is a process by which Earth's surface is worn away by forces such as wind, rain, chemicals, and the movement of ice and flowing water. Even plants can cause weathering. Plant roots and small seeds can grow into tiny cracks in rock, gradually splitting the rock apart as the roots expand.

You may have seen the effects of weathering on an old building or statue. The edges become chipped and worn, and features such as raised lettering are smoothed down. Landforms such as mountains are affected by weathering, too. The Appalachian Mountains in the eastern United States have become rounded and crumbled after millions of years of weathering by natural forces.

Erosion

Erosion is a process that works with weathering to change surface features of Earth. **Erosion** is a process by which weathered bits of rock are moved elsewhere by water, wind, or ice. Rain and moving water can erode even the hardest stone over time. When material is broken down by weathering, it can easily be carried away by the action of erosion. For example, the Grand Canyon was formed by weathering and erosion caused by flowing water and blowing winds. Water flowed over the region for millions of years, weakening the surface of the rock. The moving water carried away tiny bits of rock. Over time, weathering and erosion carved a deep canyon into the rock. Erosion by wind and chemicals caused the Grand Canyon to widen until it became the amazing landform we see today.

Weathering and erosion cause different materials to break down at different speeds. Soft, porous rocks, such as sandstone and limestone, wear away faster than dense rocks like granite. The spectacular rock formations in Utah's Bryce Canyon were formed as different types of minerals within the rocks were worn away by erosion, some more quickly than others. The result is landforms with jagged, rough surfaces and unusual shapes.

Erosion created this rock formation, named Thor's Hammer, in Bryce Canyon National Park, Utah.

▶ CRITICAL THINKING
Determining Cause and Effect
How does weathering contribute to erosion?

Stockbyte/Getty Images

Pictured is one of the tunnel-boring machines used to dig the Channel Tunnel, or Chunnel. The Chunnel is an underseas rail tunnel connecting the United Kingdom and France.

▶ CRITICAL THINKING

Describing What are the dangers when humans change the natural course of land and waterways?

Buildup and Movement

The buildup of materials creates landforms such as beaches, islands, and plains. Ocean waves pound coastal rocks into smaller and smaller pieces until they are tiny grains of sand. Over time, waves and ocean currents deposit sand along coastlines, forming sandy beaches. Sand and other materials carried by ocean currents build up on mounds of volcanic rock in the ocean, forming islands. Rivers deposit soil where they empty into larger bodies of water, creating coastal plains and wetland ecosystems.

Entire valleys and plains can be formed by the incredible force and weight of large masses of ice and snow. These masses are often classified by size as glaciers, polar ice caps, or ice sheets. A **glacier**, the smallest of the ice masses, moves slowly over time, sometimes spreading outward on a land surface. Although glaciers are usually thought of as existing during the Ice Age, glaciers can still be found on Earth today.

Ice caps are high-altitude ice masses. Ice sheets, extending more than 20,000 square miles (51,800 sq. km), are the largest ice masses. Ice sheets cover most of Greenland and Antarctica.

Science & Society Picture Library/SSPL/Getty Images

Human Actions

Natural forces are awesome in their power to change the surface of Earth. Human actions, however, have also changed Earth in many ways. Activities such as coal mining have leveled entire mountains. Humans use explosives such as dynamite to blast tunnels through mountain ranges when building highways and railroads. Canals dug by humans change the natural course of waterways. Humans have cut down so many millions of acres of forests that deadly landslides and terrible erosion occur on the deforested lands.

Pollution caused by humans can change Earth, as well. When people burn gasoline and other fossil fuels, toxic chemicals are released into the air. These chemicals settle onto the surfaces of mountains, buildings, oceans, rivers, grasslands, and forests. The chemicals poison waterways, kill plants and animals, and cause erosion. The buildings in many cities show signs of being worn down by chemical erosion.

Studies show that humans have changed the environment of Earth faster and more broadly in the last 50 years than at any time in history. One major reason is demand for food and natural resources is greater than ever, and continues to grow.

Changes to Earth's surface caused by natural weathering and erosion happen slowly. They create different kinds of landforms that make our planet unique. Erosion and other changes caused by humans, however, can damage Earth's surface quickly. Their effects threaten our safety and survival. We need to protect our environment to ensure that our quality of life improves for future generations.

Include this lesson's information in your Foldable®.

✅ **READING PROGRESS CHECK**

Describing Categorize each of the following events as a slow change or a sudden change: earthquake, glacier, tsunami, volcano eruption, wind erosion, water erosion, and plate movement.

LESSON 2 REVIEW

Reviewing Vocabulary

1. What causes the *erosion* of rocks on Earth's surface?

Answering the Guiding Questions

2. ***Identifying*** Identify Earth's seven continents.

3. ***Describing*** What evidence tells scientists that Earth's core is solid?

4. ***Distinguishing Fact From Opinion*** Is the following statement a fact or an opinion? Explain. *Earthquakes and tsunamis are caused by natural forces, so they cannot be prevented.*

5. ***Analyzing*** Explain how you think the Ring of Fire got its name.

6. ***Identifying*** Which of the following is the best evidence that plants can cause weathering and erosion to rocks?
   a. A rock has vines growing tightly around it.
   b. A rock has a crack through its center and plant roots growing through the crack.
   c. A rock is covered in thick, green moss.

7. ***Citing Text Evidence*** Give one example of how human actions can change Earth.

8. ***Argument Writing*** Write an essay that argues whether a country should be allowed to develop Earth's resources without interference from other countries. Think about why resources are developed and the effects of using them. Be sure to address arguments in your essay that oppose your point of view.

netw☺rks

There's More Online!

☑ **IMAGE** The Ocean Floor

☑ **ANIMATION** How the
Water Cycle Works

☑ **VIDEO**

ReadingHELPDESK

Academic Vocabulary

- transform

Content Vocabulary

- plateau
- plain
- isthmus
- continental shelf
- trench
- desalination
- groundwater
- delta
- water cycle
- evaporation
- condensation
- acid rain

TAKING NOTES: *Key Ideas and Details*

Describing Using a chart like this one, describe two kinds of landforms and two bodies of water.

1. 2.	1. 2.

Lesson 3
Land and Water

ESSENTIAL QUESTION • *How does geography influence the way people live?*

IT MATTERS BECAUSE
Earth's landforms and bodies of water influence our ways of life.

Land Takes Different Forms

GUIDING QUESTION *What kinds of landforms cover Earth's surface?*

What is the land like where you live? Are unique landforms located in your area? Have you ever wondered how different kinds of landforms were created? The surface of Earth is covered with landforms and bodies of water. Our planet is filled with variety on land and under water.

Surface Features on Land

Earth has many different landforms. When scientists study landforms, they find it useful to group them by characteristics. One characteristic that is often used is elevation.

Elevation describes how far above sea level a landform or a location is. Low-lying areas, such as ocean coasts and deep valleys, may be just a few feet above sea level. Mountains and highland areas can be thousands of feet above sea level. Even flat areas of land can have high elevations, especially when they are located far inland from ocean shores.

Plateaus and plains are flat, but a **plateau** rises above the surrounding land. A steep cliff often forms at least one side of a plateau. **Plains** can be flat or have a gentle roll and can be found along coastlines or far inland. Some plains are home to grazing animals, such as horses and antelope. Farmers and ranchers use plains to raise crops and livestock. A valley is a lowland area between two higher sides. Some valleys are small, level places surrounded by hills or mountains.

(l to r)©Roman Konopka/First Light/Corbis; Finnbarr Webster/Alamy; Ingram Publishing/SuperStock; Edwin Remsberg/Taxi/Getty Images

Other valleys are huge expanses of land with highlands or mountain ranges on either side. Because they are often supplied with water runoff and topsoil from the higher lands around them, many valleys have rich soil and are used for farming and grazing livestock.

Another way to classify some landforms is to describe them in relation to bodies of water. Some types of landforms are surrounded by water. Continents are the largest of all landmasses. Most continents are bordered by land and water. Only Australia and Antarctica are completely surrounded by water. Islands are landmasses that are surrounded by water, but they are much smaller than continents.

A peninsula is a long, narrow area that extends into a river, a lake, or an ocean. Peninsulas at one end are connected to a larger landmass. An **isthmus** is a narrow strip of land connecting two larger land areas. One well-known isthmus is the Central American country of Panama. Panama connects two massive continents: North America and South America. Because it is the narrowest place in the Americas, the Isthmus of Panama is the location of the Panama Canal, a human-made canal connecting the Atlantic and Pacific Oceans.

The Ocean Floor

The ocean floor is also covered by different landforms. The ocean floor, like the ground we walk on, is part of Earth's crust. In many ways, the ocean floor and land are similar. If you could see an ocean without its water, you would see a huge expanse of plains, valleys, mountains, hills, and plateaus. Some of the landforms were shaped by the same forces that created the features we see on land.

This map includes the ridges and patterns that show underwater mountain chains.

A DROP IN THE OCEAN
SALT WATER VS FRESHWATER

Earth's surface is about 70 percent water. That seems like a lot of water, but how much can we humans actually use? Hint: probably less than you think.

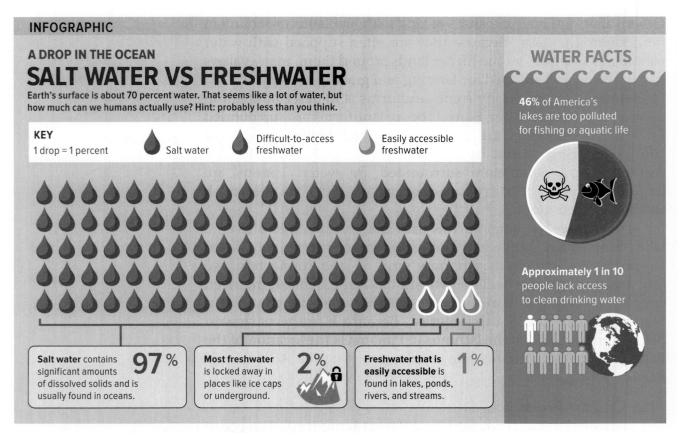

KEY
1 drop = 1 percent   Salt water   Difficult-to-access freshwater   Easily accessible freshwater

Salt water contains significant amounts of dissolved solids and is usually found in oceans. **97%**

Most freshwater is locked away in places like ice caps or underground. **2%**

Freshwater that is easily accessible is found in lakes, ponds, rivers, and streams. **1%**

WATER FACTS

46% of America's lakes are too polluted for fishing or aquatic life

Approximately 1 in 10 people lack access to clean drinking water

The surface of Earth is made up of water and land. Oceans, lakes, rivers, and other bodies of water make up a large part of Earth.

▶ **CRITICAL THINKING**

Analyzing Would you call freshwater a scarce or an abundant resource? Explain.

One type of ocean landform is the continental shelf. A **continental shelf** is an underwater plain that borders a continent. Continental shelves usually end at cliffs or downward slopes to the ocean floor.

When divers explore oceans, they sometimes find enormous underwater cliffs that drop off into total darkness. These cliffs extend downward for hundreds or even thousands of feet. The water below is so deep it is beyond the reach of the sun's light. The deepest location on Earth is the Mariana Trench in the Pacific Ocean. A **trench** is a long, narrow, steep-sided cut in the ground or on the ocean floor. At its deepest point, the Mariana Trench is more than 35,000 feet (10,668 m) below the ocean surface.

Other landforms on the ocean floor include volcanoes and mountains. When underwater volcanoes erupt, islands can form because layers of lava build up until they reach the ocean's surface. Mountains on the ocean floor can be as tall as Mount Everest. Undersea mountains can also form ranges. The Mid-Atlantic Ridge, the longest underwater mountain range, is longer than any mountain range on land.

☑ **READING PROGRESS CHECK**

Determining Word Meanings How is a valley similar to an ocean trench?

The Blue Planet

GUIDING QUESTION *What types of water are found on Earth's surface?*

Water exists around you in different forms. Water in each of the three states of matter—solid, liquid, and gas—can be found all over the world. Glaciers, polar ice caps, and ice sheets are large masses of water in solid form. Rivers, lakes, and oceans contain liquid water. The atmosphere contains water vapor, which is water in the form of a gas.

Two Kinds of Water

Water at Earth's surface can be freshwater or salt water. Salt water is water that contains a large percentage of salt and other dissolved minerals. About 97 percent of the planet's water is salt water. Salt water makes up the world's oceans and also a few lakes and seas, such as the Great Salt Lake and the Dead Sea.

Salt water supports a huge variety of plant and animal life, such as whales, fish, and other sea creatures. Because of its high concentration of minerals, humans and most animals cannot drink salt water. Humans have developed a way to remove minerals from salt water. **Desalination** is a process that separates most of the dissolved chemical elements to produce water that is safe to drink. People who live in dry regions of the world use desalination to process seawater into drinking water. But this process is expensive.

Freshwater makes up the remaining 3 percent of water on Earth. Most freshwater stays frozen in the ice caps of the Arctic and Antarctic. Only about 1 percent of all water on Earth is the liquid freshwater that humans and other living organisms use. Liquid freshwater is found in lakes, rivers, ponds, swamps, and marshes, and in the rocks and soil underground.

Water contained inside Earth's crust is called **groundwater**. Groundwater is an important source of drinking water, and it is used to irrigate crops. Groundwater often gathers in aquifers. These are underground layers of rock through which water flows. When humans dig wells down into rocks and soil, groundwater flows from the surrounding area and fills the well. Groundwater also flows naturally into rivers, lakes, and oceans.

Bodies of Water

You are probably familiar with some of the different kinds of bodies of water. Some bodies of water contain salt water, and others hold freshwater. The world's largest bodies of water are its five vast, salt water oceans.

A young girl from Gambia in West Africa pumps water from a well.

▶ CRITICAL THINKING

Describing What is groundwater? What is it used for?

Finnbarr Webster/Alamy

Humans use bodies of water for water sports and fishing.

▶ CRITICAL THINKING

Describing Describe three ways water affects the lives of people who live near it.

From largest to smallest, the oceans are the Pacific, Atlantic, Indian, Southern, and Arctic. The Pacific Ocean covers more area than all the Earth's land combined. The Southern Ocean surrounds the continent of Antarctica. Although it is convenient to name the different oceans, it is important to remember that these water bodies are actually connected and form one global ocean. Things that happen in one part of the ocean can affect the ocean all around the world.

When oceans meet landmasses, unique land features and bodies of water form. A coastal area where ocean waters are partially surrounded by land is called a bay. Bays are protected from rough ocean waves by the surrounding land, making them useful for docking ships, fishing, and boating. Larger areas of ocean waters partially surrounded by landmasses are called gulfs. The Gulf of Mexico is an example of ocean waters surrounded by continents and islands. Gulfs have many of the features of oceans but are smaller and are affected by the landmasses around them.

Bodies of water such as lakes, rivers, streams, and ponds usually hold freshwater. Freshwater contains some dissolved minerals, but only a small percentage. The fishes, plants, and other life-forms that live in freshwater cannot live in salty ocean water.

Freshwater rivers are found all over the world. Rivers begin at a source where water feeds into them. Some rivers begin where two other rivers meet; their waters flow together to form a larger river. Other rivers are fed by sources such as lakes, natural springs, and melting snow flowing down from higher ground.

A river's end point is called the mouth of the river. Rivers end where they empty into other bodies of water. A river can empty into a lake, another river, or an ocean. A **delta** is an area where sand, silt, clay, or gravel is deposited at the mouth of a river. Some deltas flow onto land, enriching the soil with the nutrients they deposit. River deltas can be huge areas with their own ecosystems.

Bodies of water of all kinds affect the lives of people who live near them. Water provides food, work, transportation, and recreation

(t)Ingram Publishing/SuperStock; (b)Edwin Remsberg/Taxi/Getty Images

to people in many parts of the world. People get food by fishing in rivers, lakes, and oceans. The ocean floor is mined for minerals and drilled for oil. All types of waters have been used for transportation for thousands of years. People also use water for sports and recreation, such as swimming, sailing, fishing, and scuba diving. Water is vital to human culture and survival.

☑ READING PROGRESS CHECK

Describing Describe three ways in which water affects your life.

The Water Cycle

GUIDING QUESTION *What is the water cycle?*

All living things need water. Humans and other mammals, birds, reptiles, insects, fishes, green plants, fungi, and bacteria must have water to survive. Water is essential for all life on Earth. To provide for the trillions of living organisms that use water every day, the planet needs a constant supply of fresh, clean water. Fortunately, water is recycled and renewed continually through Earth's natural systems of atmosphere, hydrosphere, lithosphere, and biosphere.

A Cycle of Balance

When it rains, puddles of water form on the ground. Have you noticed that after a day or two, puddles dry up and vanish? Where does the water go? It might seem as if water disappears and then new water is created, but this is not true. Water is not made or destroyed; it only changes form. When a puddle dries, the liquid water has turned into gas vapor that we cannot see. In time, the vapor will become liquid again, and perhaps it will fill another puddle someday.

Scientists believe the total amount of water on Earth has not changed since our planet formed billions of years ago. How can this be true? It is possible because the same water is being recycled. At all times, water is moving over, under, and above Earth's surface and changing form as it is recycled. Earth's water recycling system is called the **water cycle**. The water cycle keeps Earth's water supply in balance.

Water Changes Form

The sun's energy warms the surface of Earth, including the surface of oceans and lakes. Heat energy from the sun causes liquid water on Earth's surface to change into water vapor in a process called **evaporation**. Evaporation is happening all around us, at all times. Water in oceans, lakes, rivers, and swimming pools is constantly evaporating into the air. Even small amounts of water—in the soil, in the leaves of plants, and in the breath we exhale—evaporate to become part of the atmosphere.

Air that contains water vapor is less dense than dry air. This means that moist air tends to rise. As water evaporates, tiny droplets of water vapor rise into the atmosphere. Water vapor gathers into clouds of varying shapes and sizes. Sometimes clouds continue to build until they are saturated with water vapor and can hold no more. A process called **condensation** occurs, in which water vapor **transforms** into a denser liquid or a solid state.

Condensation causes water to fall back to Earth's surface as rain, hail, or snow. Hail and snow either build up and stay solid or melt into liquid water. Snow stays solid when it falls in cold climates or on frozen mountaintops. When snow melts, it flows into rivers and lakes or melts directly into the ground.

Liquid rainwater returns water to rivers, lakes, and oceans. Rainwater also soaks into the ground, supplying moisture to plants and refilling underground water supplies to wells and natural springs. Much of the rainwater that soaks into the ground filters through soil and rocks and trickles back into rivers, lakes, and oceans. In this way, water taken from Earth's surface during evaporation returns in the form of precipitation. This cycle repeats all over the world, recycling the water every living organism needs to survive.

Academic Vocabulary

transform to change

DIAGRAM SKILLS >

Condensation

Clouds

Precipitation
(snow, sleet, hail, rain)

Surface
runoff

Evaporation
from lakes
and streams

Evaporation
from ocean

Groundwater to rivers and oceans

THE WATER CYCLE
Water is constantly moving—from the oceans to the air to the ground and finally back to the oceans.

▶ **CRITICAL THINKING**
Analyzing How does water enter the air during the water cycle?

Human actions have damaged the world's water supply. Waste from factories and runoff from toxic chemicals used on lawns and farm fields has polluted rivers, lakes, oceans, and groundwater. Chemicals such as pesticides and fertilizers seep into wells that hold drinking water, poisoning the water and causing deadly diseases.

Some of the fuels we burn release poisonous gases into the atmosphere. These gases combine with water vapor in the air to create toxic acids. These acids then fall to Earth as a deadly mixture called **acid rain**. Acid rain damages the environment in several ways. It pollutes the water humans and animals drink. The acids damage trees and other plants. As acid rain flows over the land and into waterways, it kills plant and animal life in bodies of water. This upsets the balance of the ecosystem.

☑ **READING PROGRESS CHECK**

Analyzing What are the causes and effects of acid rain?

Some human activities pollute our rivers and oceans.
▶ **CRITICAL THINKING**
Describing How does acid rain affect animal and plant life?

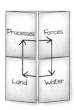

Include this lesson's information in your Foldable®.

LESSON 3 REVIEW

Reviewing Vocabulary
1. How are a *bridge* and an *isthmus* alike and different?

Answering the Guiding Questions
2. *Citing Text Evidence* Give examples of some of the landforms mentioned in the lesson by describing the landforms in your state or region.

3. *Analyzing* How is the ocean floor similar to the surface of dry land?

4. *Identifying* Identify these bodies of water as either freshwater or salt water: lake, river, ocean, pond, sea, bay, delta, gulf, groundwater.

5. *Determining Word Meanings* Explain how the processes of *evaporation* and *condensation* are both similar and different.

6. *Informative/Explanatory Writing* In your own words, explain the water cycle to someone you know. Use facts and details from the lesson in your writing.

Directions: Write your answers on a separate piece of paper.

1 Use your **FOLDABLES** to explore the Essential Question.
INFORMATIVE/EXPLANATORY WRITING Identify physical features you see in your neighborhood or community. Choose one of the features and write a description of it. Include specific details such as sights and sounds associated with the feature.

2 21st Century Skills
INTEGRATING VISUAL INFORMATION Use a variety of resources to access information about one of the four seasons. Create a poster display, a slide show, or another multimedia presentation about the season. Explain how the movement of Earth creates seasons. Describe the typical seasonal weather where you live.

3 Thinking Like a Geographer
IDENTIFYING Create a two-column chart. Use it to list Earth's layers and their composition and depth, starting with the crust and working toward the center.

4   **GEOGRAPHY ACTIVITY**

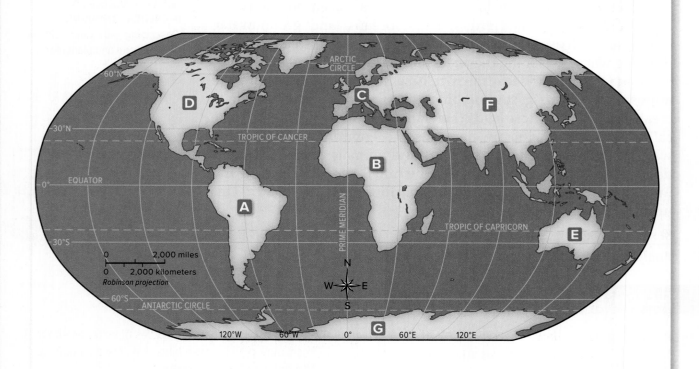

Locating Places
Match the letters on the map to the numbered continents below.

1. Africa   **3.** Europe   **5.** Asia   **7.** Antarctica

2. Australia   **4.** North America   **6.** South America

REVIEW THE GUIDING QUESTIONS

Directions: Choose the best answer for each question.

1 Earth's 24-hour cycle of day to night is caused by
   A. Earth's revolution around the sun.
   B. the pull of gravity from the moon.
   C. Earth's rotation on its axis.
   D. the sun's revolution around Earth.

2 Changes in air pressure caused by the uneven heating of Earth's surface produce
   F. ocean currents.
   G. wind.
   H. tropical storms.
   I. rain.

3 The world's largest island is
   A. Japan.
   B. Australia.
   C. Greenland.
   D. Indonesia.

4 Which forces created the Grand Canyon?
   F. wind and water
   G. snow and ice
   H. volcanoes and earthquakes
   I. glaciers and plate tectonics

5 What percentage of Earth's surface is covered in water?
   A. 40 percent
   B. 70 percent
   C. 50 percent
   D. 65 percent

6 Where is most of Earth's freshwater stored?
   F. in wells
   G. in lakes
   H. in the polar ice caps
   I. in rivers and streams

DBQ **ANALYZING DOCUMENTS**

7 IDENTIFYING In this paragraph, a science writer describes the two types of planets in our solar system.

> *"We note that the planets can be divided quite easily into two categories— the inner planets, which are small and rocky, and the gas giants that circle through the outer reaches of the solar system. Within each class, the planets bear a striking resemblance to each other, but the two classes themselves are very different."*

> —from James S. Trefil, *Space, Time, Infinity: The Smithsonian Views the Universe*

What are the two categories of planets?

A. inner and gas

B. small and rocky

C. gas and rocky

D. small and gas

8 ANALYZING Which characteristic(s) does the writer use to describe the two types of planets?

F. ability to support life

G. size and structure

H. presence of water

I. number of moons

SHORT RESPONSE

> *"There was a great rattle and jar. . . . [Then] there came a really terrific shock; the ground seemed to roll under me in waves, interrupted by a violent joggling up and down, and there was a heavy grinding noise as of brick houses rubbing together."*

> —from Mark Twain, *Roughing It*

9 IDENTIFYING What natural event do you think Mark Twain is describing? Why?

10 ANALYZING What might cause the noises Twain describes hearing?

EXTENDED RESPONSE

11 INFORMATIVE/EXPLANATORY WRITING Explain how Earth's movements affect the length of the year. How do its movements bring about day and night?

Need Extra Help?

If You've Missed Question	1	2	3	4	5	6	7	8	9	10	11
Review Lesson	1	1	2	2	1	3	1	1	2	2	1

Ancient human-like fossils tell us about our early ancestors.

Wiad74/iStock/Getty Images

8000 B.C. TO 2000 B.C.

Early Humans and the Agricultural Revolution

THE STORY MATTERS ...

Was eastern Africa the home of the earliest humans? Many scientists believe that is where the first group of human-like beings lived. Some early human skeletons found in Africa are over six million years old. Scientists estimate that this skull may be more than 3.2 million years old. It may have belonged to a three-year-old child who lived in eastern Africa. Fossils like this one tell us a lot about early humans.

Some early people may have begun moving from Africa to other regions about 1.8 million years ago. Over a period of time humans were found in Europe and as far away as China. Everywhere early humans went, they left behind clues about their lives. By studying these clues, scientists can tell us about our past.

ESSENTIAL QUESTION

• How do people adapt to their environment?

Place & Time:
Early Humans
8000 B.C. to 2000 B.C.

During the Paleolithic Age, people began to develop technology, or knowledge that is applied to help people. They created tools that helped them survive in different locations.

Step Into the Place

MAP FOCUS By about 8000 B.C., people in Southwest Asia began to stay in one place and grow crops. They also raised animals for food and clothing.

1 **LOCATION** Look at the map. Near what major body of water are Çatalhüyük and Jericho located?

2 **PLACE** Based on the map, what is the land around both settlements like?

3 **LOCATION** Describe Jericho's location in relation to the three major rivers on the map.

4 **CRITICAL THINKING** *Drawing Conclusions* Why do you think the earliest settlements developed along rivers?

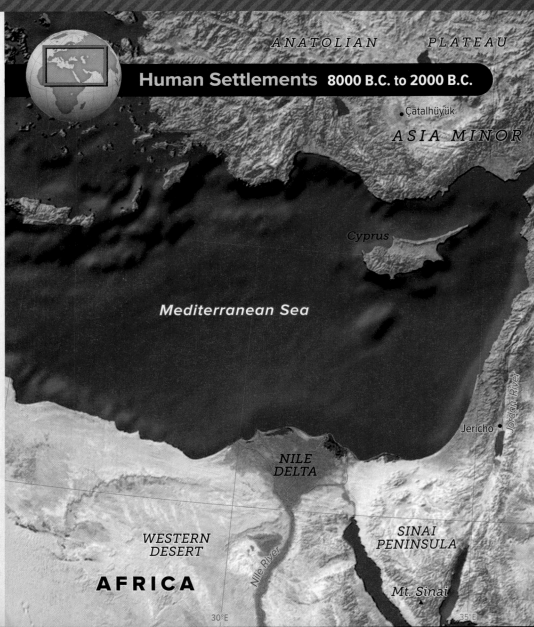

Human Settlements 8000 B.C. to 2000 B.C.

ANATOLIAN PLATEAU

Çatalhüyük

ASIA MINOR

Cyprus

Mediterranean Sea

Jordan River

Jericho

NILE DELTA

WESTERN DESERT

SINAI PENINSULA

Nile River

Mt. Sinai

AFRICA

30°E   35°E

Step Into the Time

TIME LINE Choose an event from the Early Settlements time line and write a paragraph predicting the general social or economic effects that event might have

EARLY SETTLEMENTS

THE WORLD

2.5 MILLION B.C.   100,000 B.C.

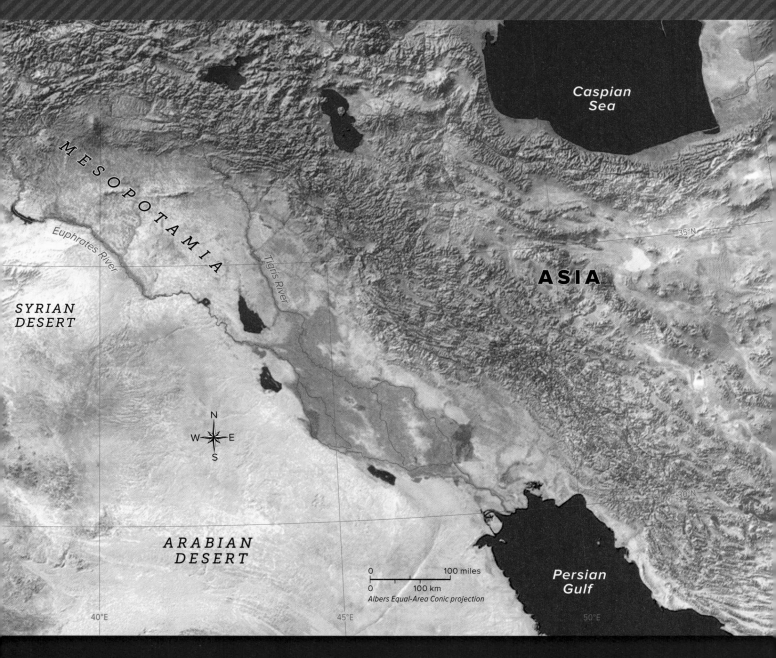

Caspian Sea

MESOPOTAMIA

Euphrates River

Tigris River

SYRIAN
DESERT

ASIA

35°N

N
W E
S

ARABIAN
DESERT

30°N

0   100 miles
0   100 km
Albers Equal-Area Conic projection

Persian Gulf

40°E   45°E   50°E

c. 6700 B.C.
Çatalhüyük established

c. 4000 B.C. Farming
established in Europe

c. 8000 B.C. Farming
begins in Southwest Asia

c. 6000 B.C. Farming begins in
Nile Valley in Egypt and in China

c. 3000 B.C. River valley civilizations emerge

8000 B.C. 7000 B.C.   6000 B.C.   5000 B.C.   4000 B.C.   3000 B.C.   2000 B.C.   1000 B.C.

LESSON 1

Hunter-Gatherers

IT MATTERS BECAUSE
Technology led to the expansion and survival of early civilization.

The Paleolithic Age

GUIDING QUESTION *What was life like during the Paleolithic Age?*

Historians call the early period of human history the Stone Age. They do this because it was the time when people used stone to make tools and weapons. The earliest part of this period was the **Paleolithic** (pay·lee·uh·LIH·thick) Age. In Greek, *paleolithic* means "old stone." Therefore, the Paleolithic Age is also called the Old Stone Age. The Paleolithic Age began about 2.5 million years ago and lasted until around 8000 B.C. Remember, that is about 4,500 years earlier than recorded time, which starts about 5,500 years ago.

Surviving in the Paleolithic Age

Try to imagine what life was like during the Paleolithic Age. Think about living in a time long before any roads, farms, or villages existed. Paleolithic people often moved around in search of food. They were **nomads** (NOH·mads), or people who regularly move from place to place to survive. They traveled in groups, or bands, of about 20 or 30 members.

Paleolithic people survived by hunting and gathering. The search for food was their main activity, and it was often difficult. They had to learn which animals to hunt and which plants to eat. Paleolithic people hunted buffalo, bison, wild goats, reindeer,

Reading **HELP**DESK

Taking Notes: *Sequencing*
Use a diagram like the one on the right to list two important inventions of Paleolithic people. Then explain why these inventions were important.

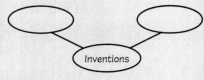

Inventions

Content Vocabulary
• Paleolithic
• nomads
• technology
• Ice Age

and other animals, depending on where they lived. Along coastal areas, they fished. These early people also gathered wild nuts, berries, fruits, wild grains, and green plants.

Finding Food

Paleolithic men and women performed different tasks within the group. Men—not women—hunted large animals. They often had to search far from their camp. Men had to learn how animals behaved and how to hunt them. They had to develop tracking methods. At first, men used clubs or drove the animals off cliffs to kill them. Over time, however, Paleolithic people developed tools and weapons to help them hunt. The traps and spears they made increased their chances of killing their prey.

Women stayed close to the camp, which was often located near a stream or other body of water. They looked after the children and searched nearby woods and meadows for berries, nuts, and grains. Everyone worked to find food, because it was the key to the group's survival.

Paleolithic people traveled in bands to hunt and gather food. Bands lived together in the open, under overhangs such as the one pictured here, or in caves.

▶ CRITICAL THINKING
Analyzing Why did these people live together in groups?

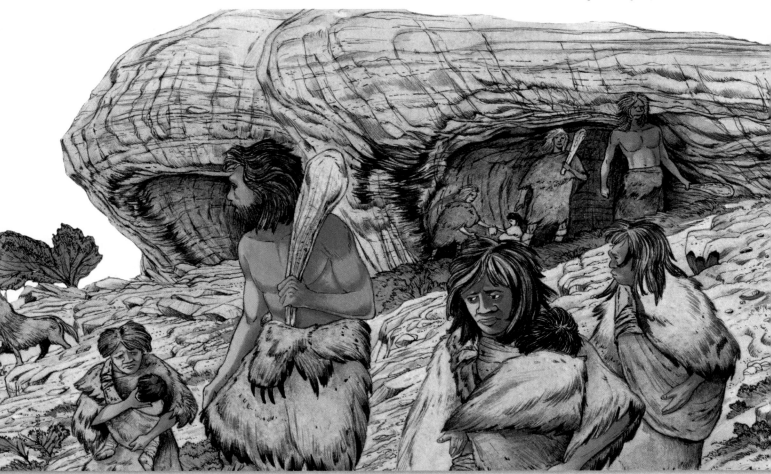

Paleolithic relating to the earliest period of the Stone Age

nomads people who move from place to place as a group to find food for themselves

Some scientists believe that an equal relationship existed between Paleolithic men and women. It is likely that both made decisions that affected the band or group. Some evidence suggests that some men and women may have hunted in monogamous pairs. This means that a man and a woman worked together to find food for themselves and their children. Such groupings became the first families.

The Invention of Tools

Culture is the way of life for a group of people who share similar beliefs and customs. The **methods** Paleolithic people used to hunt and gather their food were part of their culture, as were the tools they used.

Technology (tehk·NAHL·uh·jee)—tools and methods to perform tasks—was first used by Paleolithic people. Before this time, sticks, stones, and tree branches served as tools. Later, people made devices from a hard stone called flint. Have you ever imagined how difficult it would be to prepare or eat food without a cutting tool? Paleolithic people learned that by hitting flint with another hard stone, the flint would flake into pieces. These pieces had very sharp edges that could be used for cutting. Hand axes, for example, were large pieces of flint tied to wooden poles. Flint technology was a major breakthrough for early peoples.

Over time, early people made better, more complex tools. Spears and bows and arrows made killing large animals easier. Harpoons, or spears with sharp points, and fishhooks increased the number of fish caught. Early humans used sharp-edged tools to cut up plants and dig roots. They used scraping tools to clean animal hides, which they used for clothing and shelter.

By the end of the Paleolithic Age, people were making smaller and sharper tools. They crafted needles from animal bones to make nets and baskets and to sew hides together for clothing. This technology had a far-reaching effect. It drove the development of more advanced farming tools and influenced where people settled.

Changing to Survive

Climate affected how Paleolithic people lived. Some early people lived in cold climates and made clothing from animal skins to stay warm. They sought protection in **available** natural shelters, such as caves and rock overhangs. Remember, there

Paleolithic peoples used tools like this for many purposes. Look at this ax and decide what materials it was made of.

▶ CRITICAL THINKING
Predicting What do you think this tool was used for?

Dorling Kindersley/Getty Images

were no houses or apartment buildings as we know them in the Paleolithic Age. Gradually, humans learned to make their own shelters. People **constructed** tents and huts of animal skins, brush, and wood. In very cold climates, some people made shelters from ice and snow. In regions where wood was scarce, Paleolithic people used the large bones from dead woolly mammoths, or hairy elephant-like animals, to build frames for shelters. They then covered the bones with animal hides.

People living in warmer climates, on the other hand, needed little clothing or shelter. For the purposes of safety and comfort, however, many lived in caves and huts. These shelters provided protection against attacks by large animals.

Fire Sparks Changes

Life became less difficult for Paleolithic people once they discovered how to make fire. People learned that fire provided warmth in cold caves. It provided light when it was dark and could be used to scare away wild animals. Armed with spears, hunters could also use fire to chase animals from bushes to be killed. Eventually, people gathered around fires to share stories and to cook. Cooked food, they discovered, tasted better and was easier to chew and digest. In addition, meat that was smoked by fire did not have to be eaten right away and could be stored.

How did people learn to use fire? Archaeologists believe early humans produced fire by friction. They learned that by rubbing two pieces of wood together, the wood became heated and charred. When the wood became hot enough, it caught fire. Paleolithic people continued rubbing wood together, eventually developing drill-like wooden tools to start fires. They also discovered that a certain stone, iron pyrite, gave off sparks when struck against another rock. The sparks could then ignite dry grass or leaves— another way to start a fire.

McGraw-Hill Education

Visual Vocabulary

woolly mammoth a large, hairy, extinct animal related to modern-day elephants

Paleolithic art has been found in caves in Argentina. Early people left a message that remains today.

▶ **CRITICAL THINKING**
Identifying What subjects were most common in cave paintings?

Language and Art

Other advancements took place during the Paleolithic Age. One important advancement was the development of spoken language. Up until this time, early people **communicated** through sounds and physical gestures. Then, they began to develop language.

Ancient peoples started to express themselves in words for the same reasons we do. We use language to communicate information and emotions. Language makes it easier for us to work together and to pass on knowledge. We also use words to express our thoughts and feelings. The spoken language of early people was **constantly** growing and changing. New technology and more complicated experiences, for example, required new words.

Early people also expressed themselves through art. Some of this art can still be seen today, even though it is thousands of years old. For example, in 1879 a young girl named Maria de Sautuola wandered into a cave on her grandfather's farm near Altamira, Spain. She was startled by what she discovered on the walls of that cave:

PRIMARY SOURCE

❝ Maria entered the cave ... and suddenly reappeared all excited, shouting 'Papa, mira, toros pintados! [Papa, look, painted bulls!]' Maria had discovered one of the most famous animal-art galleries in the world. ❞

—from *Hands: Prehistoric Visiting Cards?* by August Gansser

Eduardo M. Rivero/age fotostock

Reading **HELP**DESK

Academic Vocabulary

communicate to share information with someone
constant always happening

About ten thousand years before Maria's visit, Paleolithic artists had painted mysterious signs, including what looked like a herd of animals—horses, boars, bison, and deer—on the cave's ceiling. In 1940, a cave with similar paintings to those in Spain was discovered near Lascaux (lah·SKOH) in southern France.

Paleolithic cave paintings have been found all around the world. Early artists crushed yellow, black, and red rocks and combined them with animal fat to make their paints. They used twigs and their fingertips to apply these paints to the rock walls. They later used brushes made from animal hair. Early people created scenes of lions, oxen, panthers, and other animals. Few humans, however, appear in these paintings.

Historians are not sure why early artists chose to make cave paintings. Early people may have thought that painting an animal would bring hunters good luck. Some scholars believe, however, that the paintings may have been created to record the group's history. They may have been created simply to be enjoyed.

☑ **PROGRESS CHECK**

Explaining Why was fire important for Paleolithic people?

The paintings in the Lascaux caves are the most famous examples of Paleolithic art. Scientists now believe that such paintings took thousands of years, and hundreds of generations, to produce.

▶ **CRITICAL THINKING**
Speculating Why do you think these paintings lasted so long?

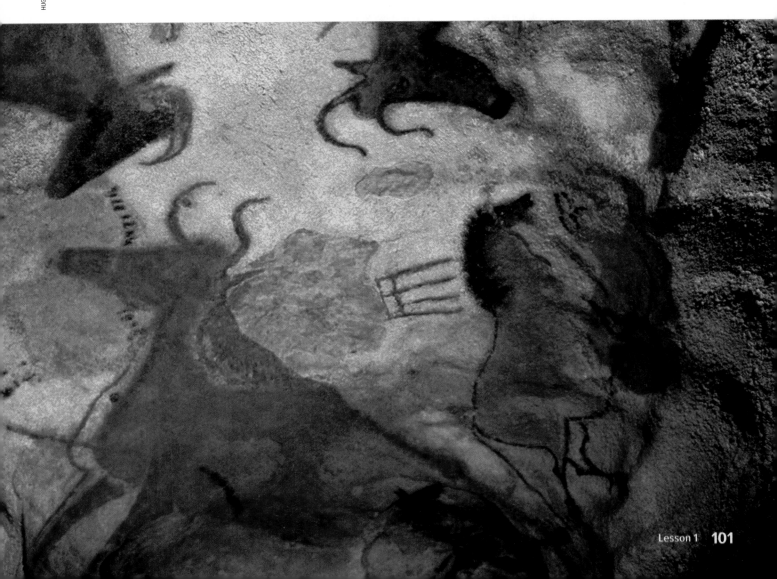

The Ice Ages

GUIDING QUESTION *How did people adapt to survive during the ice ages?*

Tools and fire were two important technological developments of Paleolithic people. Throughout history, people have used new technology to help them survive when the environment changes. The ice ages were major environmental disturbances. The changes they brought about threatened the very survival of humans.

What Changes Came With the Ice Ages?

The **ice ages** were long periods of extreme cold that affected all of Earth. The most recent Ice Age began about 100,000 years ago. Thick sheets of ice moved across large parts of Europe, Asia, and North America. As the ice sheets, or glaciers, grew larger, the water level of the oceans was lowered. The low sea

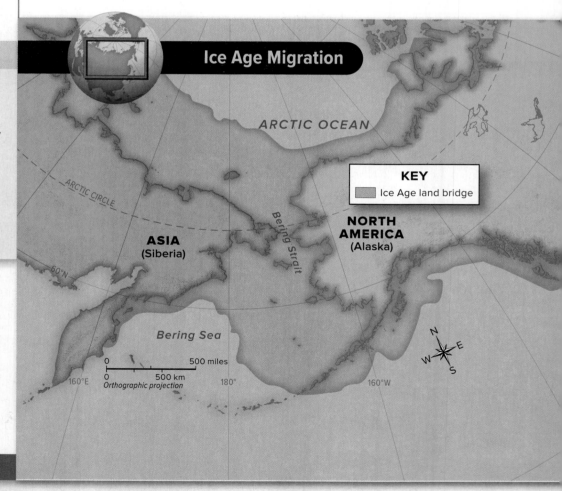

GEOGRAPHY CONNECTION

During the most recent Ice Age, a strip of land connected the continents of Asia and North America.

1 **REGIONS** How did the geography of this region change when the most recent Ice Age ended?

2 **CRITICAL THINKING**
Analyzing After people arrived in North America, what is a likely reason they moved south rather than staying near the land bridge?

Ice Age Migration

ARCTIC OCEAN

ARCTIC CIRCLE

KEY
Ice Age land bridge

ASIA
(Siberia)

Bering Strait

NORTH AMERICA
(Alaska)

60°N

Bering Sea

0   500 miles
0   500 km
Orthographic projection

160°E   180°   160°W

N E S W

ice age a time when glaciers covered much of the land

levels exposed a strip of dry land connecting the continents of Asia and North America. This strip of land was known as a land bridge. The land bridge acted as a natural highway that allowed people to travel from Asia into North America. From there, Paleolithic peoples moved southward to settle in different regions.

How Did the Ice Ages Affect Humans?

Ice age conditions posed a grave threat to human life. To survive in the cold temperatures, humans had to adapt, or change, many areas of their lives. One way they adapted their diets was by enriching meals with fat. To protect themselves from the harsh environment, they learned to build sturdier shelters. They also learned to make warm clothing using animal furs. Paleolithic people used fire to help them stay warm in this icy environment. The last Ice Age lasted about 90,000 years, ending between about 9000 and 8000 B.C.

☑ PROGRESS CHECK

Explaining How were land bridges formed?

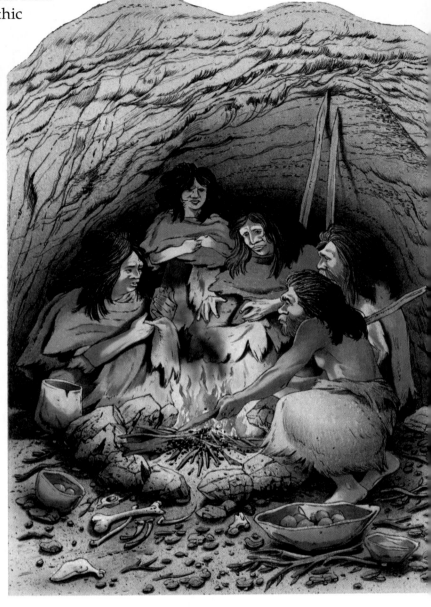

After early people controlled fire, they brought it into their shelters. At the site of some Stone Age huts, scientists have discovered an early form of a fireplace—a shallow hole lined with blackened stones.

LESSON 1 REVIEW

Review Vocabulary

1. What is another name for the *Paleolithic* Age?

Answer the Guiding Questions

2. *Describing* By what methods did Paleolithic people get food?

3. *Summarizing* How did fire help Paleolithic people survive?

4. *Determining Cause and Effect* How did the ice ages affect where people settled in the Americas?

5. *Making Connections* How does climate affect the type of house you live in or the clothes you wear?

6. **NARRATIVE** You are a mother or father who lives in the early Paleolithic Age. In a few paragraphs, describe your daily life.

LESSON 2

The Agricultural Revolution

ESSENTIAL QUESTION
• How do people adapt to their environment?

IT MATTERS BECAUSE
The Agricultural Revolution allowed people to set up permanent settlements.

Neolithic Times

GUIDING QUESTION *How did farming change people's lives?*

The earliest people were nomads who moved from place to place to hunt animals and gather plants. After the last Ice Age ended, Earth's temperatures rose. As the climate warmed, many nomads moved into areas with a mild climate and fertile land.

Another historical revolution then occurred. For the first time, people began staying in one place to grow grains and vegetables. Gradually, farming replaced hunting and gathering as the main source of food. At the same time, people began to **domesticate** (duh·MEHS·tih·kayt), or tame, animals for human use. Animals transported goods and provided meat, milk, and wool.

The Neolithic Age

This change in the way people lived marked the beginning of the **Neolithic Age** (nee·uh·LIH·thick). It began about 8000 B.C. and lasted until around 4000 B.C.—about 4,000 years. The word *neolithic* is Greek for "new stone." Calling this time period the New Stone Age, however, is somewhat misleading. Although new stone tools were made, the real change in the Neolithic Age was the shift from hunting and gathering to **systematic agriculture**. This is growing food on a regular basis.

Reading **HELP**DESK

Taking Notes: *Identifying*
Use a diagram like this to identify three advancements made during the Neolithic Age.

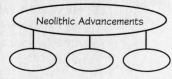

Neolithic Advancements

Content Vocabulary
- **domesticate**
- **Neolithic Age**
- **systematic agriculture**
- **shrine**
- **specialization**
- **Bronze Age**
- **monarchy**

This shift from hunting and gathering to food production, however, did not happen quickly. Even during the Mesolithic Age, or Middle Stone Age, some people continued to hunt and gather, while others began to grow their own food.

Big Changes for Humankind

Historians call this settled farming during the Neolithic Age the Agricultural Revolution. The word *revolution* refers to any change that has an enormous effect on people's ways of life. While hunter-gatherers ate wild grains that they collected, early farmers saved some of the grains to plant. Humans lived differently once they learned how to grow crops and tame animals that produced food. They now could produce a constant food supply. This allowed the population to grow at a faster rate. Nomads gave up their way of life and began living in settled communities. Some historians consider the Agricultural Revolution the most important event in human history.

GEOGRAPHY CONNECTION

Between about 7000 and 2000 B.C., farming developed on different continents.

1 **REGIONS** What crops were grown south of the Equator?

2 **CRITICAL THINKING**
Speculating Why do you think so many different crops were grown in Central America?

Early Farming

KEY

Barley	Cotton	Oats and Rye	Potatoes	Sunflowers	Wheat
Beans	Emmer	Olives	Rice	Sweet potatoes	Yams
Cocoa	Flax	Onions	Soybeans	Tea	
Coffee	Maize	Peanuts	Squash	Tomatoes	
	Millet	Peppers	Sugarcane	Vanilla	

domesticate to adapt an animal to living with humans for the advantage of humans

Neolithic Age relating to the latest period of the Stone Age

systematic agriculture the organized growing of food on a regular schedule

Widespread Farming

By 8000 B.C., people in Southwest Asia began growing wheat and barley. They also domesticated pigs, cows, goats, and sheep. From there, farming spread into southeastern Europe. By 4000 B.C., farming was an established **economic** activity in Europe.

At about the same time, around 6000 B.C., people had begun growing wheat and barley in the Nile Valley in Egypt. Farming soon spread along the Nile River and into other regions in Africa. In Central Africa, different types of crops emerged. There, people grew root crops called tubers, which included yams. They also grew fruit crops, such as bananas. Wheat and barley farming moved eastward into India between 8000 and 5000 B.C.

By 6000 B.C., people in northern China were growing a food grain called millet and were domesticating dogs and pigs. By 5000 B.C., farmers in Southeast Asia were growing rice. From there, rice farming spread into southern China.

In the Western Hemisphere, between 7000 and 5000 B.C., people in Mexico and Central America were growing corn, squash, and potatoes. They also domesticated chickens and dogs.

✔ **PROGRESS CHECK**

Explaining How did the spread of farming change the lives of nomads?

Originally, Neolithic people built large dwelling places that housed a small clan, or family group, along with their cattle and grain stores. Eventually, these were replaced by one- or two-room houses, which were usually clustered in groups.

▶ **CRITICAL THINKING**

Analyzing Why would construction methods vary depending on geographical location?

Academic Vocabulary

economy the system of economic life in an area or country; an economy deals with the making, buying, and selling of goods or services

► CRITICAL THINKING
Analyzing The village of Çatalhüyük grew into a large community. These ruins reveal well thought out construction. *Why do you think some people were happy to settle in villages?*

Life in the Neolithic Age

GUIDING QUESTION *What was life like during the Neolithic Age?*

During the Neolithic Age, people settled in villages where they built permanent homes. They **located** villages near fields so people could plant, grow, and harvest their crops more easily. People also settled near water sources, especially rivers.

Neolithic Communities

Neolithic farming villages developed throughout Europe, India, Egypt, China, and Mexico. The biggest and earliest known communities have been found in Southwest Asia. One of the oldest communities was Jericho (JAIR·ih·koh). This farming village grew in an area between present-day Israel and Jordan called the West Bank. The village of Jericho was well established by about 8000 B.C. It extended across several acres. The area of sun-dried-brick houses was surrounded by walls that were several feet thick.

Academic Vocabulary

locate to set up in a particular place

**Ötzi the Iceman
(c. 3300 B.C.)**

Mystery Man Ötzi was a Neolithic man whose remains were discovered in 1991 in the Austrian Alps. Also called the "Iceman," Ötzi presented a mystery. Did he live where he died? Did he spend his life in another location? What did he do for a living? Scientists found the same form of oxygen in Ötzi's teeth as in the water of the southern Alpine valleys. They have concluded that, even though Ötzi was found in the mountains, he lived most of his life in the valleys south of the Alps. Scientists believe Ötzi was either a shepherd or a hunter who traveled from the valleys to the mountains.

▶ **CRITICAL THINKING**
Analyzing What types of clothing or tools do you think Ötzi used?

Another well-known Neolithic community was Çatalhüyük (chah·tahl·hoo·YOOK) in present-day Turkey. Although little evidence of the community remains, historians know that between 6700 and 5700 B.C., it covered 32 acres and was home to about 6,000 people. The people lived in simple mud-brick houses that were built close together. What if, instead of a front door, your house had a roof door? In Çatalhüyük, the houses did not have front doors. Instead of going through a door in the wall, people entered their homes through holes in the rooftops. They could also walk from house to house across the roofs. People decorated the inside of their homes with wall paintings.

In addition to homes, Çatalhüyük had special buildings that were **shrines** (SHREYENZ), or holy places. These shrines were decorated with images of gods and goddesses. Statues of women giving birth have also been found in the shrines. Both the shrines and the statues show that the role of religion was growing in the lives of Neolithic people.

Farmers grew fruits, nuts, and different grains on land outside Çatalhüyük. People grew their own food and kept it in storerooms within their homes. They raised sheep, goats, and cattle that provided milk and meat. They ate fish and bird eggs from nearby low-lying wetlands called marshes. Scenes drawn on the walls of the city's ruins show that the people of Çatalhüyük also hunted.

What Were the Benefits of a Settled Life?

Neolithic people needed protection from the weather and wild animals. A settled life provided greater security. Steady food supplies created healthier, growing populations. As the population increased, more workers became available. Those individuals could grow more crops. Villagers produced more than they could eat, so they began to trade their food for supplies they could not produce themselves.

Because an abundant amount of food was produced, fewer people were needed in the fields. Neolithic people began to take part in economic activities other than farming. **Specialization** (speh·shuh·leh·ZAY·shun) occurred for the first time. People took up specific jobs as their talents allowed. Some people became artisans, or skilled workers. They made weapons and jewelry that they traded with neighboring communities. People made pottery from clay to store grain and food. They made

Marco Albonico/agefotostock

Reading **HELP**DESK

shrine a place where people worship

specialization the act of training for a particular job

baskets from plant fibers. They also used plant fibers to weave cloth. Ötzi, the Neolithic Iceman, wore a cape made from woven grass fibers. These craftspeople, like farmers, also exchanged the goods they produced for other things they did not have.

The roles of men and women changed when people moved into settlements. Men worked in the fields to farm and herd animals. They gradually became more responsible for growing food and protecting the village. Men emerged as family and community leaders. Women bore the children and stayed in the villages. They wove cloth, using the wool from their sheep. They also used bone needles to make clothing from cloth and animal skins. In addition, women managed food supplies and performed other tasks.

The growth of communities did not always bring benefits. In some places, such as settlements in present-day Jordan, rapid population growth caused resources such as wood supplies to be used up quickly. On occasion, this loss of forestation caused desert-like conditions to spread. Where this type of ecological damage occurred, many settlements were abandoned.

The End of the Neolithic Age

During the late Neolithic Age, people made more technological advances. Toolmakers created better farming tools as the need for them arose. These included hoes for digging soil, sickles for cutting grain, and millstones for grinding flour. In some regions, people began to work with metals, including copper. Workers heated rocks and discovered melted copper inside them. They then experimented with making the copper into tools and weapons. These proved to be easier to make and use than those made of stone.

Craftspeople in western Asia discovered that mixing copper and tin formed bronze. This was a technological breakthrough because bronze was stronger than copper. Bronze became widely used between 3000 and 1200 B.C. This period is known as the **Bronze Age**. Few people, however, could afford bronze and continued to use tools and weapons made of stone.

✔ PROGRESS CHECK

Explaining How did the spread of agriculture affect trade?

There's More Online! connected.mcgraw-hill.com

Thinking Like a HISTORIAN

Making Inferences

In Çatalhüyük the homes were built very close together. Each house had a door in its roof. People climbed into their homes using ladders. Use the Internet to research why the people of Çatalhüyük used this style of building. Then make an inference about the reason for the roof doors and present it to the class. For more information about making inferences, read the chapter *What Does a Historian Do?*

Bronze Age pottery shows fine details. The use of bronze for tools and weapons was another step forward for ancient peoples.

▶ CRITICAL THINKING
Analyzing Why do you think bronze tools and weapons would have been an important achievement?

Bronze Age the period in ancient human culture when people began to make and use bronze

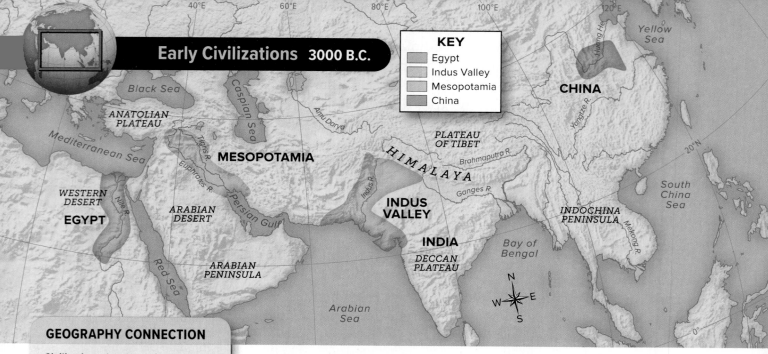

KEY
- Egypt
- Indus Valley
- Mesopotamia
- China

GEOGRAPHY CONNECTION

Civilizations developed in the river valleys of Mesopotamia, Egypt, India, and China.

1. **PLACE** Along which rivers did the early civilizations of Mesopotamia and Egypt develop?

2. **CRITICAL THINKING**
   Analyzing As these cultures became more complex, what characteristics set some of them apart as civilizations?

Civilizations Emerge

GUIDING QUESTION *What characteristics did early civilizations share?*

Humans continued to develop more complex cultures, or ways of life. By the beginning of the Bronze Age, communities were widespread. More complex cultures called civilizations began to develop in these communities. Four of the great river valley civilizations—Mesopotamia, Egypt, India, and China—emerged around 3000 B.C. All civilizations share similar characteristics.

Cities and Government

One characteristic of these early civilizations was that they developed cities and formed governments. The first civilizations developed in river valleys, where fertile land made it easy to grow crops and feed large numbers of people. The rivers provided fish and water. They also encouraged trade, which allowed the exchange of both goods and ideas. The cities that developed in these valleys became the centers of civilizations.

People formed governments to protect themselves and their food supplies. In these early civilizations, the first governments were monarchies. A **monarchy** is a type of government led by a king or queen. Monarchs created armies to defend against enemies and made laws to keep order. They also appointed government officials who managed food supplies and building projects.

Reading HELPDESK

monarchy a government whose ruler, a king or queen, inherits the position from a parent

Religions

Religions emerged in the new civilizations to help people explain their lives. For example, religions helped explain the forces of nature and the role of humans in the world.

Early people believed that gods were responsible for a community's survival. Priests performed religious ceremonies to try to win the support of the gods. Rulers claimed that their own power was based on the approval of the gods.

Social Structure

Early civilizations had social class structures. That is, people in society were organized into groups. These groups were defined by the type of work people did and the amount of wealth or power they had. Generally, rulers and priests, government officials, and warriors made up the highest social class. They set the rules and made the important decisions. Below this class was a large group of free people, including farmers, artisans, and craftspeople. At the bottom of the class structure were enslaved people, most of whom were captured from enemies during war.

Writing and Art

To pass on information, people invented ways of writing. These early systems used symbols in place of letters and words. Writing became an important feature of these new civilizations. People used writing to keep accurate records and to preserve stories.

Civilizations also created art for enjoyment and practical purposes. Artists created paintings and sculptures portraying gods and forces of nature. People designed massive buildings that served as places of worship or burial tombs for kings.

☑ **PROGRESS CHECK**

Speculating Why did early peoples form governments?

LESSON 2 REVIEW

Review Vocabulary

1. What was *systematic agriculture*?

2. How did *specialization* affect the lives of Neolithic peoples?

Answer the Guiding Questions

3. **Stating** What was the Agricultural Revolution?

4. **Identifying Cause and Effect** How did farming lead to new types of economic activities?

5. **Inferring** What are the advantages and disadvantages when a community grows?

6. **Identifying** Which groups made up the largest social class in early civilizations?

7. **ARGUMENT** You are the leader of a band of hunter-gatherers. You have seen other bands settle in river valleys and begin to farm. Write a speech to persuade your own band to settle and begin farming.

CHAPTER 4 Activities

Write your answers on a separate piece of paper.

1 Exploring the Essential Question

INFORMATIVE/EXPLANATORY How would you describe the ways people adapted to a colder environment during the Ice Age? Write an essay telling how some changes people made may have led to the development of agriculture when the last Ice Age was over.

2 21st Century Skills

ANALYZING AND MAKING JUDGMENTS Early humans made several technical advancements during the Paleolithic Age. These included the use of fire, flint tools and weapons, spoken language, and tents and wooden structures. Write a paragraph telling which of these helped them most to become more efficient hunters and why.

3 Thinking Like a Historian

COMPARING AND CONTRASTING Create a diagram like the one shown to compare and contrast the technological advancements of the Paleolithic Age with those of the Neolithic Age.

Paleolithic Age Advancements	Neolithic Age Advancements

4

GEOGRAPHY ACTIVITY

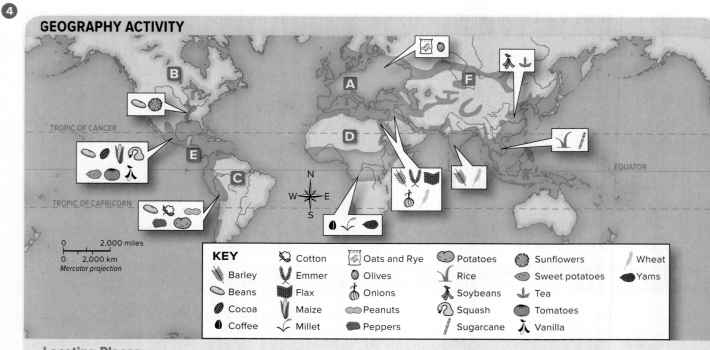

KEY

- Cotton
- Barley
- Beans
- Cocoa
- Coffee
- Emmer
- Flax
- Maize
- Millet
- Oats and Rye
- Olives
- Onions
- Peanuts
- Peppers
- Potatoes
- Rice
- Soybeans
- Squash
- Sugarcane
- Sunflowers
- Sweet potatoes
- Tea
- Tomatoes
- Vanilla
- Wheat
- Yams

Locating Places

Match the letters on the map to the numbered list of crops grown there.

1. soybeans and tea
2. beans and sunflowers
3. coffee, millet, and yams
4. oats and olives
5. beans, cotton, peanuts, peppers, and potatoes
6. beans, cocoa, corn, squash, tomatoes, sweet potatoes and vanilla

Directions: Write your answers on a separate piece of paper.

CHECKING FOR UNDERSTANDING

1 Define each of these terms as they relate to early humans.

A. nomad	**F.** Agricultural Revolution
B. technology	**G.** shrine
C. iron pyrite	**H.** Bronze Age
D. ice age	**I.** monarchy
E. Neolithic Age	

REVIEW THE GUIDING QUESTIONS

2 *Explaining* Why is the early period of human history called the Stone Age? What is the Paleolithic Age?

3 *Identifying* What was the main activity of Paleolithic people?

4 *Listing* List some of the tools developed by humans during the Paleolithic Age.

5 *Describing* How did early humans adapt to ice age conditions?

6 *Finding the Main Idea* Why is the change from hunting and gathering to farming considered a revolution?

7 *Specifying* Near what types of landforms did Neolithic peoples build their villages? Why?

8 *Identifying* In Neolithic villages, who were artisans, and what types of products did they create?

9 *Finding the Main Idea* Why did the first civilizations develop in river valleys?

10 *Identifying* In general, who belonged to the highest social class in early civilizations?

CRITICAL THINKING

11 *Contrasting* How did the roles of Paleolithic men and women differ within their groups?

12 *Recognizing Relationships* Describe the relationship between the animals hunted by Paleolithic people and how those peoples survived in harsh or difficult climates.

13 *Making Connections* What were the subjects of paintings by Paleolithic people? Why might these paintings have been created?

14 *Determining Central Ideas* Why is the term Neolithic Age a misleading name for the time period?

15 *Comparing and Contrasting* Study the map titled Early Farming in Lesson 2. Then compare and contrast the crops grown in Africa and Southwest Asia to those grown in the rest of Asia.

16 *Contrasting* Contrast the dwellings found in a Neolithic village such as Çatalhüyük with those used by Paleolithic peoples. Discuss layout, building materials, and any other relevant details.

17 *Determining Cause and Effect* How did the switch to a farming lifestyle lead to changes in technology? Describe the new types of tools that were created and the new materials being used.

18 *Evaluating* Were all the effects of the Agricultural Revolution beneficial? Explain.

19 *Explaining* Explain how the Agricultural Revolution is related to the origins of government. Describe the form of government that developed in the first civilizations in your answer.

20 *Analyzing* Consider the characteristics that were shared by early civilizations—cities and government, religion, social structure, and writing and art. Do you think these characteristics are shared by civilizations today? Explain.

Need Extra Help?

If You've Missed Question	**1**	**2**	**3**	**4**	**5**	**6**	**7**	**8**	**9**	**10**	**11**	**12**	**13**	**14**	**15**	**16**	**17**	**18**	**19**	**20**
Review Lesson	1,2	1	1	1	1	2	2	2	2	2	1	1	1	2	2	2	2	2	2	2

EXTENDED RESPONSE

Write your answer on a separate piece of paper.

21 *Narrative* You are a member of a Paleolithic group of hunter-gatherers. Write a letter to a friend describing the hunting stories you are recording in cave paintings. Explain how you think your stories might help other hunters improve their skills.

STANDARDIZED TEST PRACTICE

DBQ ANALYZING DOCUMENTS

22 *Making Connections* Study this example of one of the oldest Paleolithic cave paintings. What kind of animals does this painting appear to represent?

A. woolly mammoths
B. cattle
C. horses
D. reindeer

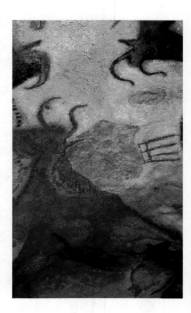

23 *Identifying* What type of tools did Paleolithic people use for painting on the cave walls?

A. wood blocks
B. paint rollers
C. pencils
D. twigs

Need Extra Help?

If You've Missed Question	**21**	**22**	**23**
Review Lesson	1	1	1

WESTERN ASIA, THE MIDDLE EAST, AND NORTH AFRICA

UNIT 2

EXPLORE the CONTINENT

ASIA is the largest continent on Earth. It extends from the Mediterranean Sea in the west to the Pacific Ocean in the east. Asia is home to about 60 percent of the world's population. Yet, at least two-thirds of the land area is too cold or too dry to support a large population. Winds called monsoons affect climate in much of Asia. They bring cool, dry weather in winter and heavy rainfall and floods in summer.

1 NATURAL RESOURCES Asia's numerous resources include petroleum, copper, rice, and fish. Growing populations and industries in cities such as Shanghai, China, demand more and more resources. Asian countries are quickly trying to meet this need.

2 LANDFORMS Asia's landforms are varied. Mountain ranges, plateaus, and plains dominate western and central areas. Hundreds of islands dot coastlines in the east. Plate movements formed many of these islands. The island country of Indonesia has about 130 active volcanoes, more than any other country on Earth.

③ BODIES OF WATER Water is plentiful in eastern and southern Asia, where many people depend on it for a living. In Sri Lanka, fishers use baitless hooks to snare mackerel and herring. In parts of western Asia, however, water is scarce. The lack of water is a major issue for countries in these areas.

FAST
FACT

Asia comprises 30 percent of the world's land area.

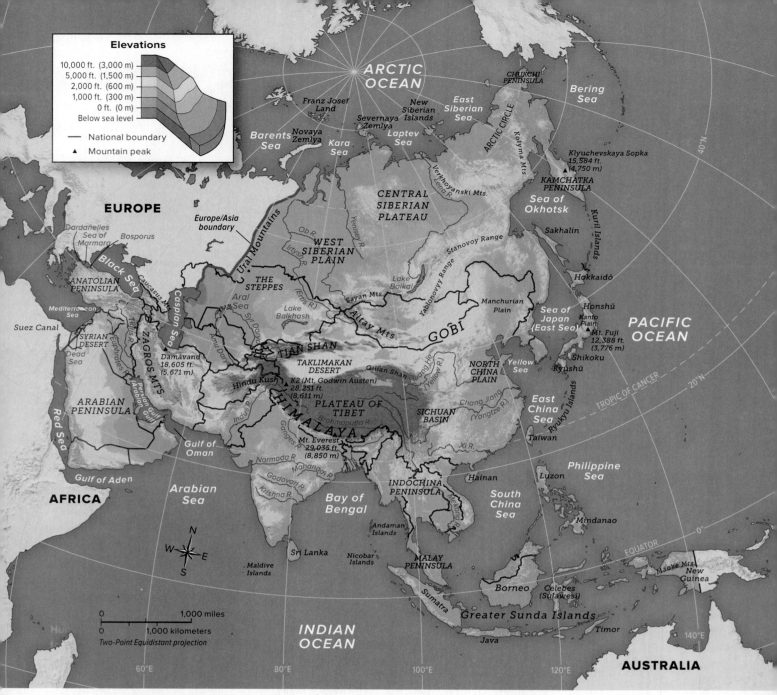

Elevations

- 10,000 ft. (3,000 m)
- 5,000 ft. (1,500 m)
- 2,000 ft. (600 m)
- 1,000 ft. (300 m)
- 0 ft. (0 m)
- Below sea level
- — National boundary
- ▲ Mountain peak

ARCTIC OCEAN

CHUKCHI PENINSULA

Bering Sea

Franz Josef Land

New Siberian Islands

East Siberian Sea

Severnaya Zemlya

Laptev Sea

ARCTIC CIRCLE

Kolyma Mts.

Klyuchevskaya Sopka 15,584 ft. ▲ (4,750 m)

40°N

Barents Sea

Novaya Zemlya

Kara Sea

CENTRAL SIBERIAN PLATEAU

KAMCHATKA PENINSULA

Sea of Okhotsk

EUROPE

Europe/Asia boundary

Ob R.

Yenisey R.

Verkhoyansk Mts.

Lena R.

Stanovoy Range

Sakhalin

Kuril Islands

WEST SIBERIAN PLAIN

Ural Mountains

Irtysh R.

Hokkaidō

Dardanelles

Sea of Marmara

Bosporus

Black Sea

Caucasus Mts.

THE STEPPES

Aral Sea

Lake Balkhash

Erti R.

Lake Baikal

Sayan Mts.

Yablonovy Range

Manchurian Plain

Sea of Japan (East Sea)

Honshū

Kanto Plain

PACIFIC OCEAN

ANATOLIAN PENINSULA

Mediterranean Sea

Suez Canal

SYRIAN DESERT

Dead Sea

Caspian Sea

ZAGROS MTS

Tigris R.

Euphrates

Amu Darya

Syr Darya

TIAN SHAN

Altay Mts.

GOBI

NORTH CHINA PLAIN

Yellow Sea

▲ Mt. Fuji 12,388 ft. (3,776 m)

Shikoku

Kyūshū

20°N

Damāvand 18,605 ft. (5,671 m)

Hindu Kush

TAKLIMAKAN DESERT

Qilian Shan

Huang He (Yellow R.)

ARABIAN PENINSULA

Persian Gulf (Arabian Gulf)

K2 (Mt. Godwin Austen) 28,251 ft. (8,611 m)

PLATEAU OF TIBET

SICHUAN BASIN

Chang Jiang (Yangtze R.)

East China Sea

Ryukyu Islands

TROPIC OF CANCER

Red Sea

Gulf of Oman

Indus R.

HIMALAYA

Brahmaputra R.

Ganges

Mt. Everest 29,035 ft. (8,850 m)

Narmada R.

Mahanadi R.

Xi R.

Taiwan

Gulf of Aden

AFRICA

Arabian Sea

Godavari R.

Krishna R.

Bay of Bengal

INDOCHINA PENINSULA

Mekong R.

Hainan

South China Sea

Philippine Sea

Luzon

N
W E
S

Sri Lanka

Andaman Islands

Nicobar Islands

MALAY PENINSULA

Mindanao

0°

Maldive Islands

EQUATOR

Maoke Mts. New Guinea

0 1,000 miles

0 1,000 kilometers

Two-Point Equidistant projection

INDIAN OCEAN

Sumatra

Borneo

Celebes (Sulawesi)

Greater Sunda Islands

Java

Timor

140°E

AUSTRALIA

60°E   80°E   100°E   120°E

ASIA

PHYSICAL

MAP SKILLS

1 PHYSICAL GEOGRAPHY What part of Asia has the highest elevation?

2 THE GEOGRAPHER'S WORLD Which ocean borders the Central Siberian Plateau?

3 PLACES AND REGIONS How would you describe the region of Southeast Asia?

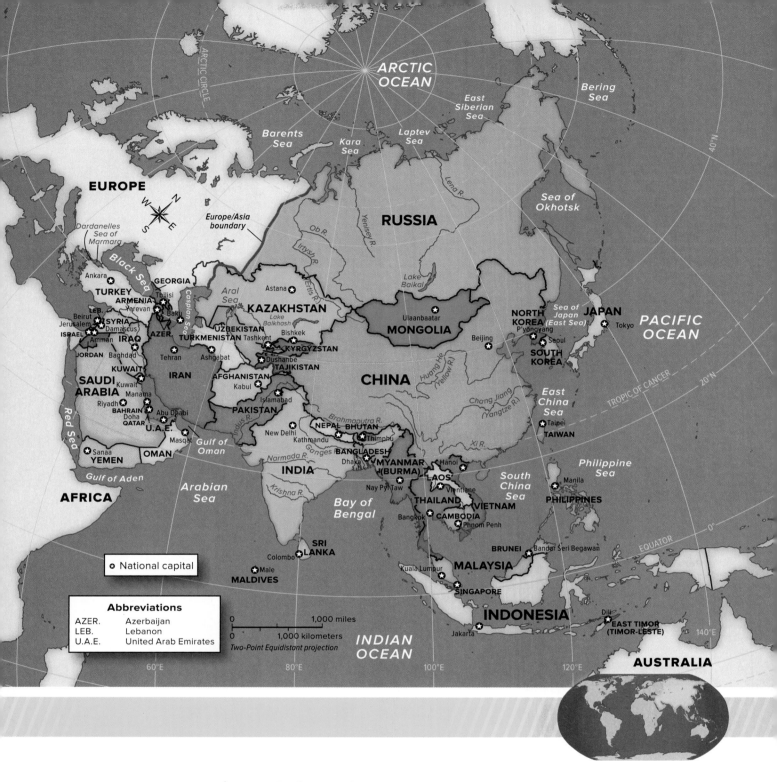

ARCTIC OCEAN

Bering Sea

East Siberian Sea

Laptev Sea

Barents Sea

Kara Sea

ARCTIC CIRCLE

EUROPE

Europe/Asia boundary

Lena R.

RUSSIA

Sea of Okhotsk

40°N

Dardanelles
Sea of Marmara

Ob R.

Yenisey R.

Irtysh R.

Lake Baikal

Black Sea

Ankara
TURKEY
GEORGIA
Tbilisi
ARMENIA
Yerevan
Baku

LEB.
Beirut
Jerusalem
ISRAEL
Amman
JORDAN

SYRIA
Damascus
IRAQ
Baghdad

AZER.

Caspian Sea

Astana

KAZAKHSTAN

Aral Sea

Lake Balkhash

UZBEKISTAN
Tashkent
TURKMENISTAN
Bishkek
KYRGYZSTAN
Dushanbe
TAJIKISTAN

Ulaanbaatar

MONGOLIA

NORTH KOREA
P'yongyang

Beijing

Sea of Japan (East Sea)

JAPAN
Tokyo

PACIFIC OCEAN

Seoul
SOUTH KOREA

KUWAIT
Kuwait

Tehran
IRAN
Ashgabat
AFGHANISTAN
Kabul

CHINA

Huang He (Yellow R.)

SAUDI ARABIA
Riyadh
Manama
BAHRAIN
Doha
QATAR
Abu Dhabi
U.A.E.
Masqat

Islamabad
PAKISTAN
Indus R.

New Delhi

Brahmaputra R.

NEPAL BHUTAN
Kathmandu
Thimphu

Chang Jiang (Yangtze R.)

Xi R.

East China Sea

TROPIC OF CANCER

20°N

Taipei
TAIWAN

Red Sea

Gulf of Oman

Narmada R.

Ganges

BANGLADESH
Dhaka

MYANMAR (BURMA)

Hanoi

Philippine Sea

Sanaa
YEMEN
OMAN

Gulf of Aden

AFRICA

Arabian Sea

INDIA

Krishna R.

Bay of Bengal

Nay Pyi Taw

LAOS
Vientiane
THAILAND
VIETNAM

South China Sea

Manila

PHILIPPINES

National capital

Bangkok
CAMBODIA
Phnom Penh

Abbreviations
AZER.   Azerbaijan
LEB.   Lebanon
U.A.E.   United Arab Emirates

Colombo
SRI LANKA

Male
MALDIVES

0   1,000 miles
0   1,000 kilometers
Two-Point Equidistant projection

INDIAN OCEAN

Kuala Lumpur
MALAYSIA
SINGAPORE

BRUNEI
Bandar Seri Begawan

EQUATOR

INDONESIA

Jakarta

Dili
EAST TIMOR (TIMOR-LESTE)

140°E

0°

60°E   80°E   100°E   120°E

AUSTRALIA

POLITICAL

MAP SKILLS

1 **PLACES AND REGIONS** Which country in the region is the largest?

2 **THE GEOGRAPHER'S WORLD** Which country is located between China and Russia?

3 **THE GEOGRAPHER'S WORLD** What body of water lies between Kazakhstan and Iran?

Cities
(Statistics reflect metropolitan areas.)

■ Over 5,000,000
□ 2,000,000–5,000,000
◉ 1,000,000–2,000,000
• 500,000–1,000,000
○ Under 500,000

POPULATION

Per sq. mi.	Per sq. km
1,250 and over	500 and over
250–1,249	100–499
63–249	25–99
25–62	10–24
2.5–24	1–9
Less than 2.5	Less than 1

0   1,000 miles
0   1,000 kilometers
Two-Point Equidistant projection

ASIA

POPULATION DENSITY

MAP SKILLS

1 THE GEOGRAPHER'S WORLD What parts of Asia are the most densely populated?

2 THE GEOGRAPHER'S WORLD Which part of the region has the lowest population density?

3 THE GEOGRAPHER'S WORLD In general, what population pattern do you see in Southwest Asia?

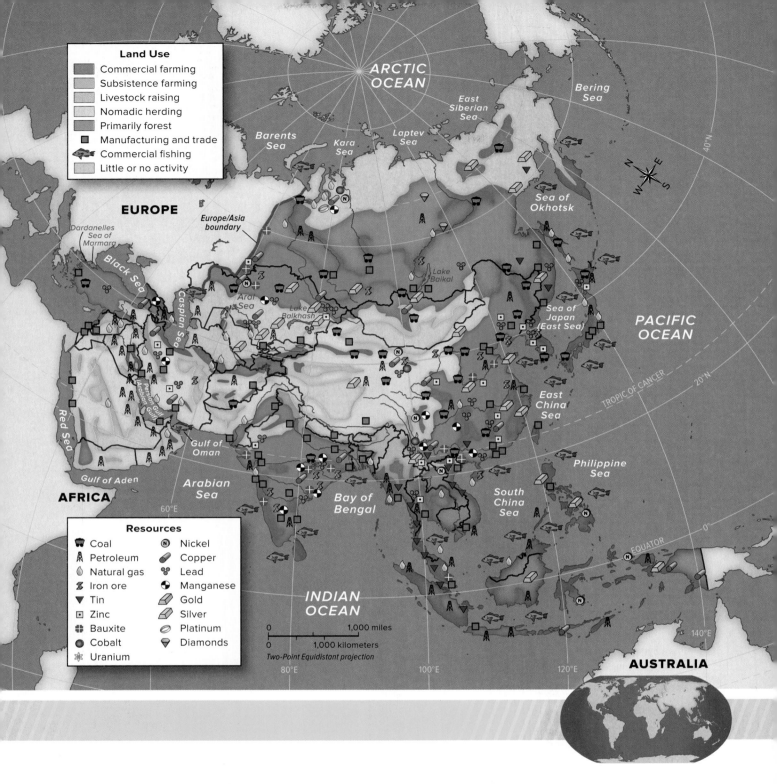

Land Use

- Commercial farming
- Subsistence farming
- Livestock raising
- Nomadic herding
- Primarily forest
- ■ Manufacturing and trade
- Commercial fishing
- Little or no activity

Resources

- Coal
- Petroleum
- Natural gas
- Iron ore
- Tin
- Zinc
- Bauxite
- Cobalt
- Uranium
- Nickel
- Copper
- Lead
- Manganese
- Gold
- Silver
- Platinum
- Diamonds

ARCTIC OCEAN

East Siberian Sea

Bering Sea

Laptev Sea

Kara Sea

Barents Sea

Sea of Okhotsk

EUROPE

Dardanelles
Sea of Marmara

Black Sea

Caspian Sea

Aral Sea

Lake Balkhash

Lake Baikal

Sea of Japan (East Sea)

PACIFIC OCEAN

AFRICA

Red Sea

Persian Gulf
(Arabian Gulf)

Gulf of Oman

Gulf of Aden

Arabian Sea

Bay of Bengal

East China Sea

South China Sea

Philippine Sea

TROPIC OF CANCER

INDIAN OCEAN

Gulf of Aden

EQUATOR

AUSTRALIA

0   1,000 miles
0   1,000 kilometers
Two-Point Equidistant projection

40°N

20°N

0°

60°E   80°E   100°E   120°E   140°E

ECONOMIC RESOURCES

MAP SKILLS

1 **PLACES AND REGIONS** What mineral resources can be found around the Persian Gulf?

2 **HUMAN GEOGRAPHY** What economic activity takes place in the South China Sea?

3 **THE GEOGRAPHER'S WORLD** In what part of Russia are gold and silver deposits found?

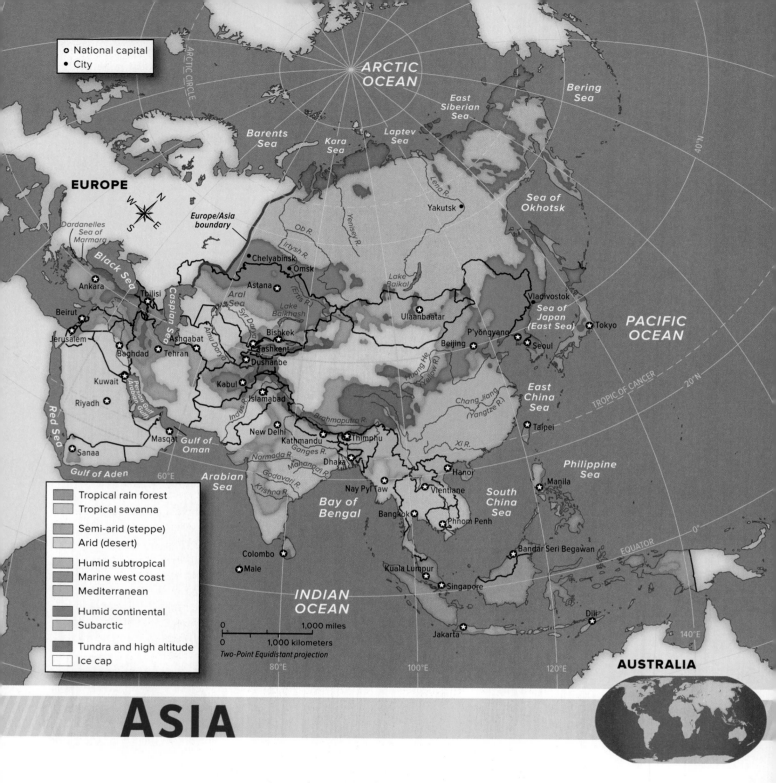

Legend — CLIMATE

- National capital
- City

Tropical rain forest
Tropical savanna
Semi-arid (steppe)
Arid (desert)
Humid subtropical
Marine west coast
Mediterranean
Humid continental
Subarctic
Tundra and high altitude
Ice cap

0 — 1,000 miles
0 — 1,000 kilometers
Two-Point Equidistant projection

Labels on map:

EUROPE

ARCTIC OCEAN
Bering Sea
East Siberian Sea
Laptev Sea
Kara Sea
Barents Sea
ARCTIC CIRCLE
40°N

Dardanelles
Sea of Marmara
Black Sea
Europe/Asia boundary
Ob R.
Yenisey R.
Irtysh R.
Lena R.
Sea of Okhotsk
Yakutsk

Chelyabinsk
Omsk
Astana
Aral Sea
Lake Balkhash
Lake Baikal
Ulaanbaatar
Vladivostok
Sea of Japan (East Sea)
PACIFIC OCEAN

Ankara
Tbilisi
Caspian Sea
Syr Darya
Bishkek
Tashkent
Dushanbe
(Irtysh R.)
Huang He (Yellow R.)
P'yŏngyang
Beijing
Tokyo
Seoul

Beirut
Jerusalem
Ashgabat
Amu Darya
Baghdad
Tehran
Kabul
Islamabad
Indus R.
Chang Jiang (Yangtze R.)
East China Sea
TROPIC OF CANCER
20°N

Kuwait
Riyadh
Persian Gulf
Arabian Gulf
New Delhi
Kathmandu
Ganges R.
Thimphu
Brahmaputra R.
Xi R.
Taipei

Red Sea
Masqat
Gulf of Oman
Narmada R.
Dhaka
Hanoi
Philippine Sea

Sanaa
Gulf of Aden
60°E
Arabian Sea
Godavari R.
Mahanadi R.
Nay Pyi Taw
Vientiane
Manila

Krishna R.
Bay of Bengal
Bangkok
South China Sea

Colombo
Male
Phnom Penh

Kuala Lumpur
Bandar Seri Begawan
EQUATOR
0°

INDIAN OCEAN
Singapore
Dili
140°E

Jakarta
120°E
100°E
80°E

AUSTRALIA

ASIA

CLIMATE

MAP SKILLS

1 PHYSICAL GEOGRAPHY How would you describe the climate zones found along the Equator?

2 PLACES AND REGIONS Which city do you think receives more rain each year—Beijing or Ulaanbaatar? Why?

3 PHYSICAL GEOGRAPHY In general, how does the climate of India's coastal areas differ from the climate of the Ganges River area?

SOUTHWEST ASIA

ESSENTIAL QUESTIONS · *How does geography influence the way people live?* · *Why do civilizations rise and fall?* · *How does religion shape society?*

Wathiq Khuzaie/Getty Images News/Getty Images

A woman in Baghdad, Iraq, displays her inked fingers, showing that she has just voted in the election.

networks

There's More Online about Southwest Asia.

CHAPTER 5

Lesson 1
Physical Geography of Southwest Asia

Lesson 2
History of Southwest Asia

Lesson 3
Life in Southwest Asia

The Story Matters...

The area between the Tigris and Euphrates Rivers in Southwest Asia is known as the Fertile Crescent. Here, fertile soil and water for irrigation supported the growth of an early civilization—Mesopotamia. Three major world religions—Judaism, Christianity, and Islam—began in this region. From ancient to modern times, the region's physical features, resources, and cultures have greatly influenced how people live.

FOLDABLES®
Study Organizer

Go to the Foldables® library in the back of your book to make a Foldable® that will help you take notes while reading this chapter.

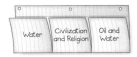

123

SOUTHWEST ASIA

Southwest Asia lies where the continents of Asia, Africa, and Europe meet. Some of the world's earliest civilizations started here.

Step Into the Place

MAP FOCUS Use the map to answer the following questions.

1 PLACES AND REGIONS
What is the capital city of Syria?

2 THE GEOGRAPHER'S WORLD
What countries border Yemen?

3 THE GEOGRAPHER'S WORLD
What body of water lies west of Saudi Arabia?

4 CRITICAL THINKING
Describing In which direction would you travel from the Persian Gulf to the city of Ankara?

BEACH RESORT People float in the Dead Sea in the Ein Bokek area of Israel. Because of the high salt content of the water, people who bathe in the Dead Sea can float on its surface without effort.

PORT CITY Modern buildings tower over the city of Jaffa, along Israel's Mediterranean coast. One of the world's oldest cities, Jaffa is known for its historic areas, fragrant gardens, and sprawling flea market.

Step Into the Time

TIME LINE Choose an event from the time line and write a paragraph explaining its effect on the region and the world.

c. 3000 B.C. The Sumerians develop early form of writing

C. A.D. 30 Jesus preaches in Jerusalem

c. 4000 B.C. People settle along the Tigris and Euphrates rivers

c. 1000 B.C. King David makes Jerusalem the capital of Israel

B.C. | A.D.

Southwest Asia

RUSSIA

Black Sea

Caspian Sea

Aral Sea

CENTRAL ASIA

40°N

★Ankara

TURKEY

Mediterranean Sea

SYRIA

Beirut

LEBANON

★Damascus

Tel Aviv-Jaffa

Jerusalem★

30°N

ISRAEL

JORDAN

A

B

Arbīl

Euphrates R.

Tigris R.

★Baghdad

IRAQ

★Tehran

IRAN

Kabul★

AFGHANISTAN

SOUTH ASIA

AFRICA

TROPIC OF CANCER

Kuwait

KUWAIT

SAUDI ARABIA

BAHRAIN

Manama★

QATAR

Persian Gulf (Arabian Gulf)

Doha★

★Riyadh

20°N

Makkah (Mecca)

Abu Dhabi

UNITED ARAB EMIRATES

Gulf of Oman

Masqat★

OMAN

○ National capital
● City

Red Sea

0   500 miles

0   500 kilometers
Lambert Azimuthal Equal-Area projection

YEMEN

★Sanaa

INDIAN OCEAN

Gulf of Aden

30°E   40°E   50°E

2003 The Iraq War begins

1290 The Ottoman Empire begins; lasts until 1922

1948 Israel is founded

1900   2010

A.D. 600s Muhammad begins preaching the teachings of Islam

1938 Oil is discovered in Saudi Arabia

1990 Persian Gulf War begins

2010 Arab Spring revolts take place in the Middle East

There's More Online!

☑ **CHART/GRAPH** Oases

☑ **MAP** Bodies of Water in Southwest Asia

☑ **ANIMATION** Why Much of the World's Oil Supply is in Southwest Asia

Reading**HELP**DESK

Academic Vocabulary

- **vary**

Content Vocabulary

- **alluvial plain**
- **oasis**
- **wadi**
- **semiarid**

TAKING NOTES: *Key Ideas and Details*

Identify As you read the lesson, complete the graphic organizer by listing the physical features found in this region.

Southwest Asia	Examples
Mountains	
Deserts	
Natural Resources	

Lesson 1
Physical Geography of Southwest Asia

ESSENTIAL QUESTION • *How does geography influence the way people live?*

IT MATTERS BECAUSE
Southwest Asia is characterized by a complex physical geography that influences its people, history, and importance in the world today.

Southwest Asia's Physical Features

GUIDING QUESTION *What are the main landforms and resources in Southwest Asia?*

Southwest Asia comprises 15 countries that lie in the area where Asia meets Europe and Africa. Similarities in physical geography help unite these countries into a single region. Mountains and plateaus formed by active plate tectonics can be seen throughout the region. Dry, desert climates are also widespread.

Mountains and Plateaus

Mountains and plateaus dominate the landscape of Southwest Asia. They have been created over the past 100 million years by collisions between four tectonic plates. This movement also caused earthquakes.

Southwest Asia's loftiest mountains rise in the Hindu Kush range, which stretches across much of Afghanistan and along Afghanistan's border with the South Asian country of Pakistan.

The Hindu Kush and neighboring ranges form natural barriers to travel and trade. As a result, mountain passes have been important in this area. One of the world's most famous passes is the Khyber Pass. It links the cities of Kabul, Afghanistan, and Peshawar, Pakistan. The pass has served as a route for trade and invading armies for thousands of years.

A vast plateau, covering much of Iran, is encircled by high mountain ranges. The mountains of western Iran merge with those of eastern Turkey. Close to the border rises Turkey's highest peak, Ararat, a massive, snowcapped volcano that last erupted in 1840. An elevated area known as the Anatolian Plateau spreads across central and western Turkey.

The Arabian Peninsula consists of Saudi Arabia, Yemen, Oman, and several other countries. It is a single, vast plateau that slopes gently from the southwest to the northwest. Long mountain ranges that parallel the peninsula's southwestern, northwestern, and southeastern coasts are actually the deeply eroded edges of the plateau.

Bodies of Water

The region of Southwest Asia has thousands of miles of coastline. Turkey has coasts on the Mediterranean and Black Seas. Syria, Lebanon, Jordan, and Israel have coasts on the Mediterranean Sea. Jordan, Saudi Arabia, and Yemen border the long, narrow Red Sea. The Red Sea has been one of the world's busiest waterways since Egypt's Suez Canal, connecting the Red Sea and the Mediterranean, was completed in 1869. To the southeast of the Arabian Peninsula lies a part of the Indian Ocean called the Arabian Sea. Yemen and its neighbor Oman have coasts along this sea.

A deadly earthquake in 1999 left widespread destruction in Turkey.

▶ CRITICAL THINKING

Describing What causes earthquakes throughout Southwest Asia?

Oil tankers pass through the Strait of Hormuz. The strait is the only sea passage from the Persian Gulf to the open ocean.

▶ CRITICAL THINKING

Analyzing Why is the Strait of Hormuz considered a strategic waterway?

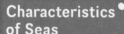

Thinking Like a Geographer

Characteristics of Seas

The word *sea* is most often used to describe a large body of salt water that is part of, or connected to, an ocean. The Black Sea and the Mediterranean Sea, both of which are connected to the Atlantic Ocean, meet this description, as does the Red Sea, a narrow extension of the Indian Ocean. The landlocked Caspian and Dead seas, however, do not. They best fit the description of *lake*. Large lakes with salty water, however, are sometimes called seas.

In the northeast, the Arabian Peninsula is shaped by the Persian Gulf, which is connected to the ocean by a strategic waterway called the Strait of Hormuz. The Persian Gulf has become tremendously important in world affairs since the middle of the 1900s.

Eight of Southwest Asia's 15 countries border the Persian Gulf: Oman, the United Arab Emirates, Saudi Arabia, Qatar, Bahrain, Kuwait, Iraq, and Iran. In the north, Iran also borders the landlocked Caspian Sea.

The Dead Sea, which lies between Israel and Jordan, is also landlocked. It is far smaller than the region's other seas. At 1,300 feet (396 m) below sea level, it ranks as the world's lowest body of water, and its shore represents the lowest land elevation.

Southwest Asia's two longest and most important rivers are the Tigris and the Euphrates, which are often considered parts of the same river system. The rivers begin within 50 miles (80 km) of each other in the mountains of eastern Turkey. In their lower courses, they flow parallel to one another across a broad **alluvial plain**, a plain created by sediment deposited during floods. The plain covers most of Iraq as well as eastern Syria and southeastern Turkey. This area has been known since ancient times as Mesopotamia, which is Greek for "land between the rivers." Thousands of years ago, one of the world's earliest civilizations took root in the fertile lands of Mesopotamia.

Deserts

Desert landscapes spread across most of Southwest Asia. The Arabian Desert, which covers nearly the entire Arabian Peninsula, is the largest in the region and one of the largest in the world. It is made up of rocky plateaus, gravel-covered plains, salt-crusted flats, flows of black lava, and sand seas, which are unbroken expanses of sand.

©Dean Conger/Corbis

In the southern part of the peninsula lies the largest sand sea in the world: the Rub' al-Khali, or Empty Quarter. Winds have sculpted its reddish-orange sands into towering dunes and long, winding ridges. The climate is so dry and hot that this starkly beautiful wilderness cannot support permanent human settlements. In some areas, nomadic people known as the Bedouin keep herds of camels, horses, and sheep.

The Arabian Desert is a harsh environment, but plants thrive in oases. An **oasis** is an area in a desert where underground water allows plants to grow throughout the year.

☑ READING PROGRESS CHECK

Analyzing How has tectonic activity—that is, movement of Earth's crustal plates—helped shape landforms in Southwest Asia?

Southwest Asia's Climates

GUIDING QUESTION *What are some ways that mountains, seas, and other physical features affect climate in Southwest Asia?*

A single type of climate dominates most of Southwest Asia. The only parts of the region with greater climatic variety lie in the northwest and northeast.

An Arid Region

Although this region is surrounded by seas and gulfs, water is a scarce resource here. Most of the region falls within an arid, or very dry, climate zone. Deserts—areas that receive less than 10 inches (25 cm) of annual rainfall—cover nearly the entire Arabian Peninsula as well as large parts of Iran. These deserts are part of a broad band of arid lands that stretch from western North Africa to East Asia. Southwest Asia's arid lands can be brutally hot in the summer. Temperatures in the Arabian Desert can soar as high as 129°F (54°C).

Mountain springs provide a constant flow of water through the Bani Wadi Khalid riverbed in northern Oman. Along the stream's course are large rock formations and shimmering pools of turquoise water.

▶ CRITICAL THINKING

Analyzing What feature makes the Bani Wadi Khalid area different from most other landscapes in the Arabian Peninsula?

OIL: RESERVES AND CONSUMPTION
KEEPING US ON THE MOVE

The countries of Southwest Asia have some of the largest reserves of oil in the world.

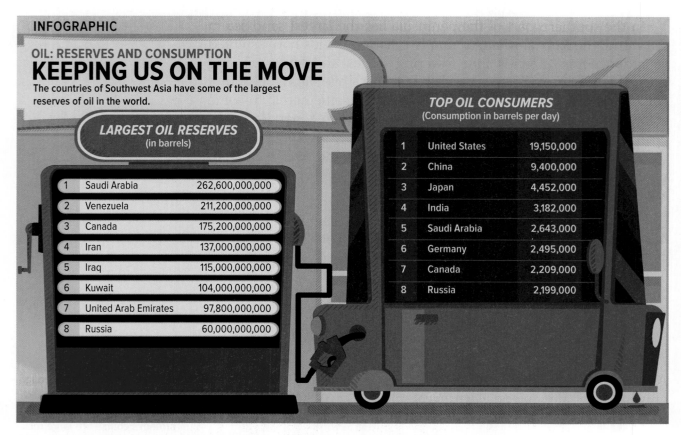

LARGEST OIL RESERVES
(in barrels)

1	Saudi Arabia	262,600,000,000
2	Venezuela	211,200,000,000
3	Canada	175,200,000,000
4	Iran	137,000,000,000
5	Iraq	115,000,000,000
6	Kuwait	104,000,000,000
7	United Arab Emirates	97,800,000,000
8	Russia	60,000,000,000

TOP OIL CONSUMERS
(Consumption in barrels per day)

1	United States	19,150,000
2	China	9,400,000
3	Japan	4,452,000
4	India	3,182,000
5	Saudi Arabia	2,643,000
6	Germany	2,495,000
7	Canada	2,209,000
8	Russia	2,199,000

Oil reserves are estimates of the amount of crude oil located in a particular economic region. Oil consumption is the amount of oil an economic region uses.

▶ **CRITICAL THINKING**

Describing Which Southwest Asian countries are among the countries with the largest oil reserves?

Although rain is scarce in this region, rainfall can quickly transform the desert landscapes. Torrents of water race through **wadis** (WAH-deez), or streambeds that are dry. Buried seeds sprout within hours, carpeting barren gravel plains in green.

At the margins of Southwest Asia's dry zones lie areas that are considered **semiarid** (seh-mee-AIR-id), or somewhat dry. These areas are found in the highlands and mountain ranges of the region.

A Mediterranean climate prevails along Southwest Asia's Mediterranean and Aegean coasts and across much of western Turkey. Winds blowing off the seas bring mild temperatures and moderate amounts of rainfall during the winter months. The summer months are warm and dry.

Mountainous areas of eastern Turkey, western Iran, and central Afghanistan have continental climates in which temperatures **vary** greatly between summer and winter. The mountains of the Hindu Kush range in far eastern Afghanistan fall within a highland climate zone, and glaciers are found among the soaring peaks.

Academic Vocabulary

vary to show differences between things

☑ **READING PROGRESS CHECK**

Identifying In what parts of Southwest Asia could farmers grow crops without irrigation?

Natural Resources

GUIDING QUESTION *How do natural resources influence the lives of people in Southwest Asia?*

Scarcity of water has shaped this region's human history and settlement patterns. Other natural resources, however, are found in abundance. The most important resources are two fossil fuels for which the world has a seemingly unquenchable thirst: oil and natural gas.

The gaseous form of petroleum is called natural gas, and the liquid form is called crude oil, or simply oil. Crude oil is refined to produce energy sources such as gasoline, diesel fuel, heating oil, and industrial fuel oil. Petroleum is also the basic raw material used to make many other products, such as plastics, bicycle tires, and cloth fibers.

The world's largest known deposits of petroleum are in Southwest Asia. Most are concentrated around and under the Persian Gulf. Together, five countries that border the gulf—Saudi Arabia, Iran, Iraq, Kuwait, and United Arab Emirates—hold more than half the oil that has been discovered in the world.

Most of the petroleum produced by these countries is exported to industrialized countries. Petroleum revenues have brought tremendous wealth to a few people in the exporting countries. But only in a relatively few areas has the wealth been used to improve the lives of the people or bring about modernization.

Southwest Asia also has a great variety of mineral resources. Large coal deposits are found in Turkey and Iran. Phosphates, used to make fertilizers, are mined in Iraq, Israel, and Syria. Between 2006 and 2010, American geologists conducting a survey of Afghanistan discovered enormous deposits of iron, copper, gold, cobalt, lithium, and other minerals such as rare earth elements used to make electronic devices.

Include this lesson's information in your Foldable®.

✓ **READING PROGRESS CHECK**

Identifying Five countries that border the Persian Gulf hold more than half the oil that has been discovered in the world. Name three of the countries.

LESSON 1 REVIEW

Reviewing Vocabulary

1. Describe the difference between a *wadi* and an *oasis*.

Answering the Guiding Questions

2. *Identifying* What makes the Dead Sea distinct?

3. *Describing* What are the major physical geography features of the Arabian Peninsula?

4. *Describing* If you were to travel across the Arabian Desert, what are two types of landscapes or landforms you might see?

5. *Citing Text Evidence* The United Nations ranks Afghanistan as one of the world's poorest countries. How might recent discoveries change that situation?

6. *Narrative Writing* Imagine that you are spending a few days exploring the area of the Arabian Desert called the Rub' al-Khali. Write a one-paragraph journal entry describing the experience.

netw⊙rks

There's More Online!

☑ **DIAGRAM** Ziggurats
☑ **IMAGES** The Kurds
☑ **MAP** Islamic Expansion
☑ **VIDEO**

Reading**HELP**DESK

Academic Vocabulary

• expand
• collapse

Content Vocabulary

• polytheism
• millennium
• monotheism
• covenant
• prophet

TAKING NOTES: *Key Ideas and Details*

Sequence As you read about Southwest Asia's history, use a time line to put key events and developments in order.

2000 B.C.   1000 B.C.   0   A.D. 1000

Lesson 2
History of Southwest Asia

ESSENTIAL QUESTION • *Why do civilizations rise and fall?*

IT MATTERS BECAUSE
Southwest Asia has played a large role in human history. The world's earliest civilization developed here, and three major religions were born. Great empires that arose in the region grew to cover parts of three continents.

Early Southwest Asia

GUIDING QUESTION *What are some of the most important advancements that occurred in Southwest Asia in ancient times?*

Mesopotamia

Throughout most of human history, people lived as hunter-gatherers. In small groups, they hunted wild animals and searched for wild fruits, nuts, and vegetables. They were nomadic, frequently moving from place to place. About 10,000 years ago, though, a dramatic change began to occur: People started practicing agriculture—raising animals and growing crops. One of the first places this agricultural revolution unfolded was in Mesopotamia. Mesopotamia was a fertile plain between the Tigris and Euphrates rivers in present-day Iraq.

With the shift to agriculture came a shift to a more settled lifestyle. Villages began to appear in Mesopotamia. Because food was plentiful, some villagers were freed up from farming and could undertake toolmaking, basket weaving, or record keeping. Over time, some villages grew into large, powerful cities that had their own governments and military forces. These cities represent the world's first civilizations.

Over thousands of years, Mesopotamian societies such as the Sumerians and the Babylonians invented sophisticated

(l to r)General Photographic Agency/Hulton Archive/Getty Images; (3)©Nik Wheeler/Corbis

irrigation and farming methods. They built huge, pyramid-shaped temple towers, and made advances in mathematics, astronomy, government, and law. Using a writing system called cuneiform (kew-NAY-ih-form), they produced great works of literature, including a poem known as the *Epic of Gilgamesh*. Mesopotamia's achievements helped shape later civilizations in Greece, Rome, and Western Europe.

Birthplace of World Religions

Southwest Asia is also a cradle of religion. Three of the world's major religions originated there. In ancient times, most people in the region worshiped many gods. This practice is known as **polytheism**. During the second millennium B.C., a new religion arose. A **millennium** is a period of a thousand years. This new religion was based on **monotheism**—the belief in just one God.

Judaism

The oldest of the three religions is Judaism. It was first practiced by a small group of people in Southwest Asia called the Israelites. The followers of Judaism today are known as Jews. We know about the early history of the Jewish people and their religion from their holy book—the Tanakh, or the Hebrew Bible.

According to the Hebrew Bible, Jews are descended from Abraham, a herder who was born in Mesopotamia about 1800 B.C. The Tanakh states that God made a **covenant**, or agreement, with Abraham. If Abraham moved to the land of Canaan, he and his descendants would be blessed. Abraham's descendants, later called the Israelites, believed they would continue to be blessed as long as they followed God's laws.

Jews believe that God revealed the most important of these laws to a **prophet**, or messenger of God, named Moses. According to the Hebrew Bible, Moses led the Israelites from slavery in Egypt to freedom. The Israelites had moved to Egypt to escape a long drought and were forced into slavery there. On their way from Egypt, at the top of Mount Sinai (SY•NY) in the desert, Moses received God's laws, including those known as the Ten Commandments. These rules differed from the laws of neighboring peoples because they were based on the worship of one God. The Israelites were not to worship other gods or human-made images. Also, all people—whether rich or poor—were to be treated fairly.

About 1000 B.C., the Israelites under King David created a kingdom in the area of present-day Israel. The kingdom's capital was the city of Jerusalem. By 922 B.C. , the Israelites kingdom had split into two states—Israel and Judah. The people of Judah came to be called Jews. In later centuries, the Jews were conquered, and many were forced to leave their homeland. Eventually, many Jewish people moved to countries in other parts of the world.

Even after leaving their homeland, Jews kept a strong connection to the land of Israel and their religion. The rabbis transformed

Judaism into a home and synagogue-based religion that could be practiced anywhere. By holding on to their religion and customs, the dispersed Jews ensured Judaism would become a worldwide religion. This migration of the Jews was called the Diaspora (dy•AS•pruh). In many areas, the Jews were treated cruelly. In other areas, they were treated with tolerance and understanding.

Christianity

Judaism gave rise to another monotheistic religion—Christianity. About A.D. 30, a Jewish teacher named Jesus began preaching in what is today Israel and the West Bank. Jesus taught that God loved all people, even those who had sinned. He told people that if they placed their trust in God, their sins would be forgiven.

Some Jews greeted Jesus as a savior sent by God to help them. This acceptance worried other Jews, as well as the Romans who ruled their land. Jesus was convicted of treason under Roman law and was crucified, or executed on a cross. Soon afterward, Jesus' followers declared that he had risen from the dead and was the Son of God.

Jesus' followers spread his message throughout the Mediterranean world. Jews and non-Jews who accepted this message became known as Christians. They formed churches or communities for worship. Stories about Jesus and the writings of early Christians—known as the New Testament— became part of the Christian Bible.

In time, Christianity spread to Europe, where it became the dominant religion, and then around the world. Today, it is the world's largest religion, with about 2.2 billion followers.

Islam

Then, in the A.D. 600s, Islam—the religion of Muslims—arose in the Arabian Peninsula. Muhammad, regarded by Muslims as the last and greatest of the prophets, announced his message in the desert city of Makkah (Mecca). Many of the teachings of Islam are similar to those of Judaism and Christianity. For example, all three religions are monotheistic and regard Abraham as the messenger of God who first taught this belief.

The religion that Muhammad preached was relatively simple and direct. It focused on the need to obey the will of Allah, the Arab word for God. It obligated followers to perform five duties, which became known as the Pillars of Islam: promising faith to God and accepting Muhammad as God's prophet, praying five times daily, fasting during the month of Ramadan (RAHM-uh-don), aiding the poor and unfortunate, and making a pilgrimage to the holy city of Makkah. Muslims later wrote down Muhammad's messages. These writings became the Quran (ku•RAN), or holy book of Islam.

Islamic Expansion

Academic Vocabulary

expand to increase or enlarge

In its first several years, Islam attracted few converts. By the time of Muhammad's death, however, in A.D. 632, it had **expanded** across the Arabian Peninsula. Under Muhammad's successors, known as caliphs (KAY-lifs), Arab armies began spreading the religion through military conquests. It was also spread by scholars, by religious pilgrims, and by Arab traders.

By about A.D. 800, Islam had spread across nearly all of Southwest Asia, including Persia (present-day Iran) and part of Turkey. It also extended into most of Spain and Portugal and across northernmost Africa. It later expanded to northern and eastern Africa, Central Asia, and South and Southeast Asia.

Islamic society was enriched by knowledge, skills, ideas, and cultural influences from many different peoples and areas. The influences contributed to a flowering of Islamic culture that lasted for centuries. During this period, great works of architecture were built, and centers of learning arose. Arab scholars made advances in math and science. This golden age was to have a lasting impact on every place it touched.

During the 1100s and 1200s, crusaders from Western Europe set up Christian states along Southwest Asia's Mediterranean coast. The Muslims fought back and gained control of these territories by 1300. However, in other areas, Muslim military power weakened.

MAP SKILLS

1 **THE GEOGRAPHER'S WORLD** How far did Islam spread by A.D. 750?

2 **PLACES AND REGIONS** Why did Muslims from Arabia conquer lands such as Syria, Persia, and Egypt?

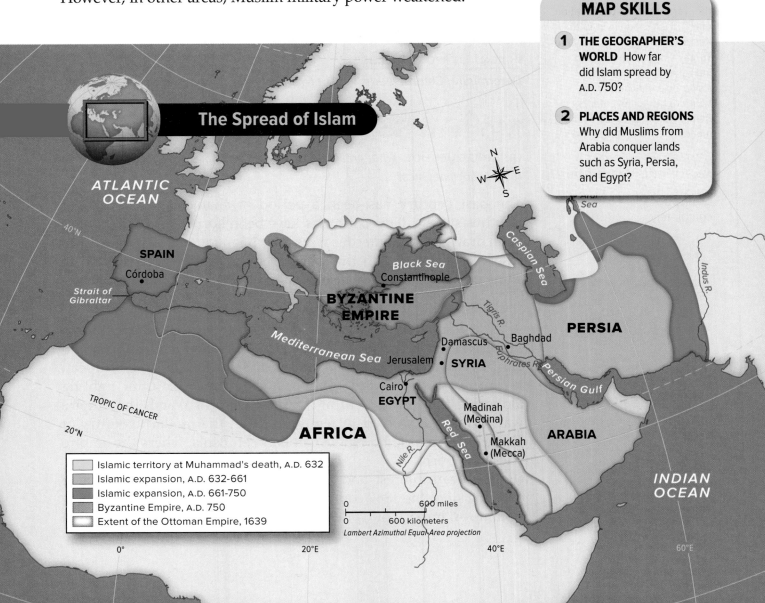

The Spread of Islam

Legend:
- Islamic territory at Muhammad's death, A.D. 632
- Islamic expansion, A.D. 632–661
- Islamic expansion, A.D. 661–750
- Byzantine Empire, A.D. 750
- Extent of the Ottoman Empire, 1639

0 — 600 miles
0 — 600 kilometers
Lambert Azimuthal Equal-Area projection

General Mustafa Kemal reviews Turkish troops during the war that led to the creation of a Turkish republic in 1923. Kemal, a military hero, became Turkey's first president and introduced reforms to modernize the country. In honor of his achievements, Kemal was later called Atatürk, meaning "Father of the Turks."

Academic Vocabulary

collapse to break down completely

In the middle of the 1200s, a Central Asian people known as the Mongols, led by the grandson of the famous leader Genghis Khan, conquered Persia and Mesopotamia. These areas became part of a vast Mongol empire that stretched across much of Eurasia.

As a result of the Mongol attacks, the Islamic world was fragmented and fell into decay. Soon, however, a new era of Islamic expansion began. At its heart were the Ottomans, a group of Muslim tribes who began building an empire on the Anatolian Peninsula in the early 1200s. By the mid-1300s, the Ottoman Empire had grown to include much of western Southwest Asia and parts of southeastern Europe and northern Africa. At its height, it was one of the world's most powerful states. It endured for six centuries before finally **collapsing** in the early 1900s.

✅ **READING PROGRESS CHECK**

Determining Central Ideas What are some ways in which Islam was spread?

Modern Southwest Asia

GUIDING QUESTION *What present-day issues facing Southwest Asia have their roots in ancient times?*

The past century has been a period of change and conflict for Southwest Asia. New countries have been born, new borders have been drawn, and numerous wars have been fought. Vast petroleum reserves discovered in this period have brought great wealth to some countries but have also created new tensions and conflicts.

Independent Countries

After reaching the peak of its power in the 1500s, the Ottoman Empire began to decline. The decline worsened in the 1800s and early 1900s. During that time, the empire lost African and European territories through wars, treaties, and revolutions. After fighting alongside the losing Central Powers in World War I, the empire was formally dissolved. A few years later, the modern country of Turkey was founded on the Anatolian Peninsula, where the empire had been born.

European interest and influence in Southwest Asia had been growing since the 1869 completion of the Suez Canal, which quickly became an important world waterway. In the peace settlement that ended World War I, Britain and France gained control over the Ottoman Empire's former territories under a mandate system. In this arrangement, the people of these territories were to be prepared for eventual independence.

Dividing up their territories, the British and French created new political boundaries that showed little regard for existing ethnic, religious, political, or historical divisions. These boundaries would take on deep importance when the territorial units became independent countries and when new discoveries of petroleum deposits were made.

Long-simmering resentment toward the European colonial powers soon grew into strong nationalist movements among Arabs, Persians, Turks, and other groups. Between 1930 and 1971, one country after another won its independence, and the map of Southwest Asia began to take its present form.

Arab-Israeli Conflict

One of the mandates received by Britain after World War I was the territory called the Palestine Mandate. It roughly corresponded to modern-day Jordan and Israel, including the Land of Israel, which was the area inhabited by the Jewish people since ancient times. Most of the people living in Palestine at the time of the mandate were Muslim Arabs. During the same period, growing numbers of Jewish immigrants seeking to escape persecution had been arriving from Europe and other parts of the world. As the Jewish population increased, tensions between Palestinian Arabs and Jews deepened.

Jewish nationalists called for the reestablishment of their historic homeland in the Palestine Mandate. This movement gained support as a result of the Holocaust—the systematic murder of 6 million European Jews by Nazi Germany during World War II. Hundreds of thousands of Jews who survived the Holocaust were now refugees in search of a place to live.

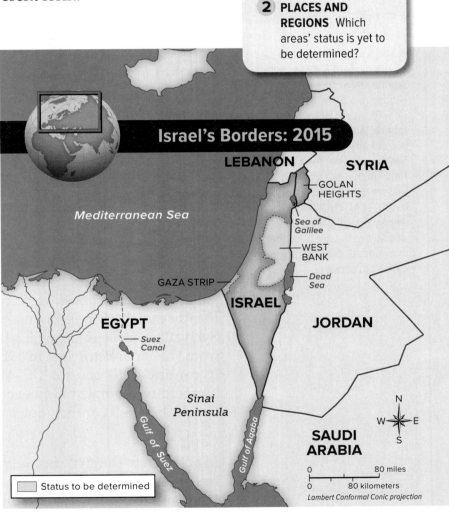

MAP SKILLS

1 **THE GEOGRAPHER'S WORLD** Describe the relative location of the Sinai Peninsula to Israel.

2 **PLACES AND REGIONS** Which areas' status is yet to be determined?

Israel's Borders: 2015

LEBANON
SYRIA
Mediterranean Sea
GOLAN HEIGHTS
Sea of Galilee
WEST BANK
Dead Sea
GAZA STRIP
ISRAEL
EGYPT
JORDAN
Suez Canal
Sinai Peninsula
Gulf of Suez
Gulf of Aqaba
SAUDI ARABIA
☐ Status to be determined

N W E S

0   80 miles
0   80 kilometers
Lambert Conformal Conic projection

Kurdish families travel by cart over a modern road in southeastern Turkey. The Kurds are a Sunni Muslim people with their own language and culture. Living in the mountains north of Southwest Asia, the Kurds have been ruled by other people throughout history.

▶ CRITICAL THINKING

Analyzing Why has the demand of the Kurds for their own independent country been difficult to achieve?

In 1947 the United Nations decided on the issue of Palestine. The United Nations voted to divide the territory into two states, one Arab and one Jewish. The proposal was rejected by the Arabs and accepted by the Jews.

On the day in 1948 that Israel, the Jewish state, declared its independence, armies from five neighboring Arab countries invaded. Hundreds of thousands of Palestinian Arabs became refugees after fleeing the violence. That war ended with a truce in 1948. Other major Arab-Israeli wars were fought, however, in the 1950s, 1960s, and 1970s.

During a brief 1967 war, Israel captured areas known as the West Bank, eastern Jerusalem, the Sinai Peninsula, the Gaza Strip, and Golan Heights. Its control of these areas was opposed by Palestinian Arabs and neighboring Arab countries, which declared shortly after the war that they would not make peace with Israel. In 1973 Egypt and Syria attacked Israel, launching the Yom Kippur War. Israel withdrew from the Sinai Peninsula in 1982 and from the Gaza Strip in 2005. It continues to control the West Bank and eastern Jerusalem. Numerous attempts have been made to find a peaceful solution to the Arab-Israeli conflict, but so far none have been successful.

Civil Wars

In addition to the strife between Arabs and Israelis, Southwest Asia has seen numerous other conflicts since World War II. Ethnic, religious, and political differences have fueled many conflicts. So has the rise of Islamist movements that consider Islam to be a political system as well as a religion. The desire to control large oil fields has also caused, or contributed to, many of the conflicts.

Civil wars have torn apart Lebanon, Afghanistan, Iraq, Syria, and Yemen. The Kurds, a fiercely independent people living in eastern Turkey, northern Iraq, northern Syria, and western Iran, have fought to gain their own country. A revolution in Iran in the late 1970s resulted in the overthrow of that country's monarchy and the establishment of an Islamic republic. Iraq invaded Iran in 1980, touching off an eight-year-long war. A decade later, Iraq invaded and annexed its small but oil-rich neighbor, Kuwait. This invasion triggered the Persian Gulf War, in which a coalition led by the United States quickly liberated Kuwait.

Conflict and Terrorism

On September 11, 2001, an Islamist organization called al-Qaeda carried out terrorist attacks on U.S. soil that killed nearly 3,000 people. The United States determined that Afghanistan's Islamist ruling group, the Taliban, was supporting al-Qaeda and sheltering its leaders. In October, forces led by the United States and the United Kingdom invaded Afghanistan and removed the Taliban from power.

Two years later, the Second Persian Gulf War began when forces from the United States and the United Kingdom invaded Iraq and overthrew the government of Saddam Hussein. Hussein was accused of possessing weapons of mass destruction, a suspicion that eventually was proved to be untrue.

Looking to the Future

Despite the many conflicts, there is hope for a more peaceful and brighter future in Southwest Asia. Revenue from petroleum has brought prosperity and modernization to oil-rich countries of the Persian Gulf. In 2010 and 2011, a popular uprising in Tunisia inspired democratic movements in Yemen, Bahrain, and Syria.

On the other hand, militant Islamic political movements limit the growth of democracy and civil rights. In addition, throughout the region, major gaps still exist in standards of living between the oil-rich countries and poorer countries.

☑ READING PROGRESS CHECK

Determining Central Ideas What event in Europe helped spur the creation of a Jewish state in Southwest Asia?

Think Again?

The Middle East and Southwest Asia are two names for the same region.

Not true. According to most authorities, the Middle East includes all or part of North Africa as well as all or most of Southwest Asia. Some authorities also consider the countries of Central Asia to be part of the Middle East.

Include this lesson's information in your Foldable®.

LESSON 2 REVIEW

Reviewing Vocabulary

1. What is the difference between *monotheism* and *polytheism*?

Answering the Guiding Questions

2. ***Identifying*** What is one of the Pillars of Islam?

3. ***Describing*** What change in Mesopotamia around 10,000 years ago resulted in a less nomadic lifestyle?

4. ***Identifying*** What are two developments that occurred during Islam's golden age?

5. ***Citing Text Evidence*** What empire represented a second period of Islamic expansion, and where did that empire begin?

6. ***Determining Central Ideas*** How did the 2001 terrorist attacks on the United States lead to a U.S. invasion of Afghanistan?

7. ***Informative/Explanatory Writing*** Some conflicts in Southwest Asia relate to the struggle for a homeland by groups such as the Jews, the Palestinians, and the Kurds. Write a short essay discussing what a homeland is and why groups are willing to fight for one.

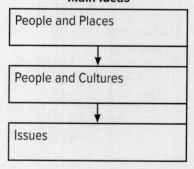

Reading HELPDESK

Academic Vocabulary

- **widespread**

Content Vocabulary

- **hydropolitics**
- **fossil water**

TAKING NOTES: *Key Ideas and Details*

Determine the Main Idea As you read the lesson, write the main idea for each section on a graphic organizer like the one below.

Main Ideas

People and Places

↓

People and Cultures

↓

Issues

Lesson 3
Life in Southwest Asia

ESSENTIAL QUESTION • *How does religion shape society?*

IT MATTERS BECAUSE
Because of its strategic location at the convergence of three continents, its huge petroleum reserves, and the deep-rooted conflicts that divide its people, Southwest Asia occupies a central place in world affairs.

People and Places

GUIDING QUESTION *In what parts of Southwest Asia do most people live?*

Southwest Asia's population is slightly greater than that of the United States, although the region is only about three-fourths as large as the United States in area. Throughout history, population patterns in Southwest Asia have been shaped largely by the availability of water. In recent times, another resource—petroleum—has also played an important role.

Population Profile

Southwest Asia is home to about 330 million people. Iran and Turkey, its most populous countries, each have about 80 million people. Some oil-rich countries around the Persian Gulf are experiencing population booms as their fast-growing economies attract foreign workers. Qatar has had one of the world's highest population growth rates in recent years.

Today, many countries of Southwest Asia are highly urbanized. In Israel, Saudi Arabia, and Kuwait, for example, more than four of every five people live in cities. In Afghanistan and Yemen, however, more than two-thirds of the people live in rural areas. However, these countries have the region's highest annual urbanization rate as people move to the cities. As a whole, the region has a rapidly growing population and a high percentage of people below 15 years of age.

Where People Live

Population is not evenly distributed across Southwest Asia. The highest densities are in the region's northern and western parts and in its southern tip. These areas include parts of Turkey, Iraq, Iran, and Afghanistan; the countries along the coast of the Mediterranean Sea; and the highlands of southern Saudi Arabia and southwestern Yemen. Most of these areas have relatively higher rainfall.

Areas with dry or somewhat dry climates are more sparsely populated. These areas include the Arabian Desert and the desert lands that spread across central and eastern Iran. Some desert areas are almost completely uninhabited. One exception is Mesopotamia, the land between the Tigris and Euphrates Rivers in Iraq. Although its climate is relatively dry, the area supports high population density because the rivers provide abundant water for irrigating crops.

Southwest Asia has metropolises, such as Istanbul, Damascus, Tehran, and Baghdad, that are home to millions of people. Gleaming modern cities, such as Dubai, Abu Dhabi, and Riyadh, rise from the sands of oil-rich Persian Gulf countries. Tel Aviv, Israel's largest city after Jerusalem, is a thriving urban center. These cities stand in sharp contrast to ancient rural villages that seem untouched by the passing of time. In some of the region's desert areas, nomads, known as Bedouins, sleep in tents and raise herds of camels, sheep, goats, and cattle.

✔ READING PROGRESS CHECK

Citing Text Evidence Why do some countries around the Persian Gulf have rapidly growing populations?

At a height of more than 2,700 feet (823 m), the Burj Khalifa (left) is the tallest building in the world. The building is located in Dubai, United Arab Emirates. (right) Adobe storage buildings stand along Al-Assad Lake, a reservoir on the Euphrates River in Syria. A network of canals carries water from the lake to irrigate land on both sides of the Euphrates.

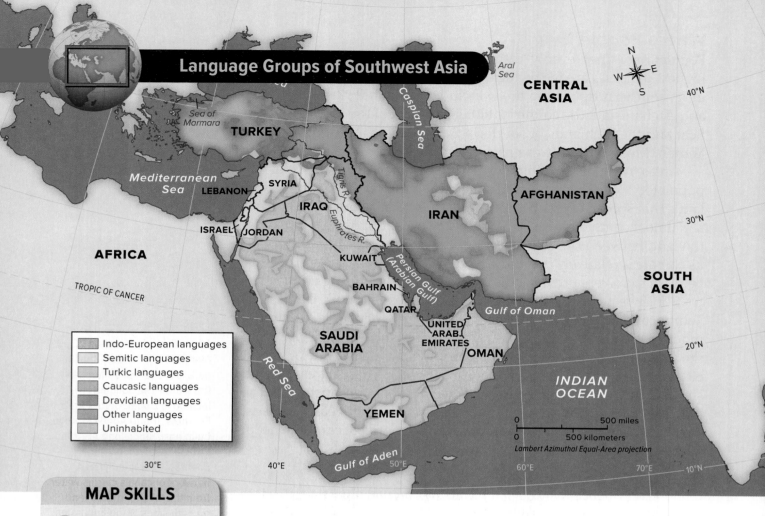

Language Groups of Southwest Asia

Legend:
- Indo-European languages
- Semitic languages
- Turkic languages
- Caucasic languages
- Dravidian languages
- Other languages
- Uninhabited

0 500 miles
0 500 kilometers
Lambert Azimuthal Equal-Area projection

MAP SKILLS

1 **THE GEOGRAPHER'S WORLD** What language group is most common in Syria?

2 **THE GEOGRAPHER'S WORLD** What two language groups are most prevalent in Iran?

Academic Vocabulary

widespread spread out

People and Cultures

GUIDING QUESTION *What cultural differences are found across Southwest Asia?*

Southwest Asia is often thought of as an Arab or an Islamic realm. The reality, however, is more complex. The region, which has always been a crossroads of humanity, is home to many different people.

Ethnic and Language Groups

Arabs represent the largest group in Southwest Asia. In Saudi Arabia, Syria, Jordan, and other countries, 9 out of 10 people are Arab. The two most populous countries in the region, however, have only small Arab populations. In Turkey, Turks form the majority. In Iran, which once was the historical region called Persia, most people are Persian.

In Israel, which was founded as a Jewish state, Jews account for about three-fourths of the population. Kurds, who have no country of their own, represent significant minorities in Turkey, Iran, and Iraq. The region they inhabit is traditionally known as Kurdistan.

Arabic, spoken by Arabs, is the most **widespread** language in Southwest Asia. Other important languages include Turkish and Farsi, the language of Persians. Hebrew is the official language of Israel, and Kurdish is spoken by Kurds.

Some of the region's countries have complex ethnic and linguistic makeup. Afghanistan, for example, is home to Pashtuns, Tajiks, Hazaras, Uzbeks, Aimaks, Turkmen, and Balochs. In addition to the official languages of Afghanistan—Pashto and Afghan Persian—the Afghani people speak Uzbek and more than 30 other languages.

The presence of so many ethnic and language groups in one country presents a challenge to national unity. Many people in Southwest Asia identify with their ethnic group more strongly than with the country they live in. This is clearly evident in countries such as Afghanistan, where people identify themselves as Pashtun or Hazari rather than as Afghani. Even in countries that are mostly Arab, such as Syria and Iraq, people identify with tribes that are based on family relationships. Tribal identity is often stronger than national identity.

Religion and the Arts

From its birthplace in the cities of the Arabian Peninsula, Islam spread across Southwest Asia some 1,300 years ago. It remains the region's dominant religion, helping to unite people of different ethnicity and languages. It is practiced by Arabs, Turks, Persians, Kurds, and many other groups.

Islam has two main branches, Sunni and Shia. Most of Southwest Asia's Muslims are Sunnis. In Iran, however, Shias—Muslims of the Shia branch—outnumber Sunnis nine to one.

Judaism is practiced by about three-fourths of the people in Israel. Christians represent about 40 percent of the population in Lebanon and 10 percent in Syria.

An Iranian woman copies the tile design on a wall at a mosque in Eşfahān, Iran. Islam discourages showing living figures in religious art, so Muslim artists often work in colorful geometric patterns, floral designs, and calligraphy. Passages from the Quran decorate the walls of many mosques.

▶ CRITICAL THINKING
Analyzing Why would Muslim artists use passages from the Quran in calligraphy?

©Jose Fuste Raga/Corbis

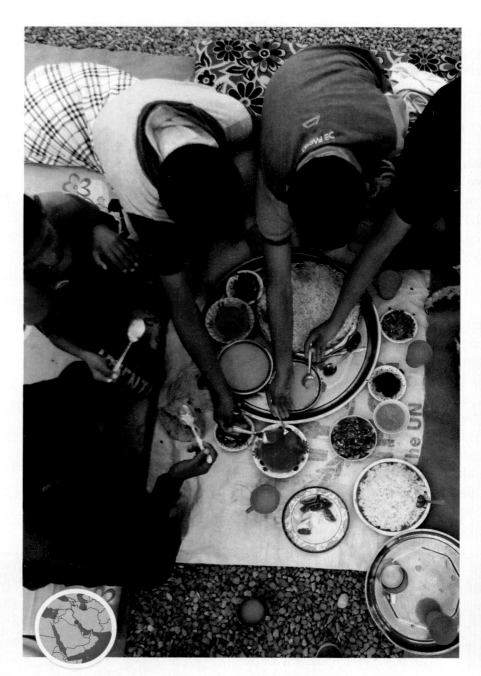

A family in Iraq eats a pre-dawn meal before fasting on the second day of the Muslim holy month of Ramadan. Muslims believe that fasting will help people focus on God and on living better lives. According to the Quran, Muhammad first received teachings from God during the month of Ramadan.

▶ CRITICAL THINKING

Describing How does religion affect daily life in Southwest Asia?

Religion and art have been closely tied in Southwest Asia throughout history. Some of the region's most magnificent works of architecture are mosques, temples, and other religious structures. Sacred texts such as the Hebrew and Christian Bibles and Islam's Quran stand as works of literature as well as guides to their followers.

The region also has other rich artistic traditions, including calligraphy, mosaics, weaving, storytelling, and poetry. Colorful, handwoven carpets from Persia, or present-day Iran, have been famous for centuries, as has the collection of folktales known as *The Thousand and One Nights*.

Daily Life

Across Southwest Asia, daily life varies greatly. Some people live in cities, some live in villages, and a few live as nomads. Throughout the region's history, most people practiced traditional livelihoods such as farming, raising livestock, or fishing. In recent times, more people have been leaving the land to work in petroleum production, food processing, auto manufacturing, textiles, and construction.

Religion plays a central role in the daily lives of many people in Southwest Asia. Islam is a complete way of life, with rules regarding diet, hygiene, relationships, business, law, and more. To Muslims, families are the foundation of a healthy society; maintaining family ties is an important duty.

Ramadan, the ninth month of the Muslim calendar, is a holy month of fasting. Between dawn and dusk, Muslims are obligated to refrain from eating and drinking. After ending their fast with prayer each evening, people enjoy festive meals. The end of Ramadan is marked by a three-day celebration called *Eid al-Fitr*, which translates as Festival of Breaking Fast.

☑ **READING PROGRESS CHECK**

Identifying What is the major ethnic group in Iran, and what language does that group speak?

Issues

GUIDING QUESTION *How have oil wealth and availability of natural resources created challenges for countries of Southwest Asia?*

The period since World War II has brought a great deal of change and conflict to Southwest Asia. Looking to the future, the region faces many difficult issues. Some of them relate to resources and others to ethnic, religious, and cultural divisions. Some are new, and others are rooted in the distant past.

Oil Dependency and Control

The discovery in the mid-1900s of vast petroleum deposits in Southwest Asia had a strong impact on the region. Exports of petroleum products have brought great wealth to countries around the Persian Gulf, where the largest deposits are found. With this wealth came modernization in some countries. In other countries, little has changed, especially for the average person.

Petroleum has brought new challenges. Many people living in modern cities in oil-producing countries grew up living in tents and practicing traditional farming and herding. Some Muslims believe that increased exposure to Western ways is corrupting the region's people. Another issue is the growing gap between rich and poor countries. Qatar and Kuwait, for example, rank among the wealthiest countries in the world; Afghanistan ranks among the poorest. The struggle to control oil has led to tension and wars. It has also resulted in increased intervention in Southwest Asia by foreign powers.

In 1991 U.S.-led forces pushed Iraqi invaders out of Kuwait. As Iraqi troops left, they set fire to more than 600 oil wells. Tons of thick oil smoke filled the air, and unburned oil spilled into the Persian Gulf. This environmental disaster took place in the area around Kuwait. The air and the soil were polluted, and animal and sea life were destroyed.

©Peter Turnley/Corbis

Because of irrigation, farming is possible in some dry areas of Saudi Arabia. This wheat farm in Saudi Arabia's Nejd region is supported by center-pivot irrigation. This method involves a long pipe of sprinklers that moves in a circle around a deep well that supplies the water.

▶ CRITICAL THINKING

Determining Central Ideas Why is fossil water valuable to Saudi Arabia?

Oil dependency is also an issue. Exporting countries thrive when oil commands high prices, but they suffer when worldwide prices drop. Further, oil is not a renewable resource, and the countries have already depleted some of their reserves. To lessen their dependency on oil, exporting countries have invested money in other industries. Countries that import oil are investigating alternatives to oil.

Changing Governments

More than six decades after it began, the Arab-Israeli conflict continues as one of the biggest issues facing Southwest Asia. At the heart of the conflict are the Gaza Strip and West Bank territories, which Israel captured in 1967. Israel withdrew its forces from Gaza in 2005. Two years later, Palestinian Arab voters in the Gaza Strip elected to power an anti-Israel Islamic group called Hamas. This group has staged terrorist attacks on and fired rockets into Israel, forcing Israel to defend itself. Eruptions of violence have limited progress toward a peaceful solution.

The years 2010 and 2011 marked the beginning of the Arab Spring, a wave of pro-democracy protests and uprisings in North Africa and Southwest Asia. Protests against authoritarian rulers broke out in Tunisia, Egypt, Libya, Yemen, Bahrain, Syria, Jordan, and Oman in early 2011.

By the end of the year, leaders in Tunisia, Egypt, Libya, and Yemen were overthrown. Protests in Bahrain were quashed by security forces, but the government later agreed to implement reforms. Syria fell into upheaval when the government used armed force to stop protests. More peaceful reform efforts are underway in Jordan and Oman.

Water Concerns

Scarcity of freshwater has plagued Southwest Asia throughout history. Dramatic population growth has produced greater demand for this precious resource, making the situation more dire and increasing the importance of **hydropolitics**, or politics related to water usage and access.

Water from the saltwater seas that surround Southwest Asia can be made into freshwater through desalination, or the removal of salt. Unfortunately, this process is expensive and therefore not practical for meeting the region's water needs.

Saudi Arabia, which has no rivers that flow year-round, has tapped into **fossil water**. This term refers to water that fell as rain thousands of years ago, when the region's climate was wetter, and is now trapped between rock layers deep below ground. By pumping the water to the surface for irrigation, Saudi Arabia has transformed areas of barren desert into productive farmland. Fossil water is not a renewable resource, however, and the underground reservoirs could soon run dry.

The region's greatest source of freshwater is the Tigris-Euphrates river system. From their sources in the mountains of eastern Turkey, the Tigris and Euphrates Rivers flow southeastward through the desert plains of Syria and Iraq.

The three countries depend heavily on the rivers and their tributaries. In recent decades, all have built dams to control flooding, to generate electricity, and to capture water for irrigation. Syria and Iraq, which are downstream from Turkey, have bitterly opposed an ambitious, decades-long dam-building project in Turkey that threatens to reduce river flow.

Include this lesson's information in your Foldable®.

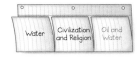

☑ **READING PROGRESS CHECK**

Describing What was the Arab Spring? What countries in Southwest Asia were involved?

LESSON 3 REVIEW

Reviewing Vocabulary

1. What is *fossil water*?

Answering the Guiding Questions

2. *Identifying* What are Southwest Asia's two most populous countries, and approximately how many people live in each country?

3. *Determining Word Meanings* What is hydropolitics?

4. *Analyzing* How might dams built on the Tigris and Euphrates Rivers in Turkey affect agriculture in Syria and Iraq?

5. *Identifying* What are the two main branches of Islam, and to which branch do most Muslims in Southwest Asia belong?

6. *Identifying Point of View* How might Persian Gulf countries be affected if oil-importing countries begin turning to alternate energy sources?

7. *Describing* Who are the Bedouin?

8. *Narrative Writing* Imagine that have you spent your whole life in a poor village somewhere in Southwest Asia. Then, one day you visit Dubai, a bustling, modern city of skyscrapers and shopping malls. Write a letter to a friend or a family member back in your village describing your experience in Dubai.

What Do You **Think?**

Are Trade Restrictions Effective at Changing a Government's Policies?

Sometimes, one country restricts trade with another country as a way to force it to change its policies. For example, if the U.S. government wants a country to give its citizens more democratic rights, it might not allow that country to sell goods in the United States. Although the U.S. government often applies trade restrictions on countries, opinions differ about their effectiveness.

Yes !

PRIMARY SOURCE

" Sanctions aimed at achieving major policy objectives have the strongest chance of success if applied by a multilateral coalition [many countries]; it helps that the multilateral approach also shares the cost. . . . Smart sanctions have their use in tightening the screws on a recalcitrant [stubborn] or defiant [openly disobedient] regime [government] without inflicting collateral [additional] damage on the population. . . . And even when sanctions don't achieve stated objectives, they nonetheless signal resolve [determination], and may in fact be essential to prepare the political ground at home and abroad for military action against the target."

—Gordon Kaplan, "Making Economic Sanctions Work"

TEXT: From "Making Economic Sanctions Work," © 2010 by Gordon Kaplan. Published by UT San Diego, August 20, 2010; PHOTO: (t)©Justin Guariglia/Corbis; (b)©Monty Rakusen/cultura/Corbis

Rows of cargo containers await shipment at Singapore, a city-state in Southeast Asia. Singapore depends on international trade for its survival. Its port is one of the busiest cargo shipping centers in the world.

No !

PRIMARY SOURCE

" Imposing sanctions . . . are not only an act of war according to international law, they are most often the first step toward a real war starting with a bombing campaign. We should be using diplomacy rather than threats and hostility. Nothing promotes peace better than free trade. Countries that trade with each other generally do not make war on each other, as both countries gain economic benefits they do not want to jeopardize. Also, trade and friendship applies much more effective persuasion to encourage better behavior, as does leading by example. "

—Ron Paul, "The Folly of Sanctions"

A port security worker checks cargo at a warehouse in London, England. Ships from all over the world pass through major international ports, such as London.

What Do You Think? DBQ

1. **Identifying Point of View** According to Kaplan, why are sanctions effective even if they do not achieve their objectives?

2. **Identifying Point of View** Why does Paul think that free trade is better than economic sanctions for promoting peace?

3. **Analyzing** Who do you think makes the stronger argument, Kaplan or Paul?

Directions: Write your answers on a separate piece of paper.

1 Use your **FOLDABLES** to explore the Essential Question.

INFORMATIVE/EXPLANATORY WRITING Choose one of the countries in this region and learn about its natural resources. Then write an essay to answer: Is the country using its resources wisely?

2 21st Century Skills

INTEGRATING VISUAL INFORMATION Working in small groups, identify one problem facing the countries of Southwest Asia. Research its effects on the people of the region and offer possible solutions. Produce a slide show or build a visual display to share your findings.

3 Thinking Like a Geographer

IDENTIFYING Identify five countries of Southwest Asia. List the countries and their capital cities. Then write one interesting fact about each country.

4 GEOGRAPHY ACTIVITY

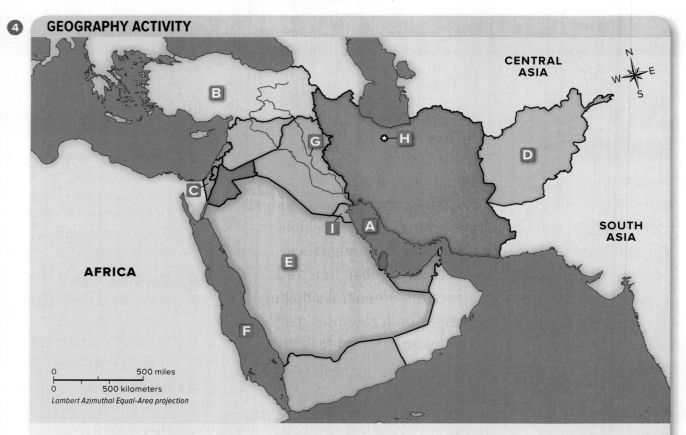

Locating Places

Match the letters on the map with the numbered places below.

1. Saudi Arabia

2. Tehran

3. Afghanistan

4. Israel

5. Red Sea

6. Kuwait

7. Persian Gulf

8. Tigris River

9. Turkey

REVIEW THE GUIDING QUESTIONS

Directions: Choose the best answer for each question.

1 Which scarce resource has most directly shaped Southwest Asia's history and settlement patterns?

A. rich soil

B. natural gas

C. water

D. forests

2 Southwest Asia's physical geography can be described as one of

F. high mountains.

G. extremes.

H. little variety.

I. sandy deserts.

3 How long ago did humans convert from living as hunter-gatherers to living in settlements and practicing agriculture?

A. a million years ago

B. 10,000 years ago

C. 50,000 years ago

D. 100,000 years ago

4 Which three major world religions originated in Southwest Asia?

F. Sikhism, Hinduism, Judaism

G. Christianity, Judaism, Hinduism

H. Islam, Judaism, Christianity

I. Judaism, Islam, Hinduism

5 What twentieth-century discovery brought great wealth to some countries in Southwest Asia?

A. the cell phone

B. vast petroleum deposits

C. gold

D. rubies and emeralds

6 The population of Southwest Asia is

F. growing rapidly.

G. declining.

H. aging.

I. leaving to find work in India.

DBQ **ANALYZING DOCUMENTS**

❼ **CITING TEXT EVIDENCE** Read the following passage about Israel's economy:

"Israel has a diversified, technologically advanced economy. . . . The major industrial sectors include high-technology electronic and biomedical equipment, metal products, processed foods, chemicals, and transport equipment. . . . Prior to the violence that began in September 2000, [Israel] was a major tourist destination."

—from U.S. State Department Background Notes, "Israel"

Which detail supports the idea that Israel's economy is technologically advanced?

A. biomedical equipment industry

B. processed food industry

C. transport equipment industry

D. tourism industry

❽ **ANALYZING** What inference can you draw about the decline of tourism to Israel after 2000?

F. Economic hard times reduced tourism to all locations.

G. Other places became more fashionable as tourist destinations.

H. Tourism declined because people were worried about their safety.

I. Lower prices for air travel would revive tourism to Israel.

SHORT RESPONSE

"One challenge the Saudis face in achieving their strategic vision to add production capacity is that their existing fields experience 6 to 8 percent annual 'decline rates' on average . . . , meaning that the country needs around 700,000 [billion barrels per day] in additional capacity each year just to [make up] for natural decline."

—from Energy Information Administration, *Saudi Arabia*

❾ **DETERMINING WORD MEANINGS** Based on this passage, what do the "decline rates" refer to?

❿ **ANALYZING** What could cause these decline rates?

EXTENDED RESPONSE

⓫ **INFORMATIVE/EXPLANATORY WRITING** Write an essay explaining why you think conflict in this part of the world since the end of World War II has increased so dramatically. Consider how conflict and wars in this part of the world affect you and your family.

Need Extra Help?

If You've Missed Question	❶	❷	❸	●	❺	❻	❼	❽	❾	❿	⓫
Review Lesson	1	1	2	2	3	3	3	3	1	1	2

NORTH AFRICA

ESSENTIAL QUESTIONS · *How do people adapt to their environment?*
· *How does religion shape society?* · *Why do conflicts develop?*

Travelscape Images/Alamy Stock Photo

Souks, or markets, such as this one in Aswan, Egypt, carry a wide assortment of goods.

The Story Matters...

Because of the fertile soil in the Nile River valley, ancient Egyptians created a farming society that developed into an empire thousands of years ago. Their great achievements had a tremendous impact on later civilizations in the region. Other waterways influenced the development of trade and communications among Africa, Asia, and Europe. Waterways and trade routes were also important to the spread of ideas and religion, including Islam.

FOLDABLES®
Study Organizer

Go to the Foldables® library in the back of your book to make a Foldable® that will help you take notes while reading this chapter.

	Know	Learned
Geography		
History		
Economy		

The countries of North Africa border the Mediterranean Sea. They make up one region of the African continent. To their south, the Sahara crosses Africa, and to the south of the Sahara lie the other regions of the second-largest continent.

Step Into the Place

MAP FOCUS Use the map to answer the following questions.

1 PLACES AND REGIONS What is the capital of Morocco?

2 THE GEOGRAPHER'S WORLD What body of water flows to the east of Egypt?

3 THE GEOGRAPHER'S WORLD Which North African country has the largest land area?

4 CRITICAL THINKING Analyzing What do the capitals of the North African countries have in common geographically?

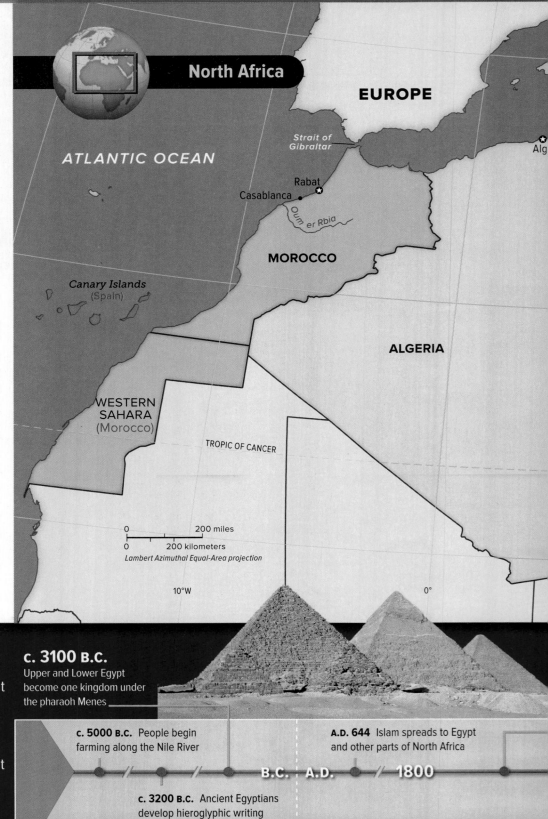

North Africa

EUROPE

ATLANTIC OCEAN

Strait of Gibraltar

Alg

Rabat
Casablanca
Oum er Rbia

MOROCCO

Canary Islands
(Spain)

ALGERIA

WESTERN SAHARA
(Morocco)

TROPIC OF CANCER

0   200 miles
0   200 kilometers
Lambert Azimuthal Equal-Area projection

10°W   0°

Step Into the Time

TIME LINE Choose an event from the time line and write a paragraph explaining the social, economic, or environmental effects of that event on the region and the world.

c. 3100 B.C. Upper and Lower Egypt become one kingdom under the pharaoh Menes

c. 5000 B.C. People begin farming along the Nile River

A.D. 644 Islam spreads to Egypt and other parts of North Africa

B.C. | A.D.   1800

c. 3200 B.C. Ancient Egyptians develop hieroglyphic writing

SOUTHWEST
ASIA

40°N

Tunis

Medjerda R.

Mediterranean Sea

TUNISIA

Tripoli

Benghazi

Alexandria

Suez
Canal

30°N

Cairo

○ National capital
● City

LIBYA

EGYPT

Nile R.

Red Sea

Aswān
High Dam

Lake
Nasser

20°N

10°E

1830
Algeria, Tunisia, and Morocco
become part of the French Empire

1969
Muammar al-Qaddafi
seizes power in Libya

2010–2011 Pro-democracy revolts known as the
Arab Spring take place in Tunisia, Egypt, and Libya

1956 Oil is discovered in Libya

1900

2000

1859–1869 The Suez Canal is built,
linking the Mediterranean and Red seas

1970 The Aswān High Dam is completed

2003 Earthquake in northern Algeria
leaves 200,000 people homeless

2011 Egyptian president
Mubarak leaves office

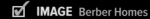

There's More Online!

☑ **IMAGE** Berber Homes

☑ **MAP** Mediterranean Climates

☑ **VIDEO**

ReadingHELPDESK

Academic Vocabulary

- **margin**
- **channel**

Content Vocabulary

- **delta**
- **silt**
- **wadi**
- **erg**
- **nomad**
- **phosphate**
- **aquifer**

TAKING NOTES: *Key Ideas and Details*

Organize Information As you read about North Africa's physical geography, take notes using the graphic organizer below. Add rows to list more features and their characteristics.

Feature	Characteristic
Atlas Mountains	

Lesson 1
The Physical Geography of North Africa

ESSENTIAL QUESTION • *How do people adapt to their environment?*

IT MATTERS BECAUSE
The Sahara, in North Africa, is the world's largest hot desert. The desert extends over almost the entire northern one-third of the continent of Africa.

Landforms and Waterways

GUIDING QUESTION *How have physical features shaped life in the region?*

Hassan is an Egyptian farmer. In winter, when temperatures are milder than during the summer, he grows wheat. Rainfall is scarce in Egypt, however. How does Hassan get the water he needs to grow his wheat? He draws it from a canal. Canals carry water from the Nile River to the country's farms around the river. Just as they did thousands of years ago, Egypt's farmers still depend on the waters of the Nile.

Countries of the Region

Egypt is the easternmost country in North Africa. The Sinai Peninsula, a triangle of land across the Red Sea from Africa, belongs to Egypt but it is considered a part of Southwest Asia.

North Africa includes five countries. All, like Egypt, sit on the southern shore of the Mediterranean Sea. Libya is to Egypt's west. Tunisia and Algeria are west of that country. Farthest west is Morocco, which has a small Mediterranean coast and a longer coast along the Atlantic Ocean. South of Morocco lies an area called Western Sahara. Morocco claims this area, although the United Nations does not recognize its ownership of this land.

(l to r)©Amar Grover/JAI/Corbis; (2)©B. Anthony Stewart/National Geographic Society/Corbis; (3)Frederic Neema/Workbook Stock/Getty Images; (4)©IStockphoto.com/hadynyah; (5)©Inge Yspeert/Corbis

North Africa is a large region. If you placed North Africa over the 48 connected states of the United States, it would reach from Maine to Washington state and cover the northern half of the country.

Coastal Plains and Mountains

In North Africa, low, narrow plains sit on the **margins**, or edges, of the Mediterranean and Atlantic coasts. In the west, the high Atlas Mountains rise just behind this coastal plain. These mountains extend about 1,200 miles (1,931 km) across Morocco and Algeria into Tunisia. They form the longest mountain chain in Africa and greatly influence the region's climate.

The Atlas Mountains are actually two sets of mountains that run alongside each other. A high plateau sits between them. The southern chain is generally higher than the one to the north. It includes Mount Toubkal in Morocco. At 13,665 feet (4,165 m), it is the highest peak in North Africa.

South of these mountains is a low plateau that reaches across most of North Africa. The land rises higher in a few spots formed by isolated mountains. In Egypt, the southern reaches of the Nile River cut through a highland area to form a deep gorge, or valley. Southeastern Egypt has low mountains on the shores of the Red Sea. The southern part of Egypt's Sinai Peninsula is also mountainous. This area includes Egypt's highest point, Gebel Katherina. It reaches 8,652 feet (2,637 m) high. Another set of low mountains lies in northeastern Libya, near the coast.

Lowlands

Northwestern Egypt has a large area of lowland. Called the Qattara Depression, it sinks 440 feet (134 m) below sea level. This area is nearly the size of New Jersey. Marshes and lakes prevent cars and trucks from passing through it.

©Amar Grover/JAI/Corbis

Academic Vocabulary

margin an edge

A village stands at the foot of a large granite formation in the Atlas Mountains of Morocco.
▶ CRITICAL THINKING
Describing How many sets of mountains make up the Atlas Mountains? What landform separates the sets of mountains?

Lush green farmland contrasts sharply with the vast desert areas that stretch for hundreds of miles on either side of the Nile River.

▶ **CRITICAL THINKING**

Analyzing How is the relationship of Egyptians to the Nile River today different from the relationship of ancient Egyptians to the river?

Academic Vocabulary

channel course

Waterways

For centuries, North Africa has been linked by the Mediterranean Sea to other lands. The sea has brought trade, new ideas, and conquering armies.

Next to the Mediterranean, the most important body of water in the region is the Nile River. At 4,160 miles (6,695 km), the mighty Nile is the longest river in the world. It begins far south of Egypt at Lake Victoria in East Africa. That lake sits on the border of Uganda and Tanzania. The river flows northward, joined by several tributaries. The most important of them is the Blue Nile, which begins in the highlands of Ethiopia.

The Nile has a massive delta at its mouth. A **delta** is an area formed by soil deposits that build up as river water slows down. Many deltas form where a river enters a larger body of water. The Nile delta is found where the Nile meets the Mediterranean Sea. Here, at the mouth of the river, the Nile's delta covers more than 9,500 square miles (24,605 sq. km)—larger than the size of New Hampshire. The river once took seven different **channels**, or courses, to reach the sea. Today, only two remain. The others have been filled with soil.

The Nile brings life to dry Egypt. In ancient times, filled by rains to the south, the Nile flooded each year. These floods left **silt**—a fine, rich soil that is excellent for farming—along the banks of the river and in the delta. Farmers used the soil to grow crops. Because they could grow large amounts of food, they were able to support the growth of a great civilization. Ancient Egypt was called "the gift of the Nile."

Today, several dams control the floods. The largest is Aswān High Dam. These dams hold back the high volume of water produced in the rainy season. The water can then be released during the year. An important benefit is that Egypt's farmers today can grow crops year-round. This is the water the farmer Hassan uses to grow his wheat. Another benefit of the dams is that people in Egypt have security from floods. One negative consequence of the dams is that the silt no longer settles on the land and enriches the soil.

Egypt controls another important waterway. This one, the Suez Canal, is human-made. The canal connects the Mediterranean Sea to the Red Sea. As a result, it links Europe and North Africa to the Indian and Pacific oceans. International trade depends on this canal. Using it enables ships traveling between Asia and Europe to avoid going all the way around Africa. The Suez Canal saves many days of travel time and much costly fuel.

☑ READING PROGRESS CHECK

Citing Text Evidence Why was ancient Egypt called "the gift of the Nile"?

Climate

GUIDING QUESTION *How do people survive in a dry climate?*

What would it be like if it hardly ever rained? That is the situation that many North Africans face. Large areas of the region receive only a few inches of rainfall each year—if that much.

A container ship passes through Egypt's Suez Canal, one of the world's most heavily used shipping lanes. Opened in 1869, the canal has been enlarged over the years to handle much bigger ships.

▶ CRITICAL THINKING

Describing What advantages does the Suez Canal provide for ship travel?

Frederic Neema/Workbook Stock/Getty Images

Causes of North Africa's Climates

The Atlas Mountains play a major role in controlling the climate in the western part of North Africa. These mountains create the rain shadow effect. Moist air blows southward from the Atlantic Ocean and the Mediterranean Sea toward the mountains. As the air rises up the northern slopes, it cools and releases rain. By the time it passes over the mountains, the air is dry. This dry air reaches the interior. Inland areas, then, remain arid.

The vast inland area of North Africa is dry for another reason. High-pressure air systems descend over areas to the south of the region for much of the year. They send hot, dry air blowing to the north. This air mass dries out the land. On the rare occasions when it does rain in the desert, the southern winds soon follow. They dry the land and leave behind **wadis**, or dry streambeds.

Desert and Semiarid Areas

Much of North Africa, then, is covered by a desert: the Sahara. Imagine a vast expanse of space, like an ocean, but covered in sand and rock. That is what the Sahara looks like. Spreading across more than 3.5 million square miles (9.1 million sq. km), the Sahara is as large as the entire United States. It covers most of North Africa and spills into three other regions of Africa, as well.

The Sahara's vast stretches of sand are called **ergs**. Strong winds blow the sand about, creating huge dust storms that choke people and animals that are caught outside. The winds also build towering sand dunes. When new winds blow, they can change the shape and size of those dunes.

Landscapes in the Sahara include rugged mountains, stony plains, and large sand dunes. A traveler (left) leads a camel caravan past towering dunes in the Moroccan part of the Sahara. Farther east, Egypt's part of the Sahara (right)—called the Libyan Desert—has rocky surfaces.

▶ CRITICAL THINKING

Describing How are sand dunes formed?

(l)©iStockphoto.com/hadynyah; (r)DEA/C.SAPPA/De Agostini/Getty Images

Ergs cover only about a quarter of the Sahara. In other areas, rocky plateaus called *hamadas* and rocks eroded by wind are common. Some areas contain oases, areas fed by underground sources of water. Plants can grow in oases and trade caravans that cross the desert stop at them for needed water. **Nomads**, people who move about from place to place in search of food, rely on these oases during their travels. They use the plants to graze herds of sheep or other animals. Some people live on oases and grow crops.

In the North African part of the Sahara, temperatures soar during the day in the summer. They can reach as high as 136°F (58°C). During the winter, though, daytime temperatures can drop as low as 55°F (13°C).

Coastal areas of North Africa have a Mediterranean climate that is well suited for growing cereal crops, citrus fruits, grapes, olives, and dates.

Mediterranean and Other Climates

North of the desert are different climate zones. A band of steppes encircle the desert immediately to the north. Temperatures here are high, and rainfall is slightly greater than in the desert. This band extends to the eastern coast. Coastal cities in Libya receive only 10 inches to 15 inches (25 cm to 38 cm) of rain per year. Alexandria, near Egypt's coast, generally receives only 7 inches (18 cm) of rainfall per year.

A Mediterranean climate dominates the western coast. This climate gives the region warm, dry summers and mild, rainy winters. More rain falls along the coast than in the dry interior. Rain amounts are higher in the west than in the east. In the west, they are higher on the mountain slopes than along the coast. Coastal areas of Morocco receive 32 inches (81 cm) or less of rain per year.

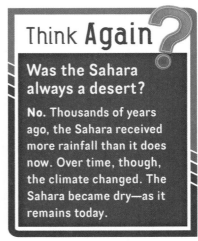

Think **Again**

Was the Sahara always a desert?

No. Thousands of years ago, the Sahara received more rainfall than it does now. Over time, though, the climate changed. The Sahara became dry—as it remains today.

nicolasdecorte/Shutterstock.com

As North Africa's population grows, the demand for water increases. This pump provides water from deep underground to people living in a Sahara environment.

▶ CRITICAL THINKING

Describing Why is so much water available underground in parts of the Sahara?

Mountain areas with highland climates also receive more rainfall—as much as 80 inches (203 cm) per year. Highland climates are found within the mountains. Morocco's Atlas Mountains often are covered by snow in the winter. As hard as it might be to believe, just a few hundred miles north of the Sahara, people can snow ski.

☑ READING PROGRESS CHECK

Analyzing Where do you think most people in North Africa live? Explain why this might be so.

Resources

GUIDING QUESTION *What resources does North Africa have?*

Oil and natural gas are resources that we use to power our cars and trucks and to generate electricity and heat. Some countries of North Africa have these resources in large quantities. All five countries in the region, though, struggle to get enough of another precious resource—water.

Oil, Gas, and Other Resources

Libya is the most oil-rich country in North Africa. Its oil reserves are ranked ninth in the world and it exports more oil than all but 15 other countries. Libya also has natural gas, but in lesser amounts. The money Libya earns from oil has fueled its economy.

Algeria has large reserves of natural gas—more than all but nine other countries. It also has large supplies of oil. These two resources make up nearly all of its exports.

Like Algeria, Egypt has larger reserves of natural gas than oil. Still, it has enough oil to supply most of what it consumes each year. Egypt even sells a small amount to other countries.

Tunisia's main resources are iron ore and phosphates. **Phosphates** are chemical compounds that are often used in fertilizers. These products are important in Morocco, as well. In addition, rich fishing grounds off Morocco's coast are a vital resource. Fish is one of that country's leading exports.

Water

Limited rainfall and high temperatures in this region leave little freshwater on the surface. Rains can be heavy when they come, but the sandy soil soon absorbs the water. Dry winds evaporate the rest. Only the Nile is a reliable source of water for farming throughout the year.

How vital is the Nile? Ninety-five out of every 100 Egyptians live within 12 miles (19 km) of the Nile River or its delta. Yet this narrow river valley and the large delta make up only a small part of Egypt's total area. Without the waters of the Nile, Egypt's people could not survive.

Outside of the Nile valley, most of the region's water needs are met with water that comes from oases and aquifers. **Aquifers** are underground layers of rock in which water collects. People use wells to tap into this water. Libya, for instance, relies on aquifers to meet almost all of its water needs. However, nearly half of Libya's people have no access to water that has been treated to be sure it meets health standards.

A growing population in this region poses problems for the future. Demand for the water in an aquifer shared by Algeria, Libya, and Tunisia has increased ninefold in recent years. In North Africa, aquifers take a long time to refill. If people continue to take water out at a high rate, the aquifers might not be able to refill quickly enough and the region's water problem will become much worse.

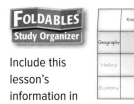

Include this lesson's information in your Foldable®.

☑ READING PROGRESS CHECK

Analyzing Why would aquifers take a long time to fill up in North Africa?

LESSON 1 REVIEW

Reviewing Vocabulary

1. In which desert feature can people live year-round, a *wadi* or an oasis? Why?

Answering the Guiding Questions

2. *Describing* How has the Mediterranean Sea affected the region?

3. *Analyzing* Does the northern or the southern chain of the Atlas Mountains receive more rainfall? Why?

4. *Determining Central Ideas* Which nations in the region are likely to import energy resources? Why?

5. *Analyzing* How can governments in the region prevent aquifers from being used up?

6. *Informative/Explanatory Writing* Write a paragraph comparing and contrasting the climates of Egypt and Morocco.

There's More Online!

- ☑ **IMAGES** Islam
- ☑ **MAP** The Punic Wars
- ☑ **ANIMATION** How the Pyramids Were Built
- ☑ **SLIDE SHOW** Egyptian Artifacts
- ☑ **VIDEO**

Reading HELP DESK

Academic Vocabulary

- project
- demonstrate

Content Vocabulary

- pharaoh
- myrrh
- hieroglyphics
- convert
- monotheism
- caliph
- regime
- fundamentalist
- civil war

TAKING NOTES: *Key Ideas and Details*

Summarize As you read about the history of North Africa, note key events and their importance using a graphic organizer like the one below.

Year, Event	Importance

Lesson 2
The History of North Africa

ESSENTIAL QUESTION • *How does religion shape society?*

IT MATTERS BECAUSE
One of the world's first civilizations arose in North Africa thousands of years ago.

Ancient Egypt

GUIDING QUESTION *Why was ancient Egypt important?*

Egypt, in North Africa, was one of the earliest known civilizations. Egyptian civilization arose along the Nile River, and Egyptians depended on the Nile for their livelihood. They built cities, organized government, and invented a writing system to keep records and create literature.

The Rise of Egypt

People have been living along the banks of the Nile River for thousands of years. As many as 8,000 years ago, people settled in the area to farm. The rich floodwaters of the Nile allowed farmers to produce enough food to support a growing population. Over time, some members of this early society began to do other things besides farming. Some made pottery. Others crafted jewelry. Some became soldiers. A few became kings.

About 5,000 years ago, two kingdoms along the Nile were united into one. For most of the next 3,000 years, kings called **pharaohs** ruled the land. The great mass of people farmed the land. They paid a share of their crops to the government. The government's leaders also made them work on important **projects**, or planned activities. These projects included building temples and other monuments. Sometimes the people had to fight in the pharaoh's armies.

The Expansion of Egypt

For centuries, Egypt traded with nearby lands. Merchants carried Egyptian grain and other products to the south. There they traded for luxury goods like gold, ivory, and incense. They also traded to the east for wood from what is now Lebanon.

Around 1500 B.C., the Egyptians decided to expand their area. They took control of lands to the south that held gold and seized areas along the Red Sea that had **myrrh**. This plant substance gives off a pleasing scent. Priests burned it in religious ceremonies. Egypt also conquered the eastern shores of the Mediterranean. That gave them control of the timber there. Egypt's kings gained wealth by taxing conquered peoples.

Religion and Culture in Ancient Egypt

The pharaoh was the head of Egyptian society. He was seen as more than a man. He was thought to be the son of the sun god. The Egyptians practiced polytheism, which is the belief in many gods. The sun god was one of the most important of their gods. His daily journey through the sky brought the warmth needed to grow crops. The pharaoh, Egyptians believed, connected them to the gods. He made sure that they would flourish as a people.

KENNETH GARRETT/National Geographic Stock

Academic Vocabulary

project a planned activity

One of the most famous Egyptian pharaohs was the boy-king Tutankhamen. At 10 years of age, Tutankhamen became ruler of Egypt, but he died unexpectedly nine years later.

▶ **CRITICAL THINKING**
Describing Based on the map, describe the area controlled by ancient Egypt.

Ancient Egypt

Mediterranean Sea

Dead Sea

NILE DELTA
LOWER EGYPT
Giza
30°N
Great Pyramid and Sphinx • Memphis

N
W E
S

Nile R.

EASTERN DESERT

WESTERN DESERT

UPPER EGYPT

Nile Valley

Red Sea

• Thebes

25°N

First Cataract

TROPIC OF CANCER

NUBIA

0   100 miles
0   100 kilometers
Lambert Azimuthal
Equal-Area projection

Second Cataract

30°E   35°E

Egyptians believed in life after death. Because of this belief, the pharaohs had vast tombs built for themselves. The tombs were filled with riches, food, and other goods. These goods were meant to support the pharaohs in the afterlife. When the pharaoh died, his body was preserved as a mummy and placed in the tomb.

At first the tombs were low structures built of bricks. Around 2600 B.C., the first pyramid was built as a tomb. These huge tombs, made of rock, were built by thousands of workers. Later, the pharaohs stopped building pyramids. Instead, workers carved their tombs out of rocky cliffs.

Historians know much about ancient Egypt because the Egyptians had a system of writing. The system, called **hieroglyphics**, used pictures to represent sounds or words.

Influence of Ancient Egypt

The Egyptians made many advances in mathematics and science. They used mathematics to measure farm fields and to figure out taxes. Their studies of the stars and planets led to advances in astronomy. They were masters of engineering as **demonstrated** by their great pyramids and temples.

Academic Vocabulary

demonstrate to show

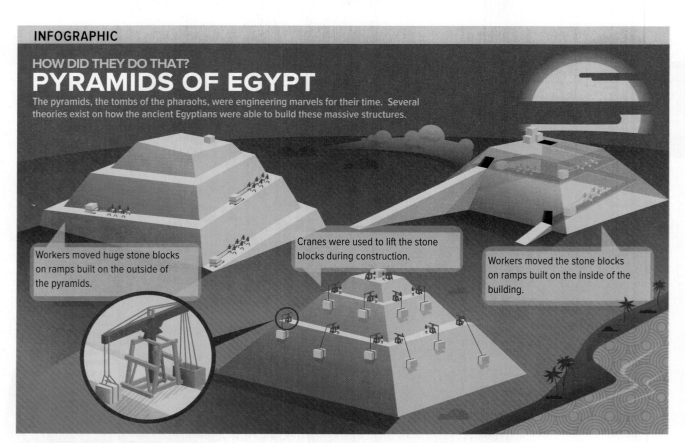

INFOGRAPHIC

HOW DID THEY DO THAT?
PYRAMIDS OF EGYPT
The pyramids, the tombs of the pharaohs, were engineering marvels for their time. Several theories exist on how the ancient Egyptians were able to build these massive structures.

Workers moved huge stone blocks on ramps built on the outside of the pyramids.

Cranes were used to lift the stone blocks during construction.

Workers moved the stone blocks on ramps built on the inside of the building.

BUILDING THE PYRAMIDS
Thousands of people were involved in building a pyramid. Much of the work was done by farmers during the Nile floods, when they could not tend their fields. Surveyors, engineers, carpenters, and stonecutters also lent their skills.

▶ CRITICAL THINKING
Analyzing How might the building of the pyramids have led to advances in science and mathematics?

Some of this knowledge was spread to other areas through trade and conquest. Later, Egypt had one of the world's earliest libraries. It was built in the 200s B.C., when Greece conquered and ruled Egypt. The library stored many important works of ancient literature.

☑ READING PROGRESS CHECK

Determining Central Ideas Why is it important to know about ancient Egypt?

The Middle Ages

GUIDING QUESTION *How was North Africa connected to other areas?*

Today, people use the Internet to contact each other anywhere in the world. In ancient times, people had to make contact in person. The people of North Africa used the Mediterranean Sea to make this contact with other peoples. Sometimes they were joined by trade. Other times they were joined by conflict.

Carthage and Rome

Western North Africa was first visited by other Mediterranean peoples in the 600s B.C. At that time, traders from what is now Lebanon sailed southwest across the Mediterranean. They built new settlements in many areas. One was a city in what is now Tunisia. They called it Carthage. Within about 200 years, the city had grown powerful. It controlled North Africa from modern Tunisia to Morocco. It also ruled parts of modern Spain and Italy.

In the 200s B.C. and 100s B.C., Carthage fought three wars with the Roman Empire. In the last war, Rome defeated Carthage and destroyed the city. Rome, then, came to control western North Africa. Eventually, Rome conquered Egypt, as well.

The waters of a Roman bath reflect the ruins of the city of Leptis Magna in Libya. The Romans made Leptis Magna one of the most beautiful cities in North Africa during the A.D. 100s.

Identifying What ancient city fought Rome for control of much of North Africa?

Guenter Fischer/Getty Images

During Roman times, many North Africans **converted**, or changed, religions. Because the Roman Empire had adopted Christianity, many North Africans converted to this religion. Others followed their native religions. Except for religion, Roman rule had little effect on native North Africans. Most people continued to live as before. Millions of Berbers who live in western North Africa today are descended from these native people.

Rise of Islam

The Roman Empire fell in the A.D. 400s. Afterward, several local kingdoms formed in North Africa. In the A.D. 600s, though, a new influence emerged in the region. The religion of Islam was founded on the Arabian Peninsula by the prophet Muhammad in A.D. 632. Followers of this religion—called Muslims—began to conquer other lands. By A.D. 642, they had conquered Egypt. By A.D. 705, they ruled all of North Africa. Islam, like Judaism and Christianity, is a monotheistic religion. **Monotheism** means belief in just one god.

Religion plays a central role in the lives of most North Africans today. These Muslim women gather for prayer in the main square of El Mansûra, a city in Egypt's Nile delta.

▶ CRITICAL THINKING

Describing How did Islam develop during the century after Muhammad?

Islamic Rule

The Muslim empire was ruled by the **caliph**. This figure had political and religious authority. Caliphs had trouble keeping control over North Africa, however. By the A.D. 800s, separate Berber kingdoms had arisen in parts of the region. These kingdoms often fought one another. Some gained control of most of North Africa. Others only ruled parts of the area.

An Islamic group known as the Fatamids arose in Egypt in the A.D. 1000s. Its rulers expanded Cairo and made it their capital. The city became a center of Muslim learning and trade.

Islamic Culture

At first, Berbers and Egyptians resisted the Islamic religion. By the A.D. 1000s, though, most of them had converted. They also adopted the Arabic language. This language and Islamic learning linked North Africa to the Muslim world. It also helped unite the cultures and people of North Africa and Southwest Asia. Considerable similarities between the regions exist to this day, more than 1,000 years later.

☑ READING PROGRESS CHECK

Identifying Point of View Did the Roman or the Islamic empire have more impact on North Africa? Why do you think so?

The Modern Era

GUIDING QUESTION *What leads people to revolt against a government?*

North Africans formed their own countries in the late 1900s. In recent decades, these countries have changed in far-reaching ways. Often, unrest accompanied the changes.

Foreign Rule

In the 1500s, North Africa began to fall under the rule of foreign armies. The Portuguese and Spanish captured parts of Morocco. The Ottoman Empire, based in modern Turkey, took the rest.

The 1800s saw Ottoman power weaken and Europeans move into North Africa. France began to conquer Algeria in 1830. Although it took several decades, by the late 1800s France controlled that area and Tunisia, too. Some Europeans who settled in these areas grew wealthy. Muslim natives, though, were largely poor. In the early 1900s, France and Spain split control of Morocco. At about the same time, Italy seized Libya.

Egypt kept its independence for much of the 1800s. Its kings tried to build a more modern state. One of the accomplishments was completing construction of the Suez Canal in 1869.

MAP SKILLS

1 **PLACES AND REGIONS**
Which North African country was the first to become independent?

2 **HUMAN GEOGRAPHY**
How was Libya governed before independence?

North African Independence

EUROPE

ASIA

ATLANTIC OCEAN

Strait of Gibraltar

Rabat

Algiers

Tunis

Medjerda R.

TUNISIA
(1956, from France)

Tripoli

Mediterranean Sea

Suez Canal

Oum er Rbia

MOROCCO
(1956, from France)

ALGERIA
(1962, from France)

Cairo

LIBYA
(1951, from United Nations trusteeship, administered by British and French governors)

EGYPT
(1922, from U.K.)

Nile R.

Red Sea

WESTERN SAHARA
(Morocco)

TROPIC OF CANCER

Lake Nasser

20°N

40°N

30°N

N
W E
S

0   500 miles
0   500 kilometers
Lambert Azimuthal Equal-Area projection

AFRICA

(1962, from France) Date of independence, ruling power

10°W   0°   10°E   20°E   30°E

In 1987 soldiers marched in a parade in Tripoli, Libya's capital, to celebrate the rule of Muammar al-Qaddafi. Opponents finally overthrew the military dictator in 2011.

▶ CRITICAL THINKING

Analyzing Why was Qaddafi able to rule Libya for so long? Why was he finally overthrown?

The Suez Canal quickly became a vital waterway. Because of the canal's importance, though, other nations wanted to control Egypt. In 1882 Britain sent troops to Egypt. Kings continued to rule, but the British were the real power in the country.

Independence

Many North Africans resented European control. Independence movements arose across the region in the early 1900s. They gained strength after World War II. Italy had been defeated in the war, and France and Britain were severely weakened.

Egypt broke free of foreign control first. In 1952 a group of Egyptian army officers revolted against the king and the British. They created an independent republic, and they put the government in charge of the economy.

Algerians had to fight long and hard for independence. They rebelled against French rule starting in 1954. Not until 1962 did they succeed in ousting the French. Many Europeans fled the country after independence was achieved.

Military leaders also took control of Libya in 1969. They were led by Muammar al-Qaddafi. He remained in control of the nation—and its oil wealth—for more than 40 years. Tunisia and Morocco have avoided military rule. Tunisia has been a republic since gaining independence in 1959. Morocco has had a monarchy since gaining freedom from France in 1956.

Recent Decades

Independence has not always led to success for the countries of North Africa. Algeria has been plagued by unrest among Islamic political groups. Tunisia's government was often accused by the U.S. government of neglecting the rights of the nation's people. Libyan leader Qaddafi had a harsh **regime**, or style of government. Dissent was suppressed, and the government controlled all aspects of life. Qaddafi angered other nations by supporting terrorist groups.

Meanwhile, other problems built up in these nations. High population growth strained their economies. Corrupt governments fueled unrest. In recent years, Muslim **fundamentalists** have led a movement for the people and government to follow the strict laws of Islam. They also reject Western influences on Muslim society.

These problems came to a head in late 2010 in a series of revolts called the Arab Spring. The revolts began in Tunisia, where widespread unrest succeeded in convincing the longtime president to step down from power early in 2011. Tunisians celebrated as a new government took office.

Emboldened by this success, many Egyptians took to the streets. For more than two weeks, thousands of Egyptians turned out every day in Cairo and other cities to protest the government. This revolt also succeeded. In February 2011, Egypt's longtime president Hosni Mubarak gave up power. A group of officers took control and promised to create a new government run by civilians. In 2012 Egyptians voted in the first free presidential election in the country's history.

Unrest also arose in Morocco. There, the king agreed to several reforms that would give more power to the people.

The Arab Spring revolt also reached Libya. The government cracked down on protests. That response angered more Libyans. A **civil war**, or a fight for control of the government, broke out. After months of fighting, the rebels succeeded in taking control of the country. In October of 2011, they killed Qaddafi, and his remaining supporters gave up.

☑ READING PROGRESS CHECK

Determining Central Ideas How did the people of North Africa react to European control of the region? Compare that reaction to how North Africans reacted to rule by the Islamic Empire.

FOLDABLES
Study Organizer

Include this lesson's information in your Foldable®.

LESSON 2 REVIEW

Reviewing Vocabulary
1. How were the *pharaohs* of ancient Egypt and the *caliphs* of the Muslim empire similar? How were they different?

Answering the Guiding Questions
2. ***Identifying Point of View*** Why did the people of Egypt not revolt against the pharaoh even though they had to pay high taxes and work on major building projects?

3. ***Integrating Visual Information*** Look at a map of the world. What routes do you think the people of North Africa traveled to trade with the people of Southwest Asia in the Middle Ages?

4. ***Determining Central Ideas*** What has caused unrest in North Africa in recent years?

5. ***Informative/Explanatory Writing*** Write a summary of the events and results of the Arab Spring.

Lesson 3
Life in North Africa

(l to r)Franz Marc Frei/Lonely Planet Images/Getty Images; (2)Andrew Woodley/Alamy; (3)©Adam Reynolds/Corbis; (4)©Claudia Wiens/Corbis; (5)©Nichole Sobecki/Corbis

ESSENTIAL QUESTION • *Why do conflicts develop?*

IT MATTERS BECAUSE
North Africa is experiencing political changes.

Culture of North Africa

GUIDING QUESTION *What is daily life like in North Africa?*

The vast majority of people in North Africa practice the Islamic religion. Five times a day, the call to prayer rings out from mosques across North Africa, and devout Muslims stop what they are doing to say prayers. Each week on Friday, millions assemble in the mosques for Friday prayer and to hear a sermon. Once a year during Ramadan, the ninth month of the Islamic calendar, Muslims fast (do not eat) from dawn to dusk.

The People

Three main groups—Egyptians, Berbers, and Arabs—make up the population of North Africa. The region has a varied culture. Egypt's ancient heritage looms over that nation just as the pyramids tower over some of its cities. French influence can be seen from Morocco to Tunisia. Although Arab Muslim culture dominates, some Berber traditions continue.

Although most people are Muslims, some Christians and Jews also live in the region. One in 10 of Egypt's people are Christians. Most of them belong to the Coptic Christian church, which formed in the A.D. 400s.

Of the North African nations, Libya has the highest rate of urbanization. More than three of every four Libyans live in an urban area. Only about half of Egypt's people are city dwellers.

Daily Life

Patterns of daily life differ between the cities and the countryside. The region's cities tend to be busy, bustling centers of industry and trade. They also are a blend of traditional cultures and modern life.

Towns and cities of North Africa show no signs of having been planned. Instead, they have grown steadily over the centuries. Streets are narrow and curving. Some built-up areas extend into the surrounding rural farming areas.

Cairo, Egypt, is by far North Africa's largest city, with more than 9.3 million people. The next three largest cities are Algiers, Algeria; Casablanca, Morocco; and Tunis, Tunisia. Combined they have fewer people than Cairo.

Cairo's buildings reflect its more than 1,000-year history. The waterfront along the Nile River boasts gleaming modern skyscrapers and parks. Throughout the city are historic mosques—Islamic places of worship. Tourists flock to the city's famous museums, though they have to endure traffic jams to get there. A jumble of old apartment buildings spreads to the west. Beyond them, a million or so people live in mud huts in a massive poor neighborhood called "the City of the Dead."

An important feature of North African cities is the **souk**, or open-air market. Here, businesspeople set up stalls where they sell food, craft products, and other goods. Singers and acrobats perform here and there in the markets, especially at night.

Life in rural areas follows a different pattern. Farming villages in rural Egypt can be as small as 500 people. Families live in homes built of mud brick with few windows. Each morning, the **fellaheen**—poor farmers of Egypt—walk to work in the fields outside the village.

Spices are among the many products sold at the Khan el-Khalili, the largest souk in Cairo, Egypt. Founded in 1382, the marketplace is a network of streets lined with shops, coffeehouses, and restaurants.

▶ CRITICAL THINKING

Describing How did cities in North Africa develop?

A family enjoys a meal at home in the town of Matmata in southern Tunisia. The Berber town is known for its dwellings that are built underground in cave-like structures. To create a home, a resident digs a wide pit in the ground and then hollows out caves around the pit's edge. The caves serve as rooms, which are connected by trench-like corridors.

Many use hand tools and rely on muscle power or animal power. At day's end, they return home.

Farms in Libya are clustered around oases. These communities are small because so little land can be farmed. In Morocco, many farmers live in the well-watered highland areas. They build terraces on steep hillsides to plant their crops.

Some rural dwellers still live like nomads. This is the same kind of life Berbers have followed for centuries. They tend herds of sheep, goats, or camels. They move from place to place in search of food and water for their herds. Some settle in one area for part of the year to grow grains.

Food

Moroccan food has gained fame around the world for its rich and complex flavors. The base of many Moroccan meals is **couscous**, small nuggets of semolina wheat that are steamed. Rich stews of meat and vegetables are poured over it. This style of cooking is also common in Algeria and Tunisia.

Sandwiches in this region are often made with flat pieces of pita bread. They might include grilled pieces of lamb, chicken, or fish. Falafel is made from ground, dried beans and formed into cakes and fried. Pigeon is also popular in Egypt and Morocco.

Arts

The arts in North Africa reflect the influence of Islam. The Islamic religion forbids art that shows the figures of animals or humans. Folk art, like weaving and embroidery, has intricate patterns but no figures. These patterns are also used to decorate buildings.

Andrew Woodley/Alamy

Many young people in North Africa are attracted to Western music and movies. This has provoked an angry response among some strict Muslims. In Algeria, some artists have left the country because of harsh criticism. Egypt has long been a center of television and film production. Its shows and movies are seen throughout the Arab world.

Languages and Literature

Arabic is the official language of all five countries in North Africa. French is prominent in Morocco, Algeria, and Tunisia. French and English are most often heard in the region's cities, but Berber languages are more common in rural areas.

As the largest Arabic-speaking country, Egypt has played an important part in the literature of the region. Egyptian writers have explored themes like the impact of influences from Western culture. Novelist Naguib Mahfouz, who wrote more than 30 novels and hundreds of stories, achieved worldwide recognition when he won the Nobel Prize for Literature in 1988.

☑ **READING PROGRESS CHECK**

Identifying What is an example of the influence of Islam on daily life in North Africa?

Challenges in North Africa

GUIDING QUESTION *What challenges face North Africa?*

Standards of living vary widely across the region and even within countries. In addition to economic issues, the region faces significant social challenges.

Economic Issues

When oil was discovered in Libya, Muammar al-Qaddafi, the leader of the country, said that a major goal was to provide social benefits to everyone. That did not happen. The income gained from selling oil did not reach most of the country's people. When Qaddafi fell from power in 2011, Libyans hoped that their lives would improve, but progress started slowly.

Algeria has tried to shift its economy away from the **emphasis** on the sale of oil and natural gas. The government keeps tight control of businesses, however. As a result, companies from other countries are not willing to invest there.

©Adam Reynolds/Corbis

Academic Vocabulary

emphasis importance

A craftsperson in Cairo, Egypt, uses copper thread to embroider Arabic writing onto fabric. Muslims prize the art of beautiful writing, which they use to express the words of the Quran, the Islamic holy book.

▶ **CRITICAL THINKING**
Determining Central Ideas
How has Islam influenced the arts of North Africa?

Morocco's economy is the most **diversified**. A diversified economy includes a mix of many different economic activities. The people of the country engage in mining, some manufacturing, farming, and tourism. Poverty and unemployment are widespread in Morocco, however.

In recent years, thousands have left the region for Europe. They move mostly to Spain and France looking for jobs. Morocco, Algeria, and Tunisia have lost the most people.

Social Issues

High population growth is a major concern in Libya and Egypt. This growth rate contributes to crowding and inadequate health care, as well as poverty. A large share of the population in the region is 14 years old or younger. This is especially true in Egypt and Libya. These countries will have to work hard to develop their economies so that today's young people can find jobs in the future.

In February 2012, U.S. Secretary of State Hillary Clinton addressed young people in Tunisia and across the region. She cited the work they did to bring about the massive changes of the Arab Spring. Clinton warned, though, that it would take a long time and hard work to build the country's economy and increase jobs for young people. The U.S. government has pledged money to several countries to help them accomplish these goals.

Another issue is literacy. Libya has the highest literacy rate in the region: 89 percent of Libyans can read and write. The literacy rate is

Workers load freight wagons at a phosphate mine in southern Tunisia. **North Africa has rich deposits of phosphates, which are mineral salts used to make fertilizer.**

▶ CRITICAL THINKING
Analyzing What social and economic challenges does North Africa face?

mediacolor's/Alamy

much lower in the other North African countries. Literacy is most serious in Morocco, where little more than one-half of Moroccans can read and write. A very low literacy rate among women is a major **factor**, or cause, for this trend. More than 65 percent of Moroccan men can read and write; less than 40 percent of that nation's women can. Literacy among women is about 20 percent lower than among men in the other four countries of the region, as well. This gap hinders the ability of the countries to build strong economies.

✔ READING PROGRESS CHECK

Identifying Point of View What might happen in North Africa if young people grow impatient with the slow rate of economic growth? Why?

North Africa's Future

GUIDING QUESTION *How will North Africa address the problems it faces?*

Powerful new social movements have swept through the region of North Africa in recent years. They have led to major political changes in three countries and put pressures on the governments of the other two.

Political Issues

Two political forces are strong in the region of North Africa. One is a push for democracy. Many North Africans have grown more and more frustrated with their leaders. They think the leaders focused more on building their own power than on building the economy and improving their countries. Many question the government's harsh treatment of people who criticize their countries' leaders. Some leaders are calling for the different groups to learn to work together to avoid the conflicts that pull societies apart.

Women students meet for class at Cairo, Egypt's Al-Azhar University, the world's chief center for Islamic learning. In Egypt, women may work outside the home, attend universities, vote, and run for office. However, opportunities for women still lag behind those for men in education and the labor market.

▶ CRITICAL THINKING
Analyzing How does the issue of women's literacy affect economies in North Africa?

Academic Vocabulary

factor a cause

©Claudia Wiens/Corbis

Young people in Benghazi, Libya, yell protest slogans against dictator Muammar al-Qaddafi. Clashes between street demonstrators and armed government forces in February 2011 led to much bloodshed. A civil war broke out, and rebel groups eventually overthrew Qaddafi.

▶ CRITICAL THINKING

Describing What happened in Libya after the fall of Qaddafi?

The second force was an increase in Islamic fundamentalism. Some strict Muslims want laws changed to conform to the rules of Islam. They want to see an end to Western influences on their culture. The political party of the Muslim Brotherhood gained a majority in Egypt's parliament in the 2011 elections. It also won a majority in Morocco and a large share of seats in Tunisia. These forces helped bring about the Arab Spring of 2010 and 2011. They have left conditions across the region uncertain.

Egypt began writing a new **constitution** in 2012. A constitution is a set of rules for a nation and its government. Egypt's new government could give more power to the parliament, the lawmaking body. It is not clear how well this new government will work or what groups will control it, though.

For nearly 20 years, Algeria has undergone brutal conflict between Islamist groups and the government and its forces. As many as 100,000 people have died in the fighting. As in Morocco, the government was able to keep power after the Arab Spring, but it had to promise to reform the political system.

By 2012, Libya's victorious rebels were working on making a new government. They also faced the need to rebuild much of the country after the civil war. In 2012, leaders in eastern Libya said they wanted self-rule in their part of the country. Although they said that they did not wish to divide the country or to keep their area's oil wealth for themselves, the move raised the possibility of continued conflict in Libya.

Islam in the Modern World

Many Muslims in the region worry about the impact of Western culture on their lands. They think that Western entertainment conflicts with Islamic values. They also disagree with Western ideas about women's rights.

Women in North Africa generally have more rights than those in other Muslim lands. In Tunisia, for instance, they can own businesses and have their own bank accounts. About half of all university students in Tunisia are women. Women may lose some of these rights if extreme Muslim leaders take control of the governments.

Several million of Egypt's Coptic Christians have grown more worried about their position in recent years as well. Some Muslim extremists have attacked them and bombed churches. Early in 2012, the longtime head of the Coptic church died. He had led the church for nearly 40 years in relative peace until near the end of his life. His death increased the uncertainty for Copts in that area.

Relations with Other Nations

Egypt broke ranks with other Muslim nations in 1979 when it signed a peace treaty with Israel. It has also developed close ties with the United States since then. That friendship has come under increasing criticism from Muslim fundamentalists. Morocco has also had close relations with the United States. Its government has been criticized for this as well.

These situations raise more questions about what will happen if Muslim conservatives gain power. Will the new governments reject close ties with the United States? Will they take steps against Israel?

The situations in Algeria and Libya also are uncertain. Will new governments there be less willing to sell oil to the United States? For what purposes will they use the money they earn from selling oil? The answers to these questions will help to shape the future of North Africa and the world.

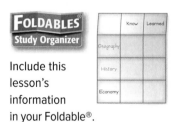

Include this lesson's information in your Foldable®.

☑ **READING PROGRESS CHECK**

Analyzing Why were the results of the Arab Spring different in Algeria and Morocco compared with the other countries of the region?

LESSON 3 REVIEW

Reviewing Vocabulary

1. Is it important for an economy to be *diversified*? Why or why not?

Answering the Guiding Questions

2. *Determining Central Ideas* Why do you think many Muslims worry about the impact of Western culture on their lands?

3. *Describing* How is the relatively young population connected to the economic issues in these nations?

4. *Analyzing* About half of Egypt's people live in rural areas. Most of them are farmers. What impact does that have on Egypt's economy? Why?

5. *Identifying Point of View* Why is the political situation in North Africa important to the United States?

6. *Argument Writing* Do you think the most serious issues facing North Africa are political, social, or cultural? Write a paragraph explaining why.

Directions: Write your answers on a separate piece of paper.

1 Use your **FOLDABLES** to explore the Essential Question.
INFORMATIVE/EXPLANATORY WRITING Briefly describe the population distribution in the region of North Africa and suggest a likely reason for the distribution.

2 **21st Century Skills**
INTEGRATING VISUAL INFORMATION With a partner, create a set of flash cards showing an outline of the five North African countries combined and outlines of the individual countries. Make five separate cards with the names of the capital cities. Devise a game using the flash cards, and exchange games with another pair of classmates. After playing both games, work with the other pair to turn the flash card games into a computer game.

3 **Thinking Like a Geographer**
INTEGRATING VISUAL INFORMATION On an outline map of North Africa, indicate the region's climates. Include the rain shadow areas on the map key.

4 **GEOGRAPHY ACTIVITY**

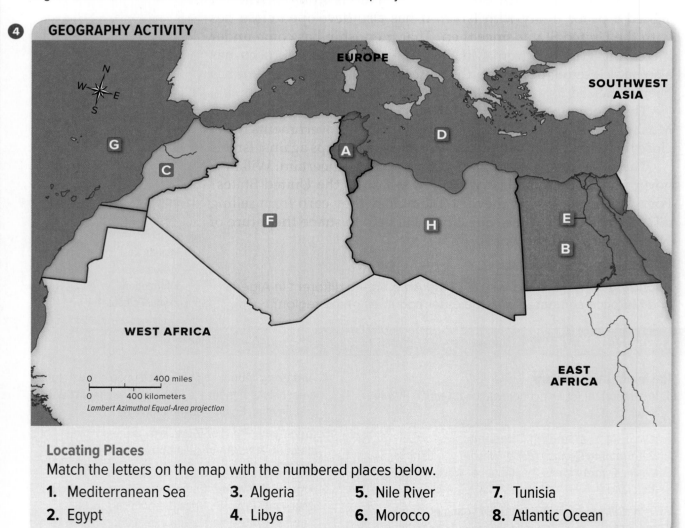

Locating Places
Match the letters on the map with the numbered places below.

1. Mediterranean Sea   3. Algeria   5. Nile River   7. Tunisia
2. Egypt   4. Libya   6. Morocco   8. Atlantic Ocean

Chapter 6 ASSESSMENT

REVIEW THE GUIDING QUESTIONS

Directions: Choose the best answer for each question.

1 One nickname for ancient Egypt was
A. serpent of the sea.
B. wadi of the floods.
C. gift of the Nile.
D. delta dawn.

2 Of the North African countries, Libya has the most
F. olives.
G. oil.
H. water.
I. cedarwood.

3 Hieroglyphics were
A. equipment used for building pyramids.
B. Muslim political and religious leaders.
C. pictures that represented sounds or words.
D. spices burned for religious ceremonies.

4 The Berbers and Egyptians became linked to the Muslim world in the A.D. 1000s by
F. the defeat at Carthage.
G. the power of the caliphs.
H. the Arabic language and Islamic learning.
I. the pharaoh's desire for more territory.

5 The official language of the five North African nations is
A. Coptic.
B. French.
C. Afrikaner.
D. Arabic.

6 Today's Islamic fundamentalists in North Africa want to
F. return to their families' farms.
G. convert the citizens of Israel.
H. end Western influence on the Islamic culture.
I. turn around the Tunisian economy.

DBQ ANALYZING DOCUMENTS

7 **CITING TEXT EVIDENCE** Read the following passage about recent changes in Libya's government:

"In March 2011, a Transitional National Council (TNC) was formed . . . with the stated aim of overthrowing the Qaddafi regime and guiding the country to democracy. . . . Anti-Qaddafi forces in August 2011 captured the capital, Tripoli. In mid-September, the [United Nations] General Assembly voted to recognize the TNC as the legitimate interim governing body of Libya."

—from CIA World Factbook, "Libya"

How did the Transitional National Council view its role in Libya?

A. as an ally of Qaddafi
C. as a temporary government

B. as supporters of Libya's former king
D. as social reformers

8 **ANALYZING** What happened to the Qaddafi government in 2011?

F. It remained in control of the country.
H. It forged an alliance with the TNC.

G. It relocated to a new capital.
I. It fell out of power.

SHORT RESPONSE

"Morocco, on account of the invasions of Arabs and the exterior adventures of Moorish kings, was strongly influenced by Middle Eastern culture and the culture of the Andaluz [Muslim-ruled Spain]. The Arabs learned [cooking] secrets from the Persians and brought them to Morocco; from Senegal and other lands south of the Sahara came caravans of spices. Even the Turks made a contribution."

—from Paula Wolfert, *Couscous and Other Good Food From Morocco* (1973)

9 **DETERMINING CENTRAL IDEAS** What is the main idea of this passage?

10 **DESCRIBING** What kinds of contact by different groups led to these influences on Moroccan culture?

EXTENDED RESPONSE

11 **INFORMATIVE/EXPLANATORY WRITING** Research the Arab Spring of 2011. Write an essay contrasting the current situation in the countries that were involved in the Arab Spring with their situation before the upheaval. Did the "spring" last? Did the citizens of these countries gain or lose what they were trying to achieve? Are their lives better or worse today than they were before 2011? Do any of them now have a stable, democratic government?

Need Extra Help?

If You've Missed Question	❶	❷	❸	❹	❺	❻	❼	❽	❾	❿	⓫
Review Lesson	1	1	2	2	3	3	2	2	2	2	2

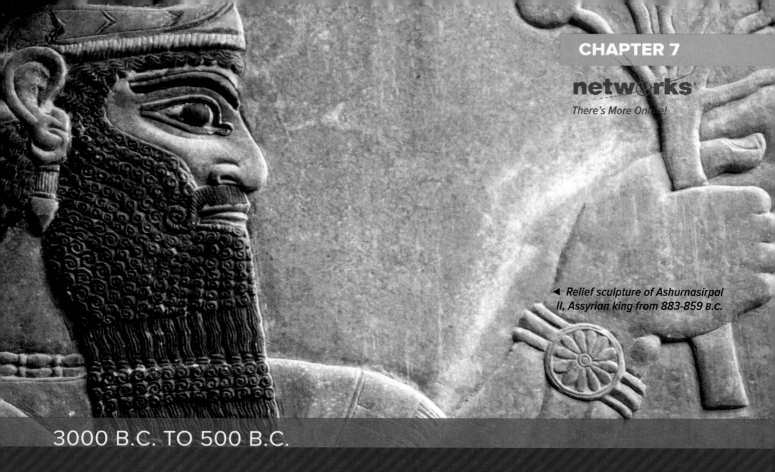

◄ *Relief sculpture of Ashurnasirpal II, Assyrian king from 883-859 B.C.*

3000 B.C. TO 500 B.C.

Mesopotamia

THE STORY MATTERS ...

Have you ever watched a large subdivision of homes being built? Did you notice solid structures beginning to appear on what was once only flat land? Assyrian King Ashurnasirpal II built such a project during his reign from 883–859 B.C. He took the small town of Nimrud and made it his capital. When he was finished, the city occupied about 900 acres. Around it, Ashurnasirpal II built a wall 120 feet thick, 42 feet high, and 5 miles long. The gates were guarded by two huge human-headed winged bulls. Parts of these gates can be seen in the New York Metropolitan Museum today. When he finished the city, the king held a festival attended by about 70,000 people. Here, he said, were "the happy people of all lands together. …"

LESSON 1
The Sumerians

LESSON 2
Mesopotamian Empires

ESSENTIAL QUESTIONS

- How does geography influence the way people live?
- Why does conflict develop?

Mesopotamia
Place & Time: 3000 B.C. to 500 B.C.

Mesopotamia extended from the Tigris River to the Euphrates River. The Sumerians were the first settlers in the region. They are the people who developed the world's first civilization. Soon several civilizations appeared in Mesopotamia. This area was called the Fertile Crescent because of its shape.

Step Into the Place

MAP FOCUS There were many Mesopotamian cities that arose along the Tigris and Euphrates Rivers.

1 PLACE What river flowed through the western side of Mesopotamia?

2 LOCATION What is the approximate distance from Nineveh to Ur?

3 MOVEMENT To what larger body of water did the people living along these rivers sail?

4 CRITICAL THINKING
Making Inferences Why do you think many cities in Mesopotamia developed near rivers?

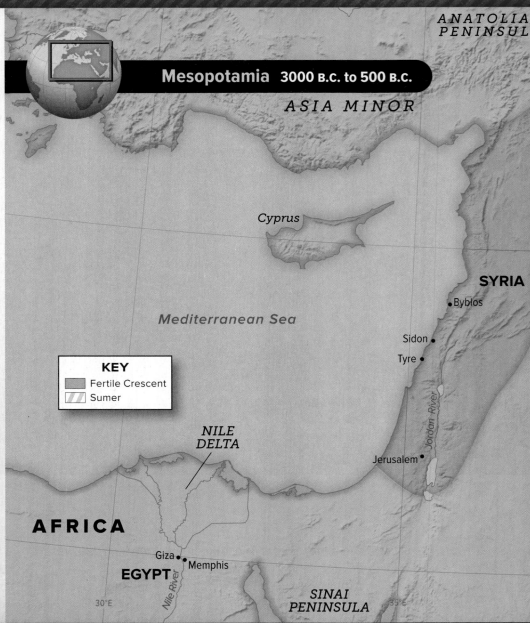

ANATOLIA PENINSULA

Mesopotamia 3000 B.C. to 500 B.C.

ASIA MINOR

Cyprus

Mediterranean Sea

SYRIA
Byblos
Sidon
Tyre

KEY
- Fertile Crescent
- Sumer

Jordan River

NILE DELTA

Jerusalem

AFRICA

Giza • Memphis

EGYPT

Nile River

SINAI PENINSULA

30°E   35°E

Step Into the Time

TIME LINE Place these events in order, starting with the earliest: Assyrians control Mesopotamia, settlements develop along the Indus River, Sumerians invent cuneiform, and first Olympic Games take place.

c. 3000 B.C. City-states arise in Sumer

c. 3200 B.C. Sumerians invent cuneiform writing system

c. 2340 B.C. Sargon conquers Sumer

c. 1792 B.C. Hammurabi becomes king of Babylonian Empire

MESOPOTAMIA
THE WORLD

3000 B.C.   2000 B.C.

c. 2700 B.C. Chinese master art of silk weaving

c. 2300 B.C. Ceramics are produced in Central America

c. 1800 B.C. Egyptians use mathematics for architecture

c. 2500 B.C. Settlements develop along Indus River

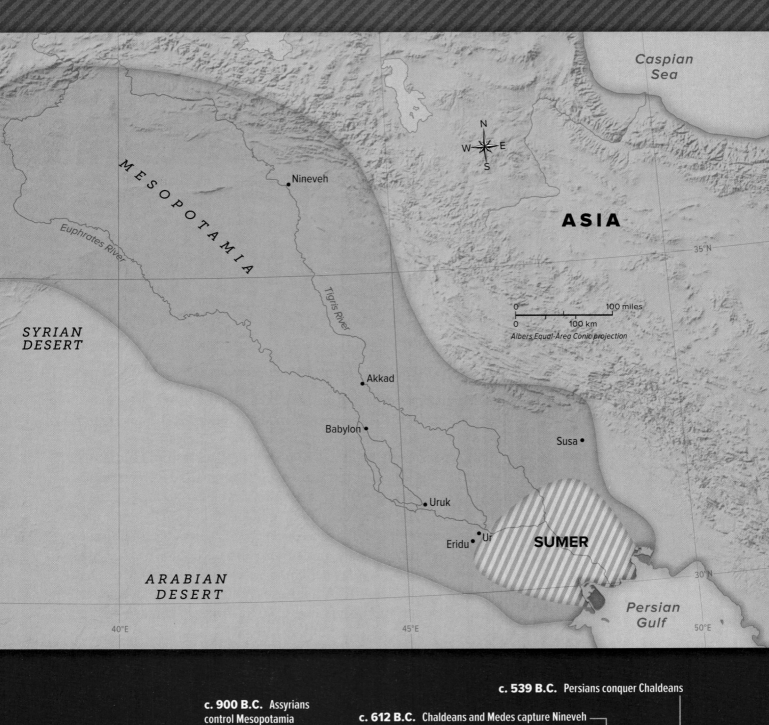

Caspian
Sea

MESOPOTAMIA

Euphrates River

Nineveh

ASIA

35°N

SYRIAN
DESERT

Tigris River

Akkad

Babylon

Susa

Uruk

ARABIAN
DESERT

Eridu • Ur

SUMER

40°E

45°E

30°N

Persian
Gulf

50°E

0   100 miles
0   100 km
Albers Equal-Area Conic projection

c. 539 B.C. Persians conquer Chaldeans

c. 900 B.C. Assyrians
control Mesopotamia

c. 612 B.C. Chaldeans and Medes capture Nineveh

1000 B.C.   900 B.C.   800 B.C.   700 B.C.   600 B.C.

LESSON 1
The Sumerians

ESSENTIAL QUESTION

• How does geography influence the way people live?

IT MATTERS BECAUSE

The Sumerians made important advances in areas such as farming and writing that laid the foundation for future civilizations.

The First Civilizations in Mesopotamia

GUIDING QUESTION *Why did people settle in Mesopotamia?*

Civilizations first developed about 3000 B.C. in the river valleys of Mesopotamia (MEH·suh·puh·TAY·mee·uh), Egypt, India, and China. Throughout history, the need to have water for drinking and growing crops influenced where people settled. Although there were differences among the early civilizations, they were alike in many ways. As these early civilizations developed, people formed social classes. The social class people belonged to partly depended on their occupations. They did specialized types of work. Using improved technology, they made more and better goods. They set up governments to pass laws, defend their land, and carry out large building projects. The people of these civilizations also developed systems of values and beliefs that gave meaning to their lives.

The Two Rivers

Mesopotamia, the earliest known civilization, developed in what is now southern Iraq (ih·RAHK). Mesopotamia means "the land between the rivers" in Greek. The civilization began on the plain between the Tigris (TY·gruhs) and the Euphrates (yu·FRAY·teez) Rivers.

Reading**HELP**DESK

Taking Notes: *Identifying*

On a diagram like this one, identify two major inventions of the Sumerians.

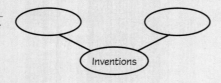

Inventions

Content Vocabulary

• silt	• city- state	• cuneiform
• irrigation	• polytheism	• scribe
• surplus	• ziggurat	• epic

These rivers are nearly **parallel** to each other and flow more than 1,000 miles (1,600 km). They run southeast from the mountains of southeastern Asia to the Persian (PUR·zhuhn) Gulf.

Mesopotamia itself was located in the eastern part of the larger Fertile Crescent. This curving strip of good farmland extends from the Mediterranean (mehd·uh·tuh·RAY·nee·uhn) Sea to the Persian Gulf. The Fertile Crescent includes parts of the modern countries of Turkey, Syria, Iraq, Lebanon, Israel, and Jordan.

Early Valley Dwellers

For thousands of years, clues to Mesopotamia's history lay buried among its ruins and piles of rubble. In the 1800s, archaeologists began to dig up many buildings and artifacts. These finds revealed much about early Mesopotamia.

Historians believe that people first settled Mesopotamia about 7000 B.C. The first settlers were hunters and herders. By about 4000 B.C., some of these groups had moved to the plain of the Tigris-Euphrates valley. They built farming villages along the two rivers.

Taming the Rivers

Early Mesopotamian farmers used water from the Tigris and Euphrates Rivers to water their fields. However, the farmers could not always rely on the rivers for their needs. Little or no rain fell in the summer. As a result, the rivers were often low. The farmers did not have enough water to plant crops in the fall.

Irrigation canals help farmers grow crops in areas that would otherwise be dry and not suitable for farming.

During the spring harvest, rains and melting snow from the northern mountains caused rivers to overflow their banks. This flooded the plains. Sometimes, unexpected and violent floods swept away crops, homes, and livestock.

Yet farmers in Mesopotamia knew that the floods were also helpful. Flooded rivers were filled with **silt**, or small particles of soil. When the floods ended, silt was left on the banks and plains. The silt proved to be a very good soil for farming.

Over time, people in Mesopotamia learned to build dams to control the seasonal floods. They dug canals that let water flow from a water source to their fields. This method of watering crops is called **irrigation** (IHR·uh·GAY·shuhn).

FLPA/Alamy

---

silt fine particles of fertile soil

irrigation a system that supplies dry land with water through ditches, pipes, or streams

Academic Vocabulary

parallel moving or lying in the same direction and the same distance apart

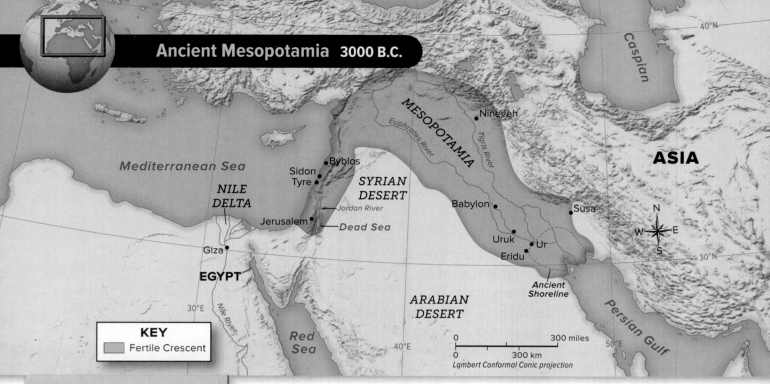

Ancient Mesopotamia 3000 B.C.

KEY
Fertile Crescent

GEOGRAPHY CONNECTION

A number of great civilizations developed in Mesopotamia.

1 LOCATION What city was located in northern Mesopotamia?

2 CRITICAL THINKING
Making Inferences Why do you think Mesopotamia was a good location for the growth of civilization?

Irrigation let these early farmers grow **surpluses** (SUHR·plus·ehz)—or extra amounts—of food. Farmers stored the surpluses for later use.

When food was plentiful, not all people needed to farm. Some became artisans, or skilled workers. They specialized in weaving cloth and making pottery, tools, and weapons.

As artisans made more goods, people's lives changed. People began to live together in places that favored trade. Small farming villages grew into cities. By 3000 B.C., several cities developed in Sumer (SOO·mer), a region in southern Mesopotamia.

✔ **PROGRESS CHECK**

Explaining How did floods sometimes help farmers?

Sumer's Civilization

GUIDING QUESTION *What was life like in Sumer?*

Sumer's people were known as Sumerians. They built the first cities in Southwest Asia, including Ur (uhr), Uruk (OO· rook), and Eridu (ER·i·doo). These cities became centers of civilization that controlled the lower part of the Tigris and Euphrates valleys.

ReadingHELPDESK

surplus an amount that is left over after a need has been met

city-state a city that governs itself and its surrounding territory

polytheism a belief in more than one god

City-States Arise

Sumer's cities were surrounded by mudflats and patches of scorching desert. The harsh landscape made it hard to travel by land and communicate with other groups. This meant that each city was largely cut off from its neighbors.

As a result, Sumerian cities became independent. The people of each city raised their own crops and made their own goods. As the cities grew, they gained political and economic control over the lands around them. By doing this, they formed **city-states**. Each city-state had its own government and was not part of any larger governing state. The population of the city-states ranged from about 5,000 to 20,000 people.

Historians think that each Sumerian city-state was protected by a large city wall. Ruins and artifacts have been found by archaeologists that support this theory. Because stone and wood were in short supply, the Sumerians used mud from the rivers as their main building material. They mixed mud with crushed reeds, formed bricks, and left them in the sun to dry. The gates of the wall stayed open during the day but were closed at night for protection. The ruler's palace, a large temple, and other public buildings were located in the center of the city.

Often, these city-states went to war with one another over resources and political borders. Sometimes, they fought to win glory or to gain more territory. During times of peace, city-states traded with each other. They also agreed to help each other by forming alliances (uh·LY·uhns·uhs) to protect their common interests.

Gods, Priests, and Kings

The Sumerian people worshipped many gods, a type of belief known as **polytheism** (PAH·lee·thee·ih·zuhm). These multiple gods played different roles in Sumerian life. The Sumerians thought that some gods had power over parts of nature, such as the rain or the wind. They also believed that some gods guided the things that people did, such as plowing or brick-making. They honored whatever god would help their activity.

Although Sumerians honored all the gods, each city-state claimed one as its own.

In areas where there was little rainfall, farmers watered their fields using irrigation channels.

▶ **CRITICAL THINKING**
Analyzing What other water sources were available in addition to the river?

The ziggurat was built to be visible throughout the city-state. The walls of the ziggurat enclosed the royal warehouses and the city's treasury.

▶ CRITICAL THINKING
Speculating Why do you think the Sumerians would want the ziggurat to be highly visible?

Thinking Like a HISTORIAN

Carved Art

The Sumerians used relief carvings in stone to commemorate feasts and construction projects. Carved cylinder seals were one of the higher art forms of the Sumerians. The cylinders were rolled over wet clay to leave stamped impressions. They also created mosaics of stone, shells, and terra cotta cones.

Reading HELP DESK

To honor its god, a city-state often included a large temple called a **ziggurat** (ZIG·oo·rat). The word *ziggurat* means "to rise high" in the ancient Akkadian (uh·KAY·dee·uhn) language. The very top of the ziggurat was a holy place. It was the god's home, and only special priests were allowed to go there. In the early days, priests of the ziggurat ruled the city-states. Groups of important men helped them govern. Later, Sumerian city-states became monarchies.

Sumerian kings claimed they received their power to rule from the city's god. The first kings were most likely war heroes. Over time, their rule became hereditary. This meant that after a king died, his son took over. In most cases, the wives of kings did not have political power. However, some controlled their own lands.

Social Groups

People in Sumer were organized into social classes. Generally, people remained in the social class into which they were born. Kings, priests, warriors, and government officials belonged to the upper class. The middle class **consisted** of merchants, farmers, fishers, and artisans. The middle class was Sumer's largest social group. Enslaved people made up Sumer's lowest class. Most of these people had been captured in war. Also, criminals and people who could not pay their debts often were enslaved. Enslaved men and women worked for the upper class.

Women and men had different roles in Sumerian society. The basic unit of society was the family. Men were the head of the home. Boys went to school and were trained for a specific job. Sumerian women ran the home, taught their daughters to do the same, and cared for the children. Women had a few civil rights. Some owned businesses. Sumerian law required parents to care for their children. The law also required adult children to care for their parents if their parents needed help.

ziggurat a pyramid-shaped structure with a temple at the top

Academic Vocabulary

consist to be made up of

Reading Strategy: *Summarizing*

When you summarize, you find the main idea of a passage and restate it in your own words. Read the paragraph under the heading "Social Groups." On a separate sheet of paper, summarize the paragraph in one or two sentences.

Farmers and Traders

If you lived in Sumer, you were most likely a farmer. Each farmer had a plot of land located in the area around a city-state. Dams and waterways ran through this farmland. Wheat, barley, and dates were the major crops. Farmers also raised sheep, goats, and pigs.

Trade was another key part of Sumer's economy. The Sumerians did not have some of the goods that they needed. For example, even though many Sumerians were skilled metalworkers, they had to trade with other peoples to obtain most of their metals. Trade routes linked Sumer to places as far away as India and Egypt.

Sumerian merchants went to other lands. They traded wheat, barley, and tools for timber, minerals, and metals. The minerals and metals were then used to make jewelry or tools. For jewelry making, Sumerians valued a red stone called carnelian from India's Indus Valley. They also searched for a blue stone known as lapis lazuli from what is now Afghanistan. Traders returned with iron and silver from present-day Turkey.

✅ **PROGRESS CHECK**

Analyzing Why do you think the Sumerians built cities with walls around them?

Sumerian Contributions

GUIDING QUESTION *What ideas and inventions did Sumerians pass on to other civilizations?*

The Sumerians created the first civilization that had a great influence on history. Later civilizations copied and improved many of the ideas and inventions that began in Sumer. As a result, Mesopotamia has been called the "cradle of civilization." It was the beginning of organized human society.

Writing

Of all the contributions made by Sumerians to the world, writing is perhaps the most important. The writing system they developed was the earliest known system in the world.

Sumerian artisans produced a variety of goods, including jewelry. This piece is made of gold and lapis lazuli.

▶ **CRITICAL THINKING**
Speculating If you were an artisan in ancient times, what would you produce?

This Royal Standard of Ur—the royal design—shows scenes of everyday life in Sumer. *Which methods of travel are shown on this standard?*

(l)DEA/A.DE GREGORIO/De Agostini Picture Library/Getty Images; (b)Fernando Fernández/Age fotostock

Sumerians needed materials for building and making tools. They sailed to other lands to trade for wood logs to take home.

Writing was a way for Sumerians to keep records of their lives and their history. Writing was also a way to share information. They could pass on their ideas to later generations.

Sumerians created a way of writing called **cuneiform** (kyoo· NEE·uh·FAWRM). The cuneiform writing system was made up of about 1,200 different characters. Characters represented such things as names, physical objects, and numbers. Cuneiform was written by cutting wedge-shaped marks into damp clay with a sharp reed. The name *cuneiform* comes from a Latin word meaning "wedge." Sumerians wrote on clay because they did not have paper. Archaeologists have found cuneiform tablets that have provided important information about Mesopotamian history.

Only a few people—mostly boys from wealthy families— learned how to read and write cuneiform. After years of training, some students became **scribes** (SKRYBS), or official record keepers. Scribes wrote documents that recorded much of the everyday life in Mesopotamia, including court records, marriage contracts, business dealings, and important events. Some scribes were judges and government officials.

Sumerians told stories orally for centuries. After developing writing, they were able to record these stories. Their tales praised the gods and warriors for doing great deeds. The world's oldest known story is from Sumer. Written more than

©Gianni Dagli Orti/Corbis

Reading HELP DESK

cuneiform a system of writing developed by the Sumerians that used wedge-shaped marks made in soft clay

scribe a person who copies or writes out documents; often a record keeper

epic a long poem that records the deeds of a legendary or real hero

4,000 years ago and still studied today, this story is called the *Epic of Gilgamesh* (GIHL·guh·MEHSH). An **epic** is a long poem that tells the story of a hero.

Technology and Mathematics

The people of Mesopotamia also made many useful inventions. For example, the Sumerians were the first people to use the wheel. The earliest wheels were solid wood circles made from carved boards that were clamped together. A Sumerian illustration from about 3500 B.C. shows a wheeled vehicle. They built the first carts, which were pulled by donkeys. They also introduced vehicles into military use with the development of the chariot.

For river travel, Sumerians developed the sailboat. They invented a wooden plow to help them in the fields. Artisans made the potter's wheel, which helped to shape clay into bowls and jars. Sumerians were also the first to make bronze out of copper and tin. They used bronze to craft stronger tools, weapons, and jewelry.

The Sumerians also studied mathematics and astronomy. They used geometry to measure the size of fields and to plan buildings. They created a place-value system of numbers based on 60. They also devised tables for calculating division and multiplication. The 60-minute hour, 60-second minute, and 360-degree circle we use today are ideas that came from the Sumerians. Sumerians watched the positions of the stars. It showed them the best times to plant crops and to hold religious ceremonies. They also made a 12-month calendar based on the cycles of the moon.

☑ **PROGRESS CHECK**

Explaining Why did the Sumerians invent a writing system?

Louvre, Paris/Bridgeman Art Library

Sumerian writing etched on stone has been found by archaeologists.

LESSON 1 REVIEW

Review Vocabulary

1. How were *polytheism* and *ziggurats* related in Sumerian civilization?

Answer the Guiding Questions

2. *Describing* Where is the Fertile Crescent located? Where is Mesopotamia located?

3. *Comparing* How were the social classes of Sumer organized?

4. *Identifying* What was the most common role for women in Sumerian society?

5. *Describing* Why were scribes important in Sumerian society?

6. **ARGUMENT** Sumerians developed many inventions. Choose the invention that you think is the most significant and explain why you made this choice.

Epic of Gilgamesh

Gilgamesh ruled Uruk in southern Mesopotamia sometime around 2000 B.C. According to mythology, he was a god and a human. It is believed that Gilgamesh was a harsh ruler until his friendship with Enkidu (EN • kee • doo) taught him to be fair and kind. In this epic poem, Gilgamesh faces many challenges. He suffers many losses and must confront his biggest fear: death. Eventually, Gilgamesh learns he cannot avoid death.

This excerpt tells the story of when Gilgamesh and his friend, Enkidu, decide to become heroes. They set out to kill Humbaba (hum • BAH • bah), a monstrous giant who ruled the cedar forest where gods lived. Humbaba has the face of a lion and his breath ignites fire, while his roar unleashes floods.

Gilgamesh (c. 2000 B.C.)

« Don't be afraid, said Gilgamesh. We are together. There is nothing We should fear.»

—*from* **Gilgamesh: A Verse Narrative**
tr. Herbert Mason

❝ Enkidu was afraid of the forest of Humbaba
And urged him [Gilgamesh] not to go, but he
Was not as strong as Gilgamesh in argument,
And they were friends:

They had **embraced** and made their vow
To stay together always,
No matter what the **obstacle**.
Enkidu tried to hold his fear …

Don't be afraid, said Gilgamesh.
We are together. There is nothing
We should fear.

I learned, Enkidu said, when I lived
With the animals never to go down
Into that forest. I learned that there is death
In Humbaba. Why do you want
To raise his [Humbaba's] anger? …

After three days they reached the edge
Of the forest where Humbaba's watchman stood.
Suddenly it was Gilgamesh who was afraid,
Enkidu … reminded him to be fearless.
The watchman sounded his warning to Humbaba.
The two friends moved slowly toward the forest gate.

When Enkidu touched the gate his hand felt numb,
He could not move his fingers or his wrist,
His face turned pale like someone's witnessing a death[.]

He tried to ask his friend for help
Whom he had just encouraged to move on,
But he could only **stutter** and hold out
His paralyzed hand. ❞

—from *Gilgamesh: A Verse Narrative*, **tr. Herbert Mason**

TEXT: A Verse Narrative: Gilgamesh by Herbert Mason. © 1970 Houghton Mifflin Harcourt
PHOTO: www.BibleLandPictures.com/Alamy

The Gilgamesh epic was written on 12 tablets and discovered in Nineveh, in present-day Iraq. The tablets were found in the library of the Assyrian king Ashurbanipal (ah • shur • BAH • nuh • puhl), who reigned 668–627 B.C.

Analyzing Literature DBQ

1 *Identifying* How many times is death mentioned in this excerpt?

2 *Describing* How do you know that Gilgamesh and Enkidu are friends?

3 *Speculating* Enkidu is left in a risky situation. What do you think happens to him?

Vocabulary

embrace to hug with arms around
obstacle something that stands in the way
stutter an uneven repetition of sounds and words

LESSON 2
Mesopotamian Empires

ESSENTIAL QUESTION

• Why does conflict develop?

IT MATTERS BECAUSE
Mesopotamia's empires greatly influenced other civilizations. Hammurabi's Code even influenced the legal codes of Greece and Rome.

The First Empires

GUIDING QUESTION *How did Mesopotamia's first empires develop?*

By 2400 B.C., Sumer's city-states were weakened by conflict. As the strength of Sumer faded, powerful kingdoms arose in northern Mesopotamia and in neighboring Syria. Seeking new lands, rulers of these kingdoms built empires. An **empire** (EHM·PYR) is a group of many different lands under one ruler. Through conquest and trade, these empires spread their cultures over a wide region.

Who Was Sargon?

The kingdom of Akkad (AK·ad) developed in northern Mesopotamia. Sargon (SAHR·GAHN) was an ambitious leader who ruled the people of Akkad, known as Akkadians (uh·KAY·dee·uhnz). About 2340 B.C., Sargon moved his well-trained armies south. He conquered the remaining Sumerian city-states one by one. Sargon united the conquered territory with Akkad and became known as the king of Sumer and Akkad. In doing so, he formed the world's first empire. Eventually, Sargon extended this empire to include all of the peoples of Mesopotamia. His Mesopotamian empire lasted for more than 200 years before invaders conquered it.

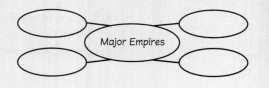

Who Was Hammurabi?

A people called the Amorites lived in the region west of Mesopotamia. In the 1800s B.C., they conquered Mesopotamia and built their own cities. Babylon (BA·buh·luhn) was the grandest of these cities. It was located on the eastern bank of the Euphrates River in what is now Iraq. Around 1792 B.C., the Babylonian king, Hammurabi (HA·muh·RAH·bee), began conquering cities controlled by the Amorites to the north and south. By adding these lands, he created the Babylonian Empire. This new empire stretched north from the Persian Gulf through the Tigris-Euphrates valley and west to the Mediterranean Sea.

Hammurabi's Code

Hammurabi was thought to be a just ruler. He is best known for creating a set of laws for his empire. He posted this law **code** for all to read. The code dealt with crimes, farming, business, marriage, and the family—almost every area of life. The code listed a punishment for each crime.

The Code of Hammurabi was stricter than the old Sumerian laws. The code demanded what became known as "an eye for an eye, and a tooth for a tooth." This means that the punishment for a crime should match the seriousness of the crime. It was meant to limit punishment and do away with blood feuds.

The code also protected the less powerful. For example, it protected wives from abuse by their husbands. Hammurabi's Code influenced later law codes, such as those of Greece and Rome.

✔ **PROGRESS CHECK**

Finding the Main Idea Why was Hammurabi's Code important?

The Assyrian Empire

GUIDING QUESTION *How did the Assyrians influence Southwest Asia?*

The Assyrian Empire arose about 1,000 years after the empire of Hammurabi. Assyria (uh·SIHR·ee·uh) was a large empire, extending into four present-day countries: Turkey, Syria, Iran, and Iraq.

The Assyrians built a large and powerful **military** to defend their hills and fertile valleys. Around 900 B.C., their army began taking over the rest of Mesopotamia.

Interfoto Scans/agefotostock

---

empire a large territory or group of many territories governed by one ruler

Academic Vocabulary

code a set of official laws
military having to do with soldiers, weapons, or war

The Assyrian Army

The army of Assyria was well trained and disciplined. In battle, the troops numbered around 50,000 soldiers. This army was made up of infantry, or foot soldiers; cavalry, or horse soldiers; and charioteers. The Assyrians fought with slingshots, bows and arrows, swords, and spears.

The Assyrians robbed people, set crops on fire, and destroyed towns and dams. They took **tribute**, or forced payments, from conquered people. The Assyrian army also drove people from their homes. Stories of Assyrian brutality spread. Sometimes people were so afraid of the Assyrians that they would surrender to them without a fight.

One of the key factors in the Assyrian successes was iron weapons. The Hittites (HIH·tyts), a people to the north, had mastered iron production, making iron stronger than tin or copper. The Assyrians learned from Hittite technology.

Kings and Government

Assyria extended from the Persian Gulf in the east to the Nile River in the west. The capital was located at Nineveh (NIH·nuh·vuh), along the Tigris River.

Assyrian kings had to be powerful leaders to rule such a large area. They divided their empire into **provinces** (PRAH·vuhn·suhs), or political districts. The government built roads that connected these provinces. The kings chose officials to govern, collect taxes, and carry out the laws in each province. Soldiers stood guard at stations along the roads to protect traders from bandits. Messengers on government business used the stations to rest and change chariot horses.

Life in Assyria

The lives of the Assyrians were built on what they learned from other Mesopotamian peoples. The Assyrians had law codes, but their punishments were harsher. Assyrians based their writing on Babylonian writing. They worshipped many of the same gods.

Assyrians built large temples and palaces filled with wall carvings and statues. They also wrote and collected stories. An ancient Assyrian king named Ashurbanipal (ah·shur·BAH·nuh·puhl) built one of the world's first libraries in Nineveh. It held 25,000 tablets of stories and songs to the gods. Historians have learned much about ancient civilizations from this library.

Hammurabi's Code was carved on stone slabs that were placed where the most people would see them. Sometimes a statue of the king was placed with it.

▶ CRITICAL THINKING
Drawing Conclusions Why was displaying the code important for Babylonians?

(l)Réunion des Musées Nationaux/Art Resource, NY; (r)akg-images

Reading**HELP**DESK

tribute a payment made to a ruler or state as a sign of surrender

province a territory governed as a political district of a country or empire

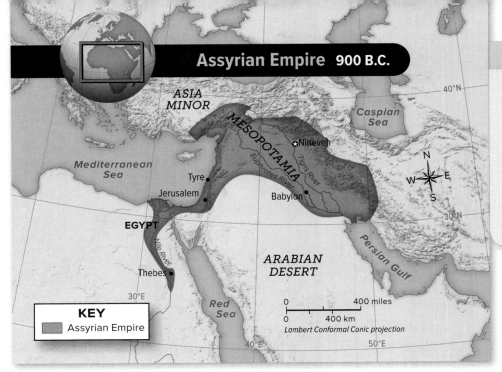

Assyrian Empire 900 B.C.

ASIA MINOR

MESOPOTAMIA

•Nineveh

Tigris River

Euphrates River

Caspian Sea

Mediterranean Sea

Tyre•

Jerusalem•

Babylon•

EGYPT

Nile River

ARABIAN DESERT

Persian Gulf

Thebes•

Red Sea

KEY
Assyrian Empire

0   400 miles
0   400 km
Lambert Conformal Conic projection

40°N

40°E

30°N

30°E

50°E

GEOGRAPHY CONNECTION

The Assyrians conquered lands from Mesopotamia to Egypt.

1 **LOCATION** What geographic feature lay to the south of the Assyrian Empire?

2 **CRITICAL THINKING**
Making Inferences Several major rivers flowed through the Assyrian Empire. Why were these rivers important?

Farming and trade were both important to the Assyrians. They brought in wood and metal from far away to supply their empire with material for building and for making tools and weapons.

✓ **PROGRESS CHECK**

Summarizing Why was Assyria's army so strong?

The Chaldean Empire

GUIDING QUESTION *Why was Babylon an important city in the ancient world?*

For 300 years, Assyria ruled the area from the Persian Gulf to Egypt. Because they were harsh rulers, people often rebelled. In about 650 B.C., fighting broke out over who would be the next Assyrian ruler. With the Assyrians in turmoil, a group of people called the Chaldeans (kal·DEE·uhns) took power.

A New Empire

Centuries before, about 1000 B.C., the Chaldean people had moved into southern Mesopotamia. At that time, the Assyrians had quickly conquered the Chaldeans' small kingdom. The Chaldeans hated their harsh new rulers and were never completely under Assyrian control.

Connections to
TODAY

Libraries

The United States Library of Congress in Washington, D.C., ranks as the largest library in the world. It holds millions of books, photographs, and other documents.

Visual Vocabulary

slingshot a weapon that is used to throw stones or other objects

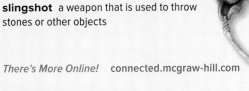

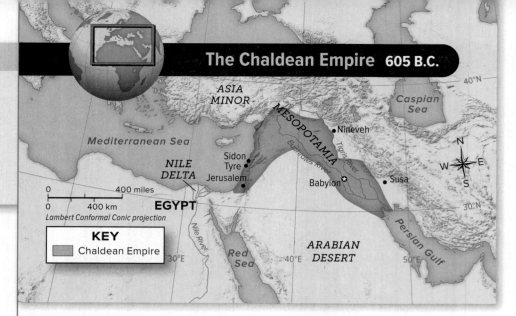

The Chaldean Empire 605 B.C.

1 **LOCATION** In which direction would someone travel from Sidon to reach the Persian Gulf?

2 **CRITICAL THINKING**
Evaluating Why do you think the Chaldeans became traders?

KEY
Chaldean Empire

Years later, when the Assyrians were fighting each other, the Chaldean king Nabopolassar (NAH·buh·puh·LAH·suhr) decided to reclaim his kingdom.

In 627 B.C., Nabopolassar led a revolt against the Assyrians. Within a year, he had forced the Assyrians out of Uruk and was crowned king of Babylonia. The Medes, another people in the **region** who wanted to break free from Assyrian rule, joined the Chaldeans. Together, they defeated the Assyrian army. In 612 B.C., they captured the Assyrian capital of Nineveh and burned it to the ground. The hated Assyrian Empire quickly crumbled.

Nabopolassar and his son, Nebuchadnezzar (NEH·byuh·kuhd·NEH·zuhr), created a new empire. Most of the Chaldeans were descendants of the Babylonians who made up Hammurabi's empire about 1,200 years earlier. Through conquest, the Chaldeans gained control of almost all of the lands the Assyrians had once ruled. The city of Babylon served as their capital. Because of this, the Chaldean Empire is sometimes called the New Babylonian Empire.

The Greatness of Babylon

King Nebuchadnezzar rebuilt Babylon, making it the largest and richest city in the world. Huge brick walls surrounded the city. Soldiers kept watch in towers that were built into the walls.

Grand palaces and temples were located in the center of Babylon. A huge ziggurat stood more than 300 feet (92 m) tall. When the sun shone, its gold roof could be seen for miles.

Reading HELP DESK

Academic Vocabulary

region a geographic area

Academic Vocabulary

complex having many parts, details, or ideas

The richness of the ziggurat was equaled by that of the king's palace. The palace had a giant staircase of greenery known as the Hanging Gardens.

Babylon's Hanging Gardens were considered one of the Seven Wonders of the Ancient World. These terraced gardens—built like huge steps—included large trees, masses of flowering vines, and other beautiful plants. A **complex** irrigation system brought water from the Euphrates River to water the gardens. It is believed that Nebuchadnezzar built the gardens to please his wife. She missed the mountains and plants of her homeland in the northwest.

For his people, Nebuchadnezzar built a beautiful street near the palace that they could visit. It was paved with limestone and marble, and lined with walls of blue glaze tile.

These ruins of the original gardens stand today as a reminder of Babylon's glory.

The grand Hanging Gardens of Babylon were watered from the top down using irrigation. Water flowed from one level to the next.

▶ CRITICAL THINKING
Making Generalizations
Why do you think ancient cities had at least one magnificent building?

King Nebuchadnezzar in the
Hanging Gardens.

Each spring, thousands of people crowded into Babylon to watch a gold statue of the god Marduk (MAHR·dook) as it was wheeled along the street. Chaldeans believed that the ceremony would bring peace and bigger crops to their empire.

The Babylonians built many new canals, making the land even more fertile. To pay for his building projects and to maintain his army, Nebuchadnezzar had to collect very high taxes and tributes. Because his empire stretched as far as Egypt, it had to have an efficient system of government.

One Greek historian in the 400s B.C. described the beauty of Babylon. He wrote, "In magnificence, there is no other city that approaches it." Outside the center of Babylon stood houses and marketplaces. There artisans made pottery, cloth, and baskets. The major trade route between the Persian Gulf and the Mediterranean Sea passed through Babylon. Merchants came to the city in traveling groups called **caravans** (KAR·uh·VANZ). They bought Babylonian goods—pottery, cloth, baskets, and jewelry. Babylon grew wealthy from this trade; under the Assyrians, the area had been fairly poor.

The people of Babylon also made many scientific advancements. The Chaldeans, like other people in Mesopotamia, believed that the gods showed their plans in the changes in the sky. Chaldean **astronomers** (uh·STRAH·nuh·muhrs)—people who study the heavenly bodies—mapped the stars, the planets, and the phases of the moon as it changed. The Chaldeans invented one of the first sundials to measure time. They also were the first to follow a seven-day week.

The Fall of the Empire

After Nebuchadnezzar died, a series of weak kings ruled the Chaldean Empire. Poor harvests and slow trade further weakened the empire. In 539 B.C., the Persians recognized

©Stapleton Collection/Corbis

Camels have been called the ships of the desert because they can live in extreme conditions. Merchants traveled to Babylon by caravan to buy and sell goods.

Christopher Boisvieux/agefotostock

that the Chaldeans had lost their strength and leadership. The Persians took advantage and captured Babylon and made Mesopotamia part of their empire. However, they allowed their newly captured land to keep its distinct culture. The Persians wisely did not want to destroy all the Chaldeans had accomplished.

☑ **PROGRESS CHECK**

Identifying Which wonder of the ancient world was located in Babylon?

LESSON 2 REVIEW

Review Vocabulary

1. How could *caravans* passing through Babylon be helped by *astronomers*?

2. How might conquered people feel about paying *tribute* to the Assyrians?

Answer the Guiding Questions

3. *Comparing* How did Hammurabi's Code differ from earlier Sumerian laws?

4. *Describing* How did the Assyrians rule their empire?

5. *Explaining* Why did the Chaldeans overthrow the Assyrians?

6. **ARGUMENT** You live in an area that the Assyrian army is attempting to conquer. Write a speech that you might give to your neighbors to persuade them either to defend themselves or to surrender without a fight.

Write your answers on a separate piece of paper.

1 **Exploring the Essential Question**
INFORMATIVE/EXPLANATORY How would you describe the influence of
Mesopotamia's physical geography on the region? Write an expository essay about how
geography influenced the way people lived in Mesopotamia. Think about the Tigris
River and the Euphrates River and the effect of flooding on the region. Include
information about how geography influenced the formation of city-states in your essay.

2 **21st Century Skills**
CREATING A COMMUNICATIONS PRODUCT Write a script for a documentary about
the technological and mathematical contributions made by the Sumerians. Divide your
script into two columns. The left column should include the narration for your
documentary. The right column should describe the images that will be shown. These
images should match with the narration in the left column. Read your script to the class,
or, if you have access to a video camera, shoot a short film based on your script.

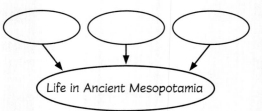

3 **Thinking Like a Historian**
IDENTIFYING Create a diagram like the one here to identify types of archeological
evidence that researchers might search for to learn about ancient Mesopotamia.

Life in Ancient Mesopotamia

4 **GEOGRAPHY ACTIVITY**

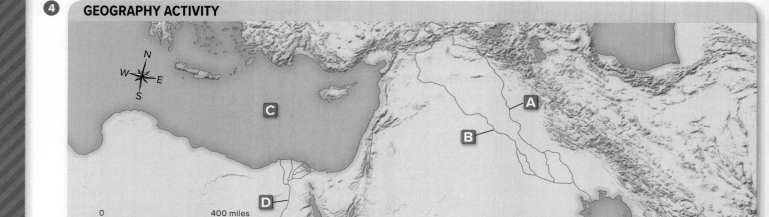

Locating Places
Match the letters on the map with the numbered places listed below.

1. Nile River   **3.** Mediterranean Sea   **5.** Persian Gulf

2. Euphrates River   **4.** Tigris River   **6.** Red Sea

Directions: Write your answers on a separate piece of paper.

CHECKING FOR UNDERSTANDING

1 Define each of these terms as they relate to Mesopotamia.
- **A.** Irrigation
- **B.** city-state
- **C.** scribe
- **D.** epic
- **E.** empire
- **F.** province

REVIEW THE GUIDING QUESTIONS

2 *Explaining* Describe the methods devised by the Mesopotamians to control the flooding of the Tigris and Euphrates Rivers and improve agriculture.

3 *Explaining* Why did the Sumerian civilization develop as a number of independent city-states?

4 *Describing* Describe the role of trade in ancient Sumer, including the products and resources that were part of that trade.

5 *Identifying* Identify one important invention that originated in Sumer and describe its uses and/or value.

6 *Describing* Describe the Code of Hammurabi. With what aspects of life did it deal? How did it treat the less powerful segment of society?

7 *Summarizing* Describe the extent of the Assyrian Empire. How did Assyrian leaders successfully rule such a large area?

8 *Identifying* What scientific advancements were made by the Chaldeans?

CRITICAL THINKING

9 *Determining Cause and Effect* How did the growth of surplus food in Mesopotamia lead to the development of Sumer's first cities?

10 *Making Connections* How were the gods worshipped by Sumerians related to everyday life?

11 *Contrasting* Contrast the social classes that developed in Sumer. What peoples/occupations belonged to each class?

12 *Evaluating* Do you think the development of writing was important to the success of Sumer as a civilization? Explain your answer.

13 *Sequencing* Describe, in order, the series of empires that developed in Mesopotamia following Sumer's fade from power.

14 *Making Generalizations* Aside from their military organization and advanced weapons, what generalization can be made about the reasons for the Assyrian Empire's military successes? Explain the reasoning for your generalization.

15 *Contrasting* During the Chaldean Empire, why did the city of Babylon grow wealthy? Why do you think this differed from when the Assyrians controlled the area?

16 *Assessing* Assess the rule of King Nebuchadnezzar of the Chaldean Empire. What were his accomplishments? Which do you consider most important?

Need Extra Help?

If You've Missed Question	**1**	**2**	**3**	**4**	**5**	**6**	**7**	**8**	**9**	**10**	**11**	**12**	**13**	**14**	**15**	**16**
Review Lesson	1,2	1	1	1	1	2	2	2	1	1	1	1	2	2	2	2

"The vast majority of the inhabitants of Babylonia, Assyria, and other Mesopotamian empires were poor and had no political power. ...Under some circumstances a person could change his or her social status. ... a trader or merchant who was uncommonly diligent or lucky in business might ... be able to afford his own plots of land."

—From *Empires of Mesopotamia* by Don Nardo

17 How might a trader improve his social status?

18 How did a person show their wealth at this time? Do you think people often improved their social status in ancient Mesopotamia? Explain your answer.

EXTENDED RESPONSE

19 *Informative/Explanatory* You are a diplomat from Egypt who is visiting Babylon around 565 B.C. The leader of your country wants information about the city, including the Hanging Gardens. How is the city organized? What do the Hanging Gardens look like? Write a report that describes your opinion about the city.

STANDARDIZED TEST PRACTICE

DBQ **ANALYZING DOCUMENTS**

This poem was written by an unknown Mesopotamian mother.

Hark the piping!
My heart is piping in the wilderness where the young man once went free.
He is a prisoner now in death's kingdom lies bound where once he lived.
The ewe gives up her lamb and the nanny goat her kid
My heart is piping in the wilderness, an instrument of grief.
—"The Mesopotamian View of Death," *Poems of Heaven and Hell from Ancient Mesopotamia*, N. K. Sanders, trans

20 **Drawing Conclusions** What has happened to the young man in the poem?
A. He has died.
B. He is in prison for life.
C. He is a successful warrior.
D. He tends a flock of sheep.

21 **Explaining** How does the mother react to what has happened?
A. She wants a chance to hug her son again.
B. She blames the king for what has happened.
C. She says she should have been tending her sheep.
D. She believes that her body is acting out her feelings.

Need Extra Help?

If You've Missed Question	17	18	19	20	21
Review Lesson	1	1	2	2	1,2

◀ *The god Osiris was respected because he represented new life and new crops.*

©Corbis

5000 B.C. TO A.D. 350

Ancient Egypt and Kush

THE STORY MATTERS ...

When you think of the most powerful person in your country, who is it? Is it the president? For ancient Egyptians, one of the most important beings was the god Osiris. Osiris controlled the power of life and death. As the god of agriculture, he controlled the very food Egyptians ate. He allowed the Nile River to flood its banks and bring fertile soil and water to the Egyptian desert. Osiris also knew death. In the underworld, the souls of the dead met the god Osiris. He did not have the power to return the dead to life, but he was a symbol of ongoing life. As you read this chapter, you will learn how the forces of life and death shaped the daily life of the ancient Egyptians and Kushites.

ESSENTIAL QUESTIONS
• How does geography influence the way people live?
• What makes a culture unique?
• Why do civilizations rise and fall?

Place & Time: Ancient Egypt and Kush 5000 B.C. to A.D. 350

The Egyptian Empire covered the northeastern corner of Africa. It centered on the mysterious Nile River valley. Egypt extended from central Africa to coastal areas along the Red and Mediterranean Seas. Despite periods of weakness, the empire expanded over the centuries of the Middle Kingdom and the New Kingdom.

Step Into the Place

MAP FOCUS Egypt's location in a river valley surrounded by deserts helped it become powerful.

1. **LOCATION** Look at the map. Is Egypt located north or south of the Mediterranean Sea?

2. **PLACE** What physical features made it possible for Egyptians to travel and trade?

3. **LOCATION** Describe the location of Egypt using cardinal directions.

4. **CRITICAL THINKING**
   Analyzing How does location near a waterway contribute to the success of a civilization?

The hot, dry climate of Egypt allowed ancient Egyptians to preserve the bodies of their dead as mummies.

These jars were used for storage during the process of making mummies. The tops of the jars show the heads of Egyptian gods.

(t)RABOUAN Jean-Baptiste/Age fotostock;
(b)SSPL/Science Museum/The Image Works

Step Into the Time

TIME LINE What events in the time line suggest that the Egyptians were unified, organized, and determined to build an empire?

c. 3000 B.C. Egyptians develop hieroglyphics

c. 2540 B.C. Great Pyramid built

c. 2600 B.C. Old Kingdom period begins

c. 3100 B.C. Narmer unites Egypt

ANCIENT EGYPT AND KUSH

THE WORLD

3000 B.C.

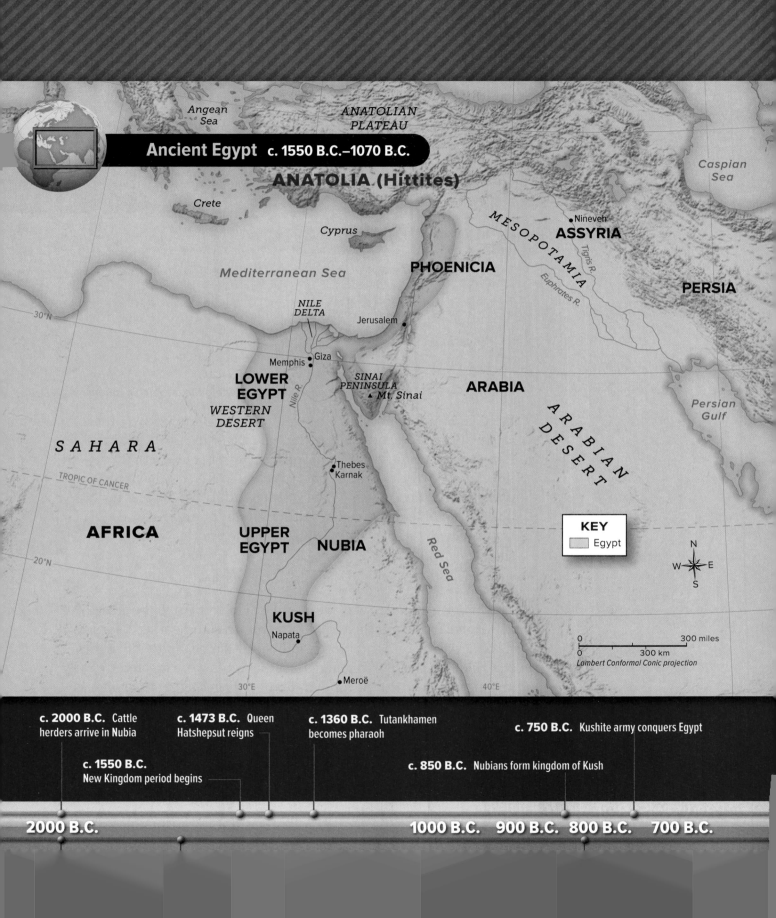

Ancient Egypt c. 1550 B.C.–1070 B.C.

Angean Sea

ANATOLIAN PLATEAU

Caspian Sea

ANATOLIA (Hittites)

Crete

Cyprus

MESOPOTAMIA

Nineveh

ASSYRIA

Mediterranean Sea

PHOENICIA

Tigris R.

Euphrates R.

PERSIA

NILE DELTA

30°N

Jerusalem

Memphis · Giza

Nile R.

SINAI PENINSULA

LOWER EGYPT

WESTERN DESERT

▲ Mt. Sinai

ARABIA

Persian Gulf

SAHARA

ARABIAN DESERT

TROPIC OF CANCER

KEY

Egypt

AFRICA

UPPER EGYPT

Thebes
Karnak

NUBIA

Red Sea

N
W   E
S

20°N

0   300 miles
0   300 km

KUSH

Napata

Lambert Conformal Conic projection

30°E

Meroë

40°E

c. 2000 B.C. Cattle herders arrive in Nubia

c. 1473 B.C. Queen Hatshepsut reigns

c. 1360 B.C. Tutankhamen becomes pharaoh

c. 750 B.C. Kushite army conquers Egypt

c. 1550 B.C. New Kingdom period begins

c. 850 B.C. Nubians form kingdom of Kush

2000 B.C.   1000 B.C.   900 B.C.   800 B.C.   700 B.C.

LESSON 1
The Nile River

• How does geography influence the way people live?

IT MATTERS BECAUSE
The Nile River was the most important factor in the development of ancient Egypt.

The Nile River Valley

GUIDING QUESTION *Why was the Nile River important to the ancient Egyptians?*

While empires flourished and fell in Mesopotamia, two other civilizations developed along the Nile River in northeastern Africa. One of these civilizations was Egypt (EE·jihpt). It developed in the northern part of the Nile River valley. The other civilization, Kush (CUSH), emerged in the far southern part of the Nile River valley. Although Egypt and Kush were **unique** civilizations, they influenced one another throughout their long histories.

Valley Civilization

The Nile River valley was ideal for human settlement because of its fertile land. As early as 5000 B.C., hunters and gatherers from the drier areas of Africa and Southwest Asia began to move into the Nile River valley. Permanent settlements were created by early groups who farmed the land and built villages along the Nile's banks. These people were the earliest Egyptians and Kushites.

The early Egyptians lived in the northern region of the Nile River valley. They called their land *Kemet* (KEH·meht), which means "black land," after the dark, rich soil. Later, this northern Nile area would be called *Egypt*. Of the world's early river valley

Reading **HELP**DESK

Taking Notes: *Identifying*
Use a web diagram like this one to identify three reasons why most ancient Egyptians lived near the Nile River.

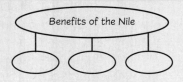

Benefits of the Nile

Content Vocabulary

• **cataract**   • **papyrus**
• **delta**   • **hieroglyphics**
• **shadoof**   • **dynasty**

civilizations, you probably are most familiar with ancient Egypt. People still marvel at its ruins located in present-day Egypt. These ruins include the enormous stone Sphinx that has the body of a lion and a human head. Archaeologists also study the wondrous pyramids and the mummies found buried in tombs once full of riches.

The Gift of the River

Many of ancient Egypt's structures survived because Egypt has a hot, dry climate. Since the region receives little rainfall, ancient Egyptians depended on the Nile for drinking and bathing. The river also supplied water to grow crops. To the Egyptians, the Nile was the "creator of all good." They praised it in a hymn:

PRIMARY SOURCE

❝ You create the grain, you bring forth the barley,

Assuring perpetuity [survival] to the temples.

If you cease your toil and your work,

Then all that exists is in anguish [suffering]. ❞

—from *"Hymn to the Nile"*

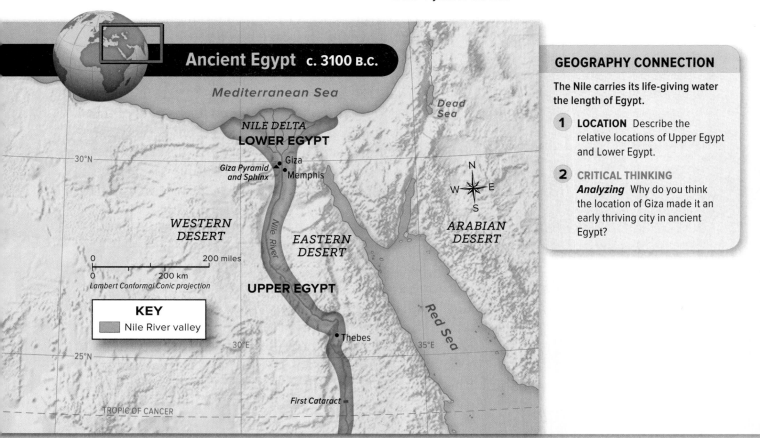

Ancient Egypt c. 3100 B.C.

Mediterranean Sea

Dead Sea

NILE DELTA
LOWER EGYPT

30°N

Giza Pyramid and Sphinx
Giza
Memphis

WESTERN DESERT

Nile River

EASTERN DESERT

ARABIAN DESERT

0   200 miles
0   200 km
Lambert Conformal Conic projection

UPPER EGYPT

Red Sea

KEY
Nile River valley

30°E   35°E
Thebes

25°N

First Cataract

TROPIC OF CANCER

GEOGRAPHY CONNECTION

The Nile carries its life-giving water the length of Egypt.

1 **LOCATION** Describe the relative locations of Upper Egypt and Lower Egypt.

2 **CRITICAL THINKING**
Analyzing Why do you think the location of Giza made it an early thriving city in ancient Egypt?

Academic Vocabulary

unique one of a kind; different from all others

Narrow cataracts on the Nile limit river travel, especially for larger ships.

Do you know which is the world's longest river? It is the Nile that flows north about 4,000 miles (6,437 km) from central Africa to the Mediterranean Sea. It has been called the "lifeblood" of Egypt.

At its source, the Nile is two separate rivers: the Blue Nile and the White Nile. The Blue Nile begins in the snowy mountains of eastern Africa. The White Nile starts in the tropics of central Africa. The two rivers join just south of Egypt to form the Nile River. There, steep cliffs and large boulders form dangerous, fast-moving waters called **cataracts** (KA·tuh·RAKTS). Cataracts make traveling by ship along the Nile difficult.

A Protected Land

As with many rivers, the Nile's flow throughout the centuries has created a valley. You can see on the map on the previous page that the Nile looks like the long winding root of a plant. Shortly before the Nile reaches the Mediterranean Sea, it splits into many branches that resemble a plant's bloom. These waterways form a fan-shaped area of fertile marshland called a **delta** (DEHL·tuh).

In the Nile River valley, we see the effect that water has on the landscape. The lush, green Nile valley and delta contrast sharply with the barren deserts that stretch out on either side of the river. The change in landscape can be so sudden that a person can stand with one foot in fertile soil and one foot in barren sand.

The Nile borders the largest deserts in the world. To the west of the Nile River is the Libyan Desert, which forms part of the Sahara (suh·HAR·uh). To the river's east lies the Eastern Desert that extends to the Red Sea. The ancient Egyptians called these deserts the "Red Land" because of their scorching heat. These large desert areas were not favorable to humans or animals. They kept Egypt **isolated,** however, from outside invaders.

In addition to the deserts, other physical features protected Egypt. To the far south, the Nile's dangerous cataracts prevented enemy ships from attacking Egypt. In the north, delta marshes stopped invaders who sailed from the Mediterranean Sea. These physical features gave the Egyptians advantages that Mesopotamians lacked. The Egyptians rarely faced the danger of invasion. As a result, Egyptian civilization developed peacefully.

The Egyptians, though isolated, were not completely cut off from other peoples. The Mediterranean Sea to the north and the Red Sea to the east provided routes for trade.

Daniela Dirscherl/WaterFrame/Age fotostock

Reading**HELP**DESK

cataract a waterfall or rapids in a river

delta a fan-shaped area of silt near where a river flows into the sea

Academic Vocabulary

isolate to separate from others

The stark contrast between watered and not watered land can be seen along the banks of the Nile.

Egyptians took advantage of the region's wind patterns so that they could travel and trade. Although the natural flow of the Nile's currents carried boats north, winds from the north pushed sailboats south.

☑ **PROGRESS CHECK**

Explaining How were the Egyptians protected by their physical environment?

People of the River

GUIDING QUESTION *How did the ancient Egyptians depend on the Nile River to grow their crops?*

We know that the Mesopotamians controlled the floods of the Tigris and Euphrates Rivers to grow crops. They developed the technology to do so, but the unpredictable rivers constantly challenged them. In Egypt, however, the flooding of the Nile River was seasonal and consistent from year to year. So the Egyptians did not face the same challenge.

Predictable Floods

As in Mesopotamia, flooding along the Nile in Egypt was common. The Nile floods, however, were more predictable and less destructive than those of the Tigris and the Euphrates. As a result, the Egyptians were not afraid that heavy floods would destroy their homes and crops. Each year, during late spring, heavy tropical rains in central Africa and melting mountain snow in eastern Africa added water to the Nile. Around the middle of summer, the Nile overflowed its banks and flooded the land. Egyptian farmers were ready to take advantage of this cycle. When the waters returned to their normal level in late fall, thick deposits of fertile soil remained.

©Michel Gounot /Godong/Corbis

Special techniques and tools—such as this shadoof—helped farmers grow crops in the dry season.

How Did Egyptians Farm?

Farmers planted wheat, barley, and flax seeds while the soil was still wet. Over time, they grew enough food to feed themselves and the animals they raised.

During the dry season, Egyptian farmers irrigated their crops. They scooped out basins, or bowl-shaped holes, in the earth to store river water. They then dug canals that extended from the basins to the fields, allowing water to flow to their crops. Raised areas of soil provided support for the basin walls.

In time, Egyptian farmers developed new tools to make their work easier. For example, farmers created a **shadoof** (shuh·DOOF), which is a bucket attached to a long pole that lifts water from the Nile and empties it into basins. Many Egyptian farmers still use this method today.

Egyptian farmers also needed a way to measure the area of their lands. When floods washed away boundary markers that divided one field from another, farmers used geometry to help them recalculate where one field began and the other ended.

Egyptians gathered **papyrus** (puh·PY·ruhs), a reed plant that grew wild along the Nile. They used the long, thin reeds to weave rope, sandals, baskets, and river rafts. Later, they used

We learn about ancient farming methods from Egyptian art murals such as this.

▶ **CRITICAL THINKING**
Describing What details about ancient farming methods can you find in this painting of farmers?

(t)Erich Lessing/Art Resource, NY; (b)Giraudon/Art Resource, NY

Reading **HELP**DESK

shadoof a bucket attached to a long pole used to transfer river water to storage basins

VERITABLE EXTRAIT DE VIANDE LIEBIG.

Histoire du papier. 2.
Fabricants de papier égyptiens.

papyrus to make paper. To do this, the Egyptians cut strips from the stalks of the papyrus plant and soaked them in water. Next, the strips were laid side by side and pounded together. They were then set out to dry, forming a large sheet of papyrus on which the Egyptians could write.

How Did the Egyptians Write?

Like the Mesopotamians, the Egyptians developed their own writing system. At first, Egyptian writing was made up of thousands of picture symbols that represented objects and ideas. A house, for example, would be represented by a drawing of a house. Later, Egyptians created symbols that represented sounds, just as the letters of our alphabet do. The combination of pictures and sound symbols created a complex writing system called **hieroglyphics** (hy·ruh·GLIH·fihks).

Few ancient Egyptians could read and write hieroglyphics. Some Egyptian men, however, attended special schools to prepare for careers as scribes in government or business. The Egyptians did not write on clay tablets like the Mesopotamians. For their daily tasks, Egyptian scribes developed a simpler script that they wrote or painted on papyrus. These same scribes carved hieroglyphics onto stone walls and monuments.

Papyrus reeds grow wild along rivers. From harvesting the reeds to final product, the process of making paper from papyrus took many days.

▶ CRITICAL THINKING
Predicting If Egyptians had not developed papyrus, what other material could they have used to write on?

✓ PROGRESS CHECK

Identifying What kind of writing system did the Egyptians develop?

papyrus a reed plant that grew wild along the Nile

hieroglyphics a writing system made up of a combination of pictures and sound symbols

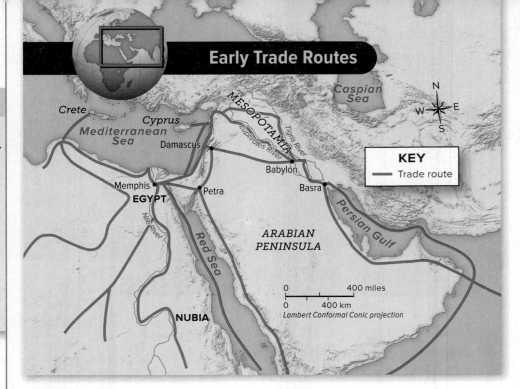

Early Trade Routes

KEY
— Trade route

0   400 miles
0   400 km
Lambert Conformal Conic projection

Uniting Egypt

GUIDING QUESTION *How did Egypt become united?*

Protected from outside attacks by desert barriers, Egyptian farmers were able to grow surpluses—extra amounts—of food. In Egypt, as in Mesopotamia, extra food meant that some people could leave farming to work in other occupations. Artisans, merchants, and traders began to play an important role in Egypt's economy. As more goods became available, villages along the Nile traded with one another. Before long, Egyptian caravans were carrying goods to Nubia (NOO•bee•uh) to the south, Mesopotamia to the northeast, and other places outside Egypt's borders. Along with the exchange of goods, Egyptian traders learned about the ways of life and governments of other societies.

Forming Kingdoms

The need for organized government became increasingly important as farming and trade increased. A government was necessary to oversee the construction and repair of irrigation ditches and dams. A government was needed to develop a process for storing and distributing grain during famines. In addition, conflicts over land ownership had to be settled.

Reading**HELP**DESK

dynasty a line of rulers from one family

Academic Vocabulary

unify to unite; to bring together into one unit

Over time, groups of villages merged to form small kingdoms. Each of these kingdoms was ruled by a king. The weaker kingdoms eventually fell under the control of the stronger ones. By 4000 B.C., Egypt was made up of two large kingdoms. One was Upper Egypt, which was located in the south-central part of the Nile River valley. The other was Lower Egypt, which was located along the Nile River's north delta.

Who Was Narmer?

Narmer (NAHR·mer) was a king of Upper Egypt. About 3100 B.C., he led his armies from the valley north into the delta. Narmer conquered Lower Egypt and married one of Lower Egypt's princesses, which **unified** the kingdoms. For the first time, all of Egypt was ruled by one king.

Narmer established a new capital at Memphis, a city on the border between Upper Egypt and Lower Egypt. He governed both parts of Egypt from this city. Memphis began to flourish as a center of government and culture along the Nile.

Narmer's kingdom lasted long after his death. The right to rule was passed from father to son to grandson. Such a line of rulers from one family is called a **dynasty** (DY·nuh·stee). When one dynasty died out, another took its place.

From about 3100 B.C. to 332 B.C., a series of 30 dynasties ruled Egypt. These dynasties are organized into three time periods: the Old Kingdom, the Middle Kingdom, and the New Kingdom. Throughout these three time periods, Egypt was usually united under a single ruler and enjoyed stable government.

✓ PROGRESS CHECK

Explaining How did the separate kingdoms of Egypt unite?

INTERFOTO/age fotostock

Egyptian art often glorified rulers. The man in the center of this carving is Narmer.

▶ CRITICAL THINKING

Analyzing How does the carving show that Narmer was a powerful leader?

LESSON 1 REVIEW

Review Vocabulary

1. Why did the Egyptians need *hieroglyphics*?

2. How does a *dynasty* work?

Answer the Guiding Questions

3. ***Identifying*** What physical feature is to the east and west of the Nile River? How did this feature help Egyptians?

4. ***Contrasting*** How did the flooding of major rivers affect both the Mesopotamians and the Egyptians?

5. ***Explaining*** What was significant about the joining of the two kingdoms under Narmer?

6. ***Analyzing*** How did the Nile River help the ancient Egyptians develop as a well-governed civilization?

7. **INFORMATIVE/EXPLANATORY** Why has the Nile River been described as the "lifeblood" of Egypt? Why was the river essential to the Egyptians? Explain your answer in the form of a short essay.

LESSON 2

Life in Ancient Egypt

ESSENTIAL QUESTION

• What makes a culture unique?

IT MATTERS BECAUSE
The Egyptian pharaohs were all-powerful rulers. Egyptians built such gigantic and sturdy pyramids in their honor that the pyramids still stand today.

Egypt's Early Rulers

GUIDING QUESTION *How was ancient Egypt governed?*

Around 2600 B.C., Egyptian civilization entered the period known as the Old Kingdom. The Old Kingdom lasted until about 2200 B.C. During these years, the Egyptians built magnificent cities and increased trade. They also formed a unified government. The Egyptians prized unity. They understood the importance of everyone working and living according to similar principles and beliefs. Therefore, they developed a government under an all-powerful ruler who controlled both religious and political affairs. A government in which the same person is both the political leader and the religious leader is called a **theocracy** (thee·AH·kruh·see).

A Political Leader
At first, the Egyptian ruler was called a king. Later, he was known as **pharaoh** (FEHR·oh). The word *pharaoh* originally meant "great house." It referred to the grand palace in which the king and his family lived.

The Egyptians were fiercely loyal to the pharaoh because they believed that a strong ruler unified their kingdom. The pharaoh held total power. He issued commands that had to

Reading**HELP**DESK

Taking Notes: *Organizing*

Use a diagram like this one to list information about ancient Egypt by adding one or more facts to each of the boxes.

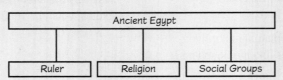

Content Vocabulary

• theocracy
• pharaoh
• bureaucrat
• embalming
• pyramid

be obeyed. Egyptians believed that a pharaoh's wise and far-reaching leadership would help their kingdom survive such disasters as war and famine.

The pharaoh appointed **bureaucrats** (BYUR·uh·kratz), or government officials, to carry out his orders. Bureaucrats supervised the construction and repair of dams, irrigation canals, and brick granaries. Granaries (GRAY·nuh·reez) were used to store grain from bountiful harvests so people would not starve during times of poor harvests.

The pharaoh owned all the land in Egypt and could use it as he pleased. The pharaoh's officials collected tax payments of grain from farmers. The pharaoh also **distributed** land to officials, priests, and wealthy Egyptians whom he favored.

A Religious Leader

Egyptians were also loyal to the pharaoh because they thought he was the son of Re (RAY), the Egyptian sun god. They believed their pharaoh was a god on earth who protected Egypt. Whenever the pharaoh appeared in public, people played music on flutes and cymbals and bowed their heads.

The pharaoh (left) had many servants to wait on him and provide him with all his needs.

Explaining What role did the pharaoh play as a political leader?

INTERFOTO/Alamy

---

theocracy government by religious leaders
pharaoh ruler of ancient Egypt
bureaucrat a government official

Academic Vocabulary

distribute to divide into shares and deliver the shares to different people

As Egypt's religious leader, the pharaoh participated in ceremonies to help the kingdom thrive. For example, the pharaoh rode a bull around Memphis because the Egyptians believed that this would help keep the soil fertile. The pharaoh was also the first person to cut the ripened grain at harvest time. Egyptians believed this action would produce abundant crops.

✅ **PROGRESS CHECK**

Analyzing How was the pharaoh a political leader and a religious leader?

Religion in Egypt

GUIDING QUESTION *What kind of religion did the ancient Egyptians practice?*

Religion influenced every aspect of Egyptian life. Like the people of Mesopotamia, ancient Egyptians worshipped many gods and goddesses. The people of Egypt, however, thought their gods were more powerful. The Egyptians believed these deities (DEE·uh·teez) controlled natural forces as well as human activities.

The Egyptians depended on the sun to grow their crops and on the Nile River to make the soil fertile. Thus, two of the most **crucial** gods were the sun god Re and the river god Hapi (HAH·pee). Another important god was Osiris (oh·SY·ruhs). According to legend, Osiris was an early pharaoh who gave the Egyptian people laws and taught them farming. His wife Isis (EYE·suhs) represented the faithful wife and mother. Osiris and Isis together ruled over the world of the dead. Thoth (THOHTH) was the god of learning. He could take human or animal form—or both—as did most gods and goddesses.

The Afterlife

The Egyptians had a positive view of the afterlife. They believed that life after death would be even better than the present life. After a long journey, the dead arrived at a place of peace.

The Egyptians gave offerings to their gods, whom they believed controlled their lives.

▶ **CRITICAL THINKING**
Speculating Why do you think the god being offered a gift has the head of a bird?

©Gianni Dagli Orti/Corbis

Reading**HELP**DESK

Reading Strategy: *Contrasting*

Look for clue words such as *however*, *but*, and *although*. These words tell you that the author is contrasting two ideas. Which sentence on this page uses a contrasting clue word? What ideas are being contrasted?

Academic Vocabulary

crucial important or significant

One of the most important writings of ancient Egypt was *The Book of the Dead*. Egyptians studied its prayers and magic spells to prepare for the afterlife. They believed that Osiris greeted those who had just died at the gate to the next world. If people had led good lives and knew the spells, Osiris would give them eternal life. This passage from *The Book of the Dead* explains what a person who enters the happy afterlife can expect:

PRIMARY SOURCE

" Wheat and barley ... shall be given unto him therein, and he shall flourish there just as he did upon earth. "

—from *Papyrus of Ani—The Egyptian Book of the Dead*

The earliest Egyptians believed that only the pharaohs could enjoy the afterlife. They thought that the pharaoh's soul **resided** in his body, and that the body had to be protected in order for the soul to complete the journey to the afterlife. There, the pharaoh would continue to protect Egypt. If the pharaoh's body decayed after death, his soul would not have a place to live. The pharaoh would not survive in the afterlife. As the centuries passed, however, Egyptians came to believe that the afterlife was not only for pharaohs. All people—rich and poor—could hope for eternal life with the help of the god Osiris. As a result, the process of **embalming** (ihm·BAHLM·ihng) emerged so that Egyptians could protect bodies for the afterlife.

Before a body was embalmed, priests removed the body's organs. The organs were stored in special jars that were buried with the body. Then the priests covered the body with a salt called natron and stored it for several days. The natron dried up the water in the body, causing it to shrink. The shrunken, dried body was then filled with burial spices and tightly wrapped with long strips of linen. The wrapped body was then known as a mummy (MUH·mee). The mummy was sealed in a coffin and placed in a decorated tomb.

The goddess Isis was the wife of the god Osiris. She was a powerful god respected on her own.

► **CRITICAL THINKING**
Inferring Why do you think the Egyptians worshipped some powerful gods that were men and others that were women?

---

embalming the process of treating a body to keep it from decaying

Academic Vocabulary

reside to be present continuously or have a home in a particular place

Preparing the pharaoh's body for burial involved a mix of science and religion. Special priests performed the process.

Explaining What do you think Egyptians learned about the human body by embalming?

Wealthy people had their mummies placed in coffins and buried in tombs. Poorer people had their mummies buried in caves or in the sand. Even animals were embalmed. Egyptians viewed animals not only as pets, but also as sacred creatures. As a result, they buried the mummies of cats, birds, and other animals at temples honoring their gods and goddesses.

Medical Skills

The Egyptians learned much about the human body from embalming. This knowledge helped them to develop basic medical skills. Egyptian doctors sewed up cuts and set broken bones. They were the first to use splints, bandages, and compresses. Egyptians also wrote down medical information on papyrus scrolls. These records were the world's first medical books.

✓ PROGRESS CHECK

Analyzing Why did Egyptians protect a person's body after death?

Wildlife Art, LTD

Reading HELP DESK

pyramid great stone tomb built for an Egyptian pharaoh

Academic Vocabulary
labor work

Pyramid Tombs

GUIDING QUESTION *Why and how were pyramids built?*

The Egyptians honored their pharaohs in a special way. They built great tombs called **pyramids** (PIHR·uh·mihds) for the pharaohs. These enormous structures were made of stone and covered the area of several city blocks. Centuries after they were built, these monuments still tower over the desert sands. The pyramids protected the bodies of dead pharaohs from floods, wild animals, and robbers. The Egyptians believed the pharaohs would be happy after death if they had their personal belongings. For that reason, they placed the pharaoh's clothing, weapons, furniture, and jewelry in the pyramids.

The pyramids preserved, or saved, these objects in relatively good condition for centuries. Today, archaeologists are able to study the pyramids and the treasures they hold to learn about life in ancient Egypt.

How Were Pyramids Built?

Thousands of workers spent years of hard **labor** to build the pyramids. Farmers did much of the work during the summer months when the Nile River flooded and they could not farm.

The Sphinx is one of the most famous Egyptian monuments. It was built to honor one of Egypt's pharaohs and stands today among the pyramids at Giza, Egypt.

Sylvain Grandadam/Getty Images

INSIDE A PYRAMID

❶ **Air Shaft**

❷ **King's Burial Chamber** The king's mummified body was placed in a room at the pyramid's center.

❸ **Grand Gallery** This tall, sloping hall held large granite blocks that sealed the tomb.

❹ **Queen's Burial Chamber** This chamber held a statue of the king, not the queen's body.

❺ **Entrance**

❻ **Underground Burial Chamber** Sometimes kings were buried here instead.

❼ **Queen's Pyramids** These smaller pyramids are believed to be tombs for the kings' wives.

❽ **Mastaba** These tombs surrounding the pyramids held royal family members and other nobles.

❾ **Valley Temple** This temple may have been used for rituals before the king was buried.

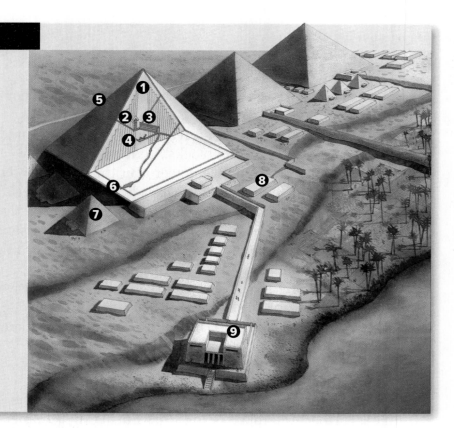

INFOGRAPHIC

The pyramids contained many rooms, each used for a different purpose.

▶ CRITICAL THINKING
Speculating Why was the king's burial chamber constructed in the middle of the pyramid and not at the top?

Reading**HELP**DESK

Surveyors, engineers, carpenters, and stonecutters also helped build the pyramids. The first great engineer who built pyramids was Imhotep (ihm·HOH·tehp). He also served as an official for the pharaoh.

Workers searched for stone in places throughout the Nile River valley or in Upper Egypt. After locating the stone, skilled artisans used copper tools to cut the stone into huge blocks. Next, workers used rope to fasten the blocks onto wooden sleds. The sleds were pulled along a path made of logs to the Nile River. There, the stones were moved onto barges that carried them to the building site. Workers unloaded the blocks and dragged or pushed them up ramps to be set in place at each new level of the pyramid.

The Egyptians faced many challenges as they built the pyramids. These challenges, however, led to important discoveries. For example, each pyramid rested on a square-shaped foundation, with an entrance facing north. To find north, the Egyptians studied the skies and developed an understanding of astronomy. With this knowledge, they invented a 365-day calendar with 12 months divided into three seasons. This calendar became the basis for our modern calendar.

Egyptians also made advancements in mathematics. Egypt's pyramid builders had to calculate how much stone was needed to build a pyramid. They had to measure angles in order to **construct** a pyramid's walls. To do this, they invented a system of written numbers based on 10. They also created fractions, using them with whole numbers to add, subtract, and divide.

An Egyptian Wonder

About the mid-2000s B.C., the Egyptians built the biggest and grandest of the pyramids—the Great Pyramid. It lies about 10 miles (16.1 km) from the modern city of Cairo. Built for King Khufu (KOO·foo), the Great Pyramid is one of three pyramids still standing at Giza on the Nile's west bank. It is about the height of a 48-story building, towering nearly 500 feet (153 m) above the desert. It extends over an area equal in size to nine football fields. More than 2 million stone blocks were used in the pyramid's construction, each weighing an average of 2.5 tons (2.3 metric tons). For more than 4,000 years, the Great Pyramid stood as the tallest structure in the world.

In this photo of the Great Pyramid, the pyramid in the center belongs to King Khafre, son of Khufu. Khafre's pyramid has a width (at its base) to height ratio of about **708:471 ft (216:143 m)**. Khufu's pyramid has a ratio of about **756:481 ft (230:147 m)**.

▶ CRITICAL THINKING
Comparing Which pyramid is larger?

✔ PROGRESS CHECK

Explaining Why did the Egyptians build the pyramids?

Academic Vocabulary

construct to build

Daily Life

GUIDING QUESTION *How was Egyptian society organized?*

At its peak, ancient Egypt was home to about 5 million people. This would be about equal to the number of people living today in the state of Colorado. Most ancient Egyptians lived in the fertile Nile valley and delta. The delta is found at the mouth of the river. These two areas, which make up only 3 percent of Egypt's land, are densely populated even today.

Egypt's Social Groups

The **roles** of the people in ancient Egypt reflected their social status, or position in society. Look at the diagram of the different social groups, or classes, in ancient Egypt. The king or pharaoh and his family held the highest social position in Egypt, followed by a small upper class of army commanders, nobles, and priests. The priests served as government officials and supervised people who worked as clerks and scribes. A larger group of traders, artisans, and scribes made up the middle class. The lowest but largest groups in Egyptian society

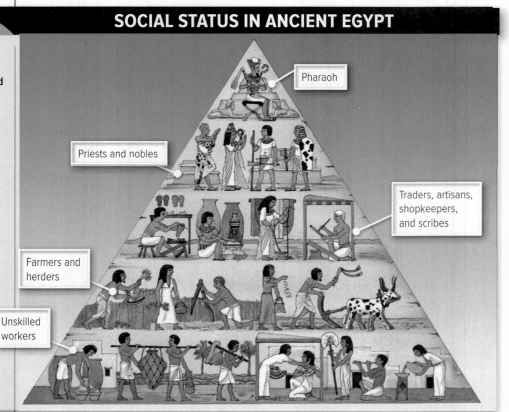

INFOGRAPHIC

People lived according to their social status and occupation. People who were ambitious could improve their status.

Identifying What level of society do you think a teacher would occupy?

SOCIAL STATUS IN ANCIENT EGYPT

Pharaoh

Priests and nobles

Traders, artisans, shopkeepers, and scribes

Farmers and herders

Unskilled workers

Reading **HELP**DESK

Academic Vocabulary

role the function or part an individual fills in society

Build Vocabulary: *Word Forms*

As a noun, *official* means "someone who holds an office or who manages the rules of a game." As an adjective, it means "authorized." The verb *officiate* means "to act in an official role."

These ancient Egyptian women are chemists. Women were educated and valued for their special skills.

▶ CRITICAL THINKING
Analyzing What social class would these women belong to?

©Bettmann/Corbis

were made up of farmers and unskilled workers. Even though there were divisions in Egyptian class structures, ambitious people in the lower classes were able to improve their social position.

How People Lived

Egypt's upper class lived in elegant homes and on estates along the Nile River. Their homes were constructed of wood and sun-dried mud bricks, and some were two or three stories tall. Surrounding their homes were lush gardens and pools filled with fish and water lilies. Men and women from the upper class dressed in fashionable white linen clothes and wore dark eye makeup and jewelry. Servants waited on them and performed household tasks.

The middle class of ancient Egyptian society was made up of people who owned businesses and held skilled jobs. These jobs included trading and working as a scribe. Artisans were also important members of the middle class. These craft-makers produced linen cloth, jewelry, pottery, and metal goods. The middle class lived in smaller homes and dressed more simply than the upper class.

Reading Strategy: *Finding the Main Idea*

Remember that each paragraph contains ideas that are related. Usually one sentence summarizes the main idea of a paragraph. Find the main idea in the last paragraph on this page.

The felucca, an ancient Egyptian river craft, sailed the Nile. Sailors today still use the same ship and sail design.

▶ CRITICAL THINKING
Analyzing Into what Egyptian social class would fishers fit?

The largest Egyptian social classes included farmers, unskilled workers, and enslaved people. Most farmers worked on land that was owned by wealthy nobles. They paid rent to the landowners, usually with a portion of their crops. Farmers lived in houses that were made of mud brick. The houses generally had only one room and a roof made of palm leaves. Farmers ate a simple diet of bread, vegetables, and fruit.

Unskilled workers performed **manual** labor, such as unloading cargo from boats and transporting it to markets. Some were fishers. Most unskilled workers settled in crowded city neighborhoods. They lived in small mud-brick houses with hard-packed dirt floors. Their houses sometimes included a courtyard. Families often gathered on the flat rooftops to socialize, play games, and sleep. Because of the hot Egyptian climate, they also did their cooking on the rooftop. This helped their homes stay cooler.

Some of these unskilled workers were enslaved people. Many of them had been captured in war, and they could earn their freedom over time. Some of these enslaved people helped build the pyramids.

Egyptian Families

The family was the most important group in ancient Egyptian society. Even the gods and goddesses were arranged in family groupings. The father was the head of the family in ancient Egypt, but women had more rights than women in other early civilizations had. Egyptian women held a legal status similar to that of men. They could own property, buy and sell goods, and **obtain** divorces.

Wealthy women even served as priests, managing temples and performing religious ceremonies. Wives of farmers often worked in the fields with their husbands. Women of the higher social classes were more likely to stay at home while their husbands worked at their jobs.

Image Source/Getty Images

Reading**HELP**DESK

Academic Vocabulary

manual involving physical effort
obtain to gain something through a planned effort

Few Egyptian children attended school. Egyptian children had time for fun, playing with board games, dolls, spinning tops, and stuffed leather balls. As in many other cultures, Egyptian children were expected to respect their parents. Mothers taught their daughters to sew, cook, and run a household. Boys learned farming or other trades from their fathers. Learning their father's trade was important, because very often the oldest son would inherit his father's business.

When boys and girls became teenagers, they were expected to get married and start families of their own. In Egyptian cities and among the upper class, people usually lived in nuclear families. A nuclear family is made up of two parents and their children. Some farm families and others in the lower class lived as extended families. In an extended family, older adults, along with their married children and their families, live together. For farm families, this provided more people to work the fields.

The oldest son, and sometimes the oldest daughter, were also responsible for taking care of their parents when the parents became too old or sick to take care of themselves. This responsibility included making sure the parents were given a proper burial after they died.

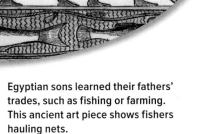

Egyptian sons learned their fathers' trades, such as fishing or farming. This ancient art piece shows fishers hauling nets.

✓ PROGRESS CHECK

Identifying What types of people made up Egypt's upper class?

North Wind/North Wind Picture Archives

LESSON 2 REVIEW

Review Vocabulary

1. Explain the role a *pharaoh* played in a *theocracy*.

2. What was the social status of a *bureaucrat* in ancient Egypt?

Answer the Guiding Questions

3. *Describing* What kind of religion did the ancient Egyptians practice? Describe at least one way that their religion was tied to agriculture.

4. *Analyzing* What was the most important purpose of the pyramids? Explain your reasoning.

5. *Comparing and Contrasting* How was life for Egyptian children similar to or different from that of children today?

6. *Defending* Why did the Egyptians spend years and many resources to build enormous tombs for their dead pharaohs?

7. **INFORMATIVE/EXPLANATORY** If you could be anyone in ancient Egypt except the pharaoh, who would you choose to be? Explain the reasons for your choice. Make sure to include the advantages and disadvantages of your social position.

LESSON 3

Egypt's Empire

ESSENTIAL QUESTION

• Why do civilizations rise and fall?

IT MATTERS BECAUSE

The leaders during the golden age of Egypt expanded the empire through war and trade. Although Egypt later declined, it greatly influenced other civilizations.

A Golden Age

GUIDING QUESTION *Why was the Middle Kingdom a "golden age" for Egypt?*

Around 2200 B.C., the ruling pharaohs in Memphis began to weaken. Ambitious nobles fought for control of Egypt. For more than 200 years, disorder and violence swept through the region. Finally, a new dynasty of pharaohs came to power. They moved the capital south to a city called Thebes (THEEBZ). These new pharaohs began a period of peace and order called the Middle Kingdom that lasted from about c. 2055 B.C. to c. 1650 B.C.

Conquests

During the Middle Kingdom, Egypt conquered new territories. Egyptian armies gained control of Nubia to the south and expanded northeast into present-day Syria. The Egyptian pharaohs added to their kingdom's wealth. They required tribute, or forced payments, from the peoples their armies had conquered.

Within Egypt, the pharaohs made many improvements. They added thousands of acres to the land already being farmed to increase crop production. They had more irrigation dams and channels built to supply more water to the population. The pharaohs also ordered the construction of a canal between the

ReadingHELPDESK

Taking Notes: *Organizing*

As you read this lesson, complete a chart like this one about the Middle Kingdom and the New Kingdom.

	Middle Kingdom	New Kingdom
Date		
Government		
Economy		

Content Vocabulary

• **incense**   • **envoy**

Nile River and the Red Sea. As a result, Egyptian traders were able to send goods south by ship through the Red Sea. From there, the ships sailed to ports along the coasts of Arabia and East Africa.

The Arts Flourish

Egyptian arts and architecture thrived during the Middle Kingdom. Painters decorated the walls of tombs and temples with colorful scenes. These tomb paintings illustrated stories about the deities, as well as scenes from everyday life. Sculptors carved hunting, fishing, and battle scenes on large stone walls. They created statues of the pharaohs, showing them as ordinary humans rather than gods.

During the Middle Kingdom, the Egyptians developed a new kind of architecture. Pharaohs no longer had pyramids built. Instead, they had their tombs cut into limestone cliffs west of the Nile River. This area became known as the Valley of the Kings.

The Hyksos

During the 1600s B.C., some Egyptian nobles challenged the power of the pharaohs. Civil war divided Egypt, ending an era of peace and prosperity. As the Middle Kingdom weakened, outsiders invaded Egypt. A people from western Asia known as the Hyksos (HIHK·sahs) swept across the desert into Egypt.

The Hyksos were powerful warriors who used methods of warfare unknown to the Egyptians. The Hyksos rode in horse-drawn chariots and fought with sturdy weapons made of bronze and iron. As a result, they overwhelmed the Egyptian soldiers and took control of the land.

For more than 100 years, Hyksos kings ruled Egypt. The Hyksos borrowed some Egyptian customs but remained separate from the Egyptian people. Meanwhile, most Egyptians hated the Hyksos and planned to overthrow them. The Egyptians learned how to steer horse-drawn chariots and use Hyksos weapons. Around 1550 B.C., an Egyptian prince named Ahmose (AH·mohs) formed an army and drove the Hyksos out of Egypt.

✔ **PROGRESS CHECK**

Analyzing How were the Egyptians able to defeat the Hyksos?

Artisans produced jewels for pharaohs and decorative objects from gold, such as this chair.

▶ CRITICAL THINKING
Differentiating What about this chair makes you think it was made for royalty?

The Hyksos introduced chariots to Egypt. Battle scenes show the advantage a soldier on a chariot has over those on foot.

Building an Empire

GUIDING QUESTION *Why was the New Kingdom a unique period in ancient Egypt's history?*

Ahmose founded a new dynasty. It began a period known as the New Kingdom, which lasted from about 1550 B.C. to 1070 B.C. During this time, Egypt prospered through trade, gained more lands through conquest, and reached the height of its power. No longer isolated, Egyptians benefited from the spread of goods, ideas, and cultures within their empire.

A Woman Pharaoh

A queen named Hatshepsut (hat·SHEHP·soot) was one of the few women to rule Egypt. She came to power in about 1473 B.C. and governed with her husband. Then, after his death, she made herself pharaoh and ruled on behalf of her young nephew.

Because the title of pharaoh was usually passed from father to son, Hatshepsut had to prove that she was a good leader. In order for the people to accept her, Hatshepsut dressed in the clothes of a male pharaoh. She even wore the false beard to copy the one worn by male Egyptian kings. She built magnificent temples and restored old monuments. Her tomb in the Valley of the Kings contains large wall carvings that illustrate some of the major events of her reign.

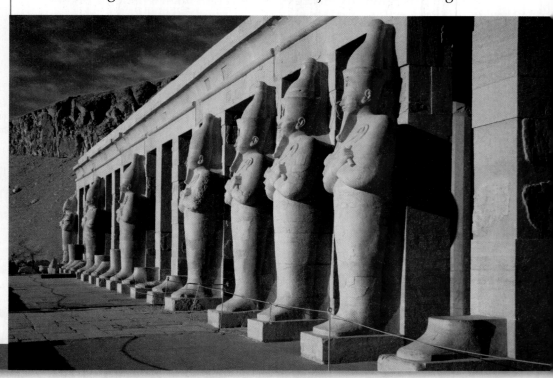

One of the few women to govern Egypt, Hatshepsut ruled with the support of her subjects. This enormous tomb stands today in honor of her reign.

Reading HELP DESK

Reading Strategy: *Sequencing*

Key words such as *then*, *later*, and *after* are clues to the order in which events happened. Which of these key words is used on this page?

Growth of Trade

Hatshepsut was more interested in promoting trade than starting wars. She made great efforts to restore trade relations that had been interrupted by the Hyksos invasion.

During the rule of Hatshepsut, Egyptian seafarers sailed to ports in Arabia and East Africa. There, Egyptian traders exchanged beads, metal tools, and weapons for gold, ivory, ebony wood, and **incense** (IN·sens), a material burned for its pleasant smell.

The Egyptians valued wood products because the Nile River valley had few trees. They needed wood to build boats, furniture, and other items. To find wood, Egyptian traders traveled to the east coast of the Mediterranean Sea where the present-day country of Lebanon is located. The people in this region were called the Phoenicians (fih·NEE·shuns). The Phoenicians had a great impact on other cultures in the region. Their invention of an alphabet and a system of writing influenced others. Phoenician trade routes and settlements also encouraged the spread of goods and ideas across a large part of the ancient world.

Trade and Politics

The Egyptians traded wheat, paper, gold, copper, tin and tools to the Phoenicians for purple dye, wood, and furniture. The traders exchanged goods they had for supplies they needed, rather than selling goods for money. The Phoenicians in turn traded Egyptian goods to other people. By trading with the Phoenicians, Egyptians spread their food and goods across Southwest Asia. Trade in the eastern Mediterranean helped make the Egyptian kingdom wealthier. Hatshepsut used some of this wealth to build monuments.

In addition to trade, New Kingdom pharaohs developed political ties between Egypt and nearby kingdoms. For example, the Egyptian dynasty became joined by treaty or marriage with ruling families in the Babylonian Empire in Mesopotamia, the Mittani (mih·TAH·nee) in Syria, and the Hittite Empire in Anatolia (ah·nuh·TOH·lee·uh).

To maintain close ties, pharaohs and the other rulers also exchanged **envoys** (EHN·voyz), or representatives. These actions marked the first time in history that a group of nations tried working together to reach common goals.

BIOGRAPHY

**Hatshepsut
(reigned 1473–1458 B.C.)**

Hatshepsut was one of the most successful rulers of Egypt. Hatshepsut chose people who were loyal to her to serve in government positions. She valued the opinions of common Egyptians and sought their support for decisions she made. After her death, Thutmose III, Hatshepsut's nephew, had her name removed from royal texts and monuments. Historians believe that he did this to show that no female ruler interrupted the royal line of males.

▶ **CRITICAL THINKING**
Drawing Conclusions What actions of hers helped make Hatshepsut a successful ruler?

---

incense a material that produces a pleasant smell when burned

envoy a government representative to another country

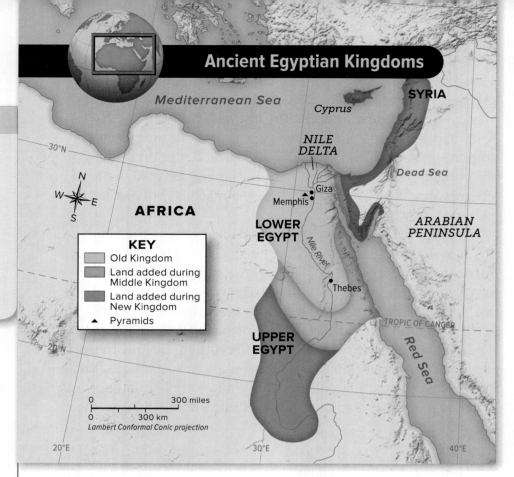

GEOGRAPHY CONNECTION

During the Middle Kingdom, the capital of Egypt was moved from Memphis to Thebes.

1 LOCATION Identify the relative location of Thebes.

2 PLACE Describe the borders of the New Kingdom.

3 CRITICAL THINKING
Comparing Which kingdom added the most territory?

KEY
- Old Kingdom
- Land added during Middle Kingdom
- Land added during New Kingdom
- ▲ Pyramids

0   300 miles
0   300 km
Lambert Conformal Conic projection

Expanding the Empire

When Hatshepsut died, her nephew, Thutmose III (thoot·MOH·suh), became pharaoh. Thutmose was a strong leader and general who expanded Egypt's control north to the Euphrates River in Mesopotamia. His troops also moved south far up the Nile and conquered Nubia, which had once thrown off Egyptian rule. Egyptian armies captured nearly 350 cities during Thutmose's reign.

As Thutmose and his armies conquered more areas, the Egyptian Empire grew wealthy, and slavery became more common. Egypt **acquired** gold, copper, ivory, and other valuable goods from conquered peoples. Egyptians captured and enslaved many prisoners of war. Enslaved people had some rights, however, including the right to own land, marry, and eventually gain their freedom.

✓ PROGRESS CHECK

Explaining Why did the Egyptians want to trade with the Phoenicians?

Reading**HELP**DESK

Academic Vocabulary

acquire to get possession of something

Two Unusual Pharaohs

GUIDING QUESTION *How did two unusual pharaohs change ancient Egypt?*

During the New Kingdom, two remarkable pharaohs came to power. One pharaoh, Amenhotep IV, tried to make dramatic changes, and one, Tutankhamen, was very young. Their actions set them apart from other rulers in Egypt's long history.

A Religious Founder

A new pharaoh named Amenhotep IV (ah·muhn·HOH·tehp) came to power in about 1370 B.C. Supported by his wife, Nefertiti (nehf·uhr·TEE·tee), Amenhotep tried to change Egypt's religion, which was based on the worship of many deities.

Amenhotep believed that Egypt's priests had grown too powerful and wealthy. He felt threatened by their power. To lessen the priests' **authority**, Amenhotep started a new religion. He introduced the worship of Aton (AHT·n), a sun god, as Egypt's only god. When Egypt's priests opposed this change, Amenhotep removed many of them from their posts, took their lands, and closed temples. He then changed his name to Akhenaton (ahk·NAH·tuhn), meaning "Spirit of Aton." The capital was moved to a new city north of Thebes called Akhetaton (ahk·heh·TAH·tuhn).

These changes unsettled Egypt. Most Egyptians rejected Aton and continued to worship many deities. In addition, the priests of the old religion resisted their loss of power. The discontent with Akhenaton's rule spread to the army leaders. They believed Akhenaton, devoted to his new religion, neglected his duties as pharaoh. Under Akhenaton's weak rule, Egypt lost most of its lands in western Asia to outside invaders.

Who Was "King Tut"?

When Akhenaton died about 1360 B.C., his son, 10-year-old Tutankhamen (too·tang·KAH·muhn), became pharaoh. The young pharaoh relied on advice from priests and officials to rule Egypt. Tutankhamen quickly restored the worship of many deities. Tutankhamen's short rule ended after only nine years, when he died unexpectedly. The cause of his death is still a mystery to historians, and he remains a fascinating figure.

King Tut is shown wearing the false beard worn by all pharaohs. Tut was a child when he became pharaoh. He died at the age of 19.

Egyptian National Museum, Cairo/SuperStock

Academic Vocabulary

authority the right or power to give orders, make decisions, or control people

Even though "King Tut" played a small role in the history of Egypt, he is the most famous of the pharaohs. British archaeologist Howard Carter attracted public attention when he discovered Tut's tomb in 1922. Carter's find was amazing because most tombs of the pharaohs had been robbed by thieves. Tut's tomb, however, contained the pharaoh's mummy and many treasures, including a brilliant gold mask of the young ruler's face.

✓ PROGRESS CHECK

Evaluating Why are Akhenaton and Tutankhamen considered unusual pharaohs?

Recovery and Decline

GUIDING QUESTION *Why did the Egyptian empire decline in the late 1200s B.C.?*

During the 1200s B.C., the pharaohs worked to restore Egypt's greatness. They fought battles for more territory, increased Egypt's wealth through trade, and built large temples and monuments.

Ramses II

The most successful of these pharaohs was Ramses II (RAM·seez), who ruled from 1279 B.C. to 1213 B.C. Ramses conquered the region of Canaan and moved north into Syria. To get this territory, he fought the Hittites, who lived in present-day Turkey. After many battles, Ramses and the Hittite king signed a peace treaty.

Age of Temples

During his 66-year reign, Ramses also devoted himself to peaceful activities. Ramses II and other New Kingdom rulers had many temples built throughout Egypt. One of the most magnificent was Karnak (KAHR·nack) at Thebes. Its huge columned hall still impresses visitors today. A poem celebrating a victory by Ramses is carved in the temple. In part of the poem, Ramses says this to his chariot driver:

" Halt! take courage, charioteer, As a sparrow-hawk swoops down upon his prey, So I swoop upon the foe, and I will slay, I will hew [cut] them into pieces, I will dash them into dust. "

—from *Pen-ta-tur: The Victory of Ramses II Over the Khita*

Most Egyptians prayed in their homes, so temples were used only for special occasions. Egyptians saw the temples as the

Few rulers reigned as long as Ramses. He reigned three years longer than England's Queen Victoria, who ruled for 63 years. What mathematical expression would tell you the length of Ramses' reign?

Reading**HELP**DESK

Academic Vocabulary

decline to become weaker

Reading Strategy: *Understanding Cause and Effect*

The word *so* indicates the effect of an event. Read the first sentence in the last paragraph above. The *effect* is that temples were used only for special occasions. What is the cause?

Still in use after more than 3,000 years, Karnak remains to honor Ramses' many achievements.

homes of their deities. Priests and priestesses performed daily rituals, washed the statues of the deities, and brought them food.

Temples were important to Egypt's economy. Priests hired people to work in temple workshops and granaries. Temples also served as banks. Egyptians used them to store valuable items, such as gold jewelry, fragrant oils, and finely woven textiles.

Why Did Egypt Decline?

After Ramses II died, Egypt **declined**. Pharaohs fought costly wars. Armies from the eastern Mediterranean attacked Egypt. By 1150 B.C., the Egyptian empire controlled only the Nile delta.

In the 900s B.C., the Libyans conquered Egypt. Then, the people of Kush seized power. Finally, in 670 B.C., Egypt was taken over by the Assyrians from Mesopotamia.

 PROGRESS CHECK

Summarizing What were the accomplishments of Ramses II?

Manuel ROMARÀS/Moment/Flickr RF/Getty Images

LESSON 3 REVIEW

Review Vocabulary

1. Why would someone want to buy *incense*?

2. What might have been the duties of an ancient Egyptian *envoy*?

Answer the Guiding Questions

3. *Describing* Discuss two reasons why the Middle Kingdom period was a "golden age" for Egypt.

4. *Explaining* Why was the New Kingdom a unique period in ancient Egypt's history?

5. *Summarizing* Describe the religious changes brought about by Akhenaton and Tutankhamen.

6. *Analyzing* In what ways were temples important to Egypt's economy?

7. **ARGUMENT** You are a scribe who works for Queen Hatshepsut. Write a brief report that explains why she is a good pharaoh and deserves the support of the people.

LESSON 4

The Kingdom of Kush

ESSENTIAL QUESTION

• Why do civilizations rise and fall?

IT MATTERS BECAUSE
The kingdoms of Nubia and Kush were influenced by Egyptian culture, and they continued many Egyptian traditions.

The Nubians

GUIDING QUESTION *How did Nubia and Egypt influence each other?*

In addition to Egypt, other civilizations flourished in Africa. One of these African civilizations was Nubia, later known as Kush. Nubia was located south of Egypt along the Nile River in present-day Sudan.

Cattle herders were the first people to settle in this region, arriving about 2000 B.C. They herded long-horned cattle on the **savannas** (suh·VA·nuhs), or grassy plains, that stretch across Africa south of the Sahara. Later, people settled in farming villages along the Nile River.

Unlike the Egyptians, the Nubians did not **rely** on the Nile floods to create fertile soil. Their land had fertile soil and received rainfall all year long. Nubian villagers grew crops such as beans, yams, rice, and grains. The Nubians also hunted for food. Their hunters and warriors excelled at using the bow and arrow.

The Rise of Kerma

Gradually, the stronger Nubian villages took over the weaker ones and formed the kingdom of Kerma (KAR·muh). The Nubians of Kerma grew wealthy from agriculture and the mining of gold. Their kingdom developed a close relationship

Reading**HELP**DESK

Taking Notes: *Sequencing*
Use a diagram like this one to list events that led up to the Kush conquest of Egypt.

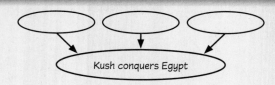

Kush conquers Egypt

Content Vocabulary
• savanna   • textile

with Egypt in the north. Kerma's central location in the Nile Valley benefited the Nubians. It made Kerma an important trade link between Egypt and the tropical areas of southern Africa. From Kerma, the Egyptians acquired cattle, gold, incense, ivory, giraffes, and leopards. They also obtained enslaved people. They hired Nubians to serve in their armies because of the Nubians' skills in warfare. Kerma's artisans produced fine pottery, jewelry, and metal goods.

Workers built tombs for Kerma's kings, usually on a smaller scale than Egyptian tombs. Like the Egyptian pharaohs, the kings of Kerma were buried with their personal belongings, including valuable gems, gold, jewelry, and pottery. These artifacts were as magnificent as those found in Egypt's royal tombs that were built during the same time period.

Egyptian Invasion

Egyptian armies invaded Nubia in the 1400s B.C. After a 50-year war, the Egyptians conquered the kingdom of Kerma and ruled it for the next 700 years.

As a result of Egyptian rule, the Nubians adopted many of the beliefs and customs of Egyptian culture. For example, the Nubians worshipped Egyptian gods and goddesses along with their own Nubian deities. They learned to use copper and bronze to make tools. The Nubians adapted Egyptian hieroglyphs to fit their own language and created an alphabet.

☑ **PROGRESS CHECK**

Analyzing Why did Kerma become an important center for trade?

The savannas of Africa are grassy and dotted with trees and herds of wildlife. The grasses can withstand long, hot periods without rain. These broad plains covered much of Nubia.

Mike D. Kock/Gallo Images/Getty Images

savanna a flat grassland, sometimes with scattered trees, in a tropical or subtropical region

Academic Vocabulary

rely to depend on someone or something

The Kushite Kingdom

GUIDING QUESTION *Why did the kingdom of Kush prosper?*

By the end of the Middle Kingdom, Egypt was weak. It could no longer govern its conquered peoples effectively, and the Nubians were able to break away from Egyptian rule.

The Rise of Kush

By 850 B.C., the Nubians had formed an independent kingdom known as Kush. Powerful kings ruled the country from its capital at Napata (NA·puh·tuh).

The city of Napata was located where trade caravans crossed the upper part of the Nile River. Caravans came from central Africa, bringing ivory and other goods. They stopped at Napata for Kushite products and then continued on to Egypt. The Egyptians traded with Kush for goods the Egyptians could not make. Such trade brought wealth to the traders and kings of Kush.

Kush Conquers Egypt

In time, Kush became powerful enough to **challenge** Egypt. About 750 B.C., a Kushite king named Kashta (KAHSH·tuh) invaded Egypt. His soldiers reached the city of Thebes. After Kashta died, his son Piye (PY) became king and completed the conquest of Egypt in 728 B.C. Piye founded the Twenty-fifth Dynasty that governed Egypt and Kush from Napata.

The kings and wealthy people of Kush continued to admire Egyptian culture. Kushites built white sandstone temples and monuments similar to those in Egypt. The Kushites also believed

©Sandro Vannini/Corbis

In this scene, Nubian royalty offer gifts to an Egyptian pharaoh. The procession shows respect for the pharaoh.

Reading **HELP**DESK

Academic Vocabulary

challenge to invite the start of a competition

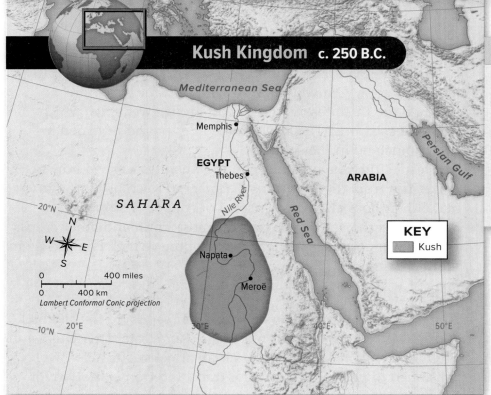

Kush Kingdom c. 250 B.C.

Mediterranean Sea

Memphis

EGYPT

Thebes

ARABIA

SAHARA

Nile River

Red Sea

Persian Gulf

20°N

N
W E
S

0   400 miles
0   400 km
Lambert Conformal Conic projection

Napata

Meroë

KEY
Kush

10°N   20°E   30°E   40°E   50°E

GEOGRAPHY CONNECTION

Trade caravans crossed the Nile near Napata, which made the city a busy trading center.

1 **LOCATION** In what direction would traders travel to get from Napata to Meroë?

2 **CRITICAL THINKING** *Analyzing* How is the Nile different south of Meroë?

Kushite artisans worked in gold, creating objects such as this statue of Amon-Re. They also made fine pottery.

in a close relationship between their rulers and their deities, many of whom were Egyptian. For example, when a king died, Kushite officials met at the temple to ask the Egyptian god Amon-Re to appoint a new leader:

PRIMARY SOURCE

❝ So the commanders of His Majesty and the officials of the palace ... [found] the major priests waiting outside the temple. They said to them, "Pray, may this god, Amon-Re ... give us our lord. ... We cannot do a thing without this god. It is he who guides us. ..." Then the commanders ... and the officials ... entered into the temple and put themselves upon their bellies before this god. They said, "We have come to you, O Amon-Re, ... that you might give to us a lord, to revive us, to build the temples of the gods, ... ❞

—from *The Selection of Aspalta as King of Kush*

The Kushites also built small, steeply sloped pyramids as tombs for their kings. Some people in Kush, however, adopted customs and styles similar to those worn by southern Africans. This included wearing ankle and ear jewelry. By this time, the people of Kush also had developed their own style of painted pottery. The elephant, a sacred animal in Kush, was used as a theme in sculpture and other arts.

INTERFOTO/Alamy

Reading Strategy: *Reading a Map*

When reading a map, first locate the key. It will help you identify what is being shown on the map. What is the key identifying on the map above?

Using Iron

Kush ruled Egypt for about 60 years. In 671 B.C., the Assyrians invaded Egypt. Armed with iron weapons, the Assyrians defeated the Kushites, who only had bronze weapons, which were not as strong. The Kushites fled Egypt and returned to their homeland in the south.

Despite their defeat in Egypt, the Kushites learned how to make iron from the Assyrians. Farmers in Kush used iron to make their hoes and plows instead of copper or stone. With better tools, they were able to grow more grain and other crops. Kushite warriors also created iron weapons, which boosted their military strength.

The Capital of Meroë

About 540 B.C., Kush's rulers moved their capital to the city of Meroë (MEHR·oh·ee), near one of the Nile's cataracts. This move made them safer from Assyrian attacks. The Nile River continued to provide a means for trade and transportation for the Kushites. Large deposits of iron ore and trees were nearby and were used to fuel furnaces for making iron. As a result, Meroë became a major center for iron production as well as a busy trading city.

Kushite kings modeled the layout and design of Meroë after Egypt's great cities. A temple dedicated to the god Amon-Re stood at the end of a long avenue lined with sculptures of rams. The walls of palaces and houses were decorated with paintings. Small pyramids stood in the royal graveyard, modeled on the larger pyramids of Egypt. Meroë, however, was different from a typical Egyptian city because it contained iron furnaces. Huge columns of smoke poured out of iron furnaces. Heaps of shiny black slag, or waste from iron making, lay around the furnaces.

The Kushites adopted pyramids as tombs. They usually built tombs that were smaller than those of the Egyptians, however.

giovanni mereghetti/Marka/Age fotostock

Modeled on Egyptian cities, Meroë had a special purpose. It was an iron-making city with smokestacks and soot.

A Trading Center

Meroë was at the heart of a large web of trade that ran north to Egypt's border and south into central Africa. Kush's merchants received leopard skins and valuable woods from the tropical interior of Africa. They traded these items, along with their own iron products, to places as far away as Arabia, India, China, and Rome. Enslaved people were also traded. In return, they brought back cotton, **textiles** (TEHK·styls), or woven cloth, and other goods. Kush's merchants used their wealth to build fine houses and public baths like ones they had seen in Rome.

Kush remained a great trading kingdom for nearly 600 years. Then, another kingdom called Axum (AHK·soom) emerged near the Red Sea in eastern Africa. Axum is located in the present-day country of Ethiopia. Axum gained its strength from its location on the Red Sea. Goods from Africa flowed into Axum. Over time, it served as a trading center for the ancient Mediterranean and East African worlds. Around A.D. 350, the armies of Axum invaded Kush and destroyed Meroë.

✓ PROGRESS CHECK

Explaining How did the use of iron affect Kush?

LESSON 4 REVIEW

Review Vocabulary

1. What are the characteristics of a *savanna*?

2. What are *textiles* used to make?

Answer the Guiding Questions

3. *Explaining* How did Nubia and Egypt influence each other?

4. *Comparing and Contrasting* How were the cities of Kush similar to and different from those of Egypt?

5. *Drawing Conclusions* How did natural resources help make Meroë a great trading city?

6. **ARGUMENT** Create an advertisement that could have been used in ancient Egypt and Kush to encourage people to use iron.

Write your answers on a separate piece of paper.

1 **Exploring the Essential Question**
INFORMATIVE/EXPLANATORY Why did the ancient Egyptian civilization fall? Write an essay that explains the events and decisions that led to the end of Egypt's role as a political, economic, and cultural power.

2 **21st Century Skills**
GIVING A PRESENTATION Prepare a presentation that identifies the key events and achievements of Egypt's Old Kingdom, Middle Kingdom, and New Kingdom. Compare and contrast the developments in each time period. End your presentation with a brief statement about the importance of the Egyptian civilization.

3 **Thinking Like a Historian**
UNDERSTANDING PROS AND CONS Create a chart like the one here to identify the pros and cons of living along the Nile River. Then, write a sentence that tells why early Egyptians settled there.

Characteristics of the Nile River	Pros	Cons
Regular flooding		
Cataracts		
Downhill flow		

4 **GEOGRAPHY ACTIVITY**

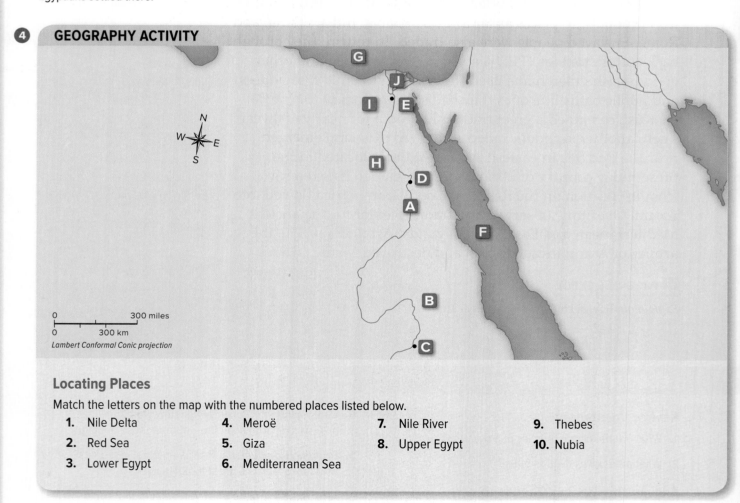

0   300 miles
0   300 km
Lambert Conformal Conic projection

Locating Places

Match the letters on the map with the numbered places listed below.

1. Nile Delta
2. Red Sea
3. Lower Egypt
4. Meroë
5. Giza
6. Mediterranean Sea
7. Nile River
8. Upper Egypt
9. Thebes
10. Nubia

Directions: Write your answers on a separate piece of paper.

CHECKING FOR UNDERSTANDING

1 Define each of these terms as they relate to ancient Egypt and Kush.

A. delta	**F.** Middle Kingdom
B. papyrus	**G.** Karnak
C. Memphis	**H.** Nubia
D. bureaucrat	**I.** Napata
E. embalming	

REVIEW THE GUIDING QUESTIONS

2 *Identifying* What bodies of water allowed Egypt to remain in contact and trade with the outside world?

3 *Describing* Describe the methods of irrigation used by Egyptian farmers along the Nile River.

4 *Explaining* How did the Egyptian form of writing advance beyond the use of symbols to represent objects and ideas?

5 *Explaining* Did Narmer's kingdom last after his death? Explain.

6 *Specifying* Why were the gods Re and Hapi especially important to the Egyptians?

7 *Identifying* Who was Imhotep, and what was his significance in ancient Egypt?

8 *Listing* List some of the items traded by the Egyptians to the Phoenicians during the New Kingdom.

9 *Explaining* How did Kerma's location benefit that kingdom?

10 *Identifying* What practice did the Kushites adopt from the conquering Assyrians? How did they use this new skill?

CRITICAL THINKING

11 *Determining Cause and Effect* What effect did the landforms surrounding the Nile Valley have on the development of Egyptian civilization?

12 *Identifying Central Issues* Why was an organized government needed in Egypt? Describe the development of government in the Nile Valley through the time of Narmer.

13 *Making Connections* How did the Egyptians' belief of an afterlife contribute to medical advancements? Describe some of those advancements in your answer.

14 *Giving Examples* Provide examples of the scientific and mathematical discoveries made by the Egyptians as they built the pyramids.

15 *Making Inferences* Study the diagram titled Social Status in Ancient Egypt in Lesson 2. What do you think the diagram tells you about relative wealth among the different classes in Egypt? Explain your reasoning.

16 *Assessing* Was the reign of Hatshepsut a successful period for the kingdom of Egypt? Explain your answer.

17 *Evaluating* Is Tutankhamen deserving of his status as the best-known Egyptian ruler? Explain.

18 *Summarizing* Summarize the events in the decline of the Egyptian kingdom.

19 *Contrasting* How did Nubian agriculture and farming practices differ from those of the Egyptians?

20 *Comparing and Contrasting* What differences and similarities existed in the societies of Egypt and Kush?

Need Extra Help?

If You've Missed Question	**1**	**2**	**3**	**4**	**5**	**6**	**7**	**8**	**9**	**10**	**11**	**12**	**13**	**14**	**15**	**16**	**17**	**18**	**19**	**20**
Review Lesson	1,2, 3, 4	1	1	1	1	2	2	3	4	4	1	1	2	2	2	3	3	3	4	4

EXTENDED RESPONSE

㉑ **_Narrative_** You are an Egyptian trader visiting the Kush city of Meroë. Write a journal entry in which you describe the city, and compare it to your Egyptian home.

STANDARDIZED TEST PRACTICE

DBQ ANALYZING DOCUMENTS

㉒ **_Drawing Conclusions_** An epic poem describes the victory of King Ramses II over the Hittites.

"Then the King spake [spoke] to his squire,
Halt! take courage, charioteer,
As a sparrow-hawk swoops down on his prey,
So I swoop upon the foe [enemy], and I will slay.'"

　　　　　—from *Pen-ta-tur: The Victory of Ramses II Over the Khita*

Which word best describes Ramses as he is depicted in the poem?

A. bird-like

B. innocent

C. uncertain

D. courageous

㉓ **_Inferring_** How might the Egyptians have reacted to this poem?

A. It made them afraid of their king.

B. It made them regret going to war.

C. It made them feel proud to be Egyptian.

D. It made them worry about losing to the enemy.

Need Extra Help?

If You've Missed Question	㉑	㉒	㉓
Review Lesson	4	3	3

TEXT: The Pyramid Builders by Virginia Morell. National Geographic Magazine November 2001. Copyright © 2001 National Geographic Society.

◀ *As a young man, David was known for his bravery and his skill in playing the lyre, a type of harp.*

1800 B.C. TO A.D. 70

The Israelites

Lebrecht Music and Arts Photo Library/Alamy

THE STORY MATTERS ...

David is considered to be the greatest Israelite king, yet he was not born into royalty. David, a shepherd, became a leader of the Israelite people. As their king, he united the Israelites and expanded their lands. He was also the author of the Psalms, or poems often used in prayer and song. David stands as the greatest among many important leaders who guided the Israelites throughout their history.

ESSENTIAL QUESTIONS

- How do religions develop?
- What are the characteristics of a leader?
- How does religion shape society?
- Why does conflict develop?

Place & Time: The Israelites 1800 B.C. to A.D. 70

The ancient Israelites struggled for centuries to build a secure homeland. This was difficult because their location in the eastern Mediterranean region was surrounded by more powerful empires. Their religion, Judaism, became a world religion. It would later influence Christianity and Islam.

Step Into the Place

MAP FOCUS The Israelites constructed the city of Jerusalem atop seven hills.

LOCATION Look at the map. Where is Jerusalem located relative to the Mediterranean Sea?

1 REGIONS Which geographic features surround Jerusalem?

2 LOCATION Where is Jerusalem located relative to Egypt?

3 CRITICAL THINKING
Analyzing Why might the Israelites have chosen Jerusalem for their capital city?

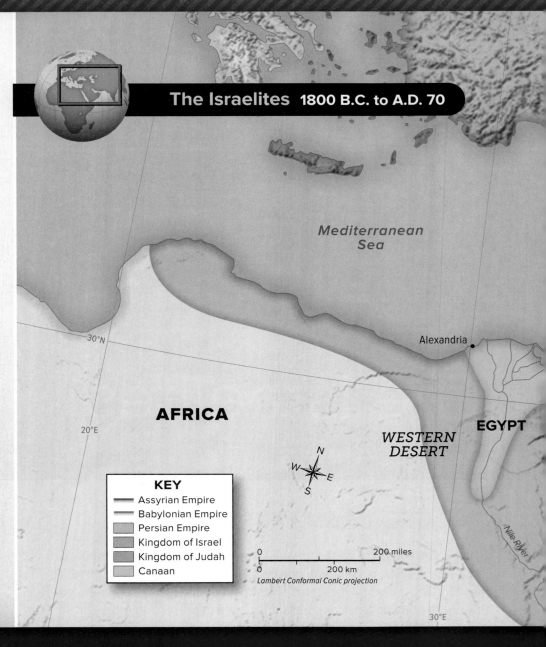

The Israelites 1800 B.C. to A.D. 70

KEY
— Assyrian Empire
— Babylonian Empire
Persian Empire
Kingdom of Israel
Kingdom of Judah
Canaan

Mediterranean Sea

AFRICA

WESTERN DESERT

EGYPT

Alexandria

Nile River

0 — 200 miles
0 — 200 km
Lambert Conformal Conic projection

Step Into the Time

TIME LINE What was happening to new ideas all over the world as Judaism grew?

c. 1290 B.C. According to the Hebrew Bible, Moses leads Israelites from Egypt

c. 1800 B.C. According to the Hebrew Bible, Abraham traveled to Canaan

THE ISRAELITES
THE WORLD

3000 B.C.   2000 B.C.

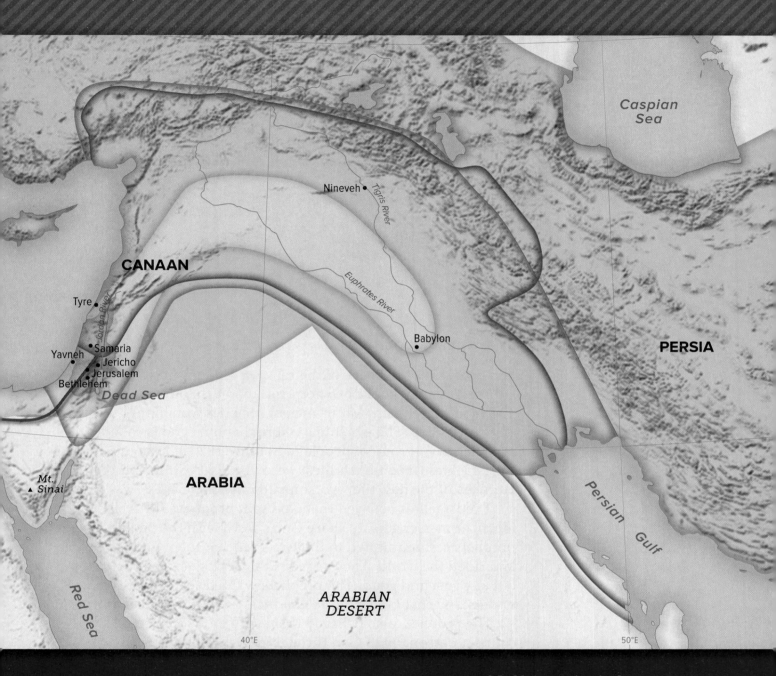

Caspian
Sea

Nineveh

Tigris River

CANAAN

Tyre

Jordan River

Euphrates River

Yavneh
Samaria
Jericho
Jerusalem
Bethlehem

Babylon

PERSIA

Dead Sea

Mt.
Sinai

ARABIA

Persian Gulf

Red Sea

ARABIAN
DESERT

40°E

50°E

c. 722 B.C. Assyrians invade northern kingdom of Israel

c. A.D. 66 Jews revolt against Rome

c. 1000 B.C. King
David rules in Jerusalem

c. 586 B.C. Chaldeans
destroy Jerusalem

c. 168 B.C.
Maccabean revolt

c. A.D. 70 Romans destroy temple
in Jerusalem

1000 B.C.   750 B.C.   500 B.C.   250 B.C.   A.D. 100   A.D. 1000

c. 700 B.C. Homer

c. A.D. 55 Paul preaches

LESSON 1
Beginnings

• How do religions develop?

IT MATTERS BECAUSE
The beliefs and early leaders of the ancient Israelites represent the foundations of Judaism.

Beginnings

GUIDING QUESTION *What did the ancient Israelites believe?*

You probably have heard of the religion of Judaism (JOO·dee·ih·zuhm). You may not know, however, that it is both an ancient and modern religion. Many ancient societies worshipped many deities, or gods. The worship of more than one god is called polytheism. A group of people in Southwest Asia known as the Israelites (IHZ·ree·ah·lites) were different. Unlike other **cultures** of the day, they worshipped only one God.

The Israelites believed that God sent **prophets** (PRAH·fehts), or messengers, to share God's word with the people. The prophets communicated to the Israelites that their God created and ruled the world. They argued that God is very powerful but also just and good. The prophets wanted the Israelites to understand that God expects goodness from his people.

The prophets also believed that every individual could connect personally to God through prayer, religious study, and good and just acts. The belief in one all-powerful, just, and personal God is called **monotheism** (MAH·nuh·thee·ih·zuhm). The practice of monotheism made Judaism unique among ancient religions.

Reading**HELP**DESK

Taking Notes: *Summarizing*
Use a diagram like this one to list at least two facts about each category.

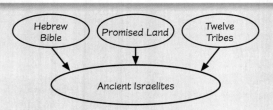

Content Vocabulary

- **prophet**
- **monotheism**
- **tribe**
- **Exodus**
- **covenant**
- **Torah**
- **commandment**
- **alphabet**

The Hebrew Bible

The Israelites recorded their beliefs and history. These writings became known as the Hebrew Bible or Tanakh (TAH·nahk). Through the Hebrew Bible, the beliefs and faith of the ancient Israelites lived on to become the religion of Judaism. The followers of Judaism are today known as Jews.

Although the original Israelite population was small, their influence was great. Judaism played an important part in the development of two other major monotheistic religions—Christianity and Islam. Christians call the Hebrew Bible the Old Testament. Christianity grew directly out of Judaism. Islam also accepted many of Judaism's beliefs and practices. Through the Hebrew Bible, Judaism influenced the values, ethics, and principles of many other societies.

Abraham

Around 1200 B.C. great changes took place in the Mediterranean region. Egypt's empire ended, and new peoples, including the Israelites, created kingdoms in the region. The early Israelites depended on herding and trading to survive. According to the Hebrew Bible, Abraham and his family migrated from Mesopotamia and settled in Canaan (KAY·nuhn) along the Mediterranean Sea. Today, the countries of Lebanon, Israel, and Jordan occupy the land that was once Canaan.

According to Jewish belief, the ancestors of the ancient Israelites were a man named Abraham and his family. The Hebrew Bible gives this account of Abraham's family and the early history of the Israelites. The Hebrew Bible states that God told Abraham to journey to Canaan, which would belong to Abraham and his descendants forever. According to the Hebrew Bible, Abraham, his wife Sarah, and their entire household accepted God's promise and settled in Canaan. The land is often called the Promised Land because of God's promise to Abraham.

The Hebrew Bible says that Abraham led his family to Canaan. In addition to his role in Judaism, Abraham is regarded as an important figure in Christianity and Islam.

Tom Lovell/National Geographic Society Image Collection

prophet a messenger sent by God to share God's word with people

monotheism a belief in one God

Academic Vocabulary

culture the beliefs and behaviors of a group of people

Moses
(c. 14th–13th century B.C.)

According to the Hebrew Bible, Moses was born in Egypt to an Israelite woman enslaved by the pharaoh. After the pharaoh demanded all newborn Israelite boys be killed, Moses's mother hid him in a basket and floated him down the Nile River. The pharaoh's daughter rescued him and adopted him.

▶ **CRITICAL THINKING**
Explaining What important leadership traits did Moses show?

Isaac and Jacob

After Abraham died, his son Isaac and later his grandson Jacob headed the family. According to the Hebrew Bible, an angel gave Jacob the new name of Israel, which means "one who struggles with God." Later Jacob's descendants were called "Israelites." As stated in the Hebrew Bible, Jacob's 12 sons became the leaders of **tribes** (TRYBS), or separate family groups. Jacob's sons were the ancestors of the Twelve Tribes of Israel.

After living in Canaan for many years, Jacob's family left because of a famine. They migrated to Egypt and lived there in peace for several generations. As the Israelite population increased, however, the Egyptian pharaoh grew uneasy. He feared that one day the Israelites would rebel. To prevent this, the Egyptians forced the Israelites into slavery.

Moses and the Exodus

The Israelites were forced to work at hard labor, so they prayed to God to be set free. According to the Hebrew Bible, an Israelite prophet named Moses turned out to be their deliverer. While tending sheep in the wilderness outside Egypt, Moses saw a bush in flames. God called to Moses from the burning bush. He told Moses to tell the pharaoh to let the Israelites go.

Moses went before the pharaoh to demand the release of the Israelites. When the pharaoh refused, the Hebrew Bible says that God sent 10 plagues upon Egypt. These plagues were events that caused problems for the Egyptians, such as **locusts** devouring the fields or outbreaks of disease. The plagues convinced the pharaoh to free the Israelites. After the Israelites left Egypt for Canaan, the pharaoh decided to send his army to pursue them.

When the Israelites reached the Red Sea, there was no way to cross the waters. According to the Hebrew Bible, God parted the Red Sea to let his people cross to the other side. When the pharaoh's army tried to follow, the waters flooded back and drowned them. The departure of the Israelites out of slavery in Egypt is known as the **Exodus** (EHK·suh·duhs). Jews celebrate a holy festival called Passover to remember their freedom from slavery.

The Covenant

On their way from Egypt, according to the Hebrew Bible, the Israelites received a **covenant** (KUHV·uh·nuhnt), or agreement with God. In the agreement, God promised to return the Israelites

Reading **HELP**DESK

tribe a social group made up of families or clans
Exodus the departure of the Israelites out of slavery in Egypt
covenant an agreement with God

Visual Vocabulary
locust a grasshopper that often migrates in large numbers

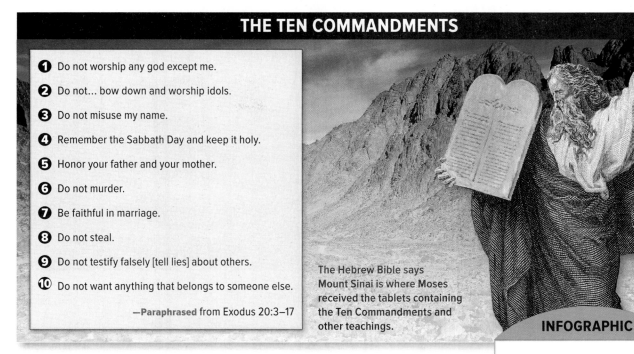

THE TEN COMMANDMENTS

❶ Do not worship any god except me.

❷ Do not... bow down and worship idols.

❸ Do not misuse my name.

❹ Remember the Sabbath Day and keep it holy.

❺ Honor your father and your mother.

❻ Do not murder.

❼ Be faithful in marriage.

❽ Do not steal.

❾ Do not testify falsely [tell lies] about others.

❿ Do not want anything that belongs to someone else.

—Paraphrased from Exodus 20:3–17

The Hebrew Bible says Mount Sinai is where Moses received the tablets containing the Ten Commandments and other teachings.

INFOGRAPHIC

1 FINDING THE MAIN IDEA
What is the main idea of the fourth commandment?

2 CRITICAL THINKING
Identifying Which commandments address family relationships?

safely to Canaan and they promised to follow God's teachings. Moses climbed to the top of Mount Sinai (SY • ny). There, as God's chosen leader, he received teachings from God. Known as the **Torah** (TAWR • uh), these teachings later became part of the Hebrew Bible.

The Torah made clear what God considered to be right and wrong. One important part of the Torah is the Ten **Commandments** (kuh•MAND•muhnts).

Loyalty to God is the central idea of the Ten Commandments. The name of God was never to be misused. The Israelites were not to worship any other gods or images. This belief that there is only one God became the basis for both Christianity and Islam.

In addition, the Ten Commandments later helped shape the moral principles of many nations. Think about the laws and rules we have today and how they might relate to these commandments. For example, the principles on which many laws are based, such as rules against stealing or killing, come from the Ten Commandments. The Ten Commandments also promoted social justice and a feeling of community. They contribute to the democratic belief that laws should apply equally to all.

✓ PROGRESS CHECK

Comparing and Contrasting How did the Israelites' beliefs differ from the beliefs of most other ancient peoples?

The Ark of the Covenant was a wooden chest, overlaid in gold, that held the tablets on which the Ten Commandments—part of God's covenant with the Israelites—appeared.

Torah teachings that Moses received from God; later became the first part of the Hebrew Bible

commandment a rule that God wanted the Israelites to follow

The Phoenicians' small, yet durable, ships influenced shipbuilding for centuries. Phoenician sailors also helped advance the use of astronomy in navigation.

▶ **CRITICAL THINKING**
Comparing and Contrasting How do the Phoenician ships appear to be similar to and different from contemporary ships?

North Wind/North Wind Picture Archives

The Land of Canaan

GUIDING QUESTION *How did the Israelites settle Canaan?*

The Hebrew Bible states that Moses died before the Israelites reached the land God had promised them. A new leader named Joshua guided the Israelites into Canaan, but they found other people living there. These peoples included the Canaanites (KAY·nuh·NYTS) and—somewhat later—the Philistines (FIH· luh·STEENS). Unlike the Israelites, these people of Canaan worshipped many gods and goddesses. They also had different ways of life.

Who Were the Canaanites?

Nomadic tribes probably settled in Canaan as early as 3000 B.C. At first, most of the people were herders. They journeyed with their flocks of sheep and other animals from pasture to pasture. Later, they settled in villages, farmed the land, and learned to trade.

Many different groups lived in Canaan. One Canaanite group was the Phoenicians (fih·NEE·shuhns). The Phoenicians lived in cities along the Mediterranean Sea in northern Canaan. Located near a major waterway, the Phoenicians were skilled sailors and talented traders. They used the sun and the stars to plot long sea voyages. Well-built Phoenician ships with oars and sails carried trade goods across the Mediterranean Sea to Greece, Spain, and even western Africa. Phoenician sailors may even have traveled as far as the British Isles in northwestern Europe.

alphabet a set of letters or other characters used to write a language

The Phoenicians soon controlled Mediterranean shipping and trade. At various ports, they exchanged cedar logs, glass, and jewelry for tin and other precious metals. One of the most valued Phoenician products was cloth colored with a beautiful purple dye. This dye was **extracted** from shellfish along the Phoenician coast.

As they traded, the Phoenicians founded settlements throughout the Mediterranean world. Carthage, a settlement on the coast of North Africa, in time became the most powerful city in the western Mediterranean.

As a result of these settlements, Phoenician ideas and goods spread to other peoples. Think what your life might be like without written language. One of the Phoenicians' important contributions was an **alphabet** (AL·fuh·beht), or a group of letters that stand for sounds. The letters could be used to spell out the words in their language. The alphabet made writing simpler and helped people keep better records.

Philistines

Another group in Canaan, the Philistines, migrated from near present-day Greece. They were one of the groups known as the "Sea People" who invaded the Mediterranean area about 1200 B.C. The Philistines set up five walled towns in southern Canaan along the Mediterranean coast. They were skilled in making iron tools and weapons, which helped them create the strongest army in Canaan. The Philistines kept their own language and religion. Still, they accepted many ideas and practices from their neighbors in Canaan.

Connections to TODAY

Alphabets

The Phoenicians began using the alphabet as a way to keep track of trade. Later, the Greeks adapted the Phoenician alphabet. From the Greek alphabet, the Romans created their alphabet. The Roman alphabet is the most widely used writing system in the world today.

EARLY ALPHABETS

INFOGRAPHIC

Modern Characters	Ancient Phoenician	Ancient Hebrew	Ancient Greek	Early Roman
A	𐤀	𐤀	ΑΑΑ	ΜΛΑ
B	𐤁	𐤁	𐤁Ε	B B
G	𐤂	𐤂	ΓΓ	C G
D	𐤃	𐤃	ΔΔΑ	Δ D
E	⊐	⊐	϶ϝϵ	E
F		Y	ϜϜϹ	F
Z	Ζ		Ι	Ζ
TH	⊗		⊙	
I	𐤉	𐤆	⅔⅔	Ι

The Phoenician alphabet contained 22 letters. Unlike the alphabet, it was written from right to left.

▶ **CRITICAL THINKING**

Making Inferences How would the lack of written language have made trade more difficult for ancient people?

Academic Vocabulary

extract to remove by a physical or chemical process

Reading in the Content Area

Tables organize information in a way that helps you remember it. To read a table, look first at the title and headings. Ask yourself questions such as "How is the information organized? What is the table trying to show me?"

Military Conquest

Because other groups lived in the region, the Israelites faced a challenge establishing Canaan as their new homeland. They believed, however, that it was God's will that they claim the land. Joshua led them in a series of battles to conquer Canaan.

The Hebrew Bible tells about the battle at the city of Jericho. There, Joshua told the Israelites to march around the city walls. For six days, they marched while priests blew their trumpets. On the seventh day, according to the account:

PRIMARY SOURCE

❝ Joshua commanded the people, "Shout, for the LORD has given you the city. … At the sound of the trumpet, when the people gave a loud shout, the wall collapsed. ❞

—from *the Hebrew Bible, the book of Joshua, 6: 16–20*

The Israelites took control of the city after the walls of Jericho crumbled.

According to the Hebrew Bible, Joshua led the Israelites in other battles. Any land they seized was divided among the 12 tribes. After Joshua died, political and military leaders called judges ruled the tribes. The judges settled disputes. They also led troops into battle. The Hebrew Bible tells of a woman judge named Deborah, who was admired for her wisdom and bravery. She told the commander Barak (Buh·RAHK) to attack the army of the Canaanite king Jabin. Deborah went to the battlefield as an adviser. With her help, Barak and 10,000 Israelites destroyed the Canaanite forces.

Mary Evans Picture Library

Jericho is one of the oldest continuously inhabited sites in the world. Here we see an illustration of the Hebrew Bible story of Joshua bringing down the walls of the city.

Life in Canaan

After many battles, the Israelite tribes won control of the hilly region of central Canaan and settled there. Most Israelites farmed and herded animals. The land was rocky and dry, with little water. So during the rainy season, farmers collected the rainwater. They stored it in small caves or under the ground. They used the stored water to irrigate crops such as olives, flax, barley, and grapes.

Imagine a rocky countryside dotted by square white houses. Most Israelites lived in houses with two levels. The walls of the houses were made of mud-brick or stone plastered with mud and white-washed. Floors were made of clay. Wooden beams supported a flat, thatched roof, covered with clay. During the day, people cooked and did household chores in the home's lower level. At night, donkeys and goats bedded down there. The family slept on the upper level.

The Tabernacle

According to the Hebrew Bible, the Israelite tribes worshipped God in a large tent-like structure called the tabernacle (TA·buhr·na·kuhl). The Israelites believed that the tabernacle housed God's presence. This structure was taken down and put away as the Israelites moved from place to place. In Canaan, they erected the tabernacle at a religious center called Shiloh.

The Hebrew Bible says that the tabernacle housed a sacred object called the Ark of the Covenant. The ark, a gold-covered wooden chest, held tablets, or stone slabs. The Israelites believed that the Ten Commandments were written on these tablets. The Israelites believed the ark was a sign of God's presence and that having it with them in battle would **ensure** victory.

The ancient tabernacle was a tent constructed from beautiful tapestries, or woven fabric, that were decorated with angels. It was an elaborate structure, containing a courtyard and two rooms. The measurements of the structure were said to have come directly from God, according to the Hebrew Bible.

☑ **PROGRESS CHECK**

Identifying Who were the Phoenicians, and what was their major contribution to world civilization?

Dorling Kindersley/Getty Images

LESSON 1 REVIEW

Review Vocabulary

1. Describe the difference between *monotheism* and *polytheism*.

Answer the Guiding Questions

2. ***Describing*** What subjects are covered in the Hebrew Bible?

3. ***Explaining*** How did the Israelites settle Canaan?

4. ***Summarizing*** What is the central theme of the Ten Commandments?

5. ***Identifying*** Which group living in Canaan included skilled sailors and traders?

6. **INFORMATIVE/EXPLANATORY** Moses was chosen to lead the Israelites out of Egypt. Write a paragraph to explain the qualities you think Moses possessed to undertake this difficult task.

LESSON 2

The Israelite Kingdom

ESSENTIAL QUESTION

• What are the characteristics of a leader?

IT MATTERS BECAUSE

The Israelites were ruled by several important kings. After this time, they were divided into two kingdoms and faced threats from neighboring empires.

Early Kings

GUIDING QUESTION *What was the role of kings in Israelite history?*

By 1100 B.C., the Israelites had settled much of the land of Canaan. They developed a prosperous culture, creating an alphabet and a calendar based on Canaanite ideas. Yet one powerful enemy—the Philistines—remained. When the Philistines moved inland from the Mediterranean Sea, they came into conflict with the Israelites. Many Israelites called for a king to unite the Twelve Tribes and lead them in battle against the Philistines.

Saul: The First King

According to the Hebrew Bible, the Israelites asked the judge Samuel to choose a king. Samuel, though, warned that a king would tax them and enslave them. The Israelites, however, still demanded a king so Samuel chose a young man named Saul (SAWL). Samuel anointed Saul as king, pouring holy oil on him to show that God had blessed him.

Under Saul's leadership, the Israelites won many battles against the Philistines. With each victory, Saul gained greater fame. Later, however, Saul lost the support of the people. According to the Hebrew Bible, Saul disobeyed some of God's commands.

Reading**HELP**DESK

Taking Notes: *Listing*

Use a chart like this one to list the achievements of King David and King Solomon.

King David	King Solomon

Content Vocabulary
• psalm   • exile
• proverb

God then instructed Samuel to choose and anoint another king. Samuel chose a young shepherd named David.

King David

Even before he became Israel's king, David had won praise for his bravery. The Hebrew Bible provides an account of David and his victory over Goliath, a giant Philistine warrior. In a bragging fashion, Goliath dared any Israelite to fight him one-on-one. Young David stepped forward with his shepherd's staff, a slingshot, and five smooth stones. With a heavy spear in hand, Goliath rushed forward. David hurled one stone straight at the giant's forehead. Goliath dropped dead.

Impressed by David's skill, King Saul placed his army under David's command. As David won more and more victories, the women of Israel sang his praises: "Saul has slain his thousands, and David his tens of thousands." Then, seized by jealousy, Saul tried to kill David, but David escaped. When Saul died in battle against the Philistines, David returned and became king.

According to the Hebrew Bible, once David was in power, he united the Israelite tribes. David and his army defeated the Philistines. He then established a capital city for Israel at Jerusalem (juh·ROO·suh·lehm). The Israelites built their capital in the hill country away from the coast. A fine musician and poet, David is believed to have written many of the sacred songs found in the Hebrew Bible's Book of **Psalms** (SALMZ)—also found in the Christian Bible. One of the most famous is Psalm 23, which begins:

The Twelve Tribes of Israel were family groups. According to the Hebrew Bible, each family descended from a son of Jacob. Scholars note that family connections and a common religion bound the tribes together long before they united under David.

According to the Hebrew Bible, David was tending sheep when Samuel arrived to anoint him.

PRIMARY SOURCE

" The LORD is my shepherd, I shall not be in want.
He makes me lie down in green pastures,
  he leads me beside quiet waters,
  he restores my soul.
He guides me in the paths of righteousness [fairness]
for his name's sake. "

—Psalm: 23:1–3

psalm a sacred song or poem used in worship

Solomon built the First Temple on a site David had selected, the Temple Mount. The spot had religious significance. It was the place, according to the Hebrew Bible, where Abraham had tried to sacrifice Isaac.

Under David's rule, the Israelites enjoyed prosperous times. Farmers cultivated the tough, dry land by building terraces on the steep hillsides. Terraced fields are strips of land cut out of a hillside like stair steps. Terraces prevented soil from washing down the hillside when it rained. After David's death, the Israelites honored him as their greatest king, as do Jews today. King David's son Solomon (SAH·luh·muhn) became the next Israelite king around 970 B.C. Through trade and treaties with other peoples, Solomon brought a long **period** of peace to the region. He constructed many cities and, according to the Hebrew Bible, built the first temple in Jerusalem. Built of fragrant cedar wood and costly stone, Solomon's temple—also called the First Temple—held the Ark of the Covenant and other sacred objects.

King Solomon was also known for his wisdom. He is believed to be the author of **proverbs** (PRAHV·uhrbz), or wise sayings, that are recorded in the Hebrew Bible. Solomon shared his proverbs in hopes of helping his people:

PRIMARY SOURCE

❝Whoever walks in integrity walks securely,
but whoever takes crooked paths will be found out.❞

—Proverbs: 10:9

Despite Solomon's accomplishments, many Israelites turned against him. They did not like working on his building projects or paying the high taxes he demanded. After Solomon's death around 922 B.C., the Israelites entered a troubled period in their history. Deep disagreements split their kingdom. In addition, powerful neighbors threatened their survival.

✓ PROGRESS CHECK

Evaluating Why did the Israelites believe David was their greatest king?

Reading**HELP**DESK

proverb a wise saying

Academic Vocabulary

period a division of time that is shorter than an era

Two Kingdoms

GUIDING QUESTION *How did neighboring empires respond to the Israelites?*

After Solomon's death, the ten northern tribes rebelled against the government in Jerusalem. These tribes **founded** a separate kingdom, Israel. Its capital was Samaria. The two tribes in the south founded the smaller kingdom of Judah (JOO·duh). Judah's capital was Jerusalem. Although split politically, the people of Israel and Judah preserved the Israelite religion.

During this time, large empires formed around Israel and Judah. As you read previously, the Assyrians and the Chaldeans built powerful empires. Their rulers wanted to control the trade routes that ran through the Israelite kingdoms. Small and weak, the kingdoms of Israel and Judah felt threatened by their powerful neighbors.

The Fall of Israel

The Assyrians spread fear throughout the region. They forced conquered peoples to pay tribute. If they did not receive tribute, the Assyrians destroyed towns, burned estates, and carried away all valuable goods. Then they forced the conquered people to move to different areas to start new settlements.

When the kingdom of Israel refused to pay tribute, the Assyrians invaded Israel in 722 B.C. The Assyrians captured major cities, including the capital at Samaria. They wanted absolute control.

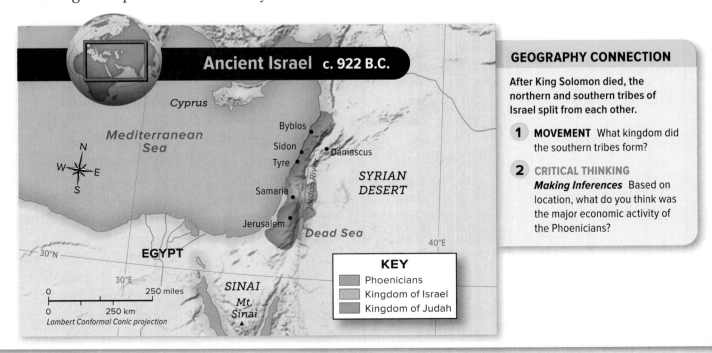

Ancient Israel c. 922 B.C.

Cyprus
Mediterranean Sea
Byblos
Sidon
Tyre
Damascus
Samaria
SYRIAN DESERT
Jordan River
Jerusalem
Dead Sea
40°E
30°N
EGYPT
30°E
0   250 miles
0   250 km
Lambert Conformal Conic projection
SINAI
Mt. Sinai ▲

KEY
Phoenicians
Kingdom of Israel
Kingdom of Judah

GEOGRAPHY CONNECTION

After King Solomon died, the northern and southern tribes of Israel split from each other.

1 **MOVEMENT** What kingdom did the southern tribes form?

2 **CRITICAL THINKING**
Making Inferences Based on location, what do you think was the major economic activity of the Phoenicians?

Academic Vocabulary

found to set up or establish

Jeremiah was one of several prophets. The Israelites believed the prophets brought them the word of God.

▶ **CRITICAL THINKING**
Comparing What do the teachings of Hosea and Jeremiah have in common?

Name	Time Periods	Teachings
Elijah	874–840 B.C.	Only God should be worshipped—not idols or false gods.
Amos	780–740 B.C.	The kingdom of King David will be restored and will prosper.
Hosea	750–722 B.C.	God is loving and forgiving.
Isaiah	738–700 B.C.	God wants us to help others and promote justice.
Micah	735–700 B.C.	Both rich and poor have to do what is right and follow God.
Jeremiah	626–586 B.C.	God is just and kind—he rewards as well as punishes.
Ezekiel	597–571 B.C.	Someone who has done wrong can choose to change.

So they forced some of the Israelites to resettle in the Assyrian Empire. Assyrians then brought in people from other parts of their empire to live in Israel. These settlers mixed with the Israelites still living there. A new mingled culture developed. These people became known as Samaritans.

The Samaritans adopted many of the Israelites' religious beliefs. They worshipped the God of Israel, read the Torah, and followed the Israelites' religious laws. The Samaritans, however, adopted religious practices that the Israelites did not accept. In time, the Samaritans and the people of Israel had little in common. Today's Judaism developed from the religious practices preserved mainly in the kingdom of Judah.

The Fall of Judah

The people of Judah **survived** the Assyrian conquests, but their freedom did not last. In 597 B.C., the Chaldeans under King Nebuchadnezzar (NEHB·uh·kuhd·NEHZ·zuhr), forced thousands of people to leave Jerusalem and live in Babylon (BAB·uh·lahn), the Chaldean capital. Nebuchadnezzar chose a new king, a Judean, to rule Judah.

At first, Judah's king did as he was told. Soon, however, he plotted to set Judah free. A prophet named Jeremiah warned that God did not want Judah to rebel, but the king refused to listen. The king led the people of Judah to revolt. The Chaldeans retook Jerusalem in 586 B.C. Nebuchadnezzar then leveled Jerusalem to the ground. He destroyed the temple, captured the king, and took him and thousands of Judah's people to Babylon.

exile a forced absence from one's home or country

Academic Vocabulary

survive to continue to live; to live through a dangerous event

In Jewish history, this time became known as the Babylonian **Exile** (EHG·zyl). When people are exiled, they are forced to leave their home or country. Psalm 137 in the Hebrew Bible describes the sadness many of Judah's people felt in living far away from their homeland:

" By the rivers of Babylon we sat and wept. . . .

How can we sing the songs of the LORD while in a foreign land?

If I forget you, O Jerusalem, may my right hand forget its skill.

May my tongue cling to the roof of my mouth if I do not remember you,

if I do not consider Jerusalem my highest joy... *"*

—Psalm 137:1–6

What Was the Prophets' Message?

The prophets had an important role in Judean life. They offered words of hope in times of despair. At other times, the prophets explained that the people were not obeying God. They urged people to change their ways and make the world a better place.

The prophet Amos said, "But let justice roll on like a river, righteousness like a never-failing stream!" This means that all people should work for a just society in which everyone is treated fairly. Dr. Martin Luther King, Jr., quoted the prophet's words in the 20th century in his "I Have a Dream" speech. The goal of a just society later became a primary part of the teachings of Christianity and Islam. Jewish prophets also stressed the importance of leading a moral life and helping others in order to connect with God.

✔ PROGRESS CHECK

Identifying What empires conquered Israel and Judah?

LESSON 2 REVIEW

Review Vocabulary

1. How might reading a series of *proverbs* affect people?

Answer the Guiding Questions

2. *Explaining* Why was it important that King David united the tribes of Israel?

3. *Explaining* How did Solomon's death affect the Israelites?

4. *Identifying* Which group mixed with the Israelites to form the Samaritan culture?

5. *Identifying* What was the Babylonian Exile?

6. **NARRATIVE** The Jews were exiled and forced to spend 70 years in Babylon. If you were forced to live far away from your homeland, how would you react to your situation? Write a journal entry describing your thoughts about being forced to live away from your homeland.

The Development of Judaism

networks
There's More Online!

IT MATTERS BECAUSE
Religion served as the basis for all daily activities for the ancient Israelites. Many of their religious beliefs and practices continue today.

Return to Judah

GUIDING QUESTION *How did the people of Judah practice their religion while in exile and in their homeland?*

The families of Judeans who were exiled to Babylon spent 70 years away from Judah. During their exile, they became known as the Jews. We call their religion Judaism.

While in Babylon, the Jews no longer had a temple in which to worship God. It is believed that small groups of Jews began to meet at **synagogues** (SIHN·uh·GAHGS), or Jewish houses of worship. They worshipped on the **Sabbath** (SA·buhth). According to **tradition**, the Sabbath lasts from sundown Friday to nightfall Saturday. During this weekly day of worship and rest, Jews prayed and talked about their religion and history. Jews still observe the Sabbath today.

Rebuilding Judah

While some Jews accepted Babylon as their permanent home, others hoped to return to Judah some day. This hope was achieved when a group of people called the Persians swept across Southwest Asia. The Persians defeated the Chaldeans and took over Babylon. In 538 B.C., the Persian king Cyrus II let Jews return to Judah.

Reading**HELP**DESK

Taking Notes: *Identifying the Main Idea*

As you read, complete a graphic organizer like this one to describe the roles of both synagogues and scribes in the survival of Judaism.

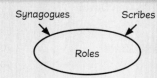

Synagogues   Scribes

Roles

Content Vocabulary
• **synagogue**   • **scroll**
• **Sabbath**   • **kosher**

Some Jews stayed in Babylon, but many returned to Judah. They rebuilt Jerusalem and constructed a new temple to replace the one destroyed by the Chaldeans. This new place of worship became known as the Second Temple.

Meanwhile, the Persians chose officials to rule the country and collect taxes from the people. They did not allow the Jews to have their own government or king. The Jews depended on religious leaders—the temple priests and scribes—to guide their society.

Many priests were religious scholars. These priests had a deep understanding of the Jewish faith. Scribes often lectured in the synagogues and taught in the schools. Led by a scribe named Ezra, the Jews wrote the five books of the Torah on pieces of parchment. They sewed the pieces together to make long **scrolls** (SKROHLZ). The Torah and writings that were added later make up the Hebrew Bible.

What Is In the Hebrew Bible?

Isn't it easier to follow rules when they are clearly explained? That is what the Hebrew Bible provided for the ancient Jews. Three parts—the Torah, the Prophets, and the Writings—make up the Hebrew Bible. It contains a series of 24 books written and collected over many centuries. The Hebrew Bible presents the laws and rules of the Israelites. It also reflects the culture of the people. Jewish history, art, literature, poetry, and proverbs are also part of the Hebrew Bible.

Genesis, the first book of the Torah, presents the Israelite view of human beginnings. It tells how God created the Earth in six days and rested on the seventh day. Genesis also describes how God punished the world for wicked behavior. In this book, God warns a man named Noah that a flood is coming and commands him to build an ark, or large boat. As the rains poured and flood waters rose, Noah, his family, and two of every animal on Earth boarded the ark. The Earth flooded and many perished. Only those on the ark escaped drowning. After the rain stopped, God placed a rainbow in the sky as a sign that the world would never again be destroyed by a flood.

Genesis also explains why the people of the world speak many different languages. It tells how the citizens of the city of Babel tried to build a tower to reach heaven.

In Jewish synagogues, the Torah is read from scrolls kept in a cabinet called the Ark of the Law. These scrolls are handled with great respect and care during worship.

©Richard T. Nowitz/Corbis

---

synagogue a Jewish house of worship

Sabbath a weekly day of worship and rest

scroll a long document made from pieces of parchment sewn together

Academic Vocabulary

tradition a custom, or way of life, passed down from generation to generation

According to the Hebrew Bible, Daniel's faith in God protected him from the lions. As a result, Daniel became a model of faith and strength to Jews facing difficult challenges.

▶ **CRITICAL THINKING**
Analyzing What lesson does the story of Daniel provide for Jewish people, especially during hard times?

God disapproved and made the people speak in different languages. The people could not **communicate** with one another. As a result, they could not work together to complete the tower. God then scattered the people across the Earth.

Later parts of the Hebrew Bible describe Jewish hopes for the future. The book of Isaiah describes what the Jews believed to be God's plan for a peaceful world. It says that the nations:

PRIMARY SOURCE

❝[W]ill beat their swords into plowshares and their spears into pruning hooks. Nation will not take up sword against nation, nor will they train for war anymore. ❞

— Isaiah 2:4

The book of Daniel explains that the Jews also believed that evil and suffering would eventually be replaced by goodness. Daniel was a trusted adviser to a Babylonian king. As a Jew, however, he refused to worship Babylonian gods. For punishment, the Chaldeans threw Daniel into a lions' den. God, however, protected Daniel from the wild beasts. The story of Daniel reminds Jews that God will rescue them. Christians and Muslims share with the Jews the hope of a better world in which good triumphs over evil.

☑ **PROGRESS CHECK**

Explaining Why did religious leaders guide Jewish society after the Jews returned from exile?

Walker Art Gallery, Liverpool, Merseyside, UK, National Museums Liverpool/Bridgeman Art Library

Reading **HELP**DESK

Academic Vocabulary

communicate to exchange knowledge or information

Jewish Daily Life

GUIDING QUESTION *How did religion shape the Jewish way of life?*

The Torah provides teachings for daily living. These teachings shaped the family life of the early Jews. The teachings gave instructions about what foods to eat and what clothes to wear. They also required Jews to help the poor, deal honestly with their neighbors, and apply laws fairly. Jewish teachings emphasized individual worth and responsibility, as well as self-discipline. It also reminded Jews of their loyalty to God.

The Jewish Family

The ancient Israelites stressed the importance of family life. The Torah identifies specific roles for the father and the mother of the house. If a father died, his sons would take his place to lead the family.

The Jewish family also stressed education—especially for young men. When sons grew old enough, fathers taught them to worship God and to learn a trade. Later, under the guidance of religious teachers, boys learned to read the Torah. Everything the students learned—from the alphabet to Jewish history—they learned from the Torah. Because reading the Torah was central to Jewish life, religious teachers became important **community** leaders.

Daughters, who were educated at home by their mothers, learned to be wives, mothers, and housekeepers. This included learning Jewish teachings about food, the Sabbath, and holidays. They also learned about the women of ancient Israel. Two of these women were Ruth and her mother-in-law, Naomi.

According to the Hebrew Bible, Naomi's husband and her two sons died. One of the sons was married to Ruth. Ruth, who was not a Jew herself, made a difficult decision. To help Naomi, Ruth chose to leave her Moabite homeland. She moved to Bethlehem to be with Naomi. Naomi had urged Ruth to stay with her own people, but Ruth responded:

Connections to
TODAY

Heroes

Stories of brave leaders like Daniel have inspired Jews to maintain their faith during times of trial and trouble. Brainstorm a list of present-day individuals or groups who inspire others with their bravery in the face of great difficulty or danger.

Sabbath comes from the Hebrew word *Shabbat*, which means "cease or desist." The Sabbath is the day of the week when, according to Jewish tradition, people stop working in order to worship. In traditional Jewish homes, the Sabbath begins with a prayer and a family meal.

Academic Vocabulary

community a group of people with common interests living in an area

Because Ruth was Naomi's daughter-in-law, she was accepted with kindness in Bethlehem.

PRIMARY SOURCE

❝ Where you go I will go, and where you stay I will stay. Your people will be my people and your God my God. Where you die I will die, and there I will be buried. **❞**

—The Book of Ruth 1:16-17

Ruth's courage and devotion to her family provided an example for Jewish girls to follow.

Dietary Laws

Jewish law tells Jews what they can eat. Ancient Jews could eat the meat of only certain animals. For example, they could eat beef and lamb but not pork. Laws about food are known as *kashrut*, which means "that which is proper." By following laws related to food, Jews believed they were showing obedience to God.

Today, food that is prepared according to Jewish dietary laws is called **kosher** (KOH·shuhr). Many items you see in a grocery store have the symbol for kosher on the label. Animals used for kosher meat must be killed in a certain way. The meat must

This symbol can be found on some food packages. It indicates that foods have been prepared according to Jewish dietary laws.

kosher prepared according to Jewish dietary law

be inspected, salted, and soaked in water. Foods that are not kosher are considered to be unclean. Dietary law prohibits Jews from eating meat and dairy products together. Jews also cannot eat shellfish, such as crab or shrimp.

Specific foods with religious significance are eaten during some meals. For example, the seder (SAY·duhr) is a special meal eaten during the festival of Passover. It is a holiday that celebrates the Exodus of the Jewish people from Egypt. Foods such as lamb, hardboiled eggs, vinegar, salt water, herbs, and flat bread called matzoh, are served at the seder. During the meal, the youngest child at the table asks a series of questions about the food and the meaning of Passover. The adults and older children at the table recite the answer to the question together. For example, they tell how the bitter herbs reflect the bitter experience of the Jews living in exile. The tradition of eating special foods at Passover and reflecting on history is sacred to the Jewish people.

✔ PROGRESS CHECK

Evaluating Why did religious teachers become important leaders in Jewish communities?

The foods of the seder are symbolic. For example, the egg is a symbol of God's kindness. Bitter herbs are dipped in fruit juice or honey to symbolize the sweetness and bitterness of life.

Identifying What is a particular food your friends or family include when you have a special dinner?

Mitch Hrdlicka/Getty Images

LESSON 3 REVIEW

Review Vocabulary

1. Use the terms *synagogue*, *Sabbath*, and *kosher* to describe traditional Jewish practices.

Answer the Guiding Questions

2. *Identifying* What are the three parts of the Hebrew Bible?

3. *Explaining* How did the people of Judah practice their religion while in exile?

4. *Comparing* How were Jewish sons and daughters educated differently?

5. *Identifying* What is one type of food that is considered unclean according to Jewish dietary laws?

6. **ARGUMENT** What do you think is the main lesson to be learned from the story of Daniel in the lions' den? Write a paragraph describing your thoughts.

LESSON 4

The Jews in the Mediterranean World

ESSENTIAL QUESTION

- Why does conflict develop?

IT MATTERS BECAUSE
The Jews experienced many significant changes under Greek and Roman rule.

The Arrival of Greek Rule

GUIDING QUESTION *What was life like for the Jews in Greek-ruled lands?*

The Jews of Judah remained under Persian rule for nearly 200 years. That is about the same amount of time as the entire history of the United States. Then, in 331 B.C., a king from Macedonia, who had conquered Greece, defeated the Persians. This king was Alexander the Great. Alexander admired Greek ways and wanted to spread them. He introduced the Greek language and culture to Judah. Alexander allowed the Jews to stay in Judah.

How Did Jewish Ideas Spread?

Under Alexander, Judah remained the center of Judaism. Many Jews at that time, however, had long lived outside Judah. Thousands had been exiled to Babylon in 586 B.C. When in 538 B.C. the conquering Persians gave them permission to return to Judah, many chose to stay in Babylon or go to other Mediterranean lands instead. These groups of Jews living outside of the Jewish homeland became known as the **Diaspora** (deye·AS·puh·ruh). *Diaspora* is a Greek word that means "scattered." Where these Jews settled, they practiced their customs, and Jewish ideas spread.

Reading **HELP**DESK

Taking Notes: *Comparing and Contrasting*

As you read, complete a diagram like this one by identifying similarities and differences between Greek rule and Roman rule.

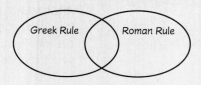

Greek Rule   Roman Rule

Content Vocabulary

- **Diaspora**   • **rabbi**

The Jews of the Diaspora remained loyal to Judaism. At the same time, many learned the Greek language and adopted features of Greek culture. A group of Jewish scholars in Egypt copied the Hebrew Bible into Greek. This Greek **version**, called the Septuagint (sehp·TOO·uh·juhnt), helped people who were not Jews to read and understand the Hebrew Bible. As a result, Jewish ideas spread throughout the Mediterranean world.

The Revolt of Maccabeus

After Alexander's death, four of his generals divided his empire into separate kingdoms. One kingdom covered much of Southwest Asia. A family known as the Seleucids (suh·LOO·suhds) ruled this kingdom. By 200 B.C., Judah was under the control of Seleucid kings.

In 176 B.C., Antiochus IV (an·TEE·uh·kuhs) came to power as the Seleucid king. As ruler of Judah, Antiochus required the Jews to worship the many Greek gods and goddesses.

GEOGRAPHY CONNECTION

The Diaspora continued throughout Alexander's Greek empire. During the first century A.D., Jews represented about 40 percent of the empire's population.

1 MOVEMENT How did the Diaspora help spread Jewish ideas?

2 CRITICAL THINKING
Analyzing How can the interaction of two cultures create benefits for both groups?

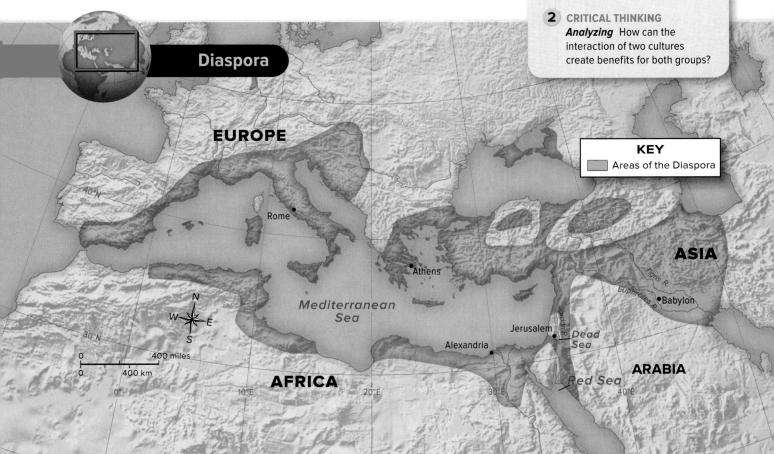

Diaspora

KEY
Areas of the Diaspora

EUROPE

40°N

Rome

Athens

Mediterranean Sea

N W E S

30°N

0 400 miles
0 400 km

AFRICA

0° 10°E 20°E 30°E 40°E

Alexandria

Jerusalem

Dead Sea

Red Sea

ASIA

Tigris R.

Euphrates R.

Babylon

ARABIA

Diaspora the groups of Jews living outside of the Jewish homeland

Academic Vocabulary

version a different form or edition; a translation of the Bible

**Judas Maccabeus
(c. 190 B.C.–160 B.C.)**

Judas Maccabeus and his followers engaged in guerrilla warfare against the Greek armies. Guerrilla warfare is irregular combat carried out by small groups of independent soldiers. This strategy helped the Maccabees succeed in battle against the Seleucids. The family of Judas Maccabeus ruled Judah and expanded its lands. With more territory surrounding it, Judah was protected and remained free until the Roman conquest.

Explaining Why is Judas Maccabeus considered a hero?

A large number of Jews, however, refused to abandon their religion. In 167 B.C., Judas Maccabeus (JOO·duhs MAK·uh·BEE·uhs), a Jewish priest, led the fight against Seleucid rule. He and his followers fled to the hills. They formed a rebel army known as the Maccabees.

After many battles, the Maccabees succeeded in capturing the Temple. They cleared it of all statues of Greek gods and goddesses. They then rededicated the temple to the worship of God. Each year, Jews recall the cleansing of the Temple when they celebrate the festival of Hanukkah (HAH·nuh·kuh).

✔ **PROGRESS CHECK**

Analyzing How did Alexander and later the Seleucids affect the people of Judah?

Roman Rule in Judaea

GUIDING QUESTION *How did the Jews react to Roman rule of their homeland?*

By 100 B.C., the Romans controlled much of the eastern Mediterranean lands. The name *Roman* came from Rome, their capital. Rome was located far to the west in what is known today as Italy. Led by powerful generals, the Romans **expanded** their empire. In 63 B.C., Roman forces conquered Judah and renamed it Judaea (joo·DEE·uh).

At first, the Romans chose a follower of the Jewish religion, Herod (HEHR·uhd), to rule as king of Judaea. Herod built many forts and cities in Judaea. The Second Temple in Jerusalem, rebuilt during Herod's reign, served as the center of Jewish worship.

Jewish Groups

After Herod's death, Roman officials ruled Judaea. At that time, disagreement grew about how Judaism should be practiced. Jews also had different views on how to deal with the Romans.

One group of Jews was known as the Pharisees (FEH·ruh·seez). The Pharisees gained the support of the common people. They taught in the synagogues and applied the teachings of the Torah to daily life. Through their teachings, the Pharisees helped to make Judaism a religion of the home and family. The Pharisees wanted to help people obey the Ten Commandments. To do this, they stressed both written and oral law. Oral law is the unwritten interpretations passed down over time by word of mouth.

Hulton Archives/Getty Images

The Pharisees wanted Judaea free of Roman rule. However, they did not urge Jews to fight the Romans. Instead, they told people to resist Roman control. They urged the people to practice the Torah's teachings with greater **devotion**.

Another Jewish group made up of wealthy noble families was the Sadducees (SA·juh·SEEZ). Many of them served as priests and scribes in the Temple. The Sadducees accepted the laws of the Torah. They were more concerned, however, with applying the laws to temple ceremonies. They also did not agree with many of the Pharisees' teachings. For example, the Sadducees emphasized the written law but rejected oral law. The Sadducees favored **cooperation** with the Romans. They wanted to keep peace and order in Judaea.

A third group was called the Essenes (ih·SEENZ). They were priests who broke away from the Temple in Jerusalem. Many Essenes lived at Qumrān, an area in the desert near the Dead Sea. They spent their lives praying and waiting for God to deliver the Jews from Roman rule. The Essenes followed only the written law of the Torah.

Centuries later, in A.D. 1947, ancient scrolls were found in caves at Qumrān. Because the caves were near the Dead Sea, the scrolls became known as the Dead Sea Scrolls. Many of the scrolls were most likely written by Essenes. The scrolls are important to historians because they reveal details of a particular place and time.

Herod was primarily responsible for developing the fortress at Masada. It was the scene of a major Roman and Jewish battle. Visitors may tour its mountainous ruins today.

Academic Vocabulary

devotion dedication, a strong commitment
cooperation working together

There are rocky cliffs along the shores of the Dead Sea. Caves in these cliffs contained the Dead Sea Scrolls.

1 **LOCATION** Describe the location of the Dead Sea in relation to the Mediterranean Sea.

2 **CRITICAL THINKING**
Drawing Conclusions Why would the discovery of the Dead Sea Scrolls be considered so significant?

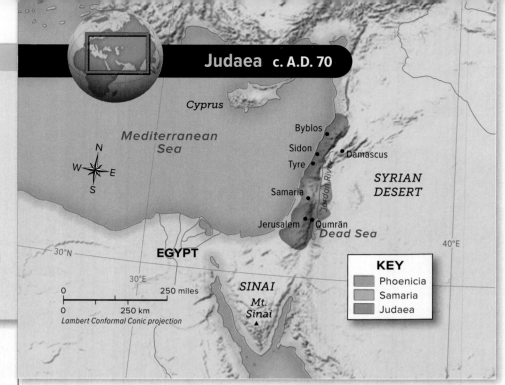

Judaea c. A.D. 70

Cyprus

Mediterranean Sea

Byblos
Sidon
Tyre
Damascus

SYRIAN DESERT

Samaria

Jordan River

Jerusalem Qumrān
Dead Sea

30°N

30°E

EGYPT

40°E

SINAI

Mt. Sinai

0   250 miles
0   250 km
Lambert Conformal Conic projection

KEY
Phoenicia
Samaria
Judaea

Locating the Dead Sea Scrolls is considered to be one of the most significant modern archaeological discoveries.

They let historians see that Judaism was not always an established religion. The scrolls show that not all followers practiced Judaism in the same way during Roman times.

Some of the scrolls tell a story about a group of Jews who, in exile, developed their own beliefs about good and evil. They saw themselves as alone in the world, surrounded by enemies. They were waiting for someone to lead them. Some scrolls describe the beliefs, holy days, and practices of other Jewish groups. The variety of the scrolls makes some historians believe that the writings were perhaps the contents of a library. The reasons for hiding the scrolls are unclear. Someone may have wanted to protect them from destruction during times of conflict with the Romans. Since their discovery, however, the scrolls have helped historians understand more about Judaism during Roman times.

A fourth Jewish group, the Zealots, lived in Judaea. They wanted to fight for their freedom against the Romans. During the A.D. 60s, Jewish hatred of Roman rule reached its peak. Hope remained in the Jewish faith, however. Many Jews were waiting for God to send a deliverer to free them from Roman rule. As **tensions** between Romans and Jews in Judaea increased, the Zealots prepared to act.

www.facsimile-editions.com

Reading**HELP**DESK

Academic Vocabulary

tension opposition between individuals or groups; stress

Jewish-Roman Wars

In A.D. 66, the Zealots revolted. They overpowered the small Roman army in Jerusalem. Four years later, Roman forces retook the city. They killed thousands of Jews and forced many others to leave. The Romans also destroyed the Second Temple in Jerusalem. Today the Western Wall still stands in Jerusalem. This structure is all that remains of the Temple complex. It is a long-standing Jewish custom to come to this wall to pray.

After a number of years passed, some Jews rebelled once again. In A.D. 132, a military leader named Simon ben Kosiba, known as Bar Kochba, led the Jews in the battle for freedom. However, three years later, Roman forces crushed the revolt. They killed Bar Kochba and many other Jewish leaders during the fighting.

With the revolt put down, the Romans imposed stricter controls and did not allow Jews to live in or even visit Jerusalem. The Romans renamed Judaea and called it Palestine. This name refers to the Philistines, whom the Israelites had conquered centuries before.

The ancient Western Wall is the only remaining structure of the Temple of Jerusalem. Coming here to pray has been a Jewish custom for hundreds of years. Those who visit the wall often leave prayers on paper stuffed into its cracks.

Explaining Why might people still come to this site to pray?

In A.D. 1947, a shepherd in the Judaean desert entered a cave along the shore of the Dead Sea. There he discovered several large clay jars. Some jars were empty, but in others he found ancient scrolls of leather, papyrus, and copper. These **documents**, written between 200 B.C. and A.D. 68, are called the Dead Sea Scrolls. The scrolls found in several caves in the area include the oldest complete copy of the Book of Isaiah and pieces of many other books of the Hebrew Bible. Among the documents are works in ancient Hebrew, Greek, and Aramaic. Most scholars believe that the scrolls were part of a library that belonged to an early Jewish community.

The Rabbis

Despite losing their struggle for independence, the Jews regrouped with the help of their **rabbis** (RA·byz), or religious leaders. The Jewish people no longer had a temple or priests. Instead, the synagogues and rabbis gained importance. The rabbis taught and explained the Torah. They provided moral guidance—accepted notions of right and wrong—to the people.

One of the most famous rabbis was Yohanan ben Zaccai (YOH·kah·nahn behn zah·KY). Ben Zaccai lived in Judaea when Jerusalem fell to the Romans in A.D. 70. He persuaded the Romans to spare the Jewish city of Yavneh. There, he founded a school to continue teaching the Torah.

Ben Zaccai helped the Judaic spirit survive the destruction of the temple and the loss of Jerusalem. He placed great importance on the study of the Torah. He also stressed acts of loving kindness and community service. Because of ben Zaccai's efforts, the school at Yavneh became a center of Torah studies and a model for other schools. Other rabbis founded Torah schools in places as far away as Babylon and Egypt.

Through the efforts of ben Zaccai and other rabbis, the basic beliefs of Judaism were preserved. Eventually, the rabbis gathered their oral discussions about Jewish law and recorded them in a work known as the Mishnah. Later, the Mishnah was combined with other Jewish legal traditions into an authoritative collection of Jewish tradition known as the Talmud. The word *Talmud* is a Hebrew term that means "instruction." The Talmud became the basis for Jewish teachings throughout the ages.

A part of the Talmud called the Mishnah began as an oral history of Jewish law passed from one generation of rabbis to another.

rabbi the official leader of a Jewish congregation

Academic Vocabulary

document an official paper used as proof or support of something

SAFRA Sylvain/Age fotostock

Even today, the Talmud remains central to Jewish teaching and is the ultimate authority on Jewish law. A prayer at the end of part of the Talmud reveals the Jewish reverence for the Torah:

Rabbis continue to educate students today. They might also perform charity or social functions for their congregations.

PRIMARY SOURCE

" Make sweet, O Lord, our God, the words of Thy Law in our mouths, and in the mouth of Thy people the house of Israel; and may we, our children, and the children of Thy people the house of Israel, all know Thy Name and learn Thy Law."

—from *The Babylon Talmud, Book 1: Tract Sabbath*

✓ **PROGRESS CHECK**

Explaining How did the rabbis help Judaism survive after the Roman conquest?

LESSON 4 REVIEW

Review Vocabulary

1. In what way did *rabbis* help the Jews during the period of Roman rule?

Answer the Guiding Questions

2. *Explaining* What was life like for the Jews in Greek-ruled lands?

3. *Identifying* Which group gained control of Judah following Alexander's death?

4. *Explaining* How did the Jews react to Roman rule of their homeland?

5. *Identifying* Who established a school for teaching the Torah at Yavneh?

6. **ARGUMENT** You are living in Judaea during the Roman conquest. Write a letter to a friend describing what action you would like to see taken to make Judaea free again.

CHAPTER 9 Activities

Write your answers on a separate piece of paper.

1 **Exploring the Essential Question**
INFORMATIVE/EXPLANATORY Write an expository essay about how key leaders
influenced the Israelites during the time periods discussed in this chapter. Identify
specific leaders who had the most significant effect. Explain how they led during times
of conflict.

2 **21st Century Skills**
CREATING A SLIDE SHOW Create a slide show about an aspect of Jewish culture
that you have studied in this chapter. When presenting, briefly introduce each image,
and offer a clear interpretation of why it is significant.

3 **Thinking Like a Historian**
COMPARING AND CONTRASTING Create a diagram like the one shown to compare
and contrast the Jewish groups that existed under Roman rule.

4 **GEOGRAPHY ACTIVITY**

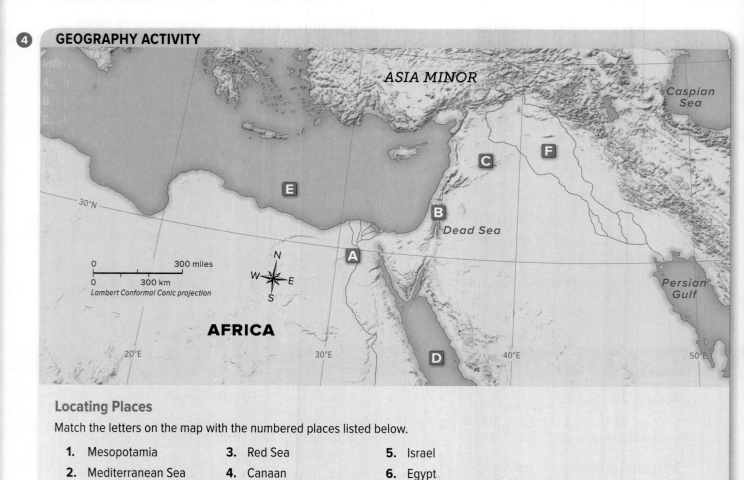

Locating Places
Match the letters on the map with the numbered places listed below.

1. Mesopotamia
2. Mediterranean Sea
3. Red Sea
4. Canaan
5. Israel
6. Egypt

Directions: Write your answers on a separate piece of paper.

CHECKING FOR UNDERSTANDING

1 Define each of these terms.

A. prophet   F. scroll
B. Exodus   G. seder
C. covenant   H. Diaspora
D. Torah   I. Zealots
E. psalm

REVIEW THE GUIDING QUESTIONS

2 *Describing* Based on the teachings of their prophets, what did the Israelites believe about God?

3 *Identifying* Name two other monotheistic religions whose development was influenced by Judaism.

4 *Listing* List the products traded by the Phoenicians in the Mediterranean area.

5 *Finding the Main Idea* Why did the Israelites in 1100 B.C. call for a king? Which of the Israelite kings fulfilled the desires of the people?

6 *Identifying* What events led to the Babylonian Exile?

7 *Explaining* What is the Jewish Sabbath? How is it observed?

8 *Describing* What basic principles about daily living are found in the teachings of the Torah?

9 *Identifying* What event does the Jewish festival of Hanukkah celebrate?

10 *Explaining* What is the Talmud, and why is it significant?

CRITICAL THINKING

11 *Making Connections* How have the Ten Commandments helped shape today's basic moral principles, laws, and democratic beliefs?

12 *Making Inferences* Why might the Ark of the Covenant have been an especially sacred object to the Israelites?

13 *Comparing and Contrasting* Compare and contrast the accomplishments of the first three kings of the Israelites.

14 *Evaluating* Explain the actions taken by the Assyrians after their invasion and conquest of Israel to gain absolute control of the area. Then evaluate the effectiveness of those actions.

15 *Making Generalizations* Study the chart on the Israelite prophets in Lesson 2. Read the teachings of the various prophets and make a generalization about their messages.

16 *Making Connections* Explain the types of information found in the 24 books of the Hebrew Bible and how the contents reflect the culture of the people. Why might such a collection of information be important to a people such as the Jews?

17 *Determining Central Ideas* Why did religious teachers become important community leaders in Jewish society? Include information about the role of religious leaders during the time of Persian control of Judah in your answer.

18 *Making Connections* How did Greek dominance in the Mediterranean help to spread Jewish ideas in that area?

19 *Contrasting* Contrast the views of the four Jewish groups—the Pharisees, Sadducees, Essenes, and Zealots—on how the Jews should deal with Roman control of Judaea.

20 *Determining Cause and Effect* What effect did the actions of the Romans after they put down the revolt of the Zealots have on the Jewish people and religion?

Need Extra Help?

If You've Missed Question	**1**	**2**	**3**	**4**	**5**	**6**	**7**	**8**	**9**	**10**	**11**	**12**	**13**	**14**	**15**	**16**	**17**	**18**	**19**	**20**
Review Lesson	1,2, 3, 4	1	1	1	2	2	3	3	4	4	1	1	2	2	2	3	3	4	4	4

DBQ SHORT RESPONSE

"The biblical King Solomon was known for his wisdom, his wealth and his writings. … Solomon's downfall came in his old age. … Within Solomon's kingdom, he placed heavy taxation on the people, who became bitter. He also had the people work as soldiers, chief officers and commanders of his chariots and cavalry. He granted special privileges to the tribes of Judah and this alienated [angered] the northern tribes."

—From *"Solomon" by Shira Schoenberg*

21 What is believed to have weakened Solomon as a king?

22 Why might Solomon granting special privileges to the tribes of Judah have displeased the other tribes?

EXTENDED RESPONSE

23 *Narrative* Write a short essay in which you compare and contrast the daily life of Jews under Greek and Roman rule. Consider how Greek and Roman rule affected the Jewish peoples' ability to practice their religion. Describe how conflicts eventually developed between the Jews and the ruling groups.

STANDARDIZED TEST PRACTICE

DBQ ANALYZING DOCUMENTS

24 *Summarizing* Which of the following best states the main purpose of the Ten Commandments?

A. to suggest ways to observe the Sabbath

B. to describe the qualifications for kings

C. to reveal warnings to Israelites

D. to provide rules for living

25 *Drawing Conclusions* The message found in the Ten Commandments can best be seen today in

A. modern biology. C. modern politics.

B. modern geography. D. modern law.

Need Extra Help?

If You've Missed Question	**21**	**22**	**23**	**24**	**25**
Review Lesson	2	2	4	1	1

The Ten Commandments

❶ Do not worship any god except me.

❷ Do not … bow down and worship idols.

❸ Do not misuse my name.

❹ Remember the Sabbath Day and keep it holy.

❺ Honor your father and your mother.

❻ Do not murder.

❼ Be faithful in marriage.

❽ Do not steal.

❾ Do not testify falsely [tell lies] about others.

❿ Do not want anything that belongs to someone else.

—*Paraphrased from Exodus 20:3-17*

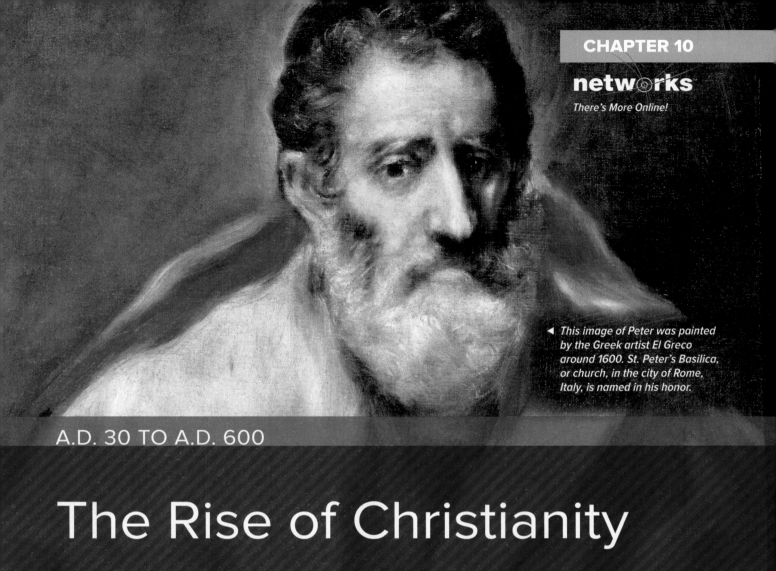

◄ *This image of Peter was painted by the Greek artist El Greco around 1600. St. Peter's Basilica, or church, in the city of Rome, Italy, is named in his honor.*

A.D. 30 TO A.D. 600

The Rise of Christianity

Scala/Art Resource, NY

THE STORY MATTERS ...

One of the chosen apostles of Jesus, Simon Peter of Galilee, was called "the rock "of the Christian church. He brought many followers to the Christian faith.

Soon after the death of Jesus, Peter, as he was called, became a leader of the early Christian church. He played an important role in spreading the teachings of Jesus and in contributing to the rise of Christianity. This painting imagines Peter as an older man.

ESSENTIAL QUESTIONS

- What are the characteristics of a leader?
- How do religions develop?
- How do new ideas change the way people live?

Place & Time: The Rise of Christianity A.D. 30 to A.D. 600

As Jesus gained followers, he alarmed Rome's rulers. They feared his growing influence and eventually executed him. Jesus' followers carried his message to many lands, and what began as a Jewish group developed into a separate religion.

Step Into the Place

MAP FOCUS Christianity began in Judaea, an area that was part of the Roman Empire. From Judaea, Christianity spread through the Mediterranean region and beyond.

1 LOCATION Look at the map. Is Rome located northwest or southeast of Jerusalem?

2 MOVEMENT To which other parts of Europe would you expect Christianity to spread most quickly?

3 CRITICAL THINKING
Analyzing How did the Mediterranean Sea make it easier for Christianity to spread?

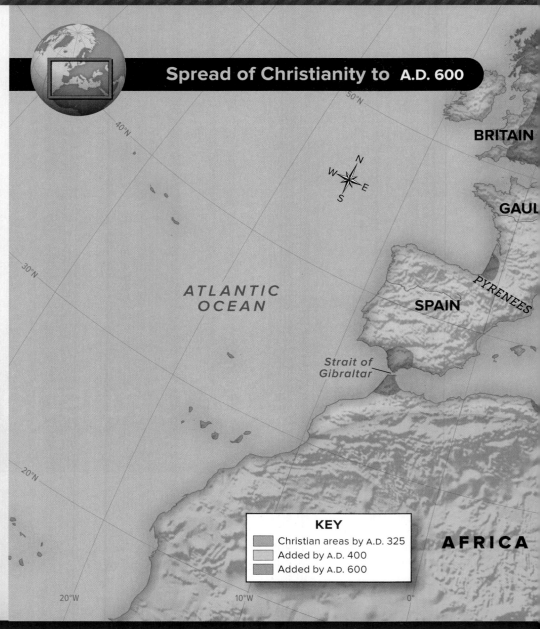

Spread of Christianity to A.D. 600

BRITAIN

GAUL

PYRENEES

SPAIN

ATLANTIC OCEAN

Strait of Gibraltar

AFRICA

KEY
- Christian areas by A.D. 325
- Added by A.D. 400
- Added by A.D. 600

Step Into the Time

TIME LINE Choose an event from the time line and write two or three sentences explaining how the ancient Romans dealt with Christianity during that time.

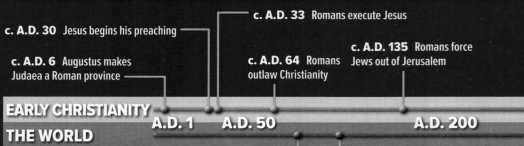

c. A.D. 30 Jesus begins his preaching

c. A.D. 33 Romans execute Jesus

c. A.D. 6 Augustus makes Judaea a Roman province

c. A.D. 64 Romans outlaw Christianity

c. A.D. 135 Romans force Jews out of Jerusalem

EARLY CHRISTIANITY

THE WORLD

A.D. 1   A.D. 50   A.D. 200

North
Sea

EUROPE

A L P S

ITALY

Rome

orsica

Sardinia

Sicily

GREECE

Constantinople

Black Sea

ASIA
MINOR

Tarsus

Antioch

SYRIA

Damascus

Nazareth

Jerusalem

JUDAEA

Alexandria

EGYPT

Red Sea

Aegean
Sea

Mediterranean Sea

Caspian Sea

Aral
Sea

ASIA

Persian Gulf

0   400 miles
0   400 km
Lambert Azimuthal Equal-Area projection

60°N

10°E   20°E   30°E   40°E   50°E

c. A.D. 312 Constantine
accepts Christianity

c. A.D. 392 Christianity becomes
official religion of Rome

c. A.D. 597 Monks
bring Christianity to Britain

A.D. 300   A.D. 400   A.D. 500   A.D. 600

LESSON 1
Early Christianity

ESSENTIAL QUESTION

• What are the characteristics of a leader?

IT MATTERS BECAUSE
Christianity is one of the world's major religions and continues to influence people around the globe.

Judaism and Rome

GUIDING QUESTION *How did the Jews respond to Roman rule?*

The Romans allowed Judaism (JOO·dee·IH·zuhm) to be practiced throughout the empire. In Judaea and Galilee, however, Romans ruled the Jews with an iron hand. Many Jews hoped that God would send a deliverer to rescue them from Roman rule. They wanted the kingdom of Israel to be restored.

Control by Romans

The Romans had taken over Judah in 63 B.C., but they allowed Jewish kings to rule it. In A.D. 6, Augustus made Judah a Roman province and called it by the Roman name of Judaea (joo·DEE·uh). Augustus replaced the Jewish ruler with a Roman governor, called a procurator (PRAH·kyuh·RAY·tuhr). Judaea was now more tightly controlled by the Roman Empire.

   The Jews disagreed among themselves over how to deal with the Romans. Some Jews wanted to avoid conflict with their rulers. They preferred to cooperate with them. Others limited their contact with Roman officials and continued to practice Jewish traditions. Some Jews completely ignored the Romans. They established communities in remote places, away from Roman rule. Jerusalem, however, remained their holy city.

Reading**HELP**DESK

Taking Notes: *Identifying*

On a graphic organizer like this one, list three things we know about the life of Jesus.

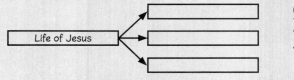

Life of Jesus

Content Vocabulary
• parable   • apostle
• resurrection   • salvation

Jewish Revolts

One group of Jews believed that they should fight the Romans for their freedom. These people, called Zealots (ZEH·luhtz), rebelled against Roman rule in A.D. 66. The Romans, however, brutally crushed the uprising. They destroyed the Jewish temple in Jerusalem and killed thousands of Jews.

The ruins of an ancient Jewish fortress called Masada (muh·SAH·duh) stand on a mountaintop in southeastern Israel. After Jerusalem fell to the Romans in A.D. 70, about 1,000 Jewish defenders overtook the Masada fortress. For almost two years, these defenders held off an army of 15,000 Roman soldiers.

In A.D. 73, the Romans broke through the walls of the fortress but found only a few Jewish survivors—two women and five children. The others had taken their own lives rather than surrender to the Romans. The fortress is now recognized as a symbol of Jewish heroism.

The Jews organized another unsuccessful rebellion in A.D. 132. In response, the Romans forced all Jews to leave Jerusalem. The Romans then declared that no Jews could ever return to the city. Many Jews, mourning the loss of their city, established communities elsewhere.

By A.D. 700, the Jews had settled in regions as far west as Spain and as far east as Central Asia. In later centuries, they settled throughout Europe and the Americas.

An armed group of Jews captured this mountain fortress of Masada from the Romans. They defended it against a Roman army that outnumbered them 15 to one.

▶ CRITICAL THINKING
Drawing Conclusions Why do you think the Jews wanted to control Masada?

Peter

Most of what we know about the disciple Peter comes from the Christian Bible. According to tradition, Peter deserted Jesus when Jesus was arrested in the garden outside Jerusalem. Later, Peter felt ashamed and regretted his lack of courage. In the years following the death of Jesus, Peter emerged as a respected leader of the earliest Christian community.

▶ **CRITICAL THINKING**
Drawing Conclusions Why do you think Peter deserted Jesus when Jesus was arrested?

Academic Vocabulary

create to bring into existence; to produce by a course of action

Although the Jews were scattered around the world, they kept their faith alive. They did this by studying and following their religious laws and traditions.

✓ **PROGRESS CHECK**

Identifying Cause and Effect How did the A.D. 132 revolt affect the Jews of Judaea?

Jesus of Nazareth

GUIDING QUESTION *Why were the life and death of Jesus of Nazareth important to his followers?*

A few decades before the first Jewish revolt, a Jew named Jesus (JEE·zuhs) grew up in a small town called Nazareth (NA·zuh·ruhth) in Galilee (GA·luh·LEE), the region just north of Judaea. In about A.D. 30, Jesus began to travel throughout Galilee and Judaea, preaching to people about his ideas. A group of 12 close followers called disciples (dih·SY·puhlz) traveled with Jesus.

What Was the Message of Jesus?

According to the Christian Bible, Jesus preached that God was coming soon to rule the world. Jesus urged people to turn from their selfish ways and welcome the kingdom of heaven. In the excerpt below, Jesus calls on his followers to joyfully accept God's coming as a precious gift:

PRIMARY SOURCE

❝ The kingdom of heaven is like a treasure buried in a field, which a person finds and hides again, and out of joy goes and sells all that he has and buys that field. ❞

—Matthew 13:54, *New American Bible*

Jesus preached that God **created** all people and loved them the way a father loves his children. Therefore, people should love God and one another. In this way, they would be obeying God.

The message of Jesus reinforced the Jewish teachings: "Love the Lord your God with all your heart and with all your soul and with all your mind and with all your strength" and "Love your neighbor as yourself."

The teachings of Jesus are summarized in his Sermon on the Mount. Jesus preached on a mountainside to a crowd of thousands.

Alan Spencer/Age fotostock

In it Jesus gave the people simple rules to live by called "The Beatitudes." He told people that it was not enough to follow religious laws. People had to love God and forgive others from the heart.

Jesus spoke using everyday language. He often preached using **parables** (PA·ruh·buhlz). These were stories about things his listeners could understand, using events from everyday life. They helped people **interpret**, or explain, the ideas Jesus taught.

In one parable, Jesus told of a Samaritan man who saw an injured traveler by the side of the road. Even though the injured man was not a Samaritan, the passerby helped him. In another parable, Jesus told the story of a father who forgave his son's mistakes. He welcomed his prodigal—or wasteful—son back into the family. Both parables taught that God is like the concerned Samaritan or the forgiving father. He loves people who have erred and will forgive them if they trust in him.

How Did Christianity Begin?

Jesus and his message sparked strong reactions from people. His followers spoke of times in which he healed the sick and performed other miracles. Stories about him were widely told.

INFOGRAPHIC **THE BEATITUDES**

The *Beatitudes* are sayings or teachings intended to guide people. They are part of Jesus' Sermon on the Mount. The Sermon includes the Lord's Prayer and nine Beatitudes for leading a better life.

1 **DOCUMENT-BASED QUESTION** Jesus says the meek—or humble—shall inherit the Earth. What do you think he meant by this?

2 **CRITICAL THINKING**
Making Generalizations
Based on what Jesus says in the Beatitudes, what kind of people is he speaking to in his sermon?

A few selected Beatitudes from the Sermon on the Mount in Matthew 5: 3-12.

"Blessed are the poor in spirit, for theirs is the kingdom of heaven.

Blessed are those who mourn, for they will be comforted.

Blessed are the meek, for they will inherit the Earth.

Blessed are those who hunger and thirst for righteousness, for they will be filled.

Blessed are the merciful, for they will be shown mercy.

Blessed are the pure in heart, for they will see God.

Blessed are the peacemakers, for they will be called sons of God."

parable a short story that teaches a principle about what is good behavior

Academic Vocabulary

interpret to explain the meaning of

The parables of the Good Samaritan (left) and the Prodigal Son (right) are shown here. In each case, one person is helping another.

▶ CRITICAL THINKING
Synthesizing What do you think of today when you hear that someone is a "good samaritan"?

Many believed he was the promised deliverer. Some Jews felt Jesus was deceiving people and opposed him. Roman rulers feared his preaching and growing influence and popularity. They viewed Jesus as a threat to law and order.

At the time of the Jewish holy days of Passover, there was growing tension between the Romans and the Jews. The Romans brought statues of the emperor into Jerusalem, the holy city of the Jews. Many Jews saw these statues as false idols and objected to their presence. The Jews had also grown weary of Roman rule and high taxes. Many Romans were angry because the Jews refused to worship statues of the Roman emperor.

In about A.D. 33, Jesus traveled to Jerusalem with his 12 disciples to celebrate the Jewish holy days of Passover. When he arrived in the city, an enthusiastic crowd greeted him as their promised deliverer. In an event known as the Last Supper, Jesus celebrated the Passover meal with his disciples.

Reading HELP DESK

Reading Strategy: *Paraphrasing*

Paraphrasing is restating what you read using your own words. Paraphrasing is a good way to check that you really understood what you read. As you finish reading a paragraph or a passage, ask yourself, "What is the main idea?" Then try to restate the main idea using your own words.

Betrayal of Jesus

After the meal, however, one of Jesus' closest followers betrayed him. Leaders in Jerusalem arrested Jesus to prevent trouble from erupting in the city. They may have charged Jesus with treason, or disloyalty to the government. He was questioned by the Roman governor and sentenced to death.

According to the Christian Bible, Jesus was crucified, or hung from a wooden cross, and died. Romans regularly crucified criminals and political rebels. The followers of Jesus were greatly saddened by his death. According to Christian belief, Jesus rose from the dead three days after his death and appeared to some of his disciples.

Early Christian writings state that Mary Magdalene, one of Jesus' followers, was the first to see him alive again. The message of Jesus' **resurrection** (REH·zuh·REHK·shuhn), or rising from the dead, led to the birth of Christianity. During this very early period, Christians were still one of the many groups that made up Judaism.

☑ **PROGRESS CHECK**

Explaining How did Jesus reinforce traditional Jewish teachings?

Who Were the Apostles?

GUIDING QUESTION *How did early Christianity spread throughout the Roman Empire?*

The early Christian leaders who spread the message of Jesus were called **apostles** (uh·PAH·suhlz). The apostles first spoke to the Jews in Judaea and Galilee. The apostles then traveled to other parts of the Mediterranean region. Small groups of Jews and non-Jews in the Greek-speaking cities of the eastern Mediterranean believed the message about Jesus.

Those who accepted Jesus and his teachings became known as "Christians" and referred to Jesus as "Jesus Christ." The word *Christ* comes from *Christos*, which is a Greek term that means "the anointed one."

The first Christians formed churches, or local groups for worship and teaching. Early Christians met in homes of men and women. At these gatherings, Christians prayed and studied the Hebrew Bible and early Christian writings. They also ate a meal similar to the Last Supper to remember the death and resurrection of Jesus.

BIOGRAPHY

Mary Magdalene

A practical, down-to-earth woman, Mary Magdalene went with Jesus during his travels throughout Galilee. Biblical accounts of the life of Jesus maintain that she was present during his crucifixion and burial. These accounts also say she and two other women went to his tomb a few days after he was placed there. Finding it empty, Mary hurried to tell the other followers. She then returned to the tomb with Peter, also a follower of Jesus.

▶ CRITICAL THINKING
Analyzing What risks did Mary Magdalene face by being loyal to Jesus?

resurrection the act of rising from the dead
apostle Christian leader chosen by Jesus to spread his message

At the end of the 1400s, the Italian artist Leonardo da Vinci created this famous painting of Jesus. Called *The Last Supper*, it was painted on a wall in Milan, Italy.

▶ CRITICAL THINKING
Analyzing What do you think is happening in this illustration of Jesus and his followers?

Early Christian Leaders

Apostles played an important part in the growth of Christianity. Peter and Paul were two important apostles in the early Christian church. Peter was a Jewish fisher from Galilee. He had known Jesus while he was alive and had been one of the 12 disciples Jesus had chosen to preach his message. According to Christian tradition, Peter helped set up a Christian church in Rome after the death of Jesus. Today, the center of the Catholic branch of Christianity is still located there.

Paul of Tarsus was another important Christian apostle. He was a well-educated Jew and a Roman citizen. He was raised as a loyal Roman who, as an adult, distrusted the Christians. Saul—his Hebrew name—at first tried to stop Christian ideas from spreading in Judaea and Galilee. The chief Jewish priest in Jerusalem then sent him to Damascus, a city in neighboring Syria. There, he was supposed to stop Christians in the city from spreading their ideas.

According to Christian belief, while he was traveling to Damascus in Syria, Paul saw a great light and heard the voice of Jesus. As a result of this encounter, Paul soon became a Christian and devoted his life to spreading the message of Jesus.

Leonardo da Vinci/The Bridgeman Art Library/Getty Images

ReadingHELPDESK

salvation the act of being saved from the effects of sin

Paul traveled throughout the eastern Mediterranean region and founded numerous Christian churches. Many of his important letters to churches in Rome, Greece, and Asia Minor are found in the Christian Bible.

What Are Basic Christian Beliefs?

The early Christians believed in one God, not the many gods of Rome. They believed that Jesus was the Son of God. They believed he had come to save people. By becoming Christians and by accepting Jesus and his teachings, people could gain **salvation** (sal·VAY· shuhn). They would be saved from their sins, or wrongdoings, and allowed to enter heaven. Like Jesus, people would be resurrected after death and join God in everlasting life.

Because of their faith in Jesus, Christians began to believe in God in a new way. Like the Jews, Christians believed in the God of Israel and studied the Hebrew Bible. However, they also believed in the Christian Trinity, which comes from a word meaning "three." In Christian belief, the Trinity refers to the three persons of God: the Father, Son, and Holy Spirit. These teachings became the basis of the Christian faith.

During the 100 years after Jesus' death, Christianity won followers throughout the world. The peace and order established by the Roman Empire gave people the ability to spread the Christian religion.

Before becoming an apostle, Paul of Tarsus tried to stop the spread of Christian ideas. After he came to believe in Jesus, Paul became one of the most influential leaders of the early Christian movement.

▶ CRITICAL THINKING
Speculating Why do you think Paul at first tried to stop the spread of the message of Jesus?

✔ PROGRESS CHECK

Identifying Why were the apostles important to early Christianity?

LESSON 1 REVIEW

Review Vocabulary

1. Why did Jesus preach using *parables*?

2. How did the *apostles* spread the message of Jesus?

Answer the Guiding Questions

3. *Explaining* How did Jewish traditions survive after A.D. 132?

4. *Describing* When Jesus said "love your neighbor as yourself," what was his message?

5. *Contrasting* How did some Jews differ in their beliefs about Jesus?

6. *Explaining* Why did Jesus have disciples?

7. **INFORMATIVE/EXPLANATORY** In a paragraph, explain why there were growing tensions between the Romans and the early Christians.

LESSON 2
The Early Church

IT MATTERS BECAUSE

The Roman Empire's system of roads, shared languages, and stability made it easier for Christianity to spread.

Christianity and the Empire

GUIDING QUESTION *How did Christianity change over time?*

As the apostles spread the message of Jesus, many people in the Mediterranean world became Christians. The Roman Empire contributed to this growth.

Christianity Spreads

Several factors helped Christianity spread throughout the empire. Areas controlled by the Romans were generally peaceful. Well-constructed roads meant Christians could easily travel from one **region** to another. Most people in the empire spoke Latin or Greek. This allowed Christians to communicate with them about the message of Jesus.

Another reason Christianity spread throughout the empire was that it had an attractive message. The official religion of Rome required people to honor the emperor and the state. This religion did not offer help to people when they experienced personal or economic problems. Christianity, however, provided comfort to people during difficult times. Christianity gave people hope that even if life was bad on Earth, there was the promise of a better afterlife.

Reading**HELP**DESK

Taking Notes: *Listing*

Use a graphic organizer like this one to list the major reasons that Christianity spread.

Reasons Christianity Spread
•
•
•
•

Content Vocabulary

- martyr
- hierarchy
- clergy
- doctrine
- gospel
- pope
- laity

Christianity also spread quickly throughout the empire because it provided its followers with security. Christians lived in **communities** where each member was responsible for taking care of the needs of others.

Why Did Romans Mistreat Christians?

As the number of Christians grew, some Romans believed that they were dangerous. They thought Christians were a threat to the empire. Romans expected everyone to worship the emperor as a god. The Christians, like the Jews, however, believed that only God could be worshipped. Christians criticized popular Roman festivals that honored the numerous Roman gods. Also, Christians did not support warfare as a way to resolve problems. As a result, they refused to serve in the Roman army. Furthermore, Christians buried their dead outside Rome in catacombs, or underground burial places. Christians could also meet there to hold memorial services.

GEOGRAPHY CONNECTION

Even though the Romans persecuted the Christians, the Christian religion continued to grow and spread its influence.

1 **LOCATION** What areas did Paul visit during his second journey?

2 **CRITICAL THINKING**
Speculating What might have prevented Christianity from spreading to more places during its first three centuries?

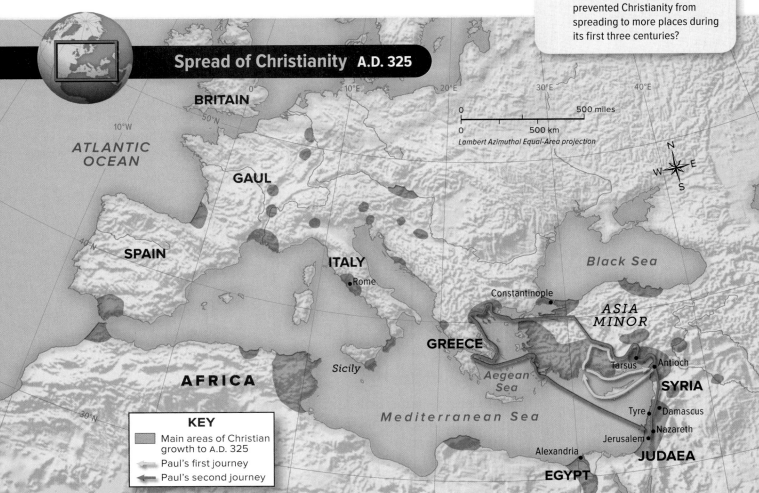

Spread of Christianity A.D. 325

KEY
- Main areas of Christian growth to A.D. 325
- Paul's first journey
- Paul's second journey

BRITAIN
ATLANTIC OCEAN
GAUL
SPAIN
ITALY
Rome
AFRICA
Sicily
Mediterranean Sea
GREECE
Aegean Sea
Constantinople
Black Sea
ASIA MINOR
Tarsus
Antioch
SYRIA
Tyre
Damascus
Nazareth
Jerusalem
JUDAEA
Alexandria
EGYPT

500 miles
500 km
Lambert Azimuthal Equal-Area projection

Academic Vocabulary

region a broad geographic area
community people living in a particular area; the area itself

Then

During the early centuries of Christianity, the Roman Catacombs were used for burials and funeral meals. Today, cemeteries are still places where we go to honor our families, experience shared history, and reflect on the sacrifices of others.

Now

▶ **CRITICAL THINKING**
Analyzing Why do you think early Christians buried their dead in hidden catacombs?

People who thought the Christians were dangerous believed that they should be punished. Some Romans blamed Christians for causing natural disasters. In A.D. 64, the emperor Nero falsely accused Christians of starting a fire that burned most of Rome. As a result, Christianity was outlawed.

Christians were often mistreated. They were arrested and beaten. Some Christians became **martyrs** (MAHR·tuhrz), or people who were willing to die rather than give up their beliefs. Despite the mistreatment, Christianity continued to flourish.

The Empire Accepts Christianity

In the early A.D. 300s, the emperor Diocletian carried out the last great persecution of Christians. But his attempt failed. Christianity had grown too strong to be destroyed by force.

In A.D. 312, the Roman emperor Constantine (KAHN·stuhn·TEEN) prepared to lead his **military** forces into battle. According to some early Christian writers, Constantine had a remarkable dream the night before the battle. In the dream he saw a flaming cross in the sky. Written beneath the cross were the Latin words that meant "In this sign you will conquer."

The next day, Constantine ordered his soldiers to paint the Christian cross on their battle shields. Constantine won the battle and believed the Christian God had helped him.

Constantine became a strong supporter of Christianity. In A.D. 313, he issued the Edict of Milan. This decree allowed all religious groups in the empire, including Christians, to practice their religions freely. Constantine attended religious meetings of Christian leaders and gave government aid to Christians. With the help of his mother, Helena (HEH·luh·nuh), he built Christian churches in Rome and Jerusalem. Christians were allowed to serve in government and were excused from paying taxes. They started to serve in the army.

One of Constantine's successors, the emperor Theodosius (THEE·uh·DOH·shuhs), banned Greek and Roman religions. In A.D. 392, he made Christianity the official religion of the Roman Empire.

Axum and Kush

At about the same time Christianity was flourishing in the Roman Empire, great trading kingdoms were rising in East Africa. The empire of Ethiopia, also known as Abyssinia, was powerful.

(t)DEA/G CARGAGNA/De Agostini Editore/Age fotostock; (b)DoD Photo by William D. Moss

Reading **HELP**DESK

martyr a person who is willing to die for his or her beliefs

Academic Vocabulary

military relating to armed forces

Its city-state of Axum served as a trading center for Mediterranean and East Asian worlds sending goods into and out of Africa. Around A.D. 300, Axum defeated neighboring Kush, another city-state. In A.D. 334, King Ezana (ah·ZAH·nah) of Axum made Christianity the official religion of Axum.

✔ PROGRESS CHECK

Evaluating How did Constantine support Christianity?

Constantine led his troops to victory at the Battle of Milvian Bridge near Rome. This triumph led Constantine to convert to Christianity.

▶ CRITICAL THINKING
Analyzing Do you think the Romans could have destroyed Christianity if Constantine hadn't been converted? Explain.

Organizing the Church

GUIDING QUESTION *How did early Christians organize their church and explain their beliefs?*

As the number of Christians grew, the church had to become more organized to unite its followers. In addition, separate Christian communities began to practice Christianity differently. The early Christian leaders had to clarify and write down their beliefs.

Church Leadership

Early Christians were familiar with how the Roman Empire was ruled. They used the empire as their model for organizing the church. Like the empire, the church came to be ruled by a **hierarchy** (HY·uh·RAHR·kee). A hierarchy is an organization with different levels of authority.

Richard Bonson/Wildlife Art, LTD

hierarchy an organization with different levels of authority

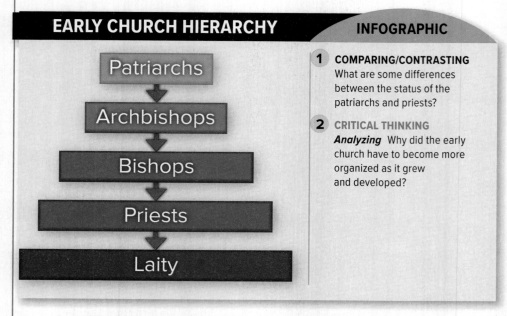

EARLY CHURCH HIERARCHY

INFOGRAPHIC

Patriarchs → Archbishops → Bishops → Priests → Laity

1 COMPARING/CONTRASTING What are some differences between the status of the patriarchs and priests?

2 CRITICAL THINKING *Analyzing* Why did the early church have to become more organized as it grew and developed?

The **clergy** (KLUHR·jee), or church officials, were the leaders of the church. The role of the clergy was different from that of the **laity** (LAY·uh·tee), or regular church members. Although women were not allowed to serve in the clergy, they were members of the church. Women cared for sick and needy church members.

By A.D. 300, individual churches were headed by clergy called priests. Priests led worship services and managed local church activities. Clergy called bishops supervised the dioceses (DY·uh·suh·suhz), or several churches grouped together. Bishops explained Christian beliefs and managed regional church affairs. A bishop in charge of an entire region was called an archbishop. The five leading archbishops—in charge of the cities of Rome, Constantinople, Alexandria, Antioch, and Jerusalem—were known as patriarchs (PAY·tree·AHRKS).

The bishops met in councils to define the teachings of the Church. They wanted to make sure that Christians practiced the same beliefs. The decisions they reached at these councils were accepted as **doctrine** (DAHK·truhn), or official church teaching. The ideas that the bishops rejected were heresies (HER·uh·seez), or teachings that did not support the Christian faith.

What Writings Shaped Christianity?

Church leaders also preserved stories about Jesus and the writings of the apostles. Jesus did not write down what he said or did. His followers, however, passed on what they remembered about him.

By A.D. 300, four accounts of the life and teachings of Jesus were widely known. Christians believed that four apostles of Jesus—Matthew, Mark, Luke, and John—wrote these accounts.

Each account was called a **gospel** (GAHS·puhl), which means "good news." Christians later included the four gospels with the writings of Paul and other early Christian leaders. Together, these works became known as the New Testament. The New Testament was added to the Greek version of the Jewish sacred writings, which Christians called the Old Testament. Together, these works formed the Christian Bible.

Other writings influenced the early church. Christian thinkers who explained church teachings became known as the Church Fathers. One of the most important Church Fathers was Augustine, a bishop in North Africa. In his writings, Augustine defended Christianity against its critics. Augustine wrote *The City of God*. This was one of the first history books written from the viewpoint of a Christian.

The Bishop of Rome

As the church grew, the bishop of Rome claimed power over the other bishops. He believed that he had received the authority from the apostle Peter. Also, his diocese was in Rome, the capital of the Roman Empire. By A.D. 600, the bishop of Rome was called by a special title—**pope** (POHP). The title is from a Latin word, *papa*, related to the word *pater*, meaning "father." Latin-speaking Christians in the western part of the empire accepted the pope as head of all the churches. The Latin churches as a group became known as the Roman Catholic Church. Greek-speaking Christians, however, would not accept the authority of the pope over them. Also claiming a link to the apostles, their churches became known as the Eastern Orthodox Church.

Augustine was one of the most important writers and thinkers in the history of Christianity. Even today, his books continue to inform and inspire.

▶ CRITICAL THINKING
Making Inferences Why do you think Augustine is remembered as one of the Church Fathers?

✓ PROGRESS CHECK

Identifying What writings are included in the New Testament?

Scala/Art Resource, NY

LESSON 2 REVIEW

Review Vocabulary

1. How did church *doctrine* help to unify early Christians?

2. How is the *pope* similar to and different from other bishops?

Answer the Guiding Questions

3. *Identifying* What were two main reasons Christianity spread during Roman times?

4. *Describing* Why were early Christians considered traitors to the Roman Empire?

5. *Comparing* Compare the responsibilities of a priest and a bishop in the early Christian church.

6. *Making Inferences* Why did bishops meet in councils?

7. **NARRATIVE** Write a journal entry that Constantine might have written after the battle he believed God helped him win.

There's More Online! connected.mcgraw-hill.com

LESSON 3
A Christian Europe

ESSENTIAL QUESTION
• How do new ideas change the way people live?

IT MATTERS BECAUSE
Christianity divided into the Roman Catholic and the Eastern Orthodox branches. Despite this division, all Christians share core beliefs that go back to Jesus of Nazareth.

Two Christian Churches

GUIDING QUESTION *What issues divided the western and eastern Christian churches?*

The Roman Catholic Church was based in Rome, the capital of the Western Roman Empire. The church was led by the very powerful pope. As the Western Roman Empire declined, the Christian church of Rome survived. At the same time, the Roman Empire in the east, which soon became known as the Byzantine Empire, thrived. The Byzantines developed their own Christian church. Their church reflected their Greek heritage. This church became known as the Eastern Orthodox Church.

Byzantine Government and Religion

The emperor of the Byzantine Empire and the officials of the Eastern Orthodox Church worked closely together. The Byzantines believed their emperor was God's representative on Earth. Beginning in the A.D. 400s, emperors were crowned in a religious ceremony. They also took an oath to defend Eastern Orthodox Christianity. They believed it was their duty to unite the empire under one Christian faith. Thus, the emperors controlled the Eastern Orthodox Church. Emperors appointed church leaders and defined how people would worship. They also controlled the wealth of the church and helped settle disputes about church beliefs.

Reading **HELP**DESK

Taking Notes: *Describing*
Create a diagram like this one, and describe how the western and eastern Christian churches viewed the authority of the pope.

Authority of the Pope	
Western Church	Eastern Church

Content Vocabulary
• icon
• iconoclast
• excommunicate
• schism
• monastery

What Are Icons?

Both Byzantine clergy and the Byzantine people discussed and often argued about religious matters. These arguments frequently became political issues and led to fights and riots.

In the A.D. 700s, a heated dispute about **icons** (EYE·KAWNZ) divided the Eastern Orthodox Church. Icons are paintings of Jesus, Mary (the mother of Jesus), and the saints, or Christian holy people. Many Byzantines **displayed** icons in their homes. They also covered the walls of their churches with them.

People who displayed icons claimed that these images symbolized the presence of God in their lives. They also believed that the images helped people understand Christian teachings. The thinker John of Damascus was the leading defender of icons.

Some Byzantines, however, did not approve of the use of icons. They thought it was a form of idol worship forbidden by God. In A.D. 726, Emperor Leo III ordered that all icons be removed from the churches. Government officials who carried out his orders were called **iconoclasts** (eye·KAH· nuh·KLASTS), or image breakers. Today, this word refers to someone who criticizes traditional beliefs or practices.

Most Byzantines, many church leaders, and even the pope in Rome disapproved of Emperor Leo's actions. The dispute over icons severely damaged the relationship between the Roman Catholic Church and the Eastern Orthodox Church. Over the next century, the argument became less heated, and icons were used once again. They are still important today.

The Great Split

Icons were only one of the issues that divided the eastern and western Christian churches. The most serious disagreement was about church authority. The pope claimed to be head of all Christian churches. He believed he was a successor, or person who follows another person, to Peter, disciple of Jesus. Peter was the first bishop of Rome. The Byzantines **rejected** the claim of the pope. They believed the patriarch of Constantinople and other bishops were equal to the pope.

This icon painted on wood shows the angel Gabriel. According to the Christian Bible, Gabriel was a messenger sent from God.

▶ **CRITICAL THINKING**
Explaining Why do you think some Byzantine people were against the use of icons?

Scala/Art Resource, NY

---

icon a representation of an object of worship
iconoclast *originally:* a person who destroys icons; *today:* a person who criticizes traditional beliefs

Academic Vocabulary

display to place an object where people can view it
reject to refuse to accept

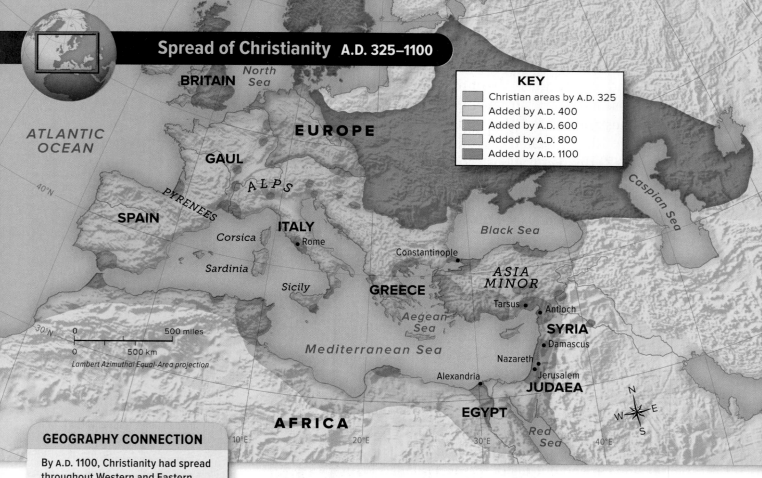

Spread of Christianity A.D. 325–1100

KEY
- Christian areas by A.D. 325
- Added by A.D. 400
- Added by A.D. 600
- Added by A.D. 800
- Added by A.D. 1100

ATLANTIC OCEAN

North Sea

BRITAIN

EUROPE

GAUL

ALPS

PYRENEES

SPAIN

ITALY

Corsica

Rome

Sardinia

Sicily

GREECE

Aegean Sea

Mediterranean Sea

Black Sea

Constantinople

ASIA MINOR

Tarsus

Antioch

SYRIA

Damascus

Nazareth

Jerusalem

JUDAEA

Alexandria

EGYPT

AFRICA

Red Sea

Caspian Sea

40°N

30°N

10°E 20°E 30°E 40°E

0   500 miles
0   500 km
Lambert Azimuthal Equal-Area projection

N E S W

GEOGRAPHY CONNECTION

By A.D. 1100, Christianity had spread throughout Western and Eastern Europe and into far northern lands.

1 UNDERSTANDING A MAP KEY Which of these two areas became Christian first: Britain or Syria?

2 CRITICAL THINKING
Analyzing Why do you think some areas took longer to convert to Christianity than others?

Military events also damaged the relationship between the pope and the patriarch of Constantinople. In the late A.D. 700s, Italy was invaded. The pope appealed to the Byzantine emperor for help, but the emperor refused. The pope then asked the Franks to help defend Rome. The Franks were a Germanic people that supported the pope as head of the Christian church.

The Franks successfully defended Italy against the invaders. To show his gratitude, the pope crowned the Frankish king, Charlemagne (SHAHR·luh·MAYN), emperor in A.D. 800. The pope's actions upset the Byzantines. They believed their ruler was the only Roman emperor.

The eastern and western churches also viewed their roles in government differently. In the Byzantine Empire, the emperor controlled both church and government. Byzantine church leaders supported the decisions of the emperor. In the West, the pope claimed he had religious and political authority over all of Europe. He often quarreled with kings about church and government affairs.

Finally, in A.D. 1054, after centuries of bitterness, the patriarch of Constantinople and the pope **excommunicated** (EHK·skuh·MYOO·nuh·KAY·tuhd) each other. To excommunicate means to declare that a person or group no longer belongs to the church. This created a **schism** (SIH·zuhm), or separation, between the two major churches of Christianity. The split between the Eastern Orthodox Church and the Roman Catholic Church still exists today.

☑ PROGRESS CHECK

Identifying What issues divided the eastern and western Christian churches?

The Spread of Christianity

GUIDING QUESTION *How did Christianity spread across Europe?*

After the fall of the Western Roman Empire, people in many parts of Europe faced disorder and violence. Many looked to the Christian church for help. They hoped that Christianity would bring peace, order, and unity.

New Christian Communities

During the A.D. 300s, devout Christians in the Eastern Roman Empire formed religious communities called **monasteries** (MAH·nuh·STEHR·eez). In the monasteries, men called monks lived apart from the world. At the same time, they performed good deeds and modeled how Christians should live.

Christian women established religious communities of their own. These women were called nuns, and they lived in convents. During this time, one of the best known nuns was a Roman widow named Paula. In the early A.D. 400s, Paula helped a scholar named Jerome translate the Christian Bible into Latin.

The Greek bishop Basil (BAY·zuhl) created a list of rules for monks and nuns. Known as the Basilian (buh·ZIH·lee·uhn) Rule, this list told people how to live and pray in Eastern Orthodox monasteries and convents.

In the West, religious communities followed another set of regulations called the Benedictine Rule. An Italian monk named Benedict (BEH·nuh·DIHKT) wrote these rules about A.D. 529. Benedictines gave up material goods. They devoted their days to work and prayer. One of their major duties was to serve as missionaries. Missionaries teach their religion to those who are not followers.

Charlemagne believed his authority to rule came from God. Inspired by the teachings of St. Augustine, he considered both the spiritual and material needs of his subjects.

▶ CRITICAL THINKING
Explaining Why do you think Charlemagne, a Frankish king, defended Rome?

Popperfoto/Getty Images

excommunicate to declare that a person or group is no longer a member of the church

schism a separation or division from a church

monastery a religious community

THE CYRILLIC ALPHABET

Cyrillic Letter	Written Name	English Sound
Б	beh	B
Г	gey	G
Ж	zheh	ZH
М	em	M
П	pey	P
С	ess	S
Ф	ef	F
Ч	cheh	CH

Cyril and Methodius quarreled with German church leaders who opposed the use of Slavic languages for preaching and worship. The Germans wanted only Latin to be used.

INFOGRAPHIC

Cyril, a Byzantine missionary, developed the Cyrillic alphabet, part of which is shown here. The original alphabet, based on Greek, had 43 letters.

1 IDENTIFYING Which Cyrillic letters make the same sounds as the letters "p" and "f" in the English alphabet?

2 CRITICAL THINKING
Applying Why did Cyril create a new alphabet for people who spoke Slavic languages?

In addition, the Rule stated that monks were to welcome outsiders who were in need of food and shelter:

TEXT: Chapter 53: The Reception of Guests. From Rule of Saint Benedict in English, edited by Timothy Fry. Copyright © 1981 by The Order of St. Benedict, Inc.; PHOTO: ©José F. Poblete/Corbis

PRIMARY SOURCE

❞ All guests who present themselves are to be welcomed as Christ, for he himself will say: I was a stranger and you welcomed me. … Once a guest has been announced, the superior and the brothers are to meet him with all the courtesy of love. … All humility [being humble] should be shown in addressing a guest on arrival or departure. ❞

—Benedictine Rule, Chapter 53: The Reception of Guests

Monks and nuns had important roles in Christian Europe. They helped the poor and ran hospitals and schools. They also helped preserve ancient Greek and Roman writings.

Christianity and the Slavs

The Byzantines wanted to bring their religion and culture to groups who lived north of their empire. Two brothers, Cyril (SIHR·uhl) and Methodius, were among the most dedicated Byzantine missionaries. Their mission was to deliver the Christian message to the Slavs, a people in Eastern Europe.

Cyril and Methodius believed that the Slavs would be more interested in Christianity if they heard about it in their own languages. About A.D. 863, Cyril invented an alphabet for the Slavic languages. It is known today as the Cyrillic (suh·RIH·lihk)

Reading**HELP**DESK

Build Vocabulary: *Word Origins*

The English word *slave* comes from the word *Slav*. In the early Middle Ages, so many Slavic people were taken into slavery that their name came to be used for anyone who was treated as the property of another and forced to work.

alphabet in honor of its inventor. The Cyrillic alphabet was based on Greek letters. It is still used today by Russians, Ukrainians, Serbs, and Bulgarians.

Christianity in Western Europe

In Western Europe, Christian missionaries sought to convert the peoples of Britain and Ireland to Christianity. Roman soldiers were stationed there also. In the A.D. 300s, Roman soldiers left Britain to defend the empire against Germanic invaders.

Beginning in the A.D. 400s, Germanic tribes from present-day Germany and Denmark invaded much of Britain. Over time, these groups united to become known as the Anglo-Saxons. They built farming villages and founded several small kingdoms. Southern Britain soon became known as Angleland, or England. The people became known as the English.

In Britain, the Anglo-Saxons pushed aside the Celts (KEHLTS), the people already living there. Some Celts fled to remote, mountainous areas of Britain. Others crossed the sea to Ireland. In the A.D. 400s, a priest named Patrick brought Christianity to Ireland. He set up churches and monasteries where monks helped preserve Christian and Roman learning.

In A.D. 597, Pope Gregory I sent about 40 monks from Rome to bring Christianity to the Anglo-Saxons of Britain. They converted King Ethelbert of Kent to Christianity. Ethelbert allowed the missionaries to build a church in his capital city of Canterbury. In about 100 years, most of England had accepted the Christian faith. Monasteries were built throughout England. As in Ireland, they became centers of religion and culture.

Pope Gregory I is also known as Gregory the Great. A former monk, he was an excellent administrator. As pope, he continued to live as a monk and tried to bring about reforms in the church.

▶ **CRITICAL THINKING**
Analyzing How might Pope Gregory's background have affected the spread of Christianity?

PROGRESS CHECK

Analyzing Why were monasteries and convents important in Christian Europe?

Giraudon/Art Resource, NY

LESSON 3 REVIEW

Review Vocabulary

1. Is an *iconoclast* someone who believes in using icons in worship or someone who opposes this practice?

2. When the early church underwent a *schism*, does that mean it changed its most important doctrines?

Answer the Guiding Questions

3. ***Comparing and Contrasting*** What different views of the role of the church in government did the Eastern and Western churches have?

4. ***Making Inferences*** Why do you think the Byzantine emperor refused to help the pope defend Rome from invaders?

5. ***Explaining*** What were monasteries and what purpose did they serve?

6. ***Identifying Cause and Effect*** How did the Cyrillic alphabet help the spread of Christianity?

7. **INFORMATIVE/EXPLANATORY** Write a paragraph to describe what happened to Ireland once Patrick brought Christianity to its lands.

CHAPTER 10 Activities

Write your answers on a separate piece of paper.

1 **Exploring the Essential Question**

NARRATIVE Imagine you are Paul of Tarsus. You want to write your thoughts about how Christianity has developed and spread. You decide to do this in the form of a letter to church leaders. What part did you play in helping Christianity develop? What challenges did you personally face? Which accomplishments are you most proud of?

2 **21st Century Skills**

RESEARCH ON THE INTERNET Find the Gospels of Luke and Matthew in an online version of the New Testament. Compare and contrast the different ways Luke and Matthew tell the story of the birth of Jesus. (In Luke, read Chapter 2, verses 1–20. In Matthew, read Chapter 1, verses 18–25 and Chapter 2, verses 1–15.) Write a report explaining the results of your research.

3 **Thinking Like a Historian**

UNDERSTANDING CAUSE AND EFFECT Create a cause-and-effect diagram like the one shown here. Fill it in with the results or effects of Emperor Constantine's conversion to Christianity.

Emperor Constantine's Conversion → Results

4 **GEOGRAPHY ACTIVITY**

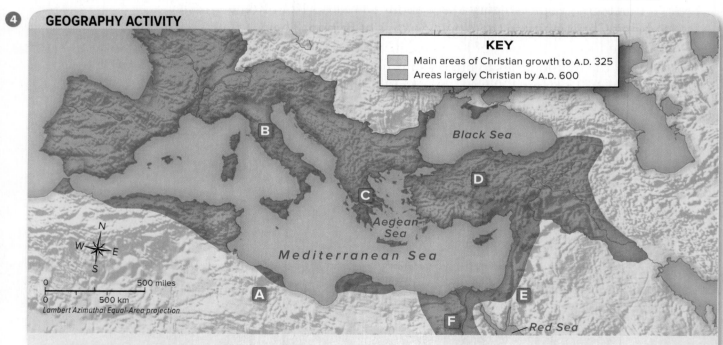

KEY
- Main areas of Christian growth to A.D. 325
- Areas largely Christian by A.D. 600

Black Sea

Aegean Sea

Mediterranean Sea

Red Sea

N W E S

0   500 miles
0   500 km
Lambert Azimuthal Equal-Area projection

Locating Places

By A.D. 600, Christianity had spread to many parts of the known world as shown on the map. Match the letters on the map with the numbered places listed below.

1. North Africa

2. Judaea

3. Asia Minor

4. Italy

5. Egypt

6. Greece

Directions: Write your answers on a separate piece of paper.

CHECKING FOR UNDERSTANDING

1 Define each of these terms as they relate to the rise of Christianity.

A. parable	**G.** laity
B. resurrection	**H.** doctrine
C. apostle	**I.** pope
D. salvation	**J.** icon
E. hierarchy	**K.** schism
F. clergy	**L.** monastery

REVIEW THE GUIDING QUESTIONS

2 *Identifying* Who were the Zealots?

3 *Stating* What did Jesus's followers believe happened to him after he died?

4 *Explaining* How did the Roman Empire contribute to the spread of Christianity?

5 *Recognizing Relationships* What is the relationship between Constantine and the spread of Christianity throughout the Roman Empire?

6 *Listing* List the hierarchy of the early Christian church in order from most to least authority.

7 *Describing* Name and describe the writings that comprise the Christian Bible.

8 *Explaining* Why did iconoclasts disapprove of the use of icons?

9 *Summarizing* How do the Eastern Orthodox Church and the Roman Catholic Church view the pope's power?

10 *Describing* How did Christianity come to England?

CRITICAL THINKING

11 *Making Generalizations* How did the Jewish people react to Roman rule?

12 *Determining Cause and Effect* What were the effects of the Zealots' rebellion against Roman rule of Judea?

13 *Giving Examples* How does Jesus's parable of the Good Samaritan reinforce his teachings?

14 *Evaluating* Who was more important in the spread and development of early Christianity: Peter or Paul? Explain your answer.

15 *Comparing and Contrasting* How was the Christian understanding of God similar to Judaism? How was it different?

16 *Predicting Consequences* How might the development of Christianity have differed if Constantine had not become a Christian himself?

17 *Identifying Central Issues* On what basis did the bishop of Rome claim authority over other bishops?

18 *Speculating* Why was early Christianity able to attract so many followers despite the threat of persecution?

19 *Making Inferences* How did the dispute over the use of icons reflect a larger issue in the early Christian church?

20 *Making Generalizations* What contributions did monks and nuns make to medieval Europe?

Need Extra Help?

If You've Missed Question	1	2	3	4	5	6	7	8	9	10	11	12	13	14	15	16	17	18	19	20
Review Lesson	1, 2,3	1	1	1, 2	2	2	2	3	3	3	1	1	1	1	1	2	2	2	3	3

DBQ SHORT RESPONSE

"Extremists among the Zealots turned to terrorism and assassination. ... They frequented [went to] public places with hidden daggers to strike down persons friendly to Rome. ... [A]t Masada in [A.D. 73] they committed suicide rather than surrender the fortress."

—Encyclopaedia Britannica, "Zealot," 2011

21 Why do you think the Zealots were so against Roman rule?

22 What effect do you think Zealot tactics had on other Jews and Romans?

EXTENDED RESPONSE

23 *Narrative* You are a young person who lives in Judaea during the time of Jesus' ministry. You have attended his Sermon on the Mount. Write a letter to your grandparents telling them about it.

STANDARDIZED TEST PRACTICE

DBQ ANALYZING DOCUMENTS

Drawing Conclusions Before becoming pope, Gregory I wrote this account of a monk who had not shared three gold coins with his fellow monks:

"When he was dead his body was not placed with the bodies of the brethren, but a grave was dug in the dung pit, and his body was flung down into it, and the three pieces of gold he had left were cast upon him, while all together cried, 'Thy money perish with thee!'"

—"Life in a Christian Monastery, ca. 585"

24 Which statement best captures the attitude of Gregory toward monks who hold on to personal property?

A. They should be pitied for their selfishness.

B. They deserve to die alone, with no one to comfort them.

C. They must be treated with scorn, even when they are dead.

D. Their sins must be punished severely to keep others from sinning.

25 *Inferring* What does Gregory's way of treating the dead monk reveal about life in an early Christian monastery?

A. Monks were expected to be cruel and hard-hearted.

B. Money was thought of as sinful and wicked.

C. Life was lived in common; all personal wealth was to be shared.

D. Monks paid a high price if they broke the rules.

Need Extra Help?

If You've Missed Question	**21**	**22**	**23**	**24**	**25**
Review Lesson	1	1	1	3	3

◄ Portrait paintings of leaders such as Suleiman II are important historical artifacts that tell us about the cultures in which the leaders lived.

A.D. 600 TO A.D. 1629

Islamic Civilization

Italian School/The Bridgeman Art Library/Getty Images

THE STORY MATTERS ...

In the 1300s, in the area now known as Turkey, a Muslim tribal chieftain named Osman gained power. He gradually took control of more lands and established the Ottoman Empire. The Ottoman Empire lasted for nearly six centuries and was ruled by Muslim leaders called sultans.

This painting of Suleiman II, sultan of the Ottoman Empire from 1687–1691, shows the elegant clothes worn by a sultan. The large turban, or headdress, indicates his status and position. For centuries, turbans were a part of dress throughout the Islamic world. An elaborate turban and richly decorated robes showed a person's high rank in society.

ESSENTIAL QUESTIONS

- How do religions develop?
- How does religion shape society?
- How do new ideas change the way people live?

Place & Time: Islamic Civilization A.D. 600 to A.D. 1629

Islamic civilization extended across Southwest Asia, North Africa, and parts of Europe. It later spread into India and Southeast Asia. Over time, Islamic rule was challenged by rivalries within Islam and by invasions of outside groups. A series of Islamic empires ruled until the early 1900s.

Step Into the Place

MAP FOCUS Arabia was a crossroads of trade and culture between East and West in the first century A.D.

1 **LOCATION** Look at the map. Is Arabia east or west of India?

2 **MOVEMENT** How did Arabia's location make it a trading crossroads between the East and the West?

3 **REGIONS** Describe all of the boundaries of Arabia.

4 **CRITICAL THINKING**
Determining Cause and Effect
How does a trading center contribute to the spread of culture and ideas?

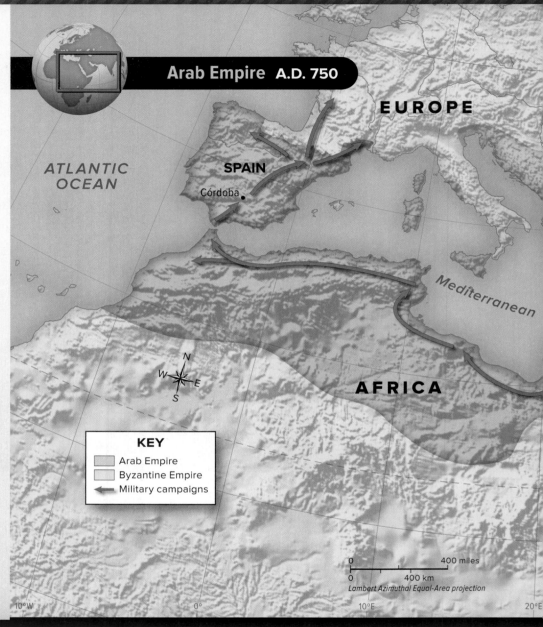

Arab Empire A.D. 750

EUROPE

ATLANTIC OCEAN

SPAIN

Córdoba

Mediterranean

AFRICA

KEY
Arab Empire
Byzantine Empire
Military campaigns

0   400 miles
0   400 km
Lambert Azimuthal Equal-Area projection

10°W   0°   10°E   20°E

Step Into the Time

TIME LINE Choose an event from the time line and write a paragraph predicting the consequences that event might have for the world.

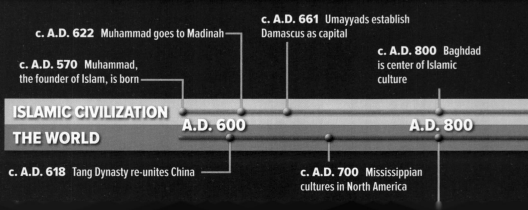

c. A.D. 622 Muhammad goes to Madinah

c. A.D. 661 Umayyads establish Damascus as capital

c. A.D. 570 Muhammad, the founder of Islam, is born

c. A.D. 800 Baghdad is center of Islamic culture

ISLAMIC CIVILIZATION

THE WORLD

A.D. 600   A.D. 800

c. A.D. 618 Tang Dynasty re-unites China

c. A.D. 700 Mississippian cultures in North America

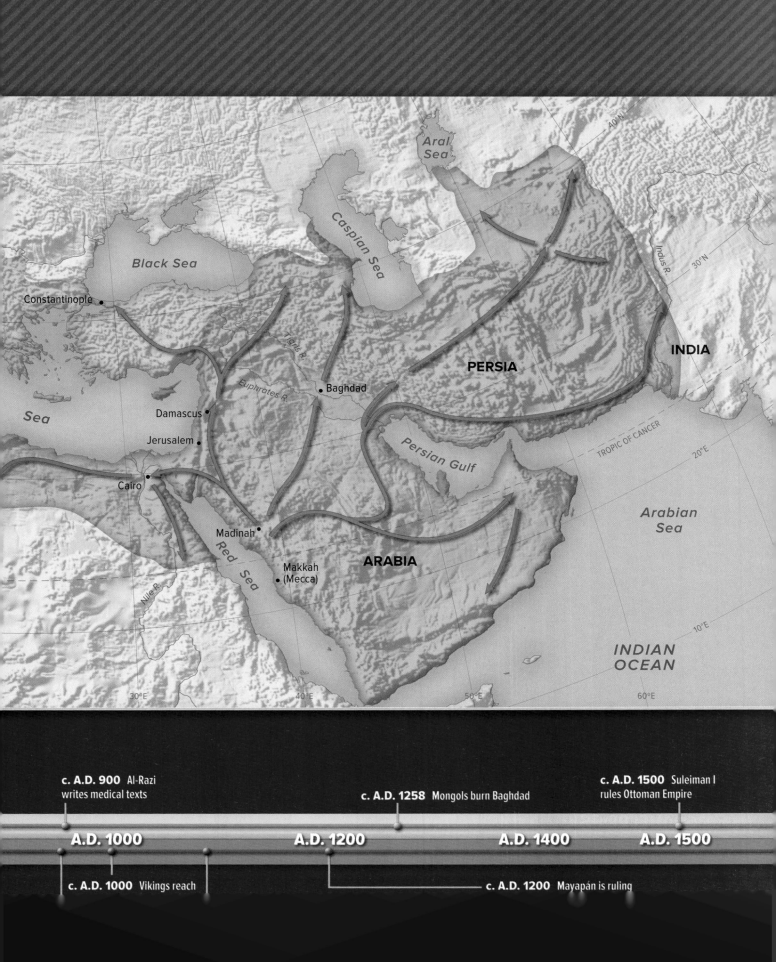

Aral
Sea

Caspian
Sea

Black Sea

Constantinople

INDIA

PERSIA

Baghdad

Damascus

Sea

Jerusalem

Persian Gulf

TROPIC OF CANCER

Cairo

Arabian
Sea

Madinah

Red Sea

Makkah
(Mecca)

ARABIA

INDIAN
OCEAN

30°E   40°E   50°E   60°E

Tigris R.

Euphrates R.

Nile R.

Indus R.

40° N

30° N

20° E

10° E

c. A.D. 900 Al-Razi
writes medical texts

c. A.D. 1258 Mongols burn Baghdad

c. A.D. 1500 Suleiman I
rules Ottoman Empire

A.D. 1000   A.D. 1200   A.D. 1400   A.D. 1500

c. A.D. 1000 Vikings reach

c. A.D. 1200 Mayapán is ruling

LESSON 1

A New Faith

• How do religions develop?

IT MATTERS BECAUSE

Islam is one of the most widely practiced religions in the world today. Approximately 25 percent of the people in the world are Muslim.

Arab Life

GUIDING QUESTION *How did physical geography influence the Arab way of life?*

Beginning in the A.D. 630s, people called Arabs created a new empire in Southwest Asia. The driving force behind their empire was the religion of **Islam** (IS·lahm). Within a century, Islam spread throughout parts of Asia, northern Africa, and Europe.

The Land of Arabia

The Arabian Peninsula, also called Arabia, is the homeland of the Arab people. It is also the center of Islam. Arabia is a huge wedge of land between the Red Sea and the Persian Gulf. Very dry plains and deserts cover most of the land. The desert heat can be intense. Summer temperatures can rise above 122° F (50° C). Water is available only at scattered springs and water holes. Such a spot is called an **oasis** (oh·AY·suhs). At an oasis, trees and other plants grow. Not all of Arabia is desert, however. There are mountains and valleys in the southwestern region. Enough rain falls in these locations for juniper and olive trees to grow.

In ancient times, the Arabian Peninsula was surrounded by many different civilizations. At various times, the Egyptian civilization was to the west, the Mesopotamian and Persian

Reading**HELP**DESK

Taking Notes: *Describing*

On a chart like this one, describe the importance of these places to the development of the religion of Islam.

The Development of Islam

Place	Importance
Arabia	
Makkah	
Madinah	

Content Vocabulary

• **Islam**
• **oasis**
• **sheikh**
• **caravan**
• **Quran**
• *shari'ah*

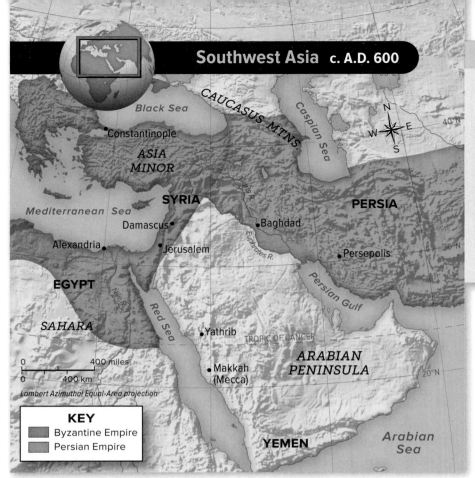

Southwest Asia c. A.D. 600

- Constantinople
- ASIA MINOR
- Black Sea
- CAUCASUS MTNS.
- Caspian Sea
- Mediterranean Sea
- SYRIA
- Damascus
- Alexandria
- Jerusalem
- Baghdad
- PERSIA
- Persepolis
- EGYPT
- SAHARA
- Nile R.
- Red Sea
- Euphrates R.
- Tigris R.
- Persian Gulf
- Yathrib
- TROPIC OF CANCER
- ARABIAN PENINSULA
- Makkah (Mecca)
- YEMEN
- Arabian Sea
- 40°N
- 30°N
- 20°N

0 400 miles
0 400 km
Lambert Azimuthal Equal-Area projection

KEY
- Byzantine Empire
- Persian Empire

GEOGRAPHY CONNECTION

The prophet Muhammad brought the message of Islam to the people of Arabia.

1 **REGIONS** Which empire was located north and west of the Arabian Peninsula?

2 **PLACE** About how far is it from Makkah to Yathrib?

3 **CRITICAL THINKING** *Analyzing* How did Makkah's location make it a center for trade?

civilizations were to the north and east, and farther north were the civilizations of the Israelites, Greeks, and Romans. Long distances and the severe Arabian climate had kept these civilizations from invading the peninsula. This **isolation,** however, was not absolute, as trade brought some outside ideas and practices to the Arab civilization.

Life in the Desert

Long ago, many Arabs were nomads who herded animals and lived in tents. These nomads are called bedouin. The bedouin raised camels, goats, and sheep and traveled from oasis to oasis. The bedouin ate mainly fresh or dried dates and drank milk. On very special occasions they ate goat or sheep meat.

To survive the harsh desert climate, early Arabs formed tribes whose members were loyal to one another. The leader of each tribe was called a **sheikh** (SHAYK). Arab tribes raided other tribes to take camels and horses. Rival tribes battled one another over land and water.

Islam a religion based on the teachings of Muhammad
oasis a green area in a desert fed by underground water
sheikh the leader of an Arab tribe

Academic Vocabulary

isolation separation from other populated areas

Bedouins value the camel as a reliable carrier. Their wide, flat feet allow the camel to move very quickly across the dunes.

Can you imagine what a camel race might be like? The bedouin enjoyed camel and horse races and other games that improved their battle skills. In the evenings, they told stories around campfires. Poets wrote and recited poems about battles, camels, horses, and love. The lines below are about an Arab warrior and a battle he must fight. He describes his reliable camel.

PRIMARY SOURCE

" My riding-camels are tractable [obedient],
they go wherever I wish;
while my intellect is my helper,
and I drive it forward with a firm order. "

—from *The Poem of Antar*

Life in Towns

By the A.D. 500s, many Arab tribes had settled around oases or in fertile mountain valleys. They set up villages, farmed or raised animals, and traded goods. Merchants carried goods by camel across the desert to different markets. For protection against bedouin raids, some made journeys in **caravans** (KEHR·uh·vanz), or groups of traveling merchants and animals.

As trade grew, Arab merchants built towns along the trade routes in Arabia. The most important town was Makkah (MAH·kuh), also known as Mecca. Makkah was located about 50 miles (80 kilometers) inland from the Red Sea. The town became a crossroads of trade. Large caravans from southwestern Arabia passed through Makkah on their way to Syria and Mesopotamia. Some caravans traveled as far away as China.

Makkah was also an important religious site. In the center of the city was the Kaaba (KAH·buh). This was a low, block-like building surrounded by statues of Arabian gods and goddesses. The people of Arabia worshipped many deities, but the most important was Allah. They believed that Allah was the creator. Arabs believed that a large stone inside the Kaaba came from heaven. Many pilgrims, people who travel to a holy place, visited the Kaaba.

✓ **PROGRESS CHECK**

Contrasting How did the lives of desert Arabs and town Arabs differ?

Reading**HELP**DESK

caravan a group of traveling merchants and animals

Reading Strategy: *Formulating Questions*

Asking questions can help you understand and remember what you read. Read about the life of Muhammad. On a separate sheet of paper, write down two or three questions that you would like answered.

Academic Vocabulary

authority power over thoughts, opinions, and behavior

Muhammad and His Message

GUIDING QUESTION *What message did Muhammad preach to the people of Arabia?*

Trade increased the contact between Arabs and other civilizations. Life in Arabia changed as people were exposed to new ideas. Arabs searched for ways to deal with these new challenges. Their search paved the way for the rise of Islam.

Who Was Muhammad?

The religion of Islam arose in the Arabian Peninsula in the A.D. 600s. Islam grew from the preachings of a man named Muhammad (moh·HAH·muhd). Muhammad was born into a merchant family in Makkah in A.D. 570. He was orphaned at the age of five or six. As a teenager, Muhammad worked as a caravan leader and eventually became a merchant.

Despite his success, Muhammad was troubled by many things he saw around him, including the greed of Makkah's wealthy citizens. He despised their dishonesty, neglect of the poor, and disregard for family life. Seeking guidance, he spent time alone praying in a cave outside the city.

Muslim tradition says that in A.D. 610, Muhammad had a vision in which a voice called him to preach Islam. Islam means "surrendering [to the will of Allah]." In the Arabic language, Allah is the word for "God." Three times the voice said, "Recite!" When Muhammad asked what he should recite, the voice said:

PRIMARY SOURCE

❝ Recite in the name of your Lord Who created, created man from a clot of congealed [thickened] blood. Recite: and your Lord is Most Generous, Who taught by the pen, taught man what he did not know. ❞

—*Quran*, Surah 96:1-5

Muhammad returned to Makkah and began preaching. He told people that there was only Allah to worship, the one true God. He said they must destroy their statues of fake gods.

Muhammad also preached that people were equal in God's sight, and the rich should share their wealth with the poor. Everywhere he went, Muhammad preached that God valued good deeds. Muhammad urged people to prepare for the Day of Judgment, when God would punish evildoers and reward the just.

Muhammad's Opponents

The first people to become Muslims, or followers of Islam, were Muhammad's family members. Slowly, Muhammad won the support of the poor, who were attracted to his message of sharing. Most wealthy merchants and religious leaders, however, thought Muhammad was trying to destroy their **authority.**

BIOGRAPHY

Muhammad (A.D. 570–632)

The tomb of the prophet Muhammad is a holy place to Muslims. During Muhammad's lifetime, he was well known for fairly resolving disputes among his followers. According to Islamic tradition, when Muhammad was asked to resolve which tribe would have the honor to place the holy black stone in the corner of the rebuilt Kaaba, Muhammad put his cloak on the ground with the stone in the center and had each tribe lift a corner to bring the stone to the correct height to be placed in the Kaaba. Muhammad's legacy has made a major impact on the world.

▶ **CRITICAL THINKING**
Drawing Conclusions Why do you think Muhammad had each tribe carry his cloak with the holy black stone?

C. Hellier/Ancient Art & Architecture Collection

Thousands of Muslim pilgrims surround the Kaaba in Makkah. A call to worship on special days draws thousands of people.

▶ **CRITICAL THINKING**

Making Inferences Why do you think the Muslim calendar begins with the year of the Hijrah?

In A.D. 622, Muhammad and his followers believed Makkah had become too dangerous. They moved to Yathrib (YA·thruhb). Muhammad's departure to Yathrib became known as the Hijrah (HIHJ·ruh). This Arabic word means "breaking off relationships." The year of the Hijrah later became the first year of the Muslim calendar. The people of Yathrib accepted Muhammad as God's prophet and their ruler. They renamed their city Madinah (mah·DEE·nah), which means "the city of the prophet."

The Islamic State

Muhammad was a skilled political and religious leader. He applied the laws he believed God had given him to all areas of life. He used these laws to settle disputes among the people. Muhammad also established the foundation for an Islamic state. The government of the state used its political power to uphold Islam. Muhammad required all Muslims to place loyalty to the Islamic state above loyalty to their tribes.

Muhammad formed an army to protect his new state. In a series of battles, Muhammad's soldiers regained Makkah and made it a holy city of Islam. The Muslims then began to expand into new areas. When Muhammad died in A.D. 632, the entire Arabian Peninsula was part of the Islamic state.

✓ **PROGRESS CHECK**

Analyzing Why did Makkah's merchants and religious leaders oppose Muhammad and his message?

Reading**HELP**DESK

Quran the holy book of Islam

shari'ah Islamic code of law

Beliefs and Practices of Islam

GUIDING QUESTION *How does Islam provide guidance to its followers?*

Islam shares some beliefs with Judaism and Christianity. Like Jews and Christians, Muslims are monotheists. Muslims believe in one all-powerful God who created the universe. They believe that God decides what is right and wrong.

Like Jews and Christians, Muslims believe that God spoke to people through prophets. For Muslims, these prophets include Adam, Abraham, Moses, Jesus, and Muhammad. In Islam, Muhammad is seen as the last and the greatest of the prophets.

The Quran

According to Muslim belief, Muhammad received messages from Allah for more than 20 years. These messages were not gathered into a written collection until after Muhammad died. This collection became the **Quran** (kuh·RAN), or holy book of Islam. Muslims believe the Quran is the written word of God. It contains accounts of events, teachings, and instructions.

For Muslims, the Quran provides guidelines for how to live. For example, the Quran instructs Muslims to be honest and treat others fairly. Muslims must respect their parents and be kind to their neighbors. The Quran forbids murder, lying, and stealing.

Islam stresses the need to obey the will of Allah. This means practicing acts of worship known as the Five Pillars of Islam. The Five Pillars are belief, prayer, charity, fasting, and pilgrimage.

Over centuries, Islamic scholars created a code of law called the *shari'ah* (shuh·REE·uh). *Shari'ah* is based on the Quran. According to *shari'ah*, Muslims may not gamble, eat pork, or drink alcoholic beverages. The *sunna* also guides Muslims. It is a set of customs based on Muhammad's words and deeds.

☑ PROGRESS CHECK

Evaluating Why is the Quran important in the daily life of Muslims?

Thinking Like a
HISTORIAN

Using a Time Line

Many important events led Muhammad to establish Islam. Select three events from his life that you consider important to his founding of Islam. Sequence them on a time line, and present your time line to the class. Be sure to explain your choices in your presentation. For more information about time lines, read *What Does a Historian Do?*

LESSON 1 REVIEW

Review Vocabulary

1. Why would the people in a *caravan* be glad to see an *oasis*?

Answer the Guiding Questions

2. *Determining Cause and Effect* How did physical geography shape life in Arabia?

3. *Explaining* Why did Muhammad and his followers move to Madinah?

4. *Describing* What is the *shari'ah* and what is it based on?

5. *NARRATIVE* Imagine that you are a bedouin. Write a letter to a friend who lives in Makkah describing a day in your life.

LESSON 2

The Spread of Islam

• How does religion shape society?

IT MATTERS BECAUSE
The religion of Islam continues to influence modern politics and society.

Founding an Empire

GUIDING QUESTION *How did the Arabs spread Islam and create an empire?*

When Muhammad died in A.D. 632, he left no instructions about who should be the next leader of Islam. Muslims knew that no person could take Muhammad's role as a prophet. They realized, however, that the Islamic state needed a strong leader to keep it united. A group of Muslim leaders chose a new type of leader called the **caliph** (KAY·luhf), or "successor."

The First Caliphs

The first four caliphs were close friends or relatives of Muhammad. The goal of the caliphs was to protect and spread Islam. Their military forces carried Islam beyond the Arabian Peninsula. Because the Muslim conquerors were Arab, the territory became known as the Arab Empire. By the 660s, the Arab Empire included all of southwest Asia and northeast Africa.

The Umayyads

Expansion continued under new caliphs known as the Umayyads (oo·MY·uhds). The Umayyads governed the Arab Empire from the city of Damascus (duh·MAS·kuhs) in Syria. They ruled from 661 to 750. Under the Umayyads, Muslim rule extended farther into Asia and Africa.

Reading **HELP**DESK

Taking Notes: *Summarizing*

On a diagram like this one, describe the ways in which the religion of Islam spread.

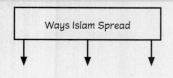

Ways Islam Spread

Content Vocabulary

• **caliph**   • **Sunni**   • **Shia**   • **sultan**

caliph a Muslim leader

A century after the death of Muhammad, Muslims had created a large and powerful empire. Arab soldiers were experienced horse riders and warriors, having raided rival tribes in the past. Now they used those same skills to fight large armies. In addition, Arab soldiers believed they had a religious duty to spread Islam.

The policies of their opponents also helped the Muslims. Byzantine and Persian rulers had tried to unite their peoples under an official religion. They often mistreated those who practiced other faiths. When Muslim armies attacked, many of these people were willing to accept Muslim rule.

After the Arabs gained control, they usually let conquered peoples practice their own religions. Islam teaches that Christians and Jews are "People of the Book," people who believe in one God and follow sacred writings. Therefore, many Muslims respect their beliefs and practices. As time passed, many of the conquered peoples in the Arab Empire became Muslims and learned the Arab language. The customs of the conquered peoples also influenced the Arab rulers. Eventually, the term *Arab* meant a speaker of Arabic, not a resident of Arabia.

Islamic Spain

Muslim warriors entered Spain from North Africa in the early 700s. They brought their religion, customs, and traditions. Spanish Muslims made the city of Córdoba a center of Islam.

Spain was home to many of Islam's greatest thinkers. Ibn Rushd (IH·buhn RUHSHT), also known as Averroës (uh·VEHR·uh·weez), practiced law and medicine in Córdoba.

GEOGRAPHY CONNECTION

After Muhammad's death, the territory of the Arab Empire expanded.

1 **MOVEMENT** What area of Europe came under Muslim control?

2 **PLACE** Describe the territories conquered by the Arabs by the year A.D. 661.

3 **CRITICAL THINKING** *Making Connections* Why do you think Muslim armies entered Europe from North Africa and not through Asia Minor?

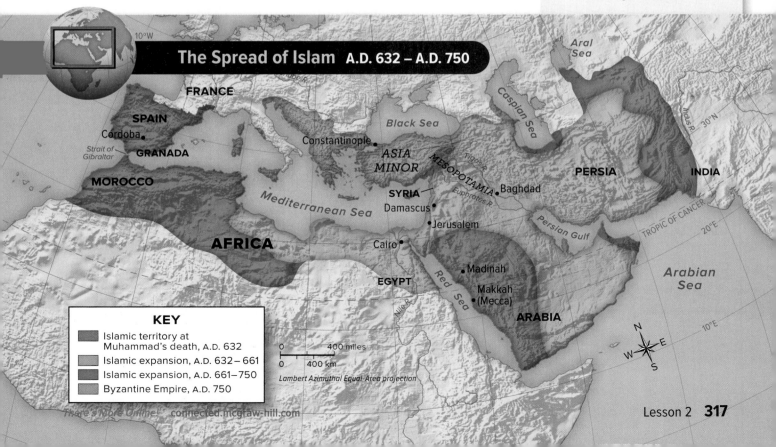

The Spread of Islam A.D. 632 – A.D. 750

FRANCE
SPAIN
Córdoba
Strait of Gibraltar
GRANADA
MOROCCO
Black Sea
Constantinople
ASIA MINOR
MESOPOTAMIA
Tigris R.
Euphrates R.
Baghdad
PERSIA
INDIA
Indus R.
Aral Sea
Caspian Sea
SYRIA
Damascus
Jerusalem
Mediterranean Sea
AFRICA
Cairo
Nile R.
EGYPT
Red Sea
Madinah
Makkah (Mecca)
ARABIA
Persian Gulf
TROPIC OF CANCER
Arabian Sea
30°N
20°E
10°E
10°W

KEY
- Islamic territory at Muhammad's death, A.D. 632
- Islamic expansion, A.D. 632–661
- Islamic expansion, A.D. 661–750
- Byzantine Empire, A.D. 750

0   400 miles
0   400 km
Lambert Azimuthal Equal-Area projection

THE FIRST FOUR CALIPHS

	Abu Bakr	Umar	Uthman	Ali
Relationship to Muhammad	father-in-law	friend	son-in-law, member of the Umayyad family	first cousin, son-in-law
Career	merchant	merchant	merchant	soldier, writer
Years as Caliph	A.D. 632–634	A.D. 634–644	A.D. 644–656	A.D. 656–661
Achievements as Caliph	spread Islam to all of Arabia; restored peace after death of Muhammad; created code of conduct in war; compiled Quran verses	spread Islam to Syria, Egypt, and Persia; redesigned government; paid soldiers; held a census; made taxes more fair; built roads and canals; aided poor	spread Islam into Afghanistan and eastern Mediterranean; organized a navy; improved the government; built more roads, bridges, and canals; distributed text of the Quran	reformed tax collection and other government systems; spent most of caliphate battling Muawiya, the governor of Syria

CHART

1 **IDENTIFYING** Which caliph ruled the longest? Whose rule was the shortest?

2 **CRITICAL THINKING** *Contrasting* How was Ali different from the other caliphs?

He is best known for his writings based on the works of the Greek philosopher Aristotle. Ibn Rushd's work influenced Christian and Jewish thinkers in Europe during the Middle Ages.

Muslims in Spain were generally tolerant, or accepting, of other cultures. In some schools, Muslims, Jews, and Christians studied medicine and philosophy together. In particular, the Jewish community in Córdoba flourished.

A Jewish scholar in Spain, Solomon ben Gabirol, wrote philosophy and poetry. His most famous book of philosophy, *The Well of Life*, shows the influence of the Greek philosophers. The book was translated from Arabic into Latin and influenced many philosophers in Christian Europe.

Another Jewish thinker called Moses Maimonides (my·MAHN·ih·deez) had to leave Spain at a very young age because it was conquered by a Muslim group that was not as accepting of other cultures. He later became a physician in the Muslim royal court in Egypt and wrote philosophy as well as a collection of Jewish laws.

Preachers and Traders

Muslim armies were not the only ones who spread Islam. Some Muslims used preaching to win followers to their religion. A group called Sufis (SOO·feez) won followers by teaching Islam.

Muslim merchants built trading posts throughout Southeast Asia and taught Islam to the people there. Today, the country of Indonesia (ihn·duh·NEE·zhuh) has more Muslims than any other nation in the world.

Some Muslim merchants crossed the Sahara to trade with powerful kingdoms in West Africa. In the 1300s, the West African city of Timbuktu (tihm·buhk·TOO) became a leading center of Muslim culture and learning.

✓ PROGRESS CHECK

Explaining Why was the Arab military successful?

Division and Growth

GUIDING QUESTION *How did the Arab Empire change after the Umayyads?*

While Arab Muslims created an empire, rival groups within Islam argued about who had the right to succeed Muhammad as caliph. Muslims divided into two groups, the **Sunni** (SU·nee) and the **Shia** (SHEE·ah). This split still divides Muslims today. Most Muslims are Sunni. Shia Muslims, however, make up most of the populations in present-day Iran and Iraq.

The Shia believed that Ali, Muhammad's son-in-law, was his rightful heir. They also believed that all future caliphs had to be Ali's descendants. According to the Shia, the Umayyad caliphs in Damascus had no right to rule. The Sunni, who outnumbered the Shia, disagreed. They recognized the Umayyad caliphs as rightful rulers, though they did not always agree with their actions.

The Shia and the Sunni agreed on the major **principles** of Islam. They both believed that there was only one God. They also believed in the Quran as Islam's holy book and the Five Pillars of Islam. In other ways, the two groups developed different religious practices and customs.

A New Dynasty

During the 700s, opposition to the Umayyad caliphs grew. Many non-Arab Muslims were angry that Arab Muslims had the best jobs and paid lower taxes. Discontent was especially strong in Mesopotamia and Persia, where Shia Islam was popular.

About 750, the Shia Muslims rebelled and won support from other Muslims throughout the empire. They overthrew the Umayyads, and the Abbasid (uh·BA·suhd) dynasty came to power. Abbasid caliphs ruled the Arab Empire until 1258.

Muslim architecture can still be found in many parts of Spain today. The high interior arches, decorative columns, and bright colors are all details of Muslim design.

▶ CRITICAL THINKING
Drawing Conclusions Why was Spain home to many of Islam's great thinkers?

Fernando Fernandez/age fotostock

Sunni group of Muslims who accepted the rule of the Umayyad caliphs

Shia group of Muslims who believed the descendants of Ali should rule

Academic Vocabulary

principle an important law or belief

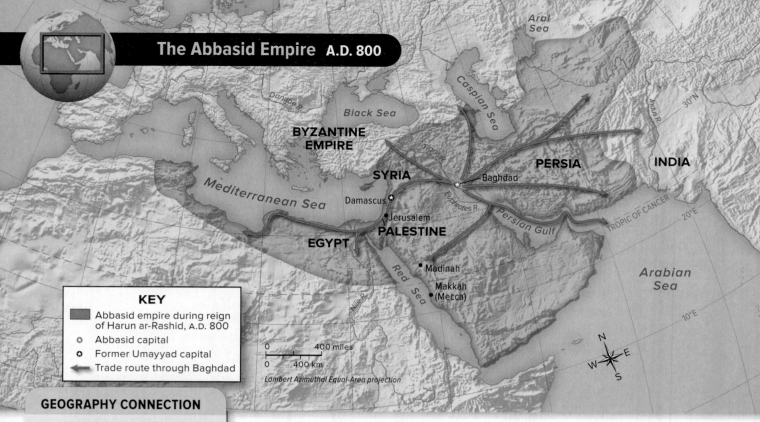

The Abbasid Empire A.D. 800

BYZANTINE EMPIRE
SYRIA
Damascus
Jerusalem
PALESTINE
EGYPT
Baghdad
PERSIA
INDIA
Madinah
Makkah (Mecca)
Mediterranean Sea
Black Sea
Caspian Sea
Aral Sea
Danube R.
Tigris R.
Euphrates R.
Persian Gulf
Red Sea
Nile R.
Indus R.
Arabian Sea
TROPIC OF CANCER
30°N
20°E
10°E

KEY

- Abbasid empire during reign of Harun ar-Rashid, A.D. 800
- ⊙ Abbasid capital
- ⊙ Former Umayyad capital
- ← Trade route through Baghdad

0   400 miles
0   400 km
Lambert Azimuthal Equal-Area projection

N E W S

GEOGRAPHY CONNECTION

Baghdad became the capital of the Abbasid empire and an important center for trade.

1 REGIONS What blocked Abbasid expansion to the northwest?

2 CRITICAL THINKING
Evaluating Does Baghdad appear to be well located for trade? Explain.

The Abbasids focused on improving trade and **culture.** They made Baghdad (BAG·dad) their capital city. Baghdad's location along the Tigris River was on trade routes that connected the Mediterranean Sea to East Asia. By the 900s, Baghdad was one of the world's most beautiful and prosperous cities.

Under Abbasid rule, the Arab Empire enjoyed a golden age. The Abbasids appreciated Persian culture and brought many Persian influences into the Arab Empire.

Who are the Seljuk Turks?

The Abbasids developed a rich culture, but they could not hold their empire together. Over time, many territories broke free from Abbasid rule. In Egypt and Spain, the Muslims set up their own caliphs. Rival rulers took over much of Persia. By the 1000s, the Abbasids ruled little more than the area around Baghdad.

Around this time, the Seljuk Turks of central Asia began moving into Abbasid territory. The Seljuk Turks were nomads and great warriors. In 1055, the Seljuks seized Baghdad. They took control of the government and army but allowed the Abbasid caliph to manage religious matters. The Seljuk ruler called himself **sultan** (SUHL·tuhn), or "holder of power."

Reading**HELP**DESK

sultan Seljuk leader

Academic Vocabulary

culture the customs, art, science, and learning of a group of people

For 200 years, Seljuk sultans ruled with the Abbasid caliphs. Then, in the 1200s, people from central Asia known as the Mongols, swept into the empire. In 1258 they stormed into Baghdad. There, the Mongols burned buildings and killed more than 50,000 people. This fierce attack brought an end to the Arab Empire.

✔ **PROGRESS CHECK**

Comparing and Contrasting How did the Sunni and Shia differ? What beliefs did they share?

Three Muslim Empires

GUIDING QUESTION *How did the Turks, Safavids, and Moguls rule their empires?*

After the Arab Empire ended, other Muslim groups created their own empires. These empires included the Ottoman Empire based in what is now Turkey, the Safavid (sah·FAH·weed) Empire in Persia, and the Mogul Empire in India.

The Ottomans

During the late 1200s, Turkish clans settled part of Asia Minor. They called themselves Ottoman Turks, after their leader named Osman. The Ottomans conquered much of the Byzantine Empire. In 1453, the Ottoman ruler Mehmet II, known as "the Conqueror," seized the Byzantine capital, Constantinople. The Ottomans renamed the city Istanbul and made it their capital.

The Ottomans then pushed into southeastern Europe, Southwest Asia, and North Africa. The Ottomans controlled much of the Mediterranean region until the late 1500s.

The Ottoman leader was called a sultan, like the leader of the Seljuks. The most famous Ottoman sultan was Suleiman I (SOO·luh·mahn). He ruled during the 1500s. He was called "The Lawgiver" because he organized Ottoman laws. Suleiman also built many schools and mosques throughout the empire.

The Shah Mosque in Isafahan, Iran, shows traditional Muslim architecture. It is known for its interior design featuring mosaic tiles.

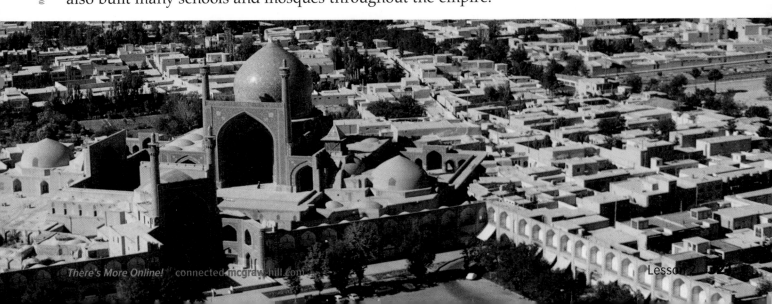

Suleiman I (1494–1566)

In 1520, at the age of 26, Suleiman I became the sultan of the Ottoman Empire. His reign is known as the Golden Age of the Ottoman Empire. He is often referred to as "Suleiman the Magnificent" or "The Lawgiver." He achieved many military successes and expanded the territory of the empire. Suleiman was responsible for the empire's greatest achievements in law, art, architecture, and literature.

▶ **CRITICAL THINKING**
Defending Why was Suleiman "magnificent"?

How Did the Ottomans Rule?

Because their empire was so large, the Ottomans ruled many peoples who practiced many religions. Islam was the empire's official religion, and Muslims enjoyed special privileges. The government passed different laws for non-Muslims. For example, non-Muslims had to pay a special tax. In return, they were free to practice their religion.

After Suleiman, the Ottoman Empire began to break down. It lost lands to the Europeans. Local rulers and conquered people broke away. The empire finally crumbled in the early 1900s.

The Safavids

In 1501, a Shia leader named Ismail proclaimed himself shah, or king, of Persia. Ismail founded the Safavid dynasty, which ruled Persia until the 1700s. During this period, Persian spread as a language of culture and trade. Urdu, a language spoken in Pakistan today, is partly based on Persian.

India's Mogul Empire

During the 1500s, the Moguls (MO·guhlz) set up a Muslim empire in India. Under Akbar (AHK·bar), the Mogul empire prospered. He allowed people to practice their religions. Later Mogul rulers, however, persecuted Hindus and Sikhs (SEEKS).

Sikhs practice the religion of Sikhism, which arose in the 1500s. The Sikhs believe in one God. They rely on one holy book, the *Adigranth*, and honor a line of teachers descending from Guru Nanak, their founder. Today, Sikhism is the world's fifth largest religion.

☑ **PROGRESS CHECK**

Identifying What is Urdu?

LESSON 2 REVIEW

Review Vocabulary

1. How did the *Sunni* feel about the Umayyad *caliphs*?

2. In addition to the Seljuks, who else used the title *sultan*?

Answer the Guiding Questions

3. ***Identifying*** What area of Europe came under Muslim control at this time?

4. ***Describing*** What changes did Abbasid rulers bring to the world of Islam?

5. ***Determining Cause and Effect*** What effect did the burning of Baghdad in 1258 have on the Islamic Empire?

6. ***Explaining*** What led to the downfall of the Ottoman Empire?

7. **INFORMATIVE/EXPLANATORY** Write a paragraph that compares how the Ottomans and Moguls each treated non-Muslims.

LESSON 3
Life in the Islamic World

ESSENTIAL QUESTION
• How do ideas change the way people live?

IT MATTERS BECAUSE
Muslim advances in mathematics, business, science, architecture, and the arts helped to create our modern society.

Daily Life and Trade

GUIDING QUESTION *How did people live and trade in the Islamic world?*

Muslim merchants controlled trade in much of Asia and Africa from the A.D. 700s until the 1400s. Their caravans traveled from Egypt and Mesopotamia to China. Their ships sailed the Indian Ocean to East Africa, India, and Southeast Asia. Muslim traders set out on their journeys with spices, cloth, glass, and carpets from their homelands. They traded these items for rubies from India, silk from China, and spices from Southeast Asia. They also traded for gold, ivory, and enslaved people from Africa. In addition, Muslim merchants sold crops such as sugar, rice, oranges, cherries, and cotton.

Why Were Muslim Traders Successful?

Muslim trade flourished for several reasons. Muslims spread the religion of Islam along with the Arabic language. As a result, Arabic became the language of business and trade in much of Asia and Africa. Muslim rulers also helped traders by providing them with coins to use for buying and selling goods. This was an easier trading method than bartering for goods.

Muslim merchants kept detailed records of their business dealings and their earnings. In time, these practices created a new industry—banking. Muslims respected merchants for their business skills and the wealth they created.

Thinking Like a HISTORIAN

Researching on the Internet

Trade was central to the success of the Islamic world. Muslim merchants traveled by land and sea routes that included the Silk Road. Imported items included gold and Ivory from Africa, grain from Western Asia, horses and livestock from the steppes, and ceramics, silk, and other luxury items from China.

Use the Internet to research the spread of culture and goods on the Silk Road.

Reading**HELP**DESK

Taking Notes: *Organizing*
Draw a diagram like this one. Fill in details about Muslim contributions in the field of science.

Muslim
Contributions
to Science

Content Vocabulary
• **mosque**   • **astrolabe**
• **bazaar**   • **minaret**

The word "bazaar" is Persian and refers to the public market district in a town. These ancient markets with many stalls and shops sold both local and imported goods from all over the world. They were the forerunners of modern shopping centers that we know today.

Now

▶ CRITICAL THINKING
Evaluating What are the advantages of having a central marketplace?

ReadingHELPDESK

mosque a Muslim house of worship

Muslim Cities and Farms

Increased trade led to the growth of cities throughout the Islamic world. Makkah, Baghdad, Cairo (KY·roh), and Damascus were located on major trade routes. Muslim cities, however, were more than places of trade. They also became centers of government, education, and culture.

Muslim cities generally had narrow streets separating closely packed buildings. The main buildings were mosques and palaces. **Mosques** (MAHSKS) are Muslim houses of worship. They also served as schools, courts, and centers of learning.

Another important feature of every Muslim city was the **bazaar** (buh·ZAHR), or marketplace. Like shopping malls today, bazaars were full of shops and stalls where goods were sold. They were often covered to protect merchants and customers from the scorching sun. Nearby inns provided travelers a place to eat and rest.

Despite the importance of cities, most Muslims, however, lived in villages and farmed the land. The dry climate and the lack of rainfall, however, made farming difficult. Muslim farmers relied on irrigation to water their crops. They raised wheat, rice, beans, cucumbers, and melons in their fields. They planted orchards that provided almonds, apricots, figs, and olives. Farmers also grew flowers for use in perfume.

Some Muslim villagers owned small farms. Most of the productive land, however, was owned by wealthy landowners. They had large estates and hired farmers from nearby villages or used enslaved people to farm the land.

How was Muslim Society Organized?

People in the Muslim world were divided into social groups based on their power and wealth. Government leaders, landowners, and wealthy merchants held the greatest power. Below them were artisans, farmers, and workers. Enslaved people held no power.

As in other civilizations, slavery was common in Muslim lands. Many enslaved people were prisoners of war. Although they faced hardships, enslaved people had some rights under Islamic law. For example, mothers and young children could not be separated, and enslaved people could buy their freedom.

Men and women had separate roles in the Muslim world. Men were in charge of government, society, and business. Women managed their families and households.

bazaar a marketplace

Women were also allowed to own property, invest in trade, and inherit wealth. Some upper-class women received an education and contributed to the arts.

✅ **PROGRESS CHECK**

Explaining Why were Muslim merchants successful?

Muslim Contributions

GUIDING QUESTION *What were Muslim contributions in mathematics, science, and the arts?*

Arabic was the most widely spoken language in the Muslim world. The use of Arabic helped with the exchange of goods and ideas among the different Islamic peoples. For example, in A.D. 830 the Abbasid caliph Mamun (mah·MOON) founded the House of Wisdom in Baghdad. At this research center, Muslim, Jewish, and Christian thinkers translated Greek, Persian, and Indian works into Arabic.

From the 700s to the 1400s, scholars in Muslim lands preserved learning of the ancient world. Europeans had lost many ancient Greek writings. In Spain, however, Jewish and Muslim scholars translated some Greek writings into Arabic. When these Arabic translations were translated into Latin, western Europeans learned about ancient Greek thinkers.

Science and Mathematics

At the Baghdad observatory founded by Mamun, Muslim astronomers studied the skies. These studies helped them create mathematical models of the universe. They correctly described the sun's eclipses and proved that the moon affects ocean tides. They gave many stars names that are still used today.

Muslim astronomers improved the Greek **astrolabe** (AS • truh • layb). Sailors used this tool to determine their location at sea. Muslim scientists used the astrolabe to measure the distance around the Earth. Based on their measurements, they **confirmed** that the Earth is round.

Other Muslim scientists experimented with metals. As a result, Muslims are considered the founders of chemistry. One of the most famous Muslim chemists was al-Razi (ahl-RAH·zee). Al-Razi was the first scientist to label substances as animal, vegetable, or mineral. This type of labeling is still used today.

©Michael Freeman/Corbis

astrolabe a tool that helps sailors navigate by the positions of the stars

Academic Vocabulary

confirm to prove that something is true; to remove doubt

There's More Online! connected.mcgraw-hill.com

Lesson 3 **325**

Islamic civilization made important contributions to science, learning, and philosophy. This astrolabe advanced the Greek invention.

Muslims also made contributions in mathematics. The Persian scholar al-Khawarizmi (ahl-khwa·RIHZ·meh) invented algebra. He and the Arab scholar al-Kindi borrowed the symbols 0 through 9 from Hindu scholars. These numbers were passed on to Europeans. Today, they are known as "Arabic numerals."

Medicine

Muslims made important medical discoveries too. Arab doctors discovered that blood circulates, or moves, to and from the heart. They also diagnosed certain diseases. Al-Razi wrote a book identifying the differences between smallpox and measles.

Muslim doctors shared their knowledge by **publishing** their findings. The Persian doctor Ibn Sina (ih·buhn SEE·nuh) produced the *Canon of Medicine*, which described how diseases spread and analyzed hundreds of different medicines.

Unlike doctors in most other places, Arab doctors had to pass a test before they could practice medicine. The Arabs created the first medical schools and pharmacies. They also built medical clinics that gave care and medicine to the sick.

Omar Khayyam—known for his poetry—was also a mathematician, philosopher, and astronomer.

Literature

Muslims wrote non-religious literature. One of the best known works is *The Thousand and One Nights*, also called *The Arabian Nights*. It includes tales from India, Persia, and Arabia. Aladdin is one of the work's well-known characters.

Another Muslim, the Persian poet Omar Khayyam (OH· MAHR ky·YAHM), wrote the *Rubaiyat* (ROO·bee·aht). Many consider it one of the finest poems ever written. In a section of the poem, Khayyam describes the human being as a mystery:

PRIMARY SOURCE

❝ Man is a cup, his soul the wine therein,
Flesh is a pipe, spirit [give life to] the voice within;
O Khayyam, have you fathomed [figured out] what man is?
A magic lantern with a light therein! ❞

—from *The Rubaiyat* by Omar Khayyam, tr. E.H. Whinfield

©Bettmann/Corbis

Reading**HELP**DESK

minaret the tower of a mosque from which Muslims are called to prayer

Academic Vocabulary

publish to produce the work of an author, usually in print

Muslim scholars studied history. During the late 1300s, the Muslim historian Ibn Khaldun (IH·buhn KAL·DOON) looked for cause-and-effect relationships to explain historical events. He was one of the first historians to study how geography and climate shape human activities.

Art and Architecture

Muslims developed forms of art based on Islam and the different cultures of the Muslim world. Opposed to idol worship, Muslim leaders discouraged artists from creating images of living creatures. Instead, Muslim art included designs entwined with flowers, leaves, stars, and beautiful writing.

Muslim cities were known for their beautiful buildings. Mosques dominated the skylines of Baghdad, Damascus, Cairo, and Istanbul. The most prominent features of a mosque are its **minarets** (mih·nuh·REHTS). These are towers from which an announcer calls Muslims to prayer five times each day.

Islamic rulers lived in large palaces with central courtyards. To cool the courtyards, architects added porches, fountains, and pools. To provide protection, they surrounded the palaces with walls. One famous example of a Muslim palace is the Alhambra (al·HAM·bruh) in Granada (gruh·NAH·duh), Spain.

Another famous Muslim building is the Taj Mahal in Agra (AH·gruh), India. The Mogul ruler Shah Jahan built it as a tomb for his wife. The Taj Mahal is made of marble and precious stones and is considered one of the world's most beautiful buildings.

It took Shah Jahan's workers and craftspeople more than 20 years to build the Taj Mahal.

▶ CRITICAL THINKING
Making Inferences What does the size and beauty of the Taj Mahal say about Shah Jahan's feelings for his wife?

©Renaud Visage/age fotostock

✔ PROGRESS CHECK

Listing What achievements were made by Muslims in medicine?

LESSON 3 REVIEW

Review Vocabulary

1. Why is a *minaret* an important feature of a *mosque*?

Answer the Guiding Questions

2. *Identifying* What groups held the greatest power in Muslim society?

3. *Explaining* What did Muslim scientists discover once they improved the astrolabe?

4. *Describing* What are the defining features of Muslim art?

5. *Summarizing* Summarize the contributions that Muslim doctors made in the field of medicine.

6. ARGUMENT What Islamic invention or development do you think has had the greatest effect on our world today? Explain your choice.

Write your answers on a separate piece of paper.

1 Exploring the Essential Question

INFORMATIVE/EXPLANATORY How does the spread of a religion change the way people live? Write an essay that discusses how the influence of Islam changed the way people lived throughout the Islamic Empire. Include the influence of Islam in daily life as well as in trade, government, and culture.

2 21st Century Skills

RECOGNIZE QUALITY SOURCES Using a computer word processing program, create a five-page report on the range of Islamic arts. Include arts that flourished in the Ottoman Empire during the reign of Suleiman I. Use primary source photos and information from reliable Internet sources such as the Metropolitan Museum of Art and national Turkish museums. Include secondary source information from encyclopedias.

3 Thinking Like a Historian

SEQUENCING EVENTS Create a time line. Place these four events in the correct order on the time line:

- Mongols burn Baghdad
- Abbasids replace the Umayyads
- Muhammad begins preaching
- Suleiman I rules the Ottoman Empire

4 GEOGRAPHY ACTIVITY

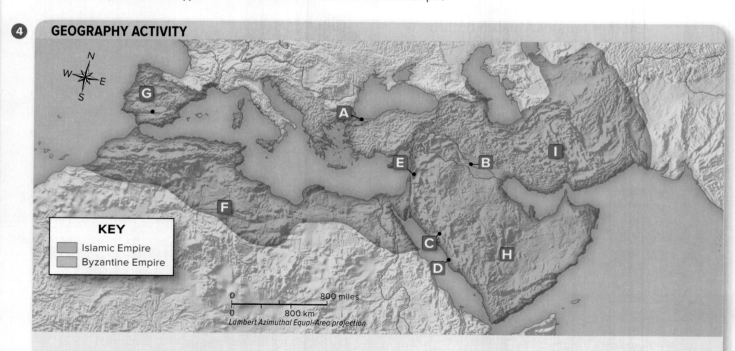

KEY
- Islamic Empire
- Byzantine Empire

0   800 miles
0   800 km
Lambert Azimuthal Equal-Area projection

Locating Places

Match the letters on the map with the numbered places listed below.

1. Africa
2. Arabia
3. Spain
4. Persia
5. Makkah
6. Baghdad
7. Constantinople
8. Damascus
9. Madinah

Directions: Write your answers on a separate piece of paper.

CHECKING FOR UNDERSTANDING

1 Define each of these terms as they relate to Islam.

A. oasis

B. sheikh

C. caravan

D. Quran

E. *shari'ah*

F. caliph

G. Sunni

H. Shia

I. mosque

J. bazaar

K. astrolabe

L. minaret

REVIEW THE GUIDING QUESTIONS

2 *Explaining* How did the geography of the Arabian Peninsula affect the lives of the people who lived there?

3 *Identifying* What was Muhammad's message to the people of Arabia?

4 *Listing* What are two ways that Islam provides guidance to its followers?

5 *Summarizing* Summarize how the Arabs were able to create an empire.

6 *Describing* What happened to the Arab Empire after the Umayyad caliphs?

7 *Discussing* How did the Ottoman Turks rule their empire?

8 *Identifying* When Muslim traders went to places like India, China, and Southeast Asia, what kinds of goods might they take? What might they bring back?

9 *Naming* What were three Muslim contributions to science? Use clear and coherent language when writing your answer.

10 *Specifying* What were some of the contributions that Muslims made to the arts and architecture? Use clear and coherent language when writing your answer.

CRITICAL THINKING

11 *Drawing Conclusions* Study the map of the Arab Empire in A.D. 750 at the beginning of this chapter. Why do you think the empire spread to Spain rather than to other parts of Europe, such as France and Germany?

12 *Making Connections* Why was a member's loyalty to his or her tribe extremely important to life in the desert?

13 *Making Connections* In Islam, how is the *shari'ah* related to the Quran?

14 *Analyzing Primary Sources* Study the image of Suleiman I in Lesson 2. What does the size of his turban tell you about his status and position?

15 *Comparing and Contrasting* How is a bazaar similar to a mosque? How is it different?

16 *Determining Cause and Effect* What factors led to trading becoming so important and widespread in the Islamic world? Use clear and coherent language in your explanation.

17 *Analyzing* Why do mosques typically contain designs such as flowers and stars rather than illustrations of people and animals?

18 *Making Decisions* If you were a merchant crossing the desert in A.D. 500, would you rather travel with one or two close friends or with a caravan of several hundred people? Explain your answer.

19 *Defending* When the Muslims conquered a new territory, they usually let the people continue to practice their own religion. Do you think this was a good idea or a bad idea? Defend your choice.

20 *Speculating* What might have happened to Greek knowledge if Jewish and Muslim scholars had not translated some Greek writings into Arabic between 700 and 1400?

Need Extra Help?

If You've Missed Question	1	2	3	4	5	6	7	8	9	10	11	12	13	14	15	16	17	18	19	20
Review Lesson	1, 2, 3	1	1	1	2	2	2	3	3	3	Opener	1	1	2	3	3	3	1	2	3

DBQ SHORT RESPONSE

*"In the 7th century [600s] Persia fell to the conquering armies of Islam. **Islamic** rule, under the **empire** of the caliphate, persisted for the next seven centuries. ... Although Islam gave the Persians a wholly new religion and altered their way of living, Persian culture remained intact [unchanged]."*

—from "Islamic Dynasties" in *Encyclopedia Britannica Kids*

21 How did Islamic rule affect the Persians?

22 How did allowing Persian culture to remain unchanged strengthen the Islamic Empire?

EXTENDED RESPONSE

23 *Narrative* You are a merchant during the era of the Umayyads. You travel the empire buying and selling goods. Write a diary entry describing one of your travels.

STANDARDIZED TEST PRACTICE

DBQ ANALYZING DOCUMENTS

Baghdad became a center of political and cultural power. A visitor, Yakut, describes the city after visiting it in A.D. 800.

"Baghdad formed two vast semi-circles on the right and left banks of the Tigris. ... Baghdad was a veritable [true] City of Palaces, not made of stucco and mortar, but of [precious] marble."

—from *Readings in Ancient History,* edited by William Stearns Davis

24 *Summarizing* Which statement best summarizes Yakut's opinion about Baghdad?
   A. Yakut is critical of Baghdad.
   B. Yakut describes Baghdad as a small city on the Tigris River.
   C. Yakut sees Baghdad as a poor city.
   D. Yakut's description paints Baghdad as a splendid city of fine buildings.

25 *Comparing and Contrasting* Why does Yakut mention building materials?
   A. All these materials were scarce throughout the Islamic Empire.
   B. The building materials show how magnificent Baghdad was.
   C. Stucco and mortar were unusual building materials.
   D. Marble was a common building material throughout the Islamic Empire.

Need Extra Help?

If You've Missed Question	**21**	**22**	**23**	**24**	**25**
Review Lesson	2	2	2	2	2

TEXT: "Persia." Student Encyclopedia. Britannica Online for Kids. Encyclopedia Britannica, 2011. Web. 4 Jan. 2011.

AFRICA

UNIT **3**

EXPLORE the CONTINENT

AFRICA

The continent of Africa covers about one-fifth of Earth's total land area. Africa is the world's second-largest continent, after Asia. For the 54 independent countries located in Africa, physical features such as the Sahara, the Congo River, and the Great Rift Valley have greatly influenced how people live in this environment.

1 NATURAL RESOURCES The region has an abundance of minerals. South Africa, Botswana, and the Democratic Republic of the Congo are among the countries that have valuable deposits of gold, uranium, diamonds, and other minerals. These miners work in one of the world's deepest gold mines in South Africa.

2 BODIES OF WATER Many of Africa's lakes lie in huge basins formed millions of years ago by the uplifting of the land. The Nile, the world's longest river, flows from the East African highlands through Egypt to the Mediterranean Sea.

(bkgd)Michael Poliza/National Geographic Stock; (t)©Tom Fox/Dallas Morning News/Corbis; (b)©Jose Fuste Raga/Corbis

③ LANDFORMS Africa's geography is made up of a variety of landforms. Step-like plateaus rise from the coasts to inland mountains. Tropical grasslands with scattered trees cover almost one half of the continent. These giraffes are among the millions of animals—zebras, gazelles, lions, and cheetahs—that roam East Africa's Serengeti, one of the world's largest plains.

FAST
FACT

Africa is three times the size of the United States.

(l)Reto Stockli, NASA Earth Observatory

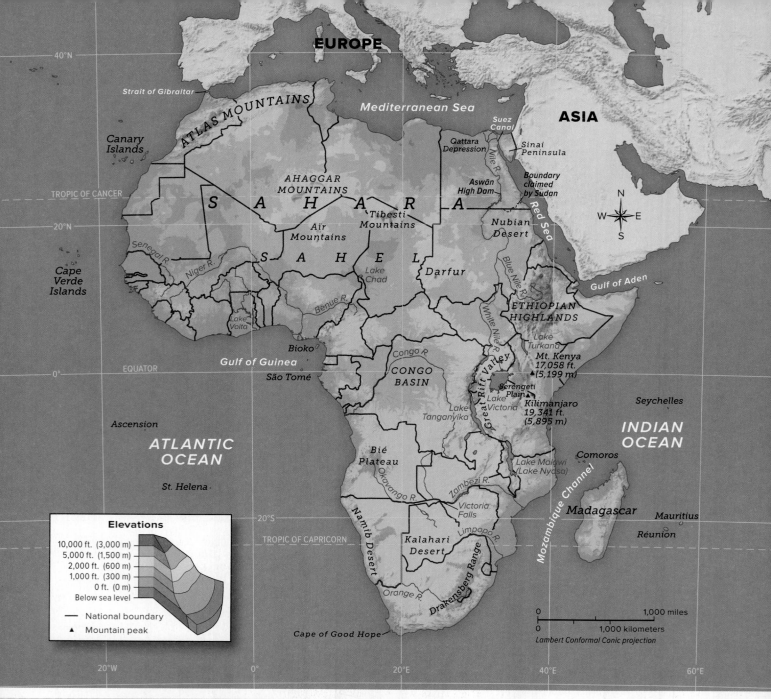

EUROPE

Strait of Gibraltar

ATLAS MOUNTAINS

Mediterranean Sea

Suez Canal

ASIA

Canary Islands

Qattara Depression

Sinai Peninsula

AHAGGAR MOUNTAINS

TROPIC OF CANCER

Aswān High Dam

Boundary claimed by Sudan

N
W   E
S

20°N

S A H A R A

Tibesti Mountains

Nubian Desert

Red Sea

Aïr Mountains

Senegal R.

Cape Verde Islands

S A H E L

Darfur

Gulf of Aden

Niger R.

Lake Chad

Blue Nile R.

Benue R.

ETHIOPIAN HIGHLANDS

Lake Volta

White Nile R.

Lake Turkana

Bioko

Mt. Kenya 17,058 ft. (5,199 m)

Gulf of Guinea

Congo R.

EQUATOR

0°

São Tomé

CONGO BASIN

Serengeti Plain

Kilimanjaro 19,341 ft. (5,895 m)

Seychelles

Ascension

Lake Tanganyika

Great Rift Valley

Lake Victoria

INDIAN OCEAN

ATLANTIC OCEAN

Bié Plateau

Comoros

St. Helena

Okavango R.

Lake Malawi (Lake Nyasa)

Madagascar

Mauritius

Zambezi R.

Réunion

20°S

Namib Desert

Victoria Falls

Mozambique Channel

TROPIC OF CAPRICORN

Kalahari Desert

Limpopo R.

Drakensberg Range

Orange R.

Cape of Good Hope

Elevations

10,000 ft. (3,000 m)
5,000 ft. (1,500 m)
2,000 ft. (600 m)
1,000 ft. (300 m)
0 ft. (0 m)
Below sea level

—— National boundary
▲ Mountain peak

0   1,000 miles
0   1,000 kilometers
Lambert Conformal Conic projection

20°W   0°   20°E   40°E   60°E

AFRICA

PHYSICAL

MAP SKILLS

1 PLACES AND REGIONS What is the major mountain range of North Africa?

2 THE GEOGRAPHER'S WORLD Which of Africa's largest lakes lies farthest to the south?

3 PHYSICAL GEOGRAPHY What is the highest mountain in Africa?

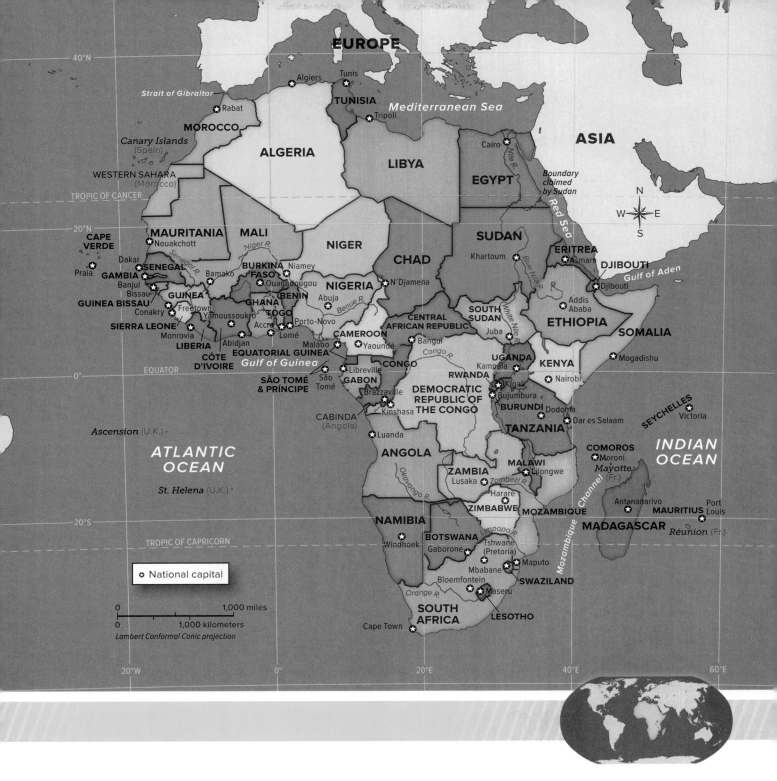

EUROPE

Strait of Gibraltar

Algiers • Tunis
TUNISIA
Tripoli •

Mediterranean Sea

• Rabat
MOROCCO

Canary Islands
(Spain)

ASIA

Cairo ⊛

ALGERIA

LIBYA

EGYPT

Nile R.

Boundary claimed by Sudan

WESTERN SAHARA
(Morocco)

TROPIC OF CANCER

Red Sea

40°N

N
W   E
S

20°N

CAPE
VERDE

MAURITANIA

MALI

⊛Nouakchott

Niger R.

Dakar

Senegal R.

Praia ⊛
GAMBIA

SENEGAL

Bamako ⊛

NIGER

CHAD

SUDAN

Khartoum ⊛

ERITREA

⊛Asmara

DJIBOUTI

Gulf of Aden

⊛Djibouti

Niamey ⊛
BURKINA
FASO
Ouagadougou ⊛

Banjul
GUINEA BISSAU   Bissau
GUINEA
Conakry ⊛

Freetown ⊛
SIERRA LEONE
Monrovia ⊛
LIBERIA

GHANA

Yamoussoukro ⊛
CÔTE
D'IVOIRE

NIGERIA

Abuja ⊛

BENIN

TOGO
Accra ⊛

Abidjan ⊛

Lomé

N'Djamena •

Benue R.

CENTRAL
AFRICAN REPUBLIC

SOUTH
SUDAN

Juba ⊛

Addis
Ababa ⊛

ETHIOPIA

SOMALIA

⊛Mogadishu

EQUATORIAL GUINEA
Porto-Novo ⊛
CAMEROON
Malabo ⊛
⊛Yaoundé

Bangui ⊛

Congo R.

UGANDA
Kampala ⊛

KENYA

⊛Nairobi

Gulf of Guinea
SÃO TOMÉ
& PRÍNCIPE   São
Tomé •
Libreville ⊛
GABON
Brazzaville ⊛
Kinshasa ⊛
CABINDA
(Angola)

EQUATOR

CONGO

RWANDA
Kigali ⊛
Bujumbura ⊛
BURUNDI

White Nile R.

Dodoma ⊛
Dar es Salaam •
TANZANIA

Blue Nile R.

SEYCHELLES

Victoria ⊛

0°

DEMOCRATIC
REPUBLIC OF
THE CONGO

Ascension (U.K.) •

ATLANTIC
OCEAN

Luanda ⊛

ANGOLA

St. Helena (U.K.) •

Okavango R.

ZAMBIA
Lusaka ⊛   Zambezi R.

MALAWI
Lilongwe ⊛

COMOROS
⊛Moroni

Mayotte
(Fr.)

INDIAN
OCEAN

Mozambique Channel

Antananarivo ⊛   Port
Louis •
MAURITIUS

20°S

Harare ⊛
ZIMBABWE
MOZAMBIQUE

MADAGASCAR   Réunion (Fr.)

TROPIC OF CAPRICORN

NAMIBIA

Windhoek ⊛

BOTSWANA
Gaborone ⊛
Tshwane
(Pretoria) ⊛
Maputo ⊛
Mbabane ⊛
SWAZILAND

⊛ National capital

0   1,000 miles
0   1,000 kilometers
Lambert Conformal Conic projection

Limpopo R.

Bloemfontein ⊛
Orange R.   ⊛Maseru
SOUTH
AFRICA   LESOTHO

Cape Town •

20°W   0°   20°E   40°E   60°E

POLITICAL

MAP SKILLS

1 **PLACES AND REGIONS** Which country in the region of North Africa is the largest in area?

2 **PLACES AND REGIONS** Name three island countries of Africa.

3 **THE GEOGRAPHER'S WORLD** Which countries border Namibia in Southern Africa?

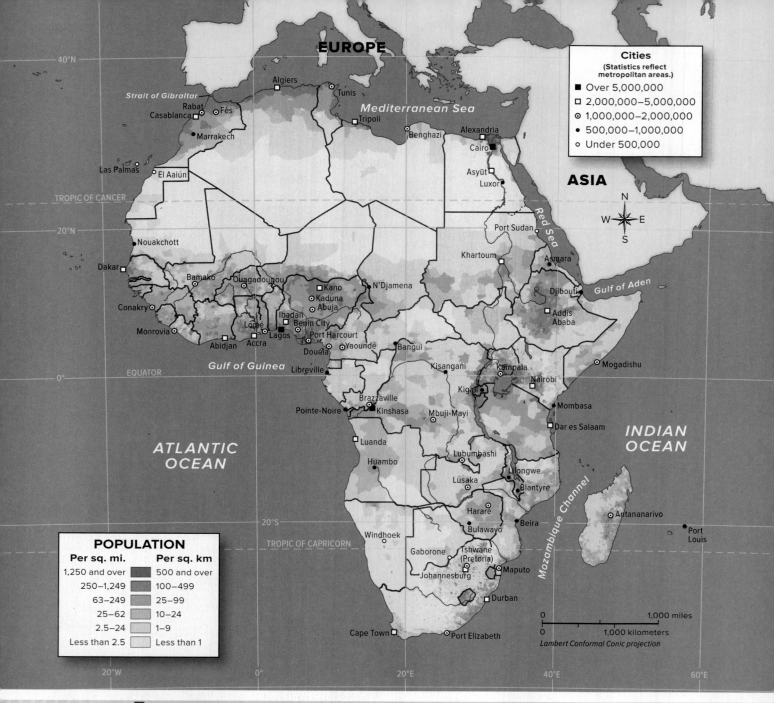

EUROPE

Strait of Gibraltar

Mediterranean Sea

Algiers
Tunis
Rabat
Fès
Casablanca
Marrakech
Tripoli
Benghazi
Alexandria
Cairo

Las Palmas
El Aaiún

ASIA

Asyūt
Luxor

Cities
(Statistics reflect metropolitan areas.)

■ Over 5,000,000
□ 2,000,000–5,000,000
◉ 1,000,000–2,000,000
• 500,000–1,000,000
○ Under 500,000

TROPIC OF CANCER

20°N

Nouakchott

Port Sudan

Red Sea

N
W E
S

Dakar
Bamako
Ouagadougou
Kano
N'Djamena
Khartoum
Asmara
Djibouti
Gulf of Aden

Conakry
Kaduna
Abuja
Addis Ababa

Monrovia
Ibadan
Benin City
Lomé
Lagos
Port Harcourt

Abidjan
Accra
Douala
Yaoundé
Bangui

Gulf of Guinea
Libreville
Kisangani
Kampala
Mogadishu

EQUATOR
0°
Nairobi
Kigali

Brazzaville
Mbuji-Mayi
Mombasa

Pointe-Noire
Kinshasa

ATLANTIC
OCEAN
Luanda
Dar es Salaam

INDIAN
OCEAN

Huambo
Lubumbashi

Lilongwe
Lusaka
Blantyre

Mozambique Channel

Harare
Antananarivo

20°S
Bulawayo
Beira

TROPIC OF CAPRICORN

Windhoek
Port Louis

Gaborone
Tshwane (Pretoria)
Maputo

Johannesburg

Durban

0   1,000 miles
0   1,000 kilometers
Lambert Conformal Conic projection

Cape Town
Port Elizabeth

20°W   0°   20°E   40°E   60°E

POPULATION

Per sq. mi.	Per sq. km
1,250 and over	500 and over
250–1,249	100–499
63–249	25–99
25–62	10–24
2.5–24	1–9
Less than 2.5	Less than 1

AFRICA

POPULATION DENSITY

MAP SKILLS

1 PLACES AND REGIONS Which areas of Africa have the lowest population density?

2 THE GEOGRAPHER'S WORLD Generalize about the areas of Africa with the highest population densities. What can you say about these places?

3 PLACES AND REGIONS What are the largest cities in Africa?

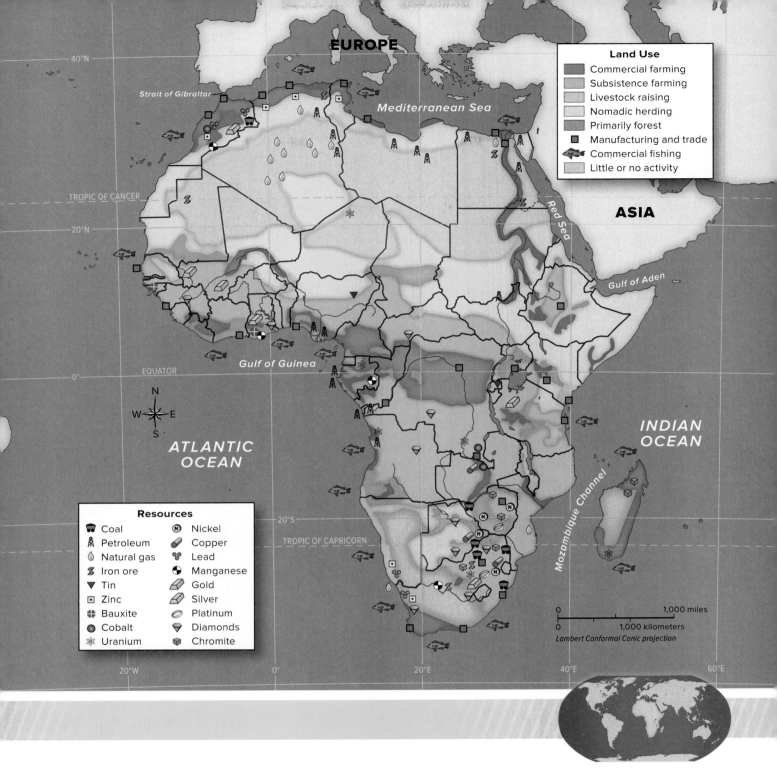

Land Use

- Commercial farming
- Subsistence farming
- Livestock raising
- Nomadic herding
- Primarily forest
- Manufacturing and trade
- Commercial fishing
- Little or no activity

Resources

- Coal
- Petroleum
- Natural gas
- Iron ore
- Tin
- Zinc
- Bauxite
- Cobalt
- Uranium
- Nickel
- Copper
- Lead
- Manganese
- Gold
- Silver
- Platinum
- Diamonds
- Chromite

0   1,000 miles
0   1,000 kilometers
Lambert Conformal Conic projection

ECONOMIC RESOURCES

MAP SKILLS

1 **ENVIRONMENT AND SOCIETY** Where are precious minerals mined in different areas of Africa?

2 **HUMAN GEOGRAPHY** What is the most common type of farming in Africa?

3 **PLACES AND REGIONS** Why do you think the Nile River valley specializes in commercial farming?

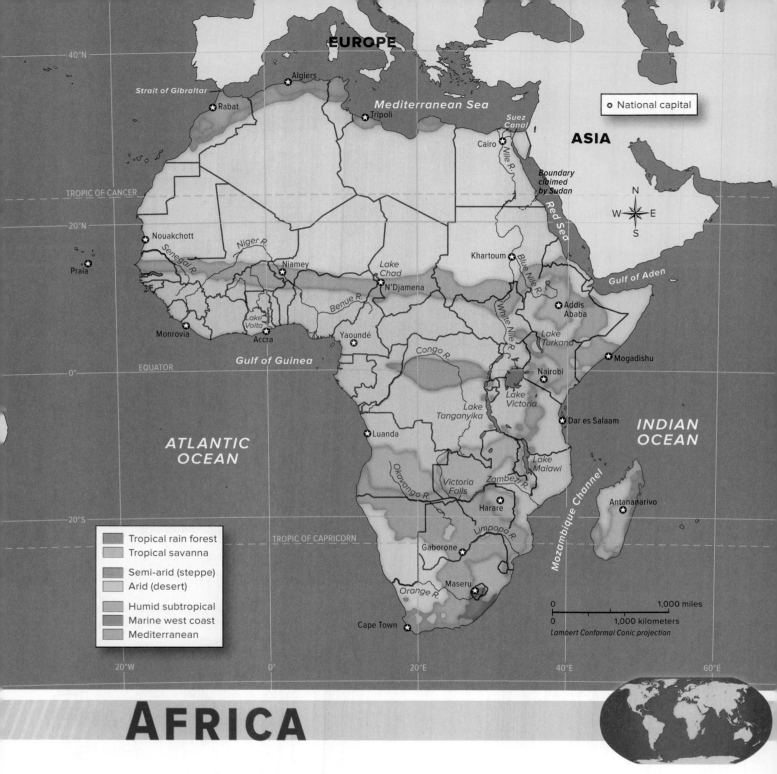

EUROPE

Strait of Gibraltar

Rabat ⭐

Algiers ⭐

Mediterranean Sea

Tripoli ⭐

Suez Canal

Cairo ⭐

ASIA

◦ National capital

Boundary claimed by Sudan

N W E S

TROPIC OF CANCER

40°N

20°N

Nouakchott ⭐

Praia ⭐

Niger R.

Senegal R.

Niamey ⭐

Lake Chad

Khartoum ⭐

Blue Nile R.

Red Sea

Gulf of Aden

N'Djamena ⭐

Benue R.

White Nile R.

Addis Ababa ⭐

Lake Turkana

Monrovia ⭐

Lake Volta

Yaoundé ⭐

Accra ⭐

Gulf of Guinea

Congo R.

Mogadishu ⭐

Nairobi ⭐

EQUATOR

0°

Lake Victoria

Lake Tanganyika

Dar es Salaam ⭐

INDIAN OCEAN

ATLANTIC OCEAN

Luanda ⭐

Okavango R.

Lake Malawi

Victoria Falls

Zambezi R.

Mozambique Channel

Antananarivo ⭐

Harare ⭐

20°S

TROPIC OF CAPRICORN

Limpopo R.

Gaborone ⭐

Maseru ⭐

Orange R.

0   1,000 miles
0   1,000 kilometers
Lambert Conformal Conic projection

Cape Town ⭐

20°W   0°   20°E   40°E   60°E

Legend

- Tropical rain forest
- Tropical savanna
- Semi-arid (steppe)
- Arid (desert)
- Humid subtropical
- Marine west coast
- Mediterranean

AFRICA

CLIMATE

MAP SKILLS

1 PLACES AND REGIONS In the area of Africa south of the Sahara, what is the predominant climate?

2 PHYSICAL GEOGRAPHY What climate types are in the area around the Congo River?

3 PLACES AND REGIONS What is the climate of Cape Town, South Africa?

EAST AFRICA

ESSENTIAL QUESTIONS · *How does geography influence the way people live?* · *Why do people trade?* · *Why does conflict develop?*

Teenage girl from the East African country of Somalia

Ariadne Van Zandbergen/Lonely Planet Images/Getty Images

networks

There's More Online about East Africa.

CHAPTER 12

Lesson 1
Physical Geography of East Africa

Lesson 2
History of East Africa

Lesson 3
Life in East Africa

The Story Matters...

Some of Africa's earliest kingdoms developed in East Africa, where trade in gold and ivory brought great wealth. Since ancient times, thriving trade has fostered interaction among different cultures, influencing language and religion and creating much ethnic diversity across the region. The landscape of East Africa also has great diversity—from the Serengeti Plain and the Great Rift Valley to the highlands in Ethiopia and Kilimanjaro in Kenya.

Go to the Foldables® library in the back of your book to make a Foldable® that will help you take notes while reading this chapter.

EAST AFRICA

Some of Africa's important early civilizations flourished in East Africa. Many of the countries have been scarred by conflict in recent years.

Step Into the Place

MAP FOCUS Use the map to answer the following questions.

1 **THE GEOGRAPHER'S WORLD** Which three East African countries share Lake Victoria?

2 **PLACES AND REGIONS** What is the capital city of Kenya?

3 **THE GEOGRAPHER'S WORLD** The Tekeze is a major river in what country?

4 **CRITICAL THINKING** **Integrating Visual Information** What country is cut off from the sea by Eritrea, Djibouti, and Somalia?

INACTIVE VOLCANO Snowcapped Kilimanjaro looms over savanna plains near the border of Tanzania and Kenya. The mountain is made up of three volcanic cones, all inactive.

WAR-TORN CITY Ruined buildings line an Indian Ocean beach in Mogadishu, the capital of Somalia. Since the early 1990s, various armed groups have fought over Somalia.

Step Into the Time

TIME LINE Using at least two events on the time line, write a paragraph describing how trade influenced the development of East Africa.

800 B.C. Kingdom of Kush develops along the Nile River

A.D. 400 Kingdom of Aksum prospers from trade

B.C. | A.D.

30,000–20,000 B.C. Ancient people live in what is now Sudan

1100s Muslim settlements multiply in East Africa

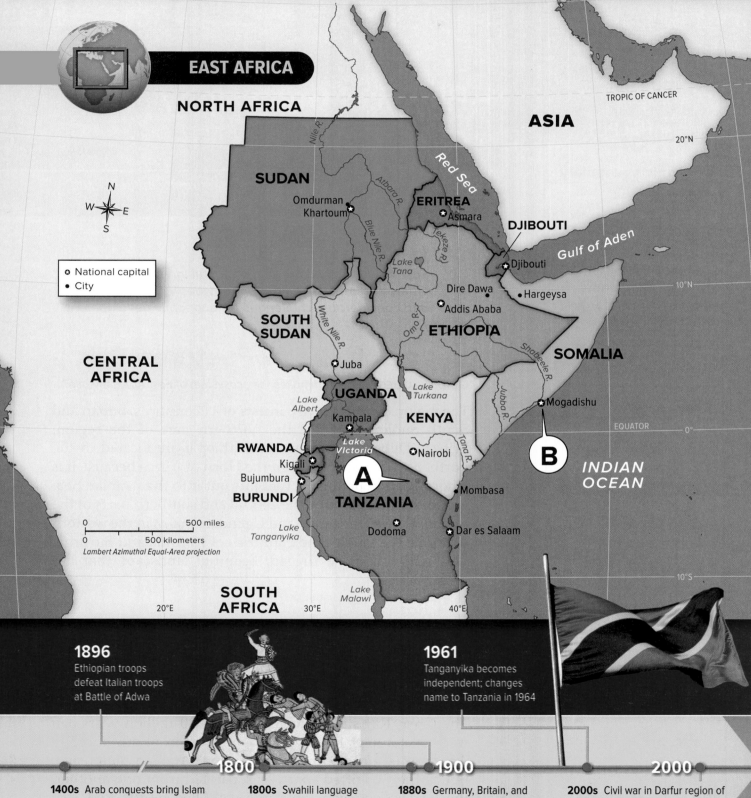

EAST AFRICA

NORTH AFRICA

ASIA

TROPIC OF CANCER

20°N

Nile R.

SUDAN

Atbara R.

Red Sea

Omdurman
• Khartoum

ERITREA
• Asmara

DJIBOUTI

Gulf of Aden

Blue Nile R.

Tekeze R.

Lake Tana

Djibouti

10°N

Dire Dawa •

• Hargeysa

○ National capital
• City

White Nile R.

SOUTH
SUDAN

• Addis Ababa

Omo R.

ETHIOPIA

SOMALIA

Shabeele R.

CENTRAL
AFRICA

Juba

UGANDA

Lake Turkana

Jubba R.

Mogadishu

EQUATOR 0°

Lake Albert

Kampala

KENYA

Tana R.

B

INDIAN
OCEAN

RWANDA

Lake Victoria

• Nairobi

Kigali

Bujumbura

A

BURUNDI

TANZANIA

• Mombasa

0   500 miles

0   500 kilometers

Lambert Azimuthal Equal-Area projection

Lake Tanganyika

Dodoma

• Dar es Salaam

10°S

SOUTH
AFRICA

Lake Malawi

20°E   30°E   40°E

1896
Ethiopian troops
defeat Italian troops
at Battle of Adwa

1961
Tanganyika becomes
independent; changes
name to Tanzania in 1964

1800   1900   2000

1400s Arab conquests bring Islam
to the area of present-day Sudan

1800s Swahili language
spreads inland

1880s Germany, Britain, and
France take control of the region

2000s Civil war in Darfur region of
Sudan kills hundreds of thousands

Reading HELPDESK

Academic Vocabulary

- **consist**

Content Vocabulary

- **rift**
- **desertification**
- **hydroelectric power**
- **geothermal energy**

TAKING NOTES: *Key Ideas and Details*

Identifying As you study the lesson, use a web diagram like this one to list information about the land and water features of the region.

Land and Water Features / Landforms / Water

Lesson 1
Physical Geography of East Africa

ESSENTIAL QUESTION • *How does geography influence the way people live?*

IT MATTERS BECAUSE
East Africa offers a rugged, beautiful landscape and different climates. The region provides variety, potential, and considerable challenges for economic development.

Land and Water Features

GUIDING QUESTION *What makes the ecosystem of East Africa diverse?*

The region of East Africa **consists** of 11 countries. Sudan and South Sudan dominate the northern part of the region. Eritrea, Djibouti, Somalia, and Ethiopia are located in the northeast. This area is called the Horn of Africa because it is a horn-shaped peninsula that juts out into the Arabian Sea. Three countries occupy the central and southern parts of the region: Kenya, Tanzania, and Uganda. Finally, in the western sector lie the landlocked countries of Rwanda and Burundi. East Africa offers a rugged, beautiful landscape that has great variety.

Landforms

The Great Rift Valley is the most unusual feature of East Africa's physical geography. Sometimes it is called the Great Rift system because it is not one single valley. Rather, it is a series of large valleys and depressions in Earth's surface. These are formed by long chains of geological faults. The Great Rift started forming about 20 million years ago when tectonic plates began to tear apart from one another. Africa was once connected to the Arabian Peninsula. But as the two **rifted** apart, or separated from one another, the land in between sank and was filled by the Red Sea.

Eventually, all of East Africa will separate from the rest of Africa, and the Red Sea will fill the rift.

The Great Rift system's northern end is in Jordan in Southwest Asia. From Jordan, it stretches about 4,000 miles (6,437 km) to its southern end in Mozambique in southeastern Africa. The rift has an average width of 30 miles to 40 miles (48 km to 64 km).

The rift system has an eastern and western branch in East Africa. The eastern Rift Valley—the main branch—runs from Southwest Asia along the Jordan River, Dead Sea, and Red Sea. It continues through the Danakil plain in Ethiopia. It is one of the hottest and driest places on Earth, and earthquakes and volcanic activity occur here regularly. Long, deep cracks develop in Earth's surface as the tectonic plates rift apart.

As the eastern Rift Valley continues south from the Danakil plain, the conditions are not as severe. It takes the form of deep valleys as it extends into Kenya and Tanzania, and down to Mozambique. The shorter western Rift Valley stretches from Lake Malawi in the south through Uganda in the north through a series of valleys. A chain of deep lakes that includes Lake Tanganyika, Lake Edward, and Lake Albert marks the western rift's northward path.

Along the branches of the Great Rift Valley, much volcanic and seismic activity occurred. The largest volcanoes are located on the eastern Rift. These include Mount Kenya and Kilimanjaro. Kilimanjaro is on the border between Kenya and Tanzania. With a summit of 19,341 feet (5,895 m), Kilimanjaro is the tallest mountain in Africa. Its summit is covered with snow year-round, even though the mountain is near the Equator.

Sudan is home to vast plains and plateaus. The northern part of the country is desert covered in sand or gravel. Somalia lies in the eastern part of the region, along the Indian Ocean.

©Hemis/Alamy

Academic Vocabulary

consist to be made up of

This aerial view shows a section of the floor of the eastern Rift Valley in Kenya. Many fault lines appear in the valley. Hardened lava from volcanoes and openings in the ground also mark the landscape.

▶ **CRITICAL THINKING**

Describing How will East Africa eventually be affected by the Rift's tectonic plate activity?

The palace of Sudan's president in Khartoum stands near where the Blue Nile joins the White Nile. The White Nile is named for the light-colored clay sediment found in its waters. The Blue Nile's name comes from the river's appearance during flood season when the water level is high.

▶ CRITICAL THINKING

Describing Where do each of the two Nile tributaries begin?

Somalia is also an extremely dry area. The country is made up largely of savanna and semidesert. To the north of Somalia lies the small country of Djibouti. Located on the coast between the Red Sea and the Gulf of Aden, Djibouti displays a highly diverse landscape. It has rugged mountains and desert plains.

South of Sudan, at the western edge of Uganda, the Ruwenzori Mountains divide that country from the Democratic Republic of the Congo. These peaks are sometimes called the "Mountains of the Moon." Mountains give way to hills in small, landlocked Rwanda. It is known as the "land of a thousand hills" for its beautiful landscape.

Bodies of Water

The longest river in the world is the Nile (4,132 miles or 6,650 km). The Nile Basin includes parts of many countries in the East African region: Tanzania, Burundi, Rwanda, Kenya, Uganda, Ethiopia, South Sudan, and the Sudan. Beginning in the 1800s, European explorers made numerous expeditions in attempts to find the source of the Nile River. The great river was discovered to have two sets of headwaters. One of them, the Blue Nile, rises in the northern highlands of Ethiopia. The other source, the White Nile, begins in Lake Victoria and runs through Lake Albert. The White Nile then passes through the swampy wetlands of central South Sudan, a huge area called the Sudd.

In northern Sudan, the Blue Nile and the White Nile meet at the city of Khartoum. The great river then runs northward through

©Michael Freeman/Corbis

Egypt and empties into the Mediterranean Sea. Other than the Nile, East Africa has few important rivers. This is due to the intermittent rainfall and the high temperatures in many areas of the region.

In the late 1970s, the swampy Sudd was the focus of a huge construction project called the Jonglei Canal. This channel was designed to avoid the Sudd. The goal was to allow the headstreams of the White Nile to flow more freely. Instead of the water spreading across the Sudd and slowly moving through it, the canal would allow more water to flow downstream and reach Sudan and Egypt. That would support more agriculture and better city services in those countries. But it would also damage the wetland environment of the Sudd. Fisheries could collapse and go extinct. Construction was suspended in 1983. The project could not continue because civil war in Sudan made it too dangerous.

Many of the lakes in East Africa are located near the Great Rift Valley. The largest lake on the continent of Africa is Lake Victoria. This lake lies between the western and the eastern branches of the Great Rift. The lake stretches into three countries: Uganda and Kenya in the north and Tanzania in the south. With an area of 26,828 square miles (69,484 sq. km), Lake Victoria is the second-largest freshwater lake in the world, after Lake Superior in the United States. For such a large body of water, Lake Victoria is relatively shallow. Its greatest known depth is about 270 feet (82 m). The lake is home to more than 200 species of fish. Of these, tilapia has the most economic value.

Another important lake in the region is Lake Tanganyika. This long, narrow body of water is located south of Lake Victoria, between Tanzania and the Democratic Republic of the Congo. The lake is only 10 to 45 miles (16 km to 72 km) wide, but very long. Measuring 410 miles (660 km) north to south, it is the world's longest freshwater lake. With a maximum depth of 4,710 feet (1,436 m), it is also the second deepest. Only Lake Baikal in Russia is deeper than Lake Tanganyika.

Farther south is Lake Malawi. It is the third-largest lake in the East African Rift Valley. The lake lies mainly in Malawi and forms part of that country's border with Tanzania and Mozambique.

☑ **READING PROGRESS CHECK**

Identifying What caused the striking physical features of the Great Rift Valley in East Africa?

Fishers leave the eastern shore of Lake Victoria by boat early in the morning to fish for tilapia and Nile perch. With its many fish species, Lake Victoria supports Africa's largest inland fishery.

©John Warburton-Lee Photography/Alamy

Climates of East Africa

GUIDING QUESTION *How does climate vary in East Africa?*

Climate varies widely in the East African region. Temperature and rainfall can be quite different from one local area to another. The major factors explaining these variations include latitude, altitude, distance from the sea, and the type of terrain, such as mountains, highlands, desert, or coastal plains.

Temperatures

The diverse physical features of East African geography are matched by an extremely varied climate. In general, temperatures tend to be warmer toward the coast and cooler in the highlands. Sudan, Djibouti, and Somalia have high temperatures for much of the year. High mountains such as Kilimanjaro and the peaks of the Ruwenzori Range have had glaciers for thousands of years. Due to climate change, however, these glaciers are melting. Some experts predict that the glaciers of Kilimanjaro will completely disappear over the next 20 years.

The climate is always spring-like in the highlands of Kenya and Uganda. As a whole, however, Kenya and Uganda display considerable variations in climate. These variations depend on factors such as latitude, elevation, wind patterns, and ocean currents.

Rainfall

In many parts of East Africa, rainfall is seasonal. This is especially true close to the Equator. Wet seasons alternate with dry ones. For example, on the tropical grasslands, or savannas, of Kenya and

The Savoia glacier is located along the border of Uganda and the Democratic Republic of the Congo. Many scientists are concerned about the effects of climate change on the Ruwenzori glaciers. Around 1900, some 43 glaciers were distributed over 6 mountains in the range. Today, fewer than half of these glaciers still exist, on only 3 of the mountains. The rest have melted.

▶ **CRITICAL THINKING**
Analyzing Why do temperatures tend to be cool in inland East Africa despite the region's closeness to the Equator?

Bruno Zanzottera/Parallelozero/Aurora Photos

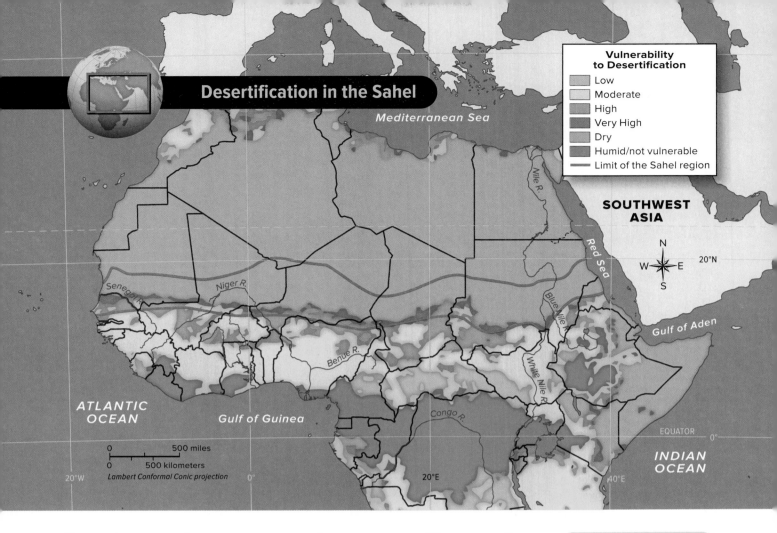

Desertification in the Sahel

Mediterranean Sea

Vulnerability to Desertification
- Low
- Moderate
- High
- Very High
- Dry
- Humid/not vulnerable
- —— Limit of the Sahel region

Nile R.

SOUTHWEST ASIA

Red Sea

20°N

N
W E
S

Senegal R.

Niger R.

Blue Nile

Benue R.

Gulf of Aden

White Nile R.

ATLANTIC OCEAN

Gulf of Guinea

Congo R.

EQUATOR 0°

INDIAN OCEAN

0 _____ 500 miles
0 _____ 500 kilometers
Lambert Conformal Conic projection

20°W   0°   20°E   40°E

Tanzania, two rainy seasons occur in most years. These are the "long rains" of April and May and the "short rains" of October and November. The months in between these periods are dry, with little or no rainfall.

Rainfall in the region, however, can be unpredictable. Sparse rainfall can result in severe drought. In 2011, for example, Somalia suffered one of the worst droughts in its history. Political instability in that country made the effects of the drought especially severe. Observers estimated that 13 million people struggled to survive in the countries of Somalia, Ethiopia, Djibouti, and Kenya.

Another urgent issue in the region is **desertification**, or the process by which agricultural land is turned into desert. This process occurs when long periods of drought and unwise land use destroy vegetation. The land is left dry and barren. During the past half century, desertification has affected much of the Sahel. The Sahel is the "edge," or border area, between the Sahara and the countries farther to the south. Two such border nations in East Africa are Sudan and South Sudan.

☑ READING PROGRESS CHECK

Determining Central Ideas What generalization can you make about the variations in temperature in East Africa?

MAP SKILLS

1 **PLACES AND REGIONS**
Based on the legend, most of the Sahel is at what level of desertification?

2 **THE GEOGRAPHER'S WORLD** What causes desertification?

Workers collect salt at Lake Assal in Djibouti. Salt covers everything, so very little vegetation is able to grow along the lake's shoreline. Located in the hot desert, the lake's area has summer temperatures as high as 126°F (52°C).

Identifying What other mineral resources are found in East Africa?

Resources of East Africa

GUIDING QUESTION *Which natural resources are important in East Africa?*

The natural resources of a region are closely linked to its economy and people's way of life. Settlement patterns in a geographical area have often been shaped by that area's natural resources. Important resources in East Africa are minerals, energy sources, landscapes, and wildlife. The ability of some countries to exploit these resources, however, has been hampered by political issues.

Mineral Resources

Mineral resources in East Africa include small gold deposits along the rifts in Kenya, Uganda, and Tanzania; gemstones like sapphires and diamonds in Tanzania; and tin in Rwanda. Ethiopia and Uganda produce lumber. Lake Assal in Djibouti, located about 500 feet (152 m) below sea level, is the world's largest salt reserve, with more than 1 billion tons of salt. This lake is located at the lowest point in Africa.

Energy Resources

Energy resources in East Africa include coal in Tanzania, as well as petroleum in Uganda, South Sudan, and northwestern Kenya. East Africa's energy potential has yet to be realized, though. For example, Sudan has the opportunity to develop **hydroelectric power**, or the production of electricity through the use of falling water. Hydroelectric power is already used in Kenya and Tanzania.

Likewise, Kenya and Djibouti are favorable locations for the development of **geothermal energy**. This type of energy comes from underground heat sources, such as hot springs and steam. In Kenya, an international group of companies is working with the government to develop geothermal energy sources. If they are successful, 30 percent of the country's energy needs could be met by geothermal energy by the year 2030.

In East Africa, management of energy resources and energy use often has been inconsistent and uneven. Major cities gobble up much of the energy that is produced. Energy is often unavailable in rural areas.

Land and Wildlife

Besides mineral and energy resources, East Africa's land and wildlife are important assets. The soils in the region are not especially rich for agriculture, and farming is reb. The breathtaking scenery of the Great Rift Valley, however, is an important tourist resource.

East Africa is also home to the greatest assemblage of wildlife in the world. Many national parks and wildlife sanctuaries are found in the region. Perhaps the most well-known wildlife reserves are located in Kenya and Tanzania. An outstanding example is the Serengeti Plain; this vast area, larger than the state of Connecticut, consists of tropical savanna grasslands. Two internationally famous national parks are located in East Africa—Serengeti National Park in Tanzania and the Masai Mara National Reserve in Kenya. These parks harbor lions, leopards, cheetahs, giraffes, zebras, elephants, and dozens of species of antelope.

Every year, thousands of tourists pour in from all over the world to see the marvel of the Great Migration. In this mass movement, more than 1 million animals travel hundreds of miles in search of fresh grazing land. The spectacular wildlife of East Africa makes an important contribution to the economy of the region.

☑ **READING PROGRESS CHECK**

Identifying What two promising alternatives might help improve energy supplies in the East African region?

Think Again?

Animals involved in the Great Migration on the Serengeti Plain travel together.

Not True. Nature employs a more sophisticated system. The three major migrating species are zebras, wildebeests, and Thomson's gazelles. These species migrate in a succession. First come the zebras. They consume crude, coarse, high grasses. Then the wildebeests follow, grazing on the lower shoots exposed by their predecessors. Last are the smaller Thomson's gazelles, antelopes that eat tender, fine shoots close to the ground.

FOLDABLES
Study Organizer

Include this lesson's information in your Foldable®.

LESSON 1 REVIEW

Reviewing Vocabulary
1. What causes the process of *desertification*?

Answering the Guiding Questions
2. *Describing* What are the differing characteristics that make Lake Victoria and Lake Tanganyika noteworthy bodies of water, both in East Africa and in the world as a whole?

3. *Analyzing* How might desertification affect the economy in a region?

4. *Identifying* How are energy supplies distributed in East Africa?

5. *Informative/Explanatory Writing* Write a letter to a friend or a relative explaining why you want to visit East Africa to see the region's wildlife.

networks

There's More Online!

☑ **IMAGE** British at Omdurman

☑ **MAP** African Trade Routes and Goods

☑ **SLIDE SHOW** Ancient Africa

☑ **VIDEO**

Reading **HELP**DESK

Academic Vocabulary

- impact

Content Vocabulary

- tribute
- imperialism
- genocide
- refugee

TAKING NOTES: *Key Ideas and Details*

Organizing As you study the lesson, use a chart like this one to list important facts about the places.

Place	Facts
Nubia/Kush	
Aksum	
Coastal City-States	

Lesson 2
History of East Africa

ESSENTIAL QUESTION • *Why do people trade?*

IT MATTERS BECAUSE
East Africa has been a center of trade since ancient times. Throughout much of its history, East Africa has attracted people from many other continents.

Kingdoms and Trading States

GUIDING QUESTION *How has the history of trade impacted the region?*

Trade was important in the ancient kingdoms in East Africa. Contact between East Africa and other areas brought together people from different civilizations. Trade also resulted in the spread of Christianity and Islam into the region.

Ancient Nubia

The ancient region of Nubia was located in northeastern Africa, below ancient Egypt. The region stretched southward along the Nile River valley almost to what is now the Sudanese city of Khartoum. The region was bounded by the Libyan Desert in the west and by the Red Sea in the east. The Nile River was the pathway by which Nubia and the powerful empire of Egypt interacted.

In about 1050 B.C., a powerful civilization arose in Nubia. This was known as Kush. The Egyptians traded extensively with the Kushites, purchasing copper, gold, ivory, ebony, slaves, and cattle. The Kushites, in turn, adopted many Egyptian customs and practices. For example, they built pyramids to mark the tombs of their rulers and nobles.

During the final centuries of their civilization, the Kushites were isolated from Egypt. As a result, they turned increasingly to other African people south of the Sahara for trade and cultural contact. Around A.D. 350, Kush was

(l to r)Nigel Pavitt/AWL Images/Getty Images; (3)©Lebrecht Music & Arts/Lebrecht Music & Arts/Corbis; (4)Sabena Jane Blackbird/Alamy; (5)©Bettmann/Corbis

conquered by Aksum, a powerful state in what is now northern Ethiopia.

Aksum

The date of Aksum's establishment is uncertain but it might have been around 1000 B.C. The people of Aksum derived their wealth and power primarily from trade. Aksum was strategically located, and it controlled the port city of Adulis on the Red Sea. At its height of power, Aksum was the most important trading center in the region. Its trading connections extended all the way to Alexandria on the Mediterranean Sea. Aksum traders specialized in sea routes that connected the Red Sea to India.

Through the port of Adulis flowed gold and ivory, as well as raw materials. It is possible that Aksum sold captives for the slave trade. Aksum traded glue, candy, and gum arabic, a substance from acacia trees that today is used in the food industry. Christianity spread from its origin in Jerusalem along the trade routes. The Aksum kings adopted Christianity as their religion.

Trade Cities

Beginning around the A.D. 900s, after the decline of Aksum, Arabs settled on the East African coast of the Indian Ocean. The religion of Islam grew steadily more important in the region. At the same time, the Arabic and Bantu languages mingled to create a new language. This language is known as Swahili. The name comes from an Arabic word meaning "coast dwellers." Swahili is widely spoken today in Tanzania and Kenya, as well as in some other countries.

Gradually, the coastal settlements formed independent trading states. From coastal Somalia southward, along the shores of Kenya and Tanzania, these city-states prospered. They included Mogadishu, Lamu, Malindi, and Mombasa.

Many of the pyramids of ancient Kush still stand in present-day Sudan. Near the pyramids, the Kushites built a capital city called Meroë. Archaeologists have uncovered some of the remains of Meroë, including a royal palace, temples, and mud-brick homes.

▶ CRITICAL THINKING
Determining Central Ideas What do the pyramids of Meroë reveal about Kushite culture?

Nigel Pavitt/AWL Images/Getty Images

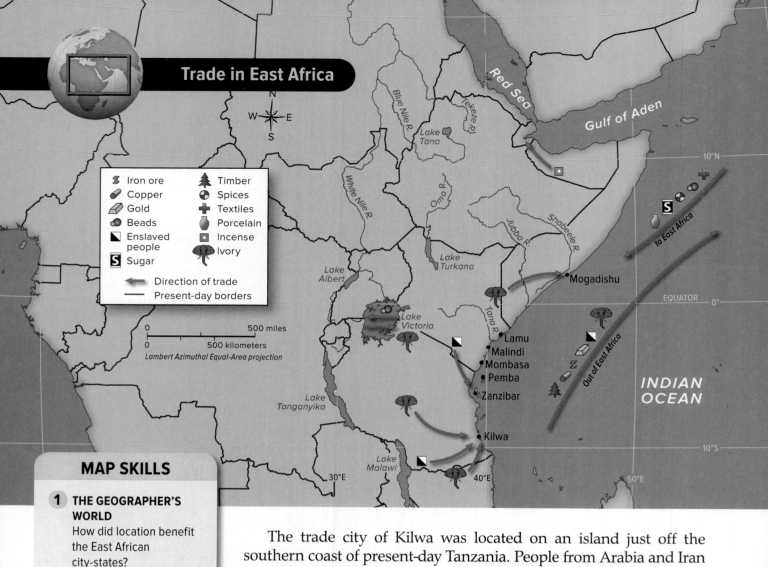

Trade in East Africa

Legend:
- Iron ore
- Copper
- Gold
- Beads
- Enslaved people
- Sugar
- Timber
- Spices
- Textiles
- Porcelain
- Incense
- Ivory

→ Direction of trade
— Present-day borders

0 — 500 miles
0 — 500 kilometers
Lambert Azimuthal Equal-Area projection

MAP SKILLS

1 THE GEOGRAPHER'S WORLD
How did location benefit the East African city-states?

2 HUMAN GEOGRAPHY
What part did inland Africa play in the region's trade?

The trade city of Kilwa was located on an island just off the southern coast of present-day Tanzania. People from Arabia and Iran founded Kilwa in the late A.D. 900s. The merchants of Kilwa dealt in copper, iron, ivory, and gold. They exchanged these goods for products from many lands, including Chinese porcelain and Indian cotton.

Kilwa was a walled city. Its ruler lived in an impressive palace. For two centuries, the city was probably the wealthiest trading center in East Africa. The fourteenth-century traveler Ibn Battuta praised Kilwa as a beautiful city. At the time of Ibn Battuta's visit, Kilwa was ruled by Abu al-Mawahib. The sultan was so generous that people called him "the father of gifts."

☑ **READING PROGRESS CHECK**

Identifying Compare the economies of the coastal city-states in East Africa to those of the kingdom of Aksum.

The Colonial Era

GUIDING QUESTION *What was the effect of colonization on East Africa?*

Until the late 1800s, most Europeans knew little or nothing about Africa. Two of the continent's most famous explorers were Henry Morton Stanley and David Livingstone. In 1878 Stanley published a popular travel book about his adventures in Africa. The book's title was *Through the Dark Continent*. The goal of Stanley's journey was to locate Livingstone, a medical missionary. Livingstone had traveled to Africa in the hope of locating the source of the Nile River.

European Traders

Just before 1500, the European age of discovery began to **impact** East Africa. Among the European countries, Portugal took the lead in overseas exploration. Along with other Europeans, the Portuguese established a sea route to India. From Europe, they sailed south along the west coast of Africa and then along the east coast of Africa. Then, they sailed along the coast of Arabia and on to India. This was a much easier and less expensive way to trade with India than any of the overland trade routes. In this way, the Portuguese were able to bring back many valuable spices from India.

As trade increased, the Portuguese began to demand **tribute**, or a regular tax payment, from the East African trading cities. The Portuguese had religious as well as economic motives; they believed that Christianity should replace Islam as the region's religion. Portuguese influence in the region did not last long, however. The Portuguese could not withstand attacks by African groups in the region. Other European countries became interested in colonizing Africa.

European Colonial Rule

In the late 1800s, European leaders set out a plan to dominate and control the continent of Africa. The action by which one nation is able to control another smaller or weaker nation is known as **imperialism**.

©Lebrecht Music & Arts/Lebrecht Music & Arts/Corbis

Academic Vocabulary

impact an effect or an influence

The Battle of Omdurman was fought in Sudan in 1898. In this battle, British and Egyptian forces—equipped with modern guns—defeated a much larger Mahdist army that used older weapons.

▶ CRITICAL THINKING
Integrating Visual Information
How does Hale's painting present the battle scene? What view of imperialism does it seem to support?

A painting in traditional Ethiopian style shows King Menelik II receiving ammunition for his army. Menelik worked to bring modern ways to Ethiopia. He especially wanted to prepare his army to successfully resist European invaders.

Africa was carved up into colonies. The reasons for colonization included economic profit, access to raw materials, and the opening of new markets. These reasons also included national pride, the protection of sea routes, the maintenance of the balance of power, and a quest to convert Africans to Christianity.

Occasional rebellions challenged European colonial rule. An especially bloody rebellion occurred against British and Egyptian domination in Sudan. Muhammad Ahmad, a religious and military leader, declared that he was the Mahdi, or redeemer of Islam. Mahdist forces succeeded in capturing Khartoum, the Sudanese capital. They established a new state there. In 1898 the British succeeded in reasserting their control of the region.

Independent Ethiopia

The revolt against foreign influence in Sudan eventually resulted in failure. In Ethiopia, however, the desire for independence prevailed. Italy had colonized the neighboring territory of Eritrea along the Red Sea coast. In 1889 the Italians signed a treaty with the Ethiopian emperor, Menelik II. Over the next few years, Italy claimed that, according to one provision of this treaty, it had the right to establish a "protectorate" in Ethiopia.

Menelik firmly denied these claims. He rejected the treaty in 1893. The Italian governor of Eritrea finally launched a major military attack in response in 1896. At the Battle of Adwa on March 1 of that year, Menelik defeated the Italian army. This conflict was one of the most important battles in African history. After the Battle of Adwa, the European powers had no choice but to recognize Ethiopia as an independent state. Physical geography played an important role in Ethiopia's ability to remain independent. Rugged mountains with difficult terrain provided a barrier that was difficult for attacking forces to overcome.

☑ READING PROGRESS CHECK

Explaining What was the significance of Menelik II's victory at the Battle of Adwa in 1896?

Independence

GUIDING QUESTION *How did the countries of East Africa gain their independence?*

After the end of World War II in 1945, a movement ensued to end colonialism in Africa, Asia, and Latin America. In East Africa, particularly, Europeans were seen as disrupting traditional life. In addition, European countries were weakened by the fighting in World War II. Because of these pressures, Europeans granted East African colonies their independence in the 1960s. However, many of the former colonies faced difficulties in establishing their own countries.

New Nations Form

The early 1960s was a turning point for East Africa. During the period from 1960 to 1963 alone, six East African countries obtained independence: Somalia, Kenya, Uganda, Tanzania, Rwanda, and Burundi.

The achievement of independence in Kenya and Tanzania was especially important. Kenya had been a British colony for about 75 years. British plantation owners dominated the economy. They disrupted the traditional East African agricultural system. Local village agriculture was replaced by the production of cash crops, such as coffee and tea, on a large scale. Native people, such as the Kikuyu, were driven off the land. The British also controlled the government.

A nationalist named Jomo Kenyatta led the political protest movement in Kenya and negotiated the terms of independence for his country. In late 1963, Kenya became independent. Jomo Kenyatta served as the country's first prime minister and later as its president.

Tanzania also sought independence. Before independence, the country was called Tanganyika.

As independent Kenya's first leader, Jomo Kenyatta brought stability and economic growth to the country. When appearing in public, Kenyatta often carried a fly whisk, a symbol of authority in some traditional African societies.

▶ CRITICAL THINKING

Describing How did Kenya win its independence from British rule?

Villagers in South Sudan try to put out fires after warplanes from neighboring Sudan raided the area in early 2012. A year earlier, South Sudan had gained independence from Sudan following years of civil war. However, tensions remained high and conflict continued.

▶ CRITICAL THINKING

Describing Why have some African countries after independence faced civil wars and conflicts with neighboring countries?

When Germany was defeated in World War I, Tanganyika came under British control. Independence was the ultimate goal for Tanganyika—a goal it reached in late 1961. Three years later, the country merged with Zanzibar, and its name was changed to Tanzania.

Highland Countries

The Highland areas had a difficult road to independence. Many ethnic groups in the former colonies were often in conflict with one another. Ethnic tensions have long simmered in Rwanda and Burundi. These countries are home to two rival ethnic groups. The Hutu are in the majority there, and the Tutsi are a minority. In the 1990s, the Hutu-dominated government of Rwanda launched an attack on the Tutsi that amounted to **genocide**—the slaughter of an entire people on ethnic grounds. Hundreds of thousands of people were killed.

Bloodshed also stained the history of Uganda after independence. From 1971 to 1979, the country was ruled by the military dictator Idi Amin. Cruelty, violence, corruption, and ethnic persecution marked Amin's regime. Human rights groups estimate that hundreds of thousands of people lost their lives under his rule. Amin was finally forced to flee into exile. He died in 2003.

The Horn of Africa

The history of Somalia since independence in 1960 offers another example of the problems East African countries have faced. Since the 1970s, Somalia has been scarred by civil war. Border disputes with Ethiopia have also increased instability. Rival clan factions have

Michael Onyiego/AP Images

engaged in bitter feuds. Drought has brought famine to much of the country. In late 1992, the United States led a multinational intervention force in an effort to restore peace to the country. The civil war in Somalia, however, remained unresolved.

The instability, misery, and violence in Somalia also have affected neighboring countries. Thousands of **refugees**, for example, have made their way into Kenya. A refugee is a person who flees to another country for safety.

Elsewhere in the Horn of Africa, more than 30 years of fighting have marked the recent history of Eritrea. This country achieved independence in 1993 after a long struggle with Ethiopia. Access to the sea was an important territorial issue in this conflict. In the years since independence, Eritrea has undertaken military conflicts with Yemen and resumed attacks on Ethiopia. The country is unable to provide enough food for its people. Furthermore, economic progress has been limited because many Eritreans serve in the army rather than in the workforce.

A New Nation

Africa's newest country emerged as a result of civil war. Sudan won independence from Egyptian and British control in 1956. Leaders in southern Sudan were angered because the newly independent Sudanese government had failed to carry out its promise to create a federal system. Southern leaders also feared that the new central government would try to establish an Islamic and Arabic state.

Religion was also an issue that generated conflict. Most people in Sudan are Muslim, but in the southernmost 10 provinces, most people follow traditional African religious practices or the Christian religion. Economic issues are also a problem. The southern provinces hold a large share of the area's petroleum deposits. As a result of the civil war, the country of South Sudan became independent from Sudan in 2011.

Include this lesson's information in your Foldable®.

✅ READING PROGRESS CHECK

Determining Central Ideas How has civil war played an important part in the recent history of East Africa?

LESSON 2 REVIEW

Reviewing Vocabulary

1. What were some of the factors that led European nations to practice *imperialism* in Africa?

Answering the Guiding Questions

2. *Identifying* Discuss two important events that occurred in the history of the Ethiopian kingdom of Aksum.

3. *Identifying* Which two countries took the lead in the European colonization of East Africa in the late 1800s?

4. *Describing* What have been some of the major problems that East African countries have faced in building their nations after achieving independence?

5. *Narrative Writing* You are a modern-day Ibn Battuta, traveling through East Africa. Write a series of journal or diary notes telling about the people you meet and the sights you see there.

ReadingHELPDESK

Academic Vocabulary

- diverse

Content Vocabulary

- **population density**
- **clan**
- **subsistence agriculture**
- **oral tradition**
- **poaching**

TAKING NOTES: *Key Ideas and Details*

Summarizing As you read about East African populations, daily life, culture, and challenges today, use a web diagram like the one here to list facts and details about each important idea.

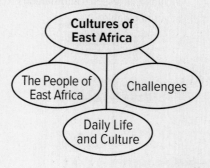

Lesson 3
Life in East Africa

ESSENTIAL QUESTION • *Why does conflict develop?*

IT MATTERS BECAUSE

East Africa is a region of great diversity in ethnicity, religion, and language—not only across the region, but also within individual countries.

The People of East Africa

GUIDING QUESTION *What ethnic groups contribute to the diversity of the population?*

East African countries typically are home to many ethnic groups. Another striking feature in this region is the split between urban and rural populations. Languages and religions make up a mosaic of many different elements.

Where People Live

The population of East Africa is split between large cities and rural areas. Many large cities are on or near the coast of the Indian Ocean (for example, Mogadishu in Somalia, Mombasa in Kenya, and Dar es Salaam in Tanzania). Some large cities, however, developed from important trading centers. Such cities include Nairobi, the capital of Kenya, and Addis Ababa, the capital of Ethiopia.

Of the 11 countries in the region, Ethiopia has the largest population (about 80 million), and Djibouti has the smallest (about 1 million). People are distributed unevenly in East Africa. **Population density** measures how many people live in a given geographical area. A thickly settled area has a high population density. In thinly settled areas, the density is low. In Tanzania, population density varies greatly from one area to another. Overall, Rwanda has the highest population density in the region. Somalia has the lowest.

In Ethiopia, the majority of people live in the central highlands. The warmer and drier areas of lower elevations are thinly inhabited. In Sudan, most people live along the Nile River. Arid parts of the country are thinly populated. In Somalia, most people are nomadic or seminomadic.

Ethnic Groups

The populations of Kenya, Tanzania, and Ethiopia are **diverse** in terms of ethnicity. Sometimes competition among different ethnic groups has led to political and economic conflict. Ethnic identity is closely linked to language and also to geography.

In Kenya, for example, the Kikuyu, Kamba, Meru, and Nyika people inhabit the fertile highlands of the Central Rift. The Luhya live in the Lake Victoria basin. The rural Luo people are located in the lower parts of the western plateau. The Masai people tend their herds of cattle in the south, along the Kenya-Tanzania border. Like the Masai, the Samburu and the Turkana are pastoralists. They live in the arid northwestern region of Kenya.

Another type of ethnic identity is the **clan**. A clan is a large group of people sharing a common ancestor in the far past. A group of related clans is called a clan family. Smaller groups of related people within a clan are called subclans. In Somalia, the basic ethnic unit is the clan.

Tom Cockrem/age fotostock

Academic Vocabulary

diverse having or exhibiting variety

Nairobi, the capital of Kenya, was founded in 1899 as a railway stop between plantations in Uganda and ports on the Kenyan coast. Today, Nairobi is one of East Africa's largest cities, with a population of about 3 million.
▶ **CRITICAL THINKING**
Describing Why are most East African cities located either along the Indian Ocean coast or in inland, highland areas?

In the A.D. 1100s, an Ethiopian king had the Church of St. George carved from solid red volcanic rock. Today, St. George and 10 similar churches in the town of Lalibela attract Ethiopian Christian worshippers as well as tourists from around the world.

Identifying What are the major religions in East Africa today?

In countries that have many diverse ethnic groups, building a sense of national identity is difficult. People often feel a stronger attachment and allegiance to their ethnic group than to their country. A Somali, for example, might feel a greater attachment to his or her clan than to the country of Somalia.

Languages

East Africa is a region where many African languages are spoken. For example, Ethiopians speak about 100 distinct languages. Kenya also has a wide variety of spoken languages. Swahili and English are used by large numbers of people to communicate. Those two languages are the official languages of the Kenyan legislature and of the courts.

Swahili is almost universal in Tanzania. The geographical location and colonial history of East African countries have often made an impact on the languages spoken there. For example, in Somalia the official language is Somali. However, Arabic is widely spoken in the northern area of the country, and Swahili is widespread in the south. In Somalia's colleges and universities, it is not uncommon to hear people speaking English or Italian. In Djibouti, Arabic and French are important languages.

Religion

Most people of East Africa follow either the Christian or Muslim faith. However, a number of traditional African religions also thrive in the region. Traders and missionaries from the Mediterranean region brought Christianity to Ethiopia in the A.D. 300s. The Ethiopian Orthodox Church is one of the world's oldest Christian churches. Today, about 60 percent of Ethiopians are Christians.

©Cameron Davidson/Corbis

In Kenya, the constitution guarantees freedom of religion. Christianity first arrived in Kenya with the Portuguese in the 1400s. But the religion was not practiced for several hundred years, until colonial missionaries arrived in Kenya in the late 1800s. Muslims are an important religious minority in Kenya. Today, Christianity is practiced by more than two-thirds of Kenya's population.

Tanzania is evenly split among Christianity, Islam, and traditional African religions. About one-third of the population follows each one of these three religious traditions.

✔ READING PROGRESS CHECK

Analyzing In a region with such diverse languages, how do you think East Africans can communicate with people outside their own language group?

Life and Culture

GUIDING QUESTION *What is daily life like for people in East Africa?*

In East Africa, traditional customs, as well as the impact of modernization, can be seen in daily life and culture. Culture in East Africa often displays a blend of African and European ways of life.

Daily Life

The rhythms of daily life are varied in East Africa. One factor is where people live: in cities or in rural areas. Most East Africans live in the countryside. But cities are growing rapidly, due to the economic opportunities they provide.

Nairobi is Kenya's capital and most important industrial city. The city is home to more than 3 million people. This makes Nairobi the most populous city in East Africa. It is a city of contrasts. High-rise business and apartment buildings sit near slums built of scrap material.

Daily life in rural areas is quite different from life in the cities. A rural family's housing, for example, might consist of a thatched-roof dwelling with very little in the way of modern or sanitary conveniences. Often, no electricity is available. Some rural people practice **subsistence agriculture**, growing crops to feed themselves and their families. Other rural people grow cash crops to sell.

A Masai mother and son (top) stand outside their home built of mud, sticks, and grass. The Masai people herd cattle on the inland plains of Kenya and Tanzania. A mosque and Islamic-style buildings (bottom) crowd the harbor of Mombasa, a city on Kenya's Indian Ocean coast.

▶ CRITICAL THINKING
Describing How do ways of life differ in East Africa depending on location and culture?

A tarab orchestra performs in Zanzibar, an Indian Ocean island that is part of Tanzania. Tarab is a form of music that began in Zanzibar and spread to other areas. The musician (left) plays a *qanun*, a stringed instrument believed to have been first used in Islamic Persia during the A.D. 900s.

▶ CRITICAL THINKING
Determining Central Ideas
What does a form of music like tarab reveal about East African culture?

In Tanzania, groups such as the Sukuma farm the land south of Lake Victoria. The Chaggas grow coffee in the plains around Kilimanjaro.

The Masai are a nomadic people who live in Tanzania and Kenya. They wander from place to place throughout the year as they tend herds of cattle. Their cattle provide the Masai with most of their diet.

The Masai have developed a unique way of living. Groups of four to eight families build a kraal, or a circular thornbush enclosure. The kraal shelters their herds of livestock. The families live in mud-dung houses inside the kraal.

The governments of Kenya and Tanzania have set up programs to persuade the Masai to abandon their nomadic lifestyle. The governments want to conserve land and protect wildlife, but the Masai have resisted. They want to preserve their way of life.

Arts and Culture

East African culture is deeply influenced by **oral tradition**. This means that stories, fables, poems, proverbs, and family histories are passed by word of mouth from one generation to the next. Folktales and fables offer good examples of oral tradition. In Kenya, the oral tradition functioned in a political way. Hymns of praise were passed on to support independence.

The small country of Djibouti is well known for its colorful dyed clothing. This includes a traditional piece of cloth that men wear around their waist like a skirt. It is common clothing for herders.

A leading novelist in East Africa is Kenya's Ngugi wa Thiong'o. His novel *Weep Not, Child* (1964) is considered the first important English-language novel written by an East African. This book is a story about the effects of conflict on families in Kenya. He also has authored works in the Bantu language of Kenya's Kikuyu people.

In Tanzania, an appealing and popular form of music is *tarab*. This type of music combines African, Arab, and Indian elements and instruments. Tarab has developed an international following. In Kenya, a popular musical style is *benga*. This pop style emerged in the 1960s in the area near Lake Victoria, which is inhabited by the Luo ethnic group.

Charles O. Cecil/Alamy

East Africa is also linked to important findings in the fields of anthropology and ecology. Evidence indicates that East Africa is where human beings originated. The earliest known human bones come from Kenya and Ethiopia. The fossil beds of Olduvai Gorge in northern Tanzania have furnished us with an important record of 2 million years of human evolution.

In the domain of ecology, the national park systems of East Africa have no equal in the world. Protected areas like the Masai Mara National Reserve and Samburu National Reserve in Kenya, the Serengeti National Park in Tanzania, Queen Elizabeth National Park in Uganda, and Volcanoes National Park in Rwanda are preserving a precious inheritance.

☑ READING PROGRESS CHECK

Describing Compare and contrast urban and rural daily life in East Africa.

Challenges

GUIDING QUESTION *How do economic, environmental, and health issues affect the region today?*

Today, the people of East Africa face many complex, challenging issues. Some of the most important challenges involve economic development, the environment, and health.

Economic Development

Agriculture is the main economic activity in East Africa. Farmers in the region, however, face difficult challenges. First, the soils in East Africa are not especially fertile. Second, climate conditions are often unpredictable. Rainfall can be intermittent. Drought can severely damage crops.

Government policies in some countries of East Africa also favor the production of cash crops such as coffee for export. Such policies harm subsistence farmers who attempt to produce enough food to meet local needs. Much of this pattern of growing cash crops results from colonialism. Even after the countries of East Africa gained independence, the practice of growing cash crops for sale continued.

Self-sufficiency is a challenge in East Africa. The region is one of the poorest in the world. In addition, the population of many countries there is growing at a faster rate than the world's average. Industrialization has come slowly for East Africa.

Students view an exhibit of African wildlife at the Kenya National Museum in Nairobi. The museum's purpose is to collect, preserve, study, and present Kenya's cultural and natural heritage.

▶ CRITICAL THINKING

Describing How do East Africans protect living wildlife?

Scores of elephant tusks, seized from illegal poachers, are burned in Kenya. The purpose of the burning was symbolic: to point out the need to keep ivory from reaching international markets and to stop the illegal killing of elephants for their tusks.

Necessary resources such as trained workers, new facilities, and equipment have been lacking. In Ethiopia, for example, manufacturing amounts to only about 10 percent of the economy. Most of Ethiopia's exports are agricultural products. Its most important export is coffee.

The emphasis on primary industries that harvest or extract raw material, such as farming, mining, and logging, is also derived from colonialism. Colonial powers developed their colonies to provide products for the powers. Even after independence, the former colonies continue to produce the same products.

In Tanzania, the economy is mostly agricultural. Many farmers practice subsistence agriculture. Corn (maize), rice, millet, bananas, barley, wheat, potatoes, and cassava are among the important crops. Coffee and cotton are the most important cash crops. Gold is Tanzania's most valuable export.

In parts of East Africa, the economy has suffered because of civil war and political instability. The economy also is linked to the availability of transportation, communication, and education. One key indicator of progress in education is a country's literacy rate. Literacy rates across the region range from a low of 38 percent in Somalia to a high of 87 percent in Kenya.

Environmental Issues

East Africa faces challenging issues related to the environment. The region's lack of electric power has quickened the pace of deforestation. People are cutting down trees to meet their energy needs at an alarming rate. They use the wood to cook food and heat their homes. Along with deforestation, desertification poses serious problems in countries like Sudan.

By setting up national parks and wildlife sanctuaries, the countries of East Africa are hoping that this will boost their economies and preserve their heritage. Ecotourism is tourism for the sake of enjoying natural beauty and observing wildlife. Revenue from ecotourism is important to the East African economy.

Wild animals such as elephants and lions also face the threat of **poaching**. Poaching is the trapping or killing of protected wild animals for the sake of profit in the illegal wildlife trade. African elephants are especially vulnerable to poaching; they are killed for their ivory tusks.

Health Issues

In East Africa, poor nutrition continues to be a difficult problem to overcome. One of the main causes of hunger and malnutrition in the region has been war. Since 1990, conflict in several East African countries has halted economic development and caused widespread starvation. Large numbers of refugees have poured across international borders.

HIV/AIDS is a serious and often fatal disease affecting people in the region. AIDS is an abbreviation that stands for "acquired immune deficiency syndrome." AIDS is caused by a virus that spreads from person to person. This disease continues to be a major health issue in Kenya, Tanzania, and Ethiopia. The resources required for medical education and treatment have put a further strain on East African economies.

Deaths from AIDS have cut the average life expectancy in East Africa. Drought and famine also have an impact on life expectancy. In East Africa, life expectancy at birth is 58 years in Rwanda and 62 years in Sudan. In Kenya, it is 63 years. By contrast, life expectancy in the United States is now about 78.5 years.

Include this lesson's information in your Foldable®.

☑ **READING PROGRESS CHECK**

Citing Text Evidence What is one major cause of deforestation in the region of East Africa?

LESSON 3 REVIEW

Reviewing Vocabulary

1. How might *poaching* affect the economies of some East African countries?

Answering the Guiding Questions

2. ***Determining Central Ideas*** What general statements can you make about the ethnic groups and where people live in East Africa?

3. ***Identifying*** Identify two ways in which trade has played a central role in the history of East Africa.

4. ***Describing*** What are two of the most important challenges confronting East Africa today?

5. ***Informative/Explanatory Writing*** Write a paragraph or two in which you explain some of the environmental issues that confront East Africa today.

Sudan Refugees and Displacement

Sudan has been involved in civil war for many years. Most people in the northern part of Sudan are Arab Muslim and live in cities. People in the southern part are African, rural farmers, and follow either African traditional religions or Christianity.

Geography Sudan is the sixteenth-largest country in the world in area and the third-largest country in Africa. It was the largest before South Sudan gained independence. Sudan's population is 33.4 million. South Sudan has approximately half that number. In land area, South Sudan ranks forty-fourth in the world.

Northern Control As an independent country, northern Sudan and its leaders controlled the government. They wanted to unify Sudan under Arabic and Islamic rule. In opposition were non-Muslims and the people of southern Sudan.

> **By the end of 2010, about 43.7 million people of the world did not have a home.**

Violence Continues When South Sudan became an independent country on July 9, 2011, many people hoped to start a new, peaceful life. However, several violent conflicts broke out, including continued conflict in Darfur.

Conflict in Darfur Darfur is a region in western Sudan. In 2003 Darfur rebel groups rose up against the Sudanese government. The rebels demanded that the government stop its unjust social and economic policies. The government reacted by raiding and burning villages. In the long conflict that followed, thousands were killed, and many were forced from their homes.

Refugees and IDPs Refugees are people who have left their country because they are in danger or have been victims of persecution. A major problem also exists with internally displaced persons (IDPs). An IDP is someone who is forced to flee his or her home because of danger, but who remains in his or her country.

World Refugee Day The United Nations (UN) World Refugee Day is observed every year on June 20. The events call attention to the problems refugees face.

People of South Sudan move to a new refugee camp to escape conflict and hunger. ▶

Paula Bronstein/Getty Images News/Getty Images

©Nichole Sobecki/Corbis

THERE'S MORE ONLINE

SEE a time line of the crisis in Darfur • *WATCH* the Red Cross help refugees

Lesson 3 **367**

These numbers and statistics can help you learn about the problems the Sudanese people face.

$1.25 a day

Although a peace agreement in 2005 brought some stability to the people of South Sudan, many terrible problems exist. More than 80 percent of the residents live on less than $1.25 a day. The country has the world's highest maternal mortality rate. About 50 percent of elementary school-age children do not attend school.

300,000

In 2003 rebellion broke out in Darfur, a region in western Sudan. Government militia attacked Darfur and the rebels. The United Nations estimates that as many as 300,000 people died in five years of conflict in Darfur. Violence still erupts at times, breaking the fragile peace.

More than 500,000

Refugees are people who have left their country because they are in danger or have been victims of persecution. In January 2011, 178,000 refugees were in Sudan, and 387,000 Sudanese who were living in other countries.

one point six million

In January 2011, more than 1.6 million Sudanese people were internally displaced.

two million

South Sudan seceded from Sudan in 2011 as a result of a peace treaty that ended decades of war that had killed 2 million people. The two countries have come close to war again. Disputes over control of territory led to armed conflict.

75%

Oil is a source of conflict between Sudan and South Sudan. About 75 percent of the oil is in South Sudan, but all the pipelines run north to Sudan. When disputes over oil erupted in 2012, Sudan bombed oil fields in South Sudan.

43.7 MILLION

By the end of 2010, about 43.7 million people of the world did not have a home. The number of refugees is the highest in 15 years.

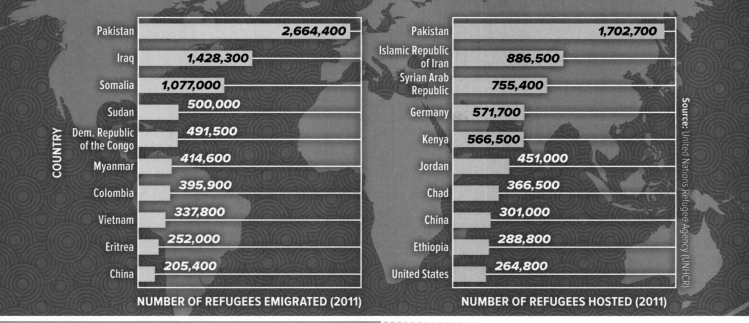

COUNTRY	NUMBER OF REFUGEES EMIGRATED (2011)
Pakistan	2,664,400
Iraq	1,428,300
Somalia	1,077,000
Sudan	500,000
Dem. Republic of the Congo	491,500
Myanmar	414,600
Colombia	395,900
Vietnam	337,800
Eritrea	252,000
China	205,400

	NUMBER OF REFUGEES HOSTED (2011)
Pakistan	1,702,700
Islamic Republic of Iran	886,500
Syrian Arab Republic	755,400
Germany	571,700
Kenya	566,500
Jordan	451,000
Chad	366,500
China	301,000
Ethiopia	288,800
United States	264,800

Source: United Nations Refugee Agency (UNHCR)

GLOBAL IMPACT

MIGRATION OF REFUGEES Refugees are people who flee to another country because of wars, political unrest, food shortages, or other problems. The graph on the left lists the 10 major source countries of refugees and the number of refugees who emigrated from those countries in 2011.

The graph on the right lists the 10 major host countries. A host country is the country a refugee moves to. For example, more than 1.7 million refugees immigrated to Pakistan in 2011.

Sudan and South Sudan

The map shows the two countries, their national capitals, and disputed areas.

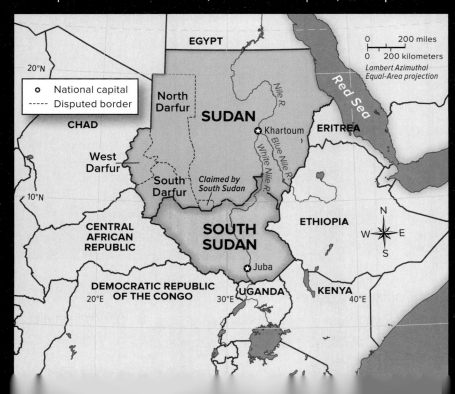

Thinking Like a
Geographer

1. **The Geographer's World** What are the major differences between Sudan and South Sudan?

2. **Human Geography** Why is oil a major factor in the conflict between Sudan and South Sudan?

3. **Human Geography** Imagine you are from Sudan and you come to live in the United States. Write a story about how you and your family learn to live in an American community.

Chapter 12 ACTIVITIES

Directions: Write your answers on a separate piece of paper.

1 Use your **FOLDABLES** to explore the Essential Question.
INFORMATIVE/EXPLANATORY WRITING Review the population map of East Africa at the beginning of the chapter. In two or more paragraphs, explain why people have settled in the locations indicated on the map.

2 **21st Century Skills**
INTEGRATING VISUAL INFORMATION Conduct research and write a paragraph about one of the national park systems in East Africa. Review a partner's paragraph using these questions to guide you: Did the paragraph include relevant details? Was there anything missing that you expected to find in the paragraph? Discuss the review of your paragraph with your partner. Revise your paragraph as needed.

3 **Thinking Like a Geographer**
IDENTIFYING Choose 1 of the 11 countries of East Africa. In a graphic organizer like the one shown, identify the capital city of the country and write two geographical facts about the country.

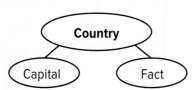

4 **GEOGRAPHY ACTIVITY**

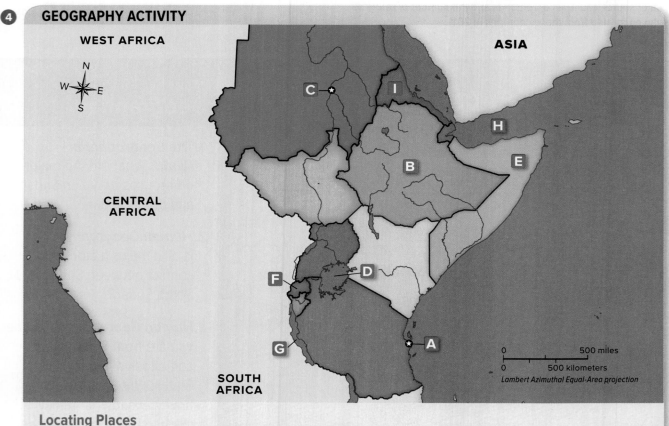

Locating Places
Match the letters on the map with the numbered places listed below.

1. Somalia
2. Eritrea
3. Lake Victoria
4. Khartoum
5. Rwanda
6. Gulf of Aden
7. Ethiopia
8. Lake Tanganyika
9. Dar es Salaam

REVIEW THE GUIDING QUESTIONS

Directions: Choose the best answer for each question.

1 The physical geography and landscape of East Africa are dominated by a series of geological faults collectively known as
A. the Ruwenzori Mountains.
B. the Great Rift Valley.
C. Kilimanjaro.
D. Jonglei.

2 Because of long periods of drought and overgrazing, agricultural land has turned into desert in a process called
F. irrigation.
G. desertification.
H. urbanization.
I. defoliation.

3 Throughout history, the countries of East Africa have been centers of
A. trade.
B. revolution.
C. oil exploration.
D. the slave trade.

4 Most countries in East Africa earned their independence from European colonial powers during which decade of the twentieth century?
F. the 1950s
G. the 1980s
H. the 1940s
I. the 1960s

5 What is the name of the nomadic people who herd cattle and build their mud-dung houses inside a kraal?
A. Samburu
B. Masai
C. Kamba
D. Meru

6 What is the main economic activity in East Africa?
F. manufacturing
G. tourism
H. agriculture
I. oil and gas production

From "Africa's Amazing Rise and What It Can Teach the World," by G. Pascal Zachary, Feb 25, 2012, http://www.theatlantic.com/international/archive/2012/02. Copyright © G. Pascal Zachary; "World's Biggest Refugee Camp in Kenya Marks 20th Anniversary," by Lisa Schlein, February 21, 2012. *Voice of America*, http://voanews.com

DBQ ANALYZING DOCUMENTS

7 ANALYZING Read the following passage about economies in Africa:

"Kenyan farmers, mostly small, are responsible for $1 billion in annual exports of fruits, vegetables, and flowers, a figure that dwarfs the country's traditional coffee and tea exports. . . . Rwanda, . . . long an importer of food, now grows enough to satisfy the needs of its people, and even exports cash crops such as coffee for the first time."

—from G. Pascal Zachary, "Africa's Amazing Rise and What It Can Teach the World" (2012)

Which statement best explains the success of Kenya's farmers?

A. They produced a variety of crops that were in demand.
B. They produced more coffee and tea.
C. They exported cash crops for the first time.
D. They imported food from Rwanda.

8 CITING TEXT EVIDENCE Which sector of Rwanda's economy has seen success?

F. agriculture
G. industry
H. mining
I. service industries

SHORT RESPONSE

"The world's biggest refugee camp, Dadaab, in northeastern Kenya marks its 20th anniversary this year. The camp, which was set up to host 90,000 people, now shelters nearly one-half million refugees. . . . The [United Nations] set up the first camps in Dadaab between October 1991 and June 1992, following a civil war[in Somalia] that continues to this day."

—from Lisa Schlein, "World's Biggest Refugee Camp in Kenya Marks 20th Anniversary" (2012)

9 DETERMINING CENTRAL IDEAS Why was a refugee camp needed?

10 ANALYZING What kinds of facilities would officials need to create to take care of tens of thousands of people?

EXTENDED RESPONSE

11 INFORMATIVE/EXPLANATORY WRITING In an essay, compare and contrast the countries of Somalia and Kenya. Use your text and Internet research to examine each country's physical geography, culture, average income, education levels, type of government, employment, and other factors that affect the way people live. Of the two, which country would you rather live in?

Need Extra Help?

If You've Missed Question	1	2	3	4	5	6	7	8	9	10	11
Review Lesson	1	1	2	2	3	3	3	3	2	2	3

CENTRAL AFRICA

ESSENTIAL QUESTIONS • *How do people adapt to their environment?*
• *How does technology change the way people live?* • *What makes a culture unique?*

A Congolese woman wears the traditional hairstyle that originated in the area long ago.

Andrew McConnell/Robert Harding World Imagery/Getty Images

The Story Matters...

The region of Central Africa straddles the Equator, which creates tropical climates that support the growth of rain forests and savannas. The Congo River—Africa's second-longest river—has so many tributaries that it forms Africa's largest system of waterways. Abundant natural resources in Central Africa greatly influenced its history. Today, the resources are vital to helping nations in the region achieve and maintain stability.

FOLDABLES
Study Organizer

Go to the Foldables® library in the back of your book to make a Foldable® that will help you take notes while reading this chapter.

Central Africa's many rivers are a source of life for people of the region. The geography of the region is dominated by the rain forest basin of the Congo River.

Step Into the Place

MAP FOCUS Use the map to answer the following questions.

1 **THE GEOGRAPHER'S WORLD** How many countries make up the region of Central Africa?

2 **THE GEOGRAPHER'S WORLD** What island country is part of the region?

3 **PLACES AND REGIONS** What is unusual about the capitals of Congo and the Democratic Republic of the Congo?

4 **CRITICAL THINKING** **Analyzing** Which cities in Gabon and Cameroon are located along the coasts? Think about their locations. What economic activities do you think are important in those cities?

ISLAND PARADISE A highway circles the scenic coast of São Tomé, a volcanic island, off the western coast of Central Africa. São Tomé forms part of São Tomé and Príncipe, a small island nation.

COURT MUSICIANS Musicians perform at the palace of one of the traditional kingdoms of Cameroon. Music and dance are an important part of ceremonies and social gatherings in Central Africa.

Step Into the Time

TIME LINE Choose at least two events from the time line to describe the cause-and-effect relationship between natural resources and the slave trade in Central Africa.

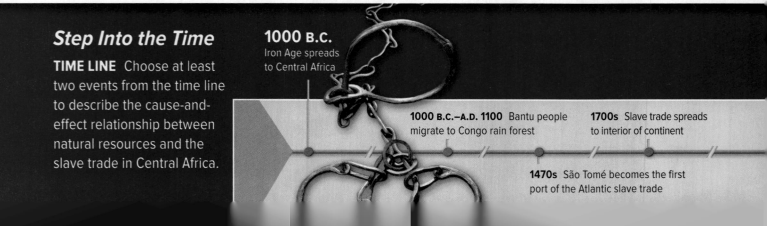

1000 B.C. Iron Age spreads to Central Africa

1000 B.C.–A.D. 1100 Bantu people migrate to Congo rain forest

1470s São Tomé becomes the first port of the Atlantic slave trade

1700s Slave trade spreads to interior of continent

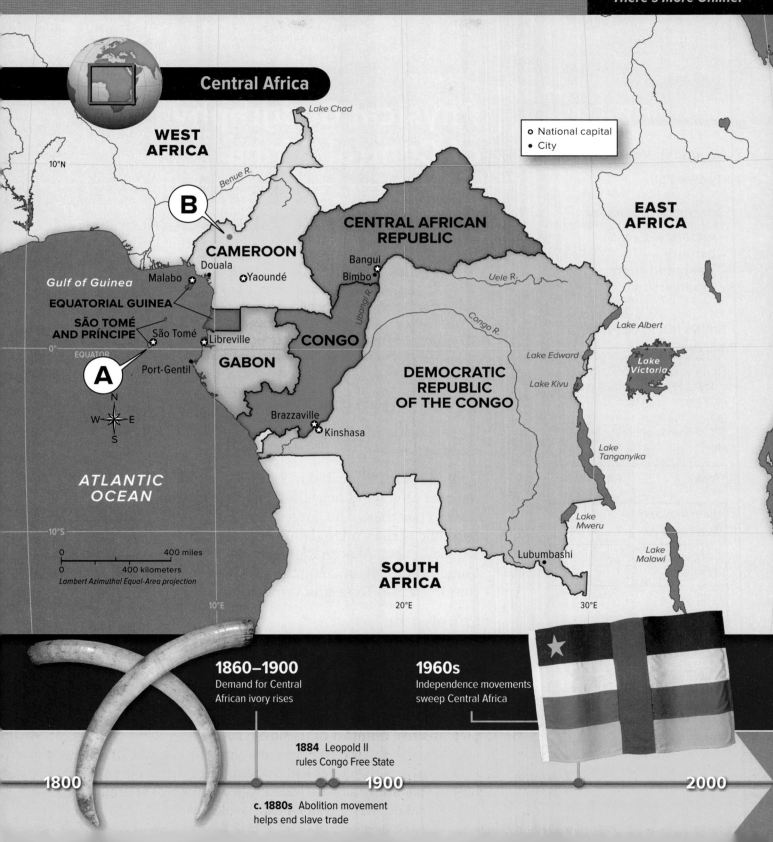

Central Africa

WEST AFRICA

EAST AFRICA

○ National capital
● City

Lake Chad

10°N

Benue R.

B

CAMEROON

CENTRAL AFRICAN REPUBLIC

Bangui
Bimbo

Uele R.

Douala

Malabo

Gulf of Guinea

Yaoundé

EQUATORIAL GUINEA

SÃO TOMÉ AND PRÍNCIPE

São Tomé

Libreville

CONGO

Ubangi R.

Congo R.

Lake Albert

Lake Edward

0° EQUATOR

Lake Victoria

Lake Kivu

A

Port-Gentil

GABON

DEMOCRATIC REPUBLIC OF THE CONGO

N
W E
S

Brazzaville

Kinshasa

Lake Tanganyika

ATLANTIC OCEAN

10°S

0   400 miles
0   400 kilometers
Lambert Azimuthal Equal-Area projection

SOUTH AFRICA

Lubumbashi

Lake Mweru

Lake Malawi

10°E

20°E

30°E

1860–1900
Demand for Central African ivory rises

1960s
Independence movements sweep Central Africa

1884 Leopold II rules Congo Free State

1800

1900

2000

c. 1880s Abolition movement helps end slave trade

networks

There's More Online!

☑ **IMAGES** Slash and Burn Agriculture

☑ **VIDEO**

Reading**HELP**DESK

Academic Vocabulary

- potential

Content Vocabulary

- watershed
- estuary
- slash-and-burn
- biodiversity

TAKING NOTES: *Key Ideas and Details*

Find the Main Idea As you study the lesson, write a main idea about each topic on a graphic organizer. Then write details that support the main idea.

Topic	Main Idea/ Detail
Landforms and Waterways	
Climate and Vegetation	
Natural Resources	

Lesson 1
Physical Geography of Central Africa

ESSENTIAL QUESTION • *How do people adapt to their environment?*

It Matters Because

Central Africa is smaller than many regions, but it holds a tremendous variety of geographic features. These features include a vast rain forest–covered basin, one of the world's greatest river systems, soaring mountains, and a deep rift valley marking the line along which Africa is splitting apart.

Landforms and Waterways

GUIDING QUESTION *What makes some landforms and waterways so important to the region?*

Central Africa is located in Earth's equatorial zone—that is, the area along and near the Equator. The region consists of seven countries. The largest of these is the Democratic Republic of the Congo (DRC). It dwarfs its neighbors, which are the Central African Republic, the Republic of the Congo, Cameroon, Gabon, Equatorial Guinea, and the island country of São Tomé and Príncipe.

Landforms

The dominant landform of Central Africa is the **watershed** of the Congo River. A watershed is the land drained by a river and its system of tributaries. At the center of the watershed is a depression called the Congo Basin. A rolling plain spreads across the center of the basin, and high plateaus rise on most of its sides.

The region's eastern edge runs along the Great Rift Valley, also known as the Great Rift System. Here, rugged mountain ranges soar above a broad, deep valley that holds several long, narrow lakes. Margherita Peak, which rises from a range

(l to r)©Per-Anders Pettersson/Corbis; (2)©Ian Nichols/National Geographic Society/Corbis; (3)©Nigel Pavitt/JAI/Corbis; (4)©FINBARR O'REILLY/Reuters/Corbis

called the Ruwenzori (ROO-un-ZO-ree), reaches the lofty height of 16,763 feet (5,109 m). Margherita Peak is the highest summit in the region and the third highest on the entire continent, ranking after Kilimanjaro and Mount Kenya.

Along the Atlantic coast of Central Africa stretches a narrow lowland. Off the coast lie several important islands. Two of these islands form the country of São Tomé and Príncipe. Two other islands, called Bioko and Pagalu, belong to Equatorial Guinea. This country also includes several smaller islands, as well as a territory on the mainland known as Mbini.

Waterways

Six of the seven countries in Central Africa have coasts on the Atlantic Ocean. The Central African Republic is the region's only landlocked country.

The Congo River and its tributaries account for most of Central Africa's inland waterways. The source of the Congo lies in East Africa between Lake Tanganyika and Lake Malawi (also called Lake Nyasa). From there, the river flows about 2,900 miles (4,667 km) to its mouth on the Atlantic Ocean. Among African rivers, only the Nile is longer than the Congo. When measured by water flow, the Congo tops every river in the world except South America's Amazon.

Difficult Navigation

No other river system in Africa offers as many miles of navigable waterways as the Congo and its tributaries. A navigable river is one on which ships and boats can travel. The Congo River is not navigable for its entire course, however. Several series of cataracts and rapids interrupt the passage of ships on the river.

Perhaps the most significant of these interruptions occurs rather close to the mouth of the Congo River. Only about 100 miles (161 km) from the Atlantic Ocean lie cataracts that block seagoing ships from traveling farther inland. The seaport city of Matadi is found here. Downstream from Matadi, in the final part of its journey, the river widens into an **estuary**, a passage in which freshwater meets salt water.

Fishers in the Democratic Republic of the Congo use bamboo supports to lower their nets into the waters along the rapids of the Congo River.

▶ CRITICAL THINKING

Describing What makes navigation difficult on parts of the Congo River?

A scientist and animal trackers analyze camera trap video of gorillas in a Central African rain forest. A camera trap is a camera equipped with a special sensor that captures images of wildlife on film, when humans are not present.

▶ CRITICAL THINKING

Analyzing How might camera traps aid in protecting Central African wildlife?

The Congo River is important to Central Africa for several reasons. First, it provides a livelihood for people who live along its banks. They use the river's water for agriculture and depend on its fish for food. Second, the river is a vital transportation artery. Although the cataracts and rapids prevent ships from navigating the entire river, ship traffic connects people and places along various sections of the river. Finally, dams on the river generate hydroelectric power.

✓ READING PROGRESS CHECK

Identifying Give two reasons for the Congo River's importance to Central Africa.

Climate and Vegetation

GUIDING QUESTION *What are the prevailing climates in Central Africa?*

Because Central Africa is centered on the Equator, the climate in much of the region is tropical. Temperatures are warm to hot, and rainfall is plentiful. The amount of rainfall generally decreases as distance from the Equator increases. In the northern and southern parts of the region, dry seasons alternate with wet seasons.

Climate Zones

The belt of Central Africa that lies along the Equator has a warm, wet climate. Because of its location, this zone experiences little seasonal variation in weather and length of daylight. The midday sun is directly or almost directly overhead every day, and daytime temperatures are always high. Rainfall is abundant throughout the year, with totals greater than 80 inches (203 cm) in some areas.

To the north and the south of the region's equatorial zone lie tropical wet-and-dry climate zones. As the name suggests, these zones have both rainy and dry seasons. There is great climate variation within the zones. In the areas nearest the Equator, the dry season typically lasts about four months. In the areas farthest from the Equator, it might last as long as seven months.

Rain Forest

A tropical rain forest, the second largest in the world, covers more than half of Central Africa. In this rain-soaked realm, closely packed trees soar as high as 15-story buildings. The forest also holds a tremendous variety of other plants, some of which are used in traditional medicines. Scientists think that only a fraction of the plant species in the forest have been identified. Most remain to be discovered.

The trees and other plants in the rain forest compete for survival. The interwoven crowns of the trees create a dense canopy, or roof, that blocks nearly all of the sunlight, leaving the lower levels in gloom. A tree seedling or sapling can only grow tall if a mature tree dies or if wind blows down some of its branches, creating an opening in the canopy. Because of the lack of sunlight, the forest floor has few of the small plants found in other types of forests. Instead, the forest floor is covered by dead leaves that decompose rapidly in the warm, wet conditions.

Savannas

In the northern and southern areas of Central Africa, rain forests give way to savannas, or areas with a mixture of trees, shrubs, and grasslands. The exact mix of vegetation depends on the length of the dry seasons. Human activity over thousands of years might be responsible for an increase in the size of the savanna areas. Experts believe that the change of forestland into savanna could be the result of clearing land through **slash-and-burn** agriculture.

This form of farming involves turning forestland into cropland. Trees and shrubs are cut down and burned in order to make the soil more fertile, at least temporarily.

Garamba National Park in the Democratic Republic of the Congo is home to the few surviving Northern white rhinoceroses.

©Nigel Pavitt/JAI/Corbis

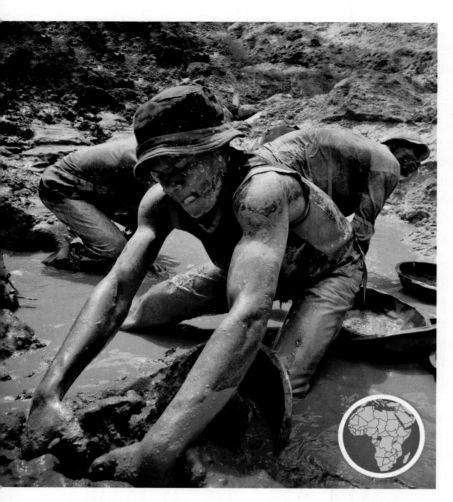

Miners search for gold in an open-pit mine in the northeastern part of the Democratic Republic of the Congo. For more than a decade, rival groups in the DRC have fought each other for control of the country's rich natural resources, such as gold, diamonds, and timber.

Within a few years, the soil becomes depleted and farmers move on. The plots of land are left so that trees and shrubs can return. Then the farmers return and repeat the process of cutting, burning, and farming. Sometimes plots remain fallow—that is, not planted—for as long as 20 years.

Slash-and-burn agriculture provides a livelihood for many people. Others, however, point out that it destroys plant and animal habitat, creates air pollution, and is causing the world's tropical forests to shrink at an alarming rate.

Those who support protecting the environment worry that activities that harm rain forests threaten biodiversity. **Biodiversity** refers to the wide variety of life on Earth. These conservationists argue that if ecosystems are wiped out, numerous valuable species will be lost forever.

✓ **READING PROGRESS CHECK**

Describing Imagine that you live in northern Cameroon. You decide to move to a location in the Republic of the Congo very near the Equator. What changes in climate can you expect?

Natural Resources

GUIDING QUESTION *Which natural resources are important in Central Africa?*

Central Africa is rich in mineral, energy, and other resources. However, many of these resources have not yet been developed.

Mineral Resources

The greatest abundance of mineral resources in Central Africa is found in the Democratic Republic of the Congo. Within that country, the area richest in mineral resources is a province called Katanga. Katanga holds deposits of more than a dozen minerals, including cobalt, copper, gold, and uranium. Minerals mined in other areas of the country include diamonds, iron ore, and limestone.

Gabon produces more than a tenth of the world's supply of manganese. This hard, silvery metal is used in the manufacture of iron and steel. The country also produces uranium, diamonds, and gold, and it holds reserves of high-quality iron ore.

Bauxite and cobalt are among Cameroon's most significant mineral resources. Equatorial Guinea has deposits of uranium, gold, iron ore, and manganese. Most of these deposits have yet to be exploited. Diamond mining is an important industry in the Central African Republic. Rich deposits of uranium, gold, and other minerals could bring the country wealth in the future.

Why have the mineral resources in some parts of Central Africa remained underdeveloped? Political instability, civil conflict, and the high costs of investment have played a role. Perhaps the most important reason, however, is that the region lacks good transportation networks. In the Democratic Republic of the Congo, for example, the Congo River still serves as the major transportation artery. The landlocked Central African Republic also must use rivers for transport. It has few paved roads and no railways. Similarly, most roads in Equatorial Guinea are unpaved and there is no railway system.

Other Resources

The region is rich in resources other than minerals. In the Democratic Republic of the Congo, for example, rapids and waterfalls on the Congo River and its tributaries offer vast **potential** for hydroelectric power. The forest reserves of the DRC are rivaled by few countries in the world. Fish from the ocean and its fresh water systems provide another important resource.

Developing these resources, however, will affect the environment. Damming rivers for hydroelectric power results in large changes to river ecosystems. Deforestation and habitat change occur when forests are cut.

In the 1990s, large reserves of petroleum and natural gas were discovered under the seafloor off Equatorial Guinea's Atlantic Coast. The export of oil and gas products have boosted the country's economy.

Likewise, petroleum has been Cameroon's leading export since 1980. The country also has natural gas deposits, but the high cost of development has kept them untapped. Nearly all of Cameroon's energy comes from dams that generate hydroelectricity.

☑ READING PROGRESS CHECK

Identifying Central Issues What are two of the factors that have slowed development of Central Africa's rich natural resources?

Academic Vocabulary

potential possible; capable of becoming

Include this lesson's information in your Foldable®.

LESSON 1 REVIEW

Reviewing Vocabulary

1. Why might *slash-and-burn agriculture* be harmful to a country's land in the long term?

Answering the Guiding Questions

2. *Analyzing* What comparisons can you make between the Congo River in Central Africa and two of the other great rivers of the world: the Nile and the Amazon?

3. *Describing* What conclusion can you make about the prevailing climate conditions in areas near the Equator?

4. *Analyzing* How would you evaluate Central Africa's hydroelectric potential?

5. *Argument Writing* Write a letter to a friend to persuade him or her to invest in mineral production in Central Africa. In your letter, use some of the information you have learned in this lesson.

(l to r)Gary John Norman/Alamy; (2)Mary Evans Picture Library/Alamy; (3)SZ Photo/Scherl/Alamy Stock Photo; (4)INTERFOTO/Personalities/Alamy

ReadingHELPDESK

Academic Vocabulary

- **foundation**

Content Vocabulary

- **millet**
- **palm oil**
- **cassava**
- **colonialism**
- **missionary**
- **coup**

TAKING NOTES: *Key Ideas and Details*

Organize Use a diagram like this one to note important information about the history of Central Africa, adding one or more facts to each of the boxes.

Topic	Information
Products	Millet Sorghum
European contact	Slave trade

Lesson 2
History of Central Africa

ESSENTIAL QUESTION • *How does technology change the way people live?*

IT MATTERS BECAUSE
Central Africa's past is a fascinating and often tragic story involving migrations, slavery, exploitation by foreign powers, and the struggle for independence, stability, and prosperity.

Early Settlement

GUIDING QUESTION *How did agriculture and trade develop in Central Africa?*

Through most of the prehistoric period, the people of Central Africa were hunters and gatherers who survived on wild game and wild plants. Eventually, climate changes forced the people to develop new ways of life.

Development of Agriculture

Around 10,000 years ago, Earth's climate entered a dry phase. Vegetation patterns changed in response and led to the movement of people. The changes also intensified the struggle for survival. The region's inhabitants were forced to find ways to get more food from a smaller area of their environment.

Gradually, a transformation that historians call the agricultural revolution swept through the region, beginning in the north. People began to collect plants—especially roots and tubers—on a more regular basis. They developed and refined tools such as stone hoes that were specially designed for digging. They discovered that if they planted a piece of a root or tuber in fertile soil, a new plant would grow from it. Over time, the hunters and gatherers turned into farmers.

Cereal farming was the next agricultural development in Central Africa. In the savannas of the north, people began cultivating **millet** and sorghum, two wild grasses that produce edible seeds. Millet proved to be especially well-suited to the area's climate. The crop thrives in high temperatures and is resistant to drought.

In addition to growing crops, Central Africa's early farmers cultivated trees and gathered their fruit. From the fruit of oil palms they made a cooking oil that was rich in proteins and vitamins. The nutrition boost provided by **palm oil** helped people to become healthier, and improved health brought about population growth.

The increase in the food supply from the practice of agriculture meant that people could live in larger, more settled communities. The agricultural revolution laid the **foundation** for village life and also for the development of items used in daily life.

Academic Vocabulary

foundation the basis of something

Using Mineral Resources

Since early times, people in Central Africa have made tools from stone. Around 3,000 years ago, they began using a new material that was far better in many ways: iron. Iron tools were expensive and could only be made by skilled artisans, but they were far more efficient and less brittle than stone tools.

In addition to iron, people in ancient Central Africa made use of other minerals, especially copper and salt. These resources played an important role in trade.

☑ READING PROGRESS CHECK

Determining Central Ideas Why was the agricultural revolution so important for the development of Central Africa as a region?

European Contact and Afterward

GUIDING QUESTION *How did colonization by foreign countries affect Central Africa?*

Regular contact with Europeans, which began in the 1400s, marked the start of a new era in Central Africa's history.

The Slave Trade

As European ships began reaching the Atlantic coast of Central Africa in the 1400s, the region began developing into one of the busiest hubs of the slave trade. The trade was driven because European colonizers demanded a large workforce for their huge plantations in the Americas. The slave trade would continue and grow for more than three centuries.

The first European country to become actively involved in the slave trade was Portugal. In the late 1400s, the Portuguese established a colony on the island of São Tomé in order to grow sugar.

A woman in Cameroon carries fruit from oil palm trees to market. The pulp from this fruit is used to make cooking oil. Some environmentalists fear that the creation of more palm oil plantations in the country will endanger the livelihood of small farmers and lead to the destruction of existing rain forests.

Gary John Norman/Alamy

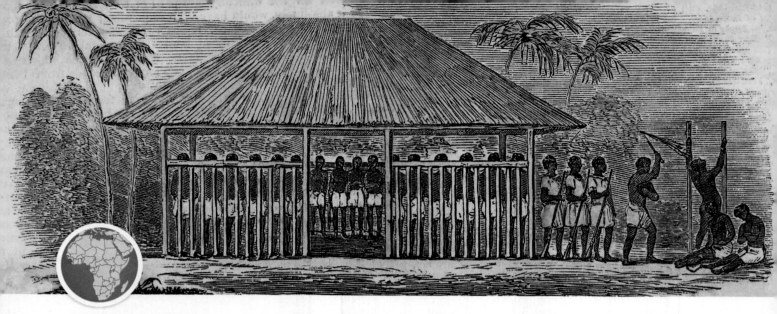

Slave traders held people who were captured for slavery in *barracoons*, or sheds. There, the captives stayed for several months before they were sold and shipped to the Americas. During imprisonment, the captives were chained by the neck and legs and often beaten.

▶ CRITICAL THINKING
Determining Word Meaning
What was the Middle Passage?

Later, this island became a staging area for the transportation of African slaves to Portugal's main conquest in the Western Hemisphere: Brazil in South America.

Gabon served as one of the most important centers of the slave trade. Slaves were gathered in the country's interior and taken on boats to a coastal inlet called the Gabon Estuary. Some of these slaves were people who had been cast out of their own societies. Others had been captured in warfare. At settlements on the estuary, the slaves were held in enclosures known as barracoons until European ships arrived.

The slave trade was part of what is sometimes called the "triangular trade," named for the triangular pattern formed by the three stages of the trade. In the first stage, ships would sail to Africa with cargoes of manufactured goods such as cloth, beads, metal goods, guns, and liquor. These goods would be traded for slaves. In the second stage, known as the Middle Passage, the ships would carry their human cargo to the Americas. There, the slaves would be exchanged for goods such as rum, tobacco, molasses, and cotton that were produced on slave-labor plantations. In the third stage, the ships would return to Europe. Ships of the time were powered by wind, and each stage followed the direction of prevailing winds.

Adoption of New Crops

After European countries established colonies in the Americas, they brought some of the native plants back to Europe and to Africa. Two plants in particular had an important effect on farming and diet in Central Africa. These were cassava and maize.

The **cassava** plant has thick, edible roots known as tubers. Rich in nutritious starch, the tubers are used to make flour, breads, and tapioca. The plant thrives in hot, sunny climates and is able to survive droughts and locust attacks. Historians believe that Portuguese ships brought cassava to Africa from Brazil. Today, cassava is a staple food for many of Africa's people.

Maize, often called corn, is one of the most important staple grains of the Western Hemisphere. Today it is the most widely grown grain crop in the Americas. Maize was domesticated in prehistoric times, probably in Central America. It was carried around the world by Europeans after their discovery of the Americas.

Colonialism

Colonialism is the political and economic rule of one region or country by another country, usually for profit. European countries began to practice colonialism in the 1500s and 1600s. They first founded colonies in the Americas for economic gain.

Colonialism came much later to Central Africa. Exploration and settlement by Europeans was impeded by the difficulty of transportation, the presence of tropical diseases like malaria, and other challenges. In the second half of the 19th century, however, European presence in the region began to grow sharply.

In 1884–1885, Germany hosted a landmark conference of European countries in the city of Berlin. The countries attending the conference agreed on a plan for dividing Africa into colonies that could be exploited for European profit.

King Leopold II of Belgium was among the strongest supporters of the conference. He believed that a fortune could be made from rubber plants. Rubber was one of the most plentiful and valuable natural resources of Central Africa. After 1885, King Leopold took over a vast area that came to be known as the Congo Free State. The king held the area as a personal possession, and he did indeed make a fortune.

Belgium's King Leopold II (oval) turned his privately owned Congo territory into a large labor camp for the harvesting of rubber. African workers (below) were overseen by European officials. Nearly 10 million Africans died of overwork or cruelty under Leopold's direct rule.

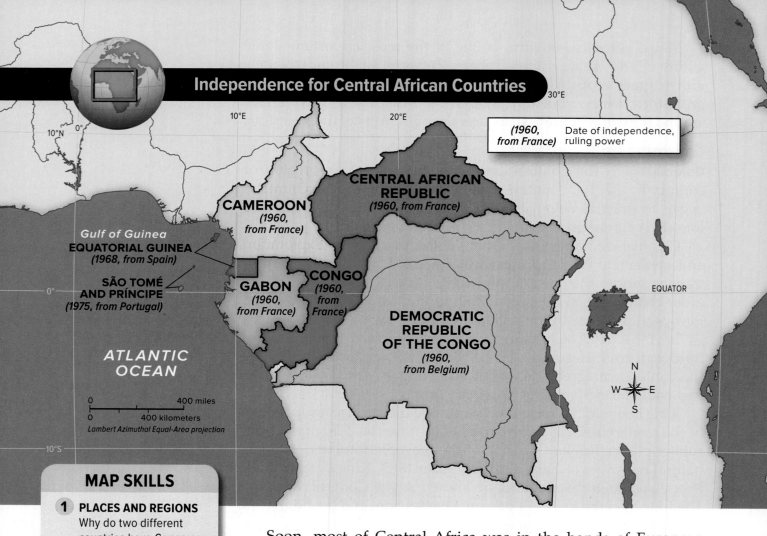

(1960, from France) Date of independence, ruling power

CENTRAL AFRICAN REPUBLIC (1960, from France)

CAMEROON (1960, from France)

Gulf of Guinea

EQUATORIAL GUINEA (1968, from Spain)

SÃO TOMÉ AND PRÍNCIPE (1975, from Portugal)

GABON (1960, from France)

CONGO (1960, from France)

DEMOCRATIC REPUBLIC OF THE CONGO (1960, from Belgium)

EQUATOR

ATLANTIC OCEAN

0   400 miles
0   400 kilometers
Lambert Azimuthal Equal-Area projection

10°N   0°   0°
10°E
20°E
30°E
0°
10°S

N W E S

MAP SKILLS

1 PLACES AND REGIONS Why do two different countries have Congo as part of their name?

2 THE GEOGRAPHER'S WORLD What country of Central Africa is landlocked?

Soon, most of Central Africa was in the hands of European colonizers. France gained control of what is now the Republic of the Congo, Gabon, and the Central African Republic. Spain colonized what is now Equatorial Guinea, while Germany ruled Cameroon. Portugal retained possession of São Tomé and Príncipe.

Europeans often justified their economic exploitation of Africa by claiming that their goal was to promote civilization and to spread Christianity. Europeans sent many **missionaries** to Africa in order to convert the native people.

At the same time, Europeans often treated the African workers under their control harshly. By the early 1900s, small revolts against French rule and the plantation-based economy were common. In the Congo Free State, the people suffered severe hardships and cruel treatment under King Leopold. Pressured by growing outrage from around the world, the Belgian parliament took over the vast area from King Leopold. It became an official colony of Belgium and was known as the Belgian Congo.

✓ READING PROGRESS CHECK

Determining Central Ideas How was Central Africa affected by a conference held in Germany in the mid-1880s?

Independent Countries

GUIDING QUESTION *What effects did gaining independence have on the countries of Central Africa?*

Near the middle of the 20th century, European countries became willing to grant independence to their African colonies. All seven of Central Africa's countries gained their independence in the period from 1960 to 1975.

A Wave of Independence

In 1960 France was the most important European colonial power in Central Africa. That year witnessed the independence of four French colonies: Gabon, the Republic of the Congo, the Central African Republic, and Cameroon, which France had gained from Germany during World War I. In the same year, the Democratic Republic of the Congo won independence from Belgium.

Many of these new countries experienced hard times after independence. Their people suffered through periods of ethnic conflict, harsh rule, and human rights abuses. In the Central African Republic, military officer Jean-Bédel Bokassa staged a **coup**. He ruled as a dictator and proclaimed himself the country's emperor. He brutally punished anyone who protested against his rule.

There have also been success stories, such as Gabon. Thanks in large part to its plentiful natural resources, Gabon has become one of the wealthiest and most stable countries in Africa.

Smaller Countries

Equatorial Guinea won independence from Spain in 1968. The country's first president, Francisco Macías Nguema, soon took over the government and became a ruthless dictator. In 1979, he was ousted by his nephew, who also ruled with an iron hand.

Portugal granted independence to São Tomé and Príncipe in 1975. With independence came great hope for the future. Like many of its neighbors, however, the country has been plagued by political instability and corruption.

☑ **READING PROGRESS CHECK**

Identifying Since the countries of the region gained independence, list at least two factors that have limited their political and economic progress.

Include this lesson's information in your Foldable®.

LESSON 2 REVIEW

Reviewing Vocabulary

1. Why was *millet* a suitable grain for planting in Central Africa?

Answering the Guiding Questions

2. ***Determining Central Ideas*** Why might tools made from iron be superior to tools made from stone?

3. ***Identifying*** What were two major motivations for the European colonization of Central Africa?

4. ***Analyzing*** In what way was the rule of Bokassa in the Central African Republic similar to the rule of Nguema in Equatorial Guinea?

5. ***Informative/Explanatory Writing*** Write a few paragraphs explaining the development of the slave trade in Central Africa.

netw⊙rks

There's More Online!

☑ **SLIDE SHOW** Types of Housing in Central Africa

☑ **VIDEO**

Reading**HELP**DESK

Academic Vocabulary

- **characteristic**
- **depict**

Content Vocabulary

- **refugee**
- **trade language**

TAKING NOTES: *Key Ideas and Details*

Find the Main Idea As you study the lesson, create a chart like this one, and fill in at least two key facts about each topic.

Topic	Fact #1	Fact #2
People		
Daily Life and Culture		

Lesson 3
Life in Central Africa

ESSENTIAL QUESTION • *What makes a culture unique?*

IT MATTERS BECAUSE
Central Africa is characterized by tremendous diversity in terms of its people, population patterns, languages, arts, and daily life.

The People of Central Africa

GUIDING QUESTION *What are some of the differences found among the people of Central Africa?*

Many different ethnic groups live in Central Africa. Each group is united by a shared language and culture.

Makeup of the Population

Central Africa is home to around 105 million people, which is roughly one-third as many as the United States has. The Democratic Republic of the Congo is by far the most populous country: It holds more than two-thirds of the region's people. Compared to other parts of the world, Central Africa does not have a large population or a high population density. However, its countries have high population growth rates. In all seven countries, the median age is below 20, which means that children and teenagers make up about half of the population. By comparison, the median age in the United States is about 37.

Life expectancy at birth for the people of the region varies considerably. In the Central African Republic, for example, life expectancy is about 50 years, while in Equatorial Guinea and São Tomé and Príncipe, it is around 63.

Hundreds of ethnic groups live in the region. Cameroon and the DRC each are home to more than 200 different groups. Some groups spread into two or more countries. One

(l to r)MJ Photography/Alamy; (2)Eye Ubiquitous/Newscom; (3)Junior D. Kannah/AFP/Getty Images; (4)©Pascal Deloche/Godong/Corbis

such group is called the Fang. Historians believe the Fang once dwelled on the savanna. In the late 18th century, they began a migration into the rain forests. Today they live in mainland Equatorial Guinea, northern Gabon, and southern Cameroon.

Another people found in the region is the Bambuti, sometimes called the Mbuti. The Bambuti live in densely forested areas of the Democratic Republic of the Congo. They are extremely short in stature: Adults average less than 4 feet 6 inches (137 cm) in height. They were probably the earliest inhabitants of an area known as the Ituri Forest. Historical records show that the Bambuti have lived in this area for at least 4,500 years as nomadic hunters and gatherers.

The population of Central Africa also includes many refugees. **Refugees** are displaced people who have been forced to leave their homes because of war or injustice. Between 1997 and 2003, for example, a brutal civil war devastated the Democratic Republic of the Congo. A huge number of refugees fled the conflict.

City and Country

Most of Central Africa's people live in the rural areas and make their living through subsistence farming. In the DRC, for example, almost two-thirds of the people live in the country.

Large urban areas dot the region, however. More importantly, the ratio of city-dwellers to rural residents is changing rapidly. For example, every year, the DRC's urban areas gain about 4.5 percent of the population. Many of the chief cities of the region are capitals of countries. Kinshasa, the capital of the DRC, has grown into a sprawling metropolis with around 9 million inhabitants. Just across the Congo River from Kinshasa sits Brazzaville, the capital of the Republic of the Congo. Brazzaville is home to about 1.6 million people.

Government buildings surround a busy central square in Brazzaville, capital of the Republic of the Congo. Brazzaville is located on the north bank of the Congo River, just across from Kinshasa, the capital of the neighboring Democratic Republic of the Congo. This is the only place in the world where two national capital cities are located on opposite sides of a river, within sight of each other.

Village women of the Hutu ethnic group prepare a meal in the eastern part of the Democratic Republic of the Congo. The Hutu are one of hundreds of ethnic groups in Central Africa.

▶ CRITICAL THINKING

Describing Why did trade languages emerge in Central Africa?

In a few countries in this region, more than half the people live in cities. In Gabon, for example, city-dwellers account for 86 percent of the total population. In the Central African Republic, the figure is 62 percent, and in Cameroon it is 58 percent. Cameroon's two major cities, Douala and Yaoundé, each have populations of around 2 million, roughly the population of Houston or Philadelphia.

Language and Religion

Because Central Africa's population is made up of hundreds of different ethnic groups, it is not surprising that hundreds of different languages are spoken across the region. Cameroon, which has been described as an ethnic crossroads, serves as an example of the region's linguistic diversity. Three main language families are used in Cameroon. In the north, where Islam has been a significant influence, the languages spoken are in the Sudanic family. The Sudanic-speaking people in this part of Cameroon include the Fulani, the Sao, and the Kanuri. The Fulani are Muslims. They began migrating into Cameroon from what is now Niger more than 1,000 years ago. In the southern part of Cameroon, people speak Bantu languages. In the west are found semi-Bantu speakers, such as the Bamileke and the Tikar.

During the colonial era, people searched for common linguistic ground, especially when they traded with one another. Certain **trade languages** emerged. Because France and Belgium had the most widespread interest in the region, French became the most common trade language of Central Africa.

Central Africa is also diverse in terms of religion. In the Democratic Republic of the Congo, for example, roughly 50 percent of the people are Roman Catholic, 20 percent are Protestant, 10 percent are Muslim, and 10 percent belong to a local sect called the Kimbanguist Church. The remaining 10 percent follow traditional African religions, which are based on a core set of beliefs, including the existence of a supreme being, the presence of spirits in the natural world, and the power of ancestors and magic.

☑ READING PROGRESS CHECK

Describing Where do most of Central Africa's people live? How do they make their living?

How People Live

GUIDING QUESTION *What are some of the key aspects of daily life and culture in Central Africa?*

In Central Africa, daily life and culture reflect the variety of influences to which the region has been exposed.

Daily Life

Daily life in Central Africa is a blend of traditional and modern **characteristics**. This combination results mainly from the impact of colonialism. It also reflects the urban-rural division of the population.

In the countryside, most people practice subsistence farming. On small plots of land, they grow crops such as cassava, maize, and millet, and they raise livestock. They strive to grow enough crops and raise enough animals to feed themselves and their families. If any surplus remains, they may sell it for small amounts of cash. Most people in the countryside live in small houses that they have built themselves. Building materials include mud, sundried mud bricks, wood, bark, and cement. For roofs, people typically use palm fronds woven together or sheets of corrugated iron.

One of the most common methods of constructing houses is known as wattle-and-daub. Poles driven into the ground are woven with slender, flexible branches or reeds to create the wattle. The finished wattle is plastered with mud or clay, known as daub. Then, a palm-frond roof is placed on top of the house.

In much of rural Central Africa, women carry out the gathering, production, and preparation of food for the household. The men hunt, trap, and fish. In addition to growing food to eat, men and women may also grow crops for sale, such as coffee, cotton, and cocoa.

Okra, corn, and yams are staple vegetables in the diets of many Central Africans. Other important foods are cassava, sweet potatoes, rice, beans, and plantains. Game is popular, as are fish-based dishes. Peanuts, milk, and poultry add protein to many dishes.

Academic Vocabulary

characteristic a quality or an aspect

Many food-related customs of Central Africa may seem surprising. In some areas, for example, males eat in one room while females eat in another. Generosity and hospitality are so deeply ingrained in some cultures that hosts might offer guests an abundance of food while remaining hungry themselves.

In many Central African cities, traditional ways of life are yielding to contemporary lifestyles. Modernization, however, has not always come easily. Central Africa has little infrastructure, which includes the fundamental facilities and systems that serve a city, an area, or a country. In the Central African Republic, for example, only a few cities and towns have modern health care facilities. Other obstacles to modernization include poor transportation and educational systems.

Culture and Arts

The visual, verbal, and performing arts are important to the cultures of many ethnic groups in Central Africa. In the southwestern part of the DRC, for example, the people known as the Kongo produce wooden statues in which nails and other pieces of metal are embedded. The Yaka create highly decorative masks and figurines. The Luba people of the southeastern part of the country are known for their skillful carvings that **depict** women and motherhood. The Mangbetu people of the northeast are known internationally for their pottery and sculpture.

In the field of literature, several modern Congolese authors are internationally recognized as poets, playwrights, and novelists. They include Clémentine Madiya Faik-Nzuji, Kama Kamanda, Ntumb Diur, and Timothée Malembe.

The DRC's capital city of Kinshasa is known around the world for its thriving music scene. The most popular style is African jazz, known as OK jazz. This style originated in the nightclubs of Kinshasa in the 1950s.

In northern Cameroon, the Fulani people decorate leather items and gourds with elaborate geometric designs. In music, the country's southern forest region is known for its drumming. In the north, the focus is on flute music.

Equatorial Guinea was formerly a colony of Spain, and Spanish influence can be tasted in the country's cuisine. In Malabo, the capital city, Spanish styles are found in the architecture. The country has produced several writers whose Spanish-language works have become known around the world.

☑ **READING PROGRESS CHECK**

Determining Word Meanings What is the main goal of subsistence farmers?

Junior D. Kannah/AFP/Getty Images

Musicians of the Congolese Symphony Orchestra perform in Kinshasa, capital of the DRC.
▶ CRITICAL THINKING
Describing Why is Kinshasa widely regarded as one of the music centers of the world?

Regional Issues

GUIDING QUESTION *What are the greatest challenges confronting Central Africa?*

Central Africa's people and governments face many complex issues. Among the issues are the economy, the environment, political stability, and population growth.

Growth and the Environment

With great population growth comes the need for economic development. The economies of many countries in the region depend heavily on agriculture, logging, and mining. Central African countries such as Gabon and Equatorial Guinea export significant amounts of valuable hardwoods, including mahogany, ebony, and okoumé.

In general, economic development depends on economic growth. Economic growth usually means that more resources are used and more pollution and waste are produced. In Central Africa, economic activities such as mining and logging are taking place in areas of high biodiversity. Some conservationists fear that this biodiversity is being lost in the rush to exploit resources.

The result is tension between the forces of economic growth and the forces of environmental conservation. In some areas, these tensions have at times led to conflict between local people and outside groups.

Development in Central Africa also raises other questions. Should the profits from economic activities go to foreign corporations and investors, or should they remain with the national governments? How should the profits and economic benefits be shared by the people?

✔ **READING PROGRESS CHECK**

Describing Why are some people critical of mining and logging activities in the region?

A nurse checks a patient's treatment chart at a clinic in Brazzaville, Republic of the Congo.

©Pascal Deloche/Godong/Corbis

FOLDABLES®
Study Organizer

Include this lesson's information in your Foldable®.

LESSON 3 REVIEW

Reviewing Vocabulary
1. Why was the use of a trade language helpful in Central Africa?

Answering the Guiding Questions
2. *Describing* What are two distinctive features of the Bambuti people, who live in the rain forests of the Democratic Republic of the Congo?

3. *Determining Central Ideas* What are some of the customs in Central Africa related to food?

4. *Analyzing* Why has the lack of political stability posed major problems for development in some Central African countries?

5. *Informative/Explanatory Writing* Write a paragraph or two in which you explain some of the economic issues confronting Central Africa.

Lesson 3 **393**

What Do You Think?

Has the United Nations Been Effective at Reducing Conflict in Africa?

The 53 independent states of Africa share one continent, but the vast land holds different people and varied resources and economies. During the past six decades, armed political conflict, either within a nation or between nations, has been the norm rather than the exception for many Africans. Since 1945, the United Nations (UN) Security Council, in its resolve to maintain international peace and security, has mounted 29 peacekeeping missions in Africa. Have the efforts of the United Nations been effective?

No !

PRIMARY SOURCE

" Africa has thus been a giant laboratory for UN peacekeeping and has repeatedly tested the capacity and political resolve of an often self-absorbed Security Council. . . . Under the loose heading of peacekeeping, the UN launched an unprecedented number of missions in the post–Cold War era. But . . . hard times appeared after disasters in Angola in 1992, when warlord Jonas Savimbi brushed aside a weak UN peacekeeping mission to return to war after losing an election; in Somalia in 1993, when the UN withdrew its peacekeeping mission after the death of eighteen U.S. soldiers; and in Rwanda in 1994, when the UN shamefully failed to halt genocide against about eight hundred thousand people and instead withdrew its peacekeeping force from the country. These events scarred the organization and made its most powerful members wary of intervening in Africa: an area generally of low strategic interest to them. "

—Adekeye Adebajo, Director, Centre for Conflict Resolution, University of Cape Town, South Africa, in *UN Peacekeeping in Africa: From the Suez Crisis to the Sudan Conflicts*

A militiaman stands guard with a machine gun in Somalia. The East African country has had political upheaval since 1991. Islamic militia forces and UN-backed government forces compete for control of Somalia.

TEXT: From UNITED NATIONS SECURITY COUNCIL SPECIAL RESEARCH REPORT NO. 2: THE PEACEBUILDING COMMISSION. 17 November 2009. <www.securitycouncilreport.org/site/c.glKWLeMTIsG/b.5604169/k.E023/Special_Research_Report_No_2brThe_Peacebuilding_Commissionbr17_November_2009.htm>; PHOTO: ©Gideon Mendel/Corbis

Troops from Thailand have contributed to UN–African Union peacekeeping efforts in the war-torn Darfur region of Sudan. In Darfur, the Thai troops conducted patrols and provided protection to civilians and humanitarian aid workers.

Yes !

PRIMARY SOURCE

" Bearing in mind the relatively young period of existence of the PBC [Peacebuilding Commission] (and the fact that inevitably it was experimenting in its first two years), Sierra Leone and Burundi—the first two countries placed on the PBC agenda—seem to have achieved some real success in consolidating peace. Burundi has made headway with its peace process, including the gains relating to its inclusive political dialogue. Sierra Leone has also chalked up significant milestones and emerged as a post conflict state on the tracks of peace consolidation, with clear reforms in socioeconomic and security sector aspects. Both countries have also had to deal with some potentially serious setbacks and in both cases it seems that the proactive involvement of the PBC has added value in overcoming those problems. "

—Security Council Report, Special Research Report No. 2, The Peacebuilding Commission, 17 November 2009

What Do You Think? | DBQ

1. **Identifying Point of View** What evidence does the Yes answer contain to support its viewpoint? What evidence does the No answer contain to support its viewpoint?

2. **Distinguishing Fact From Opinion** The two sources state facts and opinions. Identify one fact and one opinion from each source.

Critical Thinking

3. **Analyzing** Weigh the evidence. Africa has had 29 peacekeeping missions in roughly 60 years. If the United Nations has to keep going back, have the missions been effective? Why or why not?

Directions: Write your answers on a separate piece of paper.

1 Use your FOLDABLES to explore the Essential Question.

INFORMATIVE/EXPLANATORY WRITING Some geographers believe the area of Central Africa that is now savanna was at one time forestland. What might have changed the physical composition of this area? Write a short essay discussing this hypothesis. How does this relate to the concept of people adapting to the environment?

2 21st Century Skills

IDENTIFYING Use the text and the Internet to find information about one of the countries of Central Africa. List important resources for that country.

3 Thinking Like a Geographer

ANALYZING Much of Central Africa depends on agriculture as a main economic activity. Why is a good transportation system important to an agricultural society?

4 GEOGRAPHY ACTIVITY

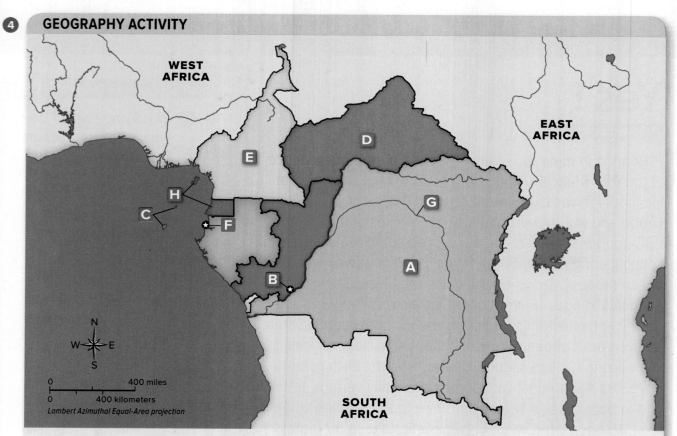

Locating Places

Match the letters on the map with the numbered places below.

1. Libreville
2. Congo River
3. Equatorial Guinea
4. Democratic Republic of the Congo
5. Brazzaville
6. Central African Republic
7. Cameroon
8. São Tomé and Príncipe

REVIEW THE GUIDING QUESTIONS

Directions: Choose the best answer for each question.

1 Choose Central Africa's primary landform.
   A. islands
   B. caves
   C. Congo River watershed
   D. steppes

2 Because Central Africa is centered on the Equator, its climate is
   F. Mediterranean.
   G. tropical.
   H. arid.
   I. mild.

3 Why were Europeans slow to establish colonies in Central Africa?
   A. The area had no worthwhile natural resources to exploit.
   B. They couldn't decide how to share the African countries.
   C. Transportation was difficult, and they feared malaria and other diseases.
   D. They didn't want to convert people.

4 The Republic of the Congo was a colony of which country?
   F. Spain
   G. France
   H. Portugal
   I. England

5 Most of the population of Central Africa makes a living by means of
   A. subsistence farming.
   B. factory labor.
   C. crafting.
   D. foreign trade.

6 Identify an obstacle to developing a modern economy in Central Africa.
   F. diverse populations
   G. commitment to traditional religions
   H. primitive housing construction
   I. insufficient infrastructure, poor transportation, and poor education

DBQ ANALYZING DOCUMENTS

7 **ANALYZING INFORMATION** Read the following passage about European colonial rule in Africa:

"The manner in which colonial administrations governed virtually ensured the failure of Africa's transition into independence. Their practice of 'divide and rule'— favoring some tribes to the exclusion of others—served to [heighten] the ethnic divisiveness that had been pulling Africa in different directions for centuries."

—from David Lamb, *The Africans* (1984)

What group does Lamb blame for the problems African nations have had creating stable governments since independence?

A. the groups that led independence movements in Africa

B. the wealthy, more-developed nations of the world today

C. European colonial governments

D. African leaders since independence

8 **IDENTIFYING POINT OF VIEW** Why would favoring some tribes over others cause problems?

F. by draining the country of valuable resources

G. by making disfavored tribes dependent on the colonial government

H. by creating inequality that becomes entrenched

I. by forcing tribes to find allies outside their country

SHORT RESPONSE

"The Congo's economy is based primarily on its petroleum sector, which is by far the country's greatest revenue earner. . . . A new potash mine . . . is expected to produce 1.2 million tons of potash . . . [used in fertilizer] per year by 2013. This will make Congo the largest producer of potash in Africa. . . . [One new iron ore mine] is thought to have ore reserves enough to be the world's third-largest iron ore mine."

—from "Republic of the Congo," State Department Background Notes

9 **DETERMINING CENTRAL IDEAS** What is the main idea of this passage?

10 **IDENTIFYING POINT OF VIEW** If oil is so valuable, why would the government of the Republic of the Congo bother developing potash and iron ore mines? Explain your answer.

EXTENDED RESPONSE

11 **ANALYZING** How was slavery in Central Africa and in the Americas similar?

Need Extra Help?

If You've Missed Question	**1**	**2**	**3**	**4**	**5**	**6**	**7**	**8**	**9**	**10**	**11**
Review Lesson	1	1	2	2	3	3	2	2	3	3	2

WEST AFRICA

Ariadne Van Zandbergen/Alamy

Young woman wears dress of traditional Kente cloth at a cultural festival in Ghana.

ESSENTIAL QUESTIONS · *How does physical geography influence the way people live?* · *How do new ideas change the way people live?* · *What makes a culture unique?*

networks

There's More Online about West Africa.

CHAPTER 14

Lesson 1
Physical Geography of West Africa

Lesson 2
The History of West Africa

Lesson 3
Life in West Africa

The Story Matters...

West Africa's diverse landscape includes desert, steppe, savanna, and tropical rain forests. Ancient rock paintings in Chad reveal details of the early herding societies who lived in this region. With rich deposits of gold and salt, trading kingdoms developed in Ghana and Mali. Trade also spread Islamic culture through much of the region. Gold attracted Europeans, whose colonial rule and slave trade impacted West Africa. Many of the independent nations of West Africa still struggle with civil war.

FOLDABLES
Study Organizer

Go to the Foldables® library in the back of your book to make a Foldable® that will help you take notes while reading this chapter.

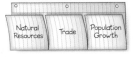

Natural Resources | Trade | Population Growth

WEST AFRICA

West Africa presents a rich variety of ethnic groups who speak many languages. Over the past 50 years, a number of the countries in the region have gained independence.

Step Into the Place

MAP FOCUS Use the map to answer the following questions.

1 **THE GEOGRAPHER'S WORLD** What are the two major lakes shown on the map?

2 **THE GEOGRAPHER'S WORLD** Which of the following countries is landlocked: Senegal, Burkina Faso, or Benin?

3 **PLACES AND REGIONS** What is the capital city of Liberia?

4 **CRITICAL THINKING** **Integrating Visual Information** If you are traveling from the capital city of Togo to the city of Bamako, in which direction are you traveling?

West Africa

TROPIC OF CANCER

MAURITANIA

• Nouakchott

Senegal R.

Dakar • SENEGAL

Banjul •

GAMBIA

Bamako •

Bissau •

GUINEA-BISSAU

GUINEA

CAPE VERDE

• Praia

ATLANTIC OCEAN

Conakry •

Freetown • SIERRA LEONE

LIBERIA

Monrovia •

10°W

⊕ National capital

Step Into the Time

TIME LINE View the time line to answer these questions: In what year did Liberia declare independence? What event occurred in 1787?

1300s Timbuktu is a center of Islamic culture

1000 B.C. Bantu people of West Africa begin migrations south and east

1000   B.C. | A.D.   1000   1300

250 B.C. Mali becomes center for trade

1324 Mansa Musa makes pilgrimage to Mecca

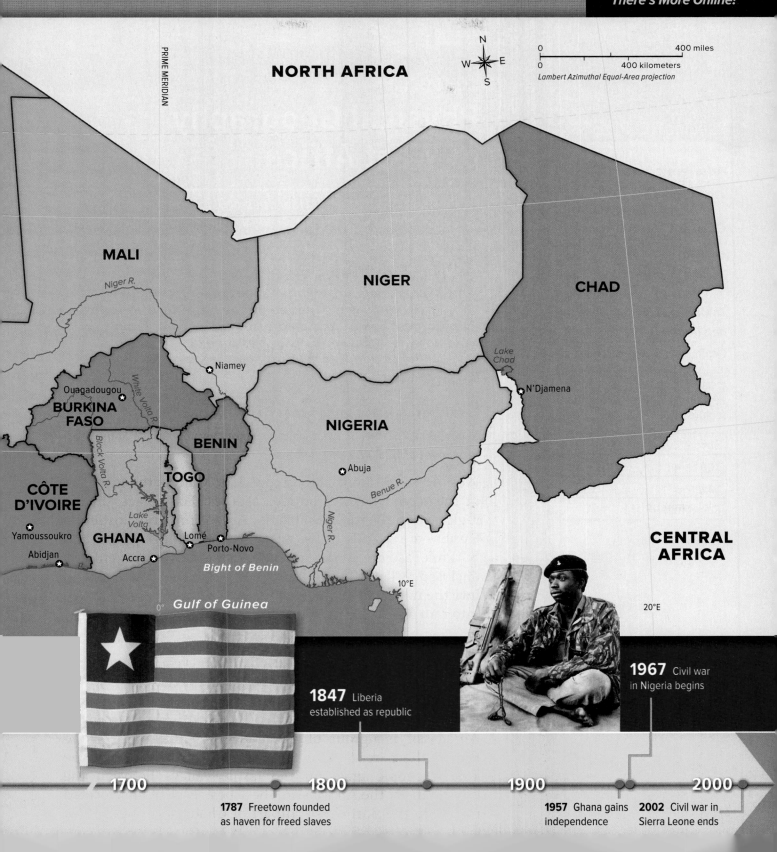

NORTH AFRICA

PRIME MERIDIAN

N
W — E
S

| 0 | | | 400 miles |
| 0 | | | 400 kilometers |

Lambert Azimuthal Equal-Area projection

MALI

NIGER

CHAD

Niger R.

Lake Chad

● Niamey

N'Djamena ★

Ouagadougou ●

White Volta R.

BURKINA
FASO

NIGERIA

BENIN

Black Volta R.

TOGO

● Abuja

Benue R.

CÔTE
D'IVOIRE

Lake
Volta

CENTRAL
AFRICA

● Yamoussoukro

GHANA

Lomé ●

Accra ★

Porto-Novo ★

Niger R.

Abidjan ●

Bight of Benin

10°E

20°E

0°

Gulf of Guinea

1967 Civil war
in Nigeria begins

1847 Liberia
established as republic

| 1700 | 1800 | 1900 | 2000 |

1787 Freetown founded
as haven for freed slaves

1957 Ghana gains
independence

2002 Civil war in
Sierra Leone ends

(l to r)George Holton/Photo Researchers; (2)NASA/Photo Researchers; (3)©FLORIN IORGANDA/X02105/Reuters/Corbis

Reading**HELP**DESK

Academic Vocabulary
- **volume**

Content Vocabulary
- **basin**
- **harmattan**

TAKING NOTES: *Key Ideas and Details*

Organize As you read the lesson, fill in a chart like this one, discussing the dryness and vegetation in these different regions.

Sahara	
The Sahel	
Savanna	
Rain forest	

Lesson 1
Physical Geography of West Africa

ESSENTIAL QUESTION • *How does physical geography influence the way people live?*

IT MATTERS BECAUSE
West Africa has a varied landscape. Its vast grasslands are bounded on the north by the world's largest desert and on the south by coastal rain forests. West Africa provides an example of how cultures adapt to different climates and landforms.

Landforms and Bodies of Water

GUIDING QUESTION *In what ways do major rivers contribute to the economies of West African countries?*

West Africa is a land of broad contrasts. Many of the countries of the region have Atlantic coastlines. Four places in the region—Cape Verde, St. Helena, Ascension, and Tristan da Cunha—are islands in the Atlantic. Mali, Niger, Chad, and Burkina Faso are landlocked countries, or countries entirely enclosed by land. The southern reaches of the Sahara extend into the northern regions of the steppe, and savannas merge into rain forests in the south.

Landforms
Erosion has worn most of the land of West Africa into a rolling plateau that slopes to sea level on the coasts. West Africa has no major mountain ranges, but it has highland regions and isolated mountains. The Air, also known as the Air Massif, is a group of mountains in central Niger, along the southern reaches of the Sahara. The livestock of the Tuareg people graze in the fertile valleys between the mountains of the Air Massif. The Tibesti Mountains, located mostly in the northwestern part of Chad, have the highest

elevations in West Africa. The highest peak is Emi Koussi, an extinct volcano standing 11,204 feet (3,415 m) above sea level.

Southeast of the Tibesti Mountains, near Chad's eastern border, is an arid desert plateau region called the Ennedi. There are abundant wild game animals in the Ennedi. These animals attract a small population of seminomadic people who live here with their livestock during the rainy season. The Jos Plateau in central Nigeria is mostly open grassland and farmland.

In central Guinea is a highland region of savanna and deciduous forest known as the Fouta Djallon. It extends southeast to become the Guinea highlands, a humid, densely forested region.

Bodies of Water

The Niger River, West Africa's longest and most important river, originates at an elevation of 2,800 feet (853 m) in the Guinea highlands. It flows northeast toward the Sahara. Just beyond the town of Mopti in Mali, the Niger River enters the "inland delta." This is an area where the river spreads out across the relatively flat land into many creeks, marshes, and lakes that are connected to the river by channels. During the rainy season, the area floods completely. In the dry season, however, the waters recede, leaving fertile farmland.

As the Niger flows past Timbuktu, along the southern edges of the Sahara, the inland delta ends and the river returns to a single channel. As it flows through Niger and Nigeria, it joins its most important tributary, the Benue River, which doubles its **volume** of water. Where the Niger River reaches the Gulf of Guinea, it forms the Niger delta. This large area is a great **basin**, a lower area of land drained by a river and its tributaries. Along its 2,600-mile (4,184-km) course, the Niger provides water for irrigation and hydroelectric power. It is the main source of Mali's fishing industry, and it serves as an important route for transporting crops and goods.

George Holton/Photo Researchers

Academic Vocabulary

volume an amount

Tuareg people lead their camels and goats to an oasis. The nomadic group tend to their livestock in the valleys of mountains. At one time, the Tuareg controlled the caravan trade routes across the Sahara.

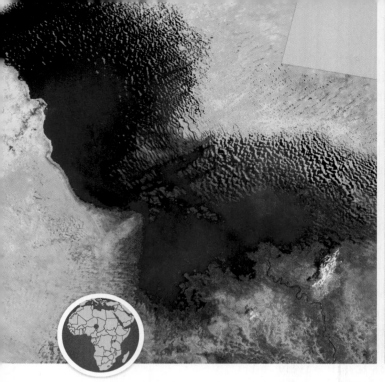
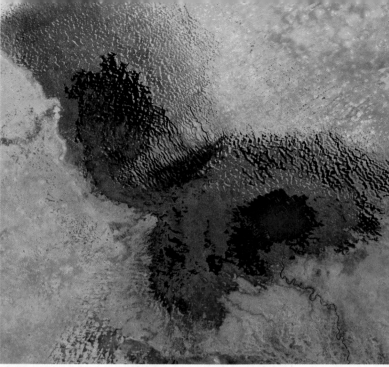

Satellite images show the Lake Chad area. Lake water is shown in blue, vegetation in red, and the surrounding desert in brown. The lake once was one of the largest bodies of water in Africa. The image on the left shows Lake Chad as it appeared in 1973. By 2007 (right), the lake had dramatically decreased in size.

▶ CRITICAL THINKING

Analyzing Taking water from the lake to use for irrigation is one reason that Lake Chad is smaller. What is another major cause of the lake shrinking in size?

The Senegal River rises in the Fouta Djallon in Guinea. Then it flows northwest to the Atlantic Ocean. For about 515 miles (829 km), the course of the Senegal River marks the border between the countries of Mauritania and Senegal.

The Black Volta River and the White Volta River originate in Burkina Faso and flow into Ghana. At a point near where the two rivers once met is the Akosombo Dam, which forms one of the world's largest artificial lakes—Lake Volta. The dam provides most of Ghana's electrical needs, and the lake provides water for irrigation.

Lake Chad covers portions of Niger, Nigeria, Chad, and Cameroon along the south part of the Sahara. The size of the lake varies from season to season, depending on the rainfall that feeds its tributaries. A series of droughts helped cause Lake Chad to shrink. Another cause was the amount of water taken from the lake and from the rivers that feed it to use for irrigating crops. People may be taking more water than water systems will be able to replace.

☑ READING PROGRESS CHECK

Describing Describe the landforms of West Africa.

Climate

GUIDING QUESTION *How do amounts of rainfall differ throughout West Africa?*

The climate of West Africa is diverse, from the harsh, arid Sahara in the north to the lush, coastal rain forests in the south. In between are vast stretches of grassland—the dry, semiarid Sahel and the lush, rainier savanna. The key characteristic of the climates throughout the region is its two distinct seasons: the wet season and the dry season.

NASA/Photo Researchers

Dry Zones

The Sahel is a semiarid region that runs between the arid Sahara and the savanna. Beginning in northern Senegal and stretching east into East Africa, the Sahel has a short rainy season. Annual rainfall ranges from only 8 inches to 20 inches (20 cm to 51 cm). This climate supports low grasses, thorny shrubs, and a few trees. The grasses are plentiful enough to support grazing livestock, such as cattle, sheep, camels, and pack oxen. It is important, however, that the herds do not grow too large. Too many animals leads to overgrazing and permanent damage to the grasslands. Overgrazing and too much farming result in desertification, the process in which semiarid lands become drier and more desert-like.

North of the Sahel is the Sahara. Daytime high temperatures are often more than 100°F (38°C) in the summer, though temperatures at night can drop by as much as 50°F. The few shrubs and other small plants that live in the Sahara must go for long periods without water. Some plants send long roots to water sources deep underground. After a rainfall, plants that have waited many months will suddenly flower, carpeting the desert with color.

From late November until mid-March, the dry, hot wind known as the **harmattan** blows through the Sahara with intensity. It carries thick clouds of dust that can extend hundreds of miles over the Atlantic Ocean, where it settles on the decks of ships. Harmattan winds contribute to the process of desertification.

Wet Zones

South of the Sahel, rains are more plentiful and feed the fuller, lusher plant life of the savanna. The savanna has two seasons—rainy and dry. The rainy season usually extends from April to September, and the rest of the year is dry. Annual rainfall reaches between 31 inches and 59 inches (79 cm and 150 cm). In some locations, though, annual rainfall can be as little as 20 inches (51 cm). This wide variability in rainfall makes human activity difficult.

The hot, dry wind that streams in from the northeast or east in the western Sahara is called the harmattan.

▶ CRITICAL THINKING
Describing During what months is the harmattan the strongest?

WEST AFRICAN ENERGY

West Africa is relatively rich in energy resources. These resources are not, however, equally developed. Also, each form of energy has benefits and drawbacks.

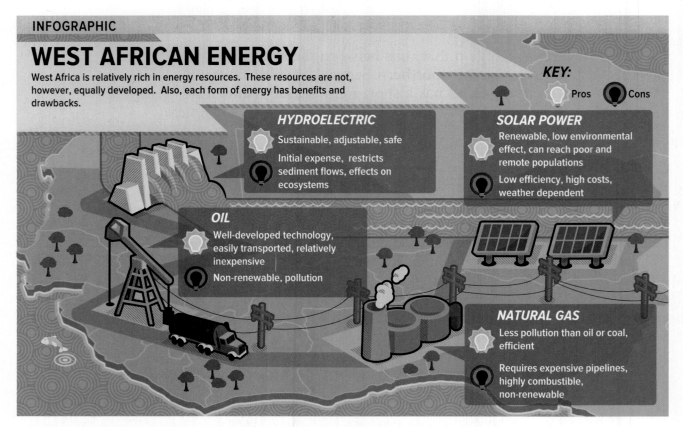

KEY:
Pros | Cons

HYDROELECTRIC
Sustainable, adjustable, safe

Initial expense, restricts sediment flows, effects on ecosystems

SOLAR POWER
Renewable, low environmental effect, can reach poor and remote populations

Low efficiency, high costs, weather dependent

OIL
Well-developed technology, easily transported, relatively inexpensive

Non-renewable, pollution

NATURAL GAS
Less pollution than oil or coal, efficient

Requires expensive pipelines, highly combustible, non-renewable

West Africa is rich in energy resources. Because of the increasing demand for energy, West Africa's importance as an energy supplier to world markets continues to grow.

▶ **CRITICAL THINKING**

Analyzing What form of energy has little or no effect on the environment?

Farther to the south, tropical rain forests cover the land. The rain forests, known for their broad-leaved evergreen trees and rich biodiversity, receive plenty of rain. Rain forests in Sierra Leone and Liberia can receive as much as 200 inches (508 cm) of rain per year.

✓ **READING PROGRESS CHECK**

Identifying What are the two major grassland areas of West Africa?

Resources

GUIDING QUESTION *How do West African countries provide for their energy needs?*

West Africa contains many resources, but some countries lack the money to develop their resources into industries.

Energy Resources

Nigeria is the region's biggest producer of petroleum. In 2010 Nigeria ranked among the top 10 in the world, producing oil at a rate of almost 2.5 million barrels per day. The petroleum industry has not been as quick to tap the country's vast natural gas reserves.

Chad has oil fields in the area north of Lake Chad. Benin has offshore oil fields, as does Ghana. The oil in Ghana was considered too expensive to extract until increases in oil prices made it profitable to drill.

Ghana's main sources of electricity are two dams on the Volta River: the Akosombo Dam and the dam at Kpong. The Organization for the Development of the Senegal River, which is made up of several countries of the region, manages the river's resources, including hydroelectric stations. The Senegal River provides about half of the energy used in Mauritania today. Hydroelectric power is vital to meeting the energy needs in Togo and Nigeria.

Other Resources

The gold trade attracted Portuguese explorers, who first visited the region in 1471. For centuries afterward, the country was simply called the Gold Coast and Europeans lived and worked there, building trading posts and forts. Gold mining remains important to the economy of Ghana, along with the mining of diamonds, manganese, and bauxite. Ghana also has unmined deposits of limestone and iron ore.

Gold is mined in Mali, Burkina Faso, and Nigeria, too. Togo mines phosphate and limestone, which are used as fertilizers and to make paper, glass, paint, and other everyday products. Togo also has promising gold deposits, but so far no gold-mining industry. Niger has a salt-mining industry. In addition to its important gold industry, Mali also mines salt and limestone, but many of Mali's mineral resources are untapped. These include iron ore and manganese, which are important in making steel.

Mauritania mines copper and iron ore, but many of the iron ore deposits have been depleted. Nigeria mines iron ore, tin, limestone, and small quantities of other minerals. Burkina Faso is one of the world's leading sources of manganese. Benin has deposits of iron ore, limestone, chromium ore, gold, and marble. Benin is a leader in the production of hardwoods, but most of the rain forests where this wood comes from have been cleared.

Include this lesson's information in your Foldable®.

☑ READING PROGRESS CHECK

Analyzing Why is Benin's hardwood industry at risk? What is another industry in this region that has faced a similar problem?

LESSON 1 REVIEW

Reviewing Vocabulary

1. How can the *harmattan* winds influence climate and vegetation?

Answering the Guiding Questions

2. ***Describing*** Why has Lake Chad changed in size over time?

3. ***Determining Central Ideas*** Why is desertification an issue in West Africa?

4. ***Identifying*** Why did the government in Ghana change its mind about its offshore oil deposits?

5. ***Informative/Explanatory Writing*** Explain how desertification occurs and why it is such an important environmental issue in West Africa.

Reading**HELP**DESK

Academic Vocabulary

- displace
- element
- revenue

Content Vocabulary

- imperialism
- secede

TAKING NOTES: *Key Ideas and Details*

Describe On a chart like this one, write at least two different facts about the three ancient empires of Ghana, Mali, and Songhai.

Ghana	Mali	Songhai

Lesson 2
The History of West Africa

ESSENTIAL QUESTION • *How do new ideas change the way people live?*

IT MATTERS BECAUSE
West Africa was under the control of a series of wealthy trading kingdoms until the late 1800s, when Europeans seized control of their lands. Regaining their independence from Europe and establishing themselves in the modern world has been a challenge.

Ancient Times

GUIDING QUESTION *What opportunities did Muslims from North Africa see in West Africa?*

Early civilizations in West Africa learned to thrive in a variety of climates and landscapes, from the Sahara to the tropical rain forests. Throughout its history, the region was open to many migrations and invasions because of its resources.

Ancient Herders

We think of the Sahara as a hot, intensely dry place where few living things can survive. Ten thousand years ago, the Sahara was a much different place. Rock drawings from 8000 B.C. depict a world that looks more like a savanna than a desert. Drawings include lakes, forests, and large animals not seen in the Sahara in modern times: ostriches, giraffes, elephants, antelope, and rhinoceroses. Seminomadic people herded cattle and hunted wild animals. As the climate grew drier, fewer species of plants and animals survived the harsh environment. Many people moved south, following the retreat of the grasslands and the rain. During this period of desertification, people discovered that camels can survive without water for longer periods than cattle, sheep, or goats. Camels also can carry heavy loads for long distances. They were perfect domesticated animals for desert dwellers.

Movement of People

The Bantu people inhabited West Africa in ancient times. They had developed farming as early as 2000 B.C. A vast migration of Bantu people out of West Africa began around 1000 B.C. and continued for hundreds of years. Their farming practices allowed them to expand rather easily into areas occupied by hunter-gatherer groups. The Bantu became the dominant population in most of East and South Africa. The Bantu might have reached the East African coast as early as the A.D. 200s. They **displaced** many of the people who had lived on these lands before them.

Wherever the Bantu moved, they spread their culture, including three vital **elements**. First, the Bantu cultivated bananas, taro, and yams, which were originally from Malaysia. These crops thrived in the humidity of the tropical rain forests. Second, the Bantu spread their languages everywhere they settled. Today, more than 500 distinct Bantu languages are spoken by 85 million Africans. Third, the Bantu brought iron-smelting technology. They could create tools and weapons unlike any the native people had ever seen.

Trade Across the Sahara

For thousands of years, the Sahara was a barrier to contact between West Africa and North Africa. By the A.D. 700s, Arab Muslims had crossed the Sahara and conquered most of North Africa. They dominated the southern Mediterranean and controlled trade in that region, as well as Saharan trade routes into West Africa. Arab geographers slowly learned about Africa south of the Sahara. They realized that the region offered opportunities, not only in trade, but also in adding converts to Islam. One of the West African kingdoms they learned about was Ghana.

Ghana controlled the gold trade in the region. It traded gold for salt that Arab traders brought in from the Sahara. Salt was a very important trade good. It was the best preserver of food, and it was rare and difficult to acquire.

The Berber people had lived in North Africa long before the Arabs arrived. The Berbers resisted Islam for a while, but in time they converted. Several groups of Islamic Berbers joined together to become the Almoravids. They were fierce fighters, and they wanted to spread their new faith.

Academic Vocabulary

displace to take over a place or position of others

element an important part or characteristic

Merchants sell slabs of salt in a market town in central Mali. Salt is plentiful in the Sahara. These conditions gave rise to the African salt trade of ancient times.

▶ CRITICAL THINKING
Describing Why was salt a valuable item for trade?

John Elk/Lonely Planet Images/Getty Images

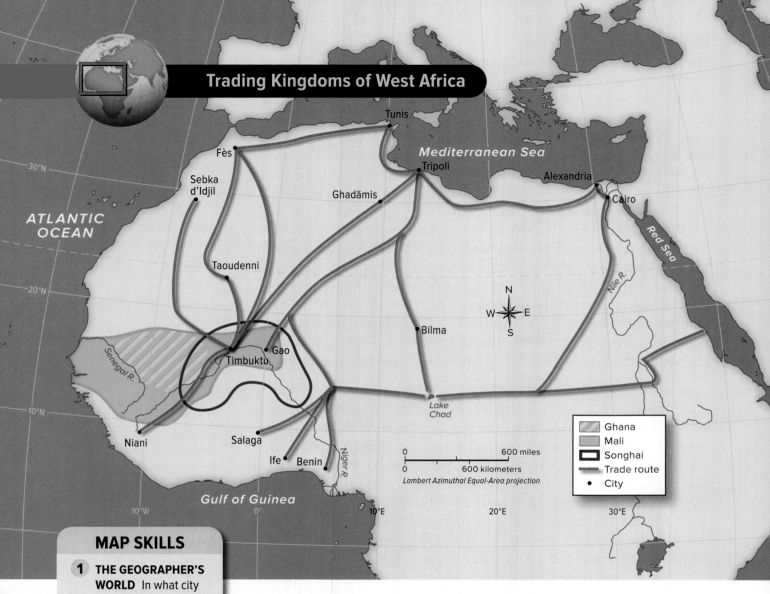

Mediterranean Sea

ATLANTIC OCEAN

Tunis
Fès
Sebka d'Idjil
Ghadāmis
Tripoli
Alexandria
Cairo
Red Sea
Nile R.
Taoudenni
Bilma
Senegal R.
Timbuktu
Gao
Lake Chad
Niani
Salaga
Ife
Benin
Niger R.
Gulf of Guinea

N
W E
S

	600 miles
0	
0	600 kilometers

Lambert Azimuthal Equal-Area projection

	Ghana
	Mali
	Songhai
—	Trade route
•	City

MAP SKILLS

1 **THE GEOGRAPHER'S WORLD** In what city did many of the trade routes merge?

2 **PLACES AND REGIONS** The early African kingdoms developed near gold-rich areas. What did a plentiful supply of gold allow them to do?

The First Trading Kingdom

The Ghana Empire was a powerful kingdom in West Africa during the Middle Ages. It had grown wealthy from its control of the gold trade. As the empire grew wealthy, it conquered many of its neighbors, including gold-rich lands to the south. Ghana built a strong trade with Muslim countries in North Africa.

In the A.D. 1000s, the Almoravids conquered Ghana. Almoravid rule over Ghana lasted only a few years, but that was long enough to damage the trade that kept the empire alive. With the arrival of so many Almoravids, there was now a larger population to feed. The dry climate could not support the sudden increase in agriculture, and this resulted in desertification: Land that at one time was fertile became desert. Ghana became weak, and its conquered neighbors began to break away.

☑ READING PROGRESS CHECK

Determining Central Ideas Why did the Ghana Empire collapse?

West African Kingdoms

GUIDING QUESTION *Why was the city of Timbuktu important to different trading kingdoms in West Africa?*

Several West African kingdoms sought to take control of the trade the fallen Ghana Empire had established in the region. Islam was taking hold in northern West Africa, and the most powerful of the new trading kingdoms were Muslim: Mali and Songhai.

Mali

The trading kingdom of Mali came after Ghana. Mali grew rich from the gold-for-salt trade. Its rulers conquered neighboring lands and built an empire.

The empire of Mali reached its height under the emperor Mansa Musa. The city of Timbuktu, which was already an important trading post, became a center for Islamic culture. Mansa Musa went on a historic pilgrimage to Mecca. By the time Mansa Musa returned home, the Islamic world knew there was a new and powerful Islamic kingdom south of the Sahara.

Songhai

After Mansa Musa's death, Songhai replaced Mali as the most powerful West African empire. A well-trained army and a navy that patrolled the Niger River made Songhai the largest of the three trading empires. Songhai now controlled the region's trade routes, had salt mines in the Sahara, and sought to turn their empire into the center for Islamic learning. The Songhai Empire eventually fell to the Moroccans, who seized the salt mines and destroyed the empire by the end of the 1500s.

Coastal Kingdoms

Slavery had been practiced in Africa for centuries. Muslims from North Africa and Asia had been buying enslaved people from south of the Sahara. As European colonists established colonies in the Western Hemisphere, they purchased enslaved people to do their labor. Small African kingdoms along the Atlantic coast became trading partners with Portugal, Spain, and Great Britain. Trade in enslaved persons became highly profitable in these kingdoms. When Europeans outlawed the slave trade, the kingdoms' economies began to fail.

✔ READING PROGRESS CHECK

Identifying How did the slave trade in West Africa change after the arrival of the Europeans?

Mansa Musa is shown sitting on his throne in this map of Africa from an atlas created in 1375.

Abraham Cresques/The Bridgeman Art Library/Getty Images

European Domination

GUIDING QUESTION *What were some of the factors that aroused European interest in exploring and colonizing Africa?*

In the late 1800s, several European countries were eager to expand into Africa with its many natural resources. After hundreds of years of self-rule, West Africans lost control of their lands to the Europeans.

Changing Trade

The British government outlawed the slave trade in 1807. Great Britain tried but could not keep other European countries from continuing to export enslaved persons. The British founded the colony of Freetown in Sierra Leone in 1787 as a safe haven for runaway or freed enslaved persons. The Americans followed suit in 1822, founding Liberia as a home for freed American enslaved persons.

The British encouraged development of the palm oil trade to make up for the loss of **revenue** from the slave trade. British traders and missionaries familiarized themselves with the trading culture of the Niger River. The British started to profit from their growing role in West African trade. Before long, France took notice.

Creating Colonies

Before the mid-1800s, the British and French posted military in North Africa, and the British and Dutch had settled in South Africa. In 1869 two events increased Europe's interest in Africa. First, the Suez Canal—an artificial waterway connecting the Mediterranean Sea to the Red Sea—opened. Second, diamonds were discovered in South Africa.

Academic Vocabulary

revenue income

Freetown, the largest city in Sierra Leone, is located in the western part of the country along the Atlantic coast.

▶ CRITICAL THINKING

Describing What is unique about how Freetown was founded?

Chris Jackson/Getty Images News/Getty Images

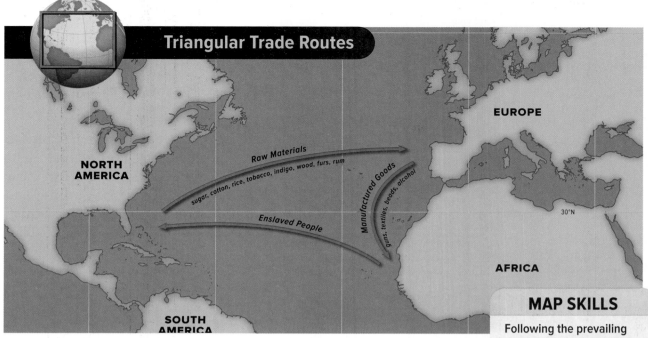

Triangular Trade Routes

Raw Materials
sugar, cotton, rice, tobacco, indigo, wood, furs, rum

Manufactured Goods
guns, textiles, beads, alcohol

Enslaved People

NORTH AMERICA

SOUTH AMERICA

EUROPE

AFRICA

30°N

MAP SKILLS

Following the prevailing winds, European ships sailed along the triangular trade route.

1 THE GEOGRAPHER'S WORLD Why were raw materials from the Americas shipped to Europe rather than to other parts of the world?

2 PLACES AND REGIONS Most European trade with Africa was conducted in West Africa. Why do you think this was so?

Before that time, Europeans had been in contact with the coastal kingdoms, but few had ventured into the interior of West Africa. This began to change as Great Britain, France, Portugal, Belgium, and the new, unified country of Germany began planning to carve out empires in Africa. Europeans followed a policy of **imperialism**, or seizing political control of other places to create an empire. At the Berlin Conference of 1884–1885, the European powers established rules for partitioning Africa.

The French and British claimed the most territory in West Africa. The modern countries of Benin, Burkina Faso, Chad, Côte d'Ivoire, Guinea, Mali, Mauritania, Niger, and Senegal were French colonies. Gambia, Ghana, Nigeria, Sierra Leone, and St. Helena were British colonies. Togo started out as a German possession, but Germany lost it in World War I.

Some colonies were ruled more harshly than others, but one thing was true about all of them: Europeans made the important decisions about how Africans lived. Settlers from Europe could set up farms on the most fertile land, even if Africans were forced off that land. Africans resisted, sometimes violently.

✔ READING PROGRESS CHECK

Describing What was the purpose of the Berlin Conference?

New Countries

GUIDING QUESTION *How does a ruler gain and hold political power?*

West African colonies began gaining independence in the late 1950s. The struggle for economic and political success was difficult because of the complex ethnic makeup of these countries.

The leader of Ghana, Kwame Nkrumah (center), meets with a citizen in 1959. Bediako Poku (standing) headed the Convention People's Party (CPP), a political party Nkrumah started. A referendum election in 1964 made the CPP the nation's only legal party, and Nkrumah was installed as president of Ghana for life. The military and police ousted Nkrumah from power in 1966.

Another factor working against political stability was the actions taken by the leaders. Often, they seized power and then used force to stay in power.

Ghana Leads the Way

The Gold Coast had been important to European trade since Portugal set up its first fort there in 1487. By the early 1800s, it was under British control, and in 1874 the Gold Coast became a British colony. The most important industries were gold, forest resources, and a newly introduced crop—the cocoa bean from which chocolate is made. By the 1920s, the Gold Coast supplied more than half the world's cocoa.

After the end of World War II, Dr. Kwame Nkrumah led protests calling for independence. Protests flared throughout the colony. In 1957 the Gold Coast gained its independence and became the Republic of Ghana. For many years, Ghana was troubled by conflict. In 1992 Ghana approved a new constitution that established a multiparty democracy. Since then, presidential elections have been peaceful, and Ghana has become a model of political reform in West Africa.

Former French Colonies

Throughout the 1950s, France made concessions to its West African colonies, many of which had instituted some form of self-rule. The independence of Ghana excited and inspired Africans, however. Cries for independence began erupting all over Africa. French Sudan and Senegal united to become the Republic of Mali, but Senegal broke away the following year, and Mali declared its own independence. In 1960 Mauritania, Niger, Côte d'Ivoire, Gambia, and Burkina Faso declared their independence. By 1961, all of France's colonies in West Africa were independent.

Nigeria

Nigeria had never been a country before the British combined two of their colonies to form the Nigerian Protectorate in 1914. Several different ethnic groups lived in this new territory. The Yoruba and Edo people had distinct territories in the south. The Hausa people were Muslims who lived in the north. The Igbo people were farmers who began to migrate east after British colonization.

When Nigeria gained its independence in 1960, tensions grew between ethnic groups. Because Britain had concentrated most of its development, including building schools, in southern Nigeria, most well-educated Nigerians lived in the south. They became leaders of the new government. Many of them were Igbo, who were mostly Christian. When they ventured north to govern the Hausa, they were met with hostility. Conflicts among the three major ethnic divisions in the country—the Hausa, the Yoruba, and the Igbo—grew violent. Thousands of Igbo living in northern Nigeria were massacred. As many as a million more fled to a region dominated by the Igbo. In 1967 the eastern region **seceded**, or withdrew formally, from Nigeria and announced that it was now the independent republic of Biafra. Nigerian forces invaded Biafra, and after more than two years of war, Biafra was in ruins. Starvation and disease may have killed more than 1 million people.

For long periods since then, the military has controlled the country's government. A new constitution was written in 1978. A year later, a democratically elected civilian government took office. That ended in a military coup in 1983. It was not until 1999 that another democratically elected president was able to rule Nigeria.

Civil War

Sometimes a military coup erupts into civil war. In late 1989, Charles Taylor led an invasion of Liberia. His aim was to depose the president, Samuel Doe. Ethnic conflict was at the heart of this struggle. Taylor and his rebels were of the Mano and Gio peoples. President Doe belonged to the Krahn people. After Doe's arrest and execution, Liberia endured seven years of civil war.

Conflict spilled over Liberia's borders into neighboring Sierra Leone. Thousands of civilians died, and many were forced to leave their homes. The civil war in Sierra Leone did not end until 2002. Estimates are that 50,000 died and another 2 million people lost their homes in the civil war. In 2012 Charles Taylor was brought to trial by a special court. He was found guilty of war crimes and crimes against humanity for his part in Sierra Leone's civil war.

✔ **READING PROGRESS CHECK**

Determining Central Ideas What reason might the French have had for letting their African colonies declare independence?

Thinking Like a Geographer

Religious Rivalry

In the A.D. 700s, Muslim people converted many West Africans to Islam. Over time, Islam became the dominant religion in northern parts of the region. Many West Africans along the coastal areas adopted Christianity after the arrival of the Europeans in the 1500s. Others continue to practice traditional African religions. Relations between these different religious groups have not always been good.

FOLDABLES
Study Organizer

Include this lesson's information in your Foldable®.

LESSON 2 REVIEW

Reviewing Vocabulary

1. How did the Berlin Conference of 1884–1885 help achieve the goals of European *imperialism*?

Answering the Guiding Questions

2. ***Determining Central Ideas*** How did the Bantu culture influence the parts of Africa to which the Bantu migrated?

3. ***Identifying*** How did the Islamic world become aware of the wealth of the Mali Empire?

4. ***Describing*** Why did the British encourage development of the palm oil trade in African kingdoms on the Atlantic coast?

5. ***Analyzing*** Why did Nigeria face so many challenges when becoming an independent country?

6. ***Argument Writing*** Write a speech to the French government in the late 1950s about how important the independence of Ghana is and why France should release its colonies.

Reading **HELP**DESK

Academic Vocabulary

- diverse

Content Vocabulary

- **pidgin**
- **creole**
- **animist**
- **extended family**
- **nuclear family**
- **kente**
- **infrastructure**

TAKING NOTES: *Key Ideas and Details*

Compare and Contrast Use a graphic organizer like the one below to show some of the differences between life in a West African city and life in a rural area of West Africa.

City	Rural
•	•
•	•
•	•
•	•

Lesson 3
Life in West Africa

ESSENTIAL QUESTION • *What makes a culture unique?*

IT MATTERS BECAUSE
West African countries have faced many challenges in the decades since they achieved independence. Even as they struggle to modernize and improve their economies, West Africans have been able to spread their artistic gifts to people around the world.

The People of the Region

GUIDING QUESTION *Why are two or more languages spoken in some West African countries?*

West Africa is the most populous region of Africa. Many different ethnic groups live here, and each group brings something unique to their country's culture.

Ethnic Groups

European countries that carved up Africa to add to their overseas empires had their own reasons for setting colonial borders where they did. They did not consider the borders of the different ethnic groups of the Africans who already lived on the land they colonized. As a result, the European colonies in Africa contained populations that were ethnically **diverse**. When African countries declared independence, the new national borders closely followed the old colonial borders, preserving that diversity.

Establishing a sense of national unity is difficult, however. Many people have a stronger identification with their ethnic group than with the country they live in. For example, the Hausa are citizens of Nigeria, but many feel closer ties to the people and culture of the Hausa than to the country of Nigeria.

Another factor working against national unity is that a West African ethnic group does not typically live in only one country. Some Yoruba people, for example, live in Nigeria. Other Yoruba live in Benin. No matter where they live, the Yoruba feel a closer connection to other Yoruba people than to Nigeria or Benin.

Languages

When West African countries achieved independence, the majority held on to the European language that had been used most in business and government during the colonial period. The European languages—English, Portuguese, and French—became the official languages of West African countries. In some cases, Arabic is also an official language.

Most ethnic groups retain their traditional languages, and many use that language more than they do the official European language. In some places, European and African languages have intermixed to form a **pidgin** language. A pidgin is a simplified language used by people who cannot speak each other's languages but need a way to communicate. Sometimes two or more languages blend so well that the mixture becomes the language of the region. This is called a **creole** language. Crioulo is the language spoken most often in Cape Verde. It is a creole language, part Portuguese and part African dialect.

Religion

Islam was introduced to North Africa in the A.D. 600s, and it spread southward with trade. It was well established in many parts of West Africa long before the arrival of Christian missionaries from Europe. Today, a sizable portion of West African populations are Muslim.

Glen Allison/Photodisc/Getty Images

Academic Vocabulary

diverse comprised of many distinct and different parts

Women talk near the Great Mosque in Djenne, Mali. The Great Mosque is the largest mud-brick building in the world. The first mosque on this site was built in the 1200s. The current mosque was built in 1907.
▶ CRITICAL THINKING
Describing In what region of Africa was Islam first introduced?

Lagos is Nigeria's largest city and ranks among the fastest-growing megacities in the world. During the 2000s, about 600,000 people have moved to Lagos every year.

▶ CRITICAL THINKING

Describing Are megacities the most common form of settlement in West Africa? Explain.

In some countries, however, Christianity is just as dominant as Islam, or more so. Even in countries where Christianity or Islam is dominant, many people still practice traditional African religions. These religions have their own rituals and celebrations that tie communities together. The beliefs are not written on paper but passed on from one generation to another. Often, the people believe in a supreme creator god and are **animists**, which means they believe in spirits—spirits of their ancestors, the air, the earth, and rivers.

Settlement Patterns

West Africa had few large towns until the colonial period. Even today, the most common settlement patterns in West Africa consist of scattered villages. Villages represent the homesteads of **extended families**, or families made up of parents, children, and other close relatives, often of more than two generations. The size of the villages and the population density depend on how much human activity the land can sustain. Water is an issue in the northern parts of West Africa, so populations are small and spread out.

Most of the largest cities in West Africa are capital cities, like Bamako, Mali, which more than tripled in population between 1960 and 1970, when droughts caused people to migrate from the countryside. The largest city in West Africa is Lagos in Nigeria, with an estimated 10.5 million people. Lagos was Nigeria's capital until 1991; Abuja is now Nigeria's capital city.

✔ READING PROGRESS CHECK

Determining Central Ideas What are two ways traditions have survived in West Africa?

Life and Culture in the Region

GUIDING QUESTION *Why are traditions more important in rural areas of West Africa than they are in West African cities?*

A variety of cultures thrive in West Africa, some of them traditional and some contemporary. Countries in the north—such as Mali, Mauritania, and Niger—are more influenced by the culture of North Africa than are their neighboring countries.

Daily Life

West Africa, with its complicated history and rich mixture of ethnicities, has a diverse culture. English or French may be the language of the cities, or of business and politics, but hundreds of other languages are still spoken. People in cities are more likely to wear Western-style clothing and to live and work in Western-style buildings. Far from the city, many people retain the traditions of their ancestors. These people are more likely to wear traditional clothing. Life in rural villages is built around the extended family. In cities, the **nuclear family**—parents with their children—is the more common family structure.

A worker weaves kente cloth in Ghana (above). The painted wood mask (below) comes from Burkina Faso.

City dwellers are far more likely to deal with a wide variety of people over the course of a day than are rural dwellers. Capital cities teem with people from different ethnic groups, races, and countries. They are more likely to speak the official language because that is the language they all have in common. In rural areas, ethnicity and tradition are still important. Devotion to traditional values keeps those languages and cultures alive even as the country is changing. The downside is that ethnic pride sometimes results in conflicts between neighboring ethnic groups.

The Arts

West Africans have created numerous unique and important works of art in many artistic fields. Traditional artwork, such as carved masks from Nigeria and Sierra Leone, are world famous. Another well-known traditional art form is **kente**, a colorful, handwoven cloth from Ghana. One of West Africa's most important artist-figures is the griot, a musical storyteller who is part historian and part spiritual advisor.

Dance is the most popular form of recreation in West Africa. Workers use dance to celebrate their skills and accomplishments; professional guilds have their own dances. Dance is used for its healing qualities, but people also dance to popular music in clubs.

Workers are on the job at a steel plant in Côte d'Ivoire. Like many other countries in the region, Côte d'Ivoire is developing its industries. Major manufacturing industries include bus and truck assembly and shipbuilding.

West African music blends a variety of many sounds, combining traditional and modern instruments. The Arabic influences of North African music mix with the music of Africa south of the Sahara, as well as with American and European rock and pop music.

West Africa has produced some of the world's finest writers. The most widely read of all African novels is *Things Fall Apart* by Chinua Achebe of Nigeria. Senegal's first president, Léopold Senghor, was a famous poet and lecturer on African history and culture.

☑ **READING PROGRESS CHECK**

Identifying Point of View Select an artistic field that you think best shows the culture of West Africa, and explain why you believe it does.

Challenges Facing the Region

GUIDING QUESTION *How did West African countries build up so much debt?*

Many West African countries face serious problems. To improve their situations, they must deal with these challenges and more: bad economies, corrupt governments, out-of-control population growth, disease, and poorly funded schools.

Government and Economics

The European powers that colonized Africa built the colonies' economies on a few key resources, such as petroleum, gold, peanuts, or copper. The **infrastructure**, or underlying framework of the colonies, was built around those key resources. Once the colonies achieved independence, it became important for them to develop a variety of different industries. Otherwise, any drop in the world price of a key resource would greatly affect a country's economy. Many foreign governments invested money in developing the

©nabil zorkot/dpa/Corbis

industrial base of the new African countries. In many cases, money from the loans was not used wisely. As a result, the invested money did not yield high returns. West African countries were not only dealing with struggling economies but also faced enormous debt.

The International Monetary Fund and the World Bank have declared that no poor or developing country should have to pay a debt it cannot possibly manage. Debt relief has been important for countries such as Ghana, which suffered from bad economic choices and political instability. Ghana is now a model for economic and political reform in West Africa. Nigeria benefited from debt relief as well, and was able to pay off the remainder of what it owed in 2006.

A major challenge for the region is that, as the population grows, the demand for food and jobs grows. An economy does not have a chance to grow if it cannot meet the needs of a growing population.

Health and Education

Thirty-four million people in the world are living with the HIV virus, and 22.9 million of them live in Africa south of the Sahara. Dealing with such a large number of HIV-infected people presents several challenges. The first challenge is to supply health care to the growing number of people who carry the virus. The second challenge is to reduce the number of new HIV infections, usually through education. The third challenge is to deal with the families and communities hurt by AIDS-related deaths.

West Africa has a high birthrate, and the population is growing quickly, but life expectancy is still short compared to other parts of the world. Health care is an issue in large cities, but it is an even greater issue in rural areas.

The population of West Africa is young. For West Africa to have a sound future, educational systems must effectively prepare young people for economic and social development. A lack of education funding means that some countries cannot afford to make updates or improvements to their schools.

Include this lesson's information in your Foldable®.

☑ READING PROGRESS CHECK

Analyzing Why is education such an important issue for the future of West Africa?

LESSON 3 REVIEW

Reviewing Vocabulary

1. How did the *infrastructure* of West African colonies lead to poor economies when they became independent countries?

Answering the Guiding Questions

2. *Analyzing* What are the advantages of a pidgin language?

3. *Describing* What is one potential downside to preserving traditional values in rural West Africa?

4. *Identifying* What are three major challenges to fighting AIDS in West Africa?

5. *Narrative Writing* Select a West African country and write a letter to the government of the country about the importance of investing in education. Explain how education will help solve the problems discussed in this lesson and how it will help preserve West African culture.

Chapter 14 ACTIVITIES

Directions: Write your answers on a separate piece of paper.

1 Use your **FOLDABLES** to explore the Essential Question.

INFORMATIVE/EXPLANATORY WRITING Choose any three countries in this region and take a closer look at how the people who live there earn their living. Use the CIA Factbook or another Internet resource to list the top five occupations in each of the three countries and the average annual wage people earn for each. Arrange your data in a chart. Are any of those occupations directly related to the physical geography of the area? Explain in one or two paragraphs.

2 21st Century Skills

INTEGRATING VISUAL INFORMATION In small groups, research the problems facing one of the countries of West Africa. Discuss possible solutions to one of the problems. Create a bulletin board display with pictures and captions to illustrate your solution to the problem.

3 Thinking Like a Geographer

DETERMINING CENTRAL IDEAS After reviewing the chapter, choose five of the most important events in the history of West Africa. Place those events and their dates on a time line.

4 GEOGRAPHY ACTIVITY

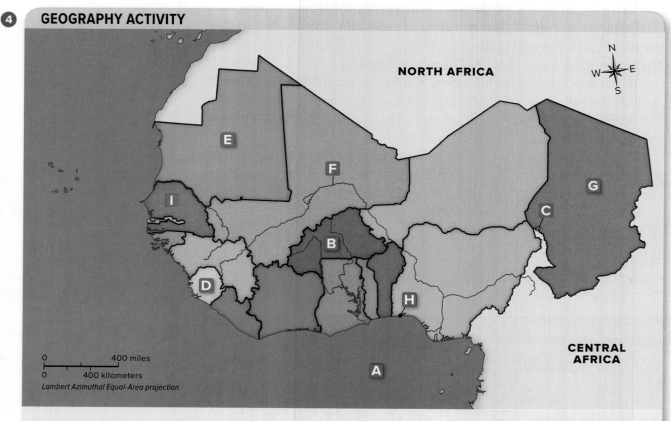

Locating Places

Match the letters on the map with the numbered places below.

1. Chad   **3.** Lagos   **5.** Mauritania   **7.** Burkina Faso   **9.** Sierra Leone

2. Niger River   **4.** Senegal   **6.** Gulf of Guinea   **8.** Lake Chad

Chapter 14 ASSESSMENT

REVIEW THE GUIDING QUESTIONS

Directions: Choose the best answer for each question.

1 The climate of northern West Africa can best be described as

   A. desert.

   B. savannah.

   C. tropical rain forest.

   D. marine west coast.

2 What attracted Portuguese explorers to Ghana in 1471?

   F. salt

   G. petroleum

   H. lithium

   I. gold

3 What did wealthy North African Muslim traders want from the people of West Africa?

   A. gold and converts to Islam

   B. salt and gold

   C. diamonds and emeralds

   D. ivory and camels

4 At the Berlin Conference of 1884–1885, France, Germany, Great Britain, Portugal, and Belgium decided to

   F. fund secondary schools and universities in West Africa.

   G. restrict the trade of enslaved people.

   H. heavily tax coffee and cocoa grown in West Africa.

   I. build empires by carving up and taking political control of African lands for themselves.

5 Traditional African religions are

   A. the dominant religions in West Africa.

   B. no longer practiced.

   C. only practiced in Mali.

   D. practiced, even in countries where Christianity or Islam is dominant.

6 When two or more languages blend and become the language of a region, the result is called a

   F. pidgin language.

   G. blended language.

   H. creole language.

   I. diverse language.

DBQ ANALYZING DOCUMENTS

❼ DETERMINING WORD MEANINGS Read the following passage about the problem of desertification:

> *"Nomads are trying to escape the desert, but because of their land-use practices, they are bringing the desert with them. It is a misconception that droughts cause desertification. Droughts are common in arid and semiarid lands. Well-managed lands can recover from drought when the rains return. Continued land abuse during droughts, however, increases land degradation."*
>
> —from United States Geological Survey, "Desertification"

What does the passage mean in saying that nomads "are bringing the desert with them"?

A. Nomads bring their desert customs wherever they move.

B. Nomads create desert in new areas because of their land-use practices.

C. Nomads have the skills they need to survive in the desert.

D. Nomads can teach their way of life to other people.

❽ IDENTIFYING What evidence does the passage give that droughts alone do not cause desertification?

F. the movement of nomads to new areas

G. the rate at which desertification takes place

H. droughts prevent desertification

I. the ability of lands to recover from drought

SHORT RESPONSE

> *"The people of Ghana have . . . put democracy on a firmer footing, with repeated peaceful transfers of power. . . . This progress . . . will ultimately be more significant [than the struggle for independence]. For just as it is important to emerge from the control of other nations, it is even more important to build one's own nation."*
>
> —from President Barack Obama, "Remarks to the Ghanian Parliament" (2009)

❾ DETERMINING CENTRAL IDEAS How do "repeated peaceful transfers of power" show that democracy in Ghana is on a "firmer footing"?

❿ IDENTIFYING POINT OF VIEW Why does President Obama think this achievement is more important than winning independence?

EXTENDED RESPONSE

⓫ ARGUMENT WRITING Ecotourism is often mentioned as a way that developing nations can use their natural resources to produce income while preserving those resources for future generations. Research the pros and cons of the topic, and decide whether or not ecotourism would be good for the countries of West Africa. Present your response in an essay.

Need Extra Help?

If You've Missed Question	❶	❷	❸	❹	❺	❻	❼	❽	❾	❿	⓫
Review Lesson	1	1	2	2	3	3	1	1	2	2	3

From "Desertification," http://pubs.usgs.gov/gip/deserts/desertification, Department of the Interior/United States Geological Survey. The USGS home page is http://www.usgs.gov.

SOUTHERN AFRICA

ESSENTIAL QUESTIONS · *How does geography influence the way people live?* · *How do new ideas change the way people live?*

Gallo Images - LKIS/Getty Images

Miner from Johannesburg,
South Africa

networks

There's More Online about
Southern Africa.

CHAPTER 15

Lesson 1
Physical Geography of Southern Africa

Lesson 2
History of Southern Africa

Lesson 3
Life in Southern Africa

The Story Matters...

From the steep slopes of the Great Escarpment to the plunging Victoria Falls, Southern Africa is filled with magnificent scenery and wildlife, which draw tourists from around the world. Southern Africa is also the continent's richest region in natural resources, including gold and diamonds. Many of Southern Africa's natural resources have become important to the global economy. Control over these vital resources has brought many great economic, political, and social changes to the region.

Go to the Foldables® library in the back of your book to make a Foldable® that will help you take notes while reading this chapter.

SOUTHERN AFRICA

Most of inland Southern Africa is rich in resources and home to a wide variety of ethnic groups. The region's coastal and island countries are struggling to develop their economies.

Step Into the Place

MAP FOCUS Use the map to answer the following questions.

1 **PLACES AND REGIONS**
Luanda is the capital city of what country?

2 **THE GEOGRAPHER'S WORLD**
What country is located on the southern tip of the African continent?

3 **THE GEOGRAPHER'S WORLD**
What countries share a border with Zimbabwe?

4 **CRITICAL THINKING**
Integrating Visual Information Which of these places is the smallest in area: Lesotho, Gabarone, or Malawi?

PROVINCIAL CAPITAL The flat-topped Table Mountain overlooks the city of Cape Town, South Africa. Cape Town serves as the capital of the Western Cape province.

DESERT MAMMAL The meerkat is a member of the mongoose family. Only about 1 foot tall (30 cm), the meerkat stands by using its long tail for balance.

Step Into the Time

TIME LINE Based on events on the time line, predict the effects of Southern Africa's colonial past on the economy, government, and culture of the region.

A.D. 900
Kingdom of Great Zimbabwe established

1400s Mutapa Empire flourishes

1652 Dutch establish Cape Colony

1800

1806 Britain gains control of Cape Colony

Southern Africa

EQUATOR

CENTRAL AFRICA

EAST AFRICA

Lake Tanganyika

SEYCHELLES

Victoria

CABINDA (Angola)

10°S

Luanda

ANGOLA

Huambo

Kitwe

ZAMBIA

Lusaka

Zambezi R.

Lilongwe

Lake Malawi (Lake Nyasa)

MALAWI

Moroni

COMOROS

Mamoudzou

Mayotte (Fr.)

Okavango R.

Rundu

Lake Kariba

Harare

ZIMBABWE

Bulawayo

MOZAMBIQUE

Mozambique Channel

MADAGASCAR

Toamasina

Antananarivo

MAURITIUS

Port Louis

Réunion (Fr.)

20°S

B

NAMIBIA

Windhoek

Francistown

BOTSWANA

Limpopo R.

TROPIC OF CAPRICORN

Gaborone

Tshwane (Pretoria)

Matola

Johannesburg

Soweto

Mbabane

Maputo

SWAZILAND

INDIAN OCEAN

ATLANTIC OCEAN

Bloemfontein

Maseru

LESOTHO

Orange R.

30°S

A

SOUTH AFRICA

Cape Town

◉ National capital
○ Departmental capital
● City

0   500 miles
0   500 kilometers
Lambert Azimuthal Equal-Area projection

20°E   30°E   40°E   50°E   60°E

1910
Boers establish independent Union of South Africa

1960s
Colonies gain independence and self-rule

1979 Birth of Zimbabwe

1900

2000

1886 World's largest gold deposits discovered

1962 Nelson Mandela sentenced to life in prison

1993 Interim constitution enumerates rights for all people

Reading**HELP**DESK

Academic Vocabulary

- **network**

Content Vocabulary

- **escarpment**
- **landlocked**
- **reservoir**
- **blood diamonds**
- **poaching**

TAKING NOTES: *Key Ideas and Details*

Summarize As you read, list important details about two countries of Southern Africa in a graphic organizer like the one below.

Country:		
Physical Geography		
Climate		
Natural Resources		

Lesson 1
Physical Geography of Southern Africa

ESSENTIAL QUESTION • *How does geography influence the way people live?*

IT MATTERS BECAUSE
Southern Africa is the world's leading producer of gold, platinum, chromium, and diamonds. Other minerals the region supplies, including uranium and copper, are also important in the global economy.

Landforms and Bodies of Water

GUIDING QUESTION *What are the dominant physical features of Southern Africa?*

The region of Southern Africa consists of the 10 southernmost countries on the African continent. It also includes four independent island countries and two French island territories in the Indian Ocean off Africa's east coast.

Southern Africa is bordered by the Indian Ocean on the east and the Atlantic Ocean on the west. The Cape of Good Hope at the southern tip of the continent is considered the place where the two oceans meet.

Several of the region's countries are fairly large. Angola and South Africa are each nearly the size of Western Europe and are the continent's seventh- and ninth-largest countries, respectively. Along with Namibia, Mozambique, Zambia, and Botswana, Angola and South Africa rank in the top 25 percent of the world's countries in land area.

The country of Madagascar occupies the world's fourth-largest island, also called Madagascar. The region's three other island countries—Comoros, Mauritius, and Seychelles—are tiny. Their combined area of 1,800 square miles (4,662 sq. km) makes them smaller than the state of Delaware.

Landforms

If Southern Africa's physical geography had to be described with one word, that word would be *high*. A series of plateaus that range in elevation from 3,000 feet to 6,000 feet (914 m to 1,829 m) cover most of the region. The northern plateaus extend from Malawi across Zambia and Angola. These plateaus are largely forested. Farther south, the plateaus are covered mainly by grasslands.

The plateau's outer edges form a steep slope called the Great Escarpment. In Angola, the **escarpment**, a steep cliff between a higher and a lower surface, runs parallel to the Atlantic Coast and continues through Namibia. Between the escarpment and the Atlantic Ocean lies a strip of desert called the Namib that is 80 miles to 100 miles (129 km to 161 km) wide. The Namib runs 1,200 miles (1,931 km) from southern Angola to western South Africa, where it merges with another desert, the Kalahari.

The Kalahari Desert is a vast, sand-covered plateau that sits some 3,000 feet (914 m) above sea level. It is bordered by even higher plateaus. The Kalahari covers much of eastern Namibia and most of Botswana. In some places, long chains of sand dunes rise as much as 200 feet (61 m) high. The sand in some areas is red because of minerals that coat the grains of sand.

South of the Kalahari Desert, much of the rest of Southern Africa is covered by a huge plateau that slopes from about 8,000 feet (2,438 m) in the east to 2,000 feet (610 m) in the west. At the southern tip of this plateau, the Great Escarpment breaks into several small, low mountain ranges. This group of ranges is known as the Cape Ranges. The ranges are separated from each other by dry basins called the Great Karoo and the Little Karoo.

As the Great Escarpment follows South Africa's coastline, it forms the Drakensberg Mountains. This is the most rugged part of the escarpment. Mountain peaks rise to more than 11,000 feet (3,353 m). A narrow coastal plain lies between the mountains and the Indian Ocean.

The Blyde River Canyon runs through the Drakensberg Mountains, the highest mountains, the highest mountain range in Southern Africa. The caves and rock shelters contain rock painting made by the San people. The San lived in the area for about 4,000 years.

As rivers spill from one plateau to the next, they create thundering waterfalls, such as the spectacular Victoria Falls.

▶ **CRITICAL THINKING**

Describing Where are the falls located?

The Drakensberg mountains parallel the Indian Ocean coastline for some 700 miles (1,127 km) through Lesotho and Swaziland, two **landlocked** countries in Southern Africa. Near Swaziland, the escarpment pulls back from the coastline to create a broad coastal plain that covers much of Mozambique. Northwestern Mozambique and the neighboring countries of Zimbabwe, Zambia, and Malawi lie at higher elevations west of the escarpment, on the plateau.

Bodies of Water

Three major river systems—the Zambezi, Limpopo, and Orange—drain most of Southern Africa. The Zambezi, which stretches for 2,200 miles (3,541 km), is the region's longest river. On the Zambia-Zimbabwe border, midway through its course, the Zambezi plunges over the spectacular Victoria Falls into a narrow gorge. Roughly a mile (1.6 km) wide and 350 feet (107 m) high, the falls are about twice the width and height of Niagara Falls in North America. Because of the heavy veil of mist that rises from the gorge, the area's indigenous people named the falls *Mosi-oa-Tunya* ("The Smoke That Thunders").

The Orange River is Southern Africa's second-longest river. It begins in the highlands of Lesotho and flows westward to reach the Atlantic Ocean. Its course marks the southern boundary of the Kalahari Desert. The region's third-longest river, the Limpopo, flows eastward in a large arc along South Africa's border with Botswana and Zimbabwe. The river then drops over the Great Escarpment to cross the plains of southern Mozambique to the Indian Ocean.

©Roger De La Harpe; Gallo Images/Corbis

These three rivers, their tributaries, and Southern Africa's other rivers have carved a **network** of canyons and gorges across the plateaus. Dams have been built in the area to store water. Lake Kariba, Southern Africa's second-largest lake, is really a **reservoir**, or an artificial lake created by a dam.

The region's largest lake—and the third largest in all of Africa—is Lake Malawi (also known as Lake Nyasa), which forms Malawi's border with Mozambique and Tanzania. It is the southernmost lake of the Great Rift Valley which stretches for thousands of miles. Lake Malawi fills a depression, or hollow, that follows one of the rifts, or tears, in Earth's crust. Because of the great depth of the depression, Lake Malawi is one of the deepest lakes in the world.

A number of flat basins, called pans, can be found in Southern Africa. The salt deposits they contain provide nourishment for wild animals. Etosha Pan, in northern Namibia, is an enormous expanse of salt that covers 1,900 square miles (4,921 sq. km). It is the largest pan in Africa, and it is the center of Etosha National Park. The park is home to some of the greatest numbers of lions, elephants, rhinoceroses, and other large animals in the world.

☑ READING PROGRESS CHECK

Identifying Which type of landform is common in Southern Africa?

Thinking Like a Geographer

Pans

Pans are believed to be the beds of ancient lakes whose water evaporated over time. They are among the flattest known landforms. Small amounts of rain can flood large areas of their surface. It is this flooding that causes and maintains their flatness. Salt deposits form as rainwater pools slowly evaporate. *Why can a small amount of rain flood a large area of a pan?*

Climate

GUIDING QUESTION *What is the climate of Southern Africa?*

Southern Africa has a wide variety of climates, ranging from humid to arid to hot to cool. Nearly all of the region's climates have distinct seasons, with certain seasons receiving most of the rain.

Tropical Zone

The Tropic of Capricorn crosses the middle of Southern Africa. This places the northern half of the region in the Tropics. Northern Angola and northern Mozambique have a tropical wet-dry climate. Each area gets as much as 70 inches (178 cm) of rain per year. Most of it falls in the spring, summer, and fall—from October to May. The high elevation makes temperatures cool.

Academic Vocabulary

network a complex, interconnected chain or system of things such as roads, canals, or computers

Zebras are among the many animals that live in the national park that is part of the Etosha Pan.

▶ CRITICAL THINKING
Describing What is unique about the Etosha Pan?

©Paul A. Souders/Corbis

People struggle to wade through the waters after a heavy rainfall in the coastal city of **Maputo** in southwestern Mozambique.

▶ **CRITICAL THINKING**

Describing How does the length of the rainy season in western Mozambique compare with the length in the northern part of the country?

Daily average temperatures range from the upper 60s°F (upper 10s°C) to the upper 70s°F (mid-20s°C). Along the coasts, temperatures are warmer.

Much of northern Mozambique's coastline is watered by rain-bearing winds called monsoons that sweep in from the Indian Ocean during the summer months. More than 70 inches (178 cm) of annual rainfall is common.

Parts of Angola and Mozambique have humid subtropical climates, as do Malawi, Zambia, and northeastern Zimbabwe. The rainy season here is shorter than in the tropical wet/dry zone, and also brings less rainfall. Most places average 24 inches to 40 inches (61cm to 102 cm) per year. Average temperatures are also slightly cooler. Nighttime frosts are not uncommon in July on the high plateaus of Zambia and Malawi. Temperatures on summer days in lowland areas, however, can exceed 100°F (38°C).

Temperate Zones

Much of South Africa, central Namibia, eastern Botswana, and southern Mozambique have temperate, or moderate, climates that are not marked by extremes of temperature. Most of these areas are semiarid. Summer days are warm—from 70°F to 90°F (21°C to 32°C), depending on elevation. Winters are cool, with frosts and sometimes freezing temperatures on the high plateaus.

Annual rainfall varies from 8 inches (20 cm) in some areas to 24 inches (61 cm) in others. Most of the rain falls during the summer, with very little the rest of the year. Droughts are common; in some places, they last for several years.

Lesotho, Swaziland, and eastern South Africa, including the Indian Ocean coastline, are much wetter. Temperatures are like those in the semiarid regions, but ocean currents and moist ocean air bring up to 55 inches (140 cm) of rain annually. Like elsewhere in the region, most of this rain falls in the summer.

Desert Regions

Western South Africa, western Namibia, and much of Botswana are arid. Along the coast, the Namib gets very little rain. In some years, no rain falls. But fog and dew provide small plants with the moisture they need to survive. Temperatures along the coast are mild, however, with daily averages ranging from 48°F to 68°F (9°C to 20°C). The aridity, the fog, and the mild temperatures result from the cold Benguela Current that flows along the coast. This area is sometimes called the "Skeleton Coast" because many ships used to lose their way in the fog and run aground. Once ashore, the sailors rarely survived because of the lack of water in the sandy desert.

In inland areas of the Namib Desert, temperatures are hotter with summer highs from the upper 80s°F to more than 100°F (30°C to 38°C). In winter, freezing temperatures sometimes occur. During wet years, desert grasses and bushes appear. Much of the time, however, the Namib is home to vast areas of barren sand.

The Kalahari's location—farther inland than the Namib—and dry air make its temperatures more extreme than in the Namib. The Kalahari also gets a little more precipitation than the Namib.

☑ READING PROGRESS CHECK

Describing Why are temperatures in Southern Africa's tropical countries generally not hot?

Natural Resources

GUIDING QUESTION *What natural resources are found in Southern Africa, and why are they important?*

Southern Africa is the continent's richest region in natural resources. Mineral resources have helped the Republic of South Africa, in particular, to build a strong economy. In other countries, like Angola and Namibia, such resources provide the only source of wealth.

The landscape of the Skeleton Coast is made up of sand dunes, rocky canyons, and mountains. Dense fogs and cool sea breezes are characteristic of the area.

▶ CRITICAL THINKING

Describing How did the Skeleton Coast get its name?

More than one-half of the world's diamonds are harvested from mines, such as this one, in Southern Africa. Diamonds were formed deep in Earth thousands of years ago under extreme heat and pressure. Volcanic pressure brings them to Earth's surface.

South Africa's Resources

The Republic of South Africa has some of the largest mineral reserves in the world. It is the world's largest producer of platinum, chromium, and gold, and one of the largest producers of diamonds—both gems and industrial diamonds, or diamonds used to make cutting or grinding tools. These resources, along with important deposits of coal, iron ore, uranium, copper, and other minerals, have created a thriving mining industry. This industry has attracted workers and investments from other countries that have helped South Africa's industries grow.

Energy Resources

The Republic of South Africa, Zimbabwe, Botswana, and Mozambique mine and burn coal from their own deposits to produce most of their electric power. Mozambique has large deposits of natural gas as well, as does Angola. Angola is also one of Africa's leading oil producers. Namibia has oil and natural gas deposits, too, and they are slowly being developed. Oil and gas must be refined, or changed into other products, before they can be used.

The region's rivers are another resource for providing power. Zimbabwe and Zambia get electricity from the huge Kariba Gorge dam on the Zambezi River. Malawi's rivers and falls generate power for that country. Deforestation, however, allows more sediment to enter the rivers, which reduces the water flow and the electricity that the rivers produce. Mozambique, Zimbabwe, and Angola have not made full use of their rivers to provide power. Economic development and the standard of living in those countries have suffered as a result.

©Herve Collart/Sygma/Corbis

Minerals and Other Resources

Namibia is one of Africa's richest countries in mineral resources. It is an important producer of tin, zinc, copper, gold, silver, and uranium. It also ranks with South Africa and Botswana as a leading world supplier of diamonds. In the 1990s, rebels captured Angola's mines and sold the diamonds to continue a 20-year-old civil war against the government. In countries outside Southern Africa, groups have also mined diamonds to pay for rebellions and other violent conflicts. Diamonds used for this purpose are called **blood diamonds**.

Gold is a leading export for Zimbabwe. Mozambique has the world's largest supply of the rare metal tantalite, which is used to make electronic parts and camera lenses. Gold, platinum, and diamonds are mined there too, as are iron ore and copper. Much of Zambia's economy is based on copper and cobalt, although gold, silver, and iron ore are also mined. Zambia has some of the largest emerald deposits in the world. A small amount of rubies, sapphires, and a variety of semiprecious gems are mined in neighboring Malawi.

Malawi's most important natural resource is its fertile soil. The country's economy is based mainly on agriculture. Tobacco is its most important export. Exporting farm products is also a major economic activity in Zimbabwe. Lesotho and Swaziland have few natural resources. Most of their people practice subsistence farming, growing only enough to meet their needs.

Wildlife

Southern Africa is known for its variety of animal life. Wildebeests, lions, zebras, giraffes, and many other animals are found across the region. They live within and outside the many national parks and wildlife reserves that nearly every country has created to protect them. Tourists come from throughout the world to see these animals. **Poaching**, or illegally killing game, is a problem. Poachers shoot elephants for their valuable ivory tusks and rhinoceroses for their horns. Others kill animals to sell their skins and meat and to protect livestock and crops.

Include this lesson's information in your Foldable®.

✔ READING PROGRESS CHECK

Describing How does deforestation affect the energy supply in the region?

LESSON 1 REVIEW

Reviewing Vocabulary

1. Why is *poaching* against the law?

Answering the Guiding Questions

2. ***Describing*** How has damming Southern Africa's rivers benefited the people and countries of the region?

3. ***Identifying*** What are the rainfall and temperature differences between Southern Africa's tropical, temperate, and arid regions?

4. ***Describing*** For what resources is Southern Africa known throughout the world?

5. ***Narrative Writing*** Create a journal entry recording your observations and experiences during one day of a photo safari at Etosha National Park.

Reading HELP DESK

Academic Vocabulary

- exploit
- grant

Content Vocabulary

- apartheid
- civil disobedience
- embargo

TAKING NOTES: *Key Ideas and Details*

Sequence Create a time line like this one. Then list five key events and their dates in the history of the region.

Lesson 2
History of Southern Africa

ESSENTIAL QUESTION • *How do new ideas change the way people live?*

IT MATTERS BECAUSE
Many of Southern Africa's resources have become important parts of the global economy. Political instability and unrest have sometimes disrupted the flow of products to world markets. Much of the instability and unrest is directly or indirectly the result of the region's colonial history.

Rise of Kingdoms

GUIDING QUESTION *What major events mark the early history of Southern Africa?*

Southern Africa's indigenous people have inhabited the region for thousands of years. Some lived as hunter-gatherers. Others farmed and herded cattle. Trade among the groups flourished. Ivory, gold, copper, and other goods moved from the interior to the east coast. There such goods were exchanged for tools, salt, and luxury items including beads, porcelain, and cloth from China, India, and Persia.

Great Zimbabwe

Around the year a.d. 900, the Shona people built a wealthy and powerful kingdom in what is now Zimbabwe and Mozambique. The capital was a city called Great Zimbabwe. (*Zimbabwe* is a Shona word meaning "stone houses.") As many as 20,000 people lived in the city and the surrounding valley.

Great Zimbabwe was the largest of many similar cities throughout the region. By the 1300s, it had become a great commercial center, collecting gold mined nearby and trading it to Arabs at ports on the Indian Ocean.

Great Zimbabwe was abandoned in the 1400s, possibly because its growing population exhausted its water and food resources. The city's ruins show the Shona's skill as builders. Some structures were more than 30 feet (9 m) high. Their large stones were cut to fit and stay in place without mortar to hold them together.

The Mutapa Empire

In the late 1400s, the Shona conquered the region between the Zambezi and Limpopo rivers from Zimbabwe to the coast of Mozambique. Like Great Zimbabwe, the Mutapa Empire thrived on the gold it mined and traded for goods from China and India.

The Portuguese arrived and took over the coastal trade in the 1500s. They gradually gained control over the empire and forced its people to mine gold for them. In the late 1600s, Mutapa kings allied with the nearby Rozwi kingdom to drive out the Portuguese. Instead, the Rozwi conquered the Mutapa's territory and ruled it until the early 1800s, when it became part of the Zulu Empire.

Other Kingdoms

The Zulu leader Shaka united his people in the early 1800s to form the Zulu Empire in what is now South Africa. He built a powerful army and used it to expand the empire by conquering neighboring people. Shaka was killed in 1828, but his empire survived until the British destroyed it in the Zulu War of 1879.

A series of kingdoms rose and fell on the island of Madagascar from the 1600s to the 1800s. Some of the early kingdoms were influenced by Arab and Muslim culture. In the early 1800s, one king allied with the British on the nearby island of Mauritius to prevent the French from taking control of Madagascar. He eventually conquered most of the island and formed the Kingdom of Madagascar. French troops invaded the kingdom in 1895 and made it a French possession.

☑ READING PROGRESS CHECK

Identifying Which outsiders traded with Southern Africans before the Europeans arrived?

Shown are remnants of the walls of the Great Enclosure of the city of Great Zimbabwe. According to historians, houses of the royal family were located within the walls.

Identifying How did Great Zimbabwe become an important center of trade?

©Christine Osborne/Corbis

European Colonies

GUIDING QUESTION *How did Southern Africa come under European control?*

Three Zulu leaders are shown holding shields and wearing traditional attire. The Zulu built a great empire, but during the 1800s, European settlers took control of their grazing and water resources. The Zulu population is about 9 million today, making them the largest ethnic group in the Republic of South Africa.

Academic Vocabulary

exploit to make use of something, sometimes in an unjust manner for one's own advantage or gain

Around 1500, Portugal and other European countries began establishing settlements along the African coast. The first settlements were trading posts and supply stations at which ships could stop on their way to and from Asia. As time passed, the Europeans grew interested in **exploiting** Africa's natural resources and, as a source of labor, its people.

Clashes in South Africa

During the 1600s till about the 1800s, Europeans set up trading posts but did not establish colonies, which are large territories with settlers from the home country. One exception was Cape Colony, founded by the Dutch in 1652 at the Cape of Good Hope on the southern tip of what is now South Africa. The Dutch became known as Boers, the Dutch word for farmers. They grew wheat and raised sheep and cattle. Enslaved people from India, Southeast Asia, and other parts of Africa provided much of the labor.

The Africans did not like the Dutch pushing into their land, and soon they started fighting over it. By the late 1700s, the Africans had been defeated. Some fled north into the desert. Others became workers on the colonists' farms.

The Union of South Africa

Wars in Europe gave Britain control of the Cape Colony in the early 1800s. Thousands of British settlers soon arrived. The Boers resented British rule. Many decided to seek new land beyond the reach of British control. Beginning in the 1830s, thousands of Boers left the colony in a migration called the Great Trek and settled north of the Orange River.

In the 1860s, the Boers discovered diamonds in their territory. Then, in 1886, they found the world's largest gold deposits. British efforts to gain these resources led to the Boer War in 1899. The Boers were defeated and again came under British control. In 1910 Britain allowed the Boer colonies to join the Cape Colony in forming an independent country—the Union of South Africa. The small African kingdoms of Lesotho and Swaziland remained under British control.

Hulton Archive/Getty Images

Colonialism in Other Areas

While the British and the Boers competed for South Africa, other European countries were competing over the rest of Africa. In 1884 representatives of these countries met in Berlin, Germany, to divide the continent among themselves.

In Southern Africa, Britain gained control over what is now Malawi, Zambia, Zimbabwe, and Botswana. The Berlin Conference decided Portugal had rights to Angola and Mozambique. Germany received what is now Namibia, although South Africa seized the colony during World War I. Besides Madagascar, France controlled what is now Comoros. Mauritius and Seychelles were British colonies.

European control in Southern Africa continued for about the next 80 years. Not until the 1960s did the region's colonies begin to gain independence and self-rule.

☑ **READING PROGRESS CHECK**

Analyzing Which European country claimed the most territory in Southern Africa in the 1800s?

Independence and Equal Rights

GUIDING QUESTION *What challenges did Southern Africans face in regaining freedom and self-rule?*

French rule in Madagascar ended in 1960, making it the first Southern African country to gain independence. Britain **granted** independence to Malawi and Zambia in 1964 and to Botswana and Lesotho in 1966. Swaziland and Mauritius gained their freedom in 1968, and Seychelles in 1976. Elsewhere, however, freedom was more difficult to achieve.

©dpa/dpa/Corbis

Academic Vocabulary

grant to permit as a right, a privilege, or a favor

Boer soldiers fight from trenches at the siege of Mafeking in 1900. The siege, lasting more than 200 days, resulted in an important victory for British forces.

▶ CRITICAL THINKING

Describing Who were the Boers? Why were the Boer Wars fought?

©David Turnley/Corbis

Laws in South Africa limited the political rights of black Africans and set up separate parks, beaches, and other public places.

▶ CRITICAL THINKING

Describing Who controlled South Africa's government until World War II? Who controlled the government beginning in 1948?

The End of Portuguese Rule

While other European nations gave up their African colonies, Portugal refused to do so. Revolts for independence broke out in Angola in 1961 and in Mozambique in 1964. The thousands of troops Portugal sent to crush these revolts failed to do so.

By 1974, the Portuguese had grown tired of these bloody and expensive wars. Portuguese military leaders overthrew Portugal's government and pulled the troops out of Africa. Angola and Mozambique became independent countries in 1975 as a result. Fighting continued, however, as rebel groups in each country competed for control. Mozambique's long civil war ended when a peace agreement was reached in 1994. Peace was not finally achieved in Angola until 2002.

The Birth of Zimbabwe

After granting Malawi and Zambia independence, Britain prepared to free neighboring Zimbabwe, then called Southern Rhodesia. The colony's white leaders, who controlled the government, instead formed a country they called Rhodesia and continued to rule.

Rhodesia's African population demanded the right to vote. When the government resisted, a guerrilla war began. In 1979 the government finally agreed to hold elections in which all Rhodesians could take part. Rebel leader Robert Mugabe was elected president, and Rhodesia's name was changed to Zimbabwe.

Equal Rights in South Africa

After independence, the growth of South Africa's mining and other industries depended on the labor of black Africans, who greatly outnumbered the country's whites. The white minority government stayed in power by limiting the black population's educational and economic opportunities and political rights.

English South Africans controlled the government until the end of World War II. Then a strike by more than 60,000 black mine workers frightened white voters into electing an Afrikaner government in 1948 that promised to take action. (Afrikaners are the descendants of the Boers. They speak a language called Afrikaans, which gives them their name.)

The new government leaders began enacting laws that created a system called **apartheid**—an Afrikaans word meaning "apartness." Apartheid limited the rights of blacks. For example, laws forced black South Africans to live in separate areas called "homelands." People of non-European background were not even allowed to vote. The African National Congress (ANC), an organization of black South Africans, began a campaign of **civil disobedience**, disobeying certain laws as a means of protest. The government's violent response to peaceful protests caused the ANC to turn to armed conflict. In 1962 ANC leader Nelson Mandela was arrested and sentenced to life in prison.

By the 1970s, apartheid-related events in South Africa had gained world attention. Countries began placing **embargos**, or bans on trade, on South Africa. Meanwhile, the struggle in South Africa grew more intense. In 1989 South Africa's president, P.W. Botha, was forced to resign. In 1990 the government, under Botha's successor, F.W. de Klerk, began repealing the apartheid laws. Mandela was released from prison in 1991. In 1993 a new constitution gave South Africans of all races the right to vote. The ANC easily won elections held in 1994, and Mandela became the country's president.

In 1995 the new government created a truth and reconciliation commission. Its task was to ease racial tensions and heal the country by uncovering the truth about the human rights violations that had occurred under apartheid.

By 1994, South Africa's policy of apartheid was officially over. Nelson Mandela became the first black person to be elected president of South Africa. Mandela is shown voting for the first time in his life on April 27, 1994.

FOLDABLES
Study Organizer

Include this lesson's information in your Foldable®.

✓ READING PROGRESS CHECK

Determining Central Ideas Why do you think South Africa's government created the apartheid system?

LESSON 2 REVIEW

Reviewing Vocabulary

1. Why might some people disapprove of *civil disobedience* as a means of protest and of achieving change?

Answering the Guiding Questions

2. ***Analyzing*** How did some of Southern Africa's early people benefit from the region's natural resources?

3. ***Identifying*** Name five present-day countries in Southern Africa that were once controlled by Britain.

4. ***Determining Central Ideas*** Why was gaining independence especially difficult for Angola and Mozambique?

5. ***Argument Writing*** Write a paragraph explaining whether actions against the governments of Rhodesia and South Africa were justified.

Lesson 2 **441**

©Louise Gubb/Corbis SABA

Lesson 3
Life in Southern Africa

ReadingHELPDESK

ESSENTIAL QUESTION • *How does geography influence the way people live?*

IT MATTERS BECAUSE
Control over Southern Africa's vast and vital natural resources has been passed on to new leadership. Great economic, political, and social changes and challenges have accompanied this transfer.

The People of the Region

GUIDING QUESTION *Where do people live in Southern Africa?*

The population of Southern Africa is overwhelmingly black African. The largest white minority is in the country of South Africa, where whites represent 10 percent of the population. In almost every other country, whites and Asians make up less than 1 percent of the population. The region's black African population is made up of many different ethnic and culture groups.

Population Patterns

Southern Africa's countries vary widely in population. Fewer than 2 million people live in the small countries of Lesotho and Swaziland. South Africa, which surrounds both of them, has the region's largest population—about 49 million.

Population depends heavily on geography and economics. For example, Botswana and Namibia are much larger than Swaziland and Lesotho, but their populations are only slightly larger. Most Batswana, as the people of Botswana are called, live in the northeast, away from their country's desert areas. Similarly, most Namibians live in the northern part of their country, away from the arid south and west.

South Africa and Angola are about the same size. South Africa, the region's most industrialized nation, has three times as many people. In both countries, most people live in cities. Angola's rural areas are thus much more thinly populated than rural areas in South Africa.

Mozambique, which is slightly smaller than Namibia and much smaller than Angola, has a population greater than those two countries combined. Most of Mozambique's 23 million people are engaged in farming, mainly along the fertile coastal plain.

Zambia is twice as big as Zimbabwe. Zimbabwe, with a population of about 12 million, has only 2 million fewer people. Both countries are largely rural, with only about one-third of their people living in cities. Large parts of Zambia are thinly populated.

Malawi is just one-third the size of Zimbabwe and one-sixth the size of Zambia, yet it exceeds both in population. With some 16 million people living in an area roughly the size of Pennsylvania, it is the region's most densely populated country. On average, every square mile holds more than 250 people.

Surprisingly, Malawi is also Southern Africa's most rural nation. Only 20 percent of its people live in cities. Its small size and large rural population mean that most of its farms are small. Most farm villages are not able to produce much more than what they need. As a result, Malawi is the region's poorest country. The average Malawian earns less than $350 per year.

MAP SKILLS

1 **PLACES AND REGIONS** What do the cities of Johannesburg, Durban, and Cape Town have in common?

2 **THE GEOGRAPHER'S WORLD** In general, which area of Southern Africa is more densely populated: eastern or western?

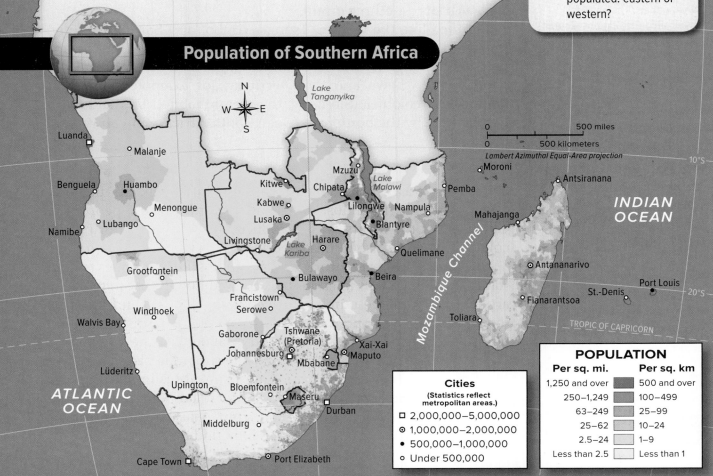

Population of Southern Africa

Cities
(Statistics reflect metropolitan areas.)
- ☐ 2,000,000–5,000,000
- ◉ 1,000,000–2,000,000
- • 500,000–1,000,000
- ○ Under 500,000

POPULATION

Per sq. mi.	Per sq. km
1,250 and over	500 and over
250–1,249	100–499
63–249	25–99
25–62	10–24
2.5–24	1–9
Less than 2.5	Less than 1

Members of the Nazareth Baptist Church in South Africa take part in their annual pilgrimage to the mountain of Nhlangakazi. The church is also called the Shembe Church after its founder, Isaiah Shembe.

Think Again?

Southern Africa's large island country of Madagascar was settled by African people.

Not true. Most of Madagascar's people speak Malagasy, a language related to those spoken in Indonesia, the Philippines, and islands in the South Pacific. The language of Madagascar indicates that the island's early inhabitants probably came from that part of the world.

Ethnic and Culture Groups

Africans are not a single people. Southern Africa is home to many ethnic and cultural groups who speak several different languages. One group, the Shona, makes up more than 80 percent of the population of the country of Zimbabwe. South Africa's 9 million Zulu make up that country's largest ethnic group. More than 7 million Xhosa also live there, as do the Khoekhoe. Some 4.5 million Tsonga people are spread among the countries of South Africa, Zimbabwe, and Mozambique.

About 4 million Tswana form the major population group in Botswana. A similar number of Ovimbundu and 2.5 million Mbundu make up approximately two-thirds of Angola's population. A smaller group, the Ambo, live in Angola and Namibia. About half of Namibia's people belong to this ethnic group. The San, a nomadic people, live mainly in Namibia, Botswana, and southeastern Angola. The Chewa are Malawi's largest ethnic group.

Groups like the Chewa, Tsonga, Ambo, and San illustrate an important point about Southern Africa's history. When Europeans divided the region, they paid little attention to its indigenous people. The Chewa and their territory, for example, were split among four colonies. Similarly, the area inhabited by the Tsonga was divided by the borders between South Africa, Zimbabwe, and Mozambique.

Religion and Languages

Southern Africa's colonial past has also influenced its people's religious beliefs. In almost every country, most of the people are Christians. Christianity was introduced to the region during the colonial era by Christian missionaries.

In Angola, however, nearly half the population continues to hold traditional indigenous religious beliefs. Traditional African religions are followed by large numbers of people in Namibia and Lesotho, too. In Zimbabwe and Swaziland, a blend of Christianity and traditional religious beliefs is followed by about half the population.

Swaziland, Zambia, Malawi, and Mozambique also have large Muslim populations. Most of Mozambique's Muslims live on the coast, where **contact** with Arab traders led long ago to the introduction of Islam. Immigration from Asia explains Zambia's Muslim population, as well as its large Hindu minority.

©STR/Reuters/Corbis

Portuguese remains the official language in Angola and Mozambique. English is an official language in most of the former British colonies. Its use, however, is mainly limited to official and business communications; nowhere is it widely spoken by the people. Instead, most speak indigenous languages. South Africa has 10 official languages besides English; Zambia has 7.

☑ READING PROGRESS CHECK
Determining Central Ideas What is the main religion practiced in Southern Africa?

Life in Southern Africa

GUIDING QUESTION *How do the various people of Southern Africa live?*

As in other regions of Africa, life differs from city to countryside. Many rural people continue to follow traditional ways of life. At the same time, urban and economic growth are challenging and changing many of the traditional ways.

Urban Life

Although most people in the region of Southern Africa live in the countryside, migration to cities grows because of job opportunities. Harare, Zimbabwe, has grown to more than 1.5 million, as have Lusaka, Zambia, and Maputo, Mozambique. Luanda, Angola's capital, is even larger: It holds some 4.5 million people. South Africa has four cities—Durban, Ekurhuleni, Cape Town, and Johannesburg—with populations of around 3 million or more.

Academic Vocabulary

contact communication or interaction with someone

Shown here is a high-rise building under construction in the city of Luanda in Angola. Luanda is the country's main seaport and government center.

Ken Gerhardt/Gallo Images/Getty Images

At an outdoor market in Lusaka, vendors come to sell handcrafted items. Food and entertainment are also available.

▶ **CRITICAL THINKING**
Describing What are periodic markets?

Urban Growth and Change

The rapid growth of some cities has strained public **utilities**—services such as trash collection, sewage treatment, and water distribution. Luanda, for example, has had many problems providing enough clean water for its many people. Outbreaks of cholera and other diseases have resulted from drinking polluted water.

The region's cities have a mix of many ethnic groups and cultures. An example is Johannesburg, where the wealth from nearby gold fields helped build one of the most impressive downtowns in all of Africa. Outside the central city are the white neighborhoods where about 20 percent of the city's population live. Some black South Africans have moved into these neighborhoods since the end of apartheid. Most, however, live in "townships" at the city's edge. These areas often have no electricity, clean water, or sewer facilities. Most of the region's large cities have shantytowns.

Johannesburg's role as a mining, manufacturing, and financial center has attracted people from around the world. Every black ethnic group in Southern Africa is present, as well. The white community is mainly English and Afrikaner. Large Portuguese, Greek, Italian, Russian, Polish, and Lebanese populations also live there. Indians, Filipinos, Malays, and Chinese live mainly in the townships. At least 12 languages are heard on city streets.

Family and Traditional Life

People who move to the cities must adjust to new experiences and a different way of life. In the countryside, traditional ways of life remain strong.

Rural villages are often small—consisting of perhaps 20 or 30 houses. Building materials, which vary by ethnic group, include rocks, mud bricks, woven sticks and twigs packed with clay, and **thatch**—straw or other plant material used to cover roofs.

In many cultures, all the people in a village are related by blood or marriage to the village's headman or chief. Men often have more than one wife. They provide a house for each wife and their children. Growing food crops is the main economic activity. Many families raise cattle as well, mainly for milk and as a symbol of wealth.

People in the countryside practice subsistence farming, growing the food they need to survive. Artwork sometimes provides a family with a source of cash. Wood and ivory carving are art forms that are generally practiced by men. Pottery-making is usually a woman's craft. In some cultures, both men and women make baskets. They sell the products in cities or at **periodic markets**—open-air trading markets held regularly at crossroads or in larger towns.

In recent times, more and more men have been leaving their villages to work at jobs in cities or mines. Although the money they send home helps support their families, this **trend** has greatly changed village life. Many villages now consist largely of women, children, and older men. Women have increasingly taken on traditional male roles in herding, family and community leadership, and other activities.

✓ **READING PROGRESS CHECK**

Citing Text Evidence Where in their countries do most Southern Africans live?

Southern Africa Today

GUIDING QUESTION *What challenges and prospects do the countries of Southern Africa face?*

Southern Africa's wealth of mineral, wildlife, and other resources may be the key to its future. Still, the region faces serious social, economic, and political challenges.

Health Issues

Life expectancy in Southern Africa is low. In the majority of countries, most people do not live beyond age 50 to 55. Lack of good rural health care is one reason, although many countries are trying to build or improve rural clinics.

ALEXANDER JOE/AFP/Getty Images

Academic Vocabulary

trend a general tendency or preference

Members of South Africa's Ndebele tribe attend a gathering of traditional leaders from all over the country in November 2009 to honor former President Nelson Mandela.

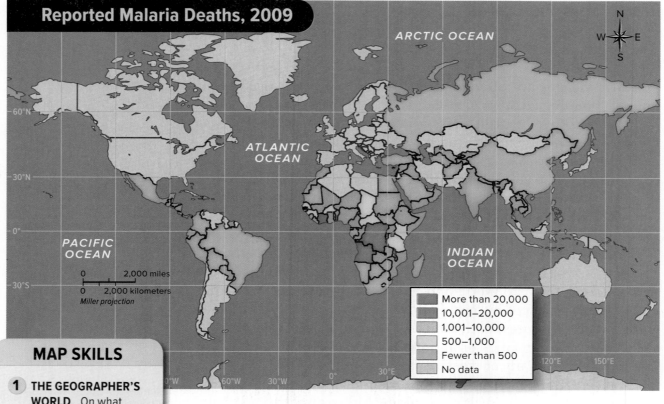

Reported Malaria Deaths, 2009

ARCTIC OCEAN

ATLANTIC OCEAN

PACIFIC OCEAN

INDIAN OCEAN

0   2,000 miles
0   2,000 kilometers
Miller projection

More than 20,000
10,001–20,000
1,001–10,000
500–1,000
Fewer than 500
No data

MAP SKILLS

1. **THE GEOGRAPHER'S WORLD** On what continent has malaria been responsible for the greatest number of deaths?

2. **THE GEOGRAPHER'S WORLD** In what regions of the world has malaria been responsible for the fewest deaths?

Disease

Malaria, a tropical disease carried by mosquitoes, is a problem in several countries. Dysentery and cholera, potentially fatal diseases caused by bacteria in water, are also widespread. So is tuberculosis. Malnutrition is a cause of death for many infants and young children.

Southern Africa has some of the highest rates of infant death in the world. In Angola, Malawi, and Mozambique, about 100 to 120 of every 1,000 children die in infancy. Elsewhere in the region, the figure is 40 to 60 per 1,000. (The infant death rate in the United States is 7 per 1,000.)

A major cause of death in children and adults is HIV/AIDS. Southern Africa has a higher HIV/AIDS rate than any other region in Africa. Swaziland, Botswana, Lesotho, and South Africa have the highest rates in the world. About one of every four adults (25 percent) in these countries is infected with this sexually transmitted disease, which women pass on to their children at birth. In the rest of the region, the adult HIV/AIDS rate averages between 11 and 14 percent. (In the United States, the rate is 0.6 percent.)

The high incidence of HIV/AIDS has disrupted the labor force by depriving countries of needed workers. It has also disrupted families through death, inability to work, or AIDS-related family issues. The disease has created millions of AIDS orphans, children whose mother and father have died from AIDS. The huge number of AIDS orphans is a major social problem.

Progress and Growth

Angola and Mozambique continue to rebuild the cities and towns, industries, railroads, and communications systems that have been damaged or destroyed by years of civil war. Oil exports in Angola and aluminum exports in Mozambique help finance this effort. So does the tourism that peace and stability have brought back to the beautiful beaches and resorts along Mozambique's coast.

Tourism at national parks has grown with the establishment of stable, democratic governments. Zambia and Malawi replaced one-party rule with more democratic forms of government in the 1990s. Botswana and Namibia have been strong democracies, respecting and protecting human rights, since independence. Only Zimbabwe and Swaziland continue to suffer economic decline and political unrest, largely due to repressive leaders.

Help From Other Countries

The United States has used economic aid to strengthen democracy in Southern Africa. Other U.S. programs have provided billions of dollars to pay for medications and care for AIDS sufferers and AIDS orphans.

Other countries and international organizations have also made huge investments in the region. Taiwan's development of a textile industry in Lesotho, for example, is giving some of that poor country's workers an alternative to employment in South Africa's mines.

Foreign investment, workers, and tourists have also returned to South Africa as it continues to recover from the effects of apartheid. South Africa remains the region's most industrial and wealthiest country. It also faces serious economic challenges. Many of its traditional African farming communities struggle in poverty, growing few if any cash crops. Its heavy reliance on the export of mineral and agricultural goods places it at risk if world demand or prices for the goods fall. These problems mirror the challenges that many other countries in Southern Africa also confront.

Include this lesson's information in your Foldable®.

✓READING PROGRESS CHECK

Analyzing Why is life expectancy in Southern Africa so low?

LESSON 3 REVIEW

Reviewing Vocabulary

1. What did rural Southern Africans use clay and *thatch* for?

Answering the Guiding Questions

2. *Determining Central Ideas* How did colonialism and contact with traders influence religious beliefs in Southern Africa?

3. *Describing* What are rural and city life like for Southern Africa's black population?

4. *Analyzing* How and why has Southern Africa benefited from the growth of democracy in the region?

5. *Argument Writing* Write a letter to the editor of a Southern African newspaper explaining whether the region should continue to work for change.

Directions: Write your answers on a separate piece of paper.

1 Use your **FOLDABLES** to explore the Essential Question.

INFORMATIVE/EXPLANATORY WRITING Write two paragraphs explaining how Southern Africa's resources place the region in a favorable position to develop trade with other countries.

2 21st Century Skills

DESCRIBING Using information from the text and online, create a brief slide show of Southern Africa's energy resources and how the region uses the resources. Narrate the slide show, identifying the different countries' means of generating power.

3 Thinking Like a Geographer

DETERMINING CENTRAL IDEAS As a geographer, would you favor setting aside more or less land for game preserves in Southern Africa? Use a T-chart to list your pro and con arguments.

4 GEOGRAPHY ACTIVITY

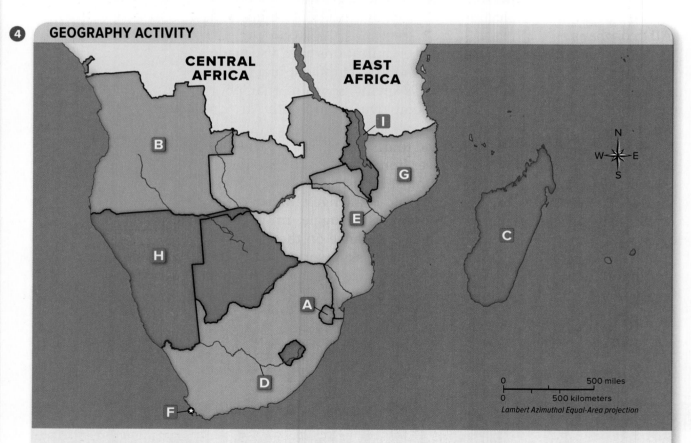

Locating Places

Match the letters on the map with the numbered places listed below.

1. Zambezi River

2. Madagascar

3. Angola

4. Cape Town

5. Orange River

6. Mozambique

7. Namibia

8. Swaziland

9. Lake Malawi (Lake Nyasa)

REVIEW THE GUIDING QUESTIONS

Directions: Choose the best answer for each question.

1. The country of Madagascar is
   A. a large plateau.
   B. Southern Africa's regional capital city.
   C. the world's fourth-largest island.
   D. the world's largest exporter of coconut milk.

2. Which is the longest river in Southern Africa?
   F. Kariba
   G. Congo
   H. Great Karoo
   I. Zambezi

3. Western South Africa, western Namibia, and Botswana have what climate zone in common?
   A. tropical
   B. desert
   C. Mediterranean
   D. steppe

4. The amount of hydroelectric power in this region has been reduced by
   F. deforestation.
   G. droughts.
   H. monsoons.
   I. civil disturbances.

5. South Africa's Afrikaners are descended from which population group?
   A. native Africans
   B. Boers
   C. Portuguese colonists
   D. Zambians

6. Which is the most densely populated country in Southern Africa?
   F. Zambia
   G. the Republic of South Africa
   H. Madagascar
   I. Malawi

DBQ ANALYZING DOCUMENTS

7 ANALYZING Read the following passage about the area around the Okavango River and the Kalahari Desert.

"During dry periods [the Okavango Delta] is estimated to cover at least 6,000 square miles, but in wetter years, with a heavy annual flood, the Okavango's waters can spread over 8,500 square miles of the Kalahari's sands. Deep water occurs in only a few channels, while vast areas of reed beds are covered by only a few inches of water."

—from Cecil Keen, *Okavango*

As described in the reading, the Okavango is a

A. desert.

B. mountain.

C. river.

D. reed bed.

8 ANALYZING What can you infer about the land of the Kalahari from this passage?

F. It is sandy because it absorbs most of the water fairly quickly.

G. It is fairly flat because more of the water is shallow than deep.

H. It is wet most of the time because it lets the floodwaters stand.

I. It tilts to the west because that is where the deep channels form.

SHORT RESPONSE

"Discouraged about the lack of results from their nonviolent campaign, Nelson Mandela and others called for an armed uprising . . . that paralleled the nonviolent resistance. That, too, failed to tear down the apartheid system, and in the end a concerted grassroots nonviolent civil resistance movement [together] with international support and sanctions [against the government] forced the white government to negotiate."

—from Lester R. Kurtz, "The Anti-Apartheid Struggle in South Africa"

9 DETERMINING CENTRAL IDEAS What were Mandela and others trying to achieve?

10 ANALYZING How did they eventually succeed?

EXTENDED RESPONSE

11 INFORMATIVE/EXPLANATORY WRITING Southern Africa has an abundance of wildlife, including animals, birds, fish, and exotic plant life. Tourists come from all over the world to see the animals, which live on animal preserves and in the wild. Do some research on travel in Southern Africa, then write an essay describing the experience of going on safari. Talk about which areas of the region you visited and what you saw, and what kind of accommodations you had on your safari.

Need Extra Help?

If You've Missed Question	❶	❷	❸	❹	❺	❻	❼	❽	❾	❿	⓫
Review Lesson	1	1	1	1	2	3	1	1	2	2	3

◄ *The African kingdom of Benin became well known for the detailed works of its artists, such as this ivory carving.*

400 B.C. TO A.D. 1500

African Civilizations

Peter Horree/Alamy

THE STORY MATTERS ...

Around A.D. 1400 the steamy rain forests of Africa were home to the kingdom of Benin. The region's steamy climate and fertile soil allowed farmers to grow surpluses of crops. Over time, communities and societies developed.

As a result, arts became very important in Benin. The kingdom became well known for the ivory and wood carvings its artists produced. An example is this rare pendant carved in ivory in honor of Queen Idia. Other artists worked with metals to produce realistic-looking masks. Today, this surviving art allows historians to learn more about the rich history and culture of early African civilizations.

ESSENTIAL QUESTIONS
- Why do people trade?
- How does religion shape society?
- How do religions develop?

Place & Time: AFRICA 400 B.C. to A.D. 1500

The earliest civilizations in Africa emerged about five thousand years ago. These early kingdoms developed rich cultures that excelled at many art forms. Later African empires were affected by the arrival of Islam and then Europeans. All had an impact creating the Africa we know today.

Step Into the Place

MAP FOCUS The vast and varied landscape of Africa influenced the development of civilizations on the continent.

1 **REGION** In which part of Africa would you find the most land that is difficult to farm?

2 **PLACE** What climate region runs along the Equator in Africa?

3 **LOCATION** Describe the location of the Mediterranean climate in Africa.

4 **CRITICAL THINKING**
Human-Environment Interaction
What impact do you think the Great Rift Valley might have had on where people settled?

The geography of Africa has determined where people settle. This aerial photo of Cape Town, South Africa, shows a coastal city. The Table Bay Harbour is visible in the foreground. Near it stands the Greenpoint Stadium, home of the 2010 men's soccer World Cup.

Wildlife abounds in Africa. Individual countries now have laws protecting their wildlife. These elephants, living near Kilimanjaro, are a protected species. Environmentalists are concerned about other types of wildlife. All over the continent, animal life is recognized as one of Africa's most valuable resources.

Step Into the Time

TIME LINE A variety of climates are found in Africa. According to the time line, where and in what climate zone did the earliest kingdoms appear?

c. 250 B.C. Mali is West Africa's largest trading center

c. A.D. 250 Bantu peoples settle south of Sahara

AFRICAN CIVILIZATIONS

THE WORLD

| 500 B.C. | A.D. 1 | A.D. 500 |

Climate Zones of Africa

40°N

ATLAS MOUNTAINS

Strait of Gibraltar

Mediterranean Sea

ANATOLIAN PLATEAU

ASIA

TROPIC OF CANCER

S A H A R A

LIBYAN DESERT

Nile R.

Red Sea

Persian Gulf

20°N

AHAGGAR MOUNTAINS

TIBESTI MOUNTAINS

ARABIAN PENINSULA

INDIA

Senegal R.

Niger R.

Lake Chad

AMHARA PLATEAU

Arabian Sea

Gulf of Aden

Lake Volta

Lake Turkana

Gulf of Guinea

Ubangi R.

EQUATOR

Congo R.

CONGO BASIN

Lake Victoria

Mt. Kenya

Kilimanjaro

0°

ATLANTIC OCEAN

Lake Tanganyika

GREAT RIFT VALLEY

INDIAN OCEAN

N
W E
S

Lake Malawi

Zambezi R.

MADAGASCAR

KEY
- Desert
- Mediterranean
- Rain forest
- Savanna

NAMIB DESERT

Limpopo R.

20°S

TROPIC OF CAPRICORN

KALAHARI DESERT

DRAKENSBERG RANGE

0   1,000 miles
0   1,000 km
Lambert Azimuthal Equal-Area projection

Orange R.

Cape of Good Hope

40°W   20°W   0°   20°E   40°E   60°E   80°E

c. A.D. 1441 First captives in European slave trade

c. A.D. 800s–900s Ghana is trading empire

c. A.D. 1493 Muhammad Ture rules Songhai

c. A.D. 1352 Ibn Battuta reaches West Africa

A.D. 1000   A.D. 1100   A.D. 1200   A.D. 1300   A.D. 1400   A.D. 1500

The Rise of African Civilizations

- Why do people trade?

IT MATTERS BECAUSE
The geography of Africa affected the development and interaction of civilizations all over the huge continent.

African Beginnings

GUIDING QUESTION *How did early peoples settle Africa?*

People have lived in Africa for a very long time. Scientists believe that the first humans appeared in eastern and southern Africa between 150,000 and 200,000 years ago. Early human groups in Africa lived as hunters and gatherers. These early peoples moved from place to place to hunt and gather food.

About seven or eight thousand years ago, hunters and gatherers in Africa began to settle in villages. They learned to tame animals and grow crops. Around 3000 B.C., as farming villages became more widespread and organized, Africa's first civilizations developed. These early civilizations were Egypt and Kush.

A Vast and Varied Landscape

The people of Africa found opportunities and challenges in the geography of the continent. First of all, Africa is very large in size. After Asia, Africa is the world's largest continent.

Most of Africa lies in the Tropics. However, this enormous continent is made up of four distinct geographic zones.

Rain forests stretch along the Equator, which slices through the middle of the continent. These forests make up about 10 percent of Africa's land **area**. The rain forest zone gets heavy rainfall, and it is warm there all year long. The dense growth of

Reading**HELP**DESK

Taking Notes: *Identifying*
On a chart like this one, list the three major West African trading kingdoms. Then add one product that each kingdom traded.

West African Kingdom	Product

Content Vocabulary
- savanna
- plateau
- griot
- dhow

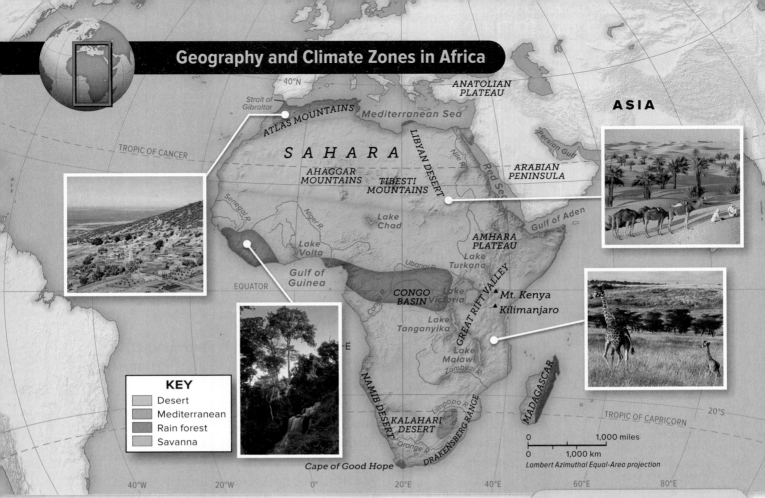

Geography and Climate Zones in Africa

KEY
- Desert
- Mediterranean
- Rain forest
- Savanna

trees and plants in the rain forest can make farming difficult. Farmers, however, clear some of the forestland to grow root crops, such as yams.

Grasslands and Deserts

Vast grasslands make up the second zone. They stretch north and south of the rain forest. **Savannas** (suh·VAN·uhs) are tropical grasslands dotted with small trees and shrubs. These flat or rolling plains cover about 40 percent of Africa's land area. The savannas have high temperatures and uneven rains. However, they get enough rainfall for farming and herding. Farmers grow grains, such as millet and sorghum (SAWR· guhm). Herders raise cattle and other animals.

In northern Africa, the savannas connect with an area of even drier grasslands known as the Sahel (SA·hil). Plants that grow there provide barely enough food for people and animals. The people of the Sahel were traditionally hunters and herders.

GEOGRAPHY CONNECTION

Differences in geographic features, such as climate, have had a strong influence on life in Africa's geographic zones.

1 LOCATION Which geographic feature covers most of East Africa?

2 CRITICAL THINKING
Making Inferences How might the geographic zones of Africa have affected interaction between people from the northeastern and northwestern parts of the continent?

---

savanna tropical grasslands dotted with small trees and shrubs

Academic Vocabulary

area the land included within a set of boundaries

Reading Strategy: *Contrasting*

When you contrast two things, you determine how they are different from each other. Read the information about savannas and the Sahel. On a separate sheet of paper, explain how these two areas differ.

	Africa	United States
Size	11,667,159 square miles (30,217,894 sq. km)	3,794,085 square miles (9,826,680 sq. km)
Population Today	about 1.03 billion people	about 308 million people
Longest River	Nile River 4,160 miles (6,693 km)	Missouri River 2,565 miles (4,130 km)
Largest Desert	Sahara 3,500,000 square miles (9,065,000 sq. km)	Mojave 15,000 square miles (38,850 sq. km)

UNITED STATES

AFRICA

Encyclopaedia Britannica OnLine s.v., "Africa," http://www.britannica.com/EBchecked/topic/7924/Africa

INFOGRAPHIC

Many areas of Africa remain mostly unpopulated. Africa's population represents only about 10 percent of the world's total population.

1 IDENTIFYING What are the longest rivers in Africa and the United States?

2 CRITICAL THINKING
Comparing and Contrasting How do Africa and the United States compare in size and population?

Deserts are Africa's third zone. They are found north and south of the grasslands. About 40 percent of the land in Africa is desert. The world's largest desert—the Sahara—stretches across much of North Africa. The Kalahari (KA·luh·HAHR·ee), another desert region, lies in southwestern Africa. For many years, the deserts limited travel and trade. People had to move along the coastline to avoid these vast seas of sand.

Small areas of mild climate—the Mediterranean—make up the fourth zone. These areas are found along the northern coast and southern tip of Africa. In these areas, **adequate** rainfall, warm temperatures, and fertile land produce abundant crops. This food surplus can support large populations.

Africa's Landforms and Rivers

Most of Africa is covered by a series of plateaus. A **plateau** (pla·TOH) is an area of high and mostly flat land. In East Africa, mountains, valleys, and lakes cross the plateau. Millions of years ago, movements of the Earth's crust created deep cuts in the surface of the plateau. This activity created the Great Rift Valley. In recent years, scientists have found some of the earliest human fossils in the Great Rift Valley.

Many large river systems are found in Africa. The civilizations of Egypt and Kush flourished along the banks of the Nile River in North Africa. The major river system in West Africa is found along the Niger (NY·juhr) River. Trade and farming led to the growth of villages and towns throughout the Niger River area.

Reading**HELP**DESK

plateau an area of high and mostly flat land

Academic Vocabulary

adequate enough to satisfy a need
transport to transfer or carry from one place to another

People living south of the Sahara also learned to make iron. This skill spread from East and Central Africa to West Africa. By 250 B.C., Djenné-jeno (jeh·NAY-JEH·noh) emerged as the largest trading center in West Africa. Its artisans produced iron tools, gold jewelry, copper goods, and pottery.

This photo shows the Great Rift Valley, a deep crack in Earth's crust that is 6,000 miles (9,659 km) long. The valley began forming 20 million years ago.

☑ **PROGRESS CHECK**

Determining Cause and Effect How did Africa's climate zones affect people's ability to raise crops?

Trading Empires in Africa

GUIDING QUESTION *How did trade develop in Africa?*

For thousands of years, the hot, dry Sahara isolated North Africa from the rest of the continent. Then, about 400 B.C., the Berber people of North Africa found ways to cross the Sahara to West Africa. Trade soon opened between the two regions.

How Did the Sahara Trade Develop?

For hundreds of years, the Berbers carried goods across the Sahara on donkeys and horses. The animals often did not survive the desert heat. The Romans introduced the central Asian camel in A.D. 200. The use of camels greatly changed trade in Africa. Camels are well suited for the desert. Their humps store fat for food, and they can travel for many days without water. The Berbers quickly adopted camels, both as a source of food and as a way to travel.

Berber traders formed caravans of many camels. These caravans crossed the Sahara between North Africa and West Africa. West African merchants sent gold mined in their region to towns bordering the Sahara. From there, caravans carried the gold northward. Some of this African gold reached Europe and Asia. Christian and Muslim rulers in these areas valued African gold.

Caravans from West Africa also carried ivory, spices, leather, and ostrich feathers. In addition, they **transported** enslaved people captured in wars. Merchants sent these captives to the Mediterranean area and Southwest Asia where they were forced to serve as soldiers or servants.

☑ **PROGRESS CHECK**

Explaining Why were camels essential for the Sahara trade?

West African Kingdoms

GUIDING QUESTION *Why did West African trading empires rise and fall?*

Caravans also headed from North Africa to West Africa. They transported cloth, weapons, horses, paper, and books. Once in West Africa, they traded for salt from mines in the Sahara.

There's More Online! connected.mcgraw-hill.com

ArCaLu/Shutterstock

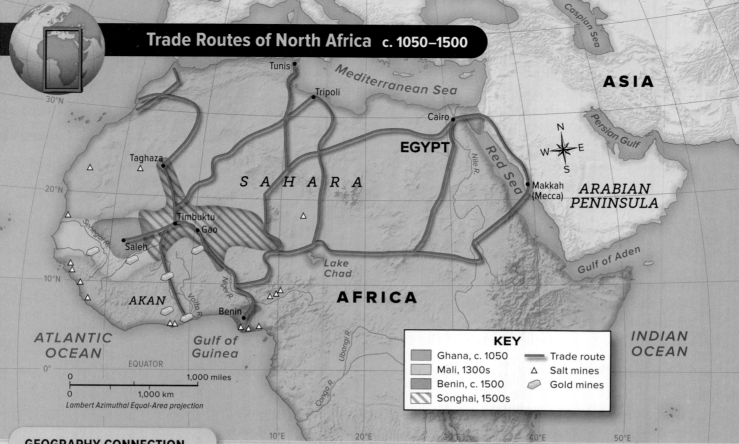

Trade Routes of North Africa c. 1050–1500

KEY
- Ghana, c. 1050
- Mali, 1300s
- Benin, c. 1500
- Songhai, 1500s
- Trade route
- △ Salt mines
- ⬭ Gold mines

Lambert Azimuthal Equal-Area projection

GEOGRAPHY CONNECTION

The opening of trade routes allowed the people of North Africa and West Africa to exchange products, such as gold and salt.

1 LOCATION What resource was found in the kingdom of Benin?

2 CRITICAL THINKING
Calculating Use the map's scale to determine how many miles a caravan might travel along a route from Tunis to Benin.

During the A.D. 700s, Berber and Arab traders brought Islam to West Africa. They established ties with West African merchants, many of whom became Muslims.

The Saharan trade brought prosperity to West Africa. As a result of trade, the population grew, and powerful city-states emerged in the region. Eventually, rulers of these city-states began to build empires. From the A.D. 500s to the A.D. 1300s, these African empires were bigger than most European kingdoms in wealth and size.

How Did Ghana Begin?

Ghana (GAH·nuh) was the first great trading empire in West Africa. It rose to power during the A.D. 400s. The kingdom of Ghana was located in the Sudan. This area was mostly grassland, stretching across north central Africa. Fertile soil and iron tools helped the farmers of Ghana produce enough food.

Ghana was located between the Sahara salt mines and gold mines near the West African coastal rain forests. As a result, Ghana became an important crossroads of trade. From Ghana, trade routes extended into North Africa to the Niger River.

Reading HELPDESK

Reading in the Content Area

When reading primary source quotes, note any words or phrases in brackets. The use of brackets provides you with additional words that help clarify the meaning of the quote.

griot traditional storytellers

They also linked to kingdoms in the Central African rain forest. Some routes reached all the way to Africa's eastern coast.

Traders interested in salt or gold had to pass through Ghana, which came at a price. Traders had no choice but to pay taxes to Ghana's kings. First, Ghana had iron ore and knew how to make iron weapons. Although Ghana owned no gold mines, it controlled the West Africans who did. Second, Ghana's kings had a well-trained army to enforce their wishes. Third, people were willing to pay any price for salt, a highly desired item used to flavor and preserve food. Berber traders wanted gold so they could buy goods from Arab countries and from Europe.

Abdullah Abu-Ubayd Al-Bakri (ehl·BEHK·ree), an Arab travelling writer in about A.D. 1067, described the way Ghana taxed merchants:

PRIMARY SOURCE

❝ The king [of Ghana] exacts the right of one dinar [of gold] on each donkey-load of salt that enters his country, and two dinars of gold on each load of salt that goes out. ❞

—from *Ghana* in 1067

Ghana reached the height of its trading power in the A.D. 800s and 900s. Muslim Arabs and Berbers involved in the salt and gold trade brought Islam to Ghana.

Rise of Mali

During the A.D. 1100s, invaders from North Africa disrupted Ghana's trade, and the empire fell. As Ghana weakened, local groups separated to form new trading states in West Africa.

In the A.D. 1200s, a small state named Mali (MAH·lee) conquered Ghana. Mali created a new empire. West African **griots** (GREE·ohz), or storytellers, credit a great king for Mali's rise. His name was Sundiata Keita (sun·dee·AH·tuh KY·tuh)—the "Lion Prince." Sundiata ruled from 1230 to 1255. He united the people of Mali.

Sundiata conquered territory extending from the Atlantic coast inland to the trading city of Timbuktu (TIHM·BUHK·TOO). His conquests put Mali in control of the gold mines in West Africa. As a result, Mali built its wealth and power on the gold and salt trade.

How Did Songhai Begin?

Mali weakened after the death of king Mansa Musa (MAHN·sah moo·SAH) in 1337. One of the states that eventually broke away from Mali's control was Songhai (SAWNG·eye). In 1464, Sunni Ali (sun·EE ah·LEE) became the ruler of Songhai. He seized control of Timbuktu. Sunni Ali used Songhai's location along the Niger River to extend his territory.

There's More Online! connected.mcgraw-hill.com

Lesson 1 **461**

©Werner Forman/Corbis

Thinking Like a
HISTORIAN

Researching on the Internet

Ghana became the first great trading empire in West Africa. In the A.D. 800s and 900s, Ghana was at the height of its trading power. Use the Internet to find reliable sources about what life was like in Ghana during this period. Write two or three sentences that summarize your findings and present your summary to the class. For more information about using the Internet for research, read *What Does a Historian Do?*

This West African sculpture is of the Queen Mother of Benin. Benin had great rulers. By the mid-1500s, the kingdom of Benin stretched from the Niger River delta to what is now Lagos.

AFRICAN TRADING EMPIRES A.D. 100–1600

	East Africa	West Africa	West Africa	West Africa	SE Africa
Location	AXUM Adulis	GHANA Saleh	MALI Timbuktu	SONGHAI Gao	ZIMBABWE Great Zimbabwe
Time Period	c. 100–1400	c. 400–1200	c. 1200–1450	c. 1000–1600	c. 700–1450
What Was Traded	ivory, frankincense, myrrh, enslaved people	iron products, animal products, salt, gold	salt, gold	salt, gold	gold, copper, ivory
Key Facts	King Ezana converted to Christianity; made it the official religion.	Taxes from traders passing through made Ghana rich.	King Mansa Musa built mosques and libraries.	Songhai gained control of West African trade by conquering Timbuktu.	Kings Mutota and Matope built huge empires.

INFOGRAPHIC

West African empires controlled trade for more than 1,000 years.

1 **IDENTIFYING** How long after the decline of Ghana did the Songhai Empire come to an end?

2 **CRITICAL THINKING**
Comparing and Contrasting
How were the goods traded by Ghana and Mali alike and different?

He took control of the river and then seized the salt mines. Songhai soon controlled the trade in salt from the Sahara and gold. By 1492, Songhai was the largest empire in West Africa. Invaders from North Africa ended the empire by A.D. 1600.

The West African kingdoms ruled the savannas. The rain forest, near the Equator, also had its own kingdoms. They included Benin, which arose in the Niger delta, and Kongo, which formed in the Congo River basin.

☑ **PROGRESS CHECK**

Identifying What were two valuable products traded through Ghana?

East African Kingdoms

GUIDING QUESTION *How did trade affect the development of East African kingdoms?*

In ancient times, powerful kingdoms also arose in East Africa. The kingdom of Kush thrived on the Nile River for hundreds of years. One of Kush's neighbors was the kingdom of Axum (AHK·SOOM) on the Red Sea.

Axum benefited from its location on the Red Sea. It was an important stop on the trade route linking Africa, the Mediterranean, and India. Axum exported ivory, incense, and enslaved people. It imported cloth, metal goods, and olive oil.

dhow sailboat using wind-catching, triangular sails

Axum fought Kush for control of trade routes to inland Africa. Around A.D. 300, King Ezana (ay· ZAHN·uh) conquered Kush. In A.D. 334, Ezana made Christianity the official religion of Axum. Islam was introduced to Axum later. Both religions had a major impact on Axum and other trading states.

Coastal States

In the early A.D. 600s, Arab traders from the Arabian Peninsula had reached East Africa. They sailed to Africa in boats called **dhows** (dowz). In the A.D. 700s, many Arab Muslim traders settled along the Indian Ocean in East Africa. They shared goods and ideas with Africans living there. By the 1300s, a string of key trading ports extended down the East African coast. They included Mogadishu (MAH·guh·DIH·shoo), Kilwa, Mombasa (mahm·BAH·suh), and Zanzibar (ZAN·zuh·BAHR).

The Rise of Zimbabwe

The Indian Ocean trade reached far inland and led to the rise of wealthy states in Central and Southern Africa. These inland territories mined rich deposits of copper and gold. During the A.D. 900s, traders from the coastal cities of Africa began to trade with the inland states. The coastal traders brought silk, glass beads, carpets, and pottery. They traded for minerals, ivory, and coconut oil. They also bought enslaved Africans for export to countries overseas.

An important trading state known as Zimbabwe (zihm·BAH· bway) arose in southeastern Africa. During the 1400s, this large empire reached from south of the Zambezi (zam·BEE·zee) River to the Indian Ocean.

A dhow usually had one or two sails. The bow, or front, of a dhow pointed sharply upward.

► CRITICAL THINKING
Making Inferences How do you think an invention such as the sails used on dhows might have benefited the Arab traders?

✔ PROGRESS CHECK

Explaining Why did Axum become a prosperous trading center?

Mary Evans Picture Library

LESSON 1 REVIEW

Review Vocabulary

1. How is a *savanna* different from a *plateau*?

Answer the Guiding Questions

2. *Explaining* What are the four main geographic zones of Africa?

3. *Identifying* What role did the cities of Mogadishu and Mombasa play in the economic life of East Africa?

4. *Naming* What products did West Africans trade?

5. *Describing* What unique factors allowed the East African trading kingdoms to expand their trade?

6. NARRATIVE You live in ancient West Africa. Your family is traveling to East Africa. In a personal journal, describe what you might experience when you arrive in East Africa. Tell about the people, land, and weather.

Africa's Governments and Religions

ESSENTIAL QUESTION
• How does religion shape society?

IT MATTERS BECAUSE
Ancient African societies showed the effects of government disputes, traditional religious beliefs, and Islam.

African Rulers and Society

GUIDING QUESTION *How did African rulers govern their territories?*

In most ancient societies, rulers were isolated from their subjects. In Africa south of the Sahara, the distance between kings and the common people was not as great. Often, African rulers would hold meetings to let their people voice complaints. In Ghana, drums called the people to the king. Anybody with a concern could address him. Before talking, subjects demonstrated their respect. They poured dust over their heads or fell to the ground. Next, they bowed and stated their business. Then they waited for their king's reply.

Kings and the People

Africans developed different ways to rule their territories. Powerful states, such as Ghana and Mali, favored strong central governments. Power rested with the rulers. They settled disputes, controlled trade, and defended the empire. They expected total loyalty from their people. Everyone benefited from the relationship. Merchants received favors from kings and paid the kings taxes in return. Local rulers held some power and gave the kings their support. This system allowed kingdoms to grow rich, control their lands, and keep the peace.

Reading **HELP**DESK

Taking Notes: *Organizing*

In a graphic organizer like this one, record at least one accomplishment of each of the leaders listed.

Leader	Accomplishments
Mansa Musa	
Muhammad Ture	
Askia Muhammad	

Content Vocabulary
• clan   • Swahili

What Was Ghana's Government Like?

The kings of Ghana were strong rulers who played active roles in running the kingdom with the help of ministers and advisors. As the empire grew, the kings divided their territory into provinces. Lesser kings often governed the provinces, which were made up of districts and governed by district chiefs. Each district was composed of villages belonging to the chief's **clan**. A clan is a group of people descended from the same ancestor.

Ghana's government had a **unique** method of transferring power from one ruler to another. "This is their custom and their habit," stated an Arab writer, "that the kingdom is inherited only by the son of the king's sister." In Arab lands, property was inherited by a man's sons. In Ghana, leadership passed to the king's nephew.

The Government of Mali

Mali had a government like that of Ghana, but on a grander scale. Mali had more territory, more people, and more trade. As a result, royal officials had more responsibilities.

Mali's kings controlled a strong central government. The empire was divided into provinces, like those of Ghana. However, the kings put generals in charge of these areas. Many people supported the generals because the generals protected Mali from invaders. Also, the generals often came from the provinces they ruled.

Mansa Musa, Mali's most powerful king, won the loyalty of his subjects by giving them gold, property, and horses. He gave military heroes the "National Honor of the Trousers." As one Arab writer said:

This king of Benin was treated with respect by his subjects. This carving shows a public gathering.

▶ CRITICAL THINKING
Analyzing How does this carving show us that the people honored their king?

PRIMARY SOURCE

❝ Whenever a hero adds to the lists of his exploits [adventures], the king gives him a pair of wide trousers. … [T]he greater the number of the knight's [soldier's] exploits, the bigger the size of his trousers. ❞

—from *Medieval West Africa: Views from Arab Scholars and Merchants*, excerpt by Ibn Fadl Allah al-'Umari

In Mali, only the king and his family could wear clothing that was sewn, like the clothes we wear today. Other people wore pieces of cloth wrapped around their bodies to form clothing. The trousers awarded to military heroes were truly a great honor.

Werner Forman/Art Resource, NY

clan a group of people descended from the same ancestor

Academic Vocabulary
unique one of a kind

The kings of Ghana taxed gold. This tax helped to control the amount of gold produced.

Government in Songhai

Songhai built on the political traditions of Ghana and Mali. It reached the height of its power under Muhammad Ture. A general and a devout Muslim, Muhammad Ture seized power in 1493 and created a new dynasty. He was a capable administrator who divided Songhai into provinces. A governor, a tax collector, a court of judges, and a trade inspector ran each province. Muhammad Ture **maintained** the peace and security of his empire with a navy and soldiers on horseback.

✓ PROGRESS CHECK

Describing Why did many people in Mali support the generals who ruled the provinces?

Traditional African Religions

GUIDING QUESTION *How did traditional religions influence African life?*

Most African societies shared some common religious beliefs. One of these was a belief in a single creator god. Many groups, however, carried out their own religious practices. These practices differed from place to place. For example, the Yoruba lived in West Africa. They believed that their chief god sent his son from heaven in a canoe. The son then created the first humans. This religion was practiced by many of the enslaved people brought by Europeans to the Americas.

In some religions, the creator god was linked to a group of lesser gods. The Ashanti people of Ghana believed in a supreme god whose sons were lesser gods. Others held that the creator god had once lived on Earth but left in anger at human behavior. This god, however, was forgiving if people corrected their ways.

Even though Africans practiced different religions in different places, their beliefs served similar purposes. They provided rules for living and helped people honor their history and ancestors. Africans also relied on religion to protect them from harm and to **guarantee** success in life. A special group of people, called diviners, were believed to have the power to predict events. Kings often hired diviners to guarantee good harvests and protect their kingdoms.

✓ PROGRESS CHECK

Explaining What was the role of diviners in African religion?

Photodisc/Getty Images

Islam Arrives in Africa

GUIDING QUESTION *How did Islam spread in Africa?*

Beginning in the A.D. 700s, traditional African religions were **challenged** by the arrival of Islam. Through trade, Berber and Arab merchants eventually introduced Muslim beliefs to West Africa. African rulers welcomed Muslim traders and allowed their people to **convert** to Islam. The rulers did not become Muslims themselves until the A.D. 1000s. By the end of the 1400s, much of the population south of the Sahara had converted to Islam.

Who Was Ibn Battuta?

Ibn Battuta (IH·buhn bat·TOO·tah) was a young Arab lawyer from Morocco. In 1325, he set out to see the Muslim world. He reached West Africa in 1352. There, he found that people had been following Islam for centuries. Yet not all West Africans were Muslims. People in rural areas still followed traditional African religions. Some rulers and traders accepted Islam only because it helped them trade with Muslim Arabs.

Ibn Battuta described in detail the people and places of West Africa. Some things amazed him. He was surprised that women did not cover their faces with a veil, as was the Muslim custom.

GEOGRAPHY CONNECTION

Today, people in Africa continue to practice a variety of religions.

1 LOCATION Which religion dominates the southern part of Africa?

2 CRITICAL THINKING
Analyzing Use the graph to compare the percentages of Africans practicing traditional religions with those practicing Islam. How do they compare?

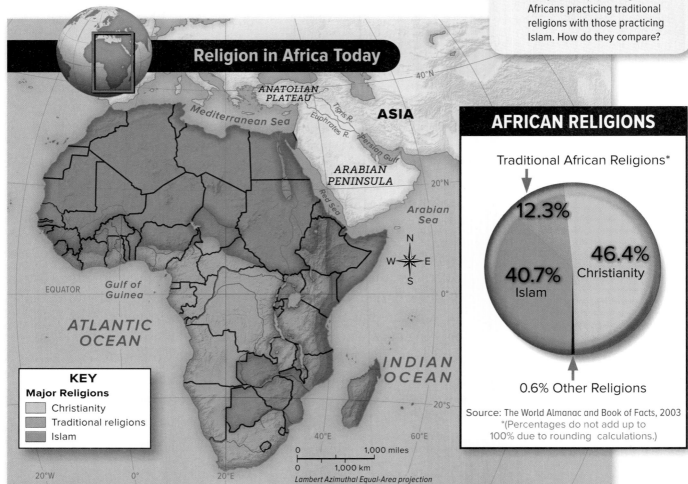

Religion in Africa Today

ANATOLIAN PLATEAU

Mediterranean Sea

ASIA

ARABIAN PENINSULA

Arabian Sea

Gulf of Guinea

EQUATOR

ATLANTIC OCEAN

INDIAN OCEAN

KEY
Major Religions
- Christianity
- Traditional religions
- Islam

0   1,000 miles

0   1,000 km

Lambert Azimuthal Equal-Area projection

AFRICAN RELIGIONS

Traditional African Religions*

12.3%

46.4% Christianity

40.7% Islam

0.6% Other Religions

Source: The World Almanac and Book of Facts, 2003
*(Percentages do not add up to 100% due to rounding calculations.)

However, he did find that West African Muslims "zealously [eagerly] learned the Quran by heart" and faithfully performed their religious duties:

Muslim architecture, such as this mosque, demonstrates the lasting influence of Islam in Africa.

PRIMARY SOURCE

❝ On Fridays, if a man does not go early to the mosque [a Muslim place of worship], he cannot find a corner to pray in, on account of the crowd. It is a custom of theirs to send each man his boy [to the mosque] with his prayer-mat; the boy spreads it out for his master in a place befitting him [and remains on it] until he comes to the mosque. Their prayer-mats are made of the leaves of a tree resembling a date-palm, but without fruit. ❞

—from Travels in Asia and Africa, by Ibn Battuta

The Journey of Mansa Musa

Ibn Battuta was impressed by Mansa Musa, Mali's most famous ruler. Mansa Musa let his subjects practice different religions. However, he was devoted to spreading Islam. Mansa Musa used his empire's wealth to build more mosques. In Timbuktu, Mansa Musa set up libraries with books from around the Muslim world.

In 1324, Mansa Musa increased the fame of Mali during a journey to Makkah (MAH·kuh). All Muslims are expected to travel to the Muslim holy city of Makkah. Mansa Musa made certain that people knew he was the ruler of a great empire.

Mansa Musa traveled in grand style. Eighty camels carried two tons of gold. Mansa Musa gave away so much gold to the poor on his journey that the price of gold fell. While in Makkah, Mansa Musa met scholars of Islam. He convinced them to return with him to Mali. They helped spread Islam in West Africa.

Islam in Songhai

Islam won followers among the Songhai people. Sunni Ali, the ruler, became a Muslim to keep the loyalty of merchants. After Sunni Ali died, his son refused to accept Islam. Muhammad Ture, a Songhai general, took over the government. With the backing of Muslim townspeople, he made himself king. He drove out Sunni Ali's family. He then took the name Askia.

Sylvain Grandadam/age fotostock

Reading**HELP**DESK

Swahili the unique culture of Africa's East Coast and the language spoken there

Academic Vocabulary

survive to continue to function or prosper

Under Askia Muhammad (moo·HAH·muhd), the Songhai created the largest empire in West Africa's history. He ordered local courts to follow Muslim laws. He also made Timbuktu an important center of Islamic learning. Askia Muhammad set up a famous university and opened schools to teach the Quran.

The Songhai Empire **survived** disputes among royal family members. It did not, however, survive the guns of Moroccan invaders. This invasion in 1591 brought down the empire.

How Did Islam Develop in East Africa?

Islam spread slowly in East Africa. Islam arrived in the A.D. 700s, but the religion did not gain many followers until the 1100s and 1200s. A new society arose known as **Swahili** (swah·HEE·lee). It was based on a blend of African and Muslim cultures. The word *Swahili* comes from an Arabic word meaning "people of the coast." By 1331, however, it referred to the culture of East Africa's coast and the language spoken there.

The African influences on the Swahili culture came from the cultures of Africa's interior. Muslim influences came from Arab and Persian settlers. The Swahili culture and language still thrive in Africa.

Islam's Effect on Africa

Islam had a far-reaching effect on much of Africa. Africans who accepted Islam adopted Islamic laws and ideas. They also were influenced by Islamic learning. Muslim schools introduced the Arabic language to their students. In addition, Islam influenced African art and its buildings. Muslim architects built beautiful mosques and palaces in Timbuktu and other cities.

☑ PROGRESS CHECK

Determining Cause and Effect What caused a unique brand of Islam to develop in Africa?

BIOGRAPHY

**Mansa Musa
(ruled 1312–1337)**

Mansa Musa attracted the attention of many nations with his famous pilgrimage, or trip, to Makkah (Mecca). Countries in Europe, as well as kingdoms in North Africa and Southwest Asia, took notice. These nations hoped to trade with Mali and gain some of its wealth. Mansa Musa expanded his empire by capturing the cities of Gao (GAH • oh) and Timbuktu. During his reign, Mali was one of the world's largest empires. Mansa Musa once boasted that traveling from the empire's northern border to its southern border would take a year.

▶ CRITICAL THINKING
Identifying Cause and Effect How did Mansa Musa's pilgrimage to Makkah benefit the kingdom of Mali?

LESSON 2 REVIEW

Review Vocabulary

1. What two meanings developed for the word *Swahili*?

Answer the Guiding Questions

2. ***Comparing*** What did all the early governments of African kingdoms have in common?

3. ***Explaining*** How did the leaders of Mali manage the grand scale of their government?

4. ***Describing*** What similar purposes did traditional African religions share?

5. ***Summarizing*** What did Ibn Battuta observe about the different religious groups in West Africa?

6. **INFORMATIVE/EXPLANATORY** Write a brief paragraph in which you explain how Mansa Musa worked to spread Islam in West Africa.

African Society and Culture

• How do religions develop?

IT MATTERS BECAUSE

The people of early Africa formed complex societies with many common characteristics. They created artistic works that reflected their beliefs and built economies.

African Society

GUIDING QUESTION *Why do people in different parts of Africa have similar traditions and cultures?*

In early Africa, most people lived in rural villages. Their homes consisted of small, round dwellings made of packed mud. Villagers generally were farmers. Africa's urban areas often began as villages with protective walls. These villages grew into larger **communities**. African towns and cities were centers of government and trade. Traders and artisans thrived in these communities. Artisans were skilled in metalworking, woodworking, pottery making, and other crafts.

Family Ties

The family formed the basis of African society. People often lived in **extended families**, or families made up of several generations. Extended families included parents, children, grandparents, and other relatives. These families ranged in size from a few individuals to hundreds of members.

Extended families were part of larger social groups known as lineage groups. Members of a lineage group could trace their family histories to a common ancestor. As in many other ancient

Taking Notes: *Finding the Main Idea*

Use a chart like this one to record and organize important ideas about the different elements of African culture.

Cultural Element	Main Idea
Art	
Music and Dance	
Storytelling	

Content Vocabulary

• **extended family**
• **matrilineal**
• **oral history**
• **sugarcane**
• **spiritual**

societies, older members had more power than younger people. Members of a lineage group were expected to support and care for each other.

Bantu Migrations

Many of Africa's social practices are a result of migrations that began in West Africa about 3000 B.C. and lasted hundreds of years. The migrants, known as the Bantu (BAN•too), shared similar languages, cultures, and technologies. The Bantu migrated from West Africa to the south and east. They spread their farming and iron-working skills, along with their languages. Today, about 220 million Africans speak hundreds of Bantu languages.

Bantu villages were also **matrilineal** (ma•truh•LIH•nee•uhl). They traced their descent, or ancestry, through mothers, not fathers. When a woman married, however, she joined her husband's family. To make up for the loss, her family received presents from the husband's family. These gifts might include cattle, goats, cloth, or metal tools.

How Did African Children Learn?

In Africa's villages, education was the duty of both the family and other villagers. Children learned the history of their people and the basic skills they would need as adults.

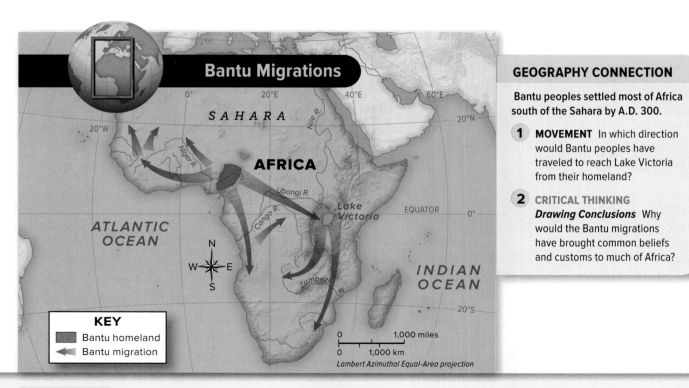

Bantu Migrations

KEY
- Bantu homeland
- Bantu migration

GEOGRAPHY CONNECTION

Bantu peoples settled most of Africa south of the Sahara by A.D. 300.

1. **MOVEMENT** In which direction would Bantu peoples have traveled to reach Lake Victoria from their homeland?

2. **CRITICAL THINKING**
Drawing Conclusions Why would the Bantu migrations have brought common beliefs and customs to much of Africa?

extended family a family made up of several generations

matrilineal tracing family descent through mothers rather than fathers

Academic Vocabulary

community a large group with common values living in an area

Some women in early Africa served as soldiers and political leaders. Queen Nzinga ruled in southern Africa.

▶ CRITICAL THINKING
Making Connections Why might European explorers have been surprised to observe women serving in these roles?

In West Africa, griots helped to teach the children. They vividly told their village's oral history . These stories were told and retold, and people passed them down from generation to generation. Many stories included a lesson about life. Lessons also were given through short proverbs. One Bantu proverb stated, "Patience is the mother of a beautiful child."

African Women

As in most other early societies, women in Africa acted mostly as wives and mothers. Men had more rights and supervised much of what women did. Visitors to Africa, however, noticed some exceptions. European explorers were amazed to learn that women served as soldiers in some African armies.

African women also served as rulers. In the A.D. 600s, Queen Dahia al-Kahina (dah·HEE·uh ahl·kah·HEE·nah) led an army against Arab invaders, who attacked her kingdom. Another woman ruler was Queen Nzinga (ehn·ZIHN·gah), who governed lands in southwestern Africa. She spent almost 30 years fighting Portuguese invaders and resisting the slave trade.

✔ PROGRESS CHECK

Describing What were families like in early Africa?

The Slave Trade

GUIDING QUESTION *How did the slave trade affect Africans?*

In 1441, a ship from the European nation of Portugal sailed down Africa's western coast. The ship captain's plan was to bring African captives back to Europe. During the voyage, the captain and crew seized 12 Africans—men, women, and boys. With its human cargo on board, the ship then sailed back to Portugal. These captives were the first Africans to be part of a slave trade that would involve millions of people.

How Was African Slavery Practiced?

Slavery was a common practice throughout the world. It had been practiced in Africa since ancient times. Bantu warriors raided nearby villages for captives to use as laborers, servants, or soldiers. Some were set free for a payment. Africans also enslaved their enemies and traded them for goods. The lives of enslaved Africans were hard, but they might win their freedom through work or by marrying a free person.

Mary Evans Picture Library

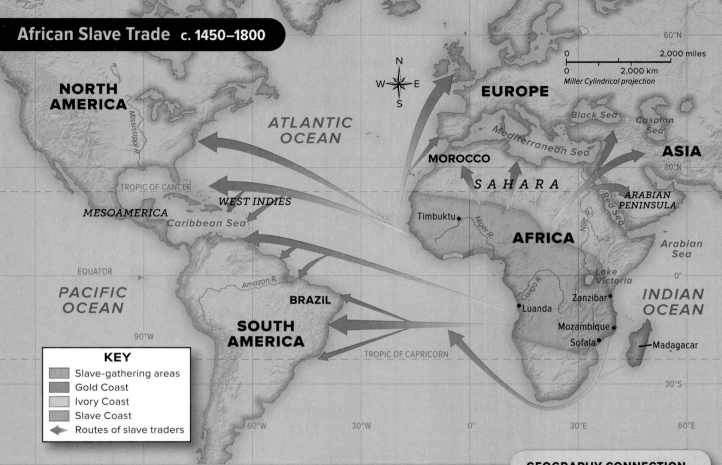

African Slave Trade c. 1450–1800

KEY
- Slave-gathering areas
- Gold Coast
- Ivory Coast
- Slave Coast
- Routes of slave traders

GEOGRAPHY CONNECTION

The slave trade carried enslaved Africans to different parts of the world.

1 **MOVEMENT** By what route is it likely a slave trader would have traveled from Mozambique to Brazil?

2 **CRITICAL THINKING** *Speculating* What developments in world history might have caused the slave trade to grow during the time period shown here?

The trade in humans grew as Africa's **contact** with the Muslim world increased. The Quran banned the enslavement of Muslims. Muslims, however, could enslave non-Muslims. Arab Muslim merchants, therefore, began to trade cotton and other goods for enslaved non-Muslim Africans.

When Europeans arrived in West Africa, a new market for enslaved Africans opened. Africans armed with European guns began raiding villages to seize captives to sell.

The European Slave Trade

In 1444, a Portuguese ship brought 235 enslaved Africans to a dock in Portugal. An official of the royal court saw the Africans being taken off the vessel. He was moved to ask:

PRIMARY SOURCE

" What heart could be so hard as not to [be] pierced with ... feeling ...? For some kept their heads low, and their faces bathed in tears. ... Others stood groaning ... crying out loudly, as if asking [for] help. ... others struck their faces. ... But to increase their sufferings still more, ... was it then needful to part fathers from sons, husbands from wives, brothers from brothers? "

—from Gomes Eannes de Zurara, as quoted in *The Slave Trade* by Hugh Thomas

This colorful blanket is made from Kente cloth. Its name comes from an African word that means "basket."

Griots, such as this woman, often accompany themselves on a stringed instrument called a kora.

▶ **CRITICAL THINKING**
Evaluating How might the tradition of oral storytelling have affected African stories over time?

Portuguese merchants now sold humans. At first, most enslaved Africans were forced to work in Portugal. Later, they were sent to the Atlantic islands of Madeira, the Azores, and Cape Verde. The Portuguese had settled these islands. The mild climate was ideal for growing **sugarcane** on plantations, or huge farms.

Harvesting sugarcane was hard work. Plantation owners could not pay high wages. Instead, they used enslaved Africans. Enslaved people received no wages. By 1500, Portugal had become the world's **major** supplier of sugar.

In the late 1400s, Europeans arrived in the Americas. They forcibly transported enslaved Africans across the Atlantic Ocean to grow sugar, tobacco, rice, and cotton.

✓ **PROGRESS CHECK**

Analyzing How did increased contact with other parts of the world affect the slave trade in Africa?

Culture in Africa

GUIDING QUESTION *Why were art forms important to Africans?*

Africans excelled in many art forms, including painting, weaving, woodcarving, poetry, dancing, and metalworking. These arts served a religious purpose. They also taught people the history of their communities.

Art in Africa

The earliest art forms in Africa were rock paintings. These paintings show the life of people in the area as they hunted animals, danced, and carried out everyday tasks.

African woodcarvers made masks and statues for religious ceremonies and teaching purposes. People believed the masks held spiritual powers. Clay and metal figures served **similar** purposes. Metalworkers in the West African region of Benin made beautiful bronze and iron statues of people and animals.

ReadingHELPDESK

spiritual a gospel song	**Academic Vocabulary**	**Reading Strategy:** *Listing*
	similar having characteristics in common	Making a list helps you organize facts presented while reading a passage. Make a list of the different types of art produced in early Africa.

Early African Music and Dance

Music and dance were connected to everyday African life. People used these arts to express their religious feelings. They also used the arts to help ease an everyday task, such as planting a field. Music and dance also had a vital role in community activities.

African music included group singing. In many African songs, a singer calls out a line, then other singers repeat it. Musical instruments, such as drums, whistles, horns, flutes, or banjos, were used to keep the beat in early African music.

Enslaved Africans relied on music to remind them of their homeland. In America, songs of hardship eventually developed into a type of music called the blues. Songs of religious faith and hopes for freedom became **spirituals**, or gospel songs. Over time, other forms of African-based music developed, such as ragtime, jazz, rock and roll, and, more recently, rap.

For many Africans, dance was a way to communicate with the spirits and express the life of a community. Lines of dancers swayed and clapped their hands. In the background, drummers sounded out the rhythm. Many African peoples had dance rituals that marked particular stages of life, such as when young boys or girls became adults.

African Storytelling

In addition to music and dance, Africans also kept alive their storytelling tradition. A few enslaved Africans escaped and shared their stories. Those who heard these stories retold them. They also retold popular stories that focused on the deeds of famous heroes.

✓ PROGRESS CHECK

Explaining What role did music and dance play in the everyday lives of early Africans?

Connections to
TODAY

West African Music Today

West African music today rocks! Amadou and Miriam are a musical group from present-day Mali. In an unusual twist, both performers lost their eyesight at a young age. Eventually, they met at a school for the visually impaired. The duo first became well known in West Africa. They later grew in popularity in France before gaining worldwide acclaim. Their songs combine the music of West Africa with influences from rock and roll and the blues.

LESSON 3 REVIEW

Review Vocabulary

1. What made a Bantu village *matrilineal*?

Answer the Guiding Questions

2. *Explaining* How did the Bantu spread their language, culture, and technology throughout Africa?

3. *Describing* What roles did women play in early African society?

4. *Identifying* Which European nation established the slave trade between Africa and Europe?

5. *Sequencing* How did art in Africa change over time?

6. **INFORMATIVE/EXPLANATORY** Describe your extended family. How might your extended family be similar to or different from extended families in early Africa?

What Do You Think?

Africa's Water Resources: Should Private Companies Control Them?

In ancient Africa, and today, the most precious natural resource is water. People worry about its availability. Many people cannot easily get clean water for daily use. Efforts are now underway to set up reliable water systems in Africa. Some local governments create their own water systems. Citizens are taxed according to their water use. Other governments cannot supply water. Then private companies agree to provide water to citizens for a fee. This system is known as *privatization*. Should control of water be left to governments or should private companies be allowed to control water?

Yes

PRIMARY SOURCE

❞ During the 1990s, it also became apparent [clear] that private participation could bring better oversight and management. The most detailed studies … concluded [found] that well designed private schemes [systems] have brought clear benefits—but not perfection. For example, in water, the most difficult sector, in cities as diverse as … Abidjan and Conakry service coverage has increased significantly…. Extended coverage tends to bring the biggest benefits to households with lower incomes, as they previously had to pay much more for the service by small informal vendors. ❞

—Klein, Michael. "Where Do We Stand Today with Private Infrastructure?" Development Outreach. March 2003. Washington, D.C.: World Bank.

Image Source/Getty Image

During the dry seasons, some areas of Africa are completely without natural water.

African governments are trying to find ways to provide clean drinking water for their people.

No

PRIMARY SOURCE

❝ Water is about life. The saying that 'water is life' cannot be more appropriate. Privatizing water is putting the lives of citizens in the hands of a corporate entity [business structure] that is accountable [responsible] only to its shareholders. Secondly, water is a human right and this means that any philosophy, scheme, or contract that has the potential to exclude [leave out] sections of the population from accessing water is not acceptable both in principal and in law. Privatization has that potential because the privateers are not charities: they are in for the profit. Price therefore becomes an important barrier to access by poor people. Water is the collective heritage of humanity and nature. . . . Water must remain a public good for the public interest. ❞

—Interview with Rudolf Amenga–Etego. "The rains do not fall on one person's roof. . ." *Pambazuka News.* 26 August 2004. Issue 171. *http://pambazuka.org/en/category/features/24190*

LYNN JOHNSON/National Geographic Stock

What Do You Think? DBQ

❶ *Describing* What is privatization?

❷ *Identifying* According to Michael Klein, where have private companies been most successful at providing water?

Critical Thinking

❸ *Analyzing* What about Michael Klein's background would cause him to believe that privatization is the best solution?

❹ *Analyzing Information* Why does Amenga-Etego mean when he says that "water is a human right. . ."?

Read to Write

❺ *Narrative* Write a paragraph describing your feelings about whether private companies have the right to make a profit by providing water to citizens.

Write your answers on a separate piece of paper.

1 **Exploring the Essential Question**

INFORMATIVE/EXPLANATORY How would you explain the ways in which trade affected the history of early African civilizations? Write a short essay in which you consider the parts of these civilizations that were affected by trade. You may choose to focus on topics such as the civilizations' growth, government, religion, or culture. Ask an adult to help you plan, revise, edit, and rewrite your essay so that it addresses the question and focuses on a unique topic.

2 **21st Century Skills**

SUMMARIZING Write a paragraph summarizing what you have learned about one of the African civilizations discussed in this chapter. Your paragraph should describe why the civilization you chose is important in African and world history. It should also include significant events, people, and accomplishments related to this civilization.

3 **Thinking Like a Historian**

GEOGRAPHY AND CIVILIZATION Create a graphic organizer that lists at least three geographic features of Africa and explains their impact on the growth of civilizations there. For instance, you might write "Sahara" on the left side of your organizer. Then, on the opposite side, you could explain that for many years the Sahara limited travel and trade in Africa.

Feature → Impact on African Civilization

4 **GEOGRAPHY ACTIVITY**

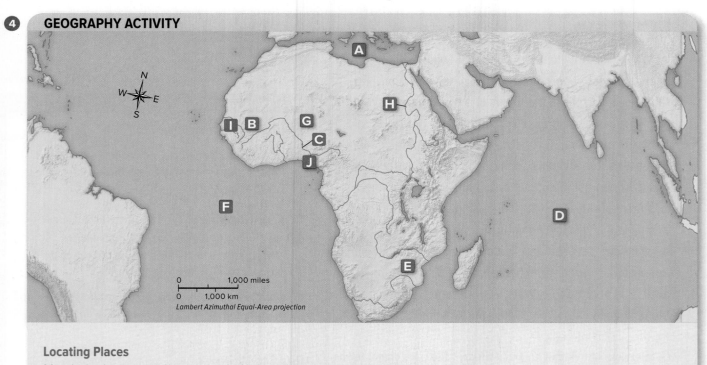

Locating Places

Match the letters on the map with the numbered places listed below.

1. Zimbabwe
2. Benin
3. Ghana
4. Mali
5. Songhai
6. Mediterranean Sea
7. Atlantic Ocean
8. Indian Ocean
9. Nile River
10. Niger River

Directions: Write your answers on a separate piece of paper.

CHECKING FOR UNDERSTANDING

1 Define each of these terms.

A. savanna	**F.** Swahili
B. plateau	**G.** extended family
C. griot	**H.** matrilineal
D. dhow	**I.** oral history
E. clan	**J.** spiritual

REVIEW THE GUIDING QUESTIONS

2 *Describing* What challenges does the environment of Africa pose to settlement there?

3 *Identifying* What natural barrier limited trade between North Africa and other parts of the continent?

4 *Explaining* How did Ghana's location help it become a great trading kingdom?

5 *Naming* What products were traded from Africa's inland territories?

6 *Identifying* Which two religions had major impacts on the development of Axum and other East African trading states?

7 *Making Comparisons* In what ways were the governments of Ghana and Mali similar?

8 *Summarizing* How was Islam introduced into West Africa?

9 *Defining* What role did griots play in early African cultures?

10 *Locating* From which part of Africa did most enslaved Africans originate?

11 *Listing* What social and cultural traditions did many African societies have in common?

CRITICAL THINKING

12 *Determining Cause and Effect* Why might raising livestock have developed in some parts of Africa before agriculture?

13 *Assessing* Which region in Africa is most suited for permanent human settlement? Explain your answer.

14 *Defending* Which African trading empire was the greatest? Explain your answer.

15 *Making Connections* In what ways did lineage groups relate to traditional African religions?

16 *Predicting Consequences* How might the pilgrimage of Mansa Musa ultimately have led to the downfall of Mali?

17 *Analyzing* Discuss the relationship between the spread of Islam and the growth of trade between Africa and Muslim traders to the east.

18 *Determining Cause and Effect* What were the most important effects of the Bantu migration?

19 *Making Generalizations* Describe the role of family in African societies.

20 *Determining Central Ideas* Explain why music, art, and dance were integral to African society.

Need Extra Help?

If You've Missed Question	**1**	**2**	**3**	**4**	**5**	**6**	**7**	**8**	**9**	**10**	**11**	**12**	**13**	**14**	**15**	**16**	**17**	**18**	**19**	**20**
Review Lesson	1,2,3	1	1	1	1	1	2	2	3	3	3	1	1	1, 2	2, 3	2	2	3	3	3

DBQ SHORT RESPONSE

"Mansa Musa was a skilled organizer and administrator who built Mali into one of the world's largest empires of the time. The empire was significant in both size and wealth. Mansa Musa encouraged the growth of trade in the empire. He also strongly supported the arts and education in Mali. He ordered the construction of mosques [Islamic temples] and established a university for Islamic studies."

—EncyclopediaBritannica Online, "Musa."
http://www.britannica.com/EBchecked/topic/398420/Musa

21 How did Mansa Musa show his support for education in Mali?

22 What traits do you think made Mansa Musa a successful ruler?

EXTENDED RESPONSE

23 *Informative/Explanatory* Write an essay in which you seek to explain the importance of the arts to early African society. What purposes did African art play in people's lives? How is the influence of early African art forms still felt today? Use details from the chapter to support your explanation.

STANDARDIZED TEST PRACTICE

DBQ ANALYZING DOCUMENTS

Ibn Battuta wrote during his travels in Mali that

"[The people of Mali] are careful to observe the hours of prayer, and assiduous [always dutiful] in attending them in congregations, and in bringing up their children to them."

—from *Travels in Asia and Africa, 1325–1354*

24 *Drawing Conclusions* Which statement best describes Ibn Battuta's impressions of the people of Mali?
   A. He praises their system for educating children.
   B. He criticizes the policies of the leaders of Mali.
   C. He criticizes the system of government used in Mali.
   D. He praises their devotion to their religious beliefs.

25 *Making Inferences* From the passage, you can infer that Ibn Battuta likely views the people of Mali with
   A. wonder.   C. respect.
   B. confusion.   D. jealousy.

Need Extra Help?

If You've Missed Question	21	22	23	24	25
Review Lesson	2	2	2	2	3

CENTRAL AMERICA, THE CARIBBEAN ISLANDS, AND SOUTH AMERICA

UNIT 4

EXPLORE the CONTINENT

SOUTH AMERICA At nearly 7 million square miles (18 million sq. km) in area, South America is the fourth-largest continent in the world. Two great rivers—the Orinoco and the Amazon—flow through Brazil and the Tropical North. The most distinctive landform in the region is the Andes mountain ranges. The Andes, 4,500 miles (7,242 km) long, is the world's longest continental mountain range.

1 NATURAL RESOURCES Farmers grow a variety of potatoes in plots located in the Peruvian Andes. El Parque de la Papa, also known as "Potato Park," is a bio-reserve that is managed by the local communities surrounding it.

2 BODIES OF WATER Oil tankers travel near the port of Maracaibo, Venezuela. Like a circulatory system, the region's many waterways serve as arteries that transport people and goods throughout the region and to the world.

(bkgd)©Frank Lukasseck/Corbis; (l)JIM RICHARDSON/National Geographic Stock;
(c)JUAN BARRETO/AFP/Getty Images; (r)Reto Stockli, NASA Earth Observatory

③ **LANDFORMS** Los Glaciares National Park in Argentina is an area of rugged mountains and many glacial lakes. Its name refers to the glaciers that are part of the Patagonian ice field. The ice field is the largest ice mantle outside Antarctica. Los Glaciares is located along Argentina's border with Chile.

FAST **FACT**

Earth's driest place is in South America.

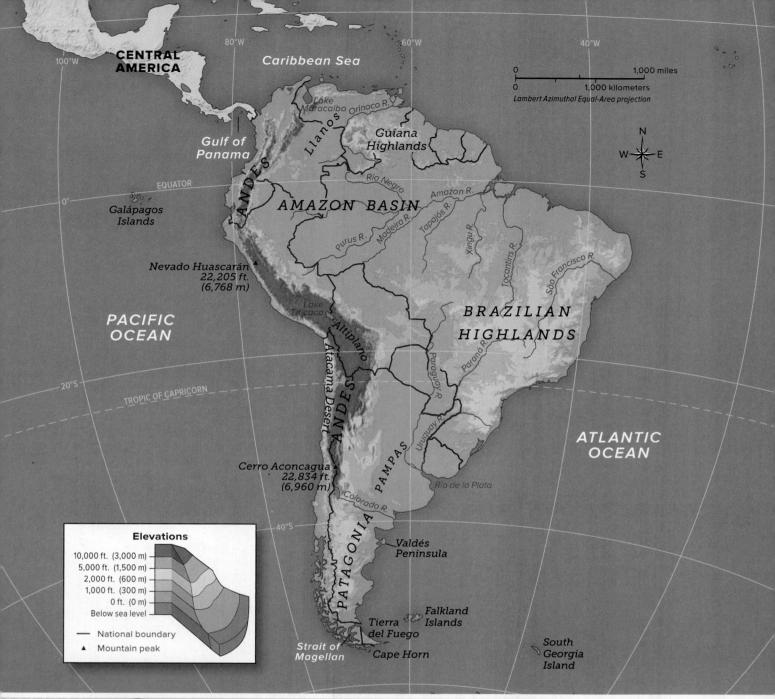

CENTRAL
AMERICA

Caribbean Sea

80°W

60°W

40°W

100°W

0   1,000 miles
0   1,000 kilometers
Lambert Azimuthal Equal-Area projection

Lake
Maracaibo   Orinoco R.

Gulf of
Panama

Llanos

Guiana
Highlands

N
W   E
S

EQUATOR

Rio Negro

Amazon R.

0°

Galápagos
Islands

AMAZON BASIN

Purus R.

Madeira R.

Tapajós R.

Xingu R.

Tocantins R.

São Francisco R.

Nevado Huascarán
22,205 ft.
(6,768 m)

PACIFIC
OCEAN

Lake
Titicaca

Altiplano

BRAZILIAN
HIGHLANDS

Paraguay R.

Paraná R.

Atacama Desert

ANDES

20°S

TROPIC OF CAPRICORN

ATLANTIC
OCEAN

Cerro Aconcagua
22,834 ft.
(6,960 m)

PAMPAS

Uruguay R.

Rio de la Plata

Colorado R.

40°S

Valdés
Peninsula

PATAGONIA

Falkland
Islands

Tierra
del Fuego

South
Georgia
Island

Strait of
Magellan

Cape Horn

Elevations

10,000 ft. (3,000 m)
5,000 ft. (1,500 m)
2,000 ft. (600 m)
1,000 ft. (300 m)
0 ft. (0 m)
Below sea level

—   National boundary
▲   Mountain peak

SOUTH AMERICA

PHYSICAL

MAP SKILLS

1 **THE GEOGRAPHER'S WORLD** What is the easternmost river in Brazil?

2 **PLACES AND REGIONS** Describe the elevation differences between western South America and eastern South America.

3 **PLACES AND REGIONS** Explain why elevation of land in the Amazon Basin makes travel easier.

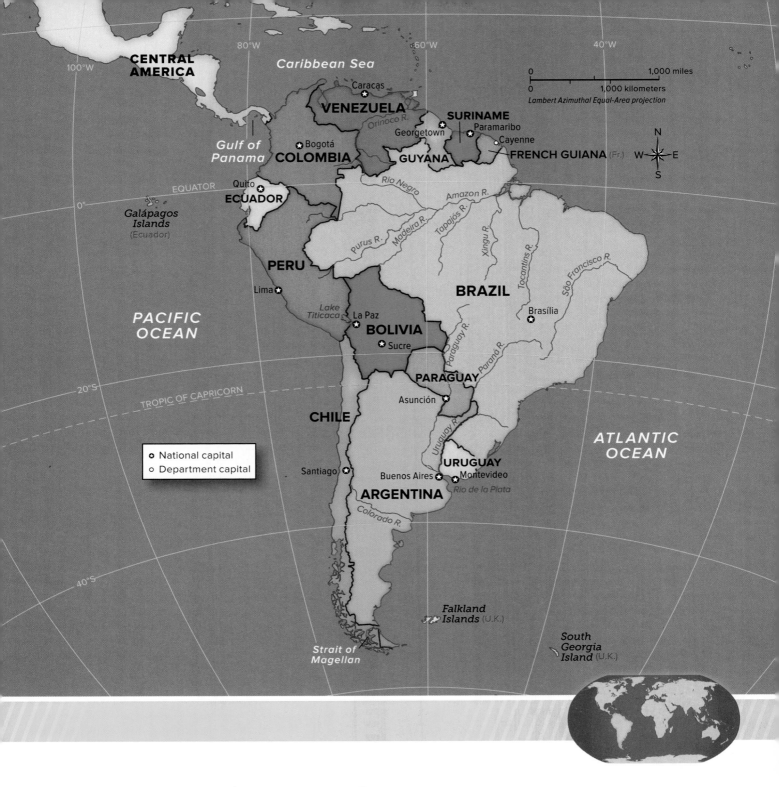

CENTRAL AMERICA

Caribbean Sea

80°W   60°W   40°W

0   1,000 miles
0   1,000 kilometers
Lambert Azimuthal Equal-Area projection

100°W

Caracas

VENEZUELA

SURINAME
Paramaribo

Orinoco R.

Georgetown

Cayenne

Gulf of Panama

Bogotá

COLOMBIA

GUYANA

FRENCH GUIANA (Fr.)

N
W   E
S

EQUATOR   Quito

ECUADOR

Rio Negro

Amazon R.

0°

Galápagos Islands (Ecuador)

Purus R.

Madeira R.

Tapajós R.

Xingu R.

Tocantins R.

São Francisco R.

PERU

BRAZIL

Lima

PACIFIC OCEAN

Lake Titicaca

La Paz

BOLIVIA

Brasília

Sucre

Paraguay R.

Paraná R.

PARAGUAY

20°S

TROPIC OF CAPRICORN

Asunción

CHILE

ATLANTIC OCEAN

Uruguay R.

National capital
Department capital

Santiago

Buenos Aires

URUGUAY
Montevideo

Rio de la Plata

ARGENTINA

Colorado R.

40°S

Falkland Islands (U.K.)

South Georgia Island (U.K.)

Strait of Magellan

POLITICAL

MAP SKILLS

1 PLACES AND REGIONS What is the capital of Uruguay?

2 PHYSICAL GEOGRAPHY Which two countries in South America do not have coastlines?

3 THE GEOGRAPHER'S WORLD Which country in South America shares its border with the most countries?

CENTRAL AMERICA

Caribbean Sea

80°W 60°W 40°W

100°W

1,000 miles
0
1,000 kilometers
Lambert Azimuthal Equal-Area projection

Barranquilla
Cartagena
Maracaibo Caracas Port-of-Spain
Valencia
Mérida Ciudad Guayana Georgetown
Medellín San Cristóbal Paramaribo
Manizales
Bogotá
Gulf of Panama
Cali
Pasto
EQUATOR
Quito Macapá
0°
Guayaquil Belém São Luís
Cuenca Manaus
Iquitos Fortaleza
Piura Teresina Natal
Trujillo Pucallpa Recife
Chimbote Río Branco Porto Velho Petrolina Maceió
Lima Huancayo Feira de Santana
Cuzco Salvador
Ica Brasília Vitória da Conquista
Arequipa Cuiabá Goiânia Montes Claros
La Paz Santa Cruz
Tacna Campo Grande Uberlândia Belo Horizonte
Ribeirão Prêto Vila Velha
Campinas
Antofagasta São Paulo Rio de Janeiro
Ponta Grossa
Salta Curitiba
San Miguel Asunción Florianópolis
de Tucumán Posadas
Caxias do Sul
San Juan Córdoba Pôrto Alegre
Santa Fe ATLANTIC OCEAN
Valparaíso Rosario Pelotas
Santiago Mendoza Buenos Aires
Concepción Montevideo
Bahía Blanca Mar del Plata

PACIFIC OCEAN

20°S

TROPIC OF CAPRICORN

40°S

Punta Arenas

N W E S

POPULATION

Per sq. mi.		Per sq. km
1,250 and over		500 and over
250–1,249		100–499
63–249		25–99
25–62		10–24
2.5–24		1–9
Less than 2.5		Less than 1

Cities
(Statistics reflect metropolitan areas.)
■ Over 5,000,000
□ 2,000,000–5,000,000
◉ 1,000,000–2,000,000
• 500,000–1,000,000
○ Under 500,000

SOUTH AMERICA

POPULATION DENSITY

MAP SKILLS

1 HUMAN GEOGRAPHY Where do most people in South America live?

2 HUMAN GEOGRAPHY About how many people live in Lima?

3 PLACES AND REGIONS What are the largest cities on South America's eastern coast?

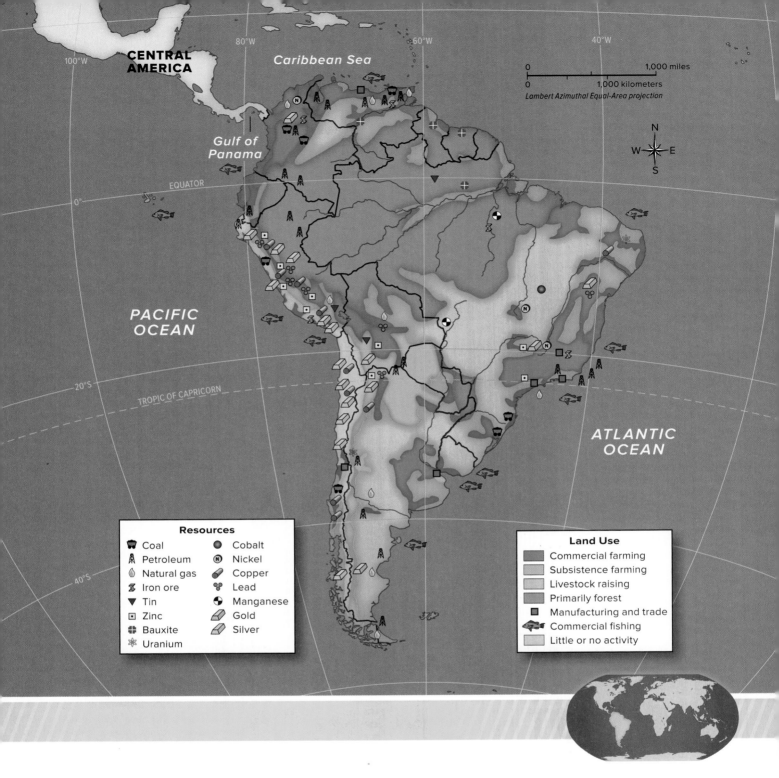

Resources

🪨	Coal	●	Cobalt
⛏	Petroleum	Ⓝ	Nickel
💧	Natural gas	⬡	Copper
⚡	Iron ore	♻	Lead
▼	Tin	◐	Manganese
▣	Zinc	◰	Gold
✚	Bauxite	▱	Silver
✳	Uranium		

Land Use

- Commercial farming
- Subsistence farming
- Livestock raising
- Primarily forest
- ■ Manufacturing and trade
- 🐟 Commercial fishing
- Little or no activity

ECONOMIC RESOURCES

MAP SKILLS

1 HUMAN GEOGRAPHY Is there more commercial farming or livestock raising in South America?

2 PHYSICAL GEOGRAPHY Where is the greatest concentration of minerals and ores?

3 ENVIRONMENT AND SOCIETY Is South America a manufacturing center?

CENTRAL
AMERICA

Caribbean Sea

Caracas

Bogotá

80°W   60°W   40°W

0   1,000 miles
0   1,000 kilometers
Lambert Azimuthal Equal-Area projection

N
W   E
S

EQUATOR

Manaus

Belém

0°

PACIFIC
OCEAN

Lima

La Paz

Brasília

Sucre

20°S

TROPIC OF CAPRICORN

Asunción

Rio de Janeiro

ATLANTIC
OCEAN

Santiago

Buenos Aires

Tropical rain forest
Tropical savanna
Semi-arid (steppe)
Arid (desert)
Humid subtropical
Marine west coast
Mediterranean
Tundra and high altitude

⊕ National capital
• City

40°S

SOUTH AMERICA

CLIMATE

MAP SKILLS

1 **PHYSICAL GEOGRAPHY** What is the most prevalent climate in South America?

2 **PHYSICAL GEOGRAPHY** Where is South America's desert climate?

3 **PLACES AND REGIONS** In which type of climate is Santiago, Chile, located?

MEXICO, CENTRAL AMERICA, AND THE CARIBBEAN ISLANDS

ESSENTIAL QUESTIONS · *How does geography influence the way people live?* · *Why does conflict develop?* · *Why do people trade?*

networks

There's More Online about Mexico, Central America, and the Caribbean Islands.

CHAPTER 17

Lesson 1
Physical Geography

Lesson 2
History of the Region

Lesson 3
Life in the Region

Girl from the highlands of Guatemala

©Sergio Pitamitz/Robert Harding World Imagery/Corbis

The Story Matters...

Early advanced civilizations developed in this region of the Americas. Their people developed economies based on farming and trade. They built planned cities and developed highly organized societies and governments. The arrival of the Spanish and other Europeans had a dramatic impact on the region and its indigenous peoples. The influence of European colonial rule and the struggles for independence can still be seen in the economies, politics, and cultures of the region today.

FOLDABLES
Study Organizer

Go to the Foldables® library in the back of your book to make a Foldable® that will help you take notes while reading this chapter.

Trade and Commerce
Civilizations
Gulf of Mexico
Mexico, Central America, and the Caribbean Islands

Mexico, Central America, and the Caribbean islands sit between North America and South America. The region is surrounded by oceans and seas and is located close to the Equator. As you study the map, look for the geographic features that make this area unique.

Step Into the Place

MAP FOCUS Use the map to answer the following questions.

1 **THE GEOGRAPHER'S WORLD** What is the largest country in this region?

2 **ENVIRONMENT AND SOCIETY** Why was the Panama Canal built where it is?

3 **THE GEOGRAPHER'S WORLD** Which of the Caribbean islands is part of the United States?

4 **CRITICAL THINKING** **Analyzing** Given their location, what might be a key economic industry of the Caribbean islands?

HISTORIC CITY Willemstad, capital of the Caribbean island of Curacao, was founded in 1634 by Dutch settlers.

MAYA RUINS Early Americans known as the Maya built cities in the rain forests of southern Mexico.

Step Into the Time

DESCRIBING Select one location on the time line and describe the impact of European colonization on the lives and environment of the people who lived there.

1325 Aztec found Tenochtitlán

1300

1492 Christopher Columbus arrives in Americas

1500

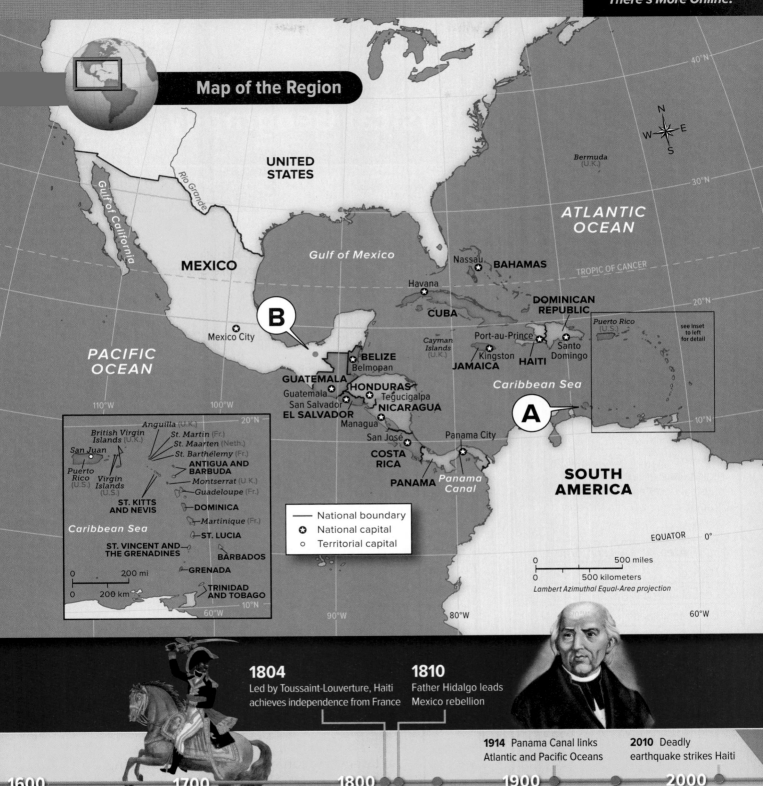

Map of the Region

UNITED STATES

Rio Grande

Gulf of California

MEXICO

Gulf of Mexico

★ Mexico City

PACIFIC OCEAN

ATLANTIC OCEAN

Bermuda (U.K.)

TROPIC OF CANCER

Nassau ★ BAHAMAS

★ Havana

CUBA

DOMINICAN REPUBLIC

Cayman Islands (U.K.)

Port-au-Prince ★ ★ Santo Domingo

★ Kingston HAITI

JAMAICA

Puerto Rico (U.S.)

see inset to left for detail

B

★ BELIZE
Belmopan

GUATEMALA

Guatemala ★ HONDURAS
San Salvador ★ Tegucigalpa
EL SALVADOR ★ NICARAGUA
Managua ★

San José ★
COSTA RICA

Caribbean Sea

A

Panama City ★
PANAMA *Panama Canal*

SOUTH AMERICA

EQUATOR 0°

40°N
30°N
20°N
10°N

110°W 100°W 90°W 80°W 60°W

Caribbean inset

Anguilla (U.K.)
British Virgin Islands (U.K.)
St. Martin (Fr.)
St. Maarten (Neth.)
San Juan ○
Puerto Rico (U.S.)
Virgin Islands (U.S.)
St. Barthélemy (Fr.)
ANTIGUA AND BARBUDA
Montserrat (U.K.)
Guadeloupe (Fr.)
ST. KITTS AND NEVIS
Caribbean Sea
DOMINICA
Martinique (Fr.)
ST. LUCIA
ST. VINCENT AND THE GRENADINES
BARBADOS
GRENADA
TRINIDAD AND TOBAGO

20°N
10°N
60°W

0 _____ 200 mi
0 _____ 200 km

--- National boundary
★ National capital
○ Territorial capital

0 _____ 500 miles
0 _____ 500 kilometers
Lambert Azimuthal Equal-Area projection

Timeline

1804 Led by Toussaint-Louverture, Haiti achieves independence from France

1810 Father Hidalgo leads Mexico rebellion

1914 Panama Canal links Atlantic and Pacific Oceans

2010 Deadly earthquake strikes Haiti

1600   1700   1800   1900   2000

1848 Mexico cedes large areas of territory to U.S.

1959 Fidel Castro takes power in Cuba

Reading **HELP**DESK

Academic Vocabulary

- **similar**
- **benefit**

Content Vocabulary

- **isthmus**
- *tierra caliente*
- *tierra templada*
- *tierra fría*
- **bauxite**
- **extinct**
- **dormant**

TAKING NOTES: *Key Ideas and Details*

Organize As you read about the region, take notes on the physical geography using a graphic organizer like the one below.

Area	Landforms
Mexico	
Central America	
Caribbean islands	

Lesson 1
Physical Geography

ESSENTIAL QUESTION • *How does geography influence the way people live?*

IT MATTERS BECAUSE
Mexico and Central America are southern neighbors to the United States.

Physical Geography of Mexico and Central America

GUIDING QUESTION *What landforms and waterways do Mexico and Central America have?*

Mexico and the seven nations of Central America act like a bridge between two worlds. Geographically, they form an isthmus that connects North and South America. An **isthmus** is a narrow piece of land that connects two larger landmasses. Culturally, they join with South America and some Caribbean islands to make up Latin America. Latin America is a region of the Americas where the Spanish and Portuguese languages, based on the Latin language of ancient Rome, are spoken. Economically, the nations have close ties to the United States. They also trade with their Latin American neighbors.

Shaped like a funnel, the region is wider in the north than in the south. To the north, Mexico has a 1,951-mile (3,140-km) border with the United States. At the southern end, the Central American country of Panama is only about 40 miles (64 km) wide.

Land Features

Mexico is the largest nation of the region, occupying about two-thirds of the land. Imagine a backwards *y* along the western and eastern coasts of Mexico, with the tail to the south. That backwards *y* neatly traces the mountain systems on Mexico's two coasts and south central region. The coastal ranges are called the Sierra Madre Occidental (Spanish for "western") and the Sierra Madre Oriental (Spanish for "eastern"). They join in the southern highlands. Coastal plains flank the western and eastern mountains. The eastern plain is wider.

Between the two arms of the y is a vast highland region called the Central Plateau. It is the heartland of Mexico. This plateau is home to Mexico City, which is the capital, and a large share of the nation's people.

Mexico has two peninsulas. The Yucatán Peninsula bulges northeast into the Gulf of Mexico. Baja California (*baja* means "lower" in Spanish) extends to the south in western Mexico.

Central America has landforms **similar** to those of south central Mexico. Mountains run down the center of these countries. Narrow coastal lowlands flank them on the east and west.

Mexico and Central America lie along the Ring of Fire that rims the Pacific Ocean. Earthquakes and volcanoes are common in the Ring of Fire. The Sierra Madre Occidental are made of volcanic rocks, but they have no active volcanoes. The mountains in the southern part of the central plateau and in Central America, however, do have numerous active volcanoes. These volcanoes bring a **benefit**. Volcanic materials weather into fertile, productive soils.

Academic Vocabulary

similar much like

benefit advantage

Mountains appear on the hazy horizon of Mexico City. Mexico's capital lies about 7,800 feet (2,377 m) above sea level.

Popocatépetl volcano stands in the background as a farmer plows the land. Popocatépetl, also known as "smoking mountain," has experienced eruptions since ancient times.

▶ CRITICAL THINKING

Explaining Why are earthquakes common in some parts of Mexico and Central America?

Earthquakes are common in the area, too. A magnitude 8.0 earthquake that hit Mexico City in 1985 killed thousands of people. One that struck El Salvador in 2001 produced another kind of disaster. A hill weakened by the earth's movement collapsed onto the town of Las Colinas. It crushed homes and killed hundreds of people.

Bodies of Water

Mexico and Central America are bordered by the Pacific Ocean to the west. The Gulf of California, an inlet of that ocean, separates Baja California from the rest of Mexico. To the east, the region is surrounded by the waters of two arms of the Atlantic Ocean. They are the Gulf of Mexico and the Caribbean Sea.

The region has few major rivers. In the northern half of Mexico, the climate is dry. This means that few rivers flow across the rocky landscape. Southern Mexico and Central America receive more rain, but the landscape is steep and mountainous, and the rivers are short. An important river is the Río Bravo. In the United States, this river is called the Rio Grande. The largest lake in the region is Lake Nicaragua, in Nicaragua.

An important waterway in the region is not a river, but a feature built by people. It is the Panama Canal, built in the early 1900s. The Panama Canal makes it possible for ships to pass between the Atlantic and Pacific oceans without journeying around South America. It saves thousands of miles of travel, which in turn saves time and money. It is one of the world's most important waterways.

Climates

Most of Mexico and Central America lie in the Tropics. Because of their location near the Equator, it might seem that the climate would be hot. Although the coastal lowlands are hot, areas with higher elevation are not. The highlands are much cooler.

Nearly the entire region can be divided into three vertical climate zones. Soil, crops, animals, and climate change from zone to zone. The *tierra caliente*, or "hot land," is the warmest zone. It reaches from sea level to about 2,500 feet (762 m) above sea level. Major crops grown here are bananas, sugarcane, and rice.

Next highest is the *tierra templada*, or "temperate land." This climate zone has cooler temperatures. Here farmers grow such crops as coffee, corn, and wheat. Most of the region's people live in this climate zone.

Higher in elevation is the *tierra fría*, or "cold land." This region has chilly nights. It can be used only for dairy farming and to grow hearty crops such as potatoes, barley, and wheat.

©iStockphoto.com/yuhirao

Think Again?

Because the Panama Canal connects the Atlantic and Pacific oceans, it must go east to west.

Not really! Central America twists to the east where Panama is located. As a result, the Panama Canal is cut from the north to the south.

Hot Springs Canyon was formed by flowing waters that have cut through the land. The Rio Bravo, or Rio Grande, carves its way through rugged countryside. It forms part of the border between Mexico and the United States.

▶ CRITICAL THINKING
Describing Why are there so few rivers in the northern part of Mexico?

CLIMATE ZONES

Although the region is located in the Tropics, many inland areas of Mexico and Central America have relatively cool climates.

▶ **CRITICAL THINKING**

1. *Identifying* What products are grown in *tierra caliente*?

2. *Analyzing* Why are many inland areas of Mexico and Central America relatively cool?

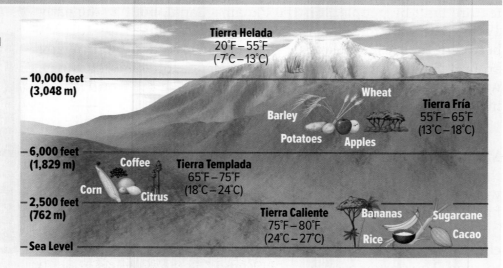

Tierra Helada
20°F – 55°F
(-7°C – 13°C)

— **10,000 feet**
(3,048 m)

Wheat

Barley

Tierra Fría
55°F – 65°F
(13°C – 18°C)

Potatoes   Apples

— **6,000 feet**
(1,829 m)

Coffee

Tierra Templada
65°F – 75°F
(18°C – 24°C)

Corn

Citrus

— **2,500 feet**
(762 m)

Tierra Caliente
75°F – 80°F
(24°C – 27°C)

Bananas   Sugarcane

Rice   Cacao

— **Sea Level**

Geographers also designate other vertical climate zones. Few human activities take place on the *tierra helada,* or "frozen land". This vertical climate zone is more common in other regions of the Americas.

Tropical Wet/Dry Climate

Much of Mexico and Central America have a tropical wet/dry climate. The climate is characterized by two distinct seasons. The wet season, during the summer months, is when most of the precipitation falls. The dry season occurs during the winter months. The dry season is longer in the areas farther from the Equator and closer to the polar regions.

The region's tropical location exposes it to another natural hazard. Ferocious hurricanes can strike in the summer and early autumn months. These storms do great damage. For example, a 1998 hurricane killed more than 9,000 people in Honduras and destroyed 150,000 homes.

Natural Resources

Oil and natural gas are Mexico's most important resources. They are found along the coast of the Gulf of Mexico and in the gulf waters. Mexico is an important oil-producing country. It has enough oil and gas to meet its own needs and still export a large amount. The exports help fuel the nation's economy. However, Mexico's oil production has declined since 2004. Many oil fields are old and are starting to run out of oil.

When Spanish explorers first came to Mexico, they were attracted to the area's gold and silver. Mexico still produces silver, which is mined in the central and north central parts of the country. Gold also is still mined in Mexico. Other minerals include copper, iron ore, and **bauxite**. Bauxite is used to make aluminum.

The seven smaller nations of Central America have few mineral resources. Nicaragua is an exception, with gold, silver, iron ore, lead, zinc, and copper. The nation is so poor, however, that it has not been able to take advantage of these deposits. Guatemala also has some oil, and its mountains produce nickel.

✔ READING PROGRESS CHECK

Analyzing Why are different climate zones found in this region, even though most of the region is in the Tropics?

Physical Geography of the Caribbean Islands

GUIDING QUESTION *How are the Caribbean islands alike and different from one another?*

Hundreds of islands dot the Caribbean Sea. The islands are home to more than 30 countries or territories belonging to other countries. Some are large, with millions of people living on them. Others are tiny and home to only thousands.

Major Islands

The Caribbean islands can be segmented into three different groups. The first group is the Greater Antilles. The four islands, the largest Caribbean islands, include Cuba, Jamaica, Hispaniola, and Puerto Rico. Cuba and Jamaica are independent countries. Hispaniola is home to two countries: Haiti in the west and the Dominican Republic

This scenic bay in the Caribbean island of Antigua provides an ideal harbor for yachts and other sailing ships. Antigua is part of the Lesser Antilles.

▶ CRITICAL THINKING

Describing What islands make up the Greater Antilles?

Pixtal/age fotostock

in the east. Puerto Rico is a commonwealth of the United States. Although it is a possession of the United States, it has its own government. The people of Puerto Rico are American citizens. They can travel freely between their island and the United States.

The second group of islands is the Lesser Antilles. Dozens of smaller islands make up this group. They form an arc moving east and south from Puerto Rico to northern South America. Most of the islands are now independent countries. At one time, they were colonies of France, Britain, Spain, or the Netherlands. Each has a culture reflecting its colonial period.

The third island group is the independent nation of the Bahamas. The islands lie north of the Greater Antilles and east of Florida. The Bahamas include more than 3,000 islands, although people live on only about 30 of them.

The Greater Antilles are a mountain chain, much of which is under water. On a map, you can see that this chain extends eastward from Mexico's Yucatán Peninsula. These islands include some mountains, such as the Sierra Maestra in the eastern part of Cuba and the Blue Mountains of Jamaica. The highest point in the Caribbean is Duarte Peak, in the Dominican Republic. The Lesser Antilles are formed by volcanic mountains. Many of the volcanoes are **extinct**, or no longer able to erupt. Some islands have **dormant** volcanoes, or ones that can still erupt but show no signs of activity.

The Caribbean Sea

The Caribbean Sea is a western arm of the Atlantic Ocean. In the past, sailing ships traveling west from Europe followed trade winds blowing east to west to reach the sea. Christopher Columbus used the winds to reach the Bahamas in 1492. There, he first sighted land in the Americas. Columbus explored the Caribbean, too. These voyages sparked European settlement of the Americas.

The warm waters of the Caribbean help feed the Gulf Stream. This current carries warm water up the eastern coast of the United States.

The Climate of the Caribbean Islands

The Caribbean islands have a tropical wet/dry climate. Temperatures are high year-round, though ocean breezes make life comfortable. Humidity is generally high, but rainfall is seasonal and varies significantly. Islands like Bonaire receive only about 10 inches (25 cm) of rain per year. Dominica, on the other hand, receives about 350 inches (899 cm) of rain each year. That is an average of almost an inch of rain every day.

Like Central America and Mexico, the Caribbean islands are prone to hurricanes. These storms are more likely to occur in the northern areas, toward the Gulf of Mexico, than to the south. On average, seven hurricanes strike the Caribbean islands each year.

Natural Resources

The waters of the Caribbean are rich in fish. Some are fished for food and others for sport. The islands have few timber resources today. People have cut down most of the trees already to use for fuel or to make farmland.

Mineral resources are generally lacking too, although some Caribbean islands have important resources. Trinidad and Tobago has reserves of oil and natural gas. The Dominican Republic exports nickel, gold, and silver. Cuba is a major producer of nickel. Jamaica has large amounts of bauxite.

Perhaps the most important resources of the Caribbean are its climate and people. Warm temperatures and gracious hosts attract millions of tourists to the region each year. Some enjoy the white sandy beaches and clear blue water. Some scuba dive to see the colorful fish darting through coral reefs.

☑ READING PROGRESS CHECK

Citing Text Evidence How did the islands of the Caribbean form?

Tourists on a boat near the French-ruled island of Guadeloupe learn to dive in Caribbean waters.

Identifying What natural resource of the Caribbean Sea benefits the region's island nations?

Include this lesson's information in your Foldable®.

Trade and Commerce
Civilizations
Gulf of Mexico
Mexico, Central America, and the Caribbean Islands

LESSON 1 REVIEW

Reviewing Vocabulary

1. What is the *tierra templada*? Why do most people in Mexico and Central America live in this vertical climate zone?

Answering the Guiding Questions

2. *Describing* How are the physical geography of Mexico and Central America similar?

3. *Analyzing* What impact does the Panama Canal have on the cost of shipping goods? Why?

4. *Determining Central Ideas* How do the locations of Mexico and Central America increase the possibility of natural hazards striking the region?

5. *Determining Word Meanings* Why are some islands in the Caribbean called the *Greater* Antilles and others called the *Lesser* Antilles?

6. *Narrative Writing* Imagine you are taking a cruise that stops at a Caribbean island, a port in Central America, and a port in Mexico. Write three diary entries describing what you would see in each place.

Lesson 2
History of the Regions

Reading**HELP**DESK

Academic Vocabulary

- **feature**
- **transform**

Content Vocabulary

- **staple**
- **surplus**
- **conquistador**
- **colonialism**
- **revolution**
- **plantation**
- **cash crop**
- **caudillo**
- **Columbian Exchange**

TAKING NOTES: *Key Ideas and Details*

Summarize As you read about the history of Mexico, take notes using the graphic organizer below.

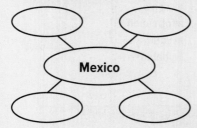

ESSENTIAL QUESTION • *Why does conflict develop?*

IT MATTERS BECAUSE
The region was home to highly developed Native American civilizations.

Mexico's History

GUIDING QUESTION *How did economic and governmental relationships between Spanish and Native Americans in Mexico change over time?*

Mexico was first inhabited by Native American groups. Later, Spanish soldiers conquered the groups and ruled them. Since the early 1800s, Mexico has been independent. Its history is long and rich, and its accomplishments are many.

Early Civilizations

Native peoples first grew corn in Mexico about 7,000 years ago. They also grew other foods that have become **staples**, or foods that are eaten regularly, such as corn, squash, chilies, and avocados. Farming allowed people to produce food **surpluses**, or more than they needed to survive. Surpluses helped people specialize in jobs other than getting food.

About 3,000 years ago, the Maya formed the major civilization in the region. They lived mainly in the lowland plains of Mexico's Yucatán Peninsula and in what is now Guatemala and Belize. One **feature** of their culture was great cities. The Maya erected pyramids with stepped sides and temples on top. They invented a complex system of writing. By studying astronomy, they were able to make accurate calendars. The height of Maya civilization was from about A.D. 300 to A.D. 900. Then their power suddenly collapsed. Archaeologists do not know exactly why.

(l to r)Jeremy Graham/dbimages/Alamy Stock Photo; Russell Kord/Alamy

The Aztec ruled the region next. They settled in central Mexico in about 1300. Their impressive capital city was Tenochtitlán. Mexico City occupies the site where it once stood. Tenochtitlán was built on an island in the middle of a lake. Causeways connected it to the mainland.

The Aztec had a complex social and religious system. They conquered many of their neighbors and made slaves of captured soldiers. Priests performed rituals to win the favor of their gods. The Aztec were also skilled farmers. They built up land in the lake to form small islands called *chinampas,* which they used to grow crops.

The Spanish Arrive

In the early 1500s, a rival power appeared. Around 1520, Hernán Cortés led a small force of Spanish **conquistadors**, or conquerors, to Mexico. Within two years, these explorers and soldiers had defeated the Aztec and taken control of their empire.

How could the Spanish conquer the Aztec with only a few hundred men? Spanish guns and armor were better weapons than Aztec spears. Another major factor was European diseases. The diseases did not exist in the Americas until Europeans unknowingly brought them. Native Americans had no resistance to them, so the diseases killed many thousands. Cortés also took advantage of the anger of other native peoples who resented Aztec rule. Several groups joined him as allies.

Winning the Aztec Empire brought Spain riches in gold and silver mines. The conquest completely **transformed** life in Mexico. Roman Catholic priests converted native peoples to Catholicism. Conquistadors forced native peoples to work on farms or in mines. Spanish rule in Mexico was an example of colonialism.

Jeremy Graham/Alamy Stock Photo

feature a characteristic
transform to change

The Aztec city of Tenochtitlán was linked by canals, bridges, and raised streets built across the water.
▶ CRITICAL THINKING
Describing How were the Aztec able to build a city and farms in an area covered by a lake?

Under **colonialism**, one nation takes control of an area and dominates its government, economy, and society. The colonial power uses the colony's resources to make itself wealthier. In colonial Mexico, settlers from Spain had the most wealth.

Independence and Conflict

After almost 300 years of Spanish rule, a priest named Miguel Hidalgo led a rebellion in Mexico in 1810. The goal of the rebellion was to win independence from Spain. Some people hoped it would also create a more nearly equal society. The Spanish captured and executed Hidalgo, but by 1821 Mexico had gained its independence. Spanish rulers, though, were replaced by wealthy Mexican landowners. Native peoples remained poor.

Through much of the 1800s, Mexico was troubled by political conflict. Rival groups fought one another for power. Most of Mexico's people remained poor.

Revolution and Stability

By the early 1900s, dissatisfaction was widespread. A revolution erupted in Mexico. A **revolution** is a period of violent social and political change. One change was the land reform plan, which divided large estates into parcels of land that were then given to poor people to farm. National public schools were established, and a new constitution was written detailing the responsibilities of the government toward the people. Only one political party, however, held power until the 1990s.

☑ READING PROGRESS CHECK

Determining Central Ideas How were the Spanish able to conquer the Aztec?

A History of Central America

GUIDING QUESTION *How did the nations of Central America develop?*

The nations of Central America developed in similar ways to Mexico. But there were differences, as well.

Early Civilizations and Conquest

The Maya had flourished in Guatemala and Belize, as well as in southern Mexico. Even after their great cities were abandoned, the Maya continued to live in the region. After conquering Mexico, the Spanish moved south. By the 1560s, Spain had seized control of most of Central America. During the early 1800s, Britain claimed the area that is now Belize.

Independence

Central America gained its independence soon after Mexico. In 1823 the territories of Central America united to form one government. By 1840, they had separated into five independent

Russell Kord/Alamy

countries: Guatemala, Honduras, El Salvador, Nicaragua, and Costa Rica. The area that is now Belize was still a British colony. Panama was part of Colombia.

Central American countries were subjected to economic colonialism. This means that foreign interests dominate a people economically. These foreign interests were large companies from other countries. They set up **plantations**, or large farms, where poorly paid workers produced cash crops. **Cash crops** are crops sold for profit. The most important were bananas, coffee, and sugarcane.

Heading the governments for much of this time were military strongmen called **caudillos**. The caudillos helped ensure the foreigners' success. In turn, the foreigners made sure that the caudillos remained in power.

Conflict in Modern Times

Around 1900, Panama gained its independence from Colombia. It was helped by the United States, which wanted to build a canal there. The United States controlled the canal until 2000. Then, by agreement, Panama took control of the canal.

The late 1900s was a time of conflict. New wealth came to the upper classes, but most people remained poor. Various groups demanded reforms. Several countries were ravaged by civil wars. Only Costa Rica and Belize remained peaceful. One of Costa Rica's presidents, Óscar Arias Sánchez, helped bring peace to the region.

✓ READING PROGRESS CHECK

Analyzing How did Central America and Mexico's history differ?

Built by the United States in the early 1900s, the Panama Canal is now owned and operated by the Republic of Panama.

Identifying Which country held Panama shortly before the United States built the Panama Canal?

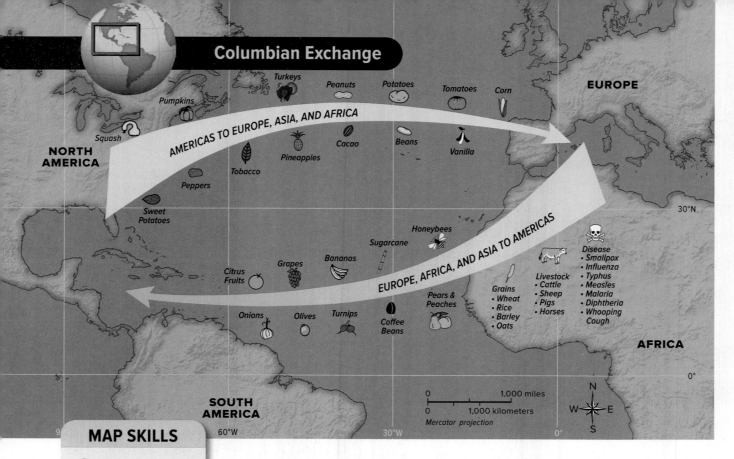

Columbian Exchange

AMERICAS TO EUROPE, ASIA, AND AFRICA

EUROPE, AFRICA, AND ASIA TO AMERICAS

NORTH AMERICA

EUROPE

AFRICA

SOUTH AMERICA

Turkeys
Peanuts
Potatoes
Tomatoes
Corn
Pumpkins
Squash
Cacao
Beans
Vanilla
Pineapples
Tobacco
Peppers
Sweet Potatoes

Honeybees
Sugarcane
Grapes
Bananas
Citrus Fruits
Onions
Olives
Turnips
Coffee Beans
Pears & Peaches

Livestock
• Cattle
• Sheep
• Pigs
• Horses

Grains
• Wheat
• Rice
• Barley
• Oats

Disease
• Smallpox
• Influenza
• Typhus
• Measles
• Malaria
• Diphtheria
• Whooping Cough

30°N
0°
60°W
30°W
0°

0   1,000 miles
0   1,000 kilometers
Mercator projection

N W E S

MAP SKILLS

1 THE USE OF GEOGRAPHY
Describe the Columbian Exchange.

2 HUMAN GEOGRAPHY
What diseases spread throughout the world as a result of the Columbian Exchange?

History of the Caribbean Islands

GUIDING QUESTION *How did the Caribbean islands develop?*

The history of the Caribbean islands is similar to that of Mexico and Central America. The islands have greater diversity, though, because several European countries ruled them as colonies.

Indigenous Peoples and European Settlers

Europeans changed the way the native peoples of the Caribbean lived. Like the Native Americans of the mainland, they suffered from diseases carried by the Europeans. This is why their numbers declined sharply soon after the arrival of the Europeans. Overwork and starvation also reduced their numbers. The Spanish set up colonies in what are now Cuba, the Dominican Republic, and Puerto Rico. Later, the French settled in what is now Haiti and on other smaller islands. The British and Dutch had some colonies, too.

Colonialism

During the 1600s, the Caribbean colonies became the center of the growing sugar industry. European landowners hoped to make money by selling the sugar in Europe. Because so many Native American workers had died, Europeans brought in hundreds of thousands of enslaved Africans to work the plantations.

The term **Columbian Exchange** refers to the transfer of plants and animals between Europe, Asia, and Africa on one side and the Americas on the other. Foods such as wheat, rice, grapes, and apples were introduced to the Americas as were cattle, sheep, pigs, and horses. At the same time, products from the Americas were introduced into Europe, Africa, and Asia. They included corn, chocolate, and the potato. The Columbian Exchange also resulted in the introduction of new diseases into different parts of the world.

Independence

The first area in the Caribbean to gain independence was Haiti, then called Saint Domingue. Led by Toussaint-Louverture, Haiti gained its independence from France in 1804. The Dominican Republic won its independence in 1844. Cuba and Puerto Rico remained Spanish until 1898. When Spain lost the Spanish-American War, it gave independence to Cuba. Puerto Rico passed into American hands. Other islands of the Caribbean did not win the right to self-government until the middle 1900s.

Turmoil in the Twentieth Century

Independence did not mean freedom or prosperity. Rule by caudillos and widespread poverty have remained a problem in Haiti and the Dominican Republic.

Cuba, too, was often subject to dictatorial rule following its independence. Then in 1959, revolutionaries led by Fidel Castro took over. Castro soon cut all ties with the United States. He said his government would follow the ideas of communism. Communism involves government control of all areas of the economy and society. His rule did not bring economic success to Cuba.

The other islands of the Caribbean have had their own difficulties. Some countries in the region are trying to improve conditions and bring economic benefits to all their citizens. Small and with few resources, they have been unable to develop strong economies. Many of the islands depend on aid from the governments that used to run them as colonies.

☑ READING PROGRESS CHECK

Analyzing What caused the population of the Caribbean islands to grow in colonial times?

FOLDABLES
Study Organizer

Include this lesson's information in your Foldable®.

LESSON 2 REVIEW

Reviewing Vocabulary

1. What is the difference between a *conquistador* and a *caudillo*?

Answering the Guiding Questions

2. *Describing* How did the Maya and the Aztec differ?

3. *Analyzing* How were relations between people with European and Native American heritage similar in Mexico during colonial times and the 1800s?

4. *Determining Central Ideas* How did economic colonialism affect the nations of Central America?

5. *Analyzing* How was the development of Cuba and of Haiti similar and different?

6. *Informative/Explanatory Writing* Write a summary of the history of Mexico, Central America, or the Caribbean islands after independence.

netw⊙rks

There's More Online!

☑ **MAP** Hispaniola

☑ **VIDEO**

Reading**HELP**DESK

Academic Vocabulary

- circumstance
- initiate

Content Vocabulary

- maquiladora
- mural
- dependence
- free-trade zone
- remittance
- reggae

TAKING NOTES: *Key Ideas and Details*

Summarize As you read about Mexico, use the graphic organizer below to take notes about its economy and culture.

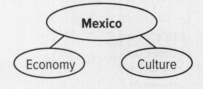

Lesson 3
Life in the Region

ESSENTIAL QUESTION • *Why do people trade?*

> **IT MATTERS BECAUSE**
> *Mexico and other countries in the region have close ties to the United States.*

Modern Mexico

GUIDING QUESTION *What is life like in Mexico today?*

When you think of Mexico, you might think of Mexican food like tacos. You might think of mariachi musicians playing lively music and wearing large sombreros. But Mexico has a rich and complex culture and is a rising economic power.

The Economy

Mexico has close economic ties to the United States and Canada. These ties are a result of joining with them in the North American Free Trade Agreement (NAFTA). About 80 percent of Mexico's exports go to NAFTA partners. More than 60 percent of Mexico's imports come from members of NAFTA. Most of this trade is with the United States.

In recent decades, Mexico has developed its manufacturing industry. Factories account for about a third of Mexico's output. Some of them are **maquiladoras**. These are factories where parts made elsewhere are assembled into products. Many of the factories are located in northern Mexico. The goods are then exported. Food processing is another major industry in Mexico. The textile and clothing industries are important, too. Mexico also has heavy manufacturing, producing iron, steel, and automobiles.

Farming remains important. Cotton and wheat are grown in the dry north using irrigation. Along the southeastern coast, farms produce coffee, sugarcane, and fruit. On the central plateau, farmers grow corn, wheat, and fruits and vegetables. In the poor south, many farmers engage in subsistence farming—growing just enough food to feed themselves and their families.

Service industries are important in Mexico. Banking helps finance economic growth. A major service industry is tourism. Visitors from around the world come to visit ancient Maya sites or to see the architecture of Spanish colonial cities. Tourists also come to relax in resorts along the warm and scenic tropical coasts.

Culture

Mexicans are proud of their blend of Spanish and native cultures. They have long celebrated the folk arts that reflect native traditions. In the early 1900s, several Mexican painters drew on these traditions to paint impressive murals celebrating Mexico's history and people. **Murals** are large paintings made on walls. The Ballet Folklorico performs Mexican dances.

Sports reflect Mexico's ties to Spain and the United States. Soccer is popular there, as it is in Spain, along with baseball.

Challenges

With nearly 9 million people, Mexico City is one of the largest cities in the world. Including the city's suburbs, it has more than 21 million people—nearly 20 percent of Mexico's population. Overcrowding is a major problem.

Pollution is another problem, particularly air pollution. Because Mexico City is at a high elevation, the air has less oxygen than at sea level. This makes breathing difficult for some people in normal **circumstances**, but conditions in Mexico City are not normal. A great deal of exhaust from cars and factories is released into the air. The polluted air is held in place by the mountains around the city.

Academic Vocabulary

circumstance a condition

Farmers sell produce at a village market in Mexico.
▶ CRITICAL THINKING
Describing What is farming like in southern Mexico?

Nicaraguan workers make clothing in a factory.
▶ CRITICAL THINKING
Identifying What types of products have Central American manufacturers recently begun to make?

Sometimes a layer of cold air high in the atmosphere keeps the pollution from rising. The result can be a serious threat to health.

Another challenge facing Mexico is the power of criminals who sell illegal drugs. Drug lords use violence to fight police and to intimidate people. Mexico has mounted a major effort to battle this problem with some success.

Poverty is yet another major challenge facing Mexico. Anywhere from one-fifth to nearly half of Mexico's people are poor. Continued economic growth would help, and seems to be working. Some economists are predicting that Mexico will overtake Brazil in the 2010s as the leading economy in Latin America.

☑ READING PROGRESS CHECK

Analyzing How have close ties with the United States helped Mexico's economy?

Modern Central America

GUIDING QUESTION *What is life like in Central America?*

The nations of Central America have fewer resources than Mexico. The region must also deal with political problems.

Central America's Economies

The countries of Central America long showed **dependence**, or too much reliance, on cash crops. In recent years, some have begun to escape this trap. A good sign is the growth of manufacturing. This consists mostly of food processing and production of clothing and textiles. Tourism has grown as well. Tourists come to Belize and Guatemala to see ancient Maya sites. They travel to Costa Rica to see the varied plants and animals in its rain forests.

Panama benefits economically from the Panama Canal. Working for additional benefit, Panama **initiated** a major building program to expand the canal so it can accept larger cargo ships.

Academic Vocabulary

initiate to begin

Christopher Pillitz/Photonica World/Getty Images

High rates of population growth create an economic challenge. The countries need to grow their economies fast to provide enough jobs. One hope for promoting growth is trade agreements between the countries of the region and other countries.

In the 2000s, the United States and the Dominican Republic signed a series of agreements with five Central American countries (Costa Rica, El Salvador, Guatemala, Honduras, and Nicaragua). The agreement, called the Central America Free Trade Agreement (CAFTA-DR), was the first agreement among the United States and smaller developing economies. CAFTA-DR creates a **free-trade zone** that lowers trade barriers between the countries. Often, however, such trade agreements help the United States more than the other countries.

Challenges Facing the Region

Another challenge to the area is natural disasters. Earthquakes and hurricanes can have a devastating effect on the region's fragile economies. Nicaragua was making some economic progress in the 1990s when Hurricane Mitch hit. The destruction set the nation's economy back significantly.

The need to solve long-standing political problems also holds the region back. The civil wars of the 1980s and 1990s are over, but some of the issues that caused them remain unsolved. If these issues again become more severe, conflict may resume.

Culture

The culture of Central America is strongly influenced by European and native traditions. Spanish is the chief language in all countries except Belize, where English is the official language. English is spoken in many cities in the region as well. In rural Guatemala, native languages are common.

The population is mainly of mixed European and native heritage. Some people of African and Asian descent live there as well. Most people of the region are Roman Catholics. In recent years, however, Protestant faiths have gained followers.

☑ READING PROGRESS CHECK

Identifying What are the causes of poverty in Central America?

A tourist descends from a tree in a rain forest in Costa Rica.
▶ CRITICAL THINKING
Identifying Point of View Why do visitors travel to Costa Rica's rain forests?

Haiti's brown, barren landscape contrasts sharply with the richly forested terrain of the neighboring Dominican Republic.

▶ CRITICAL THINKING

Analyzing Why has economic development been held back in Haiti?

The Caribbean Islands

GUIDING QUESTION *What is life like on the Caribbean islands?*

The Caribbean islands are mostly small countries with small populations and few resources. Although they have a rich and vibrant culture, they face many challenges.

Island Economies

The biggest challenge for the islands is to develop economically. Many people on the islands are poor. Even in Puerto Rico, a large share of the population lives in poverty. One reason for the poverty is high unemployment.

Cuba's economy is in poor condition after decades of communism. The government has been unable to promote economic development. It relied on aid first from the Soviet Union and more recently from Venezuela. Conditions are worse now than in the 1980s. Cubans also have little political freedom. Those who criticize the government are often arrested.

In Haiti, a history of poor political leadership has held back economic development. Haiti ranks among the world's poorest nations. Poverty is not the country's only problem. Widespread disease is another threat. In addition, as many as one in eight Haitians have left the country. Many of those who emigrated were among Haiti's most educated people. This loss hurts efforts to improve the economy. Finally, the country has not yet recovered from a deadly 2010 earthquake. Despite these problems, Haiti's people are determined to succeed.

Trinidad and Tobago has one of the more successful economies in the region. Sales of its oil and natural gas have funded economic development. Its location near Venezuela and Brazil has helped make its ports busy. The smaller Caribbean islands have had more political success than the larger ones. Governments are democratic and stable, but the economies are plagued by few resources and poverty.

Another important economic factor in the region is remittances. A **remittance** is money sent back to the homeland by people who migrated someplace else to find work. Many Dominicans came to the United States for work and send money home to support their families.

Tourism is a major part of the economy of several islands. Resorts in the Bahamas, Jamaica, and other islands invite tourists to come and relax in pleasant surroundings. The resorts often separate tourists from the lifestyle of the islanders, but they provide jobs for island citizens.

Island Cultures

The cultures of the Caribbean islands show a mix of mainly European and African influences. Large numbers of Asians also came to some of the islands in the 1800s and 1900s. Those from China went mainly to Cuba. South Asians settled in Jamaica, Guadalupe, and Trinidad and Tobago.

The languages spoken on the islands reflect their colonial heritage. English is the language of former British colonies such as the Bahamas and Jamaica. Spanish is spoken in Cuba, the Dominican Republic, and Puerto Rico. English is also taught in Puerto Rico's schools. French and Creole, a blend of French and African languages, are spoken in Haiti.

The Caribbean islands have strongly influenced world music. Much of the music blends African and European influences. Cuba is famous for its salsa, and Jamaica for reggae. Both forms of music rely on complex drum rhythms. **Reggae** has become popular around the world not only for its musical qualities but also for lyrics that protest poverty and lack of equal rights.

☑ READING PROGRESS CHECK

Citing Text Evidence How do economic conditions in Jamaica relate to the development of reggae?

Include this lesson's information in your Foldable®.

LESSON 3 REVIEW

Reviewing Vocabulary

1. What is a *free-trade zone*, and why do the nations of the region want to be in one?

Answering the Guiding Questions

2. ***Determining Central Ideas*** Do you think Mexico has a strong economy? Why or why not?

3. ***Identifying*** What challenges does Mexico face?

4. ***Describing*** How have the economies of the Central American countries changed in recent years?

5. ***Analyzing*** How do the languages of the Caribbean islands reflect their colonial history?

6. ***Argument Writing*** Take the role of a government official in one of these countries. Write a brief report to the nation's president explaining whether you think promoting tourism is good or bad for the nation's economy. Give reasons.

NAFTA
and Its Effects

The North American Free Trade Agreement (NAFTA) was created to grow trade among the United States, Canada, and Mexico to help these countries become more competitive in global markets.

Why Do Nations Trade?

No country produces all the goods and services it needs. Because most countries have more than they need of some things but not enough of others, trade is important.

Trade Barriers

Sometimes countries try to protect their industries from competition by setting up trade barriers such as tariffs and quotas. A tariff is a tax on imports. Tariffs raise the prices of imported goods so a country's own industries can produce and sell those goods at competitive prices. A quota restricts the amount of certain goods that can be imported from other countries.

Free Trade

The United States, Mexico, and Canada agreed to free trade, or getting rid of trade barriers, in 1994. The United States also has free trade agreements with 17 other nations, including Australia, Israel, and Peru.

> ❝ **No country produces all the goods and services it needs.** ❞

Disadvantages

Critics of NAFTA say that the agreement has cost U.S. jobs. Workers in Mexico are paid less. As a result, many U.S. industries moved all or part of their production to Mexico. Critics also argue that NAFTA hurt Mexican farmers. Mexico imported more corn and other grains when tariffs on those items were removed. Small farmers in Mexico could not compete with technologically advanced U.S. farms.

Advantages

Supporters of NAFTA say that it creates the largest free trade area in the world. With tariffs removed, the NAFTA countries can trade with one another at lower cost. It allows the 463 million people in the three countries greater choice in the marketplace. The three countries produced an estimated $18 trillion worth of goods and services in 2011.

A worker assembles parts at a U.S. automobile plant. Critics argued that NAFTA resulted in U.S. job losses, especially in the manufacturing industry. ▶

BIENVENIDOS NOGALES SON

THERE'S MORE ONLINE

SEE the political boundaries of the U.S., Canada, and Mexico • WATCH changes in migration patterns

These numbers and statistics can help you learn about the effects of NAFTA.

Growth Triples

In 1993, the year before NAFTA went into effect, U.S. trade with Mexico and Canada totaled $276.1 billion. In 2010 U.S. exports and imports of goods with its NAFTA partners amounted to $918 billion.

U.S. Surplus in Services

A trade deficit occurs when a nation imports (buys) more goods and services than it exports (sells). In 2010 the U.S. experienced a trade deficit of $94.6 billion in *goods* with its NAFTA partners. A trade surplus occurs when a nation exports (sells) more than it buys. In 2009 the United States had a $28.3 billion trade surplus with its NAFTA partners in the value of *services.* The main services exported are financial services and insurance.

$1 million a minute

Almost 400,000 people—truckers, businesspeople, commuters, and tourists—cross the U.S.-Canada border daily. U.S.-Canada two-way trade amounts to $1.4 billion a day. That's almost a million dollars every minute.

One-fifth

Canada is the world's largest supplier of energy to the United States. Canada provides 20 percent of U.S. oil imports and 18 percent of U.S. natural gas imports.

21,444

This is the number of U.S. Border Patrol agents in 2011. This is double the number of agents in 2003.

700,000 Jobs

Critics of NAFTA say the agreement has cost the jobs of U.S. workers. According to the Economic Policy Institute, the transfer of production to Canada, Mexico, and other countries has resulted in the loss of about 700,000 jobs in the United States since NAFTA began.

FIFTEEN THOUSAND

This is the number of workers at the new Volkswagen plant in Puebla, Mexico, making it one of the country's largest employers.

(t to b)Jae C. Hong/AP Images; Don Seabrook/The Wenatchee World/AP Images; Susana Gonzalez/Bloomberg/Getty Images

TOP 10 COUNTRIES IN EXPORTS
Countries with exports in excess of $300 billion

CHINA
U.S.
GERMANY
JAPAN
NETHERLANDS
FRANCE
ITALY
U.K.
SOUTH KOREA
RUSSIA

KEY:
- ■ $1 trillion or more
- ■ $500 billion–$999 billion
- ■ $300 billion–$499 billion

U.S. TRADE WITH OTHER NATIONS
Trade in billions of dollars
(imports and exports combined, 2011)

CANADA
$597*

CHINA
$503

MEXICO
$461*

JAPAN
$195

SOUTH KOREA
$100

NETHERLANDS
$66

GERMANY
$148

U.K.
$107

BRAZIL
$74

SAUDI ARABIA
$61

*NAFTA countries

GLOBAL IMPACT

EXPORTS AND IMPORTS Based on 2011 statistics, the exports of three countries—China, the United States, and Germany—exceeded $1 trillion in value. China's major exports to the U.S. include electrical machinery, toys, guns, and sports equipment. Top U.S. exports to China include oil seeds, fruits, vehicles, and aircraft.

The U.S. did more trade, if exports and imports are combined, with Canada in 2011 than with any other nation.

NAFTA Signing 1992

Mexican President Carlos Salinas, U.S. President George H.W. Bush, and Canadian Prime Minister Brian Mulroney look on as the chief trade representatives sign the NAFTA agreement in 1992. NAFTA was ratified by the three countries in 1993.

©Bettmann/Corbis

Thinking Like a Geographer

1. **Human Geography** What is the purpose of NAFTA?

2. **The Uses of Geography** Find a product in a store or at home that has a label in another language in addition to English. Is that language used in one of the NAFTA countries? Why would a product be labeled in more than one language?

3. **Human Geography** Hold a debate in your class on this statement: NAFTA has been good for U.S. workers and consumers.

Directions: Write your answers on a separate piece of paper.

1 Use your **FOLDABLES** to explore the Essential Question.

INFORMATIVE/EXPLANATORY WRITING Write a couple of paragraphs explaining how geographical features led the Aztec and then much later the founders of Mexico City to build their cities on the same site.

2 21st Century Skills

INTEGRATING VISUAL INFORMATION Choose a country or one of the islands mentioned in this chapter. Find out more about it by researching it on the Internet. Use the information to create a travel poster or slide show highlighting the country's or island's best features and include any places you would like to see.

3 Thinking Like a Geographer

INTEGRATING VISUAL INFORMATION Draw a graphic organizer like the one shown here and use it to record information about the islands of the Caribbean.

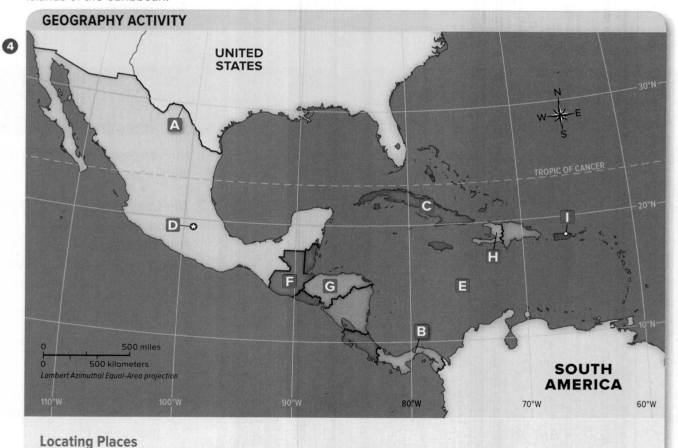

GEOGRAPHY ACTIVITY

Locating Places

Match the letters on the map with the numbered places listed below.

1. Panama Canal   **3.** Mexico City   **5.** Caribbean Sea   **7.** Guatemala   **9.** Cuba

2. Honduras   **4.** Rio Grande   **6.** Haiti   **8.** San Juan, Puerto Rico

REVIEW THE GUIDING QUESTIONS

Directions: Choose the best answer for each question.

1 What are Mexico's two most important natural resources?
A. gold and silver
B. oil and natural gas
C. iron ore and copper
D. bauxite and zinc

2 Which is one of the most important waterways in the world?
F. Lake Nicaragua
G. Río Bravo
H. Panama Canal
I. Caribbean Sea

3 A civilization that flourished in Southern Mexico, Belize, and Guatemala about 3,000 years ago and built pyramids like the Egyptians was the
A. Anasazi.
B. Olmec.
C. Aztec.
D. Maya.

4 Europeans established plantations and brought enslaved people to Cuba, Puerto Rico, and Hispaniola in order to grow
F. tobacco.
G. bananas.
H. sugar.
I. coffee.

5 Which country is Mexico's biggest trading partner?
A. Canada
B. China
C. Venezuela
D. the United States

6 What is the most serious economic challenge facing Central American countries?
F. high rate of population growth
G. fluctuating oil prices
H. food shortages
I. debt

DBQ **ANALYZING DOCUMENTS**

7 **IDENTIFYING** Read this passage about the Maya.

"About six million Maya live in Central America. Like their ancestors, many of them survive by growing maize (Indian corn) or other crops on their land, or by producing woven textiles for sale. In some villages, the men have to leave their families to find work in the cities, or on coffee and cotton plantations."

—from *How People Live*, DK Publishing

Which Maya activity today is similar to one from ancient times?

A. working in tourism

B. working in factories

C. growing maize

D. working in cities

8 **DETERMINING CENTRAL IDEAS** Which best explains why some men have to leave their villages?

F. They leave to seek wives elsewhere.

G. They're forced to do so by the government.

H. The villages are overcrowded.

I. They face a lack of jobs within the villages.

SHORT RESPONSE

"At the beginning of the 17th century the sweet crystal [sugar] transformed the Caribbean Islands into the Sugar Islands, though the islands did not turn sweet themselves. . . . Entire jungles were leveled; a slave or, later, cheap work force was massively imported from Africa and Asia; [and] a huge wave of European settlers arrived to stay."

—from Alfonso Silva Lee, *Natural Cuba/Cuba Natural*

9 **DESCRIBING** In what ways were the Caribbean islands transformed by the spread of sugar farming?

10 **DETERMINING WORD MEANINGS** What does the author of the passage mean by the phrase "the islands did not turn sweet themselves"?

EXTENDED RESPONSE

11 **INFORMATIVE/EXPLANATORY WRITING** Research and then write a brief report comparing and contrasting the cotton and rice plantations of the American South with the sugar plantations of the Caribbean islands.

Need Extra Help?

If You've Missed Question	**1**	**2**	**3**	**4**	**5**	**6**	**7**	**8**	**9**	**10**	**11**
Review Lesson	1	1	2	2	3	3	3	3	2	2	3

BRAZIL

ESSENTIAL QUESTIONS · *How does geography influence the way people live?* · *How do governments change?* · *What makes a culture unique?*

Soccer ("football") player Robinho has many fans in Brazil and around the world.

Silvia Izquierdo/AP Images

networks

There's More Online about Brazil.

CHAPTER 18

Lesson 1
Physical Geography of Brazil

Lesson 2
History of Brazil

Lesson 3
Life in Brazil

The Story Matters...

Brazil is located in the eastern half of South America. Brazil's vast land area makes it the giant of South America. Water is also important in defining the country. The great Amazon River flows through Brazil for more than 2,000 miles (3,219 km) and carries as much as one-fourth of the world's freshwater. This river drains the Amazon Basin, which stretches across the northern half of Brazil and contains the world's largest remaining tropical rain forest.

FOLDABLES
Study Organizer

Go to the Foldables® library in the back of your book to make a Foldable® that will help you take notes while reading this chapter.

Valuable Natural Resources

Urban Population

519

BRAZIL

Brazil is the largest country in South America with almost 3.3 million square miles (8.5 million sq. km) of land. It accounts for most of the eastern coast of South America. Brazil contains more than 4,665 miles (7,508 km) of coastline along the Atlantic Ocean. The Equator and the Tropic of Capricorn run through the country. As you study the map, look for the geographic features that make this area unique.

Step Into the Place

MAP FOCUS Use the map to answer the following questions.

1 **PHYSICAL GEOGRAPHY** What is the main river in Brazil?

2 **PLACES AND REGIONS** How many countries share a border with Brazil?

3 **THE GEOGRAPHER'S WORLD** Why is it significant that the Equator and the Tropic of Capricorn both run through Brazil?

4 **CRITICAL THINKING**
ANALYZING Use the scale bar on the map to measure the distance between the cities of Brasília and Rio de Janeiro.

RIO, AERIAL VIEW The huge "Christ the Redeemer" statue overlooks Rio de Janeiro. Set between beautiful mountains and the Atlantic coast, Rio de Janeiro was Brazil's capital from 1763 to 1960.

BRAZIL'S CAPITAL Brasília is a planned city, built in Brazil's central wilderness area. Brasília has been the country's capital since 1960.

Step Into the Time

IDENTIFYING How long did it take for Brazil to declare its independence from Portugal and become a republic?

1500 Cabral is first European to reach Brazil's coast

1800

1822 Brazil gains independence from Portugal

networks
There's More Online!

Brazil

Caribbean Sea

VENEZUELA
GUYANA
SURINAME
FRENCH GUIANA
(France)

COLOMBIA

ECUADOR

PERU

BRAZIL

ATLANTIC OCEAN

EQUATOR

Recife

Salvador

Brasília

São Francisco R.

Tocantins R.

Amazon R.
Madeira R.
Tapajós R.
Purus R.
Xingu R.

BOLIVIA

PACIFIC OCEAN

Paraná R.

PARAGUAY

CHILE

São Paulo
Rio de Janeiro

ARGENTINA

TROPIC OF CAPRICORN

URUGUAY

○ National capital
• City

10°N

0°

10°S

20°S

80°W   70°W   60°W   50°W   40°W

0   500 miles
0   500 kilometers
Lambert Azimuthal Equal-Area projection

1889
Brazil is proclaimed a republic

1900

1888 Slavery is abolished in Brazil

1960 Capital moves from Rio de Janeiro to Brasília

2000

2009 Rio de Janeiro chosen to host 2016 Olympic Games

2010
Dilma Rousseff elected president

Reading**HELP**DESK

Academic Vocabulary

- **area**
- **occur**

Content Vocabulary

- **tributary**
- **basin**
- **rain forest**
- **canopy**
- **plateau**
- **escarpment**
- **pampas**
- **Tropics**
- **temperate zone**

TAKING NOTES: *Key Ideas and Details*

Summarize As you read, use a graphic organizer to write a summary sentence about each topic.

Topic	Summary
Waterways	
Climate	
Resources	

Lesson 1
Physical Geography of Brazil

ESSENTIAL QUESTION • *How does geography influence the way people live?*

IT MATTERS BECAUSE
Brazil is the world's fifth-largest country in size and population.

Waterways and Landforms

GUIDING QUESTION *What are Brazil's physical features?*

Brazil is the largest country in South America. It occupies about half the continent. Rolling lowland plains and flat highland plateaus cover most of the country.

The Amazon

The Amazon River is one of Brazil's amazing natural features as well as a great natural resource. It begins high in the Andes of Peru and flows east across northern Brazil to the Atlantic Ocean. The river is the Western Hemisphere's longest river and the world's second longest, after the Nile River in Africa.

The Amazon is the largest river in terms of the amount of freshwater it carries. It moves more than 10 times the water volume of the Mississippi River. Of all the water that Earth's rivers empty into the oceans, about 25 percent comes from the Amazon. Its massive flow pushes freshwater more than 100 miles (161 km) out into the Atlantic Ocean. The river's depth allows oceangoing ships to travel more than 2,000 miles (3,219 km) upstream to unload or pick up cargo.

The Amazon Basin

One reason the Amazon carries so much water is that it has more than 1,000 **tributaries**. These smaller rivers feed into the Amazon as it flows from the Andes to the Atlantic Ocean. Several tributaries are more than 1,000 miles (1,609 km) long.

The **area** that a river and its tributaries drain is called a **basin**. The Amazon Basin covers more than 2 million square miles (5.2 million sq. km). Nearly half of Brazil's land lies within this vast region. Its wet lowlands cover most of the country's northern and western areas.

Much of the Amazon Basin is covered by the world's largest **rain forest**. A rain forest is a warm woodland that receives a great deal of rain each year. Tall evergreen trees form a **canopy**, or an umbrella-like covering. The Amazon rain forest is called the Selva. It is the world's richest biological resource. The Selva is home to several million kinds of plants, insects, birds, and other animals.

Only about 6 percent of Brazil's population live in the Amazon Basin. Most of the region contains fewer than two people per square mile. Some are Native Americans who live in small villages and have little contact with the outside world.

Brazilian Highlands

South and east of the Amazon Basin are the Brazilian Highlands. This is mainly a region of rolling hills and areas of high, flat land called **plateaus**. These highlands are divided into western and eastern parts.

(t)Manfred Gottschalk/Workbook Stock/Getty Images; (b)altrendo travel/Getty Images

Visual Vocabulary

Tributary A tributary is a smaller river or stream that flows into a larger one, or into a lake.

Academic Vocabulary

area a geographic region

South America's Amazon River and North America's Mississippi River cross vast distances and carry enormous amounts of water.

▶ CRITICAL THINKING

Comparing How are the Amazon and Mississippi Rivers similar? How are they different?

The western part of the highlands is largely grassland that is partly covered with shrubs and small trees. Farming and ranching are the major economic activities in this part of the highlands. Farther west is the Mato Grosso Plateau, a flat, sparsely populated area of forests and grasslands that extends into Bolivia and Peru.

Low mountain ranges form much of the eastern Brazilian Highlands, although some peaks rise above 7,000 feet (2,134 m). In other places, highland plateaus plunge to the Atlantic coast, forming **escarpments**, or steep slopes. These escarpments, rising from coast to highlands, have hindered development of inland areas.

Brazil's third-largest city, Brasília, is located in the Brazilian Highlands. It was built in the 1950s as Brazil's new capital to encourage settlement in the country's interior. Some 3.5 million people live in and around the city.

About 600 miles (966 km) south of Brasília is São Paulo. This huge city is located on a plateau at the highland's eastern edge, just 30 miles (48 km) from the Atlantic coast. With more than 17 million people, São Paulo is the largest city in the Southern Hemisphere. It is also South America's most important industrial city.

Farther south are grassy, treeless plains called **pampas**. The grass and fertile soil make the pampas one of Brazil's most productive ranching and farming areas.

Atlantic Lowlands

Brazil has one of the longest strips of coastal plains in South America, wedged between the Brazilian Highlands and the Atlantic Ocean. This narrow plains region, called the Atlantic lowlands, is just 125 miles (201 km) wide in the north; it becomes even narrower in the southeast. The rural parts of this region are another important area for farming.

An escarpment slopes down to an Atlantic Ocean beach near the city of São Paulo.

▶ **CRITICAL THINKING**

Describing How have escarpments affected Brazil's development?

SambaPhoto/Milton Carelo/Getty Images

Although the coastal lowlands cover only a small part of Brazil's territory, most of the nation's people live here. More than 12 million live in and around Rio de Janeiro, Brazil's second-largest city. Rio's beautiful beaches and vibrant lifestyle make it Brazil's cultural and tourist center.

☑ **READING PROGRESS CHECK**

Analyzing Why do many Brazilians live in the Brazilian Highlands?

Ranchers herd cattle on the Mato Grosso Plateau of west-central Brazil.

▶ CRITICAL THINKING

Describing What are the main features of the Mato Grosso Plateau?

A Tropical Climate

GUIDING QUESTION *What are Brazil's climate and weather like?*

Most of Brazil is located in the **Tropics**. This is the zone along Earth's Equator that lies between the Tropic of Cancer and the Tropic of Capricorn. Brazil's climate varies. In fact, the huge country has several different climates.

Wet Rain Forests

The area along the Equator in northern Brazil has a tropical rain forest climate. In this climate, every day is warm and wet. Daytime temperatures average in the 80s Fahrenheit (27°C to 32°C). It feels hotter than this because the wet rain forest makes the air humid.

E. Hanazaki Photography/Flickr/Getty Images

During periods of drought, the Amazon River carries less water, which exposes sandbars in the river and low-lying areas along the shoreline.

▶ **CRITICAL THINKING**

Identifying What type of climate is found in areas along the Amazon River?

Academic Vocabulary

occur to happen or take place

Areas along the Amazon River have a tropical rain forest climate. They experience winds called monsoons that bring a huge amount of rain—120 inches to 140 inches (305 cm to 356 cm) per year. During the monsoon season, flooding swells the Amazon River in some places to more than 100 miles (161 km) wide. These areas also have a dry season when little rain **occurs**. During the dry season, forest fires are a danger, even in a rain forest.

Tropical Wet/Dry Climate

Tropical wet/dry climates usually exist along the outer edges of tropical rain forest climates. Most of the northern and central Brazilian Highlands has a tropical wet/dry climate. This climate has just two seasons—summer, which is wet, and winter, which is dry. Daily average temperatures change very little. Summers average in the 70°F range (21°C) and winters in the 60°F range (16°C). But even this slight difference is enough to change wind patterns, which affect rainfall. Between 40 inches and 70 inches (102 cm to 178 cm) of rain fall during the summer months. Winters get almost no rain.

Dry and Temperate Climates

The northeastern part of the Brazilian Highlands has a semiarid climate. This region is the hottest and driest part of the country. The daily high temperature during the summer often reaches 100°F (38°C). Frequent and severe droughts have caused many of the region's farms to fail. Even so, the desertlike plant life supports some light ranching.

Southeastern Brazil, including São Paulo and Rio de Janeiro, is located in the **temperate zone**—the region between the Tropic of Capricorn and the Antarctic Circle. It has a temperate climate called humid subtropical. It is the same type of climate that the southeastern United States experiences.

Temperatures vary according to location and elevation in this part of Brazil. Summers are generally warm and humid, and winters are mild. Rainfall occurs year-round. In the southern parts of this climate zone, snow can fall.

✓ READING PROGRESS CHECK

Identifying What factors make farming in the northeastern part of Brazil difficult?

Natural Resources

GUIDING QUESTION *What resources are most plentiful and important in Brazil?*

Brazil has some of the world's most plentiful natural resources. Many of the resources have been developed for years, especially in the south and southeast. Recent transportation improvements have made the resources in Brazil's vast interior available to its growing industries and population. Agriculture, mining, and forestry have been important for centuries. The natural riches of Brazil attracted European settlers to the region. They found abundant trees, rich mineral resources, and fertile farmland.

River floodwaters surge through an area of the Amazon rain forest in northwestern Brazil.

▶ CRITICAL THINKING

Identifying What yearly natural event causes flooding in the Amazon Basin?

Think **Again**

Summer and winter occur at about the same time everywhere.

Not true. While American teens enjoy their summer vacation, young people in Brazil are going to school! That's because south of the Equator, the seasons are reversed. The summer months in the United States are winter months in Brazil.

Kevin Schafer/Photographer's Choice/Getty Images

A worker on a Brazilian coffee plantation picks ripe coffee berries. After picking, the coffee berries are separated for quality and packed in sacks to send to market.

▶ CRITICAL THINKING

Identifying Where are Brazil's major coffee-growing areas?

Abundant Forests

Forests cover about 60 percent of Brazil, accounting for about 7 percent of the world's timber resources. Most of the forests in the northeast and south were cleared long ago. Heavy logging continues in the Atlantic lowlands.

Logging in the Amazon Basin is increasing as more roads are built and settlement grows. The rain forest's mahogany and other hardwoods are highly desirable for making furniture. The rain forest is also a source of natural rubber, nuts, and medicinal plants. Logging, mining, and other development have become a major environmental issue. However, the rate of deforestation, or clearing land of forests or trees, has declined in recent years.

Minerals

Brazil has rich mineral resources that are only partly developed. They include iron ore, tin, copper, bauxite, gold, and manganese. At one time, most mining was done in the Brazilian Highlands. Recently, major deposits of minerals have been found in the Amazon basin. The new deposits might make Brazil the world's largest producer of many of the minerals. Brazil also has huge potential reserves of petroleum and natural gas deep under the ocean floor off its coast. Getting to the oil is a challenge, however.

Productive Farmland

Brazil is the world's largest producer of coffee, sugarcane, and tropical fruits. The country also produces great amounts of soybeans, corn, and cotton.

Brazilian farmers produce most of their country's food supply. Agriculture is also important in trade, accounting for more than one-third of Brazil's exports. It is a leading exporter of coffee, oranges, soybeans, and cassava. Cassava is used to make tapioca.

Major Crops

Production of coffee throughout the world was estimated to set an all-time high in 2012–2013, up 10 million bags from the previous year. Brazil and Vietnam accounted for most of the increase. The eastern Brazilian Highlands and the Atlantic lowlands are the main coffee-growing areas. Coffee was once Brazil's main export. Today, soybeans provide more income for the country. China is increasing its soybean imports, mostly for animal feed, and much of it comes from Brazil.

Most soybeans are grown in the south, but they are an important crop in the Brazilian Highlands, too. Farming has become easier in the highlands as farmers have begun using tractors and fertilizer to work the savanna soils.

Brazil grows one-third of the world's oranges, making it the world's leading supplier of the citrus fruit. Brazil is also the largest beef exporter in the world. Most of the country's grazing land is in the south and southeast.

In a recent year, Brazil's sugarcane production was more than two and a half times that of India, the second-leading producer. Brazilian sugarcane is used to make ethanol, which is mixed with gasoline and used as fuel for cars and trucks. For many years, the government has required cars to use ethanol. The country's car manufacturers make flexible-fuel vehicles that can use fuel with high levels of ethanol.

Include this lesson's information in your Foldable®.

☑ **READING PROGRESS CHECK**

Identifying Which two regions are Brazil's most important agricultural areas?

LESSON 1 REVIEW

Reviewing Vocabulary

1. How does Brazil's location in the Tropics affect its climate?

Answering the Guiding Questions

2. ***Determining Central Ideas*** Why is the Amazon Basin a unique region?

3. ***Analyzing*** How do a tropical rain forest climate and a tropical wet/dry climate differ?

4. ***Describing*** What resources are important Brazilian exports?

5. ***Informative/Explanatory Writing*** In which of Brazil's physical regions would you most like to live? Write a paragraph to explain why.

14.1%

Reading**HELP**DESK

Academic Vocabulary

- **comprise**
- **extract**

Content Vocabulary

- **indigenous**
- **slash-and-burn agriculture**
- **emancipate**
- **compulsory**

TAKING NOTES: *Key Idea and Details*

Sequencing As you read about Brazil's history, use the graphic organizer below to note how Brazil became a modern democratic republic.

Portugal's government moves to Brazil.

↓

↓

Lesson 2
History of Brazil

ESSENTIAL QUESTION • *How do governments change?*

IT MATTERS BECAUSE
Brazil is one of the world's leading industrial powers.

Early History

GUIDING QUESTION *How did Brazil's early peoples live?*

In 1493 Christopher Columbus returned to Spain with news of his explorations and of new lands. The Spanish worried that neighboring Portugal, a powerful seafaring rival, would try to claim these lands for itself. So they asked the pope to find a solution. The pope decided that all new lands west of a certain line should belong to Spain. Lands east of the line would belong to Portugal. The two countries agreed to this division in 1494 by signing the Treaty of Tordesillas.

Almost nothing was known of the region's geography, so neither side realized how unequal the division was. Almost all of the Americas lay west of the line, which became Spanish territory. The only exception was the eastern part of South America, which became Portuguese territory. Today, this part of South America is Brazil. That is why Brazil is the only South American country that has a Portuguese heritage.

Indigenous Populations

The first Portuguese ships stopped in Brazil in 1500. Their destination was India, so they did not stay in Brazil for long. They had peaceful encounters with some of the **indigenous**, or native, peoples who lived along the coast. The Portuguese commander, Pedro Cabral, claimed the land for Portugal. After just 10 days, the Portuguese left. They had no idea of the vast region and many peoples included in Cabral's claim.

(l to r)Mike Goldwater/Alamy; Antonello/Flickr/Getty Images; Eraldo Peres/AP Images

The people the Portuguese met were the Tupi. They lived along the coast and in the rain forests south of the Amazon River, where they grew cassava, corn, sweet potatoes, beans, and peanuts. They hunted fish and other water animals with arrows and harpoons from large log canoes, but they did little hunting on land.

Brazil's native peoples had lived there for more than 10,000 years when the Portuguese arrived. Estimates are that the population was between 2 million and 6 million by 1500. Besides the Tupi, it included the Arawak and Carib people of the northern Amazon and coast, and the Nambicuara in the drier grasslands and highlands. These are not the names of native peoples; they were Brazil's four main language groups. Each group **comprised** many different peoples.

Daily Life

Like the Tupi, Brazil's other lowland and rain forest peoples were mainly farmers. They lived in permanent, self-governing villages and practiced slash-and-burn agriculture. This is a method of farming in forests that involves cutting down trees and burning away underbrush to create fields for growing crops. Farther south, most of the Nambicuara of the Brazilian Highlands were nomads, people who move from place to place and have no permanent home. In the dry season, they lived as hunter-gatherers, people who get their food by hunting, fishing, and collecting seeds, roots, and other parts of trees and wild plants. In the wet season, they built temporary villages and practiced slash-and-burn agriculture.

Europeans Arrive

For more than 30 years after Cabral's visit, the Portuguese did not pay much attention to Brazil. Their main focus was on their colonies and trade in Asia. Their trading ships sailed south and east around Africa on their way to Asia. Portuguese sailors established a few trading posts along Brazil's coast and collected brazilwood. The red dye **extracted** from this wood was highly valued in Europe. It was because of this trade that the Portuguese named the region Brazil.

Mike Goldwater/Alamy

Academic Vocabulary

comprise to be made up of
extract to remove or take out

An Ashaninka family fishes from a boat in Brazil's Amazon rain forest.
▶ CRITICAL THINKING
Describing How did indigenous peoples make a living when the first Europeans arrived in Brazil?

Diego Frichs Antonello/Getty Images

The church of São Miguel das Missões was built about 1740 as the center of a Jesuit mission village in southern Brazil.

▶ **CRITICAL THINKING**
Explaining Why did the Jesuits build mission villages in Brazil and other parts of South America?

The valuable brazilwood trade made other Europeans more interested in Brazil. French traders began collecting the wood and shipping it to France. To bring Brazil under tighter Portuguese control, Portugal's King John III established a permanent colony and government there. The first Portuguese settlers arrived in 1533.

✔ **READING PROGRESS CHECK**

Determining Central Ideas Why did the Portuguese colonize Brazil?

Colonial Rule

GUIDING QUESTION *How did the Portuguese colony in Brazil develop?*

Portugal's rule of Brazil lasted more than 300 years. During that time, Portuguese settlements spread all along the coast. Explorers and others traveled up rivers and deep into Brazil's interior. The expansion brought wealth to Portugal, though much of it came at great cost to Brazil's indigenous peoples.

The Portuguese Conquest

King John III gave wealthy supporters huge tracts of land in Brazil. These tracts extended west from the coast about 150 miles (241 km) inland. In return, the people who received a land grant were responsible for developing it. They founded cities and gave land to colonists to farm.

Because the colonists could not do all the work that was required, they soon began enslaving nearby native peoples as laborers. Many of them resisted and were killed. Thousands more died from exposure to European diseases to which they had no natural resistance. Others fled into Brazil's interior. These conditions and other complaints caused King John to end the land-grant system in 1549. He put Brazil under royal control and sent a governor from Portugal to rule the colony.

Spread of Christianity

The new governor brought more colonists with him. They included a number of Jesuit Catholic priests who belonged to a missionary group called the Society of Jesus. The king asked the Jesuits to go to Brazil to help the native peoples and convert them to Christianity. Those who converted were settled in special Jesuit villages and were protected from slavery.

Those Portuguese colonists who held enslaved people complained to the king about the Jesuits' work. In 1574 he ruled that native peoples who did not live in Jesuit villages could be enslaved only if they were captured in war. This ruling sent Jesuits into Brazil's interior to protect and convert peoples there. Slave hunters also moved into the interior to attack and enslave the native peoples. Cattlemen and prospectors followed, slowly spreading development inland.

Sugar and Gold

As Brazil's sugar industry expanded, cattlemen needed new land. The rise of large sugarcane plantations, mainly in the northeast, pushed ranching westward.

Plantation workers carry sugarcane into a Brazilian mill, 1845.
▶ CRITICAL THINKING
Identifying Besides sugarcane, what else did large plantations grow?

Hulton Archive/Getty Images

In the 1600s, sugar became Brazil's main export and Portugal's greatest source of wealth. Coffee and cotton plantations also developed. The discovery of gold in the eastern highlands in the 1690s further boosted the development of the interior. Towns sprang up as thousands of colonists rushed to the area. Large numbers of new colonists arrived from Europe, as well. The discovery of diamonds in the region in the 1720s added to the population boom.

Plantation agriculture and mining required large numbers of workers. This increased the need for enslaved workers. When native populations could not fill the need, the Portuguese began importing large numbers of enslaved Africans. By the 1780s, more than 150,000 enslaved Africans worked in the mining districts. This was twice the size of the Portuguese population. By 1820, some 1.1 million enslaved people accounted for nearly one-third of Brazil's total population.

✓ READING PROGRESS CHECK

Determining Central Ideas Why did King John III send Jesuits to Brazil?

MAP SKILLS

1 PLACES AND REGIONS Where did the Portuguese settle in South America?

2 HUMAN GEOGRAPHY Why was the division of South America between Spain and Portugal so unequal?

Languages in South America

ATLANTIC OCEAN

EQUATOR

Amazon R.

Treaty of Tordesillas (1494)

PACIFIC OCEAN

Salvador (1549)

São Paulo (1554)

Rio de Janeiro (1565)

Cananéia (1531)

São Vicente (1532)

TROPIC OF CAPRICORN

0   800 miles
0   800 kilometers
Lambert Azimuthal Equal-Area projection

Portuguese-speaking countries
Spanish-speaking countries

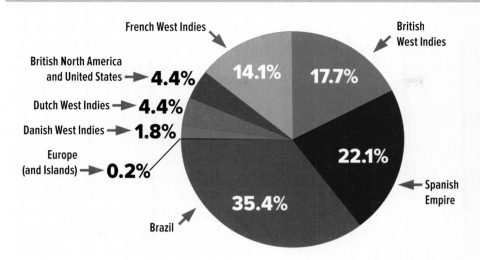

French West Indies

British North America and United States → **4.4%**

Dutch West Indies → **4.4%**

Danish West Indies → **1.8%**

Europe (and Islands) → **0.2%**

British West Indies

14.1% **17.7%**

22.1% ← Spanish Empire

35.4%

Brazil

THE SLAVE TRADE
More than one of every three enslaved Africans who were transported to the Americas were brought to Brazil.

▶ **CRITICAL THINKING**

1. *Identifying* What percentage of enslaved Africans were transported to the Spanish Empire?

2. *Integrating Visual information* What is the combined percentage of enslaved Africans brought to the West Indies?

Independent Brazil

GUIDING QUESTION *How did Brazil gain independence and become a democracy?*

Brazil gained independence from Portugal in an unusual way. It came gradually, fairly easily, and with little bloodshed. It was also the indirect result of the actions of the French emperor Napoleon Bonaparte.

Independence and Monarchy

In 1805, Britain joined by its allies Russia, Austria and Sweden, went to war with France to crush Napoleon. Instead, Napoleon defeated them and conquered much of Europe. In 1807 Napoleon invaded Portugal. As the French army closed in on Portugal's capital city of Lisbon, ruler Dom João, the royal family, and other government leaders fled to Brazil. Rio de Janeiro became the new capital of the Portuguese Empire. Brazil's status within the empire changed from a colony to a kingdom. This action gave Brazil equal status with Portugal within the empire.

After Napoleon was defeated, the Portuguese people wanted their king back. In 1821 Dom João and the rest of the government returned to Portugal. He left his son Pedro to rule Brazil. In 1822 Portugal's legislature restored Brazil's status as a colony and ordered Pedro to return. Pedro refused to give up the Brazilian throne. He declared independence and crowned himself Emperor Pedro I. Most other independent American nations became republics, but independent Brazil became a constitutional monarchy. In this form of government, a king, a queen, or an emperor acts as head of state.

Most Brazilians had supported independence from Portugal, but they soon tired of Pedro's harsh rule. In 1831 he was forced to turn over the throne to his five-year-old son.

As in the United States, voters in Brazil elect a president every four years.

▶ CRITICAL THINKING

Identifying Which group controlled the election of Brazil's president in the early republic?

A series of advisers ruled in the boy's name until he was old enough to rule on his own. In 1840, at age 14, he became Emperor Pedro II.

Pedro II ruled Brazil for nearly 50 years. His reign was marked by great progress. Brazil's population grew from 4 million to 14 million during his rule. He offered land to attract large numbers of Germans, Italians, and other European immigrants to Brazil. Sugar, coffee, and cotton production rose. Brazil's first railroads were built to get these and other products to the coast for export.

In 1850 Brazil stopped importing enslaved people from Africa. In the 1860s, a new movement began to **emancipate**, or free, the enslaved. Pedro II opposed slavery, but he thought it should be ended gradually. An 1871 law granted freedom to all children born to people in slavery. An 1885 law freed enslaved people who were over age 60. Finally, in 1888, all remaining enslaved people were freed.

The Brazilian Republic

Brazil's powerful plantation owners were angered by the loss of their enslaved workers. In 1889 they supported Brazil's army in overthrowing Pedro II. A new government was established, with a constitution based on the Constitution of the United States. Brazil became a republic, a system in which the head of state is an elected ruler instead of a king, a queen, or an emperor. In this republic, the right to vote was limited to wealthy property owners. In 1910, for example, out of a population of 22 million, only 627,000 people could vote.

Most of the power in the early republic was held by the governors of Brazil's southeastern states. Governors were elected by their state's wealthy voters. State governors controlled the election of Brazil's president, who usually came from the highly populated, coffee-rich states of São Paulo and Minas Gerais (General Mines).

These presidents followed economic policies that benefited southeastern Brazil. Coffee became Brazil's main export. By 1902, Brazil was supplying 65 percent of the world's coffee. São Paulo, Minas Gerais, and Rio de Janeiro also became the country's industrial and commercial centers. Over time, some people became unhappy with government policies that continued to favor the coffee growers and other rich Brazilians. In 1930 Getúlio Vargas overthrew the newly elected "coffee president" and seized power. He ruled for the

Eraldo Peres/AP Images

next 15 years. Vargas's reforms made him a hero to most Brazilians. He raised wages, shortened work hours, and let workers form labor unions. Yet for much of his rule, Vargas governed as a dictator. He dissolved the legislature and banned political parties. In 1945 military leaders forced Vargas to resign.

Brazil Under Military Rule

Vargas was elected president again in 1950, but again was forced from office by the military in 1954. For over 30 years, government in Brazil alternated between dictators and elected leaders. Manufacturing thrived throughout this period. Foreign investments brought rapid growth in the steel, auto, and chemical industries.

Industrial growth was accompanied by changes and unrest in Brazilian society. As a result, the military took control of Brazil in 1964, and a series of generals became the heads of government. An elected legislature was allowed, but the army controlled the elections. People who opposed the government were arrested. Many others were frightened into silence. The military gave up power in 1985 and allowed the election of a civilian president.

Modern Brazil

Today Brazil is a democratic republic in which people elect a president and other leaders. In Brazil, voting is **compulsory**. This means that citizens have no choice in deciding whether or not to vote. People from ages 18 to 70 are required by law to vote.

Because Brazil has a high number of well-supported political parties, coalition governments are common. A coalition government is one in which several political parties cooperate to do the work of government. In 2003 a democratically elected president replaced another democratically elected president for the first time in more than 40 years. In 2010 voters elected Dilma Vana Rousseff as the thirty-sixth president of Brazil. She is the first woman president in the country's history.

 READING PROGRESS CHECK

Identifying Central Ideas Why did Brazil's monarchy come to an end?

Include this lesson's information in your Foldable®.

LESSON 2 REVIEW

Reviewing Vocabulary
1. What kind of agriculture did some *indigenous* farmers practice?

Answering the Guiding Questions
2. *Analyzing* How were the Nambicuara similar to and different from the other main indigenous peoples of early Brazil?

3. *Identifying* Why did African slavery increase in Brazil before it was abolished completely in 1888?

4. *Describing* What were the main steps in Brazil's transition from a colony to a democratic country?

5. *Argument Writing* Take the role of a Brazilian living in 1889. Write a letter to the editor of your local newspaper supporting or opposing the establishment of the republic. Be sure to state the reasons for your opinion.

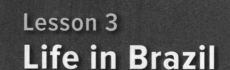

Reading**HELP**DESK

Academic Vocabulary

- diverse
- unique

Content Vocabulary

- hinterland
- metropolitan area
- central city
- favela

TAKING NOTES: *Key Ideas and Details*

Organize As you read the lesson, use the graphic organizer below to organize information about Brazil by adding one or more facts to each box.

Lesson 3
Life in Brazil

ESSENTIAL QUESTION • *What makes a culture unique?*

IT MATTERS BECAUSE
Brazil's cultures have influenced many people around the world.

People and Places

GUIDING QUESTION *What cultures are represented by Brazilians?*

With some 200 million people, Brazil is the world's fifth-largest country in population. Only China, India, the United States, and Indonesia are home to more people. About half of all South Americans live in Brazil.

Brazil's Diverse Population

Brazil is a mix of several cultures. Many people have a combination of European, African, and native American ancestry. Many are of Portuguese origin or immigrants from Germany and Italy. To a lesser degree, people came from Russia, Poland, and Ukraine. São Paulo, in particular, has a **diverse** population, including a large Japanese community.

Nearly 40 percent of Brazilians have mixed ancestry. This is largely because marriages between people of different ethnic groups have been more acceptable in Brazil than in many other countries. The largest group of multiethnic Brazilians are persons with European and African ancestors. People of European and Native American ancestry are a smaller group.

The smallest multiethnic group is persons of African and Native American descent. About 4 million Africans had been enslaved and brought to Brazil by the 1800s. Many escaped into the **hinterland**, the often remote inland regions, far from the coasts. The Africans lived there with the indigenous Native Americans or formed their own farming communities.

Today, about 80 percent of Brazilians live within 200 miles (322 km) of the Atlantic coast. After slavery ended, many formerly enslaved people left their homes and settled in other agricultural areas or towns. The northeast, however, still has Brazil's highest African and mixed populations. They also form the major population groups in coastal cities and towns north of Rio de Janeiro.

Most Brazilians of European descent live in southern Brazil. Indigenous Native Americans live in all parts of the country. The Amazon rain forest holds the greatest number, but about half of Brazil's Native Americans now live in cities.

Crowded Cities

For most of Brazil's history, the majority of Brazilians lived in rural areas, mainly on plantations, on farms, or in small towns. In the 1950s, millions of people began migrating to cities to take jobs in Brazil's growing industries. By 1970, more Brazilians lived in urban areas than in rural ones. Today, 89 percent of Brazilians live in and around cities.

São Paulo, Brazil's industrial center, is one of the world's largest cities. Some 17 million people live in its **metropolitan area**, or the city and built-up areas around the central city. The **central city** is the largest or most important city in a metropolitan area. São Paulo and Brazil's other large cities look much like cities in the United States. Skyscrapers line busy downtown streets. Cars and trucks jam highways in the mornings and evenings as people travel to and from their jobs. People work in office buildings, shops, and factories. Many own small businesses.

Favelas

Many middle-class urban dwellers live in apartment buildings. Others live in small houses in the suburbs, which are largely residential communities on the outskirts of cities. Wealthy Brazilians live in luxury apartments and mansions.

Most of Brazil's large cities also have shantytowns called **favelas**. Favelas are makeshift communities located on the edges of the cities.

Stuart Dee/Photographer's Choice RF/Getty Images

Academic Vocabulary

Academic Vocabulary

diverse differing from one another; varied

Sugarloaf Mountain looms above Rio de Janeiro's Copacabana Beach.

▶ CRITICAL THINKING

Explaining What has led to the growth of Brazil's cities since the 1950s?

The Estaiada Bridge, opened in 2008, is one of São Paulo's landmarks. It is known for its curved appearance and X-shaped tower.

▶ CRITICAL THINKING

Describing What role does São Paulo play in Brazil's economy?

Favelas arose as millions of poor, rural Brazilians with few skills and little education migrated to cities to seek better lives. These people could not afford houses or apartments. Instead, they settled on land they did not own and built shacks from scraps of wood, sheet metal, cinder blocks, and bricks. Some favelas lack sewers and running water. In many, disease and crime are widespread.

São Paulo and Rio de Janeiro have the most and largest favelas. Rio has about 1,000 of them. About one of every three of the city's residents live in a favela. Rio officials have tried to deal with this problem by offering favela dwellers low-cost housing in the suburbs. Many do not want to move because the long commute from the suburbs to jobs in the city can take hours.

☑ READING PROGRESS CHECK

Analyzing Why does Brazil have such a large percentage of people with multiethnic ancestry?

People and Cultures

GUIDING QUESTION *What is it like to live in Brazil?*

Brazilians get along well for a country whose population includes such a variety of racial and ethnic groups. This is largely due to Brazilians' reputation for accepting other people's differences. Personal warmth, good nature, and "getting along" are valued in Brazilian culture. These attitudes and behaviors are an important part of what is known as the "Brazilian Way."

Tensions exist in Brazilian society, but they involve social and economic issues more than ethnic or cultural ones. Ethnicity still plays a factor, though, because Brazilians of European origins have often had better educational opportunities. They hold many of the better jobs as a result.

Ethnic and Language Groups

Until the late 1800s, nearly all European immigrants to Brazil were from Portugal. After slavery ended, large numbers of Italians arrived to work on the coffee plantations.

During the same period, settlers from Germany started farming colonies in southern Brazil. In the early 1900s, the first Japanese arrived to work in agriculture in the Brazilian Highlands. Many of their descendants moved to cities. The first Middle Easterners, mainly Lebanese and Syrians, arrived at about the same time. They became involved in commerce in cities and towns around the country.

The diversity of Brazil's people has given the country a **unique** culture. Portuguese is Brazil's official language. Almost all Brazilians speak it. Brazilian Portuguese is quite different from the language spoken in Portugal. In fact, many Brazilians find it easier to understand films from Spanish-speaking countries in South America than films from Portugal. This is because Brazil's many ethnic groups have introduced new words to the language. Thousands of words and expressions have come from Brazil's indigenous peoples. Dozens of Native American languages are still spoken throughout Brazil.

Religion and the Arts

About two-thirds of Brazilians are Roman Catholics, but only about 20 percent attend services regularly. Women go to church more often than men, and older Brazilians are more active in the Church than the young.

Academic Vocabulary

unique unlike anything else; unusual

Most of the rest of Brazil's population follows the Protestant faith. Those who practice Islam and Eastern religions such as Buddhism are growing in numbers. Many Brazilians blend Christian teachings with beliefs and practices from African religions.

Other African influences on Brazilian culture include foods, popular music, and dance, especially the samba. Brazilians blended samba rhythms with jazz to introduce the world to music called bossa nova. Several Brazilian writers have gained world fame for their books exploring regional and ethnic themes. Brazilian movies and plays also have gained worldwide attention.

Each February, Brazilians celebrate a four-day holiday called Carnival. Millions of working-class and middle-class Brazilians spend much of the year preparing for it by making costumes and building parade floats. Nearly all city neighborhoods are strung with lights. Rio de Janeiro's Carnival is the largest and is world famous. Elaborately costumed Brazilians ride equally elaborate floats in dazzling parades. They are accompanied by thousands of costumed samba dancers moving to the lively music.

Rural Life

Family ties are strong in Brazil. Family members usually live close to one another. They hold frequent reunions or gather at a family farm or ranch on weekends and holidays. Life in rural Brazil has changed little over the years. Most rural families are poor. They work on plantations or ranches or own small farms. They live in one- or two-room houses made of stone or adobe—clay bricks that are dried and hardened in the sun. Their chief foods are beans, cassava, and rice. A stew of black beans, dried beef, and pork is Brazil's national dish.

Urban Life

Many city dwellers are poor, too, and they eat a similar diet. For those who can afford it, U.S. fast-food chains are rapidly expanding in larger Brazilian cities. In general, people in the industrial cities of southern Brazil have a better life than people in the more rural northeast.

Life in Brazil's cities moves at a faster pace. Government services and modern conveniences are available there. Many workers have good jobs and enjoy a decent quality of life. Most middle-class families have cars. Poor families rely on buses to get to work and to the beach or countryside on weekends.

Soccer ("football") is Brazil's most popular sport. It is played nearly everywhere on a daily basis. Matches between professional teams draw huge crowds in major cities. Brazil's national team is recognized as one of the best in the world.

☑ READING PROGRESS CHECK

Describing Describe one element of Brazil's culture. Explain why that element of culture is important to Brazilians.

Contemporary Brazil

GUIDING QUESTION *What challenges does Brazil face?*

Brazil has the world's seventh-largest economy. It ranks among the leaders in mining, manufacturing, and agriculture. These activities have produced great wealth for some people and a growing middle class. However, only 10 percent of Brazilians receive about half the country's income, while the bottom 40 percent receive only 10 percent of the total income. At the same time, 1 in 10 Brazilians is forced to live on less than $2 a day. About 1 in 5 workers is employed in agriculture, mainly on large farms and ranches owned by corporations or wealthy Brazilians.

Brazil is a member of several organizations designed to promote free trade. MERCOSUR, established in 1991, is South America's leading trading bloc. In 2008 the leaders of 12 South American nations created the Union of South American Nations (UNASUR).

Education and Earning a Living

Education is an important key to success in Brazil. College graduates earn twice as much as high school graduates do, and high school graduates earn four times as much as those with little or no schooling.

Soccer ("football") players scramble for the ball during a match at a Rio de Janeiro stadium.

▶ CRITICAL THINKING

Describing How important is football to Brazilians?

Buda Mendes/LatinContent WO/Getty Images

Boys read in front of the class at a public school in Brazil's Amazon area.

▶ CRITICAL THINKING

Describing How well educated are most Brazilians?

School is free up to age 17. Yet 60 percent of Brazilians have only four years of schooling or less. These people have a hard life. They work long hours for low pay. In 2011 the government launched "Brazil Without Poverty," a program aimed at raising the standard of living and improving access to education and health care.

Seeking to create a skilled workforce, Brazil's government is trying to improve education at all levels. It has increased funds to build better primary and secondary schools. At the university level, Brazil has introduced the "Science Without Borders" program, which aims to send thousands of students to universities abroad, including to colleges in the United States.

Connections and Challenges

Improving citizens' quality of life is just one of the challenges facing Brazil. The government is sponsoring a program to colonize the country's sparsely populated interior. Several highways have been built across the country. The most important is the Transamazonica Highway, from the coastal city of Recife to the border with Peru. To relieve poverty and overcrowding, poor rural Brazilians have been offered free land in the Amazon if they will develop it. Thousands have followed new roads into the Amazon Basin to take advantage of this offer.

Brazilians also have worked to develop the energy resources the country needs for continued economic development. Large power plants along several major rivers use water power to produce most of Brazil's electricity. In the 1970s, the high cost of oil caused the government to develop a program that substitutes ethanol, a fuel made from sugarcane, for gasoline. Recent discoveries of oil and natural gas off Brazil's coast provide the country with the energy it needs.

Environmental Concerns

Programs to develop Brazil's interior have resulted in great concern for the future of the Amazon rain forest. Logging has long been a problem, as trees are cut down to sell as wood. The Transamazonica Highway and other new roads have increased this destruction by making it easier to get into the rain forest and to get the logs out.

The farmers, ranchers, miners, and other settlers the roads have brought into the region have become cause for even greater concern. About 15 percent of the rain forest is already gone, and the rate of its destruction has attracted worldwide attention.

It is easy to think that good soils must lie underneath tropical rain forests. However, this is often not true. The heat and moisture of the area keep the nutrients in the biosphere, that is, in the living organisms, particularly the plants. As a result, the soil is poor. When the forest is cleared for farming, the soil cannot support crops.

A highway cuts through Brazil's Amazon rain forest.

▶ CRITICAL THINKING

Explaining How do new roads benefit and harm Brazil's development, especially in rain forest areas?

Include this lesson's information in your Foldable®.

✔ READING PROGRESS CHECK

Identifying What are reasons for allowing development in the rain forest?

LESSON 3 REVIEW

Reviewing Vocabulary

1. What is Brazil doing to develop some of its *hinterlands*?

Answering the Guiding Questions

2. ***Identifying*** In what parts of Brazil do most of its population live?

3. ***Determining Central Ideas*** How has Brazil's African heritage affected its culture today?

4. ***Analyzing*** How do education issues contribute to economic inequalities in Brazil?

5. ***Argument Writing*** Choose one challenge Brazil faces today and write a short essay suggesting how to solve it.

Rain Forest
Resources

Many medicines that we use today come from plants found in rain forests. From these plants, we derive medicines to treat or cure diabetes, heart conditions, glaucoma, and many other illnesses and physical problems.

Largest Rain Forests The world's largest rain forests are located in the Amazon Basin in South America, the Congo Basin in Africa, and the Indonesian Archipelago in Southeast Asia. The Amazon rain forest makes up more than half of Earth's remaining rain forest.

The Planet's Lungs Rain forests are often called the "lungs of the planet" for their contribution in producing oxygen, which all animals need for survival. Rain forests also provide a home for many people, animals, and plants. Rain forests are an important source of medicine and foods.

> **Every year, less and less of the rain forest remains. Human activity is the main cause of this deforestation.**

The Yanomami People
An ancient indigenous people, the Yanomami live in the Amazon rain forest regions of Brazil and Venezuela. For many years, the Yanomami lived in isolation. They rely on their environment for their food, shelter, and medicine.

Deforestation Every year, less and less of the rain forest remains. Human activity is the main cause of this deforestation. Humans cut rain forests for grazing land, agriculture, wood, and the land's minerals. Deforestation harms the native peoples who rely on the rain forest. The loss of rain forests also has an extreme impact on the environment because the rich biological diversity of the rain forest is lost as the trees are cut down.

Preserving Rain Forests More and more people realize that keeping the rain forests intact is critical. Groups plant trees on deforested land in the hope that forests will eventually recover. More companies are operating in ways that minimize damage to rain forests.

More Research Thirty years ago, very little research on the medicines of the rain forest was being done. Today, many drug companies and several branches of the U.S. government, including the National Cancer Institute, are taking part in research projects to find medicines and cures for viruses, infections, cancer, and AIDS.

Ashaninka children are at play in the rain forest. The Ashaninka comprise one of the largest indigenous groups in South America. ▶

THERE'S MORE ONLINE

HEAR why the rain forest is important • *SEE* the loss of the rain forest • *WATCH* plants become medicine

These numbers and statistics can help you learn about the resources of the rain forest.

1.4 Billion Acres

The Amazon rain forest covers 1.4 billion acres (2,187,500 sq km). If the rain forest were a nation, it would be the 13th-largest country in the world.

OVER SEVEN PERCENT

Tropical rain forests make up about 7 percent of the world's total landmass. But found within the rain forest are half of all known varieties of plants.

40 Years

In 1950 rain forests covered about 14 percent of Earth's land. Rain forests cover about 7 percent today. Scientists estimate that, at the present rate, all rain forests could disappear from Earth within 40 years.

80%

About 80 percent of the diets of developed nations of the world originated in tropical rain forests. Included are such fruits as oranges and bananas; corn, potatoes, and other vegetables; and nuts and spices.

120

Today, 120 prescription drugs sold worldwide are derived from rain forest plants. About 65 percent of all cancer-fighting medicines also come from rain forest plants. An anticancer drug derived from a special kind of periwinkle plant has greatly increased the survival rate for children with leukemia.

50,000 Square Miles

When rain forests are cleared for land, animal and plant life disappears. Almost half of Earth's original tropical forests have been lost. Every year, about 32 million acres—50,000 square miles (129,499 sq. km)—of tropical forest are destroyed. That's roughly the area of Nicaragua or the state of Alabama.

EIGHTY PERCENT

For centuries, people who live in rain forests have used the plants and trees to meet their health needs. The World Health Organization (WHO) estimates that about 80 percent of the indigenous peoples still rely on traditional medicine.

ONE PERCENT

Although ingredients for many medicines come from rain forest plants, less than 1 percent of plants growing in rain forests have been tested by scientists for medicinal purposes.

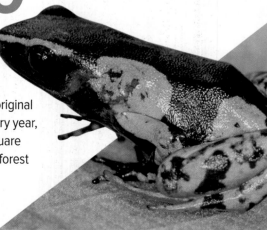

The World's Rain Forests

ARCTIC CIRCLE

60°N

EUROPE

ASIA

NORTH
AMERICA

30°N

TROPIC OF CANCER

AFRICA

0°
EQUATOR

PRIME MERIDIAN

SOUTH
AMERICA

TROPIC OF CAPRICORN

30°S

AUSTRALIA

Rain forest

N
W   E
S

0   2,000 miles
0   2,000 kilometers
Robinson projection

60°S

ANTARCTIC CIRCLE

ANTARCTICA

120°W   60°W   0°   60°E   120°E

GLOBAL IMPACT

THE WORLD'S RAIN FORESTS   Rain forests are located in a belt around Earth near the Equator. Abundant rain, relatively constant temperatures, and strong sunlight year-round are ideal conditions for the plants and animals of the rain forest.

Rain forests cover only a small part of Earth's surface. The Amazon Basin in South America is the world's largest rain forest area.

Rain Forest Research

Laboratories provide a research base for scientists to conduct environmental research. This laboratory in Mumbai attracts rain forest scientists from around the world.

Thinking Like a Geographer

1. *Environment and Society*
   Why do you think scientists only know about a small fraction of potential medicines from the rain forest?

2. *Environment and Society*
   How do you think native doctors in the Amazon rain forest discovered medical uses for plants?

3. *Human Geography* List two reasons to explain why some people support saving rain forests. List two reasons to explain why some people support cutting down rain forests. Write a paragraph to state which position you support. Include facts to support your position.

Lesson 3 **549**

Directions: Write your answers on a separate piece of paper.

1 Use your FOLDABLES to explore the Essential Question.

INFORMATIVE/EXPLANATORY Write an essay explaining how the Brazilians' conversion of rain forest land to farmland may affect the environment of the rest of the world.

2 21st Century Skills

IDENTIFYING POINT OF VIEW Given what you have learned about the benefits of rain forests, do you think Brazil has an obligation to maintain what remains of them? Write two or three paragraphs to explain your viewpoint.

3 Thinking Like a Geographer

DESCRIBING On a graphic organizer, note important differences between Brazilians who live in the major cities and those who do not. Add other categories you think are important in describing the differences.

	City dwellers	Country dwellers
Wealth		
Housing		
Work		

4 **GEOGRAPHY ACTIVITY**

Locating Places

Match the letters on the map with the numbered places below.

1. Brasília   **3.** Amazon River   **5.** Recife   **7.** São Francisco River

2. Atlantic Ocean   **4.** São Paulo   **6.** Pacific Ocean   **8.** Amazon Basin

Chapter 18 ASSESSMENT

REVIEW THE GUIDING QUESTIONS

Directions: Choose the best answer for each question.

1 Brazil is the world's largest exporter of

A. beef.

B. clocks.

C. peanut butter.

D. tropical plants.

2 Most of Brazil's population lives in

F. the rain forest.

G. the coastal lowlands.

H. the Amazon Basin.

I. northeastern Brazil.

3 The first Portuguese explorer to lay claim to Brazil was

A. Ferdinand Magellan.

B. a Jesuit priest.

C. Getúlio Vargas.

D. Pedro Cabral.

4 When Napoleon invaded Portugal in 1807 and the Portuguese royal family and government leaders fled to Brazil, which city became the new capital of the Portuguese Empire?

F. São Paulo

G. Campinas

H. Rio de Janeiro

I. Brasília

5 Brazil's largest metropolitan area, or city and surrounding suburbs, is

A. Brasília.

B. Buenos Aires.

C. São Paulo.

D. Rio de Janeiro.

6 The official language of Brazil is

F. Spanish.

G. Brazilian.

H. Portuguese.

I. English.

DBQ ANALYZING DOCUMENTS

❼ IDENTIFYING POINT OF VIEW Read the following news report:

"Brazilian farmers meanwhile have been demanding the country's Congress ease environmental laws in the Amazon region. They support a bill that would let them clear half the land on their properties in environmentally sensitive areas. Current law allows farmers to clear just 20 percent of their land in the Amazon zone."

—from Marco Sibaja, "Amazon Deforestation in Brazil Increases"

Why do Brazilian farmers want to be able to clear more land?

A. They oppose any environmental protection laws.

B. They want more land for crops to increase their profits.

C. They plan to sell the cleared land for new housing developments.

D. They hope to drive Native Americans from the land.

❽ ANALYZING What is likely to happen if the bill the farmers support becomes law?

F. Brazil's economy will suffer from too much emphasis on agriculture.

G. Agriculture in Brazil will decline because the land is unproductive.

H. Deforestation in the Amazon will increase at a faster rate.

I. Environmentalists will stop fighting over deforestation.

SHORT RESPONSE

"Exploiting vast natural resources and a large labor pool, [Brazil] is today South America's leading economic power. . . . Highly unequal income distribution and crime remain pressing problems."

—from *CIA World Factbook*

❾ ANALYZING How has Brazil's economy benefited from the nation's large size?

❿ IDENTIFYING Why is unequal income distribution in Brazil a problem?

EXTENDED RESPONSE

⓫ INFORMATIVE/EXPLANATORY WRITING Compare and contrast the cultures of the United States and Brazil, including political, economic, and social factors.

Need Extra Help?

If You've Missed Question	❶	❷	❸	❹	❺	❻	❼	❽	❾	❿	⓫
Review Lesson	1	1	2	2	1	3	3	3	1	3	3

THE TROPICAL NORTH

ESSENTIAL QUESTIONS • *How does geography influence the way people live?* • *Why does conflict develop?* • *What makes a culture unique?*

©Pablo Corral V/Corbis

Farmer Juan Lucas harvests palms in Ecuador's tropical coastal lowlands.

networks

There's More Online about The Tropical North.

CHAPTER 19

Lesson 1
Physical Geography of the Region

Lesson 2
History of the Countries

Lesson 3
Life in the Tropical North

The Story Matters...

The countries of the Tropical North are home to some of the most ethnically diverse populations in the world. Native Americans, Europeans, Africans, and Chinese are among those who live in this subregion of South America. It is also home to some of the most diverse environments in the world. Landscapes include jungles, towering mountain ranges, broad river plains, plunging waterfalls, and an archipelago renowned for its unique animal life.

FOLDABLES
Study Organizer

Go to the Foldables® library in the back of your book to make a Foldable® that will help you take notes while reading this chapter.

THE TROPICAL NORTH

Ecuador, Colombia, Venezuela, Guyana, Suriname, and French Guiana are the lands that make up South America's Tropical North.

Step Into the Place

MAP FOCUS Use the map to answer the following questions.

1. **THE GEOGRAPHER'S WORLD** Which country in the Tropical North is connected to Central America?

2. **THE GEOGRAPHER'S WORLD** In which direction would you go if you were traveling from French Guiana to Suriname?

3. **PLACES AND REGIONS** Why do you think the Galápagos Islands belong to Ecuador?

4. **CRITICAL THINKING**
   DESCRIBING Use the map to help you describe how Guyana and Suriname are similar geographically.

A

RIVER TRAVEL Indigenous peoples, such as the Makushi, live in small villages on the banks of rivers that wind their way through Guyana's rain forests.

B

URBAN CENTER With about 4 million people, Caracas is the capital and largest city of Venezuela.

Step Into the Time

DESCRIBING Choose one event from the time line and write a paragraph describing the social, political, or environmental effect that event had on the region and the world.

1821 Simón Bolívar frees Venezuela from Spanish rule

1667 The Netherlands acquires Suriname from Britain

1800

1835 English naturalist Charles Darwin arrives on Galápagos Islands

The Tropical North

TROPIC OF CANCER

20°N

ATLANTIC OCEAN

GUATEMALA
HONDURAS

EL SALVADOR
NICARAGUA

ANTIGUA AND BARBUDA

ST. KITTS AND NEVIS

DOMINICA

Caribbean Sea

ST. LUCIA
BARBADOS

GRENADA
ST. VINCENT AND THE GRENADINES

COSTA RICA

Barranquilla

Maracaibo
Valencia
Caracas

B

Maracay

TRINIDAD AND TOBAGO

10°N

PANAMA

Gulf of Panama

Atrato R.

Lake Maracaibo

Orinoco R.

Medellín

Cauca R.

Magdalena R.

VENEZUELA

Georgetown

Paramaribo

GUYANA

Cayenne

Bogotá

SURINAME

FRENCH GUIANA (Fr.)

Cali

COLOMBIA

A

Galápagos Islands (Ecuador)

EQUATOR

BRAZIL

0°

Quito

ECUADOR

Guayaquil
Guayas R.

National capital
Department capital
City

N
W E
S

PACIFIC OCEAN

PERU

0   400 miles
0   400 kilometers
Lambert Azimuthal Equal-Area projection

10°S

90°W   80°W   70°W

BOLIVIA

Timeline

1935 Ecuador declares part of Galápagos Islands a wildlife sanctuary

1998 Hugo Chávez is elected president of Venezuela

1966 Guyana gains independence from Britain

1900

2000

1978 UNESCO adds the Galápagos Islands to the World Heritage List

1990s Ecuadoran Indians protest for rights

555

netw⊙rks

There's More Online!

☑ **GRAPHIC ORGANIZER**

☑ **MAP** Tropical North

☑ **SLIDE SHOW** Emeralds

☑ **VIDEO**

Lesson 1
Physical Geography of the Region

ESSENTIAL QUESTION • *How does geography influence the way people live?*

(l to r)Fabio Filzi/Vetta/Getty Images; Ecuadorpostales/Shutterstcock.com; ©Last Refuge/Robert Harding World Imagery/Corbis

Reading HELP DESK

Academic Vocabulary

• **exceed**
• **despite**

Content Vocabulary

• **elevation**
• **trade winds**
• **cash crop**

TAKING NOTES: *Key Ideas and Details*

Identify As you read the lesson, use a graphic organizer like this one to record the important resources of each of these countries.

Country	Resources
Ecuador	
Colombia	
Venezuela	
Guyana	
Suriname	

IT MATTERS BECAUSE

The land and waters of the Tropical North provide oil, bauxite, and emeralds, along with shrimp and other food products that people and industries in the United States and around the world need or want.

Landforms and Waterways

GUIDING QUESTION *What are the major physical features of the Tropical North?*

South America's Tropical North consists of five countries and a colony. From west to east, they are Ecuador, Colombia, Venezuela, Guyana, Suriname, and French Guiana.

Colombia is the Tropical North's largest country, and Venezuela is the second largest. Each is more than twice the size of California. Ecuador and Guyana, the third and fourth largest, are about the size of Colorado and Kansas, respectively. Suriname is about the size of Washington State; French Guiana, the smallest, is the size of Maine. Together, the countries of the Tropical North total only about one-third the size of nearby Brazil.

Landforms of the Tropical North

Ecuador, Colombia, and Venezuela have the region's most diverse physical geography. The Andes mountain ranges, which extend the length of western South America, run through each country. Some of the peaks have **elevations**, or height above the level of the sea, that **exceed** 18,000 feet (5,486 m)—almost 3.5 miles (5.6 km) high. Many peaks are covered with snow year-round. About 40 peaks are volcanoes.

Cotopaxi in Ecuador, at 19,347 feet (5,897 m), is the world's highest active volcano. In Colombia, the Sierra Nevada de Santa Marta mountains along the Caribbean coast are the world's highest coastal range.

Colombia is the only country in South America with coastlines on both the Pacific Ocean and the Caribbean Sea. The mountains make travel between the coasts difficult. So does the Darién, a wilderness region of deep ravines, swamps, and dense rain forest along Colombia's border with Panama.

West of the Andes, Colombia and Ecuador have narrow lowlands that border their Pacific coasts. East of the mountains, more lowlands extend into Peru, Brazil, and Venezuela. The southern half of the lowlands is part of the Amazon Basin. The northern half is a grassy plain called the Llanos. This plain also covers most of northern Venezuela.

Southern Venezuela contains a heavily forested region of rolling hills, low mountains, and plateaus called the Guiana Highlands. Along the border with Brazil, groups of forest-covered mesas called *tepuis* rise to heights of 9,000 feet (2,743 m) in places. The Guiana Highlands extend east into Guyana, Suriname, and French Guiana. Rain forest covers most of this region except for a narrow band of low and sometimes swampy plains along the Atlantic coast.

Abundant Waterways

Rivers flow across much of northern South America. The 1,300-mile-long (2,092 km) Orinoco River is the continent's third-longest river. Its more than 400 tributaries form the north's largest river system. The Orinoco crosses Venezuela in a giant arc, dropping from the Guiana Highlands through the Llanos to the Atlantic Ocean. One of its tributaries flows over Angel Falls, the world's highest waterfall. Angel Falls is more than 20 times higher than Niagara Falls. From the top of a *tepui,* the water plunges more than a half-mile to the fall's base.

(t)©Last Refuge/Robert Harding World Imagery/Corbis; (b)Ecuadorpostales/Shutterstock.com

Visual Vocabulary

Mesa A mesa is a small, elevated area of land that has a flat top and sides that are usually steep cliffs.

Wild horses graze on the slopes of the Cotopaxi volcano in Ecuador.
▶ CRITICAL THINKING
Analyzing Why is there snow on Cotopaxi even though the volcano lies close to the Equator?

The waters of Venezuela's Angel Falls drop from such a height that they are vaporized by the wind and turn into mist before reaching the ground.
▶ CRITICAL THINKING
Identifying Angel Falls is part of what major river system?

The Tropical North region has coastlines on three bodies of ocean water. Ecuador and western Colombia lie along the Pacific Ocean. Northern Colombia and Venezuela lie along the Caribbean Sea. The Atlantic Ocean washes the shores of Guyana, Suriname, and French Guiana.

Colombia's two main rivers, the Magdalena and the Cauca, flow north across Andes plateaus and valleys to the Caribbean Sea. These rivers form important routes into the country's agricultural and industrial interior. Both can be navigated by commercial ships for much of their length.

Other rivers that begin in the Andes flow west to the Pacific. Of these, Ecuador's Guayas River is the most important because it has made Guayaquil the country's largest city and a major port.

Rivers in Guyana, Suriname, and French Guiana flow north and empty into the Atlantic. Most are shallow, slow moving, and responsible for the region's swampy coastline. They are not useful for long-distance transportation into the interior.

Galápagos Islands

The Galápagos Islands lie in the Pacific, about 600 miles (966 km) west of Ecuador. They consist of 13 major islands, six smaller ones, and many tiny islands called islets. These rocky islands, which were formed by underwater volcanoes, are owned by Ecuador. Most have no human population.

The islands' isolation makes them home to many unusual animals, such as lizards that swim and birds with wings although they do not fly. In the 1800s, British scientist Charles Darwin studied the islands' animals to develop his theory of evolution. Today, the islands are tourist attractions. Many are protected as national parks.

✔ READING PROGRESS CHECK

Analyzing How do Colombia's rivers help the nation's economy?

Climates

GUIDING QUESTION *How and why do climates vary in the Tropical North?*

South America's Tropical North lies along the Equator. **Despite** its location, the region has a variety of climates. Many of the variations result from differences in elevation and location, and from the influence of ocean currents and winds.

Tropical Climates

The region's coasts, interior lowlands, plains, and highlands all have some type of tropical climate. This means warm temperatures throughout the year.

Fabio Filzi/Vetta/Getty Images

Much of the coastal and eastern lowlands of Ecuador and Colombia have a tropical monsoon climate, with a short, dry season and a long, wet season of heavy rainfall. In Colombia's coastal Chocó region, which includes the rugged Darién, it rains more than 300 days per year. This produces more than 400 inches (1,016 cm)—about 33 feet (10 m)—of rainfall each year, making it one of the wettest places on Earth.

The Llanos of Colombia and Venezuela have a tropical wet-dry climate, with an annual rainfall of 40 inches to 70 inches (102 cm to 178 cm). Most rain falls between May and October. Average daily temperatures are above 75°F (24°C) throughout the year. The Guiana Highlands have a tropical monsoon climate in some places. In other areas, a tropical rain forest climate (which has no dry season) is normal.

Guyana, Suriname, and French Guiana have the same climate as Venezuela's highlands. Yearly rainfall ranges from 70 inches to 150 inches (178 cm to 381 cm). Their coasts are not as hot as might be expected because of the **trade winds**, steady winds that blow from higher latitudes toward the Equator. The Caribbean coast of Venezuela and Colombia is also cooler. It has a semiarid climate, receiving less than 20 inches (51 cm) of rain per year.

Cooler Highlands

Mountain climates depend on elevation. From 3,000 to 6,500 feet (914 m to 1,981 m) is the *tierra templada,* or "temperate land." This zone has moderate rainfall and temperatures with daily averages between 65°F (18°C) and 75°F (24°C). Next is the *tierra fria,* or "cold land," reaching to about 10,000 feet (3,048 m). A colder zone called the *páramo* begins at about 10,000 feet (3,048 m); daily average temperatures in this zone are below 50°F (10°C). Wind, fog, and light drizzle are common in this zone. Vegetation is mainly grasses and hardy shrubs. Above 15,000 feet (4,572 m), the ground is permanently covered with snow and ice.

✓ READING PROGRESS CHECK

Identifying How do the climates of the Pacific coast, the Atlantic coast, and the Caribbean coast differ?

Natural Resources

GUIDING QUESTION *Which natural resources are most important to the economies of the Tropical North's countries?*

Tropical rain forests cover much of the North, but lack of roads and the region's physical geography have made it difficult for any of its countries to exploit this natural resource. The North's largest countries, Venezuela and Colombia, are its richest and most diverse in other resources, as well.

Think Again ?

Angel Falls was named after a pilot.

True. The falls are called Salto Ángel in Spanish. They are named for Jimmie Angel, a Missouri-born pilot who was the first person to fly over the falls in a plane in 1933. In 2009, however, Venezuelan president Hugo Chávez declared that the falls should be known as Kerepakpai Merú, which means "waterfall of the deepest place" in the language of the local Pemón people. He believed that Venezuela's most famous natural wonder should have an indigenous name. At the time of Chávez's death in early 2013, the name of the falls remained in dispute.

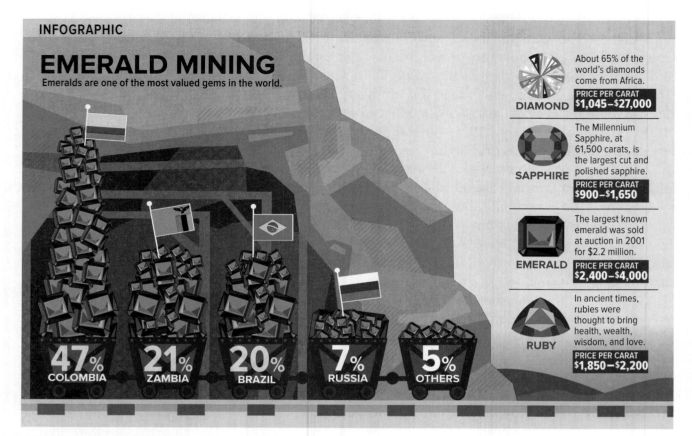

EMERALD MINING

Emeralds are one of the most valued gems in the world.

47% COLOMBIA

21% ZAMBIA

20% BRAZIL

7% RUSSIA

5% OTHERS

DIAMOND
About 65% of the world's diamonds come from Africa.
PRICE PER CARAT
$1,045–$27,000

SAPPHIRE
The Millennium Sapphire, at 61,500 carats, is the largest cut and polished sapphire.
PRICE PER CARAT
$900–$1,650

EMERALD
The largest known emerald was sold at auction in 2001 for $2.2 million.
PRICE PER CARAT
$2,400–$4,000

RUBY
In ancient times, rubies were thought to bring health, wealth, wisdom, and love.
PRICE PER CARAT
$1,850–$2,200

Emeralds were first mined in South America by indigenous peoples centuries ago. Later, the Spanish mined emeralds and shipped them to Europe as part of the valuable treasure from their American empire.

▶ CRITICAL THINKING

Analyzing Why do you think emeralds, gold, and diamonds are considered to be valuable?

Fossil Fuels

Oil is found across much of the Tropical North. Venezuela is South America's top producer of oil and ranks eleventh in the world. Some of the world's largest known reserves are in the Llanos, at the mouth of the Orinoco River, and offshore in the Caribbean. Large amounts also exist around Lake Maracaibo, South America's largest lake, along the country's northwestern coast. Venezuela has some of the world's largest natural gas deposits and is South America's second-largest coal producer. Most of the coal lies along the country's southwestern border with Colombia.

Colombia is South America's largest coal producer, with major deposits in its lowlands. It is also South America's third-largest oil producer (Brazil is second), with deposits in the Amazon lowlands, the Llanos, and the Magdalena River valley.

Ecuador produces less oil than Colombia, but it accounts for 40 percent of Ecuador's exports. It is piped over the Andes from oil fields in the east. Suriname and Guyana also have oil resources, but they do not produce enough to even meet their needs.

Minerals and Gems

Gold is found throughout the Tropical North. The largest deposits are in Colombia's mountains, eastern Ecuador, and Venezuela's

Guiana Highlands. In Ecuador, thousands of miners live in remote jungle regions and do dangerous work in tunnels that sometimes collapse in heavy rains.

Diamonds are mined from Colombia to Suriname, but Colombia is better known for high-quality emeralds and is the world's leading emerald producer. Guyana is one of the world's largest producers of bauxite, a mineral used to make aluminum. Venezuela and Suriname also have major bauxite deposits. In addition, the four countries have important deposits of copper, iron ore, and other minerals. Except for gold, Ecuador's mineral resources are limited, and French Guiana has no important mining industries.

Agriculture and Fishing

The differing elevations and climates in Ecuador and Colombia allow farmers to grow a variety of crops. Both countries export bananas from their tropical lowlands and coffee from the *tierra templada*. Ecuador's agriculture, however, is not well developed. The amount of farmland is limited, and most rural Ecuadorans grow only enough to feed their families. Corn, potatoes, beans, and cassava are common crops in both countries. Colombia produces rice, wheat, sugarcane, and cattle for sale, as well as cotton for the country's large textile industry.

Coffee is Venezuela's main **cash crop**, a product raised mainly for sale. Venezuela's main food crops are corn and rice. Most farming takes place in the northwest, and most ranching happens on the Llanos. Only about 10 percent of Venezuelans are farmers or ranchers, and much the same is true of Venezuela's neighbors to the east. Guyana, Suriname, and French Guiana have little farming because much of the land is covered by rain forest. Any farming takes place mainly along the coast.

Fishing is not a major economic activity in the Tropical North, which is unusual for countries that border the sea. The region's people do not eat much fish. The major catch of its small fishing industry is shrimp, most of which is exported.

✔ READING PROGRESS CHECK

Identifying Which fossil fuel, mineral, and gem are most widespread in the Tropical North?

Include this lesson's information in your Foldable®.

LESSON 1 REVIEW

Reviewing Vocabulary

1. What *cash crops* are important to the economy of the Tropical North?

Answering the Guiding Questions

2. *Analyzing* Why are Venezuela's Orinoco and Colombia's Magdalena rivers so important?

3. *Identifying* How are climate and elevation related in the Tropical North?

4. *Analyzing* Why is agriculture more important in Colombia than elsewhere in the Tropical North?

5. *Informative/Explanatory Writing* Which of the Tropical North's countries would you most like to visit? Write a paragraph to explain why.

Reading HELPDESK

Academic Vocabulary

- conflict
- stable

Content Vocabulary

- immunity
- *encomienda*
- hacienda

TAKING NOTES: *Key Ideas and Details*

Analyze As you read the lesson, write summary sentences about five important events in the history of the Tropical North on a graphic organizer like the one below.

Important Events
• Native Americans settle in villages along the region's coast.
•
•
•
•

Lesson 2
History of the Countries

ESSENTIAL QUESTION • *Why does conflict develop?*

IT MATTERS BECAUSE
The countries of the Tropical North export products that are sought after and highly valued by the rest of the world.

Early History and Colonization

GUIDING QUESTION *How did Europeans colonize the Tropical North?*

The Tropical North's indigenous peoples lived there for thousands of years before encountering Spanish explorers. These explorers invaded the region in the early 1500s. Less than 50 years later, the Spanish had conquered and colonized most of the region.

Early Peoples of the Tropical North

The Native Americans of the Tropical North included Carib, Arawak, and other hunter-gatherer peoples. They settled in villages along the Caribbean and Atlantic coasts.

To the west, the Cara and other peoples built fishing villages along the Pacific coast. Over time, groups like the Chibcha and Quitu moved inland to mountain valleys in the Andes. There they created advanced societies that farmed, made cloth from cotton and ornaments of gold, and traded with the Inca, an advanced civilization that developed to the south. In the late 1400s, some of the groups were conquered by the Inca and became part of the Inca Empire.

Arrival of the Europeans

In the early 1500s, Spanish adventurers landed on the Caribbean and Atlantic coasts, seeking gold and enslaving native peoples. When they met resistance and found no gold, they lost interest. The first Spanish settlements did not appear on the Caribbean coast—in Venezuela and Colombia—until 1523 and 1525. The Spanish made no effort to colonize east of Venezuela.

On the Pacific coast, the Spanish conquered the Inca in 1530 and seized their silver and gold. Driven by hunger for more wealth, they invaded Ecuador in 1534. By the mid-1500s, the conquest of the area that is now Ecuador, Colombia, and Venezuela was complete.

Spanish Colonies

To control their new colonies, the Spanish set up governments. Bogotá, which the Spanish founded in 1538, became the capital of Colombia in 1549. The Spanish placed Ecuador's government at the native town of Quito in 1563. Caracas, which the Spanish founded in 1567, eventually became Venezuela's capital. The Spanish located these cities where Native Americans already had settlements. Most were located inland, in the higher elevations where climates are milder than on the tropical coasts. For many years, Venezuela was ruled from Peru. In the 1700s, Spain placed Venezuela, Ecuador, and Colombia under a single government located at Bogotá.

Native American peoples suffered greatly under the Spanish. As in Brazil, thousands died from European diseases to which they had no natural **immunity**, or protection against illness. Others found themselves forced to work for the Spanish under a system called **encomienda**. This system allowed Spanish colonists to demand labor from the Native Americans who lived in a certain area.

The *encomienda* provided workers for Spanish mines and for the large estates, called **haciendas,** that developed in some rural areas. Native Americans in remote regions, such as Venezuela's Llanos and the rain forests of eastern Ecuador and Colombia, came under the control of Roman Catholic missionaries who were trying to convert them to Christianity.

Under Spanish rule, the Native American village of Teusaquillo became known as Bogotá. Life in Spanish Bogotá focused on the main plaza, or square, surrounded by a cathedral and government buildings.

▶ CRITICAL THINKING

Describing What role did location play in the selection of Bogotá and other cities as centers of government in northern South America?

Most haciendas became plantations that grew coffee, tobacco, sugarcane, or other cash crops. Others, mostly on the Llanos, were cattle ranches. As the hacienda system grew, the Spanish brought in thousands of enslaved Africans to provide more labor. African slavery was most common in Venezuela.

European Colonization

The French, British, and Dutch fought over and colonized Guyana, Suriname, and French Guiana. The British and the Dutch established sugar plantations and brought the first enslaved Africans to the area. Control of these colonies changed hands several times in the 1600s and 1700s. Eventually, what is now Guyana became British Guiana. Suriname was called Dutch Guiana, and French Guiana became a colony of France.

✓ **READING PROGRESS CHECK**

Identifying Which European nations founded colonies in the Tropical North, and which countries did each nation colonize?

Simón Bolívar, also known as "the Liberator," led the movement that won freedom for several countries in the Americas.

Independence

GUIDING QUESTION *How did Spain's colonies become independent countries?*

By the late 1700s, many Spanish colonists who were born in the Americas wanted independence from their Spanish rulers. Their chance came in 1808, when the French ruler Napoleon invaded and conquered Spain. Spain found it difficult to fight the French in Europe and to rule its colonies. Some of the colonists in the Americas took this opportunity to fight for independence from Spain.

Overthrow of Colonial Rule

Ecuadorans rose up against Spanish rule in 1809. Colombians and Venezuelans soon followed. A long war began, at first mainly between groups who remained loyal to Spain and those who favored independence. After the Spanish expelled the French from Spain in 1814, Spain's king sent troops to South America to try to restore Spanish control. In the south, resistance to the Spanish was led by Argentine general José de San Martín. In the north, Venezuela's Simón Bolívar led the revolt.

Spanish forces were not finally defeated until 1823. In 1819, however, Bolívar united Venezuela, Colombia, Panama, and Ecuador to form an independent republic called Gran Colombia. He became its first president.

©Bettmann/Corbis

Independent Countries

Gran Colombia broke apart after Bolívar's death in 1830. Ecuador and Venezuela formed independent countries. Colombia and Panama remained united as one country. In the early 1900s, Panama separated from Colombia and became independent.

Independence and self-government did not bring democracy and peace. Wealthy landholders competed with wealthy city businesspeople for control of the government. **Conflict** over the Catholic Church's role in society added to the unrest. The tensions resulted in civil wars in Colombia and Venezuela. Throughout the history of Ecuador, Colombia, and Venezuela, military or civilian leaders often ruled as dictators.

Labor and Immigration

While Ecuador, Colombia, and Venezuela struggled with self-government, British, Dutch, and French Guiana remained colonies. The British abolished slavery in their colony in 1838. The French and the Dutch followed in 1863.

To replace the once-enslaved workers, British and Dutch plantation owners recruited laborers from India and China. The Dutch also imported workers from their colony in Indonesia. The immigrants had to work on their colony's sugar, rice, coffee, or cacao plantations for a required length of time. At the end of their contract, they were free. Many stayed in the colony and, like the formerly enslaved people they replaced, founded towns along the coast.

In 1852 France began sending convicted criminals to its colony. More than 70,000 convict laborers arrived between 1852 and 1939. The worst convicts were imprisoned off the coast on notorious Devil's Island.

✓ READING PROGRESS CHECK

Determining Central Ideas How did British, Dutch, and French colonists find workers after slavery ended in their colony?

British and Dutch colonial rulers recruited foreign workers from India, China, and other parts of Asia to harvest various tropical crops in their South American colonies. The prison on Devil's Island (above) housed convict laborers.

▶ CRITICAL THINKING

Describing How did the arrival of foreign workers in British Guiana and Dutch Guiana change these territories in a way that made them different from other parts of South America?

Academic Vocabulary

conflict a serious disagreement

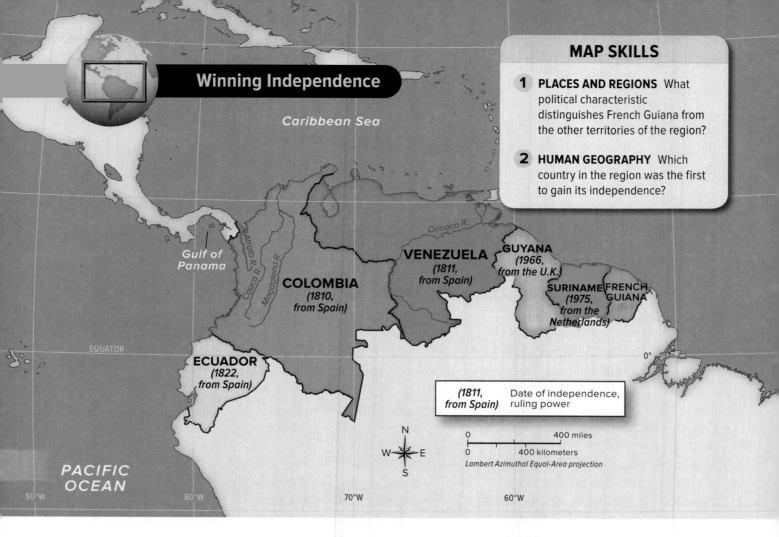

Winning Independence

Caribbean Sea

MAP SKILLS

1 **PLACES AND REGIONS** What political characteristic distinguishes French Guiana from the other territories of the region?

2 **HUMAN GEOGRAPHY** Which country in the region was the first to gain its independence?

Orinoco R.

Gulf of Panama

Atrato R.

Cauca R.

Magdalena R.

COLOMBIA *(1810, from Spain)*

VENEZUELA *(1811, from Spain)*

GUYANA *(1966, from the U.K.)*

SURINAME *(1975, from the Netherlands)*

FRENCH GUIANA *(Fr.)*

EQUATOR

0°

ECUADOR *(1822, from Spain)*

(1811, from Spain) — Date of independence, ruling power

N
W E
S

0 ____ 400 miles
0 ____ 400 kilometers
Lambert Azimuthal Equal-Area projection

PACIFIC OCEAN

90°W   80°W   70°W   60°W

Challenges and Change

GUIDING QUESTION *What challenges do the countries of the Tropical North face?*

The political and social problems that plagued Ecuador, Colombia, and Venezuela after independence continued through most of the twentieth century. Venezuela, for example, did not achieve a peaceful transfer of power between opposing groups until 1969. Meanwhile, the region's other countries, which gained independence in the twentieth century, experienced similar issues and challenges.

Gaining Independence

Independence came slowly for Guyana and Suriname. The British granted their colony limited self-government in 1891. In 1953 all colonists were given the right to vote and allowed to elect a legislature. Guyana finally gained independence in 1966.

Colonists in Dutch Guiana obtained the right to vote in 1948 and self-government in 1953. The colony became the independent country of Suriname in 1975.

The people of French Guiana became French citizens and gained the right to vote in 1848. In 1946 French Guiana's status changed from a colony to an overseas department, or district, of the country of France. French Guiana remains part of France and has representatives in France's national legislature.

Revolutions and Borders

The Tropical North's lack of strong, **stable** governments has resulted in major unrest in its countries, as well as conflicts between them. In Colombia, assassinations and other violence between feuding political groups took as many as 200,000 lives between 1946 and 1964. In the 1960s and 1970s, small rebel groups began making attacks throughout the country in hopes of overthrowing the government.

Ecuador's government has not maintained control over its remote region, which lies in the Amazon Basin, to the east of the Andes. In the 1940s, Peru seized some of this land. The two countries often clashed, until a settlement was finally reached in 1968. In 2008 tensions between Ecuador and Colombia were strained after Colombian forces attacked a Colombian rebel camp in Ecuador's territory. In 2010 Colombia accused Venezuela of allowing Colombian rebels to live in its territory. War was narrowly avoided.

Guyana's independence renewed an old border dispute with Venezuela that arose when Guyana was a British colony. The dispute was not settled until 2007. Another dispute arose on Guyana's eastern border after Suriname gained independence in 1975. Several clashes took place before that boundary was settled in 2007. Guyana also experienced years of social and political unrest as its African and South Asian populations competed for power.

Like Guyana, Suriname has faced internal unrest since independence. The military removed civilian leaders in 1980 and again in 1990. Meanwhile, rebel groups of Maroons, the descendants of escaped slaves, disrupted the country's bauxite mining in an effort to overthrow the government. The army responded by killing thousands of Maroon civilians. Thousands more fled to safety in French Guiana.

☑ **READING PROGRESS CHECK**

Identifying Which of the region's nations have experienced serious internal unrest since gaining independence?

stable staying in the same condition; not likely to change or fail

Include this lesson's information in your Foldable®.

LESSON 2 REVIEW

Reviewing Vocabulary

1. How were the *encomienda* and the *hacienda* related?

Answering the Guiding Questions

2. ***Analyzing*** Why were the Spanish more interested in colonizing Ecuador, Colombia, and Venezuela than Guyana, Suriname, and French Guiana?

3. ***Identifying*** How did conflicts in society lead to independence for Spain's colonies and cause unrest afterward?

4. ***Determining Central Ideas*** Why do the Tropical North's nations have a history of tense relations and internal unrest?

5. ***Argument Writing*** Write a short speech calling for or opposing independence for French Guiana. Support your view.

(l to r)John Coletti/AWL Images/Getty Images; Rob Francis/age fotostock; Kymri Wilt/DanitaDelimont.com "Danita Delimont Photography"/Newscom

Lesson 3
Life in the Tropical North

ESSENTIAL QUESTION • *What makes a culture unique?*

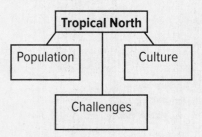

IT MATTERS BECAUSE

Many nations of the world, including the United States, have important trade relations with countries of the Tropical North.

People and Places

GUIDING QUESTION *What ethnic groups populate the Tropical North, and where do they live?*

People of European, African, Native American, and mixed descent are the major population groups of the countries that border the Pacific and Caribbean coasts. African, South Asian, and ethnically mixed peoples form the majority in the Atlantic coast countries.

Population Groups

Ecuador has the Tropical North's greatest indigenous population. About one in four Ecuadorans is Native American. If mestizos, or people of white and Native American descent, are added, the **ratio** becomes 9 of every 10 Ecuadorans.

Venezuela and Colombia have the opposite distribution. Some 20 percent of their populations are white, and 1 to 2 percent are Native American. Colombia's native population is the lowest of any Andean country. Mestizos are the largest group, accounting for more than two-thirds of Colombians and Venezuelans. The African populations of Venezuela, Ecuador, and Colombia are small, although some 15 percent of Colombians have mixed African and European ancestry.

The descendants of contract laborers from India are Suriname's largest group, making up nearly 40 percent of the population. An equal number are people of African and mixed-African descent. A large Indonesian population is also present. Whites and Native Americans total less than 5 percent of Surinam's population.

Neighboring Guyana is home to more Native Americans; this group makes up almost 10 percent of the country's population. Ethnic Africans make up one-third of the population, and East Indians account for more than 40 percent. The country has no significant white population. About one in six Guyanese is of mixed ancestry.

People of mixed descent make up most of French Guiana's population. Small groups of French, Native Americans, Chinese, East Indians, Laotians, Vietnamese, Lebanese, Haitians, and Africans also live in French Guiana.

Where People Live

Guyana's population remains largely rural. Elsewhere in the Tropical North, most people live in cities. Bogotá, Colombia's capital on a high Andes plateau, is home to almost 5 million people. It is the North's largest city and the fifth largest in South America.

Colombia's Caribbean lowlands are home to about 20 percent of its people, mainly in Cartagena and other port cities along the coast.

John Coletti/AWL Images/Getty Images

Academic Vocabulary

ratio the relationship in amount or size between two or more things

The Iglesia de San Francisco, built by Catholic missionaries in about 1560, is the oldest restored church in Bogotá, Colombia.

▶ **CRITICAL THINKING**

Describing How important is the city of Bogotá in the Tropical North region today?

The country's Pacific coast is sparsely settled. Most of the people there are descendants of enslaved Africans who worked on plantations near the Caribbean Sea. As they were freed or they escaped, they migrated into remote areas in western Colombia. The Llanos, where cattle ranching is the main activity, is another area with few people.

Quito, Ecuador, is another mountain capital city, with nearly 2 million people. Most of Ecuador's Native Americans live in or around Quito, or they farm rural mountain valleys nearby. Most other Ecuadorans live along the coast. Guayaquil, the country's largest city and major port, is located there.

Most Venezuelans live along the coast. As in Colombia and Ecuador, Venezuelans began **migrating** to cities in the mid-1900s for the jobs and opportunities they offered. Today, more than 90 percent of the country's people live in Caracas, the capital city of 3 million, and other cities on or near the coast.

The countries of Guyana, Suriname, and the territory of French Guiana are sparsely populated. The population of the three combined totals only about half the population of Caracas. The interior of French Guiana has few roads and is largely uninhabited. In Suriname, small groups of Native Americans live in the Guiana Highlands. Nearly everyone else lives along the coast. Suriname's capital, Paramaribo, a city of 260,000, is home to more than half the country's population.

Most Guyanese also live on the coast, mainly in small farm towns. Each town's farmlands extend inland for several miles. The country's interior is home to a few groups of Native Americans and scattered mining and ranching settlements.

☑ **READING PROGRESS CHECK**

Determining Central Ideas Where do the greatest number of people in the Tropical North live?

People and Cultures

GUIDING QUESTION *What is the Tropical North's culture like?*

Despite its largely Spanish heritage, no one culture unifies the Tropical North. Instead, its culture can be defined by the wide variety of ethnic groups that populate the region.

Language Groups

Spanish is the official language of Ecuador, Colombia, and Venezuela. There are differences in Ecuadoran Spanish because of the influence of Native American languages in each region of the country. More than 10 native languages are spoken in Ecuador. More than 25 native languages are spoken in Venezuela and some 180 in Colombia. Colombians, however, have taken great care to preserve the purity of the Spanish language.

Academic Vocabulary

migrate to move from one place to another

Rob Francis/age fotostock

Languages in Guyana, Suriname, and French Guiana reflect their colonial heritage as well as their ethnic populations. **Creole**, a group of languages that enslaved people from various parts of Africa developed to communicate on colonial plantations, is widely spoken. Most people in Guyana speak English. In Suriname, the official language, Dutch, is spoken only as a second language. Native American languages, Hindi, and other South Asian languages are heard in both countries.

Religion, Daily Life, and the Arts

Ecuador, Colombia, and Venezuela are overwhelmingly Roman Catholic. No more than 10 percent of the people in these countries practice other religions. The religions practiced in Guyana, French Guiana, and Suriname reflect the variety of ethnic groups that live there. Suriname's population is made up of about equal numbers of Roman Catholics, Protestants, Hindus, and Muslims. Guyana's population is largely Protestant and Hindu, with sizable Catholic and Muslim minorities. In all countries, some Native Americans practice indigenous religions.

Each country's foods, music, and other cultural elements reflect its ethnic and religious makeup. Venezuela, Colombia, and Ecuador celebrate Carnival, though the festivities are not as colorful or as lively as those in Brazil. Regional religious festivals are celebrated in many Andes communities.

Whether they come from the region's rural or urban areas, many people enjoy a celebration called Carnival. This festival is celebrated just before the beginning of Lent, the Christian holy season that comes before Easter.

A girl in the Andes of Ecuador plays a pan flute, one of the most popular instruments of Andean music.

▶ CRITICAL THINKING

Describing In addition to music, what other cultural traditions are practiced by people in the region?

Culture often differs by geographic area. Native Americans in mountain regions weave baskets and cloth using designs that are hundreds of years old. They play Andean music using drums, flutes, and other traditional instruments. Along the coast of Colombia and Venezuela, a dance called the *cumbia* blends the region's Spanish and African heritages. Other Venezuelan coastal music and dance, such as salsa and merengue, show Caribbean island influences. Maracas and guitars are used to perform the music of the Llano.

☑ **READING PROGRESS CHECK**

Analyzing What language and religion are most common in the region?

Ongoing Issues

GUIDING QUESTION *What challenges do the countries of the Tropical North face?*

Many people who live in the Tropical North are poor, although natural resources in the region are plentiful. For generations, those resources have mostly benefited only a wealthy few. This situation has created tensions within and between countries.

Trade Relations

Many South American leaders believe that one way to strengthen their countries' economies is to expand trade. In 2008 the countries in the Tropical North joined with the rest of South America to form the Union of South American Nations (UNASUR). One of the organization's goals is ending **tariffs**—taxes on imported goods—on trade between member nations. Another goal is adopting a uniform currency, similar to the euro.

A Northern Neighbor

Another challenge is improving the region's relationship with the United States. The relationship has sometimes been rocky in the past, as when the United States helped Panama gain independence from Colombia in the early 1900s. Relations between the United States and Colombia have improved greatly. The United States and the Colombian government are working together to stop the flow of illegal drugs.

Challenges in Venezuela

In 1998 Venezuelans elected Hugo Chávez, a former military leader, as president. Chávez frequently criticized the United States and became friendly with anti-U.S. governments in Cuba and Iran.

After his election, Chávez promised to use Venezuela's oil income to improve conditions for the country's poor. Among other actions that angered U.S. leaders, in 2009 he seized control of U.S. companies that were developing oil resources in Venezuela. His strong rule split Venezuela into opposing groups. Working-class people supported Chávez, but middle-class and wealthy Venezuelans opposed his policies.

Struggles in Colombia and Ecuador

Colombia has undergone a long and bitter struggle between the country's government and a Colombian organization called the Revolutionary Armed Forces of Colombia (FARC). One of FARC's goals is to curtail the role of foreign governments and businesses in Colombia's affairs. Another goal is to provide help and support for the nation's poor farmers. FARC is funded through various means, including the production and sale of illegal drugs.

In Ecuador, indigenous peoples protested for rights and blamed President Rafael Correa for not keeping his promises. Correa had promised to rewrite Ecuador's constitution. Among other things, he pledged to extend the rights of the people. Disappointed when Correa did not act, indigenous peoples organized to win rights for access to land, basic services, and political representation.

✔ **READING PROGRESS CHECK**

Determining Central Ideas How did Hugo Chávez increase tensions between Venezuela and the United States?

Include this lesson's information in your Foldable®.

LESSON 3 REVIEW

Reviewing Vocabulary

1. Why did enslaved Africans create *Creole*?

Answering the Guiding Questions

2. ***Identifying*** Why is the Tropical North home to so many ethnic groups?

3. ***Analyzing*** Why are there Hindu and Muslim populations in northern South America?

4. ***Analyzing*** How and why is UNASUR likely to affect the economies and people of the Tropical North's countries?

5. ***Informative/Explanatory Writing*** Choose one of the challenges the Tropical North faces, and write a short essay suggesting how to solve it.

Directions: Write your answers on a separate piece of paper.

1 Use your **FOLDABLES** to explore the Essential Questions.

INFORMATIVE/EXPLANATORY WRITING Choose one of the region's countries or colonies. Compare the physical and population maps found at the beginning of the unit. Then write at least two paragraphs explaining how the physical geography affects where people live and work.

2 21st Century Skills

ANALYZING Working in small groups, choose one of the countries or the colony found in the region and research the most common occupations practiced by its people. Are any of those jobs unique to that country and its culture? Present your findings to the class in a slideshow or a poster.

3 Thinking Like a Geographer

IDENTIFYING Create a two-column chart. List the name of the Tropical North country or colony in the first column. List the primary languages spoken in the second column.

4 GEOGRAPHY ACTIVITY

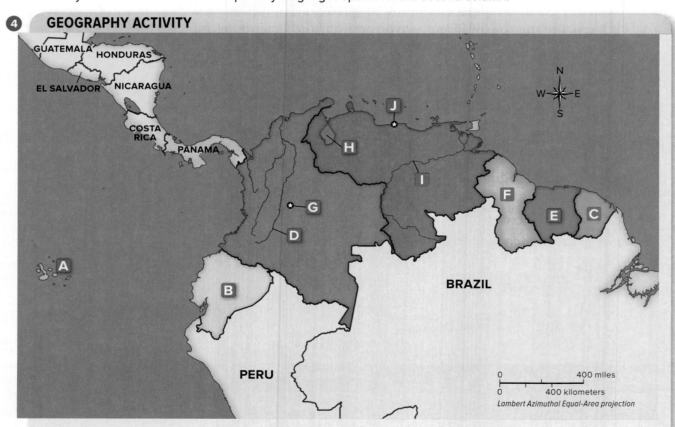

Locating Places
Match the letters on the map with the numbered places listed below.

1. Lake Maracaibo
2. Ecuador
3. French Guiana
4. Caracas
5. Orinoco River
6. Guyana
7. Bogotá
8. Galápagos Islands
9. Suriname
10. Magdalena River

REVIEW THE GUIDING QUESTIONS

Directions: Choose the best answer for each question.

1 The Galápagos Islands were the site of
   A. Christopher Columbus's second landing in the Americas.
   B. an outpost of the Incas.
   C. Charles Darwin's study that resulted in the theory of evolution.
   D. Ecuador's largest volcanic eruption.

2 The world's leading producer of emeralds is
   F. Venezuela.
   G. Colombia.
   H. Ecuador.
   I. French Guiana.

3 South America's native populations were forced into laboring for the Spanish under a system called
   A. *encomienda*.
   B. immunity.
   C. hacienda.
   D. Quito.

4 The transition from colonial governments to independence in the Tropical North of South America
   F. happened suddenly in 1550.
   G. took place slowly over a period of more than 100 years.
   H. began in Brazil.
   I. was a result of the War of 1812.

5 The most populous spot in the Tropical North is
   A. Ecuador.
   B. Bogotá.
   C. the Llanos.
   D. Cartagena.

6 Of the languages used in the Tropical North countries, Spanish is used in its purest form in
   F. Ecuador.
   G. French Guiana.
   H. Venezuela.
   I. Colombia.

DBQ ANALYZING DOCUMENTS

❼ **CITING TEXT EVIDENCE** Read the following passage:

"With one of the highest deforestation rates in Latin America, Ecuador is losing 200,000 hectares (494,211 acres) of forest every year . . . Although most of the forests of the country are public lands, an important percentage of what is left is in the hands of indigenous people and farmers, among the country's poorest citizens."

—from Steve Goldstein, "A Grand Plan: Ecuador and 'Forest Partners'" (2008)

What group in Ecuador controls the forests on public lands?

A. indigenous people   C. the government

B. farmers   D. businesses

❽ **ANALYZING** Which most likely explains why the indigenous people and the farmers might be willing to sell their land?

F. to enjoy a better way of life

G. so they can buy more productive land

H. so they can move to the city

I. to rid themselves of the burden of the land

SHORT RESPONSE

"Latin American pop superstar Shakira will be at this weekend's gathering of the Western Hemisphere's leaders advocating for [promoting] her favorite issues: early childhood development and universal education."

—from Gregory M. Lamb, "Shakira Advocates for Children at the Summit of the Americas" (2012)

❾ **IDENTIFYING POINT OF VIEW** How would improving child development and education benefit the countries of the region?

❿ **ANALYZING** What step do you think nations in this region should take to improve child development? Why?

EXTENDED RESPONSE

⓫ **INFORMATIVE/EXPLANATORY WRITING** What is school like for children who live in the Tropical North of South America? Research and then describe the educational system in this part of the world in a detailed report. Find out how many months of the year school is in session, how long the typical day is, and what kinds of subjects are taught. You might also want to find out how education is funded. Then compare the results with your school experience.

Need Extra Help?

If You've Missed Question	❶	❷	❸	❹	❺	❻	❼	❽	❾	❿	⓫
Review Lesson	1	1	2	2	3	3	1	3	3	3	3

ANDES AND MIDLATITUDE COUNTRIES

ESSENTIAL QUESTIONS · *How does geography influence the way people live?* · *Why do civilizations rise and fall?* · *What makes a culture unique?*

iStockphoto.com/hadynyah

Woman in traditional dress from the area of Oruro in west central Bolivia

networks

There's More Online about Andes and Midlatitude Countries.

CHAPTER 20

Lesson 1
Physical Geography of the Region

Lesson 2
History of the Region

Lesson 3
Life in the Region

The Story Matters...

Running the length of the Pacific coast of South America, the Andes define the countries of Peru, Bolivia, and Chile. For the people who have made the Andes their home, the grandeur of the high mountain peaks often contrasts sharply with the challenges of life in such a rugged location. And yet, it was in this very location of mountains, high plateaus, plains, and deserts that the ancient Inca built their powerful and highly developed civilization.

FOLDABLES Study Organizer

Go to the Foldables® library in the back of your book to make a Foldable® that will help you take notes while reading this chapter.

The world's longest mountain system runs parallel to the Pacific coast of South America. The Andes stretch about 4,500 miles (7,242 km) and include many high mountain peaks. As you study the map, look for other geographic features that make this area unique.

Step Into the Place

MAP FOCUS Use the map to answer the following questions.

1 **PLACES AND REGIONS** Which country has two capitals? Name them.

2 **THE GEOGRAPHER'S WORLD** Which two bodies of water does the Strait of Magellan connect?

3 **THE GEOGRAPHER'S WORLD** What is Uruguay's capital city?

4 **CRITICAL THINKING** **ANALYZING** Why do you think Chile has such a unique shape?

RUGGED TERRAIN Gigantic cacti dot the hilly landscape on Bolivia's Incahuasi Island. The island is in the middle of the world's largest salt flats.

HANDICRAFTS The people of the small island of Taquile on Lake Titicaca are known for making some of Peru's highest-quality handwoven clothing.

Step Into the Time

TIME LINE Which event on the time line discusses natural resources? Write a paragraph explaining positive and negative effects on a country's colony that holds valuable resources.

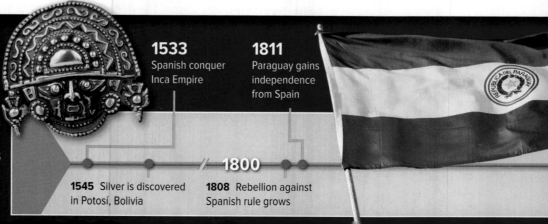

1533 Spanish conquer Inca Empire

1811 Paraguay gains independence from Spain

1800

1545 Silver is discovered in Potosí, Bolivia

1808 Rebellion against Spanish rule grows

Andes and Midlatitude Countries

ECUADOR

PERU

BRAZIL

Ucayali R.

Lima

Cuzco

Beni R.

Mamoré R.

Lake Titicaca

La Paz

Sucre

BOLIVIA

A

B

PARAGUAY

Paraná R.

CHILE

ARGENTINA

Elqui R.

Asunción

Paraguay R.

URUGUAY

Uruguay R.

PACIFIC OCEAN

Santiago

Colorado R.

Bío-Bío R.

Buenos Aires

Montevideo

Río de la Plata

ATLANTIC OCEAN

EQUATOR   0°

TROPIC OF CAPRICORN   20°S

40°S

N
W E
S

⊛	National capital
○	Territorial capital
●	City

0   1,000 miles
0   1,000 kilometers
Albers Equal-Area Conic projection

Falkland Islands (U.K.)

Stanley

South Georgia Island (U.K.)

Strait of Magellan

Scotia Sea

South Sandwich Islands (U.K.)

2006 Michelle Bachelet elected first woman president of Chile

1946 Juan Perón becomes president of Argentina

2007 Earthquake in southwest Peru leaves 200,000 people homeless

1900

2000

1900s Foreign companies run mining operations in the region

2009 Bolivia's new constitution empowers indigenous peoples

There's More Online!

☑ **SLIDE SHOW** Landforms: Andean Region

☑ **IMAGES** Uses of Wool

☑ **MAP** Comparing Mountain Ranges

☑ **VIDEO**

Reading**HELP**DESK

Academic Vocabulary

- **isolate**

Content Vocabulary

- **cordillera**
- **altiplano**
- **pampas**
- **estuary**
- **altitude**

TAKING NOTES: *Key Ideas and Details*

Integrate Visual Information
As you read, use a graphic organizer like this one to identify significant physical features of the region.

```
┌──────────┐
│ Physical │ ───
│ Features │ ───
└──────────┘ ───
```

Lesson 1
Physical Geography of the Region

ESSENTIAL QUESTION • *How does geography influence the way people live?*

IT MATTERS BECAUSE
Much of the terrain of the southern and western part of South America is extremely rugged. The geography of the area presents unique challenges to the people who live there.

Andes Countries

GUIDING QUESTION *What are the physical features of the Andean region?*

Three countries make up the bulk of the Andean region in South America. They are Peru, Bolivia, and Chile. From north to south, these countries span from the Equator to the southern tip of the continent of South America. The physical landscape includes towering mountains, sweeping plains, and significant waterways.

The Andes

On a map of South America, one of the first features you might notice is the system of mountain ranges running parallel to the continent's Pacific coast. These are the Andes, the longest continuous group of mountain ranges in the world and the tallest in the Western Hemisphere. The Andes include high plateaus and high plains, with even higher mountain peaks rising above them. The entire series of the Andes range stretches for 4,500 miles (7,242 km).

The peaks that make up the Andes are not arranged in one neat line. Instead, they form a series of parallel mountain ranges. The parallel ranges are called **cordilleras**. The rugged terrain of the cordilleras makes travel difficult. These ranges **isolated** human settlements from one another for centuries.

In Peru and Bolivia, the two main branches of the Andes border a high plain called the **altiplano**. In fact, *altiplano* means "high plain" in Spanish. About the size of Kentucky, the altiplano has an elevation of 11,200 feet to 12,800 feet (3,414 m to 3,901 m) above sea level.

The Andes mountain ranges are the result of collisions between tectonic plates. This kind of geologic activity comes as no surprise. After all, the Andes are part of the Ring of Fire. All around the rim of the Pacific Ocean, plates are colliding, separating, or sliding past each other. Those forces make earthquakes and volcanic eruptions a part of life throughout much of the Andes.

Plains and Deserts

The Andes run parallel to the Pacific coast but lie 100 miles to 150 miles (161 km to 241 km) inland from the coast. The land between the Andes and the coast averages more than 3,500 feet (1,067 m) above sea level. In most places, the land rises steeply from the ocean. The area has tall cliffs and almost no areas of coastal plain. In Peru and northern Chile, the area between the Pacific and the Andes is a coastal desert. On the Atlantic side of South America, broad plateaus and valleys spread across Uruguay and eastern Argentina.

Academic Vocabulary

isolate to separate

Spectacular mountains are part of Torres del Paine National Park in southern Chile.
▶ CRITICAL THINKING
Describing How were the Andes mountain ranges formed?

The Illimani mountains tower over a small village in the plains of western Bolivia.

▶ **CRITICAL THINKING**

Describing What are the main economic activities in the area?

This plain is called the **pampas**. Its thick, fertile soils come from sediments that have eroded from the Andes. The pampas, like North America's Great Plains, provide land for growing wheat and corn and for grazing cattle.

Coastal Peru and Chile and most of southern Argentina have deserts. Wind patterns, the cold Peru Current, and high elevations are the causes of the low precipitation. The Atacama Desert in Peru and northern Chile is so arid that in some places no rainfall has ever been recorded. The Patagonia Desert in Argentina lies in the rain shadow of the Andes.

Waterways

The Paraná, the Paraguay, and the Uruguay Rivers combine to create the second-largest river system in South America, after the Amazon. This river system drains much of the eastern half of South America. The system is especially important to Paraguay, because Paraguay is a landlocked country. The river system provides transportation routes and makes possible the production of hydroelectric power. Along the Paraguay River is the Pantanal, one of the world's largest wetlands. This area produces a diverse ecosystem of plants and animals.

The Paraná-Paraguay-Uruguay river system flows into the Río de la Plata (Spanish for "river of silver"). This river then empties into the Atlantic Ocean on the border of Argentina and Uruguay. The Río de la Plata meets the ocean in a broad estuary. An **estuary** is an area where the ocean tide meets a river current.

South America has few large lakes. The largest lake in the Andean region is Lake Titicaca. It lies on the border between Bolivia and Peru. Lake Titicaca is on the altiplano at 12,500 feet (3,810 m) above sea level. It is the world's highest lake that is large enough and deep enough to be used by small ships.

☑ **READING PROGRESS CHECK**

Analyzing How do you think the geography of the Andean region affects the lives of the people who live there?

Climate Diversity

GUIDING QUESTION *How does climate affect life in the Andean region?*

Climate is part of a region's physical geography. The varying mountains, plains, and other landforms in the Andean region and midlatitude countries of South America mean that the region's climate is extremely diverse.

The Effect of Altitude

The main factor that determines climate in the Andes is **altitude**, or height above sea level. The higher the altitude, the cooler the temperatures are. This is true even in the warm tropics. Conditions in the region can range from hot and humid at lower elevations to freezing in the mountain peaks.

Farming is a challenge in the rugged Andean region. Farmers have successfully terraced the hillsides to grow crops such as potatoes, barley, and wheat.

Visitors to the Andes may find the altitude at the higher elevations hard to handle. Oxygen is thin. This results in heavy breathing and tiring easily. The region's inhabitants are adapted to the thinner air, as are various native species of plants and animals.

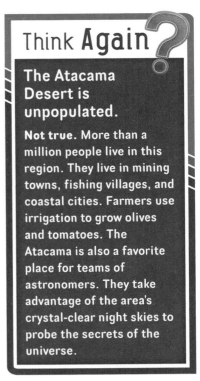

Think Again

The Atacama Desert is unpopulated.

Not true. More than a million people live in this region. They live in mining towns, fishing villages, and coastal cities. Farmers use irrigation to grow olives and tomatoes. The Atacama is also a favorite place for teams of astronomers. They take advantage of the area's crystal-clear night skies to probe the secrets of the universe.

Midlatitude Variety

Climates of the midlatitude countries of South America are quite different from the Andean region. These countries enjoy a generally temperate, or moderate, climate. In Uruguay, for example, the average daily temperature in the middle of winter are a mild 50°F to 54°F (10°C to 12°C). In mid-summer, the average daily temperatures reach a comfortable 72°F to 79°F (22°C to 26°C). There is no wet or dry season—rainfall occurs throughout the year. Inland areas, however, are drier than the coast.

Argentina is much larger than Uruguay and includes a greater variety of landforms. As you might expect, Argentina's climate is extremely diverse. It varies from subtropical in the north to tundra in the far south. Northern Argentina has hot, humid summers. Southern Argentina has warm summers and cold winters with heavy snowfall, especially in the mountains.

Paraguay presents yet a different climate. Paraguay is a landlocked country. The climate is generally temperate or subtropical. Strong winds often sweep the pampas in Paraguay because the country lacks mountain ranges to serve as wind barriers.

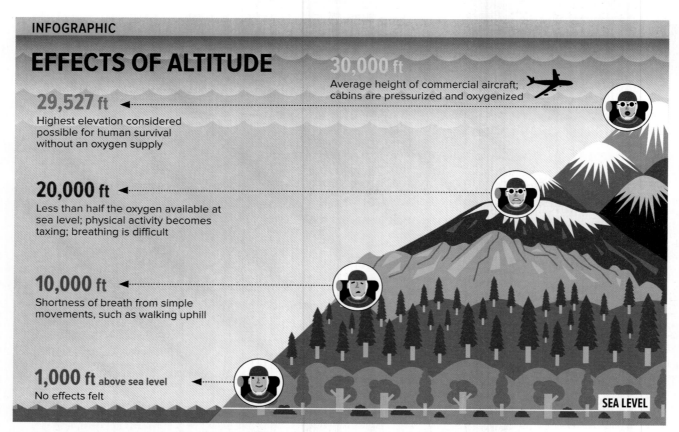

INFOGRAPHIC

EFFECTS OF ALTITUDE

30,000 ft
Average height of commercial aircraft; cabins are pressurized and oxygenized

29,527 ft
Highest elevation considered possible for human survival without an oxygen supply

20,000 ft
Less than half the oxygen available at sea level; physical activity becomes taxing; breathing is difficult

10,000 ft
Shortness of breath from simple movements, such as walking uphill

1,000 ft above sea level
No effects felt

SEA LEVEL

At all latitudes, altitude, or the height above sea level, influences climate. Earth's atmosphere thins as altitude increases. Thinner air retains less heat.

▶ **CRITICAL THINKING**

Describing What happens to temperatures as altitude increases? How do higher elevations affect humans?

Climate Extremes

Extremes of climate can be experienced in the Andean countries without changing latitude. Altitude is all that has to change. The climate changes tremendously in the Andes from the lower to the higher elevations. The *tierra caliente,* or "hot land," is the land near sea level. The hot and humid conditions do not change much from month to month. In this zone, farmers grow bananas, sugarcane, cacao, rice, and other tropical crops.

From 3,000 feet to 6,000 feet (914 m to 1,829 m), the air is pleasantly cool. Abundant rainfall helps forests and a great variety of crops grow. This zone is the *tierra templada,* or "temperate land." It is the most densely populated area. Here, farmers grow a variety of crops, such as corn, coffee, cotton, wheat, and citrus fruits.

Higher up, the climate changes. This is the *tierra fría,* or "cold land." It extends from 6,000 feet to 10,000 feet (1,829 m to 3,048 m). The landscape is a combination of forests and grassy areas. Farmers here grow crops that thrive in cooler temperatures, including potatoes, barley, and wheat.

The land at the highest altitude is the *tierra helada,* or "frozen land." Here, above 10,000 feet (3,048 m), conditions can be harsh. The winds blow cold and icy, and temperatures fall well below freezing. Vegetation is sparse, and few people live in this zone.

Mining (left), especially copper mining, is an important part of the Chilean economy. Mining can be dangerous. Miners celebrate their rescue on October 12, 2010 (right), after being trapped underground for 69 days.

Identifying Besides minerals and metals, what natural resources are abundant in the Andean and midlatitude countries?

Llamas are camelids, relatives of camels. They are bred and raised for food, wool, and as pack animals for pulling carts.

Identifying What other camelids are common in the region?

El Niño and La Niña

Every few years, changes in wind patterns and ocean currents in the Pacific Ocean cause unusual and extreme weather in some places in South America. One of these events is called El Niño. During an El Niño, the climate along the Pacific coast of South America becomes much warmer and wetter than normal. Floods occur in some places, especially along the coast of Peru.

El Niños form when cold winds from the east are weak. Without these cold winds, the central Pacific Ocean grows warmer than usual. More water evaporates, and more clouds form. The thick band of clouds changes wind and rain patterns. Some areas receive heavier-than-normal rains. Other areas, however, have less-than-normal rainfall.

Scientists have found that El Niños occur about every three years. They also found that in some years, the opposite kind of unusual weather takes place. This event is called La Niña. Winds from the east become strong, cooling more of the Pacific. When this happens, heavy clouds form in the western Pacific.

☑ READING PROGRESS CHECK

Identifying Why is the *tierra templada* the most populated climate zone by altitude in the Andean region?

Imágenes del Perú/Flickr/Getty Images

Natural Resources

GUIDING QUESTION *Which natural resources are important to the region?*

The Andean and midlatitude countries are rich in natural resources. Energy sources are especially important. Bolivia holds the second-largest reserves of natural gas in South America, trailing behind only Venezuela. Bolivia also has extensive deposits of petroleum. Paraguay's hydroelectric power plants produce nearly all the country's electricity. The governments want to use these resources to develop and strengthen their economies.

Minerals and Metals

Besides energy resources, the region has a number of mineral resources. Most of the area's mines are in the Andes. Chile leads the world in exports of copper. Tin production is important to the Bolivian economy. Bolivia and Peru have deposits of silver, lead, and zinc, and Peru also has gold.

Wildlife

The region's varied geography and climate support a variety of wildlife, including many species of birds and butterflies. The ability of plants and animals to thrive in the region varies with altitude.

A group of mammals called camelids is especially important in this region. Camelids are relatives of camels, but they do not have the typical humps of camels. Two kinds of camelids are the llama and the alpaca. The llama is the larger of the two. Llamas serve as pack animals and are a source of food, wool, and hides. Native Americans throughout the Andes tend herds of llamas. These animals are used to carry goods or pull carts. They are also raised for food, hides, and wool.

Alpacas are found only in certain parts of Peru and Bolivia. The animal's thick, shaggy coat is an important source of wool. Alpaca wool is strong yet soft and repels water. It is used for all kinds of clothing and as insulation in sleeping bags.

Include this lesson's information in your Foldable®.

✓ READING PROGRESS CHECK

Analyzing What metal is important to Chile's economy?

LESSON 1 REVIEW

Reviewing Vocabulary

1. Why is *altitude* an important feature in the Andean region?

Answering the Guiding Questions

2. *Determining Central Ideas* Why do earthquakes and volcanoes occur in the Andes?

3. *Analyzing* Why is the climate wet on the western slopes of the Andes in southern Argentina but dry on the eastern slopes?

4. *Describing* How does the climate of the Andes countries compare with that of the midlatitude countries?

5. *Identifying* Give a specific example of how a family living in the Andes might use llamas.

6. *Narrative Writing* You are living with a relative for a month somewhere in the Andes. Choose the country and the area where you are staying. Then write a letter to a friend describing where you are and what you did yesterday.

networks

There's More Online!

☑ **MAP** Native American Civilizations

☑ **VIDEO**

Reading **HELP**DESK

Academic Vocabulary

- **hierarchy**

Content Vocabulary

- **smallpox**
- **guerrilla**
- **multinational**
- **coup**

TAKING NOTES: *Key Ideas and Details*

Describe As you read this lesson, use a graphic organizer like this one to write an important fact about each topic.

Topic	Fact
Inca Empire	
Spanish rule	
Independence movements	

Lesson 2
History of the Region

ESSENTIAL QUESTION • *Why do civilizations rise and fall?*

IT MATTERS BECAUSE
In the Andean and midlatitude countries of South America, history and government have developed in very different ways.

Early History and Conquest

GUIDING QUESTION *How has history influenced the region?*

Native Americans and European colonizers made major contributions to the history of this region of South America. The actions and achievements of both groups continue to influence life today. Almost all the countries in the region have been independent for nearly two centuries. Still, their history continues to influence their culture.

Rise and Fall of the Inca Empire

Before the rise of the Inca in the 1100s, the Andean region was the home of small Native American societies such as the Moche, the Mapuche, and the Aymara. These societies were based primarily on agriculture. The Moche settled on the arid coastline of northern Peru. Archaeological finds show that they were talented at engineering and irrigation. They used a complex irrigation system to grow corn (maize), beans, and other crops.

The Inca developed a highly sophisticated civilization. They first settled in the Cuzco Valley in what is now Peru. It was not until their fifth emperor, Capac Yupanqui, that they began to expand outside the valley. In the 1400s, under the rule of Pachacuti Inca Yupanqui, the Inca made extensive conquests. By the early 1500s, the Inca ruled a region stretching from northern Ecuador through Peru and then southward into Chile. Historians estimate that the area was

(l to r) HUGHES Hervé©/hemis.fr/Getty Images; ©Werner Forman/Corbis; DEA/G. DAGLI ORTI/De Agostini/Getty Images; Keystone-France/Gamma-Keystone/Getty Images

home to 12 million people. This population included dozens of separate cultural groups, who spoke many different languages.

The Inca state was called Tawantinsuyu. The name means "the land of the four quarters." The imperial capital was located where the four quarters, or provinces, of the Inca Empire met, at Cuzco. Inca society was highly structured. At the top of the **hierarchy** were the emperor, the high priest, and the commander of the army. The nobility served the emperor as administrators. At the bottom of the social pyramid were farmers and laborers.

Inca technology and engineering were highly advanced. The Inca built extensive irrigation systems, roads, tunnels, and bridges that linked regions of the empire to Cuzco. Today you can still see the remains of Inca cities and fortresses. Some of the most impressive ruins are at Machu Picchu, located about 50 miles (80 km) northwest of Cuzco.

The Inca had no written language. Instead, they created a counting system called quipu for record keeping. A quipu was a series of knotted cords of various colors and lengths.

Messengers carrying quipu could travel as far as 150 miles (241 km) per day on the roads. The Inca became extremely wealthy because of their vast natural resources of gold and silver.

Spain Conquers Peru

Unfortunately for the Inca, however, their advanced culture could not turn back the invasion that led to the empire's downfall. The Spanish conquests in Mexico encouraged them to move into South America. In 1532 a Spanish adventurer named Francisco Pizarro landed in Peru with a small band of soldiers.

(tr) ©Werner Forman/Corbis; (b) HUGHES Hervé©/hemis.fr/Getty Images

hierarchy a classification that is arranged by rank

Visual Vocabulary

quipu The quipu was an Inca counting device.

The ruins of the city of Machu Picchu are high in the Andes.
▶ **CRITICAL THINKING**
Describing How did the Inca build a large empire?

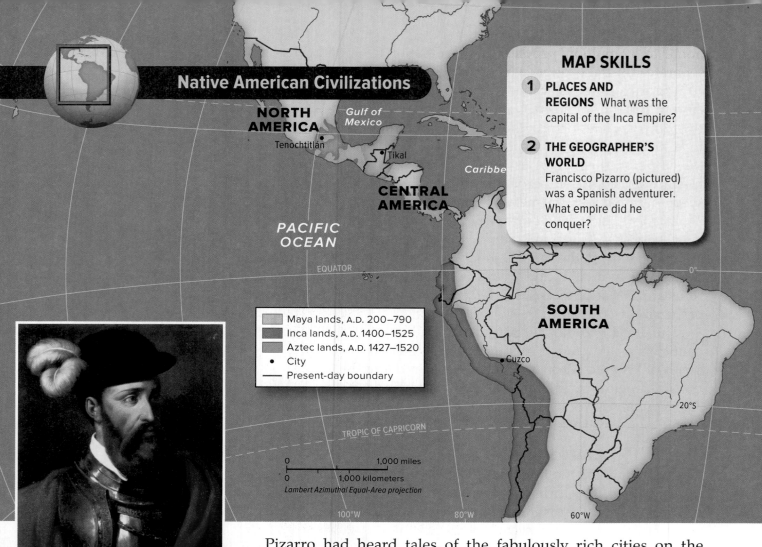

Native American Civilizations

NORTH AMERICA

Gulf of Mexico

Tenochtitlán

Tikal

CENTRAL AMERICA

Caribbe

PACIFIC OCEAN

EQUATOR

SOUTH AMERICA

Cuzco

20°S

TROPIC OF CAPRICORN

0°

80°W

60°W

100°W

| Maya lands, A.D. 200–790 |
| Inca lands, A.D. 1400–1525 |
| Aztec lands, A.D. 1427–1520 |
| • City |
| — Present-day boundary |

0   1,000 miles
0   1,000 kilometers
Lambert Azimuthal Equal-Area projection

MAP SKILLS

1 **PLACES AND REGIONS** What was the capital of the Inca Empire?

2 **THE GEOGRAPHER'S WORLD** Francisco Pizarro (pictured) was a Spanish adventurer. What empire did he conquer?

Spanish conquistador Francisco Pizarro conquered the empire of the Inca.

Pizarro had heard tales of the fabulously rich cities on the Pacific coast of South America. He also learned that the Inca empire had been badly weakened by a civil war from which the new emperor, Atahualpa, had emerged victorious. When the Spanish confronted Atahualpa, the Inca army, unprepared to face Spanish artillery, was nearly destroyed. Within a few years, the Spanish controlled the entire empire. The Spanish also seized control of the region's precious metals. The road system that the Inca developed became an important transportation route for Spanish goods. The Inca are the ancestors of the Native Americans who live in the Andes region today.

The Spanish also branched out from Peru to create colonies in Argentina, Chile, and other parts of South America. The Spanish military victors were called conquistadors, from the Spanish word for "conqueror." The Spanish colonies became sources of wealth for Spain. Some Spanish settlers prospered from gold and silver mining. Spanish rule of the Andean and midlatitude areas in the region continued for nearly 300 years.

After the Inca lost their empire to the Spanish, they and other Native Americans in the region endured great hardships. Their numbers declined drastically as a result of **smallpox**, a highly infectious disease introduced by the Europeans. The introduction of epidemic diseases also affected numerous Native American groups in North America.

✔ READING PROGRESS CHECK

Analyzing How were the Spanish, under conquistador Francisco Pizarro, able to conquer such a mighty empire as the Inca?

Independent Countries

GUIDING QUESTION *How did the countries of the Andean region gain their independence?*

By the early 1800s, most of South America had been under Spanish control for nearly 300 years. History was about to change once again. The reasons for this shift were local as well as international.

Overthrow of Spanish Rule

In the early 1800s, revolution and liberation movements were occurring around the world. The United States threw off British rule, and the French replaced the monarchy with a republic. Struggles for independence also occurred in Mexico and the Caribbean. People in South America were encouraged by these events. It was exactly the right time for two South American revolutionary leaders to lead the fight against Spanish rule. These two leaders were Simón Bolívar and José de San Martín.

The two leaders were able to rally support for independence. San Martín pioneered many elements of **guerrilla** warfare—the use of troops who know the local landscape so well that they are difficult for traditional armies to find. By the mid-1800s, many South American countries had gained independence.

Power and Governance

After the Spanish left South America, several different countries formed. Their borders mostly followed the divisions set in place by the Spanish colonizers. But despite gaining independence, political and economic hardships continued on the continent.

In contrast to the United States, there was no strong momentum for unity in South America. In fact, the rulers of many of the newly independent countries were wealthy aristocrats, powerful landowners, or military dictators. Their mindset was more European than South American. In addition, communication between countries was difficult because of the mountainous terrain.

The new countries lacked a tradition of self-government. The British colonies in North America had elected representatives in their colonial legislatures. The new countries of South America, however, did not have a structure in place for a government to function. The newly independent countries drafted constitutions.

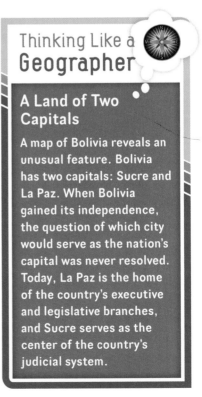

Thinking Like a **Geographer**

A Land of Two Capitals

A map of Bolivia reveals an unusual feature. Bolivia has two capitals: Sucre and La Paz. When Bolivia gained its independence, the question of which city would serve as the nation's capital was never resolved. Today, La Paz is the home of the country's executive and legislative branches, and Sucre serves as the center of the country's judicial system.

The enormously uneven distribution of wealth between rich and poor, however, resulted in social and economic instability. Several countries engaged in bloody conflicts over boundary disputes and mineral rights. These conflicts led to much loss of life and weakened economies.

☑ READING PROGRESS CHECK

Describing Why are Simón Bolívar and José de San Martín important in the history of the region?

History of the Region in the Modern Era

GUIDING QUESTION *What challenges did the countries of the region face in the late 1800s and 1900s?*

The Andean and midlatitude countries continued to face challenges during the late 1800s and 1900s. With military backing, dictators seized power, and they ignored democratic constitutions. Economies were still dependent on outside powers.

Eva Perón was married to Juan Perón, president of Argentina. She won admiration for her efforts to support the woman suffrage movement and to improve the lives of the poor.

▶ CRITICAL THINKING

Identifying How was Juan Perón removed from office? Who ruled Argentina after Perón?

Economic Challenges

The countries of the region faced economic challenges. Among the challenges were developing and controlling resources, building roads and railroads, and establishing trade links. Before independence, the countries of the region depended economically on Spain and Brazil. After independence, the economies of the region remained tied to countries outside South America.

Rapidly industrializing countries in Europe exploited the region for its raw materials. Wealthy landowners, cattle grazers, and mining operators refused to surrender their ties to European investors. Beginning in the early 1900s, large U.S. and European **multinational** firms—companies that do business in several countries—started mining and smelting operations in the region. As the economies expanded, profits grew for wealthy landowners and multinational companies. But many workers and farmers and their families remained mired in poverty.

Political Instability

Economic woes led to calls for reform. Political leaders promised changes for the better. In 1946 Argentinians elected General Juan Perón as the nation's president. Perón and his wife, Eva, were popular with the people. The new government enacted economic reforms to benefit the working people. However, the Perón government limited free speech, censored the press, and added to the country's debt. After Perón was overthrown in 1955, the military government ruled Argentina.

The new government moved to put an end to unrest. The rulers imprisoned thousands of people without trial. Some were tortured or killed. Others simply "disappeared." Argentina was also troubled by conflict over the Falkland Islands. Argentina and Great Britain both claimed the Falklands. After a brief war in 1982, Argentina was defeated, and the Falklands remain a British territory.

Significant changes were also taking place in the country of Chile. In the presidential election of 1970, Chileans elected a socialist candidate named Salvador Allende. Allende took action to redistribute wealth and land. The government took over Chile's copper industry and banking system. Allende's economic reforms were popular with workers but angered the upper classes. In 1973 Chilean military officers staged a **coup**, an illegal seizure of power, and killed Allende. A military dictatorship, headed by General Augusto Pinochet, ruled Chile for the next 16 years.

Movements for Change

In recent years, democracies have replaced dictatorships. Yet the countries in the region are still struggling to end corruption in government, shrink the gap between rich and poor, provide jobs, and protect human rights.

Voters also have elected new leaders. In 2005 Bolivians elected Evo Morales, the country's first indigenous president. Morales introduced a new constitution and land reforms, brought industries under government ownership, and moved to limit U.S. corporate involvement in the country's politics. In 2006 Chileans elected the country's first female president, Michelle Bachelet. A year later, Cristina Fernández de Kirchner became Argentina's first elected female president. Both female leaders started efforts to improve human rights and equal opportunity.

Include this lesson's information in your Foldable®.

☑ **READING PROGRESS CHECK**

Determining Central Ideas After independence, why did the countries in this region continue to experience economic hardship?

LESSON 2 REVIEW

Reviewing Vocabulary

1. What is one advantage of *guerrilla* warfare?

Answering the Guiding Questions

2. *Identifying* What were some of the strengths and achievements of the Inca culture?

3. *Describing* What were two events in North America and Europe that set the stage for the independence movement in the Andes and midlatitude countries?

4. *Determining Central Ideas* What can you infer about democratic government based on what you learned about Juan Perón in Argentina and Salvador Allende in Chile?

5. *Argument Writing* You are either Simón Bolívar or José de San Martín. The year is 1822, when the two men met face to face in Guayaquil (now located in Ecuador). Write a paragraph or two in which you urge your fellow leader to pursue the struggle for independence from Spain.

Inca road system
Pan-American highw

Lesson 3
Life in the Region

ESSENTIAL QUESTION • *What makes a culture unique?*

ReadingHELPDESK

Academic Vocabulary

• impact
• contemporary

Content Vocabulary

• pueblo jóven

TAKING NOTES: *Key Ideas and Details*

Describe As you read this lesson, use a graphic organizer like this one to write an important fact about each topic.

Topic	Fact
People and Places	
People and Cultures	
Ongoing Issues	

IT MATTERS BECAUSE
The population of the Andean and midlatitude countries is ethnically diverse. People, places, and cultures have been shaped by physical geography, urban growth, migration, and immigration.

People and Places

GUIDING QUESTION *What are the major population patterns in the Andean region?*

The population of the Andean region is not evenly distributed. Population patterns in this region reflect the changing **impact** of politics, economics, and the availability of natural resources and jobs.

Population Density and Distribution
The people of the region came from many different places. Three centuries of colonization by Spain have left their mark on the population. Enslaved Africans were brought as laborers, especially in Peru; this was less common in other countries of the region. After independence, immigrants from many European countries traveled to settle in South America. Immigrants also came from Asia.

Today, Bolivia and Peru have large Native American populations. Argentina and Chile have many people of European ancestry, including Spanish, Italian, British, and German backgrounds. Peru has descendants of people from Europe, but also people with origins in Japan and Southwest Asia.

In the Andean and midlatitude countries, as with the whole continent, the population is densest in the coastal areas. This area is sometimes called the "population rim." The rugged, mountainous areas and the tropical rain forest have discouraged settlement in many inland areas. Transportation is difficult, and communication can be slow or nonexistent. Coastal regions offer fertile land, favorable climates, and easy transportation.

Large Cities and Communities

The largest city in the region is Buenos Aires, the capital of Argentina. This is a bustling port and cultural center. It resembles a European city with its parks, buildings, outdoor cafes, and wide streets. About 2.8 million people live in the central city of Buenos Aires, but the metropolitan area includes 11.5 million people. This is more than one-fourth of Argentina's entire population. Although Argentina as a whole is not densely populated, the area in and around Buenos Aires is.

Buenos Aires and many other large cities in the region have shantytowns. These makeshift communities often spring up on the outskirts of a city. Poor people migrate here from remote inland areas to seek a better life. They cannot afford houses or apartments in the city or suburbs, so they settle in the shantytowns. They build shacks from scraps of sheet metal, wood, and other materials. Shantytowns often lack sewers, running water, and other services. They tend to be dangerous places with widespread crime.

In Lima, the capital and largest city in Peru, the shantytowns are called **pueblos jóvenes**. The name means "young towns." One pueblo jóven was home to María Elena Moyano. She worked to improve education, nutrition, and job opportunities in the pueblo jóven. She refused to give in to the demands of the government or to the communist rebels, who assassinated her in 1992. She has become recognized as a national hero for her courage.

☑ READING PROGRESS CHECK

Analyzing What limits the population in many inland areas?

WINFIELD PARKS/National Geographic Stock

Academic Vocabulary

impact an effect

Shacks made of metal, wood, and other materials stand in front of high-rise apartments in Buenos Aires.

▶ CRITICAL THINKING
Describing What challenges do people living in the shantytowns face?

People and Cultures

GUIDING QUESTION *How do ethnic and religious traditions influence people's lives?*

The Andean and midlatitude regions are home to a wide range of ethnic groups. Although many people trace their ancestry back to Europe, Asia, and Africa, Native American groups still thrive in parts of the region.

Ethnic and Language Groups

The Guarani is a Native American group that lives mainly in Paraguay, but people of Guarani descent also can be found in Argentina, Bolivia, and Brazil. The Guarani lived in tropical forests and practiced slash-and-burn agriculture—cutting and burning small areas of forest to clear land for farming. After a few years, the soil's nutrients were used up, and the people moved to a new area.

Today, Guarani customs and folk art are an important part of the culture in Paraguay. Guarani is one of the country's official languages. A related language is Sirionó. The Sirionó live in eastern Bolivia. In Peru, Quechua, a surviving language of the central Andes, is still widely spoken, along with Spanish.

Traditional Medicine

In Bolivia, the custom of Kallawaya medicine is widespread. The word *Kallawaya* might come from the Aymara word for "doctor." Kallawaya healers use traditional herbs and rituals in their cures. Many Bolivians seek the help of Kallawayas when they get sick, either because they prefer these healers or because they cannot afford other doctors. In fact, 40 percent of the Bolivian population relies on the natural healers, who travel from place to place.

Religion and the Arts

During the centuries of Spanish colonization, the Roman Catholic Church was one of the region's most important institutions. The influence of the Catholic Church continues. Millions of people practice mixed religions. Many of the native peoples of the Andes combine their indigenous rituals and beliefs with Roman Catholicism. Others have adopted Protestant religions.

Traditional arts, crafts, music, and dance thrive in the Andean and midlatitude countries. In literature, two Chilean poets, Gabriela Mistral and Pablo Neruda, have won the Nobel Prize for Literature. The works of writers from Argentina,

Kallawaya healers use traditional methods in efforts to cure the sick. The customs and languages of the indigenous peoples are an important part of the culture of the region.

▶ CRITICAL THINKING
Identifying What are some of the languages that are spoken in the region?

©David Mercado/Reuters/Corbis

including Jorge Luis Borges and Manuel Puig, are popular with readers around the world. Isabel Allende from Chile, a cousin of the country's former president Salvador Allende, is a **contemporary** writer of great distinction. Many writers have been praised for their use of magic realism. This style combines everyday events with magical or mythical elements. It is especially popular in Latin America.

Academic Vocabulary

contemporary living or happening now

Daily Life

In large cities and towns and in wealthier areas, family life revolves around parents and children. In the countryside, extended families are more common. In the region, the *compadre* relationship is still valued. This relationship is a strong bond between a child's parents and other adults who serve as the child's godparents.

In a megacity like Buenos Aires, people can wander through large, modern shopping malls. They may dine in outdoor cafes or fancy restaurants. They may work in modern office buildings. Traditional Andean foods of the countryside include *pachamanca* in Peru. This is a mixture of lamb, pork, and chicken baked in an earthen oven. Pachamanca dates back to the time of the Inca Empire.

Soccer, or football, is the most popular sport in the region. Football is Argentina's national game, and its teams have won several World Cup titles. Equestrian sports, or sports featuring riders on horseback, are popular in the region. Argentina's polo teams have long dominated international competition. The Argentina team won the first ever Olympic polo gold medal in 1924.

The Larcomar Shopping Mall in Lima, Peru, is a popular attraction for international tourists.

Football is also the national sport for many of the other countries in the region. The top professional league, the American Football Confederation, is made up of teams from 10 South American nations. League teams are eligible for the World Cup and the America Cup. Other popular sports include basketball, golf, boxing, and rugby. Social life focuses on family visits, patriotic events, religious feast days, and festivals.

✔ READING PROGRESS CHECK

Analyzing How is Kallawaya medicine different from the modern medicine that is practiced in most Western countries?

©Paul Thompson/Corbis

The Pan-American Highway

— Inca road system
— Pan-American highway

0°EQUATOR
ANDES
Ucayali R.
Amazon R.
10°S
Marañon R.
ANDES
Beni R.
Lake Titicaca
Mamore R.
20°S
TROPIC OF CAPRICORN
ANDES
Paraguay R.
Parana R.
PACIFIC
OCEAN
30°S
Uruguay R.
Rio de la Plata
0   500 miles
0   500 kilometers
Albers Equal-Area
Conic projection
Bio Bio R.
Colorado R.
40°S
90°W   80°W   70°W   60°W   50°W

N
W—E
S

MAP SKILLS

1 THE GEOGRAPHER'S WORLD Why did the Inca road system extend into many areas of South America?

2 THE GEOGRAPHER'S WORLD Why do you think the Pan-American Highway links many capital cities?

Ongoing Issues

GUIDING QUESTION *How are economic and environmental issues affecting the region?*

The population growth rate in the Andean and midlatitude countries is generally not high. However, population is growing enough in some places to add to today's challenges of earning a living.

Earning a Living

It is difficult to build strong economies in the Andean region largely because of the rugged terrain. Many countries rely heavily on agriculture, which is limited and difficult in the mountains. About one-third of Peruvians, for example, are farmers. They grow potatoes, coffee, and corn on terraces built into the mountain slopes. Farms in the valleys along the coast produce sugarcane, asparagus, mangoes, and many other crops.

Mining and fishing are other important economic activities in Peru. Mines in the mountains produce silver, zinc, copper, and other minerals. Peru also produces oil and natural gas. The country's coastal waters are rich fishing grounds. Much of the fish catch is ground into fishmeal for animal feed and fertilizer.

Management of natural resources presents many important issues and challenges. An example is conflict between countries over gas reserves. Bolivia has the second-largest reserve of natural gas in Latin America. Bolivia is landlocked. So, to export the gas, it must move through Peru or Chile.

In 2003 the Bolivian government proposed moving the natural gas through Chile, because it would be cheaper than an alternate plan to go through Peru. The Bolivian people turned out in huge numbers to protest. In Bolivia, suspicion and anger against Chile are widespread. These feelings date back to the Pacific War of the early 1880s, when Chile took over Bolivia's former coastal lands.

As the economies in the region develop, the primary economic activities of agriculture, mining, and fishing remain important. Other activities have become important as well. About 20 percent of the workers in the region are employed in the secondary, or manufacturing, sector. They work in factories making products.

About 65 percent find jobs in the tertiary, or services, sector. They work in a wide variety of occupations, ranging from transportation and retail sales to banking and education.

Transportation and Trade

This region has many geographic and regional barriers. The Andes limit construction of roads and railroads. Yet highways do link large cities. The Pan-American Highway, for example, runs from Argentina to Panama, then continues northward after a break in the highway. A trans-Andean highway connects cities in Chile and Argentina. Peru and Brazil are building the Transoceanic Highway. Parts of it opened in 2012. Eventually, this road will link Amazon River ports in Brazil with Peruvian ports on the Pacific Ocean. Unlike other countries, Argentina has an effective railway system.

Trade also connects countries. In 1991 a trade agreement, known as MERCOSUR, was signed by Argentina, Paraguay, Uruguay, and Brazil. In 2011 MERCOSUR merged into a new organization—the Union of South American Nations (UNASUR). The Union set up an economic and political zone modeled after the European Union (EU). Its goals are to foster free trade and closer political unity.

Addressing Challenges

Looking toward the future, the Andean and midlatitude countries must address many challenges. Environmental issues are among the most important. Air and water pollution is a major problem, especially in the shantytowns of urban areas, where the lack of sewage systems and garbage collection increases disease.

Disputed borders have presented challenges for years. For example, Bolivia and Paraguay long disputed rights to a region thought to be rich in oil. In 1998 Peru and Ecuador finally settled a territorial dispute after years of tensions marked by episodes of armed conflict. Border wars use up resources of people, money, time, and brainpower that could be used to address economic development and environmental concerns.

☑ READING PROGRESS CHECK

Determining Central Ideas How does the physical landscape hamper transportation? What actions are being taken to improve transportation?

Include this lesson's information in your Foldable®.

LESSON 3 REVIEW

Reviewing Vocabulary

1. Why might someone live in a *pueblo jóven*?

Answering the Guiding Questions

2. ***Describing*** How are the populations of Peru and Bolivia different from the populations of Argentina and Chile?

3. ***Analyzing*** Why might the Kallawaya of Bolivia have an important influence on people's lives?

4. ***Identifying*** What are two important industries in Peru today?

5. ***Informative/Explanatory Writing*** Write a paragraph or two to explain what you think is the most pressing problem facing the people who live in shantytowns.

What Do You **Think?**

Is Globalization Destroying Indigenous Cultures?

Globalization makes it easier for people, goods, and information to travel across borders. Customers have more choices when they shop. Costs of goods are sometimes lower. However, not everyone welcomes these changes. Resistance is particularly strong among indigenous peoples. They see the expansion of trade and outside influences as a threat to their way of life. Is globalization deadly for indigenous cultures?

TEXT: From "CULTURAL LIBERTY IN TODAY'S DIVERSE WORLD" from Human Development Report 2004; United Nations Development Programme, http://hdr.undp.org; PHOTO: Robert van der Hilst/Corbis

No !

PRIMARY SOURCE

" Indigenous people have struggled for centuries to maintain their identity and way of life against the tide of foreign economic investment and the new settlers that often come with it. ... But indigenous groups are increasingly assertive. Globalization has made it easier for indigenous people to organize, raise funds and network with other groups around the world, with greater political reach and impact than before. The United Nations declared 1995–2004 the International Decade for the World's Indigenous People, and in 2000 the Permanent Forum on Indigenous Issues was created. ... Many states have laws that explicitly recognize indigenous people's rights over their resources. ... Respecting cultural identity [is] possible as long as decisions are made democratically—by states, by companies, by international institutions and by indigenous people. "

—Report by the United Nations Development Programme (UNDP)

A Quechuan family shops at an open air market in a Peruvian village. The Quechua is the term for several native groups who speak a common language. They live in many countries throughout the region.

TEXT: Jerry Mander is Distinguished Fellow of International Forum on Globalization. This quote is from Web Site: http://www.ifg.org/.
PHOTO: Martin Mejia/AP Images

A woman carries water home in a mining town in central Peru. Protesters contend that aggressive mining practices contaminate the environment and destroy the way of life of indigenous people.

Yes !

PRIMARY SOURCE

" Globalization ... is a multi-pronged attack on the very foundation of [indigenous people's] existence and livelihoods. ... Indigenous people throughout the world ... occupy the last pristine [pure and undeveloped] places on earth, where resources are still abundant [plentiful]: forests, minerals, water, and genetic diversity. All are ferociously sought by global corporations, trying to push traditional societies off their lands. ...

Traditional sovereignty [control] over hunting and gathering rights has been thrown into question as national governments bind themselves to new global economic treaties. ... Big dams, mines, pipelines, roads, energy developments, military intrusions all threaten native lands. ... National governments making decisions on export development strategies or international trade and investment rules do not consult native communities. ... The reality remains that without rapid action, these native communities may be wiped out, taking with them vast indigenous knowledge, rich culture and traditions, and any hope of preserving the natural world, and a simpler ... way of life for future generations. "

—International Forum on Globalization (IFG), a research and educational organization

What Do You Think? DBQ

1 **Citing Text Evidence** According to the IFG, why are indigenous people at risk?

2 **Describing** According to the United Nations report, how has globalization given indigenous people more power?

Critical Thinking

3 **Identifying** One effect of globalization is that more tourists are visiting remote places such as rain forests in South America and wildlife areas in Africa. How do you think indigenous peoples feel about the growth of tourism in their communities?

Directions: Write your answers on a separate piece of paper.

1 Use your **FOLDABLES** to explore the Essential Questions.

INFORMATIVE/EXPLANATORY WRITING Write a short essay to answer the question: Why are people who live in the Andes more likely to follow a traditional way of life than those who live in cities?

2 21st Century Skills

DESCRIBING Write a radio script for a two-minute segment about what people do for recreation in one of this region's countries. Research the topic, and outline the information you want to include in your script. Share your notes with an adult, and ask: (a) Is my outline clear and well-organized? (b) Does the outline have too much or too little information? Revise your outline as needed, and then use it to write the script. Exchange scripts and compare your script with a classmate's. Discuss strong and weak points in each script.

3 Thinking Like a Geographer

ANALYZING Think about why industrialization requires good transportation and communication systems. Then, describe obstacles that slow the development of these systems.

4 GEOGRAPHY ACTIVITY

Locating Places

Match the letters on the map with the numbered places below.

1. Rio de la Plata
2. Bolivia
3. Lima
4. Falkland Islands (Malvinas)
5. Santiago
6. Chile
7. Paraguay
8. Uruguay
9. Uruguay River
10. Buenos Aires

REVIEW THE GUIDING QUESTIONS

Directions: Choose the best answer for each question.

1 The ocean tide meets a river current at a(n)
A. cordillera.
B. altiplano.
C. estuary.
D. *tierrra templada.*

2 Chile leads the world in exports of
F. emeralds.
G. copper.
H. lead.
I. gold.

3 The Inca became extremely wealthy because of
A. the system called quipu.
B. rich farmland.
C. huge deposits of gold and silver.
D. a lucrative fur trade.

4 The broad plain that spreads across Uruguay and eastern Argentina is called
F. the pampas.
G. the Atacama.
H. the Rio Blanco.
I. the Río de la Plata.

5 The group of South American animals called camelids includes
A. horses and donkeys.
B. sheep and goats.
C. llamas and alpacas.
D. mules and llamas.

6 The Spanish explorer who took the Inca emperor Atahualpa hostage was
F. Pizarro.
G. Columbus.
H. Magellan.
I. Fernandez.

DBQ ANALYZING DOCUMENTS

7 CITING TEXT EVIDENCE Read the following passage:

"[Argentina's] President [Cristina] Kirchner . . . announce[d] the nationalization of the Argentine oil company. . . . The move . . . raised concerns that this may be the first of many expropriations [government takeovers] of privately run companies."

—from Jonathan Gilbert, "The Next Venezuela?" (2012)

What does the writer say that Argentina's government might do in the future?

A. break the nation's dependence on imported oil

B. take over other companies

C. replace nuclear power with oil as the main source of energy

D. end high unemployment in Argentina

8 IDENTIFYING What impact will Argentina's action probably have on foreign companies doing business there?

F. They probably will try to sell their businesses to the government.

G. They will expect to have lower costs when oil prices fall.

H. They are likely to fear that their companies will be taken over, too.

I. They will seek to buy the oil company from the government.

SHORT RESPONSE

"Visitors to modern Cuzco frequently marvel at the exquisite [very fine] workmanship of its many Inca walls. The . . . impression is that a great deal of Inca Cuzco has survived. . . . [Actually,] new streets have been created, ancient ones lost, and the bulk of the city's former palaces, halls, temples, and shrines [holy places] have been demolished."

—from Brian S. Bauer, *Ancient Cuzco: Heartland of the Inca* (2004)

9 DETERMINING CENTRAL IDEAS Is the impression visitors have that much of Inca Cuzco has survived correct? Why or why not?

10 IDENTIFYING Who do you think was responsible for these changes to ancient Cuzco? Why?

EXTENDED RESPONSE

11 INFORMATIVE/EXPLANATORY WRITING Think about what you have read about the physical geography of the Andes and midlatitude countries. What geographic factors influence where people have settled in the region?

Need Extra Help?

If You've Missed Question	❶	❷	❸	❹	❺	❻	❼	❽	❾	❿	⓫
Review Lesson	1	1	2	1	1	2	3	3	2	2	1

Jonathan Gilbert, BA (Hons), PgDip. This article first appeared in THE CHRISTIAN SCIENCE MONITOR. http://CSMonitor.com; From ANCIENT CUZCO: HEARTLAND OF THE INCA, by Brian S. Bauer, Copyright © 2004. By permission of the University of Texas Press.

◄ *Xiuhtecuhtli was also known as "The Turquoise Lord." This mask is made of wood and covered with turquoise mosaic. The teeth are made from shells.*

1500 B.C. TO A.D. 1600

The Americas

THE STORY MATTERS ...

Why do the seasons change? What causes thunder? Today, we look to science to answer these questions. Ancient people told stories.

The native people of Central America told a story to explain the origin of the sun. According to the legend, Nanahuatzin (nah • nah • WAHT • zeen), an Aztec god, had warts, or bumps, all over his face. At the time the world was created, Nanahuatzin threw himself into a great fire. Rather than dying in the flames, Nanahuatzin arose and became the sun.

This mask was made in Mexico about 600 years ago. Some historians believe it is a mask of Nanahuatzin. Other historians believe this represents Xiuhtecuhtli (zhee • ooh • tay • COOT • lee), the Aztec god of fire.

ESSENTIAL QUESTIONS

• How does geography affect the way people live?
• What makes a culture unique?

LESSON 1
The First Americans

LESSON 2
Life in the Americas

Werner Forman/Art Resource, NY

The Americas
Place & Time: 1500 B.C. to A.D. 1600

Early people in the Americas depended on natural resources to survive. The development of farming and trade allowed them to build complex cultures. The Maya, Inca, and Aztec Empires ruled over large parts of Mesoamerica and South America.

Early American mountain dwellers lived on wide plateaus such as this, found in mountain ranges. The level areas provided land for settlements and farming.

Step into the Place

MAP FOCUS The geography and climates in North and South America influenced early people who lived there and caused them to develop different cultures.

1 **LOCATION** Look at the map. Is Cahokia located north or south of the Amazon River?

2 **PLACE** How did the location of Tenochtitlán affect Aztec trade?

3 **LOCATION** Use cardinal directions to locate Cuzco compared to Cahokia.

4 **CRITICAL THINKING** *Analyzing* How does location affect the strength of an empire?

The Navajo are known for their complex religious ceremonies. Many of these ceremonies take place within buildings that are constructed so that the entrance faces east—toward the rising sun. When a fire is built inside the building, the opening at the top allows smoke to escape.

(t)Judith Lienert/Shutterstock.com; (b)Robert F. Sisson/National Geographic/Getty Images

Step Into the Time

TIME LINE Choose an event from the time line and write a paragraph predicting the general social, political, or economic consequence that event might have for the

c. A.D. 500 Maya cities flourish in Mesoamerica

THE AMERICAS
THE WORLD

| A.D. 500 | A.D. 600 | A.D. 700 | A.D. 800 | A.D. 900 |

North and South American Groups

NORTH AMERICA

ROCKY MOUNTAINS

Missouri R.

Cahokia

Mesa Verde

Chaco Canyon

Mississippi R.

APPALACHIAN MTS.

Rio Grande

Gulf of Mexico

ATLANTIC OCEAN

TROPIC OF CANCER

20°N

Teotihucacán

Chichén Itzá

Tenochtitlán

YUCATÁN PENINSULA

VALLEY OF MEXICO

Caribbean Sea

PACIFIC OCEAN

EQUATOR

Amazon R.

SOUTH AMERICA

Machu Picchu • Cuzco

ANDES

0°

20°S

TROPIC OF CAPRICORN

40°N

160°W   140°W   120°W   100°W   80°W   60°W   40°W

KEY
- Aztec Empire
- Maya Empire
- Inca Empire
- Olmec civilization
- Anasazi culture
- Mound Builders

Robinson projection

0   1,000 miles
0   1,000 km

N W E S

c. A.D. 1400 Aztec Empire reaches its height

c. A.D. 1100 Inca found city of Cuzco

c. A.D. 1325 Aztec build Tenochtitlán

c. A.D. 1438 Pachacuti builds Inca Empire

c. A.D. 1570 Eastern Woodland peoples form Iroquois Confederacy

A.D. 1000   A.D. 1100   A.D. 1200   A.D. 1300   A.D. 1400   A.D. 1500   A.D. 1600

Civil war divides

LESSON 1

The First Americans

ESSENTIAL QUESTION

• How does geography affect the way people live?

IT MATTERS BECAUSE
Early people in the Americas built the beginnings of several civilizations.

Geography of the Americas

GUIDING QUESTION *How did geography shape the ways people settled in the Americas?*

About 15,000 years ago, prehistoric hunters left northeastern Asia and arrived in what is today Alaska. They are believed to be among the first people to settle the region called the Americas. Their descendants are called Native Americans. Over the centuries, Native American groups adopted different ways of life. Each group's way of life was based on local resources.

A Diverse Region

The Americas stretch north to south nearly 11,000 miles (almost 18,000 km). This vast region begins north at the Arctic Circle. It reaches south to Tierra del Fuego (tee•EHR•eh del FWAY•goh). Tierra del Fuego is a group of islands located off the coast of Chile and Argentina, at the southern tip of South America.

The four geographical areas of the Americas are North America, South America, Central America, and the Caribbean. North America and South America are both continents and make up most of the Americas. Central America is an **isthmus** (IHS•muhs), a narrow piece of land that connects two larger areas of land. East of Central America is the Caribbean Sea, where the Caribbean islands spread across to the Atlantic Ocean.

Reading**HELP**DESK

Taking Notes: *Summarizing*

Use a chart like the one here to record the climates and mountain ranges of the four main areas of the Americas.

	Climate	Mountains
North America		
South America		
Central America		
Caribbean		

Content Vocabulary

• **isthmus**   • **maize**

isthmus a narrow piece of land linking two larger areas of land

Within the vast expanse of the Americas you can find many different geographic features and climates. North America lies north of the Equator and has climates that range from cold to tropical.

Central America and the Caribbean islands are also north of the Equator. South America extends both north and south of the Equator. Most of these areas have a warm, rainy climate. A broad range of plants grows in the three areas.

Towering Mountains

In the west, rugged mountain chains run nearly the entire length of the Americas. They separate coastal plains near the Pacific Ocean from broad eastern plains that sweep toward the Atlantic Ocean.

The Rocky Mountains and the Pacific coastal ranges are in western North America. These mountains contain passes, or low areas. Even with these passes, overland travel across the mountains could be difficult.

In eastern North America, a range of mountains—the Appalachians—runs near the Atlantic coast. The Appalachians are lower than the Rockies and Pacific coastal ranges. Early Americans had no difficulty traveling over the Appalachians.

The Andes are the world's longest mountain system. These mountains stretch along the Pacific coast of South America. Valleys and plateaus (plah·TOES) lie between the mountain chains. Plateaus are large areas of raised land that have a flat surface.

Denali (Mount McKinley) is the tallest mountain in North America. It stands in Denali National Park, Alaska.

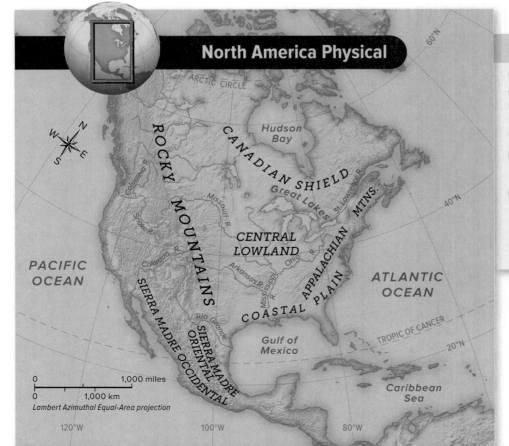

North America Physical

GEOGRAPHY CONNECTION

North America is the third-largest continent on Earth. It is mostly surrounded by water. Mountain ranges take up more than one-third of the total land area.

1 **PLACE** Which mountain range is closest to where you live?

2 **CRITICAL THINKING**
Analyzing What would have made travel across North America difficult for early Americans?

Rolling Plains

North America has many coastal and inland plains. The rolling grasslands of central North America are known as the Great Plains. The Great Plains have fertile soil for farming and raising cattle.

South America also has large areas of plains. In the northeast, the tropical Amazon Basin covers about 2.7 million square miles (7.0 million sq km). It is home to the world's largest rain forest.

Additional lowland plains are located north and south of the Amazon Basin. Tropical grasslands stretch across the northwest. Another area of plains called the Pampas lies in the south. The mild climate of the Pampas makes them a good place for growing grains. Many ranchers herd cattle there as well.

Rushing Rivers

Large river systems drain the Americas. They begin in the mountain ranges and flow through interior plains to the oceans. Today, the many waterways of the Americas transport people, goods, and ideas.

In North America, the largest river system is the Mississippi. It flows 2,350 miles (3,782 km), from present-day Montana and Minnesota to the Gulf of Mexico. The Mississippi is the major waterway for the central part of North America.

The Amazon is South America's largest river system. It starts in the Andes and flows about 4,000 miles (6,437 km) to the Atlantic Ocean. The Amazon carries the highest **volume** of water of any river on Earth.

✓ PROGRESS CHECK

Describing Which four separate areas make up the Americas?

The land surrounding the Amazon is home to the greatest variety of plants on Earth. As many as 250 species of trees may grow in one acre of the Amazon River basin.

▶ CRITICAL THINKING
Analyzing How might early Americans have used the Amazon River?

Erik Sampers/Stock Image/Getty Images

ReadingHELPDESK

Academic Vocabulary

volume amount included within limits
link to connect

Settling the Americas

GUIDING QUESTION *How did prehistoric people reach the Americas and form settlements?*

How did prehistoric people come to the Americas? Today, the Americas are not **linked** to the world's other landmasses, but they were long ago.

Reaching the Americas

Some scientists think that people walked across a land bridge from Asia into the Americas during the last Ice Age. Evidence of ancient tools and other artifacts reveals that these first Americans were hunters following herds of animals.

Other scientists argue that the first Americans arrived by boat. They passed by Alaska and sailed south along the Americas' Pacific coast. The travelers first explored coastal areas. They then journeyed inland where they set up campsites.

Once they arrived, the first Americans did not stay in one place. They moved south and east. They travelled in boats to islands in the Caribbean. In time, there were people living in different groups in North, Central, and South America.

Hunters and Gatherers

How did the first Americans survive? Historians believe it is likely that the first people in the Americas lived in small groups. These early Americans moved from place to place to find food.

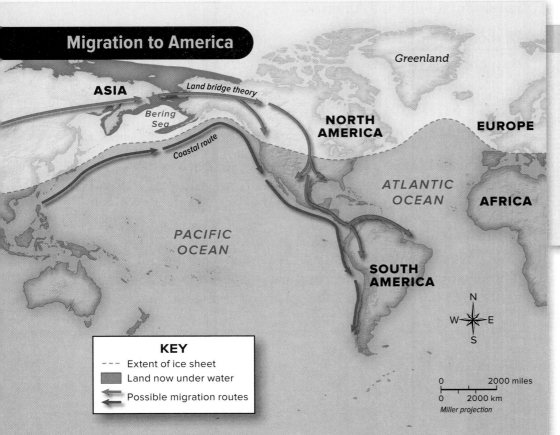

Migration to America

Greenland

ASIA

Land bridge theory

Bering Sea

Coastal route

NORTH AMERICA

EUROPE

ATLANTIC OCEAN

AFRICA

PACIFIC OCEAN

SOUTH AMERICA

N
W · E
S

KEY
- - - Extent of ice sheet
▬ Land now under water
⬅ Possible migration routes

0   2000 miles
0   2000 km
Miller projection

GEOGRAPHY CONNECTION

Over thousands of years, prehistoric people migrated southward through the Americas.

1 **MOVEMENT** How do scientists think prehistoric people got to North America from Asia?

2 **CRITICAL THINKING**
Analyzing Why do you think prehistoric people moved from one place in the Americas to another?

Early Americans used corn in many forms. The corn grinding stone like this Anasazi tool developed out of necessity.

▶ CRITICAL THINKING
Predicting How do you think early Americans used ground corn?

Archaeologists have unearthed evidence of early American ways of life. This evidence includes heaps of shells, rounded grinding stones, and bone fishhooks.

Hunter-gatherers in the Americas used natural resources for food, clothing, and shelter. People living along seacoasts collected shellfish and snails. People who lived inland fished in rivers and gathered roots, nuts, and fruits in forests. Early Americans also hunted large animals, which provided meat, hides for clothing, and bones for tools.

The Beginnings of Agriculture

As the last Ice Age ended, the climate grew warmer. People in the Americas learned to plant the seeds of grains and other plants. The seeds would grow into crops that could be eaten. This activity became the start of farming in the Americas.

Farming began in Mesoamerica (meh·zoh·uh·MEHR·ih·kuh) 9,000 to 10,000 years ago. *Meso* comes from the Greek word for "middle." This region includes lands stretching from central Mexico to Costa Rica in Central America.

The geography of Mesoamerica was suited for farming. Much of the area had rich, volcanic soil and a mild climate. The first crops that early Americans grew included peppers, pumpkins, squash, gourds, beans, and potatoes. Corn, also known as **maize** (mayz), took longer to develop. However, it became the most important food in the Americas.

☑ PROGRESS CHECK

Describing What were the first crops grown in the Americas?

First American Societies

GUIDING QUESTION *How did farming make civilization possible in the Americas?*

Growing and trading crops helped early Americans form more **complex** societies. The first American cultures emerged in Mesoamerica and along the western coast of South America.

Olmec Culture

About 1200 B.C., a people called the Olmec (OHL·mehk) built what may be the oldest culture in Mesoamerica. Based on farming and trade, the Olmecs lasted about 800 years.

Harald Sund/Riser/Getty Images

Reading**HELP**DESK

maize corn

Academic Vocabulary

complex made up of many related parts

Civilizations of Mesoamerica

MEXICO

Lake Texcoco

Tula

Teotihuacán

Tenochtitlán

Tlaxcala

VALLEY OF MEXICO

La Venta

Gulf of Mexico

Chichén Itzá

YUCATÁN PENINSULA

Palenque

Tikal

Copan

PACIFIC OCEAN

0   300 miles
0   300 km
Bipolar Oblique projection

KEY
- - - - Olmec c. 500 B.C.
▮ Maya c. A.D. 750
- - - - Toltec c. A.D. 1200
▮ Aztec c. A.D. 1500

GEOGRAPHY CONNECTION

Mesoamerican societies developed in Mexico and Central America.

1 PLACE Which culture occupied the Yucatán Peninsula?

2 CRITICAL THINKING
Making Inferences The Olmec built a pyramid of clay and sand at La Venta. Why do you think they did not use stone?

The Olmec set up farms in the tropical lowlands along the Gulf of Mexico. They grew beans and produced salt. The Olmec traded with people living inland. They exchanged salt and beans for jade and obsidian, or volcanic glass. Olmec artisans used the jade for jewelry. They made sharp knives from the obsidian.

The Olmec created centers for religious ceremonies. In these areas, they built pyramids and other stone monuments.

First Planned Cities

About 400 B.C., the Olmec culture collapsed. A group of inland peoples rose to power in central Mexico. This group built one of the first planned cities in the Americas, Teotihuacán (tay•oh•tee•wuh•KAHN), or "Place of the Gods." It lasted from about A.D. 250 to A.D. 800. Around 120,000 to 200,000 people lived in Teotihuacán. Temples and palaces lined its main street, which led to the Pyramid of the Sun.

A people called the Zapotec (ZAH•poh•tehk) built farms and cities in south central Mexico. Their magnificent capital, Monte Albán (MON•teh AL•bahn), had a main square surrounded by stone temples, monuments, and tombs. In addition to farming, the Zapotec created pottery and traded with Teotihuacán and other places in Mesoamerica. The Zapotec developed a writing system based on hieroglyphs (HIGH•roh•glifz).

Another people called the Maya (MY•uh) prospered in the steamy rain forests of the Yucatán Peninsula (yoo•kuh•TAN). Like the Zapotec, the Maya traded throughout Mesoamerica. From their central location, the Maya spread into southern Mexico and Central America.

One of the things the Olmecs are most famous for is colossal heads made out of rock. Some were more than seven feet high. How they managed to get them to the sites where they remain to this day is unknown.

De Agostini/Getty Images

Teotihuacán and the Zapotec flourished between the A.D. 300s and A.D. 500s. Then, they declined. Historians are not sure why this happened. The causes for decline might have been a severe drought—a long period with little rainfall—or revolts by populations that had used up the natural resources of the area. Whatever the reason, the cities were **abandoned**.

Who Were the Toltec?

After the collapse of these cities, the Toltec (TOHL•tehk) rose to power in central Mexico. The warlike Toltec conquered much of Mexico and northern Central America. Their empire reached the height of its power between A.D. 950 and A.D. 1150.

The Toltec grew crops of beans, maize, and pepper in irrigated fields. They also built pyramids and palaces. Toltec artisans introduced metalworking to Mesoamerica.

Around A.D. 1125, the Toltec Empire began to decline. Within a few decades, groups of invaders, including Aztec (AZ•tek) people, attacked and burned the Toltec city of Tollan (toh•lahn). For nearly 200 years, there was no ruling group in central Mexico.

Early Cultures in South America

In South America, several different early civilizations thrived along the Pacific coast. About 900 B.C., the Chavín developed a civilization in the coastal areas of present-day Peru and Ecuador. They built a large temple with stones from nearby hills. Part of a ceremonial center, the temple was surrounded by pyramids and stone figures of different deities, or gods. For unknown reasons, they declined around 200 B.C. The Moche (MOH•cheh), developed around A.D. 100 in the dry coastal desert of Peru. The Moche built canals to bring water from rivers in the Andes foothills to their desert homeland to grow food. Much about Moche culture is known from their arts and crafts.

In spite of everything they **achieved**, the Chavín and the Moche did not build empires. The first empire in South America was built by another people called the Inca (IHNG•kuh).

✔ PROGRESS CHECK

Explaining Why did early American cultures decline?

The story of the Moche culture is told through their artwork, such as this pottery figure of an alpaca.

▶ CRITICAL THINKING
Analyzing Visuals What can you tell about the Moche based on this example of art?

©Nathan Benn/Corbis

Reading**HELP**DESK

Academic Vocabulary

abandon to leave, often because of danger
achieve to successfully complete a task; to gain something by working for it

Pueblo Bonito, located in present-day New Mexico, was a four-story sandstone village.

▶ CRITICAL THINKING
Analyzing How did the location near cliffs help people living in Pueblo Bonito survive?

Early Cultures in North America

GUIDING QUESTION *Why did a large number of societies develop in North America?*

North of Mesoamerica, other early Americans developed their own ways of living. Despite their cultural differences, many of these groups learned the same farming methods as their Mesoamerican neighbors. Farming spread to the American Southwest and then along the coasts and up the Mississippi, Missouri, and Ohio Rivers. As farming developed in these areas, so did new cultures.

Peoples of the Southwest

The scorching desert of what is now Arizona was home to the Hohokam (hoh·hoh·KAHM). About A.D. 300, the Hohokam planted gardens on lands between the Salt and Gila rivers. They dug hundreds of miles of irrigation canals to carry river water to their fields. They grew corn, cotton, beans, and squash. The Hohokam also made pottery, carved stone, and etched shells.

Another group called the Anasazi (ah·nuh·SAH·zee) lived about the same time as the Hohokam. The Anasazi settled in the canyons and cliffs of the Southwest. Like the Hohokam, they practiced farming. To water their crops, they gathered the water that ran off cliffs and sent it through canals to their fields.

The Anasazi built large stone dwellings that the Spanish explorers later called pueblos (PWEH·blohs). They also built dwellings in the walls of steep cliffs. Cliff dwellings were easy to defend and offered protection from winter weather.

The Anasazi and the Hohokam both prospered until the early A.D. 1000s. At that time, they faced droughts that killed their crops. The two groups eventually abandoned their settlements.

The Anasazi were skilled at making pottery and jewelry.

(l)Martin Gray/Getty Images; (b)©Dewitt Jones/Corbis

Build Vocabulary: *Prefixes*

Meso is a prefix that means "middle." Another, more common prefix meaning middle is "mid." *Midterm* is the middle of the school term. *Midway* is halfway between two places. What other words with the prefix *mid* can you think of?

The Mound Builders

East of the Mississippi River, another early American civilization arose. It began about 1000 B.C. and lasted until about A.D. 400. Its founders built huge mounds of earth that were used as tombs or for ceremonies. These constructions gave these people their name—Mound Builders.

The Mound Builders were mostly hunters and gatherers, but they began to practice farming. Two major groups made up the culture—the Adena people and the Hopewell. Scientists believe that the Mound Builders domesticated many wild plants, such as sunflowers, gourds, and barley. Corn became another popular crop after it was introduced to the region about A.D. 100.

The Great Serpent Mound, made by the Mound Builders, still exists in southern Ohio. This mound may have been used in religious ceremonies.

▶ CRITICAL THINKING
Analyzing Why do you think the Great Serpent Mound has maintained its shape?

Who Were the Mississippians?

By A.D. 700, a new people known as the Mississippians arose. Their name came from their location in the Mississippi River Valley. The Mississippians were able to produce enough corn, squash, and beans to become full-time farmers. They also built mounds and lived in cities.

Their largest city was Cahokia (kuh•HOH•kee•uh). It may have had 16,000 to 30,000 residents. Mississippian government was centered there between A.D. 850 and 1150. Cahokia was the site of the largest Mississippian mound. Cahokia and the Mississippian society collapsed during the A.D. 1200s.

✔ PROGRESS CHECK

Explaining How were early Americans able to grow crops in desert areas of the Southwest?

LESSON 1 REVIEW

Review Vocabulary

1. Which main area of the Americas is an *isthmus*?

2. How did *maize* help early people in the Americas?

Answer the Guiding Questions

3. *Explaining* How did mountain ranges affect the way people lived in the Americas?

4. *Summarizing* How did prehistoric people reach the Americas?

5. *Comparing* In what ways did early civilizations in North America produce food?

6. **INFORMATIVE/EXPLANATORY** Write a two-paragraph essay that describes the ways of life of the Olmec and the Zapotec.

LESSON 2
Life in the Americas

ESSENTIAL QUESTION
• What makes a culture unique?

IT MATTERS BECAUSE
Long before the arrival of Europeans, people in the Americas created complex societies.

The Maya

GUIDING QUESTION *How did the Maya live in the rain forests of Mesoamerica?*

In A.D. 1839, archaeologists John Lloyd Stephens and Frederick Catherwood discovered an ancient city, hidden for centuries by vines and trees. The people who had built the city were called the Maya. These early Americans were the ancestors of the millions of Maya who live in present-day Mexico, Guatemala, Honduras, El Salvador, and Belize.

Maya Communities

About A.D. 300, the Maya developed a complex culture in parts of southern Mexico and Central America. The ancient Maya faced many challenges in the area that they settled, which was called Petén (peh·TEHN). Thick forests nearly blocked out sunlight. Stinging insects filled the air. Yet, the ancient Maya prospered.

Swamps and sinkholes gave the Maya a year-round source of water. A **sinkhole** is an area where the soil has collapsed into a hollow or depression. Sinkholes gave the Maya access to a network of underground rivers and streams.

The Maya began to develop a society. They worked together to clear forested areas. They planted fields of corn and other crops and built cities under government direction.

Reading **HELP**DESK

Taking Notes: *Organizing*
Use a pyramid like the one here to place the Aztec social classes in order. Begin at the top level of the pyramid and list classes from highest to lowest.

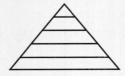

Content Vocabulary
• **sinkhole**   • **hogan**

The Maya Today

Modern-day descendants of the Maya speak about 70 different languages. They typically live on farms and grow corn, beans, and squash. As weaving and spinning have become less common, most present-day Maya, especially women, wear traditional clothing made of cloth produced in a factory.

Maya artists often portrayed Chac seated, waiting to receive the arrival of captives.

The Maya set up more than 50 independent city-states. The Maya city-states were connected by culture, political ties, and trade. However, they often fought each other for control of territory.

What Was Maya Society Like?

Each Maya city-state was ruled by a king, who claimed he was descended from the sun god. As god-kings, Maya rulers expected people to serve them. The greatest Maya king was Pacal II. He ruled the city-state of Palenque (puh•LENGH•KAY) for 67 years in the A.D. 600s. Pacal II built many structures considered to be some of the best examples of Maya architecture.

The Maya city-states had a strict class system. Nobles and priests assisted kings in governing the city-states. Below them were farmers, artisans, and hunters. People of this class paid taxes and worked on large building projects.

The Maya believed that the gods controlled everything that happened on Earth. Priests performed ceremonies to please the gods. These ceremonies sometimes included human sacrifice.

When the Maya fought battles, they wanted captives and they wanted land. When drought came and threatened their crops, Maya priests tried to please Chac (CHOCK), the god of rain, by offering the lives of their captives.

Women played a significant role in the Maya city-states. In the city-state of Calakmul (kah•lahk•MOOL), at least two women served as ruling queens. One of them may have helped to found the city.

Royal Maya women often married into royal families in other Maya city-states. This practice increased trade. It also helped form alliances—political agreements between people or states to work together.

Maya Achievements

Maya rulers turned to priests for advice. The priests thought the gods revealed their plans through movements of the sun, moon, and stars. By watching the sky, the priests learned about astronomy. They developed calendar systems to **predict** eclipses and to schedule religious festivals.

Toño Labra/Age fotostock

Reading HELP DESK

sinkhole a depression or hollow where soil has collapsed

Academic Vocabulary

predict to describe something that will happen in the future

In Maya society, a birth in the royal family called for a musical celebration, such as the one depicted above.

▶ **CRITICAL THINKING**
Drawing Conclusions Why do you think most early people developed music?

They also used calendars to decide when to plant and harvest crops. The Maya had two major calendars. They used a 260-day calendar for religious events. They used a 365-day calendar for events related to the seasons and agriculture.

The Maya developed a system of mathematics. They invented a method of counting based on 20, and they used the concept of zero. They also developed a written language to record numbers and dates. Like the Zapotec, they used hieroglyphics. They carved hieroglyphics on stone monuments and used them in books.

About A.D. 900, the Maya civilization collapsed. Historians do not know why this happened. Some evidence shows that conflict and warfare increased among city-states. Also, erosion and overuse of the soil may have caused a drop in food production. Too little food would have led to illnesses and starvation.

✅ **PROGRESS CHECK**

Explaining How were the Maya governed?

The Aztec

GUIDING QUESTION *How did the Aztec establish their society in central Mexico?*

The Aztec came to power in Mesoamerica during the A.D. 1300s. The early Aztec were hunters and warriors. About A.D. 1200, they moved into central Mexico.

Rise of the Aztec

For many years, the Aztec had been searching for a home they believed had been promised to them by their sun god—the feathered serpent Quetzalcoatl (KWEHT·suhl·kuh·WAH·tuhl). In A.D. 1325, the Aztec took refuge on a swampy island in Lake Texcoco (tehs·KOH·koh). Although the land was hardly welcoming, the Aztec chose this site to be their new home.

This shield made of feathers most likely belonged to an Aztec emperor.

▶ CRITICAL THINKING
Analyzing What do you think the animal represented here is holding in its mouth?

Aztec priests declared that the gods demanded they build a great city upon this spot. Laborers worked around the clock. They built bridges to the mainland with soil dug from the lake bottom. Floating gardens dotted the surface of the lake. The wondrous city they built was Tenochtitlán (tay•nawch•teet•LAHN).

For the next 100 years, Aztec workers built temples, palaces, and homes in Tenochtitlán. The city eventually became the largest city in Mesoamerica. It was the center of a web of trade routes that reached throughout Mexico.

The Aztec **relied** on strong kings, or emperors, who claimed to be descended from the gods. A council of priests, nobles, and warriors usually named a new emperor from the ruling family. Council members wanted someone skilled in warfare who could lead troops into battle.

Montezuma I (MAHN•tuh•ZOO•muh) was perhaps the most powerful Aztec ruler. He governed from A.D. 1440 to A.D. 1469. Montezuma used his armies to expand the empire to the Gulf of Mexico. He also built temples, aqueducts, and roads.

By A.D. 1500, Aztec armies had conquered much of what is today Mexico. The new empire was a collection of partly independent territories governed by local leaders. The Aztec ruler supported these leaders in return for tribute—goods or money paid by conquered peoples to their conquerors.

Aztec Life

The emperor was at the top of Aztec society. There were four classes of people under the emperor. These were nobles, commoners, unskilled workers, and enslaved people. Most of the Aztec were commoners, who worked as farmers, artisans, or merchants.

From an early age, boys in Aztec society were taught to be warriors. Girls were trained to work at home, weave cloth, and prepare for motherhood. Although not equal to men, Aztec women could own and inherit property.

Priests played an important role in Aztec society. Some sacrificed captives to please the gods. Death was considered honorable. The Aztec believed that those sacrificed would be rewarded in the afterlife.

Aztec priests also worked to preserve the religion, history, and literature of their people. Priests recorded these in books that historians still refer to today. Like the Maya, the Aztec

INTERFOTO/Alamy Stock Photo

Academic Vocabulary
rely to depend on

developed two different calendars. They used a religious calendar with 260 days to keep track of important ceremonies and festivals. They also had a 365-day calendar for everyday use and for marking the time for planting and harvesting crops.

Much of Mexico was not suited for farming. The Aztec overcame this difficulty by irrigating and fertilizing the land. Aztec crafts, as well as fruit, vegetables, and grain from Aztec farms, passed through markets and along trade routes. The trade in these goods and the tribute from conquered peoples helped make the Aztec Empire wealthy.

✅ PROGRESS CHECK

Explaining Why did the Aztec develop two different calendars?

The Inca

GUIDING QUESTION *How did the Inca organize their government and society?*

In the late A.D. 1300s, the Inca were only one of many groups that fought over scarce fertile land in the valleys of the Andes Mountains. From their capital of Cuzco, the Inca raided nearby groups and seized territory. Within 100 years, the Inca had created a powerful empire.

Inca Rulers

A series of strong emperors helped build the Inca Empire. Pachacuti (PAH•chah•KOO•tee) was the first of these rulers. In the A.D. 1430s, he launched a campaign of conquest. The two emperors who followed continued this expansion, building the largest empire in the Americas.

According to Aztec legend, in 1325 an eagle was seen atop a cactus with a snake in its mouth. This event fulfilled an Aztec prediction. As a result, this location became the capital of the Aztec Empire, Tenochtitlán.

DEA/G. DAGLI ORTI/Getty Images

**Pachacuti
(ruled A.D. 1438–1471)**

As emperor, Pachacuti concentrated on expanding the Inca Empire. When he wanted to conquer a kingdom, he first sent messengers to tell the local rulers all the benefits of being part of the Inca Empire. Pachacuti then asked the other rulers to join his empire. If they accepted willingly, they were treated with respect and given some rights. If they refused, the Inca attacked with brutal force.

▶ **CRITICAL THINKING**
Analyzing What do you think would be the advantages and disadvantages of joining the Inca Empire?

Reading**HELP**DESK

Academic Vocabulary

distribute to hand out or deliver, especially to members of a group

To hold the empire together, Inca rulers created a strong central government. They set up tax bureaus, legal courts, military posts, and other government offices. Inca emperors required people to learn Quechua (KEH•chuh•wuh), the language spoken by the Inca. People also had to work for the government for several weeks each year.

Inca Projects

The Inca had people work on projects such as a system of roads. When finished, these roads connected all parts of the empire. This large network helped the Inca overcome geographic barriers. The roads helped move soldiers, goods, and information quickly over the coastal deserts and high mountains.

The Inca also used irrigation and fertilizers to improve the soil. Inca engineers developed terrace farming. Terrace farming uses a series of wide steps built into a mountainside. Each step creates level farmland. Inca farmers grew potatoes and quinoa, a protein-rich grain. Government officials stored food when there were good harvests and **distributed** it when harvests were poor.

How Was Inca Society Organized?

The Inca believed their rulers had the protection of the sun god Inti (IHN•tee). As divine rulers, Inca emperors controlled the lives of their subjects. They owned all the land and set rules for growing crops and distributing food.

Below the emperor and his family were the head priest and the leading commander of the army. Next came regional army leaders. Below them were temple priests, local army commanders, and skilled workers. At the bottom were farmers, herders, and ordinary soldiers.

Like the Aztec Empire, the Inca Empire was built on war. All young men were required to serve in the army, which made it the largest and best armed military force in the region.

Culture of the Inca

The Inca believed in many gods. Unlike the Aztec, the Inca rarely sacrificed humans to honor their gods. They did, however, build large stone structures to please these dieties. They had no system of writing, no wheels, and no iron tools. Yet they built places like Machu Picchu (mah•choo PEE•choo), a retreat for Inca emperors. Constructed of white granite and thousands of feet high, Machu Picchu was located in the Andes.

Building enormous structures like Machu Picchu required the Inca to develop a method for doing mathematics. The Inca used a **quipu** (KEE•poo), a rope with knotted cords of different lengths and colors. This was a useful tool for both mathematics and for record keeping.

The Inca were also skilled engineers. Inca workers fit stones so tightly together that they needed no mortar. Because the stone blocks could slide up and down during earthquakes, many Inca structures have survived.

The ruins of Machu Picchu draw thousands of visitors. Research suggests that this monument was used as a home for the royal family and as a center for celebrations.

✅ **PROGRESS CHECK**

Describing What building projects did the Inca carry out?

North American Peoples

GUIDING QUESTION *What were the societies of North American peoples like?*

By A.D. 1500, many different groups of Native Americans lived north of Mesoamerica. They spoke about 300 languages and called themselves by thousands of different names. As they spread across North America, these peoples adapted to the different environments.

How Did People Live in the Far North?

The first people to reach the far northern areas of North America called themselves the Inuit (IH•new•weht), which means "the people." The Inuit settled along the coasts of the tundra (TUN•drah) region, the treeless land south of the Arctic.

The Inuit adapted well to their cold environment. They used dogsleds on land and seal-skin kayaks (KEYE•ackz) at sea. In winter, they built homes from stone and blocks of earth. When they traveled, they built igloos, **temporary** homes made from cut blocks of hard-packed snow.

The Inuit were skilled hunters. They used spears made from animal antlers or tusks to hunt seals, walruses, caribou, and polar bears. Blubber, or fat, from seals and whales was a food that provided needed calories and furnished oil for lamps.

(t)Jeremy Horner/Getty Images; (b)Werner Forman/Art Resource, NY

Academic Vocabulary

temporary not permanent; lasting for a limited period

Visual Vocabulary

quipu a tool used in mathematics and as a system of historical record keeping. The quipu used knots to represent numbers and items.

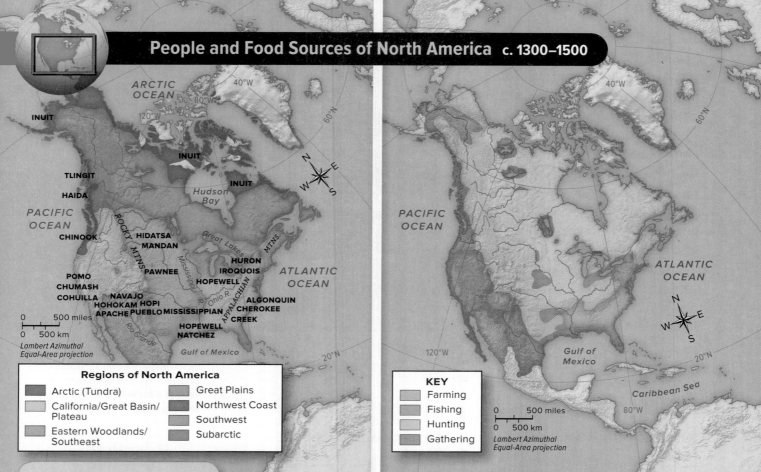

People and Food Sources of North America c. 1300–1500

Regions of North America
- Arctic (Tundra)
- California/Great Basin/Plateau
- Eastern Woodlands/Southeast
- Great Plains
- Northwest Coast
- Southwest
- Subarctic

Lambert Azimuthal Equal-Area projection

KEY
- Farming
- Fishing
- Hunting
- Gathering

Lambert Azimuthal Equal-Area projection

GEOGRAPHY CONNECTION

Certain groups lived in different North American regions. Depending on the geography of their region, North Americans found food in different ways.

1 **PLACE** What was the most common method for obtaining food on the Atlantic coast?

2 **CRITICAL THINKING**
Analyzing Why do you think fishing was more common along the Gulf of Mexico and Florida than along the northern Atlantic coast?

West Coast Life

The Pacific coast of North America had a mild climate and reliable food sources. As a result, this was the most heavily populated region north of Mesoamerica.

In the Pacific Northwest, peoples such as the Tlingit (TLIHNG·kuht), Haida (HEYE·deh), and Chinook (shuh·NOOK) used cedar trees to build wooden houses and canoes. They hunted and fished for otters, seals, whales, and their main food—salmon.

More than 500 early American cultures thrived in the area that is now California, including the Chumash (choo·MASH), the Cahuilla (kuh·WEE·uh), and the Pomo (POH·moh).

In the Southwest, the Hopi (HOH·pee), the Acoma (AHK·eh·meh), and the Zuni (ZOO·nee) built apartment-like homes from sun-dried mud bricks called adobe (uh·DOH·bee). The Southwest peoples dug irrigation canals to bring water to their fields. Their major crops were corn, beans, squash, and melons. They developed a trade network that spread into Mesoamerica.

Reading**HELP**DESK

hogan a square wooden home

In the A.D. 1500s, two new groups—the Apache (uh·PAH·chee) and the Navajo (NAH·vah·hoe)—settled in the Southwest. The Apache and Navajo were hunters and gatherers. In time, the Navajo became farmers and settled in villages made up of square wooden homes called **hogans** (HOH·gahns). The Apache, however, remained hunters.

Life on the Great Plains

Native Americans living on the Great Plains were nomads. They set up temporary villages that lasted for only one or two growing seasons. Their homes were cone-shaped skin tents called tepees. Farming on the Great Plains was not easy. Peoples like the Mandan (MAHN·dahn) and Pawnee (paw·NEE), however, planted gardens in the fertile soil along rivers.

Plains women grew beans, corn, and squash. Before the arrival of the horse, men hunted by driving herds of antelope, deer, and bison over cliffs to their deaths. Plains peoples had many uses for the bison. They ate the meat, used the skins for clothing and tepees, and made tools from the bones.

How Did People Live in the Eastern Woodlands?

The land east of the Mississippi River was known as the Eastern Woodlands because of its dense forests. Farming was widely practiced in the southeast. The most important crops were corn, beans, and squash. In the cooler northeast, people depended more on hunting animals, such as deer, bear, rabbits, and beaver.

The people of the Eastern Woodlands formed complex societies with different kinds of governments. One plan was formed in the 1500s to end fighting among five groups. The Iroquois (IHR·uh·kwoy) Confederacy created the first constitution, or plan of government, in what is now the United States.

✔ **PROGRESS CHECK**

Explaining Why did the Iroquois form a confederacy?

Thinking Like a HISTORIAN

Comparing and Contrasting

Early Americans adapted to the environments in which they settled. As a result, many different cultures and ways of life developed. As you read, note the similarities and differences among Native Americans living in the far north, the Pacific Coast, the Southwest, the Great Plains, and the Eastern Woodlands. Share your findings with the class. For more information on comparing and contrasting, read the chapter *What Does a Historian Do?*

LESSON 2 REVIEW

Review Vocabulary

1. How did *sinkholes* help the Maya?

2. How did a *hogan* differ from a tepee?

Answer the Guiding Questions

3. *Evaluating* What were the advantages and disadvantages for the Maya of living in the rain forest?

4. *Contrasting* How did Native American groups on the Pacific Coast differ from those in the Southwest?

5. *Drawing Conclusions* How did establishing a confederacy benefit Woodlands Native Americans?

6. **NARRATIVE** Describe daily life in a Maya city-state from the point of view of a Maya priest.

Write your answers on a separate piece of paper.

① **Exploring the Essential Question**

INFORMATIVE/EXPLANATORY How did geography affect the societies and cultures that developed in the early Americas? Choose two early civilizations or cultures that developed in different parts of the Americas. Write an essay describing how each adapted to its environment. Describe their food, shelter, government, and religion.

② **21st Century Skills**

DEBATING Which civilization that you read about in this chapter do you think had the greatest achievements? Choose a civilization and list its achievements as well as the reasons those achievements are important. Then, debate the issue with a fellow classmate who chose a different civilization.

③ **Thinking Like a Historian**

SEQUENCING Create a time line like the one shown. Fill in significant dates and events in the history of the Maya Empire.

A.D. 300
Maya develop civilization in southern Mexico and Central America

④ **GEOGRAPHY ACTIVITY**

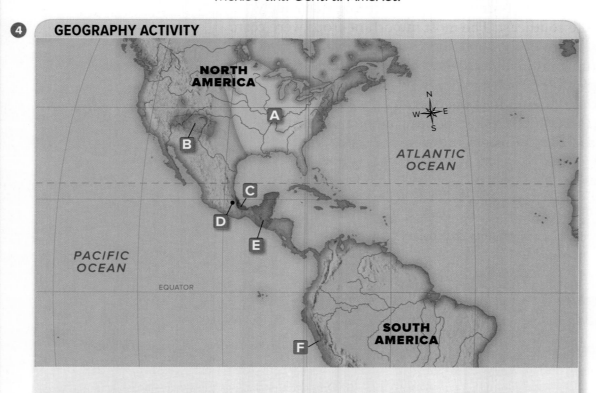

Locating Places

Match the letters on the map with the numbered groups listed below.

1. Anasazi
2. Aztec
3. Chavín
4. Maya
5. Mound Builders
6. Olmec

CHAPTER 21 Assessment

Directions: Write your answers on a separate piece of paper.

CHECKING FOR UNDERSTANDING

1 Match the following terms with their descriptions.
1. isthmus
2. maize
3. sinkhole
4. hogan

A. corn
B. a narrow piece of land that connects two larger areas of land
C. a square wooden home
D. an area where the soil has collapsed into a hollow or depression

REVIEW THE GUIDING QUESTIONS

2 *Identifying* Based on the geography of the Great Plains, what advantages did people settling in that area have?

3 *Describing* In what two ways do scientists think prehistoric people reached the Americas?

4 *Explaining* Why was it necessary for people to become farmers in order for civilization to begin?

5 *Summarizing* Use your own words to summarize why so many different societies developed in North America.

6 *Specifying* What steps did the Maya take to make the rain forests livable?

7 *Paraphrasing* Use your own words to describe how the Aztec established their society in central Mexico.

8 *Listing* What were the different levels of Inca society?

9 *Discussing* What kind of society did the Inuit create?

CRITICAL THINKING

10 *Analyzing* Why were bison important to Native Americans living on the Great Plains?

11 *Speculating* Why do you think the first planned cities were built in areas such as central Mexico rather than in areas such as the northeast region of North America?

12 *Contrasting* How was farming in Costa Rica different from farming in North America's Southwest?

13 *Drawing Conclusions* Why do you think the Maya had two types of calendars? Give specific reasons for your answer.

14 *Giving Examples* What are two examples of how the people of the Pacific Northwest adapted to their environment?

15 *Integrating Visual Information* Study the image of the mask on the first page of this chapter. Based on this mask and what you have learned about the Aztec's religion, what conclusions can you draw about the mask?

16 *Determining Cause and Effect* What were two reasons that the Anasazi built their homes in the walls of steep cliffs?

17 *Predicting Consequences* What do you think might have happened if the Inca had not had a complex system of roads?

18 *Reasoning* Why do you think salt was an important item that the Olmec traded with people living inland?

19 *Recognizing Relationships* How was the location of Tenochtitlán related to the Aztec religion?

20 *Defending* Do you think it is more likely that the first people who came to the Americas from Asia arrived by boat or walked across a land bridge to Alaska? Give reasons for your opinion.

Need Extra Help?

If You've Missed Question	1	2	3	4	5	6	7	8	9	10	11	12	13	14	15	16	17	18	19	20
Review Lesson	1,2	1	1	1	1	2	2	2	2	2	1	1,2	2	2	2	1	2	1	2	1

EXTENDED RESPONSE

21 *Narrative* You are an early American. Write a journal entry describing an encounter with a Native American people in one of the regions described in the chapter. Describe their daily life. Focus on the unique characteristics of their culture.

STANDARDIZED TEST PRACTICE

DBQ ANALYZING DOCUMENTS

The author of the following creation myth of the Inca is unknown:

> *"Thus our imperial city . . . was divided into two halves: . . . [Upper] Cuzco was founded by our king and . . . [Lower] Cuzco by our queen . . . There existed only one single difference between them, . . . that the inhabitants of Upper-Cuzco were to be considered as the elders . . . [they] had been brought together by the male, and those below by the female element."*

22 *Analyzing* Which statement best describes how the imperial city was separated?

A. The citizens in Upper-Cuzco chose to be independent.

B. A council of elders decided to divide the city into four kingdoms.

C. Invaders captured the lower half of the city.

D. The king founded one half of the city and the queen founded the other.

23 *Evaluating* Why were the inhabitants of Upper-Cuzco considered to be elders?

A. They were located to the north.

B. They had founded their city first.

C. Their city was founded by a male.

D. They had defeated the citizens of Lower-Cuzco.

Need Extra Help?

If You've Missed Question	**21**	**22**	**23**
Review Lesson	1, 2	2	2

Using **FOLDABLES** is a great way to organize notes, remember information, and prepare for tests. Follow these easy directions to create a Foldable® for the chapter you are studying.

CHAPTER 2: THE GEOGRAPHER'S WORLD

Describing Make this Foldable and label the top *Geographer's View* and the bottom *Geographer's Tools*. Under the top fold, describe three ways you experience geography every day. Under the bottom fold, list and describe the tools of geography and explain how a map is a tool. In your mind, form an image of a map of the world. Sketch and label what you visualize on the back of your shutter fold.

Step 1
Bend a sheet of paper in half to find the midpoint.

Step 2
Fold the outer edges of the paper to meet at the midpoint.

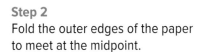

CHAPTER 3: PHYSICAL GEOGRAPHY

Identifying Make this Foldable and label the four tabs *Processes*, *Forces*, *Land*, and *Water*. Under *Processes*, identify and describe processes that operate above and below Earth's surface. Include specific examples. Under *Forces*, give examples of how forces are changing Earth's surface where you live. Finally, under *Land* and *Water*, identify land and water features within 100 miles (161 km) of your school and explain how they influence your life.

Step 1
Fold the outer edges of the paper to meet at the midpoint. Crease well.

Step 2
Fold the paper in half from side to side.

Step 3
Open and cut along the inside fold lines to form four tabs.

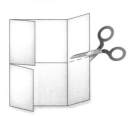

Step 4
Label the tabs as shown.

Foldables® Library

CHAPTER 5: SOUTHWEST ASIA

Describing On your Foldable, label the three tabs *Water*, *Civilization and Religion*, and *Oil and Water*. Under *Water*, describe the role of freshwater and salt water in the development of Southwest Asia. Under *Civilization and Religion*, explain why this region in called the "cradle of civilization." Under *Oil and Water*, describe and compare the importance of oil and water to the economy of the region.

Step 1
Fold a sheet of paper in half, leaving a ½-inch tab along one edge.

Step 2
Then fold the paper into three equal sections.

Step 3
Cut along the folds on the top sheet of paper to create three tabs.

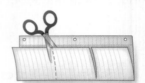

Step 4
Label your Foldable as shown.

CHAPTER 6: NORTH AFRICA

Organizing Label the rows *Geography*, *History*, and *Economy*. Label the columns *Know* and *Learned*. Use the table to record what you know and what you learn about the geography, history, and economy of North Africa.

Step 1
Fold the paper into three equal columns. Crease well.

Step 2
Open the paper and then fold it into four equal rows. Crease well. Unfold and label as shown.

CHAPTER 12: EAST AFRICA

Analyzing Write the chapter title on the cover and label the tabs *"Great" Things; Past Affects Present*; and *Daily Life, Literacy, and Health*. Under the first tab, describe the Great Rift Valley and the Great Migration and their impact on the economy of the region. Under the second tab, give examples of historical events that affect the region's current economy and politics. Under the third tab, compare two countries in East Africa using literacy rates and life expectancy.

Step 1
Stack two sheets of paper so that the back sheet is 1 inch higher than the front sheet.

Step 2
Fold the paper to form four equal tabs.

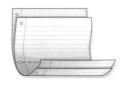

Step 3
When all tabs are an equal distance apart, fold the papers and crease well.

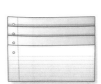

Step 4
Open the papers and then glue or staple them along the fold.

CHAPTER 13: CENTRAL AFRICA

Describing Label the four tabs *Rain Forests*, *Savannas*, *Triangular Trade*, and *Rural vs. Urban*. Under the *Rain Forests* and *Savannas* tabs, differentiate between the climate and vegetation of rain forests and savannas. Under *Triangular Trade*, describe the three stages of the triangular trade route and explain why each was profitable for merchants. Under *Rural vs. Urban,* explain why you think the capital cities of many of the countries within this region are becoming huge metropolises.

Step 1
Fold the outer edges of the paper to meet at the midpoint. Crease well.

Step 2
Fold the paper in half from side to side.

Step 3
Open and cut along the inside fold lines to form four tabs.

Step 4
Label the tabs as shown.

CHAPTER 14: WEST AFRICA

Analyzing Label the first tab *Natural Resources,* and identify which resources you think should be protected and which should be developed. Label the second tab *Trade.* Summarize the importance of trade to the region and list three valuable trade goods. Finally, label the third tab *Population Growth.* Describe how and why rapid population growth is negatively affecting the economy of the region.

Step 1
Fold a sheet of paper in half, leaving a ½-inch tab along one edge.

Step 2
Then fold the paper into three equal sections.

Step 3
Cut along the folds on the top sheet of paper to create three tabs.

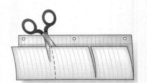

Step 4
Label your Foldable as shown.

CHAPTER 15: SOUTHERN AFRICA

Organizing Cut notebook paper into eighths to make small note cards that fit in the pockets. Sketch an outline of Southern Africa on the back of the Foldable and label geographic features of the region. On the front, label the pockets *Geography*, *History*, and *Economy*. On the note cards, record information about major geographic features, important historical events, and economic and political events that occurred in the region.

Step 1
Fold the bottom edge of a piece of paper up 2 inches to create a flap.

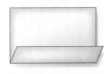

Step 2
Fold the paper into thirds.

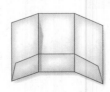

Step 3
Glue the flap on both edges and at both fold lines to form pockets. Label as shown.

CHAPTER 17: MEXICO, CENTRAL AMERICA, AND THE CARIBBEAN ISLANDS

Analyzing Make the Foldable below. Write the chapter title on the cover tab, and label the three small tabs *Gulf of Mexico*, *Civilizations*, and *Trade and Commerce*. Under *Gulf of Mexico*, explain how the gulf has affected life in the region. Include information on weather, tourism, and the economy. Under *Civilizations*, sequence and describe the major civilizations that developed in this region and their cultural influences. Finally, under *Trade and Commerce*, compare and contrast trade events that are important to the economy of the region.

Step 1
Stack two sheets of paper so that the back sheet is 1 inch higher than the front sheet.

Step 2
Fold the paper to form four equal tabs.

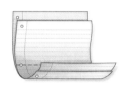

Step 3
When all tabs are an equal distance apart, fold the papers and crease well.

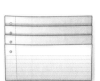

Step 4
Open the papers, and glue or staple them along the fold.

CHAPTER 18: BRAZIL

Organizing Create the Foldable below. On the back, write the chapter title and sketch a map of Brazil. Label the two front tabs *Valuable Natural Resources* and *Urban Population*. On your sketch, label Brazil's major geographic features. Under *Valuable Natural Resources*, outline when and where valuable natural resources were discovered and how the discoveries affected the native and colonial populations. Under *Urban Population*, discuss the impact of the population distribution.

Step 1
Bend a sheet of paper in half to find the midpoint.

Step 2
Fold the outer edges of the paper to meet at the midpoint.

Foldables® Library

CHAPTER 19: THE TROPICAL NORTH

Identifying Create the Foldable below. Label the cover *The Tropical North* and the layers *Geography*, *Foreign Influences and Resources*, and *Trade*. Under *Geography*, explain how geography and resources affect the countries and people of the region. Under *Foreign Influences and Resources*, explain how resources and foreign countries have impacted the Tropical North. Under *Trade*, explain how countries in the region are trying to expand trade and why.

Step 1
Stack two sheets of paper so that the back sheet is 1 inch higher than the front sheet.

Step 2
Fold the paper to form four equal tabs.

Step 3
When all tabs are an equal distance apart, fold the papers and crease well.

Step 4
Open the papers, and then glue or staple them along the fold.

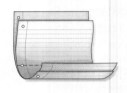
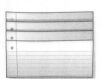

CHAPTER 20: ANDES AND MIDLATITUDE COUNTRIES

Describing Make the Foldable below, and then label the top of the sections *Geography*, *Culture*, and *Economy*. Under *Geography*, explain how the Andes Mountains affect the lives of the people who live near or around them. Under *Culture*, describe the rise and fall of the Inca Empire and what it tells about the history of the region. Finally, under *Economy*, explain how the terrain and the resources available affect the way people live.

Step 1
Fold a sheet of paper into thirds to form three equal columns.

Step 2
Label your Foldable as shown.

GAZETTEER

Gazetteer

A gazetteer (ga·zuh·TIHR) is a geographic index or dictionary. It shows latitude and longitude for cities and certain other places. Latitude and longitude are shown in this way: 48°N 2°E, or 48 degrees north latitude and two degrees east longitude. This Gazetteer lists many important geographic features and most of the world's largest independent countries and their capitals. The page numbers tell where each entry can be found on a map in this book. As an aid to pronunciation, most entries are spelled phonetically.

A

Abidjan [AH·BEE·JAHN] Capital of Côte d'Ivoire. 5°N 4°W (p. RA22)

Abu Dhabi [AH·BOO DAH·bee] Capital of the United Arab Emirates. 24°N 54°E (p. RA24)

Abuja [ah·BOO·jah] Capital of Nigeria. 8°N 9°E (p. RA22)

Accra [ah·KRUH] Capital of Ghana. 6°N 0° longitude (p. RA22)

Addis Ababa [AHD·dihs AH·bah·BAH] Capital of Ethiopia. 9°N 39°E (p. RA22)

Adriatic [AY·dree·A·tihk] **Sea** Arm of the Mediterranean Sea between the Balkan Peninsula and Italy. (p. RA20)

Afghanistan [af·GA·nuh·STAN] Central Asian country west of Pakistan. (p. RA25)

Albania [al·BAY·nee·uh] Country on the Adriatic Sea, south of Serbia. (p. RA18)

Algeria [al·JIHR·ee·uh] North African country east of Morocco. (p. RA22)

Algiers [al·JIHRZ] Capital of Algeria. 37°N 3°E (p. RA22)

Alps [ALPS] Mountain ranges extending through central Europe. (p. RA20)

Amazon [A·muh·ZAHN] **River** Largest river in the world by volume and second-largest in length. (p. RA17)

Amman [a·MAHN] Capital of Jordan. 32°N 36°E (p. RA24)

Amsterdam [AHM·stuhr·DAHM] Capital of the Netherlands. 52°N 5°E (p. RA18)

Andes [AN·DEEZ] Mountain system extending north and south along the western side of South America. (p. RA17)

Andorra [an·DAWR·uh] Small country in southern Europe between France and Spain. 43°N 2°E (p. RA18)

Angola [ang·GOH·luh] Southern African country north of Namibia. (p. RA22)

Ankara [AHNG·kuh·ruh] Capital of Turkey. 40°N 33°E (p. RA24)

Antananarivo [AHN·tah·NAH·nah·REE·voh] Capital of Madagascar. 19°S 48°E (p. RA22)

Arabian [uh·RAY·bee·uhn] **Peninsula** Large peninsula extending into the Arabian Sea. (p. RA25)

Argentina [AHR·juhn·TEE·nuh] South American country east of Chile. (p. RA16)

Armenia [ahr·MEE·nee·uh] European-Asian country between the Black and Caspian Seas. 40°N 45°E (p. RA26)

Ashkhabad [AHSH·gah·BAHD] Capital of Turkmenistan. 38°N 58°E (p. RA25)

Asmara [az·MAHR·uh] Capital of Eritrea. 16°N 39°E (p. RA22)

Astana Capital of Kazakhstan. 51°N 72°E (p. RA26)

Asunción [ah·SOON·see·OHN] Capital of Paraguay. 25°S 58°W (p. RA16)

Athens Capital of Greece. 38°N 24°E (p. RA19)

Atlas [AT·luhs] **Mountains** Mountain range on the northern edge of the Sahara. (p. RA23)

Australia [aw·STRAYL·yuh] Country and continent in Southern Hemisphere. (p. RA30)

Austria [AWS·tree·uh] Western European country east of Switzerland and south of Germany and the Czech Republic. (p. RA18)

Azerbaijan [A·zuhr·BY·JAHN] European-Asian country on the Caspian Sea. (p. RA25)

B

Baghdad Capital of Iraq. 33°N 44°E (p. RA25)

Bahamas [buh·HAH·muhz] Country made up of many islands between Cuba and the United States. (p. RA15)

Bahrain [bah·RAYN] Country located on the Persian Gulf. 26°N 51°E (p. RA25)

Baku [bah·KOO] Capital of Azerbaijan. 40°N 50°E (p. RA25)

Balkan [BAWL·kuhn] **Peninsula** Peninsula in southeastern Europe. (p. RA21)

Baltic [BAWL·tihk] **Sea** Sea in northern Europe that is connected to the North Sea. (p. RA20)

Bamako [BAH·mah·KOH] Capital of Mali. 13°N 8°W (p. RA22)

Bangkok [BANG·KAHK] Capital of Thailand. 14°N 100°E (p. RA27)

Bangladesh [BAHNG·gluh·DEHSH] South Asian country bordered by India and Myanmar. (p. RA27)

Bangui [BAHNG·GEE] Capital of the Central African Republic. 4°N 19°E (p. RA22)

Banjul [BAHN·JOOL] Capital of Gambia. 13°N 17°W (p. RA22)

Barbados [bahr·BAY·duhs] Island country between the Atlantic Ocean and the Caribbean Sea. 14°N 59°W (p. RA15)

Beijing [BAY·JIHNG] Capital of China. 40°N 116°E (p. RA27)

Beirut [bay·ROOT] Capital of Lebanon. 34°N 36°E (p. RA24)

Belarus [BEE·luh·ROOS] Eastern European country west of Russia. 54°N 28°E (p. RA19)

Belgium [BEHL·juhm] Western European country south of the Netherlands. (p. RA18)

Belgrade [BEHL·GRAYD] Capital of Serbia. 45°N 21°E (p. RA19)

Belize [buh·LEEZ] Central American country east of Guatemala. (p. RA14)

Belmopan [BEHL·moh·PAHN] Capital of Belize. 17°N 89°W (p. RA14)

Benin [buh·NEEN] West African country west of Nigeria. (p. RA22)

Berlin [behr·LEEN] Capital of Germany. 53°N 13°E (p. RA18)

Bern Capital of Switzerland. 47°N 7°E (p. RA18)

Bhutan [boo·TAHN] South Asian country northeast of India. (p. RA27)

Bishkek [bihsh·KEHK] Capital of Kyrgyzstan. 43°N 75°E (p. RA26)

Bissau [bihs·SOW] Capital of Guinea-Bissau. 12°N 16°W (p. RA22)

Black Sea Large sea between Europe and Asia. (p. RA21)

Bloemfontein [BLOOM·FAHN·TAYN] Judicial capital of South Africa. 26°E 29°S (p. RA22)

Bogotá [BOH·GOH·TAH] Capital of Colombia. 5°N 74°W (p. RA16)

Bolivia [buh·LIHV·ee·uh] Country in the central part of South America, north of Argentina. (p. RA16)

Bosnia and Herzegovina [BAHZ·nee·uh HEHRT·seh·GAW·vee·nuh] Southeastern European country bordered by Croatia, Serbia, and Montenegro. (p. RA18)

Botswana [bawt·SWAH·nah] Southern African country north of the Republic of South Africa. (p. RA22)

Brasília [brah·ZEEL·yuh] Capital of Brazil. 16°S 48°W (p. RA16)

Bratislava [BRAH·tih·SLAH·vuh] Capital of Slovakia. 48°N 17°E (p. RA18)

Brazil [bruh·ZIHL] Largest country in South America. (p. RA16)

Brazzaville [BRAH·zuh·VEEL] Capital of Congo. 4°S 15°E (p. RA22)

Brunei [bru·NY] Southeast Asian country on northern coast of the island of Borneo. (p. RA27)

Brussels [BRUH·suhlz] Capital of Belgium. 51°N 4°E (p. RA18)

Bucharest [BOO·kuh·REHST] Capital of Romania. 44°N 26°E (p. RA19)

Budapest [BOO·duh·PEHST] Capital of Hungary. 48°N 19°E (p. RA18)

Buenos Aires [BWAY·nuhs AR·eez] Capital of Argentina. 34°S 58°W (p. RA16)

Bujumbura [BOO·juhm·BUR·uh] Capital of Burundi. 3°S 29°E (p. RA22)

Bulgaria [BUHL·GAR·ee·uh] Southeastern European country south of Romania. (p. RA19)

Burkina Faso [bur·KEE·nuh FAH·soh] West African country south of Mali. (p. RA22)

Burundi [bu·ROON·dee] East African country at the northern end of Lake Tanganyika. 3°S 30°E (p. RA22)

C

Cairo [KY·roh] Capital of Egypt. 31°N 32°E (p. RA24)

Cambodia [kam·BOH·dee·uh] Southeast Asian country south of Thailand and Laos. (p. RA27)

Cameroon [KA·muh·ROON] Central African country on the northeast shore of the Gulf of Guinea. (p. RA22)

Canada [KA·nuh·duh] Northernmost country in North America. (p. RA6)

Canberra [KAN·BEHR·uh] Capital of Australia. 35°S 149°E (p. RA30)

Cape Town Legislative capital of the Republic of South Africa. 34°S 18°E (p. RA22)

Cape Verde [VUHRD] Island country off the coast of western Africa in the Atlantic Ocean. 15°N 24°W (p. RA22)

Caracas [kah·RAH·kahs] Capital of Venezuela. 11°N 67°W (p. RA16)

Caribbean [KAR·uh·BEE·uhn] **Islands** Islands in the Caribbean Sea between North America and South America, also known as West Indies. (p. RA15)

Caribbean Sea Part of the Atlantic Ocean bordered by the West Indies, South America, and Central America. (p. RA15)

Caspian [KAS·pee·uhn] **Sea** Salt lake between Europe and Asia that is the world's largest inland body of water. (p. RA21)

Caucasus [KAW·kuh·suhs] **Mountains** Mountain range between the Black and Caspian Seas. (p. RA21)

Central African Republic Central African country south of Chad. (p. RA22)

Chad [CHAD] Country west of Sudan in the African Sahel. (p. RA22)

Chang Jiang [CHAHNG jee·AHNG] Principal river of China that begins in Tibet and flows into the East China Sea near Shanghai; also known as the Yangtze River. (p. RA29)

Chile [CHEE·lay] South American country west of Argentina. (p. RA16)

China [CHY·nuh] Country in eastern and central Asia, known officially as the People's Republic of China. (p. RA27)

Chişinău [KEE·shee·NOW] Capital of Moldova. 47°N 29°E (p. RA19)

Colombia [kuh·LUHM·bee·uh] South American country west of Venezuela. (p. RA16)

Colombo [kuh·LUHM·boh] Capital of Sri Lanka. 7°N 80°E (p. RA26)

Comoros [KAH·muh·ROHZ] Small island country in Indian Ocean between the island of Madagascar and the southeast African mainland. 13°S 43°E (p. RA22)

Conakry [KAH·nuh·kree] Capital of Guinea. 10°N 14°W (p. RA22)

Gazetteer

Congo [KAHNG•goh] Central African country east of the Democratic Republic of the Congo. 3°S 14°E (p. RA22)

Congo, Democratic Republic of the Central African country north of Zambia and Angola. 1°S 22°E (p. RA22)

Copenhagen [KOH•puhn•HAY•guhn] Capital of Denmark. 56°N 12°E (p. RA18)

Costa Rica [KAWS•tah REE•kah] Central American country south of Nicaragua. (p. RA15)

Côte d'Ivoire [KOHT dee•VWAHR] West African country south of Mali. (p. RA22)

Croatia [kroh•AY•shuh] Southeastern European country on the Adriatic Sea. (p. RA18)

Cuba [KYOO•buh] Island country in the Caribbean Sea. (p. RA15)

Cyprus [SY•pruhs] Island country in the eastern Mediterranean Sea, south of Turkey. (p. RA19)

Czech [CHEHK] **Republic** Eastern European country north of Austria. (p. RA18)

D

Dakar [dah•KAHR] Capital of Senegal. 15°N 17°W (p. RA22)

Damascus [duh•MAS•kuhs] Capital of Syria. 34°N 36°E (p. RA24)

Dar es Salaam [DAHR EHS sah•LAHM] Commercial capital of Tanzania. 7°S 39°E (p. RA22)

Denmark Northern European country between the Baltic and North Seas. (p. RA18)

Dhaka [DA•kuh] Capital of Bangladesh. 24°N 90°E (p. RA27)

Djibouti [jih•BOO•tee] East African country on the Gulf of Aden. 12°N 43°E (p. RA22)

Dodoma [doh•DOH•mah] Political capital of Tanzania. 6°S 36°E (p. RA22)

Doha [DOH•huh] Capital of Qatar. 25°N 51°E (p. RA25)

Dominican [duh•MIH•nih•kuhn] **Republic** Country in the Caribbean Sea on the eastern part of the island of Hispaniola. (p. RA15)

Dublin [DUH•blihn] Capital of Ireland. 53°N 6°W (p. RA18)

Dushanbe [doo•SHAM•buh] Capital of Tajikistan. 39°N 69°E (p. RA25)

E

East Timor [TEE•MOHR] Previous province of Indonesia, now under UN administration. 10°S 127°E (p. RA27)

Ecuador [EH•kwuh•dawr] South American country southwest of Colombia. (p. RA16)

Egypt [EE•jihpt] North African country on the Mediterranean Sea. (p. RA24)

El Salvador [ehl SAL•vuh•dawr] Central American country southwest of Honduras. (p. RA14)

Equatorial Guinea [EE•kwuh•TOHR•ee•uhl GIH•nee] Central African country south of Cameroon. (p. RA22)

Eritrea [EHR•uh•TREE•uh] East African country north of Ethiopia. (p. RA22)

Estonia [eh•STOH•nee•uh] Eastern European country on the Baltic Sea. (p. RA19)

Ethiopia [EE•thee•OH•pee•uh] East African country north of Somalia and Kenya. (p. RA22)

Euphrates [yu•FRAY•teez] **River** River in southwestern Asia that flows through Syria and Iraq and joins the Tigris River. (p. RA25)

F

Fiji [FEE•jee] **Islands** Country comprised of an island group in the southwest Pacific Ocean. 19°S 175°E (p. RA30)

Finland [FIHN•luhnd] Northern European country east of Sweden. (p. RA19)

France [FRANS] Western European country south of the United Kingdom. (p. RA18)

Freetown Capital of Sierra Leone. (p. RA22)

French Guiana [gee•A•nuh] French-owned territory in northern South America. (p. RA16)

G

Gabon [ga•BOHN] Central African country on the Atlantic Ocean. (p. RA22)

Gaborone [GAH•boh•ROH•nay] Capital of Botswana. (p. RA22)

Gambia [GAM•bee•uh] West African country along the Gambia River. (p. RA22)

Georgetown [JAWRJ•town] Capital of Guyana. 8°N 58°W (p. RA16)

Georgia [JAWR•juh] European-Asian country bordering the Black Sea south of Russia. (p. RA26)

Germany [JUHR•muh•nee] Western European country south of Denmark, officially called the Federal Republic of Germany. (p. RA18)

Ghana [GAH•nuh] West African country on the Gulf of Guinea. (p. RA22)

Great Plains The continental slope extending through the United States and Canada. (p. RA7)

Greece [GREES] Southern European country on the Balkan Peninsula. (p. RA19)

Greenland [GREEN•luhnd] Island in northwestern Atlantic Ocean and the largest island in the world. (p. RA6)

Guatemala [GWAH•tay•MAH•lah] Central American country south of Mexico. (p. RA14)

Guatemala Capital of Guatemala. 15°N 91°W (p. RA14)

Guinea [GIH•nee] West African country on the Atlantic coast. (p. RA22)

Guinea-Bissau [GIH•nee bih•SOW] West African country on the Atlantic coast. (p. RA22)

Gulf of Mexico Gulf on part of the southern coast of North America. (p. RA7)

Guyana [gy·AH·nuh] South American country between Venezuela and Suriname. (p. RA16)

H

Haiti [HAY·tee] Country in the Caribbean Sea on the western part of the island of Hispaniola. (p. RA15)

Hanoi [ha·NOY] Capital of Vietnam. 21°N 106°E (p. RA27)

Harare [hah·RAH·RAY] Capital of Zimbabwe. 18°S 31°E (p. RA22)

Havana [huh·VA·nuh] Capital of Cuba. 23°N 82°W (p. RA15)

Helsinki [HEHL·SIHNG·kee] Capital of Finland. 60°N 24°E (p. RA19)

Himalaya [HI·muh·LAY·uh] Mountain ranges in southern Asia, bordering the Indian subcontinent on the north. (p. RA28)

Honduras [hahn·DUR·uhs] Central American country on the Caribbean Sea. (p. RA14)

Hong Kong Port and industrial center in southern China. 22°N 115°E (p. RA27)

Huang He [HWAHNG HUH] River in northern and eastern China, also known as the Yellow River. (p. RA29)

Hungary [HUHNG·guh·ree] Eastern European country south of Slovakia. (p. RA18)

I

Iberian [eye·BIHR·ee·uhn] **Peninsula** Peninsula in southwest Europe, occupied by Spain and Portugal. (p. RA20)

Iceland Island country between the North Atlantic and Arctic Oceans. (p. RA18)

India [IHN·dee·uh] South Asian country south of China and Nepal. (p. RA26)

Indonesia [IHN·duh·NEE·zhuh] Southeast Asian island country known as the Republic of Indonesia. (p. RA27)

Indus [IHN·duhs] **River** River in Asia that begins in Tibet and flows through Pakistan to the Arabian Sea. (p. RA28)

Iran [ih·RAN] Southwest Asian country that was formerly named Persia. (p. RA25)

Iraq [ih·RAHK] Southwest Asian country west of Iran. (p. RA25)

Ireland [EYER·luhnd] Island west of Great Britain occupied by the Republic of Ireland and Northern Ireland. (p. RA18)

Islamabad [ihs·LAH·muh·BAHD] Capital of Pakistan. 34°N 73°E (p. RA26)

Israel [IHZ·ree·uhl] Southwest Asian country south of Lebanon. (p. RA24)

Italy [IHT·uhl·ee] Southern European country south of Switzerland and east of France. (p. RA18)

J

Jakarta [juh·KAHR·tuh] Capital of Indonesia. 6°S 107°E (p. RA27)

Jamaica [juh·MAY·kuh] Island country in the Caribbean Sea. (p. RA15)

Japan [juh·PAN] East Asian country consisting of the four large islands of Hokkaido, Honshu, Shikoku, and Kyushu, plus thousands of small islands. (p. RA27)

Jerusalem [juh·ROO·suh·luhm] Capital of Israel and a holy city for Christians, Jews, and Muslims. 32°N 35°E (p. RA24)

Jordan [JAWRD·uhn] Southwest Asian country south of Syria. (p. RA24)

Juba [JU·buh] Capital of South Sudan. 5°N 31°E (p. RA22)

K

Kabul [KAH·buhl] Capital of Afghanistan. 35°N 69°E (p. RA25)

Kampala [kahm·PAH·lah] Capital of Uganda. 0° latitude 32°E (p. RA22)

Kathmandu [KAT·MAN·DOO] Capital of Nepal. 28°N 85°E (p. RA26)

Kazakhstan [kuh·ZAHK·STAHN] Large Asian country south of Russia and bordering the Caspian Sea. (p. RA26)

Kenya [KEHN·yuh] East African country south of Ethiopia. (p. RA22)

Khartoum [kahr·TOOM] Capital of Sudan. 16°N 33°E (p. RA22)

Kigali [kee·GAH·lee] Capital of Rwanda. 2°S 30°E (p. RA22)

Kingston [KIHNG·stuhn] Capital of Jamaica. 18°N 77°W (p. RA15)

Kinshasa [kihn·SHAH·suh] Capital of the Democratic Republic of the Congo. 4°S 15°E (p. RA22)

Kuala Lumpur [KWAH·luh LUM·PUR] Capital of Malaysia. 3°N 102°E (p. RA27)

Kuwait [ku·WAYT] Country on the Persian Gulf between Saudi Arabia and Iraq. (p. RA25)

Kyiv (Kiev) [KEE·ihf] Capital of Ukraine. 50°N 31°E (p. RA19)

Kyrgyzstan [s·gih·STAN] Central Asian country on China's western border. (p. RA26)

L

Laos [LOWS] Southeast Asian country south of China and west of Vietnam. (p. RA27)

La Paz [lah PAHS] Administrative capital of Bolivia, and the highest capital in the world. 17°S 68°W (p. RA16)

Latvia [LAT·vee·uh] Eastern European country west of Russia on the Baltic Sea. (p. RA19)

Lebanon [LEH·buh·nuhn] Country south of Syria on the Mediterranean Sea. (p. RA24)

Gazetteer

Lesotho [luh•SOH•ᴛᴏʜ] Southern African country within the borders of the Republic of South Africa. (p. RA22)

Liberia [ly•BIHR•ee•uh] West African country south of Guinea. (p. RA22)

Libreville [LEE•bruh•ᴠɪʜʟ] Capital of Gabon. 1°N 9°E (p. RA22)

Libya [LIH•bee•uh] North African country west of Egypt on the Mediterranean Sea. (p. RA22)

Liechtenstein [LIHKT•uhn•ѕʜᴛʏɴ] Small country in central Europe between Switzerland and Austria. 47°N 10°E (p. RA18)

Lilongwe [lih•LAWNG•ɢᴡᴀʏ] Capital of Malawi. 14°S 34°E (p. RA22)

Lima [LEE•mah] Capital of Peru. 12°S 77°W (p. RA16)

Lisbon [LIHZ•buhn] Capital of Portugal. 39°N 9°W (p. RA18)

Lithuania [ʟɪʜ•thuh•WAY•nee•uh] Eastern European country northwest of Belarus on the Baltic Sea. (p. RA21)

Ljubljana [lee•oo•blee•AH•nuh] Capital of Slovenia. 46°N 14°E (p. RA18)

Lomé [loh•MAY] Capital of Togo. 6°N 1°E (p. RA22)

London Capital of the United Kingdom, on the Thames River. 52°N 0° longitude (p. RA18)

Luanda [lu•AHN•duh] Capital of Angola. 9°S 13°E (p. RA22)

Lusaka [loo•SAH•kah] Capital of Zambia. 15°S 28°E (p. RA22)

Luxembourg [LUHK•suhm•ʙᴜʜʀɢ] Small European country bordered by France, Belgium, and Germany. 50°N 7°E (p. RA18)

M

Macao [muh•KOW] Port in southern China. 22°N 113°E (p. RA27)

Macedonia [ma•suh•DOH•nee•uh] Southeastern European country north of Greece. (p. RA19). Macedonia also refers to a geographic region covering northern Greece, the country Macedonia, and part of Bulgaria.

Madagascar [ᴍᴀ•duh•GAS•kuhr] Island in the Indian Ocean off the southeastern coast of Africa. (p. RA22)

Madrid Capital of Spain. 41°N 4°W (p. RA18)

Malabo [mah•LAH•boh] Capital of Equatorial Guinea. 4°N 9°E (p. RA22)

Malawi [mah•LAH•wee] Southern African country south of Tanzania and east of Zambia. (p. RA22)

Malaysia [muh•LAY•zhuh] Southeast Asian country with land on the Malay Peninsula and on the island of Borneo. (p. RA27)

Maldives [MAWL•ᴅᴇᴇᴠᴢ] Island country southwest of India in the Indian Ocean. (p. RA26)

Mali [MAH•lee] West African country east of Mauritania. (p. RA22)

Managua [mah•NAH•gwah] Capital of Nicaragua. (p. RA15)

Manila [muh•NIH•luh] Capital of the Philippines. 15°N 121°E (p. RA27)

Maputo [mah•POO•toh] Capital of Mozambique. 26°S 33°E (p. RA22)

Maseru [MA•zuh•ʀᴏᴏ] Capital of Lesotho. 29°S 27°E (p. RA22)

Masqat [MUHS•ᴋᴀʜᴛ] Capital of Oman. 23°N 59°E (p. RA25)

Mauritania [ᴍᴀᴡʀ•uh•TAY•nee•uh] West African country north of Senegal. (p. RA22)

Mauritius [maw•RIH•shuhs] Island country in the Indian Ocean east of Madagascar. 21°S 58°E (p. RA3)

Mbabane [uhm•bah•BAH•nay] Capital of Swaziland. 26°S 31°E (p. RA22)

Mediterranean [ᴍᴇʜ•duh•tuh•RAY•nee•uhn] **Sea** Large inland sea surrounded by Europe, Asia, and Africa. (p. RA20)

Mekong [MAY•KAWNG] **River** River in southeastern Asia that begins in Tibet and empties into the South China Sea. (p. RA29)

Mexico [MEHK•sih•KOH] North American country south of the United States. (p. RA14)

Mexico City Capital of Mexico. 19°N 99°W (p. RA14)

Minsk [MIHNSK] Capital of Belarus. 54°N 28°E (p. RA19)

Mississippi [ᴍɪʜ•suh•SIH•pee] **River** Large river system in the central United States that flows southward into the Gulf of Mexico. (p. RA11)

Mogadishu [ᴍᴏʜ•guh•DEE•shoo] Capital of Somalia. 2°N 45°E (p. RA22)

Moldova [mawl•DAW•vuh] Small European country between Ukraine and Romania. (p. RA19)

Monaco [MAH•nuh•ᴋᴏʜ] Small country in southern Europe on the French Mediterranean coast. 44°N 8°E (p. RA18)

Mongolia [mahn•GOHL•yuh] Country in Asia between Russia and China. (p. RA23)

Monrovia [muhn•ROH•vee•uh] Capital of Liberia. 6°N 11°W (p. RA22)

Montenegro [ᴍᴀʜɴ•tuh•NEE•groh] Eastern European country. (p. RA18)

Montevideo [ᴍᴀʜɴ•tuh•vuh•DAY•oh] Capital of Uruguay. 35°S 56°W (p. RA16)

Morocco [muh•RAH•ᴋᴏʜ] North African country on the Mediterranean Sea and the Atlantic Ocean. (p. RA22)

Moscow [MAHS•ᴋᴏᴡ] Capital of Russia. 56°N 38°E (p. RA19)

Mount Everest [EHV•ruhst] Highest mountain in the world, in the Himalaya between Nepal and Tibet. (p. RA28)

Mozambique [ᴍᴏʜ•zahm•BEEK] Southern African country south of Tanzania. (p. RA22)

Myanmar [MYAHN•ᴍᴀʜʀ] Southeast Asian country south of China and India, formerly called Burma. (p. RA27)

N

Nairobi [ny·ROH·bee] Capital of Kenya. 1°S 37°E (p. RA22)

Namibia [nuh·MIH·bee·uh] Southern African country south of Angola on the Atlantic Ocean. 20°S 16°E (p. RA22)

Nassau [NA·saw] Capital of the Bahamas. 25°N 77°W (p. RA15)

N'Djamena [uhn·jah·MAY·nah] Capital of Chad. 12°N 15°E (p. RA22)

Nepal [NAY·pahl] Mountain country between India and China. (p. RA26)

Netherlands [NEH·thuhr·lundz] Western European country north of Belgium. (p. RA18)

New Delhi [NOO DEH·lee] Capital of India. 29°N 77°E (p. RA26)

New Zealand [NOO ZEE·luhnd] Major island country southeast of Australia in the South Pacific. (p. RA30)

Niamey [nee·AHM·ay] Capital of Niger. 14°N 2°E (p. RA22)

Nicaragua [NIH·kuh·RAH·gwuh] Central American country south of Honduras. (p. RA15)

Nicosia [NIH·kuh·SEE·uh] Capital of Cyprus. 35°N 33°E (p. RA19)

Niger [NY·juhr] West African country north of Nigeria. (p. RA22)

Nigeria [ny·JIHR·ee·uh] West African country along the Gulf of Guinea. (p. RA22)

Nile [NYL] **River** Longest river in the world, flowing north through eastern Africa. (p. RA23)

North Korea [kuh·REE·uh] East Asian country in the northernmost part of the Korean Peninsula. (p. RA27)

Norway [NAWR·way] Northern European country on the Scandinavian Peninsula. (p. RA18)

Nouakchott [nu·AHK·shaht] Capital of Mauritania. 18°N 16°W (p. RA22)

O

Oman [oh·MAHN] Country on the Arabian Sea and the Gulf of Oman. (p. RA25)

Oslo [AHZ·loh] Capital of Norway. 60°N 11°E (p. RA18)

Ottawa [AH·tuh·wuh] Capital of Canada. 45°N 76°W (p. RA13)

Ouagadougou [WAH·gah·DOO·goo] Capital of Burkina Faso. 12°N 2°W (p. RA22)

P

Pakistan [PA·kih·stan] South Asian country northwest of India on the Arabian Sea. (p. RA26)

Palau [puh·LOW) Island country in the Pacific Ocean. 7°N 135°E (p. RA30)

Panama [PA·nuh·MAH] Central American country on the Isthmus of Panama. (p. RA15)

Panama Capital of Panama. 9°N 79°W (p. RA15)

Papua New Guinea [PA·pyu·wuh NOO GIH·nee] Island country in the Pacific Ocean north of Australia. 7°S 142°E (p. RA30)

Paraguay [PAR·uh·GWY] South American country northeast of Argentina. (p. RA16)

Paramaribo [PAH·rah·MAH·ree·boh] Capital of Suriname. 6°N 55°W (p. RA16)

Paris Capital of France. 49°N 2°E (p. RA18)

Persian [PUHR·zhuhn] **Gulf** Arm of the Arabian Sea between Iran and Saudi Arabia. (p. RA25)

Peru [puh·ROO] South American country south of Ecuador and Colombia. (p. RA16)

Philippines [FIH·luh·PEENZ] Island country in the Pacific Ocean southeast of China. (p. RA27)

Phnom Penh [puh·NAWM PEHN] Capital of Cambodia. 12°N 106°E (p. RA27)

Poland [POH·luhnd] Eastern European country on the Baltic Sea. (p. RA18)

Port-au-Prince [POHRT·oh·PRIHNS] Capital of Haiti. 19°N 72°W (p. RA15)

Port Moresby [MOHRZ·bee] Capital of Papua New Guinea. 10°S 147°E (p. RA30)

Port-of-Spain [SPAYN] Capital of Trinidad and Tobago. 11°N 62°W (p. RA15)

Porto-Novo [POHR·toh·NOH·voh] Capital of Benin. 7°N 3°E (p. RA22)

Portugal [POHR·chih·guhl] Country west of Spain on the Iberian Peninsula. (p. RA18)

Prague [PRAHG] Capital of the Czech Republic. 51°N 15°E (p. RA18)

Puerto Rico [PWEHR·toh REE·koh] Island in the Caribbean Sea; U.S. Commonwealth. (p. RA15)

P'y ngyang [pee·AWNG·yahng] Capital of North Korea. 39°N 126°E (p. RA27)

Q

Qatar [KAH·tuhr] Country on the southwestern shore of the Persian Gulf. (p. RA25)

Quito [KEE·toh] Capital of Ecuador. 0° latitude 79°W (p. RA16)

R

Rabat [ruh·BAHT] Capital of Morocco. 34°N 7°W (p. RA22)

Reykjavík [RAY·kyah·veek] Capital of Iceland. 64°N 22°W (p. RA18)

Rhine [RYN] **River** River in western Europe that flows into the North Sea. (p. RA20)

Riga [REE·guh] Capital of Latvia. 57°N 24°E (p. RA19)

Rio Grande [REE·oh GRAND] River that forms part of the boundary between the United States and Mexico. (p. RA10)

Riyadh [ree·YAHD] Capital of Saudi Arabia. 25°N 47°E (p. RA25)

Gazetteer

Rocky Mountains Mountain system in western North America. (p. RA7)

Romania [ru•MAY•nee•uh] Eastern European country east of Hungary. (p. RA19)

Rome Capital of Italy. 42°N 13°E (p. RA18)

Russia [RUH•shuh] Largest country in the world, covering parts of Europe and Asia. (pp. RA19, RA27)

Rwanda [ruh•WAHN•duh] East African country south of Uganda. 2°S 30°E (p. RA22)

S

Sahara [suh•HAR•uh] Desert region in northern Africa that is the largest hot desert in the world. (p. RA23)

Saint Lawrence [LAWR•uhns] **River** River that flows from Lake Ontario to the Atlantic Ocean and forms part of the boundary between the United States and Canada. (p. RA13)

Sanaa [sahn•AH] Capital of Yemen. 15°N 44°E (p. RA25)

San José [SAN hoh•ZAY] Capital of Costa Rica. 10°N 84°W (p. RA15)

San Marino [SAN muh•REE•noh] Small European country located on the Italian Peninsula. 44°N 13°E (p. RA18)

San Salvador [SAN SAL•vuh•DAWR] Capital of El Salvador. 14°N 89°W (p. RA14)

Santiago [SAN•tee•AH•goh] Capital of Chile. 33°S 71°W (p. RA16)

Santo Domingo [SAN•toh duh•MIHNG•goh] Capital of the Dominican Republic. 19°N 70°W (p. RA15)

São Tomé and Príncipe [sow too•MAY PREEN•see•pee] Small island country in the Gulf of Guinea off the coast of central Africa. 1°N 7°E (p. RA22)

Sarajevo [SAR•uh•YAY•voh] Capital of Bosnia and Herzegovina. 43°N 18°E (p. RA18)

Saudi Arabia [SOW•dee uh•RAY•bee•uh] Country on the Arabian Peninsula. (p. RA25)

Senegal [SEH•nih•GAWL] West African country on the Atlantic coast. (p. RA22)

Seoul [SOHL] Capital of South Korea. 38°N 127°E (p. RA27)

Serbia [SUHR•bee•uh] Eastern European country south of Hungary. (p. RA18)

Seychelles [say•SHEHL] Small island country in the Indian Ocean off eastern Africa. 6°S 56°E (p. RA22)

Sierra Leone [see•EHR•uh lee•OHN] West African country south of Guinea. (p. RA22)

Singapore [SIHNG•uh•POHR] Southeast Asian island country near tip of the Malay Peninsula. (p. RA27)

Skopje [SKAW•PYAY] Capital of the country of Macedonia. 42°N 21°E (p. RA19)

Slovakia [sloh•VAH•kee•uh] Eastern European country south of Poland. (p. RA18)

Slovenia [sloh•VEE•nee•uh] Southeastern European country south of Austria on the Adriatic Sea. (p. RA18)

Sofia [SOH•fee•uh] Capital of Bulgaria. 43°N 23°E (p. RA19)

Solomon [SAH•luh•muhn] **Islands** Island country in the Pacific Ocean northeast of Australia. (p. RA30)

Somalia [soh•MAH•lee•uh] East African country on the Gulf of Aden and the Indian Ocean. (p. RA22)

South Africa [A•frih•kuh] Country at the southern tip of Africa, officially the Republic of South Africa. (p. RA22)

South Korea [kuh•REE•uh] East Asian country on the Korean Peninsula between the Yellow Sea and the Sea of Japan. (p. RA27)

South Sudan [soo•DAN] East African country south of Sudan. (p. RA22)

Spain [SPAYN] Southern European country on the Iberian Peninsula. (p. RA18)

Sri Lanka [SREE LAHNG•kuh] Country in the Indian Ocean south of India, formerly called Ceylon. (p. RA26)

Stockholm [STAHK•HOHLM] Capital of Sweden. 59°N 18°E (p. RA18)

Sucre [SOO•kray] Constitutional capital of Bolivia. 19°S 65°W (p. RA16)

Sudan [soo•DAN] East African country south of Egypt. (p. RA22)

Suriname [SUR•uh•NAH•muh] South American country between Guyana and French Guiana. (p. RA16)

Suva [SOO•vah] Capital of the Fiji Islands. 18°S 177°E (p. RA30)

Swaziland [SWAH•zee•land] Southern African country west of Mozambique, almost entirely within the Republic of South Africa. (p. RA22)

Sweden Northern European country on the eastern side of the Scandinavian Peninsula. (p. RA18)

Switzerland [SWIHT•suhr•luhnd] European country in the Alps south of Germany. (p. RA18)

Syria [SIHR•ee•uh] Southwest Asian country on the east side of the Mediterranean Sea. (p. RA24)

T

Taipei [TY•PAY] Capital of Taiwan. 25°N 122°E (p. RA27)

Taiwan [TY•WAHN] Island country off the southeast coast of China; the seat of the Chinese Nationalist government. (p. RA27)

Tajikistan [tah•JIH•kih•STAN] Central Asian country east of Turkmenistan. (p. RA26)

Tallinn [TA•luhn] Capital of Estonia. 59°N 25°E (p. RA19)

Tanzania [TAN•zuh•NEE•uh] East African country south of Kenya. (p. RA22)

Tashkent [tash•KEHNT] Capital of Uzbekistan. 41°N 69°E (p. RA26)

Tbilisi [tuh•bih•LEE•see] Capital of the Republic of Georgia. 42°N 45°E (p. RA26)

Tegucigalpa [tay•GOO•see•GAHL•pah] Capital of Honduras. 14°N 87°W (p. RA14)

Tehran [TAY•uh•RAN] Capital of Iran. 36°N 52°E (p. RA25)

Thailand [TY•LAND] Southeast Asian country east of Myanmar. 17°N 101°E (p. RA27)

Thimphu [thihm•POO] Capital of Bhutan. 28°N 90°E (p. RA27)

Tigris [TY•gruhs] **River** River in southeastern Turkey and Iraq that merges with the Euphrates River. (p. RA25)

Tiranë [tih•RAH•nuh] Capital of Albania. 42°N 20°E (p. RA18)

Togo [TOH•goh] West African country between Benin and Ghana on the Gulf of Guinea. (p. RA22)

Tokyo [TOH•kee•OH] Capital of Japan. 36°N 140°E (p. RA27)

Trinidad and Tobago [TRIH•nuh•DAD tuh•BAY•goh] Island country near Venezuela between the Atlantic Ocean and the Caribbean Sea. (p. RA15)

Tripoli [TRIH•puh•lee] Capital of Libya. 33°N 13°E (p. RA22)

Tshwane [ch•WAH•nay] Executive capital of South Africa. 26°S 28°E (p. RA22)

Tunis [TOO•nuhs] Capital of Tunisia. 37°N 10°E (p. RA22)

Tunisia [too•NEE•zhuh] North African country on the Mediterranean Sea between Libya and Algeria. (p. RA22)

Turkey [TUHR•kee] Country in southeastern Europe and western Asia. (p. RA24)

Turkmenistan [tuhrk•MEH•nuh•STAN] Central Asian country on the Caspian Sea. (p. RA25)

U

Uganda [yoo•GAHN•dah] East African country south of Sudan. (p. RA22)

Ukraine [yoo•KRAYN] Eastern European country west of Russia on the Black Sea. (p. RA25)

Ulaanbaatar [oo•LAHN•BAH•TAWR] Capital of Mongolia. 48°N 107°E (p. RA27)

United Arab Emirates [EH•muh•ruhts] Country made up of seven states on the eastern side of the Arabian Peninsula. (p. RA25)

United Kingdom Western European island country made up of England, Scotland, Wales, and Northern Ireland. (p. RA18)

United States of America Country in North America made up of 50 states, mostly between Canada and Mexico. (p. RA8)

Uruguay [YUR•uh•GWAY] South American country south of Brazil on the Atlantic Ocean. (p. RA16)

Uzbekistan [uz•BEH•kih•STAN] Central Asian country south of Kazakhstan. (p. RA25)

V

Vanuatu [VAN•WAH•TOO] Country made up of islands in the Pacific Ocean east of Australia. (p. RA30)

Vatican [VA•tih•kuhn] **City** Headquarters of the Roman Catholic Church, located in the city of Rome in Italy. 42°N 13°E (p. RA18)

Venezuela [VEH•nuh•ZWAY•luh] South American country on the Caribbean Sea between Colombia and Guyana. (p. RA16)

Vienna [vee•EH•nuh] Capital of Austria. 48°N 16°E (p. RA18)

Vientiane [vyehn•TYAHN] Capital of Laos. 18°N 103°E (p. RA27)

Vietnam [vee•EHT•NAHM] Southeast Asian country east of Laos and Cambodia. (p. RA27)

Vilnius [VIL•nee•uhs] Capital of Lithuania. 55°N 25°E (p. RA19)

W

Warsaw Capital of Poland. 52°N 21°E (p. RA19)

Washington, D.C. Capital of the United States, in the District of Columbia. 39°N 77°W (p. RA8)

Wellington [WEH•lihng•tuhn] Capital of New Zealand. 41°S 175°E (p. RA30)

West Indies Caribbean islands between North America and South America. (p. RA15)

Windhoek [VIHNT•HUK] Capital of Namibia. 22°S 17°E (p. RA22)

Y

Yamoussoukro [YAH•MOO•SOO•kroh] Second capital of Côte d'Ivoire. 7°N 6°W (p. RA22)

Yangon [YAHNG•GOHN] City in Myanmar; formerly called Rangoon. 17°N 96°E (p. RA27)

Yaoundé [yown•DAY] Capital of Cameroon. 4°N 12°E (p. RA22)

Yemen [YEH•muhn] Country south of Saudi Arabia on the Arabian Peninsula. (p. RA25)

Yerevan [YEHR•uh•VAHN] Capital of Armenia. 40°N 44°E (p. RA25)

Z

Zagreb [ZAH•GREHB] Capital of Croatia. 46°N 16°E (p. RA18)

Zambia [ZAM•bee•uh] Southern African country north of Zimbabwe. (p. RA22)

Zimbabwe [zihm•BAH•bway] Southern African country northeast of Botswana. (p. RA22)

Gazetteer

GLOSSARY/GLOSARIO

- Content vocabulary words are words that relate to world geography content.
- Words that have an asterisk (*) are academic vocabulary. They help you understand your school subjects.
- All vocabulary words are **boldfaced** or <mark>highlighted in yellow</mark> in your textbook.

abandon • archaeology

ENGLISH	A	ESPAÑOL

*abandon to leave and not return; to leave, often because of danger (p. 614)

*abandonar salir y no regresar; dejar, con frecuencia debido al peligro (pág. 614)

absolute location the exact location of something (p. 45)

localización absoluta ubicación exacta de algo (pág. 45)

*accurate without mistakes or errors (p. 68)

*exacto sin faltas o errores (pág. 68)

*achieve to succeed; to gain something as the result of work; to successfully complete a task (p. 614)

*lograr tener éxito; obtener algo como resultado del trabajo; completar una tarea con éxito (pág. 614)

acid rain rain that contains harmful amounts of poisons due to pollution (p. 89)

lluvia ácida lluvia que contiene cantidades nocivas de venenos debido a la polución (pág. 89)

*acquire to get possession of something; to get as one's own (p. 234)

*adquirir tomar posesión de algo; tomar como propio (pág. 234)

*adequate enough for a particular requirement (p. 458)

*adecuado suficiente para un requisito en particular (pág. 458)

alphabet a set of letters or other characters used to write a language (pp. 254–255)

abecedario conjunto de letras o de otros caracteres usados en la lengua escrita (págs. 254–255)

altiplano the high plains (p. 581)

altiplano meseta elevada (pág. 581)

altitude the height above sea level (p. 583)

altitud altura sobre el nivel del mar (pág. 583)

animist a person who believes in spirits that can exist apart from bodies (p. 418)

animista persona que cree en espíritus que viven por fuera del cuerpo (pág. 418)

anthropology the study of human culture and how it develops over time (pp. 22–23)

antropología estudio de la cultura humana y su desarrollo a lo largo del tiempo (págs. 22–23)

apartheid the system of laws in South Africa aimed at separating the races (p. 441)

apartheid sistema jurídico de Sudáfrica que establecía la segregación racial (pág. 441)

apostle Christian leader chosen by Jesus to spread his message (p. 289)

apóstol líder cristiano elegido por Jesús para difundir su mensaje (pág. 289)

aquifer an underground layer of rock through which water flows (p. 163)

acuífero estrato rocoso subterráneo por donde corre el agua (pág. 163)

archaeology the study of objects to learn about past human life (p. 22)

arqueología estudio de objetos para conocer el pasado de la vida humana (pág. 22) *area a geographic location (p. 523)

*area the land included within a set of boundaries (pp. 456–457)

artifact an object made by people (pp. 22–23)

astrolabe a tool that helps sailors navigate using the positions of the stars (p. 325)

astronomer a person who studies planets and stars (p. 202)

atmosphere the layer of gases surrounding Earth (p. 68)

*authority the right or power to give orders, make decisions, or control people; power over thoughts, opinions, and behavior (p. 235; pp. 312–313)

*available ready to be used (p. 98)

axis an imaginary line that runs through Earth's center from the North Pole to the South Pole (p. 66)

*área territorio geográfico (pág. 523)

*área terreno incluido dentro de un conjunto de límites (págs. 456–457)

artefacto objeto elaborado por las personas (págs. 22–23)

astrolabio instrumento que ayuda a los marineros a navegar mediante la ubicación de las estrellas (pág. 325)

astrónomo persona que estudia los planetas y las estrellas (pág. 202)

atmósfera capa de gases que rodea la Tierra (pág. 68)

*autoridad derecho o facultad de dar órdenes, tomar decisiones o controlar a las personas; poder sobre los pensamientos, las opiniones y el comportamiento (pág. 235; págs. 312–313)

*disponible listo para usarse (pág. 98)

eje línea imaginaria que atraviesa el centro de la Tierra desde el Polo Norte hasta el Polo Sur (pág. 66)

B

basin an area of land that is drained by a river and its tributaries (p. 523)

bauxite the mineral ore that is used to make aluminum (p. 496)

bazaar a marketplace (p. 324)

*benefit an advantage (p. 493)

bias an unreasoned, emotional judgment about people or events (p. 26)

biodiversity the wide variety of life on Earth (p. 380)

blood diamonds diamonds that are sold on the black market, with the proceeds going to provide guns and ammunition for violent conflicts (p. 435)

Bronze Age the period in ancient human culture when people began to make and use bronze (p. 109)

bureaucrat a government official (p. 219)

cuenca área de terreno drenada por un río y sus afluentes (pág. 523)

bauxita mineral metalífero que se utiliza para producir aluminio (pág. 496)

bazar mercado (pág. 324)

*beneficio ventaja (pág. 493)

parcialidad juicio emotivo o que no tiene fundamento racional acerca de personas o eventos (pág. 26)

biodiversidad variedad amplia de vida en la Tierra (pág. 380)

diamantes sangrientos diamantes que se venden en el mercado negro y cuyas ganancias se utilizan para adquirir armas y municiones en conflictos violentos (pág. 435)

Edad del Bronce periodo de la cultura humana antigua en el cual las personas comenzaron a fabricar y usar el bronce (pág. 109)

burócrata funcionario del gobierno (pág. 219)

Glossary/Glosario **645**

Glossary/Glosario

C

caliph a Muslim leader (p. 316)

caliph the successor to Muhammad (p. 168)

canopy the umbrella-like covering formed by the tops of trees in a rain forest (p. 523)

caravan a group of merchants traveling together for safety, usually with a large number of camels; a group of traveling merchants and animals (p. 202; p. 312)

cash crop a farm product grown for sale (p. 503)

cassava a tuberous plant that has edible roots (p. 384)

cataract a waterfall or rapids in a river (p. 212)

caudillo a person who often ruled a Latin American country as a dictator and was generally a high-ranking military officer or a rich man (p. 503)

central city the densely populated center of a metropolitan area (p. 539)

*challenge to invite the start of a competition; to present with difficulties (p. 240; pp. 466–467)

*channel a course for a river to flow through (p. 158)

characteristic a quality or an aspect (p. 391)

*circumstances conditions (p. 507)

city-state a city that governs itself and its surrounding territory (pp. 188–189)

civil war a fight between opposing groups for control of a country's government (p. 171)

clan a group of people descended from the same ancestor (p. 465)

clan a large group of people who have a common ancestor in the far past (p. 359)

clergy church officials (p. 295)

climate the average weather in an area over a long period of time (p. 47)

califa líder musulmán (pág. 316)

califa sucesor de Mahoma (pág. 168)

manto cubierta en forma de sombrilla formada por las copas de los árboles en una selva tropical (pág. 523)

caravana grupo de mercaderes que viajan juntos por seguridad, usualmente con un gran número de camellos; grupo de mercaderes y animales que viajan (pág. 202; pág. 312)

cultivo comercial producto agrícola que se cultiva para la venta (pág. 503)

yuca planta tuberosa de raíces comestibles (pág. 384)

catarata cascada o rápidos de un río (pág. 212)

caudillo persona que gobernaba un país latinoamericano como dictador; por lo general, era un oficial de alto rango o un hombre pudiente (pág. 503)

ciudad central centro densamente poblado de un área metropolitana (pág. 539)

*desafiar invitar para que se dé inicio a una competencia; presentarse con dificultades (pág. 240; págs. 466–467)

*canal curso artificial por donde fluye un río (pág. 158)

característica cualidad o aspecto (pág. 391)

*circunstancias condiciones (pág. 507)

ciudad-estado ciudad que se gobierna a sí misma y el territorio que la rodea (págs. 188–189)

guerra civil lucha entre grupos opositores por el control del gobierno de un país (pág. 171)

clan grupo de personas que descienden del mismo ancestro (pág. 465)

clan agrupación extensa de personas que tienen un ancestro común en el pasado remoto (pág. 359)

clero funcionarios de la Iglesia (pág. 295)

clima tiempo atmosférico promedio en una zona durante un periodo largo (pág. 47)

*code a set of official rules; a system of principles or rules (p. 197)

*collapsing falling or breaking down (p. 135)

colonialism a policy based on control of one country by another (p. 502)

Columbian Exchange the transfer of plants, animals, and people between Europe, Asia, and Africa on one side and the Americas on the other (p. 504)

commandment a rule that God wanted the Israelites to follow (p. 253)

*communicate to share information with someone; to exchange knowledge or information (p. 100; p. 266)

*community a group of people with common interests and values living in an area; people living in a particular area; an area (p. 267; p. 293; pp. 470–471)

compass rose the feature on a map that shows direction (p. 52)

*complex having many parts, details, or ideas; made up of many related parts; complicated (pp. 200–201; p. 612)

*component a part of something (p. 47)

compulsory mandatory; enforced (p. 537)

conclusion a decision reached after examining evidence (p. 14, 28)

condensation the result of water vapor changing to a liquid or a solid state (p. 88)

*confirm to prove that something is true; to remove doubt (p. 325)

*conflict a serious disagreement (p. 565)

conquistador a Spanish explorer of the early Americas (p. 501)

*consist to be made up of (p. 342)

*consist to be made up of (p. 190)

*constant always happening (p. 100)

constitution a document setting forth the structure and powers of a government and the rights of people in a country (p. 178)

*código conjunto de leyes oficiales; sistema de principios o reglas (pág. 197)

*colapsar caer o derrumbarse (pág. 135)

colonialismo política que se basa en el control o dominio de un país sobre otro (pág. 502)

intercambio colombino traslado de plantas, animales y personas entre Europa, Asia y África, de un lado, y América, del otro (pág. 504)

mandamiento regla que Dios quería que los israelitas cumplieran (pág. 253)

*comunicar compartir información con alguien; intercambiar conocimientos o información (pág. 100; pág. 266)

*comunidad grupo de personas con intereses y valores comunes que viven en un área; personas que viven en un área en particular; un área (pág. 267; pág. 293; págs. 470–471)

rosa de los vientos convención de un mapa que señala la dirección (pág. 52)

*complejo que tiene muchas partes, detalles o ideas; que consta de muchas partes relacionadas (págs. 200–201; pág. 612)

*componente parte de algo (pág. 47)

compulsivo obligatorio; forzoso (pág. 537)

conclusión decisión que se toma luego de examinar evidencias (pág. 14, 28)

condensación cambio del vapor de agua a un estado líquido o sólido (pág. 88)

*confirmar demostrar que algo es verdadero; despejar dudas (pág. 325)

*conflicto desacuerdo grave (pág. 565)

conquistador explorador español de América en sus inicios (pág. 501)

*consistir estar hecho de (pág. 342)

*constar estar formado de (pág. 190)

*constante que siempre sucede (pág. 100)

constitución documento que establece la estructura y los poderes de un gobierno así como los derechos de las personas en un país (pág. 178)

Glossary/Glosario

*construct to build by putting parts together; to build; to create (pp. 98–99; p. 225)

*contact communication or connection; interaction with other people (pp. 472–473)

*contact communication or interaction with someone (p. 444)

**contemporary of the present time; modern (p. 597)

continental shelf the part of a continent that extends into the ocean in a plateau, then drops sharply to the ocean floor (p. 84)

continent a large, unbroken mass of land (p. 76)

*convert to accept a new belief; to bring from one belief to another (pp. 466–467)

*convert to change from one thing to another (p. 51); to change religions (p. 168)

*cooperation working together (p. 273)

coup an action in which a group of individuals seize control of a government (p. 593)

couscous a small, round grain used in North African and Southwest Asian cooking (p. 174)

covenant an agreement with God (p. 133, p. 252)

*create to make or produce something; to bring something into existence; to produce by a course of action (p. 286)

credentials something that gives confidence that a person is qualified for a task (p. 33)

creole a group of languages developed by enslaved people on colonial plantations that is a mixture of French, Spanish, and African (p. 571); two or more languages that blend and become the language of the region (p. 417)

*crucial important or significant (p. 220)

*culture the set of beliefs, behaviors, and traits shared by a group of people (pp. 250–251; p. 320)

*construir formar uniendo las partes; edificar; crear (págs. 98–99; pág. 225)

*contacto comunicación o conexión; interacción con otras personas (págs. 472–473)

*contacto comunicación o interacción (pág. 444)

*contemporáneo perteneciente al tiempo presente; moderno (pág. 597)

plataforma continental parte de un continente que se adentra en el océano en forma de meseta y luego desciende abruptamente hasta el fondo oceánico (pág. 84)

continente extensión de tierra grande e ininterrumpida (pág. 76)

*convertir aceptar una nueva creencia; llevar de una creencia a otra (págs. 466–467)

*convertir cambiar de una cosa a otra (pág. 51); cambiar de religión (pág. 168)

*cooperación trabajar juntos (pág. 273)

golpe (de Estado) acción mediante la cual un grupo de individuos se apodera del control de un gobierno (pág. 593)

cuscús cereal pequeño y redondo que se utiliza en la cocina de África del Norte y el Sudeste Asiático (pág. 174)

alianza acuerdo con Dios (pág. 133, pág. 252)

*crear hacer o producir algo; hacer que algo exista; producir mediante una serie de acciones (pág. 286)

credenciales algo que brinda confianza con respecto a las cualificaciones de una persona para una tarea (pág. 33)

criollo grupo de lenguas desarrollado por las personas esclavizadas en las plantaciones coloniales, que consiste en una mezcla de francés, español y africano (pág. 571); dos o más lenguas que se mezclan y convierten en la lengua de una región (pág. 417)

*crucial importante o relevante (pág. 220)

*cultura conjunto de creencias, comportamientos y características que comparte un grupo de personas (págs. 250–251; pág. 320)

cuneiform writing developed by the Sumerians that used wedge-shaped marks made in soft clay (p. 192)

cuneiforme sistema de escritura desarrollado por los sumerios que consta de marcas en forma de cuña hechas sobre arcilla blanda (pág. 192)

D

*****data** information, usually facts and figures (p. 34)

*****datos** información, por lo general hechos y cifras (pág. 34)

*****decade** a group or set of 24; period of 24 years (p. 19)

*****década** grupo o conjunto de diez; periodo de diez años (pág. 19)

*****decline** to become weaker; to move toward a weaker condition; to decrease in importance (pp. 236–237)

*****decaer** debilitarse; moverse hacia una condición de mayor fragilidad; perder importancia (págs. 236–237)

delta a fan-shaped area of silt near where a river flows into the sea (p. 212)

delta área cenagosa en forma de abanico cercana al punto donde un río desemboca en el mar (pág. 212)

delta an area where sand, silt, clay, or gravel is dropped at the mouth of a river (pp. 86)

delta área donde se deposita arena, sedimento, lodo o gravilla en la desembocadura de un río (págs. 86)

*****demonstrate** to show (p. 166)

*****demostrar** probar (pág. 166)

dependence too much reliance (p. 508)

dependencia confianza excesiva (pág. 508)

*****depict** to describe or to show (p. 392)

*****representar** describir o mostrar (pág. 392)

desalination a process that makes salt water safe to drink (p. 85)

desalinización proceso que elimina la sal del agua para hacerla potable (pág. 85)

desertification the process by which an area turns into a desert (p. 347)

desertización proceso por el cual un área se transforma en un desierto (pág. 347)

*****despite** in spite of (p. 558)

*****a pesar de** no obstante (pág. 558)

*****devotion** dedication, a strong commitment (p. 273)

*****devoción** dedicación, compromiso sólido (pág. 273)

dhow sailboat using wind-catching, triangular sails (pp. 462–463)

dhow velero que usa velas triangulares para atrapar el viento (págs. 462–463)

Diaspora groups of Jews living outside of the Jewish homeland (pp. 270–271)

diáspora grupos de judíos que viven fuera de su territorio natal (págs. 270–271)

*****displace** to take over a place or position of others (p. 409)

*****desplazar** tomar el lugar o la posición de otros (pág. 409)

*****display** to place an object where people can view it (p. 299)

*****exponer** colocar un objeto donde las personas puedan verlo (pág. 299)

*****distort** to change something so it is no longer accurate (p. 51)

*****distorsionar** cambiar algo de modo que ya no es correcto (pág. 51)

*****distribute** to divide into shares and deliver the shares to different people; to give or deliver to members of a group (p. 219; p. 622)

*****distribuir** dividir en partes y repartirlas entre diferentes personas; dar o repartir a los miembros de un grupo (pág. 219; pág. 622)

*diverse composed of many distinct and different parts (p. 538)

*diverso compuesto de muchas partes distintivas y diferentes (pág. 538)

diversified increased variety to achieve a balance (p. 176)

diversificado variedad incrementada para lograr un equilibrio (pág. 176)

doctrine official church teaching (p. 296)

doctrina enseñanza oficial de la Iglesia (pág. 296)

*document an official paper used as proof or support of something; a piece of writing (p. 276)

*documento texto oficial que se usa como prueba o respaldo de algo; escrito (pág. 276)

domesticate to adapt an animal to live with humans for the advantage of the humans (pp. 104–105)

domesticar adaptar a un animal para que viva con los seres humanos para provecho de estos (págs. 104–105)

dormant still capable of erupting but showing no signs of activity (p. 498)

inactivo que aún es capaz de entrar en erupción pero no muestra señales de actividad (pág. 498)

*dynamic always changing (p. 44)

*dinámico en permanente cambio (pág. 44)

dynasty a line of rulers from one family (pp. 216–217)

dinastía línea de gobernantes de una familia (págs. 216–217)

E

earthquake an event in which the ground shakes or trembles, brought about by the collision of tectonic plates (p. 78)

terremoto suceso en el cual el suelo se agita o tiembla como consecuencia de la colisión de placas tectónicas (pág. 78)

*economy the system of economic life in an area or country; an economy deals with the making, buying, or selling of goods and services (p. 106)

*economía sistema de la vida económica en un área o un país; la economía se relaciona con la elaboración, compra y venta de productos o servicios (pág. 106)

edu the ending of a URL of a Web site for an educational institution (p. 34).

edu parte final del URL (por sus siglas en inglés) del sitio web de una institución educativa (pág. 34).

*element an important part or characteristic (p. 409)

*elemento parte o característica importante (pág. 409)

elevation the measurement of how much above or below sea level a place is (p. 53)

elevación medida de cuánto más alto o más bajo está un lugar respecto del nivel del mar (pág. 53)

emancipate to make free (p. 536)

emancipar liberar (pág. 536)

embalming the process of treating a body to prevent it from decaying (p. 221)

embalsamamiento proceso que consiste en tratar un cuerpo para evitar que se descomponga (pág. 221)

embargo a ban on trade with a particular country (p. 441)

embargo prohibición de comerciar con un país específico (pág. 441)

embrace to hug someone (p. 195)

abrazar estrechar entre los brazos a alguien (pág. 195)

*emphasis an expression that shows the importance of something (p. 175)

*énfasis expresión que muestra la importancia de algo (pág. 175)

empire a large territory or group of many territories governed by one ruler (pp. 196–197)

imperio gran territorio o grupo de muchos territorios a cargo de un gobernante (págs. 196–197)

Glossary/Glosario

encomienda the Spanish system of enslaving Native Americans and making them practice Christianity (p. 563)

encomienda sistema español de esclavizar a los indígenas americanos y obligarlos a profesar el cristianismo (pág. 563)

*ensure to make certain or make sure of (pp. 256–257)

*asegurar tener certeza o garantizar (págs. 256–257)

environment the natural surroundings of a place (p. 47)

medioambiente entorno natural de un lugar (pág. 47)

envoy a government representative to another country (p. 233)

enviado representante de un gobierno ante otro país (pág. 233)

epic a long poem that records the deeds of a legendary or real hero (pp. 192–193)

epopeya poema largo que registra las hazañas de un héroe legendario o real (págs. 192–193)

Equator a line of latitude that runs around the middle of Earth (p. 45)

ecuador línea de latitud que atraviesa la mitad de la Tierra (pág. 45)

equinox one of two days each year when the sun is directly overhead at the Equator (p. 70)

equinoccio uno de dos días al año cuando el sol se halla situado directamente sobre el ecuador (pág. 70)

era a large division of time (p. 19)

era gran división de tiempo (pág. 19)

erg a large area of sand (p. 160)

erg zona extensa de arena (pág. 160)

erosion the process by which weathered bits of rock are moved elsewhere by water, wind, or ice (p. 79)

erosión proceso por el cual fragmentos desgastados de rocas son llevados a otra parte por acción del agua, el viento o el hielo (pág. 79)

escarpment a steep cliff at the edge of a plateau with a lowland area below (p. 524)

escarpado acantilado pendiente, al borde de una meseta, que tiene debajo un área de tierras bajas (pág. 524)

estuary an area where river currents and the ocean tide meet (p. 583)

estuario área donde convergen corrientes fluviales y la marea oceánica (pág. 583)

evaporation the change of liquid water to water vapor (p. 87)

evaporación cambio del agua en estado líquido a vapor (pág. 87)

evidence something that shows proof or an indication that something is true (pp. 24–25)

evidencia algo que proporciona pruebas o indicios de que algo es cierto (págs. 24–25)

*exceed to go beyond a limit (p. 556)

*exceder traspasar un límite (pág. 556)

excommunicate to declare that a person or group is no longer a member of the church (p. 301)

excomulgar declarar que una persona o un grupo ya no son miembros de la Iglesia (pág. 301)

exile a forced absence from one's home or country (pp. 262–263)

exilio ausencia obligada del propio hogar o país (págs. 262–263)

Exodus the departure of the Israelites out of slavery in Egypt (p. 252)

éxodo salida de los israelitas de Egipto que puso fin a su esclavitud (pág. 252)

*expand to enlarge; to spread out; to increase the number, volume, or scope (p. 272)

*ampliar agrandar; extender; aumentar el número, el volumen o el alcance (pág. 272)

*expand to spread out; to grow larger (p. 134)

*expandir extender; agrandar (pág. 134)

extended family a family made up of several generations (pp. 470–471)

familia extendida familia compuesta por varias generaciones (págs. 470–471)

extended family a unit of related people made up of several generations, including grandparents, parents, and children (p. 418)

familia extensa unidad de personas emparentadas conformada por varias generaciones, incluidos abuelos, padres e hijos (pág. 418)

extinct describing a volcano that is no longer able to erupt (p. 498)

extinto volcán que ya no puede entrar en erupción (pág. 498)

*extract to remove by a physical or chemical process (p. 255)

*extraer eliminar mediante un proceso físico o químico (pág. 255)

*extract to remove or take out (p. 531)

*extraer remover o sacar (pág. 531)

F

fault a place where two tectonic plates grind against each other (p. 78)

falla lugar donde dos placas tectónicas chocan entre sí (pág. 78)

favela an overcrowded city slum in Brazil (p. 539)

favela tugurio urbano superpoblado de Brasil (pág. 539)

*feature a noteworthy characteristic (p. 500)

*rasgo característica notable (pág. 500)

fellaheen the peasant farmers of Egypt who rent small plots of land (p. 173)

fellaheen campesinos de Egipto que arriendan pequeñas parcelas (pág. 173)

*finite limited; having boundaries (p. 14, 28)

*finito limitado; que tiene límites (pág. 14, 28)

fossil water water that fell as rain thousands of years ago and is now trapped deep below ground (p. 147)

agua fósil agua que cayó en forma de lluvia hace miles de años y ahora se encuentra atrapada en las profundidades del subsuelo (pág. 147)

fossil plant or animal remains that have been preserved from an earlier time (pp. 22–23)

fósil restos vegetales o animales que se han preservado desde una época anterior (págs. 22–23)

*found to create or set up something such as a city; to set up or establish; established or took the first steps in building; (p. 20; p. 261)

*fundar crear o instituir algo, como una ciudad; establecer o formar (pág. 20; pág. 261)

free-trade zone an area where trade barriers between countries are relaxed or lowered (p. 509)

zona de libre comercio área donde las barreras comerciales entre los países se distienden o reducen (pág. 509)

fundamentalist a person who believes in the strict interpretation of religious laws (p. 171)

fundamentalista persona que cree en la interpretación estricta de las leyes religiosas (pág. 171)

G

geography the study of Earth and its peoples, places, and environments (p. 42)

geografía estudio de la Tierra y de sus gentes, lugares y entornos (pág. 42)

geothermal energy the electricity produced by natural, underground sources of steam (pp. 349)

energía geotérmica electricidad producida por fuentes naturales de vapor subterráneas (págs. 349)

glacier a large body of ice that moves slowly across land (p. 80)

glaciar masa de hielo enorme que se mueve lentamente sobre la tierra (pág. 80)

gospel the accounts that apostles wrote of Jesus' life (pp. 296–297)

evangelio relato que los apóstoles escribieron sobre la vida de Jesús (págs. 296–297)

gov the ending of an Internet URL of a government Web site (p. 34).

gov parte final del URL de un sitio web del gobierno (pág. 34).

*grant to allow as a right, privilege, or favor (p. 439)

*conceder permitir como un derecho, privilegio o favor (pág. 439)

griot traditional storyteller (pp. 460–461)

griot narrador tradicional (págs. 460–461)

groundwater the water contained inside Earth's crust (p. 85)

agua subterránea agua contenida en el interior de la corteza terrestre (pág. 85)

guarantee to promise (p. 466)

garantizar prometer (pág. 466)

guerrilla a member of a small, defensive force of irregular soldiers (p. 591)

guerrillero miembro de una fuerza pequeña y defensiva de soldados irregulares (pág. 591)

H

hacienda a large estate (p. 563)

hacienda gran propiedad rural (pág. 563)

harmattan a wind off the Atlantic coast of Africa that blows from the northeast to the south, carrying large amounts of dust (p. 405)

harmattan viento de la costa atlántica de África que sopla del nordeste al sur, arrastrando consigo grandes cantidades de polvo (pág. 405)

hemisphere each half of Earth (p. 50)

hemisferio cada mitad de la Tierra (pág. 50)

*hierarchy a ruling body arranged by rank or class (p. 589)

*jerarquía cuerpo de gobierno organizado por rango o clase (pág. 589)

*hierarchy an organization with different levels of authority; a classification into ranks (p. 295)

*jerarquía organización con diferentes niveles de autoridad; clasificación en categorías (pág. 295)

hieroglyphics a writing system made up of a combination of pictures and sound symbols (p. 215)

jeroglíficos sistema de escritura formado por una combinación de imágenes y símbolos que representan sonidos (pág. 215)

hieroglyphics the system of writing that uses small pictures to represent sounds or words (p. 166)

jeroglífico sistema de escritura que representa sonidos o palabras con dibujos pequeños (pág. 166)

hinterland an inland area that is remote from the urban areas of a country (p. 538)

hinterland zona interior distante de las áreas urbanas de un país (pág. 538)

hogan a square wooden home of Native Americans (pp. 624–625)

hogan casa cuadrada de madera de los indígenas americanos (págs. 624–625)

Glossary/Glosario

Glossary/Glosario

hydroelectric power the electricity that is created by flowing water (p. 348)

energía hidroeléctrica electricidad producida por agua en movimiento (pág. 348)

hydropolitics the politics surrounding water access and usage rights (p. 147)

hidropolítica política relativa al acceso al agua y los derechos de su uso (pág. 147)

I

Ice Age a time when glaciers covered much of the land (p. 102)

Era de Hielo tiempo en el cual los glaciares cubrían la mayor parte de la Tierra (pág. 102)

iconoclast originally: a person who destroys icons; today: a person who criticizes traditional beliefs (p. 299)

iconoclasta originalmente, persona que destruye íconos; hoy, persona que critica las creencias tradicionales (pág. 299)

icon a representation of an object of worship (p. 299)

ícono representación de un objeto de adoración (pág. 299)

immunity the ability to resist infection by a particular disease (p. 563)

inmunidad capacidad de resistir la infección provocada por una enfermedad específica (pág. 563)

*impact an effect or influence (p. 594)

*impacto efecto o influencia (pág. 594)

imperialism a policy by which a country increases its power by gaining control over other areas of the world (p. 353)

imperialismo política mediante la cual un país aumenta su poder ejerciendo control sobre otras áreas del mundo (pág. 353)

incense a material that produces a pleasant smell when burned (p. 233)

incienso material que produce un aroma agradable al quemarlo (pág. 233)

infrastructure a system of roads and railroads that allow the transport of materials (p. 420)

infraestructura sistema de carreteras y ferrocarriles que permite el transporte de materiales (pág. 420)

*initiate to begin (p. 508)

*iniciar comenzar (pág. 508)

*integral essential, necessary (pp. 18–19)

*integral esencial, necesario (págs. 18-19)

*intense strong (p. 78)

*intenso poderoso (pág. 78)

*interpretation an explanation of the meaning of something (pp. 14, 28–29)

*interpretación explicación del significado de algo (págs. 14, 28–29)

*interpret to explain the meaning of (p. 287)

*interpretar explicar el significado de algo (pág. 287)

irrigation a system that supplies dry land with water through ditches, pipes, or streams (p. 187)

irrigación sistema que abastece de agua los terrenos secos mediante zanjas, tuberías o corrientes (pág. 187)

Islam a religion based on the teachings of Muhammad (pp. 310–311)

islam religión basada en las enseñanzas de Mahoma (págs. 310–311)

*isolate to separate from others; to separate from other populated areas; to set apart from others (p. 212; p. 311)

*aislar separar de otros; separar de otras áreas pobladas; apartar de otros (pág. 212; pág. 311)

isthmus a narrow piece of land linking two larger areas of land (p. 608); isthmus a narrow strip of land that connects two larger land areas (p. 83)

istmo porción estrecha de tierra que une dos áreas más grandes de tierra (pág. 608); **istmo** franja estrecha de tierra que conecta dos áreas de tierra más grandes (pág. 83)

K

kente the colorful, handwoven cloth produced in Kenya (p. 419)

kente tela tejida de vivos colores que se fabrica en Kenia (pág.419)

key the feature on a map that explains the symbols, colors, and lines used on the map (p. 52)

clave elemento de un mapa que explica los símbolos, colores y líneas usados en este (pág. 52)

kosher prepared according to Jewish dietary law (p. 268)

kosher preparado de acuerdo con la ley judía sobre la alimentación (pág. 268)

L

*****labor** the ability of people to do work; work; the tasks that workers perform (pp. 222–223)

*****mano de obra** capacidad de las personas para trabajar; tareas que los trabajadores realizan (págs. 222-223)

laity regular church members (p. 295)

laicado miembros regulares de la Iglesia (pág. 295)

landform a natural feature found on land (p. 47)

accidente geográfico formación natural que se encuentra sobre la tierra (pág. 47)

landlocked having no border with an ocean or a sea (p. 430)

sin salida al mar que no limita con un océano o un mar (pág. 430)

landscape the portions of Earth's surface that can be viewed at one time from a location (p. 43)

paisaje partes de la superficie terrestre que se pueden observar a un mismo tiempo desde una ubicación (pág. 43)

latitude the lines on a map that run east to west (p. 45)

latitud líneas sobre un mapa que van de este a oeste (pág. 45)

*****link** a connecting element or factor; to connect; to join (pp. 610–611)

*****vínculo** elemento o factor que conecta; el término en inglés "link" también significa "conectar"; "unir" (págs. 610–611)

*****locate** set up in a particular place (p. 107)

*****localizarse** establecerse en un lugar en particular (pág. 107)

longitude the lines on a map that run north to south (p. 45)

longitud líneas sobre un mapa que van de norte a sur (pág. 45)

M

*****maintain** to keep in the same state; to continue (p. 466)

*****mantener** conservar en el mismo estado; continuar (pág. 466)

maize corn (p. 612)

maíz elote (pág. 612)

*****manual** involving physical effort; work done by hand (p. 228)

*****manual** que implica esfuerzo físico; trabajo elaborado a mano (pág. 228)

map projection one of several systems used to represent the round Earth on a flat map (p. 52)

proyección cartográfica uno de los varios sistemas que se usan para representar la esfera terrestre en un mapa plano (pág. 52)

maquiladora a foreign-owned factory where workers assemble parts (p. 506)

maquiladora fábrica de propiedad extranjera donde los obreros ensamblan partes (pág. 506)

***margin** an edge (p. 157)

***margen** borde (pág. 157)

martyr a person who is willing to die for his or her beliefs (p. 294)

mártir persona dispuesta a morir por sus creencias (pág. 294)

matrilineal tracing descent through mothers rather than fathers (p. 471)

matrilineal linaje que se traza teniendo en cuenta la línea materna, no la paterna (pág. 471)

***method** a way of doing something; a procedure or process (p. 98)

***método** manera de hacer algo; procedimiento o proceso (pág. 98)

metropolitan area an area that includes a city and its surrounding suburbs (p. 539)

metropolitan área área que incluye una ciudad y los suburbios que la rodean (pág. 539)

***military** of or relating to soldiers, arms, or war; the armed forces (p. 197)

***militar** relativo a los soldados, las armas o la guerra; las fuerzas armadas (pág. 197)

millennium a period of a thousand years (p. 133)

milenio periodo de mil años (pág. 133)

millet a grass that produces edible seeds (p. 383)

mijo especie de pasto que produce semillas comestibles (pág. 383)

minaret the tower of a mosque from which Muslims are called to pray (pp. 326–327)

alminar torre de una mezquita desde la cual se convoca a los musulmanes a orar (págs. 326–327)

missionary someone who tries to convert others to a certain religion (p. 386)

misionario persona que trata de convertir a otras a una religión específica (pág. 386)

monarchy a government whose ruler, a king or queen, inherits the position from a parent (p. 110)

monarquía gobierno cuyo jefe, un rey o una reina, hereda el cargo de uno de sus padres (pág. 110)

monastery a religious community (p. 301)

monasterio comunidad religiosa (pág. 301)

monotheism a belief in one God (p. 133, pp. 250–251,)

monoteísmo creencia en un solo Dios (pág. 133, págs. 250–251,)

mosque a Muslim house of worship (p. 324)

mezquita casa musulmana de culto (pág. 324)

multinational a company that has locations in more than one country (p. 592)

multinacional compañía que tiene oficinas en más de un país (pág. 592)

mural a large painting on a wall (p. 507)

mural pintura de gran tamaño hecha sobre un muro (pág. 507)

myrrh a sweet perfume used as medicine in ancient times (p. 165)

mirra perfume dulce que antiguamente se empleaba como medicamento (pág. 165)

— **N** —

Neolithic Age relating to the latest period of the Stone Age (pp. 104–105)

Era Neolítica relativo al último periodo de la Edad de Piedra (págs. 104–105)

*****network** a complex, interconnected chain or system of things such as roads, canals, or computers (p. 431)

*****red** cadena o sistema complejo e interconectado de carreteras, canales o computadoras, entre otros (pág. 431)

nomads people who move from place to place as a group to find food (pp. 96–97)

nómadas personas que viajan de un lugar a otro en búsqueda de alimento (págs. 96–97)

nomad a person who lives by moving from place to place to follow and hunt herds of migrating animals or to lead herds of grazing animals to fresh pastures (p. 161)

nómada persona que vive trasladándose de un lugar a otro para seguir y cazar manadas de animales migratorios o para conducir rebaños de animales de pastoreo hacia pastos frescos (pág. 161)

nuclear family the family group that includes only parents and their children (p. 419)

familia nuclear grupo familiar que solo incluye a padres e hijos (pág. 419)

— **O** —

oasis a green area in a desert fed by underground water (pp. 310–311)

oasis área verde en el desierto que se alimenta de agua subterránea (págs. 310–311)

obstacle something that stands in the way (p. 195)

obstáculo algo que se interpone en el camino (pág. 195)

*****obtain** to gain something through a planned effort; to acquire or receive something; to take possession of (p. 228)

*****obtener** conseguir algo mediante un esfuerzo planificado; adquirir o recibir algo; tomar posesión de (pág. 228)

*****occur** to happen or take place (p. 526)

*****ocurrir** suceder o acontecer (pág. 526)

oral history stories passed down from generation to generation (p. 472)

historia oral historias transmitidas de generación en generación (pág. 472)

oral tradition the process of passing stories by word of mouth from generation to generation (p. 362)

tradición oral forma de transmitir historias de generación en generación, mediante la palabra hablada (pág. 362)

orbit to circle around something (p. 66)

orbitar moverse en círculo alrededor de algo (pág. 66)

org the ending of an Internet URL for an organization (p. 34).

org parte final del URL de una organización (pág. 34).

— **P** —

Paleolithic relating to the earliest period of the Stone Age (pp. 96–97)

Paleolítico relativo al periodo más antiguo de la Edad de Piedra (págs. 96–97)

paleontology the study of fossils (pp. 22–23)

paleontología estudio de los fósiles (págs. 22–23)

Glossary/Glosario

Glossary/Glosario

palm oil an oil that is used in cooking (p. 383)

pampas the treeless grassland of Argentina and Uruguay (p. 524)

papyrus a reed plant that grows wild along the Nile River (pp. 214–215)

parable a short story that teaches moral lesson (p. 287)

***parallel** moving or lying in the same direction and the same distance apart (p. 187)

periodic market an open-air trading market that springs up at a crossroads or in larger towns (p. 447)

***period** a division of time that is shorter than an era (p. 260)

pharaoh ruler of ancient Egypt (pp. 218–219)

pharaoh the name for a powerful ruler in ancient Egypt (p. 164)

phosphate a chemical salt used to make fertilizer (p. 163)

pidgin a language formed by combining parts of several different languages (pp. 417)

plagiarize to present someone's work as your own without giving that person credit (pp. 34–35)

plain a large expanse of land that can be flat or have a gentle roll (p. 82)

plantation a large farm (p. 503)

plateau a flat area that rises above the surrounding land (p. 82)

plateau an area of high and mostly flat land (p. 458)

poaching illegal fishing or hunting (pp. 365, 435)

point of view a personal attitude about people or life (p. 26)

polytheism a belief in more than one god (p. 133, pp. 188–189)

pope the title given to the Bishop of Rome (pp. 296–297)

aceite de palma un aceite que se usa para cocinar (pág. 383)

pampas praderas sin árboles de Argentina y Uruguay (pág. 524)

papiro planta hueca que crece a lo largo del río Nilo (págs 214–215)

parábola historia corta que enseña una lección moral (pág. 287)

***paralelo** que se mueve o se extiende en la misma dirección y a la misma distancia (pág. 187)

mercado ambulante mercado al aire libre que se instala en una aldea o en pueblos más grandes (pág. 447)

***periodo** división de tiempo más corta que una era (pág. 260)

faraón emperador del antiguo Egipto (págs. 218-219)

faraón nombre dado a un poderoso gobernante en el Antiguo Egipto (pág. 164)

fosfato sal química utilizada para producir fertilizantes (pág. 163)

pidgin lengua formada por la combinación de partes de varias lenguas distintas (págs. 417)

plagiar presentar el trabajo de otra persona como propio sin darle ningún crédito a esa persona (págs. 34–35)

llanura gran extensión de tierra plana o con ligeras ondulaciones (pág. 82)

plantación granja grande (pág. 503)

meseta área plana que se eleva por encima del terreno circundante (pág. 82)

meseta área alta y en su mayoría plana (pág. 458)

caza furtiva pesca o caza ilegal (págs. 365, 435)

punto de vista actitud personal acerca de la vida o las personas (pág. 26)

politeísmo creencia en uno o más dioses (pág. 133, págs. 188–189)

papa título dado al obispo de Roma (págs. 296–297)

potential the possibility (p. 381)

precipitation the water that falls on the ground as rain, snow, sleet, hail, or mist (p. 72)

*precise exact (p. 20)

*predict to describe something that will happen in the future (p. 618)

primary source firsthand evidence of an event in history (pp. 24–25)

Prime Meridian the starting point for measuring longitude (p. 45)

*principle an important law or belief; rules or a code of conduct (p. 319)

*project a planned activity (p. 164)

prophet a messenger sent by God to share God's word with people (pp. 250–251)

prophet messenger of God (p. 133)

proverb a wise saying (p. 260)

province a territory governed as a political district of a country or empire (p. 198)

psalm a sacred song or poem used in worship (p. 259)

*publish to produce the work of an author, usually in print (p. 326)

pueblo jóven shantytown with poor housing and little or no infrastructure built outside a large metropolitan area (p. 595)

pyramid a great stone tomb for an Egyptian pharaoh (pp. 222–223)

potencial posibilidad (pág. 381)

precipitación agua que cae al suelo en forma de lluvia, nieve, aguanieve, granizo o rocío (pág. 72)

*preciso exacto (pág. 20)

*predecir describir algo que sucederá en el futuro (pág. 618)

fuente primaria evidencia de primera mano de un hecho histórico (págs. 24–25)

primer meridiano punto de partida para medir la longitud (pág. 45)

*principio ley o creencia importante; reglas o código de conducta (pág. 319)

*proyecto actividad planificada (pág. 164)

profeta mensajero enviado por Dios para compartir su palabra con las personas (págs. 250–251)

profeta mensajero de Dios (pág. 133)

proverbio refrán sabio (pág. 260)

provincia territorio gobernado como distrito político de un país o imperio (pág. 198)

salmo canción o poema sagrado que se usa en el culto (pág. 259)

*publicar producir la obra de un autor, por lo general de manera impresa (pág. 326)

pueblo jóven barrio marginal con viviendas precarias y poca o ninguna infraestructura, construido en las afueras de una gran área metropolitana (pág. 595)

pirámide gran tumba de piedra para los faraones egipcios (págs. 222–223)

Q

quipu a tool with a system of knots used for mathematics (p. 623)

Quran the holy book of Islam (pp. 314–315)

quipu instrumento con un sistema de nudos usado para las matemáticas (p.623)

Corán libro sagrado del Islám (págs. 314–315)

Glossary/Glosario

R

rabbi the official leader of a Jewish congregation (p. 276)

rabino líder oficial de una congregación judía (pág. 276)

rain forest a dense stand of trees and other vegetation that receives a great deal of precipitation each year (p. 523)

selva tropical formación densa de árboles y otra vegetación que recibe una gran cantidad de precipitación todos los años (pág. 523)

rain shadow an area that receives reduced rainfall because it is on the side of a mountain facing away from the ocean (p. 73)

sombra pluviométrica zona que recibe pocas precipitaciones porque se halla en la ladera de una montaña que está en el lado contrario al océano (pág. 73)

*ratio the relationship in amount or size between two or more things (p. 568)

*ratio relación en cantidad o tamaño entre dos o más cosas (pág. 568)

reggae a traditional Jamaican style of music that uses complex drum rhythms (p. 511)

reggae género musical tradicional de Jamaica que utiliza complejos ritmos de tambor (pág. 511)

regime a style of government (p. 171)

régimen estilo de gobierno (pág. 171)

*region a broad geographic area with similar features (p. 200; pp. 292–293)

*región área geográfica amplia con características similares (pág. 200; págs. 292–293)

region a group of places that are close to one another and that share some characteristics (p. 46)

región agrupación de lugares cercanos que comparten algunas características (pág. 46)

*reject to refuse to accept or consider (p. 299)

*rechazar negarse a aceptar o considerar (pág. 299)

relative location the location of one place compared to another place (p. 44)

localización relativa la ubicación de un lugar comparada con la de otro (pág. 44)

relief the difference between the elevation of one feature and the elevation of another feature near it (p. 53)

relieve diferencia entre la elevación de una formación y la de otra formación cercana (pág. 53)

*rely to depend on someone or something; to be dependent; to count on for help; to contribute to (pp. 238–239; p. 620)

*confiar depender de alguien o de algo; ser dependiente; contar con la ayuda de alguien (págs. 238–239; pág. 620)

remittance the money sent back to the homeland by people who have gone somewhere else to work (pp. 511)

remesa dinero enviado al país de origen por personas que se han ido a trabajar a otro lugar (págs. 511)

remote sensing the method of getting information from far away, such as deep below the ground (pp. 56)

detección remota método para obtener información muy lejana, como de las profundidades del subsuelo (págs. 56)

reservoir an artificial lake created by a dam (p. 431)

embalse lago artificial creado por una presa (pág. 431)

*reside to be present continuously or have a home in a particular place; to live (p. 221)

*residir estar presente de manera continua o tener un hogar en un lugar determinado; vivir (pág. 221)

resource a material that can be used to produce crops or other products (p. 47)

recurso materia prima que se puede utilizar para obtener cultivos u otros productos (pág. 47)

resurrection the act of rising from the dead (p. 289)

revolution a complete trip of Earth around the sun (p. 66); a period of violent and sweeping change (p. 502)

rift to separate two pieces from one another (p. 342)

Ring of Fire a long, narrow band of volcanoes surrounding the Pacific Ocean (p. 78)

*role the function or part an individual fills in society; something that plays a part in the process (p. 226)

resurrección acción de levantarse de entre los muertos (pág. 289)

revolución recorrido completo de la Tierra alrededor del Sol (pág. 66); periodo de cambio violento y radical (pág. 502)

escindir separar dos partes entre sí (pág. 342)

Cinturón de Fuego banda larga y estrecha de volcanes que rodean el océano Pacífico (pág. 78)

*rol función o papel que un individuo cumple en la sociedad; algo que desempeña un papel en el proceso (pág. 226)

S

Sabbath a weekly day of worship and rest (pp. 264–265)

salvation the act of being saved from the effects of sin (pp. 290–291)

savanna a flat grassland, sometimes with scattered trees, in a tropical or subtropical region (pp. 238–239; p. 457)

scale bar the feature on a map that tells how a measured space on the map relates to the actual distance on Earth (p. 52)

scale the relationship between distances on the map and on Earth (p. 53)

schism a separation or division from a church (p. 301)

scholarly concerned with academic learning or research (p. 14, 28)

scribe a person who copies or writes out documents; often a record keeper (p. 192)

scroll a long document made from pieces of parchment sewn together (p. 265)

secede to withdraw from a group or a country (p. 415)

secondary source a document or written work created after an event (p. 25)

semiarid having lower temperatures and cooler nights than hot, dry deserts (p. 130)

shadoof a bucket attached to a long pole used to transfer river water to storage basins (p. 214)

sabbat día semanal de culto y descanso (págs. 264–265)

salvación acción de salvarse de los efectos del pecado (págs. 290–291)

sabana pradera llana en una región tropical o subtropical, algunas veces con árboles dispersos (págs. 238–239; pág. 457)

escala numérica elemento cartográfico que muestra la relación entre un espacio medido sobre el mapa y la distancia real sobre la Tierra (pág. 52)

escala relación entre distancias en un mapa y en la Tierra (pág. 53)

cisma separación o división de una Iglesia (pág. 301)

erudito relacionado con el aprendizaje académico o la investigación (pág. 14, 28)

escriba persona que copia o escribe documentos; con frecuencia, quien lleva los archivos (pág. 192)

rollo documento largo elaborado con pedazos de pergamino unidos (pág. 265)

separarse retirarse de un grupo o un país (pág. 415)

fuente secundaria documento o trabajo que se escribe después de que ocurre un evento (pág. 25)

semiárido que tiene temperaturas más bajas y noches más frías que los desiertos cálidos y secos (pág. 130)

cigoñal cubeta atada a una pértiga larga que se usa para pasar agua del río a vasijas de almacenamiento (pág. 214)

Glossary/Glosario

shari'ah Islamic code of law (pp. 314–315)

sheikh the leader of an Arab tribe (p. 311)

Shia group of Muslims who believed the descendants of Ali should rule (p. 319)

shrine a place where people worship (p. 108)

silt fine particles of fertile soil (p. 187); small particles of rich soil (p. 158)

***similar** having things in common; having characteristics in common (p. 474); having qualities in common (p. 493)

sinkhole a depression or hollow where soil has collapsed (pp. 617–618)

slash-and-burn agriculture a method of farming that involves cutting down trees and underbrush and burning the area to create a field for crops (p. 531)

smallpox an often-fatal disease that causes a rash and leaves marks on the skin (p. 590)

solstice one of two days of the year when the sun reaches its northernmost or southernmost point (p. 69)

souk a large, open-air market in North African and Southwest Asian countries (p. 173)

***source** a document or reference work (pp. 24–25)

spatial Earth's features in terms of their places, shapes, and relationships to one another (p. 42)

specialization the act of training for a particular job (p. 108)

species a class of individuals with similar physical characteristics (pp. 22–23)

***sphere** a round shape like a ball (p. 50)

spiritual a gospel song (pp. 474–475)

***stable** staying in the same condition; not likely to change or fail (p. 567)

staple a food that is eaten regularly (p. 500)

sharia código jurídico islámico (págs. 314–315)

jeque líder de una tribu árabe (pág. 311)

chiíta grupo musulmán que creía que los descendientes de Alá debían gobernar (pág. 319)

templo lugar donde la gente rinde culto (pág. 108)

limo partículas finas de suelo fértil (pág. 187); pequeñas partículas de suelo fértil (pág. 158)

***similar** que tiene cosas en común; que tiene características en común (pág. 474); que tiene cualidades en común (pág. 493)

sumidero depresión u hoyo donde el suelo ha colapsado (págs. 617–618)

agricultura de tala y quema método agrícola que consiste en talar árboles y rastrojos y quemar el área despejada para crear un campo de cultivo (pág. 531)

viruela enfermedad, por lo general mortal, que causa sarpullido y deja marcas en la piel (pág. 590)

solsticio uno de dos días al año cuando el sol alcanza su máxima declinación norte o sur (pág. 69)

zoco mercado grande al aire libre propio de África del Norte y los países del Sudoeste Asiático (pág. 173)

***fuente** documento u obra de referencia (págs. 24–25)

espaciales características de la Tierra en cuanto a sus lugares, formas y relaciones entre sí (pág. 42)

especialización acción de capacitarse para un trabajo específico (pág. 108)

especie clase de individuos con características físicas semejantes (págs. 22–23)

***esfera** figura redonda como una pelota (pág. 50)

espiritual canción de música gospel (págs. 474–475)

***estable** que permanece en la misma condición; algo que es improbable que cambie o decaiga (pág. 567)

alimento básico alimento que se consume habitualmente (pág. 500)

stutter an uneven repetition of sounds and words (p. 195)

subsistence farming/agriculture a type of farming in which the farmer produces only enough to feed his or her family (p. 361)

sugarcane a grassy plant that is a natural source of sugar (pp. 472–473)

sultan Seljuk leader (p. 320)

Sunni group of Muslims who accepted the rule of the Umayyad caliphs (p. 319)

surplus an amount that is left over after a need has been met (p. 188); extra; more than needed (p. 500)

*****survive** to continue to live; to live through a dangerous event; to continue to function or prosper (p. 262; pp. 468–469)

Swahili the unique culture of Africa's East Coast and the language spoken there (pp. 468–469)

synagogue a Jewish house of worship (pp. 264–265)

systematic agriculture the organized growing of food on a regular schedule (pp. 104–105)

tartamudeo repetición irregular de sonidos y palabras (pág. 195)

agricultura de subsistencia tipo de agricultura en el que los granjeros producen apenas lo suficiente para alimentar a su familia (pág. 361)

caña de azúcar planta herbácea que es una fuente natural de azúcar (págs. 472–473)

sultán líder seléucida (pág. 320)

sunita grupo musulmán que solo acepta el mandato de los califas Umayyad (pág. 319)

excedente cantidad que queda luego de satisfacer una necesidad (pág. 188); sobrante; más de lo que se necesita (pág. 500)

*****sobrevivir** seguir viviendo; vivir luego de haber tenido una experiencia peligrosa; continuar funcionando o prosperar (pág. 262; págs. 468–469)

swahili cultura exclusiva de la costa este de África y lengua que se habla allí (págs. 468–469)

sinagoga casa judía de culto (págs. 264–265)

agricultura sistemática cultivo organizado de alimentos de acuerdo con un calendario habitual (págs. 104–105)

T

tariff a tax added to the price of goods that are imported (p. 572)

technology any way that scientific discoveries are applied to practical use (p. 54); the use of advanced methods to solve problems; an ability gained by the practical use of knowledge (p. 98;)

tectonic plate one of the 40 pieces of Earth's crust (p. 77)

temperate zone a region with a climate that is neither too hot nor too cold (p. 527)

*****temporary** not permanent; lasting for a limited period (pp. 622–623)

arancel impuesto añadido al precio de los productos importados (pág. 572)

tecnología cualquier forma en que los descubrimientos científicos se aplican para un uso práctico (pág. 54); uso de métodos avanzados para solucionar problemas; habilidad obtenida mediante el uso práctico del conocimiento (pág. 98)

placa tectónica uno de las 40 partes de la corteza terrestre (pág. 77)

zona templad región cuyo clima no es ni muy frío ni muy caliente (pág. 527)

*****temporal** que no es permanente; que dura un periodo limitado (págs. 622–623)

tensions opposition between individuals or groups; stress (p. 274)

textile woven cloth (pp. 242–243)

thatch a bundle of twigs, grass, and bark (p. 447)

thematic map a map that shows specialized information (p. 54)

theocracy a government of religious leader(s) (pp. 218–219)

tierra caliente the warmest climate zone, located at lower elevations (p. 495)

tierra fría a colder climate zone, located at higher elevations (p. 495)

tierra templada a temperate climate zone, located at mid-level elevations (p. 495)

Torah teachings that Moses received from God; later became the first part of the Hebrew Bible (p. 253)

trade language a common language that emerges when countries trade with each other (p. 390)

trade winds the winds that blow regularly in the Tropics (p. 559)

*tradition a custom, or way of life, passed down from generation to generation (pp. 264–265)

*transform to change something completely (p. 88)

*transport to transfer or carry from one place to another; to convey or carry (pp. 458–459)

trench a long, narrow, steep-sided cut on the ocean floor (p. 84)

*trend a general tendency or preference (p. 447)

tribe a social group made up of families or clans (p. 252)

tribute money paid by one country to another in surrender or for protection (p. 353); payment made to a ruler or state as a sign of surrender; payment to a ruler as a sign of submission or for protection (p. 198)

tensiones oposición entre individuos o grupos; presión (pág. 274)

textil tela tejida (págs. 242–243)

techo de paja armazón de ramas, pasto y corteza (pág. 447)

mapa temático mapa que muestra información especializada (pág. 54)

teocracia gobierno de uno o más líderes religiosos (págs. 218–219)

tierra caliente la zona climática más cálida, ubicada en elevaciones bajas (pág. 495)

tierra fría zona climática fría, ubicada entre elevaciones altas (pág. 495)

tierra templada zona de clima templado, ubicada entre elevaciones medias (pág. 495)

Tora enseñanza que recibió Moisés de Dios; llegó a ser la primera parte de la Biblia hebrea (pág. 253)

lenguaje comercial lenguaje común que surge cuando los países comercian entre sí (pág. 390)

vientos alisios vientos que soplan regularmente en los trópicos (pág. 559)

*tradición costumbre, o forma de vida, que se transmite de una generación a otra (págs. 264–265)

*transformar cambiar algo por completo (pág. 88)

*transportar transferir o llevar de un lugar a otro; comunicar o llevar (págs. 458–459)

fosa depresión larga, estrecha y profunda del fondo oceánico (pág. 84)

*tendencia inclinación o preferencia general (pág. 447)

tribu grupo social conformado por familias o clanes (pág. 252)

tributo dinero que un país paga a otro por sometimiento o para obtener protección (pág. 353); pago hecho a un gobernante o Estado en señal de rendición; pago a un gobernante como señal de sumisión o para obtener protección (pág. 198)

Glossary/Glosario

Tropics an area between the Tropic of Cancer and the Tropic of Capricorn that has generally warm temperatures because it receives the direct rays of the sun for much of the year (p. 525)

trópicos zona entre el trópico de Cáncer y el trópico de Capricornio que generalmente tiene temperaturas cálidas porque recibe los rayos directos del sol la mayor parte del año (pág. 525)

tsunami a giant ocean wave caused by volcanic eruptions or movement of the earth under the ocean floor (p. 78)

tsunami gigantesca ola oceánica provocada por erupciones volcánicas o movimientos de la tierra bajo el lecho oceánico (pág. 78)

U

*unify to bring together in one unit; to join; to make into one group (pp. 216–217)

*unificar juntar en una unidad; unir; formar un grupo (págs. 216–217)

*unique one of a kind; different from all others (pp. 210–211; p. 465)

*exclusivo único en su clase; diferente de los demás (págs. 210–211; pág. 465)

*unique unusual (p. 541)

*único inusual (pág. 541)

URL the abbreviation for uniform resource locator; the address of an online resource (p. 34)

URL abreviatura de uniform resource locator (localizador uniforme de recursos); dirección de un recurso en línea (pág. 34)

utility the infrastructure provided by companies or governments such as electricity, water, and trash removal (p. 446)

servicios públicos infraestructura que proveen algunas compañías o gobiernos, como electricidad, agua y recolección de basuras (pág. 446)

V

*version a different form or edition; a translation of the Bible (p. 271)

*versión formato o edición diferentes; traducción de la Biblia (pág. 271)

*violate to disobey or break a rule or law; to break, to treat with disrespect (pp. 34–35)

*violar desobedecer o incumplir una regla o ley; romper, tratar de manera irrespetuosa (págs. 34–35)

*volume amount included within limits (p. 610); an amount (p. 403)

*volumen cantidad incluida dentro de los límites (pág. 610); cantidad (pág. 403)

W

wadi a dry riverbed that fills with water when rare rains fall in a desert (p. 130)

vado lecho seco de un río que se llena de agua cuando ocasionalmente llueve en un desierto (pág. 130)

water cycle the process in which water is used and reused on Earth, including precipitation, collection, evaporation, and condensation (p. 87)

ciclo del agua proceso en el cual el agua se usa y reutiliza en la Tierra; incluye la precipitación, recolección, evaporación y condensación (pág. 87)

Glossary/Glosario

weathering the process by which Earth's surface is worn away by natural forces (p. 79)

meteorización proceso mediante el cual la superficie terrestre se deteriora por la acción de fuerzas naturales (pág. 79)

*widespread commonly occurring (p. 142)

*extendido que ocurre con frecuencia (pág. 142)

Z

ziggurat a pyramid-shaped structure with a temple at the top (p. 190)

zigurat estructura en forma de pirámide, en cuya punta se encuentra un templo (pág. 190)

The following abbreviations are used in the index: *m=map, c=chart, p=photograph or picture, g=graph, crt=cartoon, ptg=painting, q=quote*

— **A** —

Index 669

Index

---D---

Index

Index

Index

Index

Index

Index

O

P

Index

pueblos, *p615,* 615; Pueblo Bonito, *p615,* 615
Pueblos jóvenes, 595
Puerto Rico, *m491,* 497, 498; independence of, 505; Spanish colonies in, 504. *See also* Caribbean Islands
Puig, Manuel, 597
pyramids, 211, 223–225, *ptg224, p225,* 228, 241, *p242, q246, c248,* 613, 614; in the Americas, 613, 614; Great Pyramid, *c208,* 225, *c248;* Pyramid of the Sun, 613
pyramids, Ancient Egypt, 166; Ancient Kush (Sudan), *p351;* making of, *i166*

Qatar, Persian Gulf border, 128; population of, 140; as wealthy country, 145
Qattara Depression, 157
Qin dynasty, 25
Quechua language, 596
Quechuan family, *p600*
Queen Elizabeth National Park, 363
quipu, 589, *p589,* 623, *p623*
Quito, Ecuador, 563, 570
Quitu people, 562
Quran, 144, *p175, q313,* 315, 319, 468, 469, 473

rabbis, 276–277, *p277*
rain forest, 546–549, *m549;* as biome, 74; in Central Africa, 378–379; climate and, 75. *See also* Amazon rain forest; tropical rain forest; defined, 523
rain forests, 453, *m455,* 456–457, *m457,* 460, 610
rain shadow, *d72,* 73
rainfall, Australia; Central Africa, 378; East Africa, 346–347; North Africa, 156, 159–162; Sierra Leone and Liberia, 406; Southern Africa, 432; Southwest Asia desert, 130; West Africa, 404–406. *See also* monsoon
rainwater, 88
Ramadan, 134, *p144,* 145
Ramses II, pharaoh of Egypt, 236, *p236,* 237, 246, *q246*
Re, 219, 220
Red Sea, 212, 230–231, *m244,* 252, 310, 312, 462; parting of the, 252
Red Sea, Adulis on, 351; Ancient Egyptian control along, 165; Ancient Nubia and, 350; Eritrea, 354; Great Rift Valley and, 343; mountains on shores of (Egypt), 157; in Southwest Asia, 127–128; Suez Canal and, 159
refugees, in Central Africa, 389; Somolian, 357; Sudanese, 366–369
reggae music, 511

regime, 171
region, 46, *c48*
relative location, 44–45
relief, on physical maps, 53
religion, 20–21, 198, 262; African, 462–463, 466, 467, *m467,* 474–475; in the Americas, 606, 613; ancient Egypt, 165–166; birthplace of, 133; Brazil, 541–542; calendars and, 20–21; Central Africa, 390–391; Chaldean, 201, 202; common beliefs of Judaism, Christianity, and Islam, 251, 266, 314; of early humans and civilizations, 108, 110–111, 606, 613; Egyptian, 207, 208, 218–223, *ptg220, p221, ptg222,* 228, 235, 236–237; influence on modern law, 253; in Kush, 239, 241, *q241;* in medieval Europe, 317–319, 327; Mesopotamian, 189–190, 192, 194, 197, 198, 201, 202; monotheism, 250, 251, 291; polytheism, 189, 250; rivalry in West Africa, 415; Roman, 292–294; Sikhism, 322; spread of, 316–322; Southern Africa, 444–445; Southwest Asia, 143–144; Sumerian, 189–190; theocracy, 218–219. *See also* Buddhism; Tropical North, 571 Christian Church; Christianity; gods and goddesses; Hinduism; Islam; Jainism; Judaism; missionaries; Roman Catholic Church; Zoroastrianism
remittance, 511
remote sensing, 56
Republic of Mali, 414
Republic of South Africa, 434. *See also* Southern Africa
Republic of the Congo, 386; as independent nation, 387; Republic of Ghana, 414; State Department Background Notes about, *q398*
reservoir, 431
resources, defined, 47
resurrection, 289
revolution, 502; of Earth around the sun, 66–67
Revolutionary Armed Forces of Colombia (FARC), 573
rhinoceroses, 431, 435
Rhodesia, 440. *See also* Zimbabwe
rice, 106, *q114;* in China, 106
rifted, 342–343
Ring of Fire, Andes mountains in, 581; defined, 78; Mexico and Central America in, 493, 498
Rio Bravo, 494, *p495*
Rio de Janeiro, Brazil, 525, 527, 535; Carnival in, 542; "Christ the Redeemer" statue, *p520;* favelas in, 539–540; Sugarloaf Mountain and Copacabana Beach in, *p539*
Rio Grande River, 494
rivers, freshwater, 86; liquid water in, 85; mouth of, 86
Riyadh, 141

Robinho (Brazilian soccer player), *p519*
Roman bath, *p167*
Roman Catholic Church, 290, 297, 298–301; excommunication, 301; heresy, 296; schism in, 299–301
Roman Catholic Church, in Brazil, 541
Roman civilization, 311, *c454;* culture, *q31;* emperors, 292, 293; gods and goddesses, 293; Latin, 21, 292, 297; literature and theater, 302; religion, 292–294
Roman Empire, *q31,* 167–168, 459; Christianity, 282, *c282, c283,* 284–286, 292–297; division of, *c283;* Eastern Roman Empire, 301; expansion of, 272; influence in the modern world, 20; Jewish revolt against, *c249,* 274–275, 285; Judaism and, 272–275, *c278,* 282, *c282,* 284–286, 287–291; military, 293, 294, *ptg295,* 303; road system, 292, *c454;* rule of Judaea, 272–275, *c282;* Western Roman Empire, 298, 301
Roman Republic, Julius Caesar, 20, *c454*
Rome, *p19,* 243, *c249,* 272, 281, 291, 294, 298; founding of, 20
Roughing It (Twain), *q92*
Rousseff, Dilma (President of Brazil), *p521,* 537
Rozwi kingdom, 437
Rub' al-Khali (Empty Quarter), 129
Rubaiyat (Khayyam), 326, *q326*
rubber, 385
Ruth, 267, *q268, ptg268*
Ruwenzori Mountains, 344, 346, 377
Rwanda, ethnic tensions in, 356; genocide in, 394; independence of, 355; as landlocked country, 344; life expectancy, 365; mineral resources of, 348; population density of, 358; Volcanoes National Park, 363
Río de la Plata, 583

Sabbath, *c253,* 264, 267, *p267*
Sadducees, 273
Safavid Empire, 321, 322
Sahara, 212, 238, *c454,* 458, 459–460, 462, 464, 467
Sahara desert, harmattan winds in, 405; landscapes in, *p160;* the Sahel and, 347; size of, 160; temperatures in, 161; trade across, 409–410; in West Africa, 402–403, 408
Sahel, 347, 405
Saint Domingue, 505
salt and salt trade, *p409;* in Central Africa, 383; gold-for-salt (Mali), 411; in Lake Assal, 348, *p348;* in Southern Africa, 431, 436
salt water, 85; freshwater vs., *i84*

Index

Index